Microsoft® Dynamics CRM 2011 Administration Bible

Microsoft® Dynamics CRM 2011 Administration Bible

Matthew Wittemann and Geoff Ables

WILEY

Wiley Publishing, Inc.

Microsoft® Dynamics CRM 2011 Administration Bible

Published by
Wiley Publishing, Inc.
10475 Crosspoint Boulevard
Indianapolis, IN 46256
www.wiley.com

Copyright © 2011 by Wiley Publishing, Inc., Indianapolis, Indiana

Published by Wiley Publishing, Inc., Indianapolis, Indiana

Published simultaneously in Canada

ISBN: 978-0-470-56814-9

Manufactured in the United States of America

10 9 8 7 6 5 4 3 2 1

For general information on our other products and services or to obtain technical support, please contact our Customer Care Department within the U.S. at (877) 762-2974, outside the U.S. at (317) 572-3993 or fax (317) 572-4002.

Library of Congress Cataloging-in-Publication Data is available from the Publisher upon request

About the Authors

Matthew Wittemann

Five-time Microsoft MVP award recipient Matthew Wittemann is the CRM practice director at C5 Insight, a CRM and SharePoint consultancy that has been helping companies improve their use of technology in sales, marketing, and service since 2001. Matthew is a frequent contributor to CRM industry publications and user communities. Since 2004 he has authored the ICU-MSCRM blog, a website dedicated to Microsoft Dynamics CRM, for which he was recently ranked 22nd among the top 100 most influential figures in the Microsoft Dynamics industry. With a diverse background in web technologies, he has led the development of numerous complex and award-winning CRM deployments, and has recently turned much of his focus towards using Microsoft CRM and SharePoint technologies as a rapid application development platform.

Geoff Ables

Geoff Ables is a speaker, author, and Managing Partner of C5 Insight, a Microsoft Dynamics CRM, SharePoint and Salesforce.com consulting company. He has more than 20 years of experience consulting with businesses in process design, customer relationship management, database marketing, business intelligence, and collaboration. Geoff also founded or co-founded two additional startups and launched new business divisions for two organizations. Geoff's insights have been seen and heard through many international venues, including: *BusinessWeek,* National Public Radio, *USA Today*, The International Journal of CRM, EuroForum, and The New Zealand Direct Marketing Journal. Mr. Ables was named as one of Charlotte, North Carolina's prestigious "40 Under 40" in recognition of his business accomplishments and commitment to the community.

For Elizabeth and June

Credits

Senior Acquisitions Editor
Stephanie McComb

Project Editor
Beth Taylor

Technical Editor
Ronald Lemmen and Sander Bockting

Copy Editor
Beth Taylor

Editorial Manager
Rosemarie Graham

Editorial Director
Robyn Siesky

Business Manager
Amy Knies

Senior Marketing Manager
Sandy Smith

Vice President and Executive Group Publisher
Richard Swadley

Vice President and Executive Group Publisher
Bob Ipsen

Vice President and Executive Publisher
Barry Pruett

Project Coordinator
Patrick Redmond

Graphics and Production Specialists
Andrea Hornberger
Julie Trippetti

Quality Control Technicians
John Greenough
Lauren Mandelbaum

Proofreading and Indexing
Christine Sabooni
BIM Indexing & Proofreading Services

Foreword

There is no question about two things. CRM and Social CRM are here to stay as both a burgeoning industry that has measurable and direct benefits for companies and something that companies have decided they need as a necessity of their business strategies and programs. That's the first.

The second is that Matt Wittemann is not only eminently qualified to write a significant guidebook to Microsoft Dynamics CRM; he also knows CRM inside and out.

That combination is why I'm writing the foreword to this book.

Over the past couple of decades, customer relationship management (CRM) and its evolutionary sibling social customer relationship management (SCRM) have, after a very rocky start, shown substantial positive benefits when it comes to the operational effectiveness of the customer facing departments, like sales, marketing, and customer service. Most companies, according to recent Gartner Group, Forrester Research and IDC studies, are at least somewhat satisfied, and at times, wildly enthused by the results of their CRM deployments. Minimally, they recognize they need CRM systems to enable their customer programs and they get what are generally pretty solid technology systems for their agility and their operational effectiveness. The standard median response in these studies is that the CRM implementation met enough of each respondent's objectives that it was worth the company's investment. The number that keeps appearing is approximately 70 percent of the goals and objectives were met — and a roughly 70 percent satisfaction rate. This is a far cry from the 2002 Gartner Group study of CRM satisfaction — a report that is now somewhat iconic — that found that 55 to 70 percent of CRM implementations failed. In contract, the recent studies show that 70 percent of implementations succeed to the satisfaction of the owners of the initiative.

What might be the reasons that 30 percent still don't succeed? That's a legitimate question because after all, you're buying a book on Microsoft Dynamics CRM — a great book, I might add — for any number of possible reasons:

1. You're already implementing Microsoft Dynamics CRM 2011 and want some useful practical tips and hints.

2. You're considering an implementation of Microsoft Dynamics CRM 2011 and want to see what it does either on its own or in comparison to some other package you might be contemplating.

3. You are thinking long term and just want to see what Microsoft is offering in their new package.

4. Something else I doubt I can even fathom or want to.

There are a myriad of reasons that CRM implementations fail that range from the failure to get the users' buy-in from the beginning to poor planning and underfunding, to ignoring the cultural and organizational change necessary to succeed at using the CRM system. Also, it can be simply because the organizations didn't understand what the applications and services they were buying truly did and didn't do.

Which is where Matt Wittemann comes in.

See, if there's one thing that Matt knows its what Microsoft Dynamics CRM does and doesn't do. Not only that, the man is ruthlessly honest about it so that even though you'll be reading a handbook that can walk you through the basics of Microsoft Dynamics CRM 2011, you aren't buying a bit of marketing fluff when it comes to what the products are capable of.

Let me explain.

I met Matt in 2008, when I had challenged Microsoft and salesforce.com to a shootout over the claim that Steve Ballmer had made about the simplicity of the Microsoft development platform. This was going to be a contest to see whether Microsoft or salesforce.com met the claims being made and who did it better. There would be a winner and a loser. Blood sport. Matt wrote me and told me that he would be happy to help because his firm implements both salesforce.com and Microsoft Dynamics CRM. I was so taken by his obvious knowledge and his confidence, that I made him a judge in the contest. He worked tirelessly and came up with a set of technical specs and requirements for the contestants that were just THAT good.

The contest, due to varying reasons, didn't happen, but my appreciation for what Matt brings to the table did. Matt is an expert at his craft. He knows Microsoft Dynamics CRM. He's studied it, played with it, planned it, and implemented it. Simply put, the man is a star when it comes to Microsoft Dynamics CRM and there is no better person to write this book.

We've reached a real nodal point when it comes to the maturity of CRM. When I wrote the first edition of CRM at the Speed of Light released back in 2001 (it's now in its 4th edition, released in early 2010), CRM was not that mature and was something that was seen as a useful option. Many of the applications were clunky, overly difficult to implement, expensive and even harder to deliver. Microsoft didn't even have a CRM offering. Now as we get to 2011, most of the significant vendors have applications that are quite good and do what they are expected to do. Microsoft is going through its 5th iteration of CRM. Additionally, we have seen a real evolution of CRM to a far more social format that takes into account not just customer transactions and operations, but customer interactions and measurable experiences. The vendors providing CRM solutions are now beginning to provide the functionality to support the social inputs and outputs that are required by these more demanding, newly empowered social customers.

Microsoft Dynamics CRM 2011 is a big leap forward for Microsoft and its partners, its customers and future prospects. It takes a team like Matt and Geoff to navigate you through it. But, with these two being thorough and engaging, the ride will actually be fun. So hop on if you've bought the book and get ready to roll. If you're reading this to decide to buy the book, just do it. It's SO worth it.

Paul Greenberg

Author, CRM at the Speed of Light, 4th Edition

Acknowledgments

A project of this scope is always the result of the efforts of many, many people — and this book was no exception. We are grateful to have played the role of the authors on this particular project. Many others supported that role by covering our responsibilities at home or in the office; and others contributed time and knowledge to this project.

Matt Wittemann's Acknowledgments

When I was approached by Wiley about writing this book I called Paul Nielsen, author of the SQL Server Bible to get his advice. Like some of the other authors I've spoken to, he warned me about the amount of work, time, and commitment a book of this magnitude would require. He also shared some great insight about how to organize the book's contents and start to tackle the subject matter.

In spite of this helpful advice, as I started this endeavor I didn't give enough consideration to the amount of work, time, and commitment that would be required of my family, co-workers, and friends in order to make this book possible. So I'd like to rectify this oversight in some small measure by thanking the following very supportive people:

My fantastic, loving, patient, beautiful, and patient (did I say that already?) wife, Elizabeth: Thank you. Aleksandr and Sofia: Thanks for being glad to see me when I made my infrequent and fleeting re-emergences into your lives, and for not driving your mother too crazy while I was writing.

Brian Goddard, thank you for suggesting that I look into this new-fangled CRM thing that Microsoft was introducing back in 2003.

Paul Greenberg, author of *CRM at the Speed of Light*: Thanks for the super foreword, and for your helpful insights into the CRM marketplace and social CRM.

My fellow MVPs and CRM industry insiders, especially Jerry Weinstock of CRM Innovation, Jeffry van de Vuurst at CWR Mobility, Aaron Zupancic of Experlogix: Thanks to all of you.

I'd also like to thank my friends at Microsoft, particularly Jim Glass, as well as the many other members of the CRM product group who helped us out in so many ways.

Geoff Ables' Acknowledgments

First of all, thanks to Matt Wittemann for asking me to be your co-author for this book (I think).

Thanks to my wife June for patiently enduring many weekends and evenings with no husband during this effort. I promise, no more books . . . for a while. And to my beautiful, brilliant and wonderful daughters Mallorie and Lauren — you always make me proud to be your Dad. The three of you make all the work worthwhile.

Thanks to Mom and Dad. You guys are my inspiration for always trying to do everything with excellence and integrity. Thank you.

Our Collective Acknowledgments

Throughout this project, a number of individuals worked with both of us in different capacities. Our collective thanks go out to these individuals.

Curtis Hughes, for contributing the SharePoint integration appendix to this book, and to our other co-workers at C5 Insight, for encouraging us and picking up our slack around the office: Thank you.

Stephanie McComb at Wiley, and Beth Taylor our tenacious editor: Thanks for making sure everything came together and met your high standards. Ronald Lemmen and his colleague Sander Bockting: Thanks for the technical editing and suggestions.

And there were many other individuals at Microsoft who helped us with technical questions, suggestions and pointers to help fine-tune the content of the book. We'd particularly like to thank Steve Blazevich, Andrew Bybee, Corey Hanson, Mike Ming-Shen Lin, Ravindra Upadhya, and Tarry Wang.

Introduction

This is an exciting time to be working in the CRM industry, and in particular, to be working with Microsoft Dynamics CRM. The pace of change and the scope of business challenges have never been greater. With innovations like cloud hosting, declarative design and platform development, Dynamics CRM is an ideal medium for creative technologists to employ as they tackle these challenges.

Dynamics CRM, like few other software products, offers a limitless variety of solutions to these challenges. Implementing Dynamics CRM, however, can demand a full spectrum of technical skill levels and familiarity with a wide range of technologies. From simple drag-and-drop form design to deep .NET development, from Word mail merges to SQL Server Reporting Services, and from mobile device management to integration with ERP systems, you will have no shortage of interesting challenges as you plan, implement, and maintain Dynamics CRM.

While we made every attempt to ensure accuracy and completeness, this book was written based on pre-release versions of the software. Our goal for this book is to equip you, the reader, with the broadest range of tools and knowledge so you can make the most of Dynamics CRM for your organization or your customers.

Contents at a Glance

Contents

Contents

Contents

Contents

Contents

Contents

Contents

Contents

Part VI: Customizing Dynamics CRM with Custom Code   481

Chapter 19: Understanding the Other Customization Options 483

Chapter 20: Understanding the Development Options 497

Contents

Contents

Part I

Laying a Solid Foundation

What is CRM and why is it cropping up in more and more businesses? CRM systems have been around for a couple of decades now, starting in large corporations like banks and insurance companies that needed a simple way to store and retrieve large volumes of customer information.

As software technologies have evolved during that time, CRM systems have evolved along with them, and along the way they've started to find their way into the center of more and more types of organizations. From small non-profits to government service departments, and everything in between, CRM software is a growing part of the IT landscape.

Microsoft entered the marketplace several years ago, and with its release of Microsoft Dynamics CRM 2011, the company is making a big splash in the industry. And because of the ubiquitous nature of Microsoft's software, more and more technology professionals are finding themselves involved in one way or another with Dynamics CRM implementations.

Perhaps you are one of these technologists who is being exposed for the first time to both the generic concepts surrounding customer relationship management and the specific Microsoft flavor of CRM software. Or perhaps you're a seasoned CRM professional looking for an inside path to mastering Microsoft Dynamics CRM 2011.

Familiarizing Yourself with CRM

Welcome to the world of CRM! This chapter introduces you to the concepts of customer relationship management (CRM) without getting into many of the specifics about Dynamics CRM. If you are a long-time Dynamics CRM administrator, then you can focus on the XRM section of this chapter. If you have administered or used other CRM systems, but not Dynamics CRM, then you may want to skim the entire chapter, focusing on the areas that are new to you. On the other hand, if Microsoft Dynamics CRM 2011 is your first significant CRM project, then plan to invest some time into reading this chapter — doing so can give you a strong foundation for understanding the remainder of the content in this book.

IN THIS CHAPTER

Managing customers with CRM

XRM: Extending CRM

Planning for a successful CRM project

Managing Customers with CRM

To define CRM (or customer relationship management), first think about how a one-person company might manage customer relationships. For example, think of a fictitious personal fitness training company called Able Body Solutions (ABS) as an example. The owner of ABS is old-fashioned and keeps a list of customers and prospects in a handwritten address book. She listens carefully, keeping a journal of conversations, and prides herself on giving personal attention to the individuals with whom she does business. With prospects, she asks about training goals (they vary from losing weight to dropping clothing sizes to improving how they feel) and she helps them understand how her services can help them realize those goals. For customers, she crafts a personalized fitness program based on their specific situation and goals and helps them to track progress. Over time, she has fine-tuned her sales and her training services based on what has and has not worked.

Do You Need CRM?

Some signs that a business should get serious about their CRM strategy include:

- Leads that submit their names on your Web site don't hear back from you for hours (or even days).
- Sales and service reps have no visibility into each other's activities.
- Customers complain that their issues are not resolved in a timely manner.
- Marketing cannot track the bottom line return on investment for their campaigns.
- Management has a difficult time improving sales and service processes because existing processes are not tracked and are inconsistent.
- Employees are spending too much time searching for customer information.
- Executives cannot see more than 30–90 days into the sales pipeline.

Without touching a computer, the owner of ABS has done a perfectly acceptable job of practicing the core tenets of customer relationship management! Specifically, she has done the following:

- Captured customer data (into an address book and a personal journal)
- Analyzed the information to better understand her customers and prospects
- Engaged with customers in a dialog that is relevant to their needs
- Tracked her results and made improvements based on what she has learned

Understanding complex customer relationships

The concept of CRM is simple, but in companies with even just a few employees it can be difficult to pull off. Many businesses frequently "drop the ball" with seemingly simplistic customer management challenges. Figure 1.1 illustrates how complex managing customer relationships can become when many employees interact with many customers across many communication channels regarding a diverse range of products and services.

Managing all of these complexities requires a clearly defined set of processes and the appropriate technology to manage and automate them. Tools like Dynamics CRM provide a database of customer (and prospect) information, the ability to view and analyze that information across the organization, activity management for engaging in relevant dialog, and reporting tools (often becoming known as dashboards or business intelligence) to track results. Moreover, Dynamics CRM provides powerful workflow rules that enable businesses to ensure that consistent processes and best practices are being applied across all customer relationships.

FIGURE 1.1

The complexities of managing customer interactions

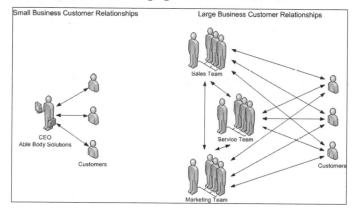

A practical definition for CRM is the processes, and supporting technologies, that a business uses to capture information about customers (and prospects), analyze the information, make the information available to others in the business, engage with customers, and measure results.

Understanding where CRM ends and ERP begins

Traditionally, CRM systems were designed to handle the sales process up until an opportunity was won. After an opportunity had been won, the enterprise resource planning (ERP) system would be used to handle processing orders, sending invoices, tracking accounts receivable, and so on. In recent years, however, the line between ERP and CRM has become increasingly blurred.

Businesses began to realize that they needed to reengineer many of their processes to work the way their customers wanted to work — and CRM systems were well positioned to handle this challenge. ERP systems are optimized to handle *business facing* activities such as processing transactions, not *customer facing* activities such as tracking activities. ERP systems are complex to work with and require far more training and expertise than do most CRM systems. Finally, the flexibility of Dynamics CRM (see the XRM section, below) has made it possible to move even more functions that are typically found in ERP systems into Dynamics CRM. As a result, many businesses are handling customer transactions all the way up to sending the invoice in their CRM system.

Where should CRM end and ERP begin? The answer to that question varies for every organization. The following questions can help you make an informed decision for your business. For each step of your process, ask:

- Is the customer directly involved with this step or impacted by this step?
- Are the individuals involved in this step typically interacting with customers?

- Will the customer want to have visibility into the information that is generated during this step?
- By getting the customer more involved with this step of the process, could we improve our competitive position in the market?

Getting Acquainted with CRM: Concepts and Terminology

If you're new to the concept of CRM, the first step is to understand some of the basic concepts and terminology that are used in all CRM applications and in particular in Dynamics CRM. These concepts are used throughout this book, so it's a good idea to carefully read this section if you are new to CRM in general and to at least scan this section if you already know the fundamentals of CRM, but Dynamics CRM is new to you.

Figure 1.2 shows the functional areas that make up a CRM system. In this chapter, we focus only on the basic terminology that is used extensively within CRM. Subsequent chapters define additional terms as needed.

FIGURE 1.2

The core components of a CRM system

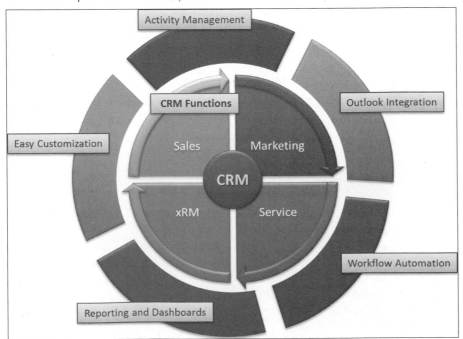

Understanding basic terminology

These basic terms are used across all functional areas of CRM. Getting comfortable with these terms can help you to work more efficiently everywhere within the CRM application.

Users

Users are individuals that have permission to log into CRM. Users can "own" various records (for example, if a user owns an activity record, then it is that user's responsibility to complete the activity). A user can be assigned to a business unit and to one or more security roles to govern which functionality he is allowed to access and what information that he is allowed to create, read, update, or delete.

Accounts and contacts

Accounts and contacts are organizations or individuals (respectively) that are involved with your organization. Note that their involvement with your organization can vary widely. For example, they may be customers, prospects, vendors, competitors, partners, distributors, or any of a number of roles related to your business.

Accounts and contacts are typically related to one another, enabling you to see all of the organizations that are involved with your organization and all of the contacts that work in those organizations. This is known as a one-to-many relationship (one account is related to many contacts). The concept of a one-to-many relationship is illustrated in Figure 1.3.

Customers

In Dynamics CRM customers can be either an account or a contact. As noted above, an account or contact may not really be a customer, but a partner, prospect, or other role. If your organization generally sells directly to consumers, then customers will usually be contacts. On the other hand if your organization typically sells to other organizations, then customers will usually be accounts.

Note

A customer is typically thought of as someone who is actively engaged in transacting with a business. However, in Dynamics CRM, a customer can be any person (contact) or organization (account) that is involved with your organization. This can include customers, prospective customers, partners, suppliers, distributors, media contacts, or any number of others. When we use the term customer in this book, we are referring to this broader definition of a customer.

Activities and history

Activities are actions that a user plans to take. If you are already using Microsoft Outlook, then you are probably familiar with activities that appear in your Inbox (e-mails), calendar (appointments), and to do list (tasks). Activities in Dynamics CRM are very similar to Outlook activities, but Dynamics CRM includes additional activity types such as phone calls, letters, faxes, and others. In fact, Dynamics CRM activities can synchronize with your Outlook activities — more on that in future chapters.

FIGURE 1.3

One account record associated with many contact records

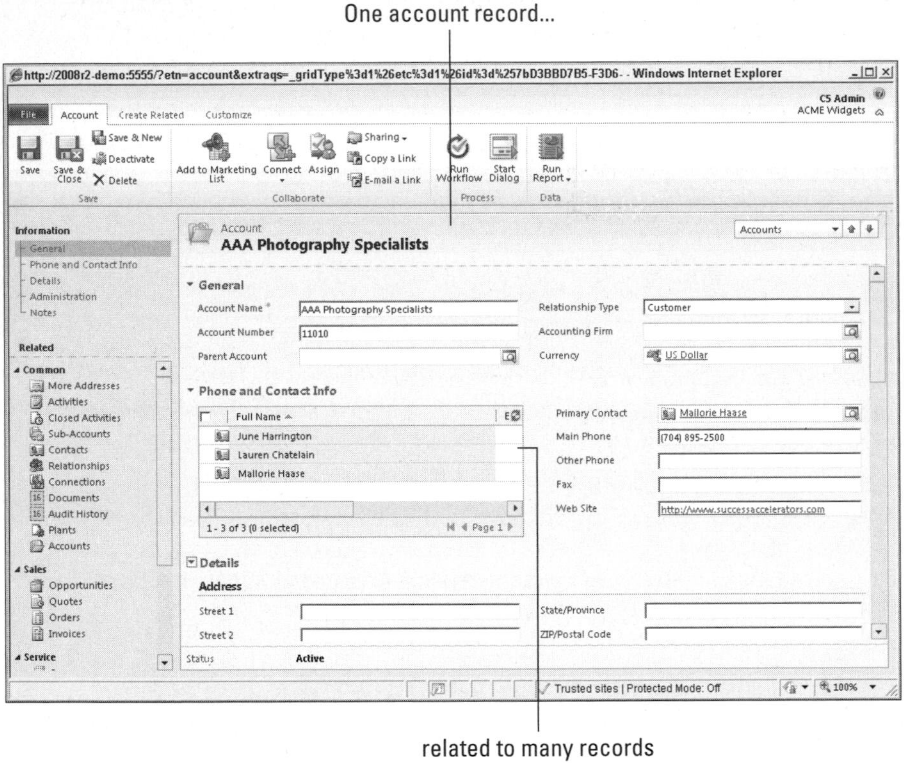

One account record...

related to many records

In Dynamics CRM, activities can be linked to other records, such as accounts and contacts. For example, you can schedule a phone call activity regarding a contact that you met at a trade show. When you open the phone call activity, you can immediately see the link to the contact so you will know the context for this activity.

Activities appear under the records that they are regarding. So, for example, if you navigate to an account, you can see all of the activities that are regarding that account. This feature gives business people the ability to see the full communication history with a customer because all of the activities for all users are visible under each account record.

Activities in Dynamics CRM typically appear in two buckets. Activities that are not yet completed appear in the list of activities. Activities that have been marked complete appear in the list of history.

Understanding sales terminology

CRM solutions provide a diverse range of sales functionality. Sales people use this functionality to ensure that important contacts don't slip through the cracks. Management leverages the sales functions in CRM to coach their sales people and manage the sales pipeline. Central to the sales functions in CRM is the concept of managing leads and opportunities.

Leads

Leads are records that you have not yet qualified as desirable prospects for your organization. For example, if someone visits your Web site and submits a "contact us" form, your organization may want to follow up and qualify them. Once qualified, a lead is converted into an account, a contact, and possibly an opportunity. Leads that are disqualified are kept in the database for reporting purposes but are otherwise hidden from standard views.

Depending on your situation, you may find that your organization makes heavy usage of leads or does not need to use leads at all. Organizations that spend a lot of time trying to filter out unqualified leads (those that they do not wish to do business with) typically find that leads are an important part of CRM. Organizations that have a captive audience of qualified leads and customers (such as a public utility) may not need to use leads at all.

Opportunities

Opportunities are potential transactions that your organization may engage in with a targeted customer. They are linked to the customer (an account or contact) to which they are related.

Organizations often struggle with understanding the difference between a lead and an opportunity. Leads are a way to track prospects that you are not yet sure if you have an interest in pursuing. Some businesses generate a large number of leads through acquiring lists, attending trade shows, and so forth. These organizations don't want to clutter up their list of qualified prospects and active customers with these unqualified leads. Leads also lend themselves to business processes designed specifically for the purpose of lead qualification and nurturing. Opportunities, on the other hand, are typically used to represent active sales deals that are being considered by the prospect and that can be reliably included in a sales forecast.

Understanding service and call center terminology

Included with most CRM solutions is functionality to support the service and/or call center. These functions are designed to improve the quality and timeliness of customer service interactions. Organizations that use these functions also experience an improvement in the quality of communication between their sales and service groups. Internal helpdesks often use this functionality to support employees as well.

Cases

Cases are service requests that have been received from clients. Other CRM systems some-times refer to these as *trouble tickets* or *issues*. In Dynamics CRM cases are very flexible and can be used for a variety of different purposes. You can think of them as mini-projects that may require multiple steps and activities to complete.

Cases are designed to ensure that customers receive a response to every request that they make. In addition, cases can be combined with other functionality built into CRM to:

- **Create service queues:** Cases can be assigned to a queue that is visible to all service representatives. The first available representative can check the queue and claim the highest priority case.
- **Auto-assign cases:** Workflow rules can be developed to automatically assign cases to specific representatives. For example, high-priority customers can be assigned to a senior service representative.
- **Escalate cases:** Managers can be alerted to cases that have not been worked within a designated period of time.

Knowledge Base

The Knowledge Base is a list of articles that can solve frequent problems that your customers experience. Think of the Knowledge Base as a dynamic library that expands and changes to meet the needs of your customers. Knowledge Base articles can be used to handle phone-based support, can be sent to customers via e-mail, and can be made available via your corporate Web site. This speeds up the process of resolving customer issues, delivers a more consistent customer experience, and enables organizations to track which articles are the most useful in resolving customer issues.

Understanding marketing terminology

A properly implemented CRM system can aid in bridging the gap that often exists between sales and marketing business units. Marketers often complain that Sales does not work their leads, use their collateral, or provide them with useful feedback on how they can improve. Similarly, sales people often complain that leads and collateral from Marketing are not useful for their sales process. Marketing functionality empowers businesses to connect the dots between marketing activities and sales results.

Campaigns

Campaigns are marketing programs executed by your organization. Dynamics CRM provides the capability to manage the information, planning tasks and campaign activities associated with all of your marketing campaigns. Campaigns also include the ability to track campaign responses (individuals who have responded to a campaign) and convert them into opportunities. By using the campaign functionality built into CRM, you can generate financial reports and dashboards to link marketing campaigns to bottom-line profits.

Terminology Review: A Day in the Life of a Customer

Walk through a day (or, more realistically, a few months) in the life of a customer so that you can put the terms into context. Doing this gives you an overview of how Dynamics CRM works and the kind of benefits that it can provide to your organization.

1. A prospective customer visits your Web site and completes the contact us form.

2. The information captured on the Web site is automatically pushed into CRM as a lead.

3. A rule setup in CRM automatically assigns the lead to a user based on their address information.

4. CRM also automatically creates an activity to remind the user to call the lead within the next 24 hours.

5. The user makes the call and finds that this individual is qualified to do business with your organization and has requested a quote, so the user converts the lead into an account, a contact and, an opportunity.

6. The user find some sales literature that may be of interest to the contact so they create an e-mail activity, attach the sales literature to it, and send it to the contact.

7. Two weeks later, the client signs the quote and places an order with you. The sales rep sets the opportunity to won.

8. Shortly after that, the customer experiences an issue with your product and calls your service department who creates a case to track the issue.

9. The service rep finds an answer to the issue in the knowledge base and creates an e-mail activity with the knowledge base article attached to it and sends it to the customer.

10. A few months later, while on your Web site, the customer opts into a list to receive special offers by e-mail. The customer is automatically added to a marketing list called "special offers" and later that month is added to an e-mail campaign advertising a special discount.

11. Any user who has permission to see this customer record in CRM can see all of the interactions that the organization has had with the customer including activities, cases, marketing lists, campaigns, opportunities, and so on. Any manager can view all the activities of the users who report to them.

Marketing lists

Marketing lists are sets of leads, accounts or contacts that are filtered by criteria specified by the user. Marketing lists are dynamic in that they allow additional records to be added as members of the list over time. So, for example, you can maintain a list of individuals subscribed to a company newsletter as a marketing list.

Marketing lists can also be associated with campaigns, can be exported for direct mail or e-mailing purposes, or can be used to create quick campaigns. Marketing lists also include a very flexible approach for adding and removing members. This capability is important for multi-wave campaigns in which you may want to remove responders in one wave from receiving contact in subsequent waves.

Sales literature

Sales literature is a library of documents that can be used to enable the sales process. In most organizations, it is the job of the marketing department to create and manage the literature that the sales group requires for customer interactions. Dynamics CRM provides a means to store sales literature electronically, manage the lifecycle of each piece of literature, and make it easy to search for literature and to make the literature available for sales to attach to outgoing e-mails.

Understanding What Makes Microsoft Dynamics CRM Unique

Many options are on the market for a CRM solution. Microsoft has made a number of decisions in the development of Dynamics CRM that have differentiated it from most other available solutions today. As a result, Dynamics CRM has enjoyed rapidly growing market share and since Version 3.0 has consistently been identified by industry analysts among the top available options for businesses of all sizes.

Using CRM with Microsoft Office

One of the biggest challenges facing CRM projects is user adoption — that is, the willingness of users to change their work habits and to become disciplined users of the CRM system. During the development of Dynamics CRM, Microsoft placed a heavy amount of emphasis on the ease of use. As one may expect, Microsoft also did a superlative job of integrating Dynamics CRM with the Microsoft Office product line including Outlook, Excel, and Word. As a result, Dynamics CRM is consistently rated as one of the top CRM solutions in terms of ease of use.

Microsoft Outlook

Microsoft Outlook has become the communications hub for business people everywhere. It is the first thing that people look at in the morning, what they monitor throughout the day, and what they check on their wireless devices when away from the office. As unified communications and social media continue to evolve, it appears that Outlook may emerge as the application that is used to unify those communication channels as well. As a result, every serious CRM solution provider puts a tremendous amount of effort into synchronizing data from their CRM application with Microsoft Outlook. Microsoft has taken this one step further and has completely integrated Microsoft Outlook with Dynamics CRM in the following three areas:

- **Synchronization:** Data created in Outlook can be tracked in Dynamics CRM and data created in Dynamics CRM can be automatically pushed to Outlook. Once data between the applications is linked, it is automatically kept in sync regardless of where changes are made. Because Outlook syncs with mobile devices, CRM data is visible (and can be updated) on these devices as well. Synchronization can be utilized with e-mail messages, tasks, activities, and contacts.

- **Integration:** Dynamics CRM is available fully integrated with Microsoft Outlook. What this means to the user is that they can fully utilize Dynamics CRM without ever having to leave the native Outlook application. Learning a new application can be an intimidating and time-consuming experience. Making Dynamics CRM available directly within Outlook reduces the learning curve. Many businesses select Dynamics CRM based on this factor alone — its team uses Outlook so heavily that this integration with Dynamics CRM is a must-have capability.

- **Offline Availability:** For users who travel and need to have access to CRM data while on the road, Microsoft has built an offline version of Dynamics CRM directly into Outlook. Using Dynamics CRM offline is very similar to using Outlook offline. Users can still access their Dynamics CRM data inside of Outlook while offline, and changes that they make are synchronized when they reconnect to their office network. Most other CRM systems that provide an offline version require users to access it by using a different application. Microsoft has made the offline experience seamless, so there is no learning curve between the offline and online versions.

Microsoft Excel

The No. 1 tool in the world for data analysis is Microsoft Excel. Dynamics CRM is designed to make it easy for users to extract their data into Excel for reporting and analysis. Moreover, Dynamics CRM allows users to save their Excel files back to CRM as reports that can be rerun with up-to-date data whenever needed.

In most CRM applications, reporting and data analysis is a complex task that requires a power user (or even IT expert) to get involved. The integration between Microsoft Excel and Dynamics CRM puts reporting and data analysis within the reach of everyday CRM users.

Microsoft Word

If you've ever handled a mail merge using Microsoft Word, you find that there is almost no learning curve using Dynamics CRM to handle mail-merge activities. The integration between Dynamics CRM and Microsoft Word means that you can set up a template and launch mail-merge project without having to go through complex data export steps.

Mail-merge templates can be made easily available to all Dynamics CRM users. So one individual can set up them, and the whole team can use them. Mail-merge templates can also be used in marketing campaigns to create bulk correspondence out of Dynamics CRM.

Users of many CRM systems complain that they spend a great deal of time rekeying information that has already been keyed into CRM into letters, quotes, proposals, or other correspondence. Integration with Microsoft Word is one way that Dynamics CRM reduces this burden.

Other Microsoft product integration

Dynamics CRM integrates with a broad range of other products from Microsoft to make it an even more flexible and easy-to use-solution. The tools listed below form a framework to extend Dynamics CRM:

- **SharePoint:** SharePoint is a Web portal development, collaboration, document management, and business intelligence framework developed by Microsoft. Microsoft Dynamics CRM 2011 includes the ability to integrate CRM with SharePoint document libraries. Using this functionality, businesses can easily create document management functionality for customers, opportunities, proposals or a variety of other CRM processes — and these document libraries can be shared with customers or partners through the SharePoint Web site. Custom integration to SharePoint can also be developed to further enhance CRM functionality for searching, collaborating, social media, and providing corporate business intelligence dashboards. Microsoft has made the entry level version of SharePoint (called SharePoint Foundation 2010) freely available.

- **SQL Server:** Microsoft SQL Server is the database that holds all of the information for Dynamics CRM. Built into SQL Server is a powerful reporting engine called SQL Server Reporting Services (SSRS), and a powerful report design tool called Business Intelligence Design Studio (BIDS). These tools give organizations using Dynamics CRM the ability to develop an unlimited range of reports and dashboards that can enhance the usefulness of the application. SQL Server is required in order to install Dynamics CRM on-premise and is included with Dynamics CRM Online. So you have access to the SQL Server reporting tools at no additional cost as a part of your investment in Dynamics CRM.

- **Visual Studio:** Dynamics CRM was built using Visual Studio .NET programming languages, and Microsoft has created an interface that allows it to be extended using .NET code. What this means is that, if there is a specific function not available in the application, it can be created by writing .NET code that is linked to the Dynamics CRM application. This also means that an active community of developers has been releasing add-ons that can provide more extensions to the Dynamics CRM environment. Although .NET coding is not for everyone, it delivers the ability to create any breadth or depth of customization that an organization may need. Entry level versions of Visual Studio are available for download at no cost from the Microsoft Web site.

Customizing Dynamics CRM

It is the goal of every business to differentiate itself from competitors. In the pursuit of differentiation, organizations have found that customer-facing processes are one of the most visible areas to focus on. Therefore, CRM solutions must provide a flexible framework that can be changed to work the way the business does — rather than forcing the business to change the way that it works to fit with a one-size-fits-all CRM process.

Dynamics CRM delivers a broad range of tools that enable organizations to customize features. Virtually every portion of the application can be customized. Forms can be changed to capture unique data. Entirely new entities (also known as tables or lists) can be created to capture other business information. Workflows can be triggered to ensure that users are following consistent practices across the organization. Security roles can ensure that users can see only the data that they have permission to view. And this is just a sample of the customization toolkit included with Dynamics CRM.

In fact, Microsoft CRM is so flexible that many organizations are using it as a framework for creating entirely new applications. This topic is covered in more detail in the XRM section.

Caution

Having so much flexibility comes with some risk. Some organizations have added so much new functionality that they make it more difficult for users to adopt the application. When users are overwhelmed by many menu options or fields on a page, they have no idea where to start. To mitigate this risk, it is important for organizations to develop an initial plan, focus on simplifying the application initially, and have a strong governance process to make sure the application does not quickly devolve into a confusing set of fields and functions.

One interesting area of flexibility in Dynamics CRM is the ability to seamlessly handle both business and consumer relationships. Most CRM solutions were created for either business relationships (account management) or consumer relationships (contact management). However, Dynamics CRM does an equally good job of handling either type of relationship. Moreover, Dynamics CRM can handle both types of relationships at the same time.

Much of this book is dedicated to familiarizing you with the tools that deliver this flexibility to administrators of Dynamics CRM. As you reference other chapters in this book, you will become familiar with the many options open to you to make CRM work the way your organization works.

Supporting Dynamics CRM

Dynamics CRM delivers a framework that is easy to support. This is important for organizations because it lowers the cost of the IT personnel required to support the application and reduces the amount of time required to configure changes to the system.

Dynamics CRM administration

Although other CRM solutions are capable of being customized, most of them require significant technical knowledge in order to make even simple changes. When using Dynamics CRM, most of the configuration changes that any organization will need to make are built right into the user interface. This includes a drag-and-drop form editor, visual workflow designer, interactive query builder, and a range of other tools.

Dynamics CRM server management

Organizations that are already supporting other servers using Microsoft products (such as Windows Server, Exchange, SQL Server, or SharePoint) will find that Dynamics CRM fits in well with their corporate architecture. Microsoft CRM leverages components of the Microsoft networking architecture (such as Active Directory) and uses standard SQL Server databases to handle data. Therefore, routine server maintenance for Dynamics CRM can be easily folded into existing IT maintenance procedures for your network administrators.

For organizations that are not supporting servers, Microsoft offers other hosting options (described in the section "User choice") that eliminate the need for server management entirely.

Scaling CRM to different organizations

Scalability is the ability for an application to support the ever-growing number of records and increasingly complex workflows that are the result of an expanding organization. Dynamics CRM has been used in organizations ranging from just a few users and a small amount of data, up to large organizations with many thousands of users, millions of records, and complex workflow processes. Implementations of Dynamics CRM can be found from small family businesses to many of the Fortune 500.

In addition to providing scalability, Dynamics CRM provides full functionality to businesses of all sizes. Because Dynamics CRM is sold as a single package (rather than a range of versions or modules), a small business has access to the same level of functionality that a large enterprise does.

Choosing how to use CRM

Different organizations have different models for how they purchase software. Different users have different preferences for how they access their software. Microsoft has focused on giving businesses and users the ability to choose the right arrangement for their needs.

User choice

Users can choose the way that they access Dynamics CRM and update their data. On the desktop, Dynamics CRM can be accessed from within Outlook, via Internet Explorer, or both. Users can also access Dynamics CRM via their mobile device by using Mobile Express (included with Dynamics CRM). Because Dynamics CRM integrates with Outlook and Outlook integrates with most mobile devices, users can also access much of their data via their standard mobile device.

Hosting choice

Dynamics CRM is available through a variety of hosting options:

- **Microsoft hosted:** Dynamics CRM can be hosted by Microsoft (this offering is called Microsoft Dynamics CRM Online and is also often referred to as "cloud hosted" or "software as a service"). For more on cloud computing, see the section "Cloud Computing and CRM" later in this chapter.

- **On-premise hosted:** Dynamics CRM can be hosted on-premise at the location of the organization using it. For organizations that maintain their own computer servers, this option can offer a cost savings, more diverse customization options, and more control over the IT environment.

- **Partner hosted:** Dynamics CRM can be hosted by a third-party Microsoft partner. This option provides more customization options than the CRM Online option but without requiring the cost of internal IT support required for the on-premise option.

Leveraging the Microsoft connection

Because Dynamics CRM is backed by Microsoft, organizations can expect ongoing improvements and strong product support.

Since soon after the release of Microsoft Dynamics CRM 4, Microsoft established a cycle of releasing Update Rollups to the software every two months. These Update Rollups included both bug fixes as well as new functionality. Microsoft also released an increasingly robust set of support tools through the CRM software development kit (SDK). Expect to see the rhythm of these releases continue with Microsoft Dynamics CRM 2011.

In addition to the Update Rollups, Microsoft has also been releasing an ongoing set of Solution Accelerators. Solution Accelerators are open-source projects that can be freely downloaded from `http://crmaccelerators.codeplex.com`. Solution Accelerators provide a framework for functionality that can be customized and expanded to meet the specific needs of businesses. A few of the Solution Accelerators that Microsoft has released include Social Networking Accelerator, Customer Portal Accelerator, Partner Relationship Management Accelerator, and Analytics Accelerator.

Microsoft has chosen to develop a community of partners to aid in implementing and extending their software solutions. There are a large number of specialized and local Dynamics CRM implementation partners around the globe. Independent software vendors have developed an ever-growing set of add-on tools that extend the functionality of Dynamics CRM. With the new solution management framework introduced in Microsoft Dynamics CRM 2011, expect to see even more expansion in the number of third-party add-ons available for Dynamics CRM.

XRM: Extending CRM

Nothing in a business changes faster than customers. As a result, CRM software needs to be adaptable to change. To keep up with user demands Microsoft has made Dynamics CRM more flexible with each subsequent release of the software. It is now so flexible that organizations have started to develop a variety of applications that go far beyond the scope of traditional CRM projects.

Note

This concept of developing entirely new applications built on the Dynamics CRM framework has frequently been called extended relationship management (or XRM). It is also being called platform development and is even being rolled into the term cloud computing or cloud platform development in some cases. Throughout this book, we refer to this simply as XRM.

Figure 1.4 illustrates Microsoft's shift in their marketing strategy for CRM. It appears that they are increasingly positioning it as the XRM development framework with the tagline "xRM: One Platform. Many Applications. Infinite Possibilities." For those of you who dive into writing code to extend Dynamics CRM, you will note that the coding framework is now referred to as the XRM framework or the XRM model.

FIGURE 1.4

Microsoft's XRM positioning

Dozens of applications have emerged built on the Dynamics CRM foundation. The list below provides a sense of the variety of applications that can be developed but is by no means comprehensive:

- **Expense Management:** To capture employee expense reports, auto-submit reports to managers for approval and route to accounting for reimbursement.

- **Asset Tracking:** To track assets (such as equipment) from the production line, to shipping, to acceptance by the customer, to service history and resale to subsequent owners.

- **Human Resources and Recruiting:** To manage employee and applicant information, administer paid time off and other benefits, store policy documents, track personnel complaints, and ensure legal compliance.

- **R&D:** To create R&D projects, track granular project findings, submit results to project managers for review and approval, and report findings in Word documents for presentation.

- **Project Management:** To auto-create projects after winning an opportunity, manage alerts and project steps, and track time spent on each project activity.

- **Appraisal and Environmental Risk Assessment:** For bankers to request appraisals via Web portals, manage project acceptance and alerts for deliverable dates, and track historical projects for future usage.

Understanding why Dynamics CRM is a good choice for development

Using a Dynamics CRM as a framework can reduce the need for technical expertise, provide faster response to changing customer demands, shorten the time required to develop new applications, lower maintenance costs, and produce applications that are more in alignment with business goals. Note that Dynamics CRM is not (and may never be) a complete replacement for custom application development — but it is replacing much of what used to require custom application development.

Development foundation

Many development projects require rebuilding the same elements such as login routines, security roles, form design standards, and so on. The Dynamics CRM platform already includes most of the "plumbing" that has to go into developing any new application.

Additionally, many of the other elements built into Dynamics CRM are highly desirable for most business applications. Items such as Outlook integration, contact management, task tracking, and appointment setting are needed in a large number of business applications. Each of these areas of functionality can require a significant amount of time to re-create if they were to be built from scratch.

Some functionality in Dynamics CRM lends itself to be repurposed for other business applications. For example: cases can be used to track legal cases, leads can be used to track candidate inquiries, and campaigns can be used to track events.

Customer centricity

To remain competitive, businesses have had to become increasingly "customer-centric." This has been a challenge because most business systems tend to be "transaction-centric." Dynamics CRM has been designed to keep the customer at the center of every piece of information that is tracked. Creating new applications that link information to customer records is relatively straightforward in Dynamics CRM.

Business agility

The pace of business continues to increase. Using Dynamics CRM as a development framework significantly shortens the amount of time that it takes to go from concept to functioning application. It also enables businesses to learn faster and adapt their applications to a changing marketplace more quickly.

Although it is a subtle advantage, business agility may be the most important reason to consider Dynamics CRM as a development framework. Consider a business that can only roll out one update to an application in a given year versus a company that can move faster and roll out three updates to the same application in a year. The business that can roll out three updates is moving three times faster than their competitor. In three years, they will have made nine updates to their application while their competitor will have made only three. The more agile business will outmaneuver their competitor on an increasingly frequent basis, eventually stealing most of their market share.

Empower developers to develop

In most businesses the demand for application development exceeds the supply of developers. Dynamics CRM delivers two benefits to mitigate this situation:

- Because Dynamics CRM is so easy to customize, much of the development effort does not require a developer at all. By having a "power user" or Business Analyst handle much of the customization, the work can be done by someone who has a deep understanding of the project requirements but little development skill. This delivers a completed solution, faster.

- Because developers don't have to work on projects that can be handled by others, they can spend more time focusing on a smaller number of development projects requiring their specific expertise. Developers are able to focus on the highest and best use of their time.

The Microsoft ecosystem

Microsoft products are supported by millions of developers and product experts around the world. Organizations that are using Dynamics CRM can tap into the global community of talent that is available to support their projects.

Dynamics CRM, SharePoint, SQL Server, and .NET as a development framework

The Dynamics CRM platform includes a diverse set of tools. When combined with other tools available from Microsoft, as illustrated in Figure 1.5, it is an even more powerful solution for developing custom applications. Microsoft recognizes this and has begun to position Dynamics CRM as part of a larger application development framework that includes SharePoint, Visual Studio .NET, and SQL Server. Each of these tools is available either as a part of Dynamics CRM, as entry level versions that are freely distributed by Microsoft, or as paid versions with enhanced functionality.

SharePoint and Dynamics CRM

SharePoint is another product from Microsoft that delivers a framework that can be customized to handle many different needs. SharePoint excels at managing unstructured data and business processes such as document management, collaboration (including social networking), and Web portals. Dynamics CRM excels at managing highly structured data and business processes. So the two applications are quite complimentary to one another.

SharePoint and CRM can be integrated in a variety of ways to provide a richer user experience. By integrating these two applications, a business will have a framework that will typically meet 90 percent or more of their application development needs without having to write code. Table 1.1 illustrates the complementary nature of Dynamics CRM and SharePoint as development tools.

FIGURE 1.5

The Microsoft development "stack"

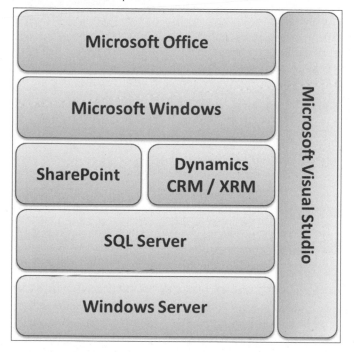

TABLE 1.1

Dynamics CRM and SharePoint: Complementary Development Tools

SharePoint	Unstructured & Semi-Structured Data	Social Engagement & Collaboration	Information Evolution & Storage	Information Rules	Enterprise Search	Across Teams & Domains
Dynamics CRM (XRM)	Structured Relational Data	Interactions, Activities, & Tasks	Information Generation & Analytics	Formalized Processes	Data Query & Filter	Within Teams & Domains

SQL Server and Visual Studio

As strong as the Dynamics CRM and SharePoint frameworks are, they won't be able meet every potential need that a business experiences. For those cases, Microsoft has integrated these tools with their other development tools including Visual Studio .NET and SQL Server. SQL Server provides a set of tools for reporting, data visualization, and data integration. Visual Studio .NET provides a comprehensive development environment to develop a limitless set of extensions to SharePoint and Dynamics CRM.

Cloud computing with Dynamics CRM

Applications available over the Internet are now being defined as cloud applications. You are probably already using cloud applications for things like personal e-mail (Gmail and Hotmail), file sharing (SkyDrive), or even accounting (QuickBooks online). Two of the highest demand cloud applications are both from Microsoft — Windows Update and Xbox Live. Businesses can choose to have other businesses host their applications in the cloud (commonly referred to as the *public cloud*) or they can choose to host them in their own data center (commonly called the *private cloud*).

Experts are predicting that cloud computing (in particular the public cloud) will grow at an accelerated rate in the coming years. This is because businesses are realizing that cloud computing can bring them many benefits, including:

- **Cost management:** Businesses that host their own applications must manage the costs of the personnel and hardware required to maintain their applications, including hardware support, backups, and other administrative maintenance. They must also manage the risk of bringing in outside experts if their applications go down and their internal teams are not able to bring them back online. These costs are even higher for desktop applications. Cloud computing gives businesses a smooth and predictable monthly payment structure for their applications, something that CFOs like to see.

- **Focus on core business value:** Although most businesses need IT to function, they do not consider IT to be the value that they deliver to their customers. In fact, most businesses find that managing IT functions can be a time-consuming distraction. Cloud computing enables businesses to eliminate computer hardware and IT personnel that do not contribute to the core mission of the business.

- **Maintaining software:** Computer applications that are maintained in the cloud can be updated more frequently and cost effectively. When a new desktop application is introduced, it can be quite time consuming for a business to roll out the update to all users. Similarly, upgrading server-based applications can be complex, time-consuming, and expensive. Cloud applications are updated by their manufacturers, and the upgrades are built into the monthly pricing agreements without adding any incremental cost. Users log in one morning and a new version of the software is available.

- **Ease of delivering add-ons:** Applications that are hosted in the cloud are easier to extend than applications hosted internally. Every business has a unique IT architecture and security protocols. Add-on applications installed on business servers need to be tailored to the unique situation of each individual business. Because cloud applications use a consistent architecture across all users, it is less costly to develop add-on applications for these applications, and it is faster to deploy them into a business.

Think of cloud computing as electricity. Businesses could choose to purchase their own generators to provide a source of power for their operations. However, it is much more practical for businesses to purchase their electricity from other providers. This keeps their costs predictable, enables them to focus on their core business, removes the distraction of having to maintain their electrical equipment, and gives them a foundation where they can literally just plug in new add-ons. Outsourcing application hosting to the cloud brings similar benefits to businesses as outsourcing electricity generation does.

From the very beginning, Dynamics CRM has been an Internet application that organizations could host in their own data centers. Microsoft began to offer hosted Dynamics CRM under the name "CRM Online" beginning with Microsoft Dynamics CRM 4 Online, but it included some functional limitations. With Microsoft Dynamics CRM 2011 Online, organizations have access to the full range of CRM functionality in the cloud. Microsoft has also introduced a range of other hosted offerings including SharePoint, Exchange, and Azure (hosted Microsoft .NET applications).

Developing business applications with the Dynamics CRM framework

Just because it is easy to develop custom applications in Dynamics CRM does not mean that you should jump right in and start developing an application right away. In fact, starting to develop an application without a road map can lead to a lot of frustration.

There are a number of standardized approaches for developing applications. If your organization already uses a specific approach, then you should review it and decide how it should be adapted to work with Dynamics CRM. Figure 1.6 represents a simple "Four P" process you can use if this is your first development project.

Cross-Reference
See Chapter 27 for example application development walk-through scenarios to get familiar with developing applications in Dynamics CRM.

FIGURE 1.6

A simple process for developing business applications in CRM

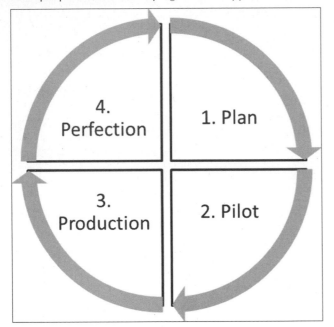

Plan

Every development project should begin with a plan. This step helps you to define exactly where you want to be at the conclusion of your project. An application plan can be as short as a few pages or as long as a few hundred pages. Regardless of the length, there are some consistent items that should be included in your plan:

- **Goals.** Having a written overview of what your application should accomplish is always helpful. Start by writing this section first and then come back and refine it after you are done with the rest of the plan.

- **Inputs.** Define the information that will be required as inputs in order to achieve your targeted goal.

- **Process and Stages.** Use flowcharting tools to diagram exactly how your business will use this application to get work done. In addition, define the different stages of the process. Almost every record in a database goes through various stages in its lifetime (for example, a quote may be in a draft, active, approved, and won/lost stage during its lifetime). Define the stages that you expect your records to go through. For each stage, define the process steps and the data that must be gathered.

- **Outputs.** Capture the outputs of your process. What information or results will be delivered as a final result of the process, and to whom? If reports will be required, then use Excel to develop a draft of what they will look like.

- **Data.** Review the plan to determine exactly what data will be required for your application and how it should be organized. Document the data that will be needed in your plan.

On the Web Site

We have included a sample planning document in the Planning folder. Use this as a starting point to create your own version of this tool.

Caution

When planning a Dynamics CRM project, your goal should be to maximize what you develop using the user interface and minimize what you have to write custom code for. This results in an application that is less costly to maintain. Business users who are communicating requirements will often insist that the way they do things now must be emulated exactly in Dynamics CRM — but there are often better ways to accomplish the same goals by using functionality natively available in CRM. For this reason, it is a good idea to work with an individual who has deep insight into the capabilities of CRM and the leadership to negotiate with business users on the best possible way to implement their requirements.

Pilot

After you get started developing your custom application, you should plan to review it with users prior to making it available in production. Dynamics CRM includes a number of tools that enable you to develop customizations prior to publishing them for all users to access. For larger organizations, you can also set up complete development and test environments for your applications.

During the pilot phase, you should plan meetings with a group of users to review the work you have done and solicit their feedback prior to going live. Repeat this process as many times as it takes to get an application that you and the users are comfortable will deliver on the goals you set for the project. Remember that your goal is not perfection but a first step that will deliver value to your business — fine-tuning comes later.

Cross-Reference

See Chapter 16 for information on setting up Dynamics CRM with solutions and publishers to manage your custom solution. See Chapter 17 for information on testing your customizations prior to publishing them for all users.

Production

After you have finished gathering feedback and adjusting your application, you are ready to go live and put it into production. Depending on what kind of customizations you have made, this may be as easy as clicking a button to publish your application. More complex applications may involve custom entities, reports, dashboards, workflows, and .NET applications. Remember to build time into this step of the process to train your new users on the application.

A Failed XRM Application

We were asked to evaluate a custom application developed in CRM that had started out working well, but users had slowly stopped using the application. We reviewed the application with the client and noticed that there were dozens of fields on the custom form that they had developed. When asking about the fields, we were told that various different users had asked for the fields over a period of time. We then interviewed some of the users and found that many of the fields were requested only by a single user, and in some cases we could not find any users who remembered what some fields were used for.

The ultimate problem was that the form was so intimidating and time consuming to fill out that users simply stopped using the application. In the spirit of providing good service, the implementation team had been highly responsive to user requests. Unfortunately, this led to the ultimate demise of the application.

This situation can be avoided by establishing governance procedures to ensure that all user requests are reviewed, accepted or rejected, and prioritized prior to implementation. This needs to be balanced with clear communication procedures to make sure that users do not feel that their requests are vanishing into a black hole.

Perfection

Perfection is a goal that you should continuously pursue but will never attain with an application. The good news is that applications developed with Dynamics CRM are easy to fine-tune. Expect to spend some intensive time soliciting feedback from users and implementing their requests in the first few weeks after you launch into production. Over time, the requests for changes will subside, but don't be surprised if your users continue to suggest other ways to improve the application even years after you have put it into production.

Caution

You may be tempted to add every request made by users into your application. Although this level of responsiveness may feel helpful, it can also lead to over complicating your applications. See the "A Failed XRM Application" sidebar for a real-life example of a custom application that did not work out.

Planning a Successful CRM Project

The experts tell us that somewhere between 33 percent and 70 percent of customer relationship management projects fail regardless of which CRM technology a business selects. The high rate of failure is a sobering reality for businesses that are considering making a significant investment into a CRM project for their organization. The success or failure of a CRM project is most often determined in the earliest stages of the project — selecting a team and developing a plan. Frequently organizational leaders have lofty expectations for CRM, but jump in with little or no planning while delegating responsibility to individuals who have little knowledge of how the sales, service, and marketing groups work.

Think of your goals for CRM as a house. Think of Dynamics CRM as a toolbox and the raw materials for building a house. When you are building a house, you need more than just tools and raw materials (no matter how good your tools might be). You need a seasoned architect to listen to your expectations and draw up a plan that you agree to prior to starting work. You need skilled masons, electricians, carpenters, and plumbers to build the house. If it's a large project, you might need a general contractor to manage the team.

CRM is no different. Every organization should work with someone who has expertise in CRM strategies to aid them with drawing up a plan. And every organization should do a diligent job of selecting a team that represents all of the expertise required to deliver a solid result. Few people would risk building a new home on their own or even putting it into the hands of a trusted general handyman — you shouldn't make the same mistake with your CRM project.

Implementing CRM: A sample methodology

In this section, we provide a simple five-step methodology you can use to guide your CRM project. There are many good project methodologies being used today, and, depending on who you select to lead your team, you may determine to use a different methodology. Microsoft has developed an implementation methodology known as Sure Step that many Microsoft partners use in their CRM implementations. In any event, you should be certain to use a methodology that takes into account the structure and subtleties of a CRM project. A full discussion on the intricacies of project management is beyond the scope of this book, but this section will give you a gentle push in the right direction.

Cross-Reference

Though similar, there are subtle differences between a CRM project and an XRM project. See the section in this chapter titled "Developing business applications with the Dynamics CRM framework" for a general overview of extending CRM with custom applications. In some cases you may have a CRM project that includes some elements of XRM. In those cases, you should be sure to blend these approaches, using the best approach at each step of the project.

1: Select the team

One of the first steps of the project should be to select the right team. Your team should be structured to include a Project Sponsor, Project Manager (possibly from both your business and from any outside partner you are working with), as well as the project participants, outlined below.

- **Business Users:** A sampling of the individuals who will be using the CRM solution to get their job done once it is in production. Users from each line of business involved with the project (typically sales, service, and marketing) should be included in the project team. Selected individuals should be those who have deep insight into how the business engages with customers in these processes.

- **Managers:** A sampling of individuals who manage the business users (above). Selected individuals should be those who are motivated to better manage the business through reports and dashboards available in CRM, and in empowering their teams with tools that provide greater efficiency and visibility into customer information.

Lessons from Failed CRM Projects _____

When businesses begin considering a CRM project for the first time, the first decision that they typically try to make is the software. Factors that they evaluate include:

- Does it have the functions they want?
- How much does it cost?
- How easy is it to use?

Much farther down the list of priorities is their decision about the partner that they will work with to review their processes and get the software implemented in their organization. Businesses that have an unsuccessful initial CRM project and come back to restart their project take a different approach. While questions about the software are still important, their top priorities are questions about their partner:

- What is their performance track record?
- What kind of support can they count on from them?

Learn a lesson from the second timers. The software is important, but a tool doesn't get the job done unless it is in the hands of a skilled craftsman. Find the right partner to make your project a success.

- **Information Technology:** Individuals from the IT department who will be responsible for maintaining the CRM system. Selected individuals should be those who understand the technology architecture and security standards for the organization. If your CRM solution will be integrated with other IT systems, then individuals who understand the inner workings of these other systems should also be included on the team.

- **Voice of Customer:** Remember to keep the "C" in CRM. Make sure that the voice of the customer is heard as a part of your project. Although your goals may be to improve sales, service, or marketing, none of those can be accomplished without the cooperation of your customers. You can get the customer's voice involved in your project by conducting won/lost sales interviews, measuring customer satisfaction, providing marketing performance metrics, and conducting primary research with existing customers.

- **CRM Subject Matter Experts:** Make sure that your team includes individuals who have both a strategic and technical understanding of CRM. These should be individuals who will understand the best practices in CRM processes and the technical aspects of Dynamics CRM.

2: Develop a plan

Take the time to develop your blueprint for how CRM will work in your organization. The time you spend on this step will vary widely depending upon the size of your organization and the complexity of your project. Small businesses with simple needs may require only a half-day session. Large enterprises with complex processes may spend a number of months developing their plan.

Planning workshops

To develop a solid plan, you need to meet with your project team. You can do this as a single meeting with the entire team, or as a series of meetings with different members participating in different meetings. Regardless of how your meetings are structured, we have outlined some goals and best practices that you should follow below (note that they are in the preferred sequence, but this is not a hard and fast rule).

1. **Start with Objectives:** In every project, it is always a best practice to know where you want to go before you start mapping out how to get there. Executive input is important to ensure business leader's vision for CRM is captured. Remember that the more measurable you can make your objectives, the better your chances will be of meeting them.

2. **Map Current Processes:** The workshops should include ample time to fully document your current processes. This is where you may want to break the meeting up into separate groups to cover different processes. You can use some of the questions posed in the "Don't Think You Need a Plan?" sidebar to help you with these meetings. Have whiteboards handy so participants can visually map out their processes. Users should be very involved in these workshops — management is often disconnected with the processes that are being used on the front lines and some of the best ideas come from the individuals who work directly with customers.

3. **Review a Proof-of-Concept Demo:** We have found that it is very difficult for participants to envision how their process can be improved with Dynamics CRM until they've gotten a close look at exactly how it works. After you have mapped current processes, a demo can be provided that is tailored to show some concepts of how your business processes can work inside of CRM. This gives the group a good framework to begin to brainstorm on the next item for your workshops.

4. **Envision Improved Processes:** Most businesses implement a CRM solution with a vision of "paving the cow paths" (automating the same processes they have always used). Dynamics CRM can certainly help you automate existing processes. Perhaps more importantly, however, it also delivers the capability to improve processes that may boost customer satisfaction, revenues, or business planning. Take the time to discuss ideas for improvement with the team.

5. **Review Current Data:** You will also need to evaluate the data that will be associated with CRM. Data that is in other systems that you will need to migrate in to CRM should be reviewed in detail, with mappings of exactly where the data will be moved and which records will be retained. Most businesses also want CRM to share data with their accounting system and sometimes with other systems (such as their Web site) — this is a process called systems integration. This can be a tedious step that will be tempting to gloss over, but incomplete planning here is a key source of cost overruns and missed expectations.

Don't Think You Need a Plan?

Many business leaders say that their process is simple, and a formalized planning workshop is not necessary for their CRM project. Here is a simple test to help you understand the importance of scheduling ample time for planning. Put three people who will be involved with the CRM project into a room together. Ask them to agree upon answers to the following five groups of questions. See the variety of answers you get and the amount of discussion required. These are a small subset of the questions you should cover in your planning.

Sales Questions

- List the stages of the sales process.
- For each stage define tasks that must be completed, data that must be gathered, who owns the step, and performance metrics for tracking results.
- What is the organization's definition for a customer, a prospect, an opportunity, and a lost customer?

Service Questions

- What types of service inquiries do we receive?
- Do you need to capture every inquiry in CRM, or just some? How will service reps know which ones to track?
- Who handles which inquiries under which circumstances? What do we do if an issue is not resolved quickly enough?

Marketing Questions

- What tools (collateral, etc.) does the marketing department provide to sales?
- How do these tools relate to the various stages of the sales process?
- What is the role of marketing in lead generation, and when should leads get handed off to sales?

Data Visualization Questions

- What decisions does management want to make by pulling reports out of CRM? Include specific details about the content of reports. Does management understand the implications of asking users to key in the data required to produce the reports that they wish to see?
- Under what circumstances should users receive alerts via e-mail (such as when a lead has not been worked for a certain amount of time)? Does the group understand how many of these alerts may be generated and how this may impact the productivity of users?
- What reports are important for users to see in order to know that they are meeting expectations and to ensure that no opportunities or issues are slipping through the cracks?

Technology Questions

- What permissions should users have to create, read, update, or delete data in CRM?
- Which data should be mapped into CRM? Will we drop some records? Will some records be categorized as leads and some as contacts? If so, what will the rules be to determine what is dropped and how the remaining records are categorized?
- What is our plan for identifying and managing duplicate records?
- How will CRM interact with our Web site to make it easier to capture leads, manage service inquiries, or share prospect information with our partners?

The project blueprint

After your workshops are complete, the findings should be documented in a blueprint for the project. Your blueprint should contain a long-term framework that may be somewhat high level and a short-term plan that should be highly detailed. The more detail you can place into your blueprint, the more swiftly your team will be able to move through the implementation stage of the project. Make liberal usage of flowcharting tools to visually document your current processes and your proposed future processes. We have found that Six Sigma process mapping tools can be quite useful for the blueprint document. When the blueprint is done, it should be validated by reviewing it with your project team, prior to moving into the next phase of the project.

3: Implement

Now that a clear plan has been defined, you are ready to begin implementing CRM. The remainder of this book defines many aspects of implementing Dynamics CRM, so we won't go into a great amount of detail about that here. There are, however, a few pointers you should keep in mind as you work on implementation:

- Go through implementation in the right sequence. All CRM solutions should be implemented in a specific sequence. This book has been sequenced to walk you through the Dynamics CRM implementation in the appropriate order.
- Set your sights on making Dynamics CRM work the way you do. In the old days of CRM, businesses would buy software and then have to figure out how to change their business to work the way the software forced them to work. Microsoft has made Dynamics CRM flexible so you can configure it to work the way your business does. This reduces learning curves and can help you to differentiate your business.
- On the other hand, you should also understand the functionality that is built into CRM. Some businesses expend a tremendous amount of effort trying to configure CRM to work exactly the way that their antiquated processes work. In many cases, however, CRM has built-in functionality that businesses can leverage that is less time consuming and costly to implement and can modernize their processes at the same time.

4: Validate

No matter how good the team was that wrote the plan, there will always be items that were missed which should be addressed before going live. This can be as simple as sitting down with a set of users and walking through the application and getting their feedback each step of the way.

Keep in mind that Steps 3 and 4 may be iterative. Validate and gather feedback, do more implementation work, and validate again — until users are satisfied that the application is ready for general usage. If you are in a large organization, you may want to take this a step further by having a pilot group work with Dynamics CRM to iron out some of the wrinkles prior to a general rollout.

Skipping the validation step may be tempting; however, the risks associated with doing so are significant. The organization takes the time to train users and get them started using CRM. Then, when they find it does not meet their needs, they may discontinue using it. By the time the issues are resolved they will have forgotten much of their training and will need to be retrained. After a few iterations of this, the CRM project suffers from a tarnished reputation, and it can become very difficult to get users to try to change their work habits and attempt using CRM again.

5: Manage Change

The final step of the project is to manage the change associated with a new customer relationship management system. This step includes going live, training users, monitoring usage, and making ongoing improvements to the system. We have called this step "manage change" because most organizations treat this step as a one-time event rather than an ongoing process. It will take time and effort to get users fully trained and comfortable with CRM and to fine-tune it to meet your changing needs. Go into this step with an expectation that you will need to spend plenty of time initially handling training, support, and improvements. Stay in this step with the understanding that nothing changes faster than your customers, and you will be called upon to make the CRM system change with them.

Avoiding common mistakes

Many mistakes commonly made when implementing a CRM system have already been outlined earlier in this chapter, so we won't repeat them here. There are, however, a few principles that you can add to the list above that will help you on your way to a successful project with Dynamics CRM (or any CRM solution, for that matter).

- **Plan your work and work your plan.** We've stressed how important planning is in your CRM project. But it bears repeating. Getting the team to participate in developing a good plan, in writing, is essential. Carve out the time to make this happen. Getting some of your most senior people and many of your customer-facing people together in a room for a number of days may appear to be a costly investment. The budget, time, and training involved with a failed CRM project, however, is much higher.

- **Start simple.** You don't have to execute your vision for CRM all at once. In fact, it can be a benefit to start with only a very small piece of your CRM project. Most first phase projects that we work on tend to focus more on hiding much of the default functionality built into CRM than on creating new functionality. This way, your new users won't be overwhelmed by a large number of options and can focus on doing just a few things very well. Over time additional functionality can be rolled out.

- **Stay simple.** Although you want to continually improve your Dynamics CRM system and adapt it to changing conditions, you should also balance this with a goal of keeping it simple and efficient to use. Adding every field that each user requests to a form may add little incremental value but may make it much more complicated and time consuming to use.

- **Get the process right. Get the technology right.** We are frequently asked to perform "CPR for CRM" for organizations that have had a failed CRM project. The reason for failure almost always comes down to an incomplete understanding of their business processes, or an incomplete understanding of the specific CRM technology (regardless of which CRM system the client is using). Set yourself up for success by making sure you have a team that understands your CRM goals at a strategic level and that has in-depth knowledge of Dynamics CRM.

- **Differentiate.** Dynamics CRM gives you an opportunity to deliver an experience to your customers that differentiates you from your competitors. Take the time to configure it to deliver something unique and valuable to your customers that they're not going to find anywhere else. As you continue to make improvements, focus on your customers and how you can deliver something to them that they can't find anywhere else.

Summary

This chapter covered the fundamentals of customer relationship management (CRM) including some new terms and concepts that are important to understand. At the heart of CRM are customers. CRM systems are designed to put customers at the center of your business. They enable you to capture customer information, share it across the organization, more effectively engage in selling and servicing customers, and track the results of customer interactions.

Dynamics CRM is highly customizable, so much so that organizations have used it as a framework to develop entirely new applications that don't resemble basic CRM (including Human Resources management, for example). The practice of using CRM to create whole new applications is called extended relationship management (XRM). Businesses that have developed XRM applications have experienced lower costs and faster development cycles and are able to center more of their business on the customer than their competitors.

Success with a CRM project is not guaranteed. It is important that you develop a good plan, select the right team, and follow good project management practices in order to be successful.

Taking a Tour of Dynamics CRM

Microsoft Dynamics CRM has come a long way since Microsoft's initial foray into the customer relationship management market in 2003. Driven by a competitive marketplace and the rapid evolution of cloud-based offerings, Microsoft has delivered a significantly enhanced feature set with industry-leading sales, marketing, and customer service functionality, as well as a compelling development platform.

In this chapter, we explore the new features and functionality in Microsoft Dynamics CRM 2011, and the different ways you can deploy and access Dynamics CRM. Along the way, we take a look at the hardware and software required to get the most out of Dynamics CRM. The purpose of this chapter is to help you get comfortable with some of the most important features and deployment considerations.

IN THIS CHAPTER

Discovering new features for customizers and users in Microsoft Dynamics CRM 2011

Deciding between hosted or on-premise deployment

Required hardware and software

Dynamics CRM client overview

Looking at What's New in Microsoft Dynamics CRM 2011

Microsoft has made significant architectural changes to Dynamics CRM in order to provide its customers with the same breadth of customization and control, whether they subscribe to the company's Dynamics CRM Online offering or purchase the software for traditional, on-premise installation.

A number of significant changes to the application's architecture are meant to more closely align Dynamics CRM with the software maker's overall stack of operating systems and development frameworks.

64-bit only architecture

For starters, the Dynamics CRM server software, like many other recent releases from Microsoft, now runs solely on a 64-bit infrastructure. While this takes advantage of the trend toward the higher-performing 64-bit operating systems and hardware, it does provide some complications for organizations upgrading from earlier 32-bit implementations.

Cross-Reference

Chapter 3 contains a recommended strategy for upgrading your Dynamics CRM server from a 32-bit environment. Microsoft Dynamics CRM 2011 includes the ability to import a Version 4.0 organization database directly into a Version 2011 installation.

This architectural change applies to the Dynamics CRM server and server components, all of which are now supported only in 64-bit environments. Server components include the Dynamics CRM server and Deployment Manager, E-mail Router, and SSRS Data Connector. Client applications like the Outlook add-in continue to be supported on both 32-bit and 64-bit machines. (Later in this chapter we review the hardware and software requirements for both server and client components.)

Sandbox service

The inability of customers to deploy server-side code was a major limitation of the original Dynamics CRM Online offering. Because Dynamics CRM was designed to be multitenant — that is, capable of supporting multiple organizations within a single implementation of the server software — Microsoft did not allow their customers to deploy plug-ins due to the potential impact on the performance or data integrity of a co-hosted organization. Microsoft partners who offered hosted versions of Dynamics CRM were often in the same predicament.

Microsoft has overcome this limitation for its online offering and provided an enhanced security model for hosting partners and on-premises installations alike, by incorporating a *sandbox* service, which effectively quarantines server-side code used for plug-ins. This quarantine creates a partial-trust environment which prevents plug-ins from accessing server files and processes that are outside of the Dynamics CRM application. Developers working with on-premises implementations of Dynamics CRM retain the option to deploy plug-ins outside of the sandbox in a full-trust environment.

Enhanced pipeline framework

Dynamics CRM now allows developers to tap into an enhanced plug-in framework, enabling transaction and rollback support. Transaction support is an essential ingredient in many line-of-business applications being built on the Dynamics CRM platform (see the "Transaction Support" sidebar).

Transaction Support

Transaction support means developers can group multiple, inter-dependent operations into a single transaction, so that, should any operation fail, the entire transaction can be rolled back. For example, a developer may want to deploy a plug-in that ties orders in Dynamics CRM together with an invoice in a separate accounting application. The transaction may consist of two operations: posting the order details to the accounting system and then marking the order as processed in Dynamics CRM. In the absence of transaction rollback, should the second operation fail, the order details would still have been posted to the accounting system, and it would be difficult to determine whether the order had in fact been successfully processed or not. Transaction support enables all of the operations to be rolled back if any operation fails.

Solutions and publishers

Dynamics CRM has evolved into a development platform, and Microsoft has responded by creating a customization model that allows independent software vendors (ISVs) and customers to neatly package discrete combinations of custom objects, workflows, and other resources. These packages are called *solutions,* and the ISV or customizing organization is represented in the application as a *publisher.*

Beyond simply packaging up customizations by exporting a solution, customers are now able to install and uninstall solutions quickly and cleanly without hunting around for the various bits and pieces of XML and custom code that have previously been the hallmark of Dynamics CRM customizations.

A new, clean installation of Dynamics CRM contains the Default Solution, which is the system's core set of entities, attributes, reports, and so on. You can add your own customizations directly to the default solution or create a new solution in order to modularize your changes by first creating a new "Publisher" and then configuring the new solution. Dynamics CRM solutions also enable publishers to track version numbers and installation dates, making it easier to enhance and maintain the system. Solutions can build on and complement the functionality of the default solution or other solutions or can be relatively self-contained, modular add-ons that supplement the system with new functionality.

Web resources

Web resources are solution components that allow administrators and customizers to store a variety of client-side code and extensions inside the Dynamics CRM database, from where they can later be referenced within entity forms or directly via a unique URL. Seven types of Web resources can be stored within a solution. They are:

- HTML Web pages
- JS files containing JScript

- CSS files
- Images (GIF, JPG, or PNG)
- XML code
- XSL code
- Silverlight XAP files

For HTML, JScript, CSS, XML, and XSL, the Web resources interface allows administrators and customizers to either upload files or use a built-in text editor to paste in or compose code directly. HTML Web resources also provide a rich-text editor (see Figure 2.1) that supports font styling and references to images and hyperlinks, which can in turn be other previously created Web resources or external files.

FIGURE 2.1

The Web Resources dialog with the HTML rich-text editor open. Note that you can also access the HTML source behind the rich text.

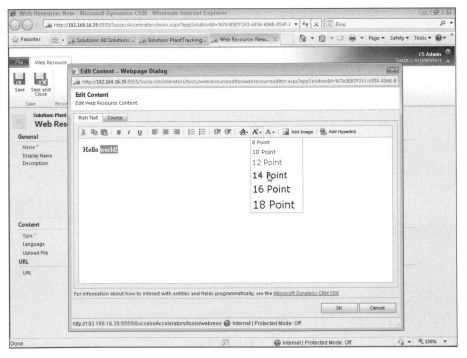

Option sets

A common requirement in many organizations is to have drop-down lists, or picklists as they are called in Dynamics CRM, which are common across different entities. For example, both Leads and Accounts have an Industry picklist that designates the type of industry in which the person or company operates. In previous versions of Dynamics CRM, separate picklists had to be maintained per entity, creating the probability that at some point the options in the different picklists would become out of synch with one another, or that the option indexes and values would be different from picklist to picklist, making it difficult to reliably work with them programmatically. Microsoft Dynamics CRM 2011 overcomes this limitation with option sets, reusable picklists that can be used throughout a solution and across multiple entities, yet maintained centrally within the solution.

Cutting-edge development platform

Microsoft Dynamics CRM 2011 incorporates many of the latest Microsoft development technologies, including the ability to leverage standard .NET types, LINQ to SQL, and ADO.NET. In addition, Dynamics CRM uses the following development tools and components:

- **.NET Framework 4.** Microsoft Dynamics CRM 2011 runs on Version 4 of the .NET Framework, Microsoft's core development framework. Version 4 of the framework provides developers with greater flexibility, convenience, and performance.

- **Visual Studio 2010.** Because Dynamics CRM now uses .NET 4, developers can take advantage of the enhanced development environment of Visual Studio 2010.

- **Windows Communication Foundation (WCF).** WCF provides an application interface to more easily develop service-oriented applications. WCF also enables Dynamics CRM to support claims-based authentication and federation.

- **No-Code Workflows.** Using the graphical design tools in Visual Studio 2010 and the Windows Workflow Foundation (WWF), developers can create powerful custom workflow automation rules and extensions and incorporate them into the Dynamics CRM application's GUI, where they can be deployed and managed by users. Workflow rules designed with the Dynamics CRM application can be exported and modified in Visual Studio 2010, again without code.

- **Azure.** For those customers who want to integrate custom Web applications hosted in the cloud, Dynamics CRM now has tighter integration with Microsoft's hosted development framework, Azure. Azure is essentially a hosted .NET runtime environment, a cloud-based operating system. The Dynamics CRM SDK makes use of AppFabric, an Azure service that allows on-premises applications to be tightly integrated with cloud-based services, enabling developers to create composite applications that combine data, workflow, and logic. More information about Azure is available at www.microsoft.com/windowsazure/.

Cross-Reference

Chapter 19 contains more detail about what Microsoft has included in the Dynamics CRM Software Development Kit (SDK) and some guidance on setting up your development environment. Chapter 21 provides tutorials for developing your first custom server-side extensions to Dynamics CRM using the new features of the development platform.

Changes to the User Experience

Microsoft focused a great deal of effort on delivering improvements for administrators and developers in this version of Dynamics CRM, yet users were not given short shrift either. Users will immediately notice a number of significant changes and improvements, like the Ribbon menus and dashboards, which are designed to minimize clicks and increase productivity. Collaboration has also taken a front seat with the ability to create ad hoc "connections" and access SharePoint document libraries natively within Dynamics CRM. There are a host of minor improvements as well, including the ability to send Sales Literature by E-mail, add images and hyperlinks to KB articles and E-mail templates, and total record counts being displayed in list views.

In the following sections, we explore some of the more significant changes to the user experience.

Wider international availability of Dynamics CRM Online

Microsoft continues to expand availability of Dynamics CRM Online to international markets in dozens of languages, with the Microsoft-hosted offering currently or soon to be available throughout North America, Northern and Western Europe, Hong Kong, India, Israel, Japan, Malaysia, New Zealand, Romania, and Singapore.

Getting Started panes

Getting Started panes made their debut in CRM Online with Version 4.0, and are now included in all deployment models. Located at the top of most system entity list views, the collapsible Getting Started panes contain links to how-to articles and videos, and helpful tools like the import wizard so users can begin making use of Dynamics CRM, even if they've had minimal introductory training.

Getting Started panes can be collapsed by default on a user-by-user basis through the users' Personal Options settings, or administrators can disable them globally in the System Settings.

Note

If the administrator disables Getting Started panes in System Settings, they are disabled for all users regardless of the users' selection in Personal Options.

Charts

Visualizations can now be found throughout Dynamics CRM's interface, from dashboards to inline charts displayed alongside entity list views. Users and customizers can create colorful, interactive charts with just a few clicks, and set them to display next to the related entities.

Similar to views and saved advanced find views, charts can be either user-owned or published across the organization, and automatically provide drill-through to explore data in more detail. Because charts make use of the security model, they can be assigned to and shared with other users or teams.

Familiar chart types include column and bar charts, line charts, pie charts, and funnels. Organization-owned charts are part of the related entity's customizations and therefore are packaged up as part of the solution to which the entity belongs.

Dashboards

Dashboards are configurable pages that can display combinations of charts, entity list views, or IFrames that can point at reports, Web resources, or any URL-addressable component. They conform to the security model, meaning they can be user-specific or organization-owned, and are packaged as part of customization solutions. Several dashboards for sales and customer service are included as part of the default installation (see Figure 2.2), and a dashboard wizard allows customizers and users with appropriate privileges to select a dashboard layout and add available components to create highly customized, interactive dashboards.

Enhanced data management tools

The wizards available to Dynamics CRM users have been made more robust and functional. The Data Import Wizard now allows new entities and fields to be created on the fly to speed data import. Additionally, this wizard now handles a variety of common file types and even zipped packages of multiple files. On-premise and partner-hosted deployments can also take advantage of the Bulk Delete Wizard (previously only available in Dynamics CRM Online), and the Duplicate Detection Wizard has been enhanced.

Ribbon menus

Ribbon menus first appeared in Office 2007 and have become an integral part of the Microsoft user experience across applications as diverse as SharePoint, Word, and now Dynamics CRM, which has a Ribbon that should be very familiar to users of SharePoint 2010 or Office 2010. The Ribbon provides users with contextual menu options grouped by functional area. Users can collapse the Ribbon menu to hide it, in which case it will remain collapsed as the user navigates from one entity to another until the user chooses to expand it again.

FIGURE 2.2

The Sales Overview Dashboard, showing several charts and the Opportunity list view. Users can drill into each chart to analyze the data in more detail.

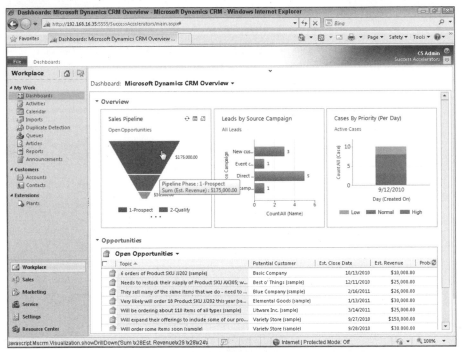

Because the Dynamics CRM user interface is role-based, the Ribbon exposes different options based on the logged-on user's privileges and access levels. This means that administrators and customizers have immediate access to form and view layout in the main application areas without having to navigate to the customizations area. The Ribbon can also be extended with custom tabs and menu options.

Navigational improvements

Microsoft has responded to user requests to reduce the number of clicks and new windows by making a multitude of both minor tweaks and substantial changes to application navigation:

- **A shortcut to recently viewed pages and views.** This shortcut, next to the new Home icon at the top of the Sitemap navigation, also allows users to "pin" recently visited items, so they remain quickly accessible with minimal clicks (see Figure 2.3).

- **Direct access to entity views from the left-hand navigation.** Hover over an entity in the Sitemap and a triangular button appears next to it, the clicking of which exposes the views available to the user as well as recently visited records for the entity.

- **Quick navigation from one record to another.** When viewing a record, a new set of navigational options appears on the top right of the record form. The first button in this group opens a small pane that previews the default view for that entity, allowing the user to quickly scroll or page through the list and select another record to open in the current window. The second set of buttons opens the next and last records above and below the current record being viewed.

- **Quick find in associated views.** Another minor improvement enables users to search through lists in associated views. For example, when viewing the contacts inside an account, there is now a search box at the top of the list of associated contacts, which helps to minimize paging and scrolling.

FIGURE 2.3

Improvements to the Dynamics CRM navigation make it easier to get to the data you want, with fewer clicks.

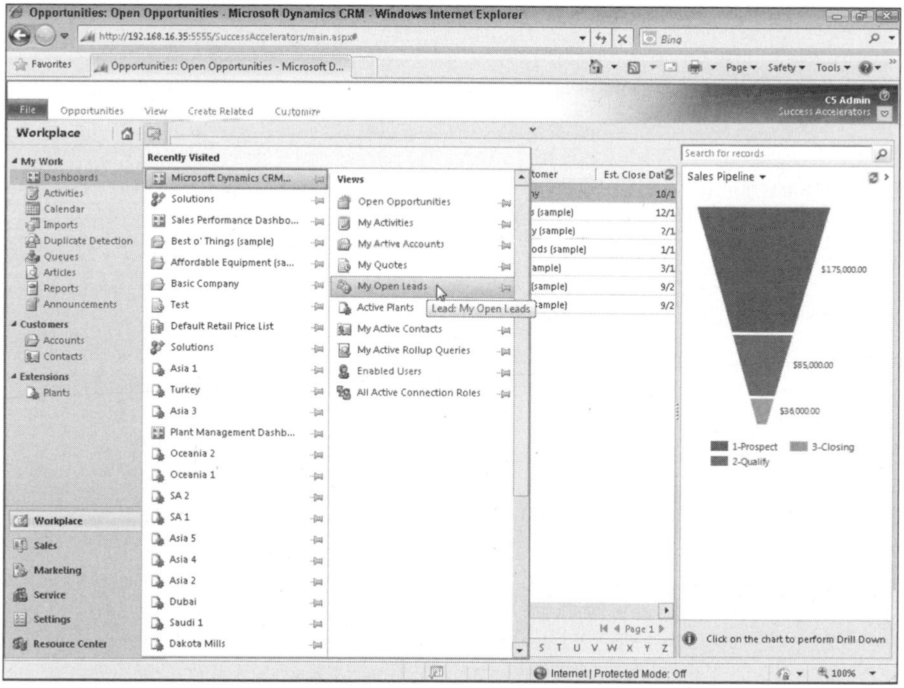

Filterable columns in views

Views can now be filtered on the fly without opening Advanced Find. Clicking the Filter button on the Ribbon menu adds a filter icon to the list view column headings. Based on a concept similar to the filtering capabilities in Excel, clicking on the filter icon on the column heading opens a small dialog in which the user can quickly select filtering criteria.

Role-based forms

Entity forms that display differently based on the logged-on user's security role represent a significant improvement in the Dynamics CRM user experience. To achieve an approximation of role-based forms in previous versions required the customizer to employ a variety of mostly unsupported JavaScript hacks to the form object model. Microsoft Dynamics CRM 2011 now provides true role-based forms tightly integrated with the existing security role scheme, a long-awaited feature.

Form customization and layout

Form customization and layout has undergone a major overhaul. Most notably, tabs have given way to collapsible form areas (though these areas are still referred to as tabs in some documentation). The immediate implication of this change is that users will now be scrolling down a form rather than clicking on tabs to access different groups of sections. This change is sure to be the source of much debate amongst longtime users of Dynamics CRM.

Other changes to the form include

- **Headers and footers.** Forms have configurable headers and footers, keeping important information visible even as the user scrolls or jumps down the form.
- **Side-by-side sections.** Two form sections can be positioned next to each other on the form, allowing more flexibility in form layout. For example, IFrames can be configured to span only one column, and a separate section with fields can be placed next to it.
- **Sub-grids displayed inline on forms.** Associated lists of related entities can be displayed inline on forms. A frequent customization utilizing custom code in previous versions of Dynamics CRM showed activity or history views on Lead or Contact forms. With this release, this functionality is part of the native form customization toolset.
- **Filtered lookups.** Limiting lookup dialogs to records related to the starting record is another feature that previously required extensive customization or a third-party add-on, and which is now a part of the form customizations in Dynamics CRM.

Team ownership of records

Teams have been given expanded capabilities in Microsoft Dynamics CRM 2011 and can now be assigned ownership of records. Teams are assigned Security Roles in the same way as users.

Field-level security

Dynamics CRM security roles have long provided highly granular control of access and privileges at the entity level. This control has now been extended down to custom fields. System fields cannot be configured to use field-level security. Field security profiles are a new construct used to define the privileges users have on selected fields.

Note

Configuring a large number of fields with field-level security can have a negative impact on performance. Due to the way that security roles and access roles are used to calculate a user's permissions on the fields, users may experience delays when attempting to open records with many secured fields. Generally speaking, this should not be an issue when only five or ten fields are secured. Careful consideration and testing should be employed when configuring field-level security.

Field changes

Fields (formerly called attributes) also have seen some significant changes, with a redefined set of data types. Customizers can also create a lookup field just as easily as creating other types of fields, and the underlying N:1 relationship is automatically created by the platform.

Recurring appointments

In addition to regular appointments, a new activity type called Recurring Appointments is available with familiar options to create weekly, monthly, or yearly recurrence. The Dynamics CRM calendar will display only the next 15 recurrences.

Custom activities

For the first time, customizers can create custom activity types just as easily as creating a new entity. Custom activities will appear in the associated activity and history views on related records and share many of the other attributes of activities. However, be aware that custom activities do not synchronize to Outlook.

Dialogs

Dialogs are designed to prompt users, such as call center representatives, as they capture information in a directed manner. In addition to configurable, branching scripts made up of interdependent statements, Dynamics CRM keeps a running log of completed and canceled dialogs in the form of Dialog Sessions. Dialogs present some interesting possibilities for businesses whose data-entry requirements follow a well-defined path or branching logic. With some creativity, Dialogs may also be combined with custom Ribbon menu items to replace standard dialogs such as the Lead conversion dialog, or the Case resolution dialog.

Auditing

Both system and custom entities can be audited, with field changes recorded in a special audit activity, visible from audit-enabled records. Auditing must be enabled at the entity level before flagging each of the desired fields for auditing.

SharePoint integration

Dynamics CRM now includes the ability to programmatically interact with SharePoint sites and document libraries (see Figure 2.4). When properly configured, Dynamics CRM can create and display integrated document libraries related to individual Dynamics CRM records. Users have full SharePoint functionality, such as check-in/check-out, document properties, and so on directly within the Dynamics CRM interface. In addition, SharePoint document libraries and folders can be created through workflow automation.

FIGURE 2.4

Seamless access to SharePoint document libraries, with full SharePoint functionality embedded in Dynamics CRM, can be a tremendous boost to productivity.

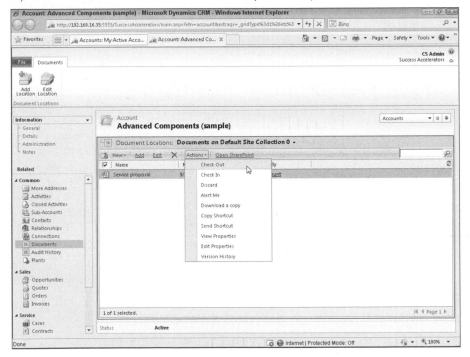

Connections

Connections allow users to create ad hoc relationships between records. This is similar to the functionality of the Relationship entity introduced in Version 3.0. Relationships though are limited to Accounts, Contacts, and Opportunities, whereas Connections can work across all entity types. Like Relationships, Connections depend on administrators setting up predefined roles. Relationships, while still functional in upgraded systems, are being deprecated and are hidden by default in new installations of Microsoft Dynamics CRM 2011.

Outlook integration

The Outlook experience has been redesigned to take advantage of the rich GUI in Outlook 2007 and 2010. While the core functions of tracking e-mail and regarding it to Dynamics CRM records remain unchanged, significant improvements have been made to the navigation and interface. One example is that records can be selected in list views and displayed in the Outlook preview pane, in just the same way as e-mail messages are previewed. The last section in this chapter, "Accessing Dynamics CRM," provides more detail on the changes to the Outlook client.

Changes to queues

Queues have been given a facelift as well, with new, clearer names for default user queues, and the ability to flexibly route records between queues. In addition, all entities can now be configured so they are assignable to queues. Note that after an entity is queue-enabled, it cannot be changed back.

Choosing a Deployment Option

"The Power of Choice." This is a phrase that has been used heavily by Microsoft to describe their strategy for Dynamics CRM, as well as other recent software products. In the case of Dynamics CRM, this choice is more powerful and more compelling than ever before. With the significant architectural changes to the program, the possibilities for extending Dynamics CRM Online are now nearly as limitless as with the On-Premise version.

Certainly, there are differences in how the online offering can be extended, but technologies like Azure and the Sandbox service have made the range of possibilities virtually identical. In this section we'll clarify the differences between the deployment options and list the factors you should consider when making this significant choice.

Understanding the differences among online, on-premise, and partner-hosted options

Microsoft Dynamics CRM 2011 is available through three deployment options:

- **Online.** Hosted in Microsoft data centers
- **On-Premises.** Installed on your company's servers
- **Partner-Hosted.** Hosted by a Microsoft partner

Microsoft Dynamics CRM Online

Microsoft's Dynamics CRM Online offering is delivered as a true on-demand service with a quick and easy sign-up, monthly billing, and all the benefits associated with software-as-a-service (SaaS), or, in Microsoft lingo, Software + Services. Dynamics CRM Online takes advantage of the multi-tenant architecture of the application — in fact, the primary reason Microsoft designed Dynamics CRM to be multitenant was so that they could offer it as an online service.

On-premises

Of course, Dynamics CRM is also available as traditional software that can be installed on your company's servers. It is available through the standard Microsoft licensing channels and comes in two basic "sizes" to fit your organization: a Workgroup edition, which is limited to five users and which allows only one tenant organization to be installed and operational at a time; and the Professional edition, which is fully multitenant.

Partner-hosted

Microsoft partners can sign a SPLA — a Services Provider License Agreement — and host Dynamics CRM in their own data centers or collocation facilities. SPLA partners may offer multitenant subscriptions or dedicated servers, depending on their business models and customer requirements. SPLA partners also offer their own payment methods.

Though the codebase is the same across the various deployment options, there are some significant differences. Table 2.1 lists some of the major differences between the Microsoft-hosted Dynamics CRM Online and the on-premises versions. Because each hosting partner is different, this table does not include a comparison of the Partner-Hosted option, though you can use it as a guide to ask questions if you are considering this option.

TABLE 2.1

Differences in Deployment Options

Feature	Online (Microsoft-hosted)	On-Premises
Multiple Organizations	No.	Yes. Multiple tenant organizations can be implemented except with the Workgroup licensing model.
Upload Custom Reports (.rdl files)	Yes. Custom reports can be created with the Report Wizard and in Visual Studio using an extension that enables connecting to and querying against the Dynamics CRM Web services.	Yes. Custom reports can be created with the Report Wizard and Visual Studio or any reporting tool capable of producing an RDL file.

Feature	Online (Microsoft-hosted)	On-Premises
Host Custom Web Applications	No. Web resources allow only straight HTML, not .ASPX or other server-side Web applications, to be hosted within the Dynamics CRM Web site. Azure is the recommended method of hosting custom Web applications for use with Dynamics CRM Online.	Yes. On-premises installations of Dynamics CRM include an "ISV" folder within the Web site root, which can be used to host custom Web applications.
Full-Trust Plug-ins	No. Plug-ins deployed to Dynamics CRM Online must reside within the Sandbox service, which gives the plug-ins only partial trust.	Yes. Developers can choose whether to deploy a plug-in outside of the Sandbox service in order to leverage full-trust.
Read-only User Licenses	No. Security roles can be configured to limit a user to read-only access, but this does not impact the cost of the licensing.	Yes. Read-only user licenses are available at approximately half the cost of full access licenses.
Device Licenses	No. Each user must be licensed and paid for.	Yes. For organizations whose employees use the same device at different times, such as shift workers, Dynamics CRM licenses can be acquired for the device.
Database Size Limits	Yes. Dynamics CRM Online organizations include 5GB of storage, with additional storage available for a per-GB fee.	No.
Maximum Number of Custom Entities	Yes. Subscribing organizations are limited to a maximum of 200 custom entities.	No.
Maximum Number of Workflows/Plug-ins	Yes. Subscribing organizations are limited to a maximum of 200 workflow rules. Plug-ins deployed to the Sandbox service count toward this limit.	No.
Authentication	LiveID, Claims-Based Authentication	Active Directory, Claims-Based Authentication
Internet-Facing Deployment (IFD)	Yes.	Yes. Your CRM server must be properly configured for access from the Internet (outside of your corporate network).
Move Between Deployment Options	Yes. Customers who start out using Dynamics CRM Online can request copies of their SQL databases for import into an on-premises installation.	No. After an organization deploys Dynamics CRM on-premises, the database cannot be imported to Dynamics CRM Online. However, options may be available from hosting partners should you wish to move your deployment into the cloud.

Deciding which deployment option is right for your organization

In addition to the differences detailed in Table 2.1, other important considerations must be made when deciding which deployment option is right for your organization.

Cost

Frequently, organizations can become focused solely on the perceived licensing and implementation costs of one deployment option compared to another. Although costs are — and must be — an important consideration, they are not the whole story and will often play a smaller role than expected in the overall success of your implementation.

When comparing licensing costs, keep in mind that although the upfront costs of an on-demand service are less than those of an on-premises implementation, they are continual for the life of your Dynamics CRM use. Have a competent partner perform a Total Cost of Ownership (TCO) analysis for your organization, and compare several different time periods: first-year costs, three- and five-year costs, and ten-year costs. These analyses will give you a better picture of the real differences over time.

Other costs that should not be overlooked include costs associated with planning your implementation and gathering requirements; customization, development, and testing; initial and ongoing user training; subsequent improvements and change management; and maintenance and upgrade costs. For many organizations, these costs exceed the licensing costs.

Long-term strategy

In conjunction with evaluating the costs to your organization, one of the most important factors to evaluate is your organization's long-term technology strategy. How rapidly will your company adopt new cloud-based applications, if at all? Are existing business applications being migrated to the cloud or co-located? If your corporate strategy is to reduce or phase out IT overhead and move to the cloud, an on-premises implementation may not make sense in the long term. If, on the other hand, IT is core to your organization's competencies and value proposition, on-premises may provide greater value.

Tip

If your organization doesn't have a documented and up-to-date strategy for its use of technology, now is the time to create one. Organizations that implement CRM systems or other types of business software without a clear understanding of how those systems fit into their long-term strategy are more likely to spend more money and get poorer results. Define and document your long-term technology strategy today!

Company culture and skillsets

These two considerations are corollaries to your company's long-term IT strategy. This factor is really about how management and users interact with IT. Is there a culture that is conducive to seeing a complex IT project through to completion? Are the right skillsets readily available, whether in-house or through a partner? Depending on your deployment choice and how complex your business needs are, the skills that can be required to implement and manage Dynamics CRM projects include Windows Server administration, SQL Server and SQL Server Reporting Services knowledge, Web and .NET development skills, business analyst and project management know-how, training delivery, and familiarity with change management.

The implementation of any business application, and the change that goes along with it, are inevitably accompanied by ups and downs, and the range of these peaks and valleys is determined by how much responsibility your organization takes on itself. Dynamics CRM Online minimizes responsibility for infrastructure and server administration, providing immediate start-up and fewer ongoing worries, whereas an on-premises installation provides greater control and more options for custom development and integration.

Your company's ability to tackle the installation, maintenance, and upgrade responsibilities for a complex application should carefully be weighed when considering an on-premises implementation versus a hosted offering.

Business requirements

Each business has unique requirements. Whether it's a distinctive sales process or regulatory compliance mandates, unique requirements are often one of the key determinants in a company's choice of deployment modes. For example, some firms' data security policies do not permit customer data to be stored off-premises, making hosted offerings a non-starter. On the other hand, if you are not bound by restrictive data policies, and the customization options of Dynamics CRM Online will suit your business requirements, an on-premises installation may be overkill. The key to evaluating these criteria is to understand the driving forces behind your company's decision to implement Dynamics CRM, and what its non-negotiable requirements are.

Integration plans

Because Dynamics CRM is a modern n-tier application with a separation between the application layer and the data layer, all inbound data integration should go through the Dynamics CRM Web services interface (as opposed to direct integration to the database layer in SQL Server). Outbound integration from Dynamics CRM can use either the Web services API or the database's filtered views.

This means that from a technical standpoint, integrating Dynamics CRM with an accounting system or another business application is possible regardless of the deployment choice. For example, Microsoft offers free integration between Dynamics CRM Online and Dynamics GP (an accounting application popular among many small to mid-sized businesses).

Cross-Reference
See Chapter 25 for an in-depth discussion of integration options and considerations.

Server Roles

Keep in mind that Dynamics CRM is an n-tier application, meaning that it can be installed on as few or as many servers as a given implementation requires. There are three basic layers: the application layer (the Dynamics CRM Web site), the platform layer (the Asynchronous service and plug-in pipeline), and the data layer housed in the SQL Server databases. All of these layers can be installed on as few as two servers, with the application and platform components on one server and the database on another; or it can be installed on a Web farm with multiple application servers, separate platform servers, and a cluster of SQL Servers. Each of these scenarios will have implications for your planning and implementation, as well as the required hardware and software to support it. Throw in the potential to combine virtual environments with physical servers, and it's easy to see how the list of requirements can change from implementation to implementation. Chapters 3 and 4 go into more detail on how to architect your system and install or upgrade the Dynamics CRM server and related components.

Depending on your business requirements — whether you'll be integrating your systems in real-time or by batch processes, the volume of data you'll be integrating, and whether you'll be synchronizing data in one or two directions — performance can often be better controlled and throughput increased with an on-premises integration. Simply put, if you'll be sending a lot of data back and forth in real-time, any cloud-based application can present an additional set of challenges for the integrator.

The appeal of on-demand software

Lastly, there is no denying the appeal to business decision makers of on-demand software: lower cost of entry, minimal maintenance overhead, and simplicity all make compelling arguments for the online delivery model. Further, today's business application users often want the latest versions of a software package rolled out to them quickly and seamlessly. Cloud-based systems like Dynamics CRM Online are worth a close look from every business considering improvements to its IT assets. Unless your organization has specific requirements that dictate an on-premises implementation, or anticipates a need to maintain the current version beyond the expected release date of the next major version, include the online offering in your consideration.

System Requirements

When speaking of Dynamics CRM it is often easy to slip into the shorthand of referring to it as an application, or a piece of software. In reality, Dynamics CRM is a true system comprised of many pieces. When Microsoft first released Microsoft Business Solutions Customer Relationship Management 1.0 (even more of a mouthful than the current name!) it was touted as their first fully .NET business software release. This was significant, because as flawed and short-lived as Version 1.0 turned out to be, it marked a milestone in the maturation of the underlying stack of .NET-enabled components: SQL Server, Internet Information Services (IIS), Active Directory, Windows Server, and of course the .NET Framework.

This is no less true today. If installed on your own servers, Dynamics CRM has its own collection of required hardware and software components (see Table 2.2 for a quick reference of system requirements) and is only available for installation on 64-bit systems, and 32-bit architecture is no longer supported.

TABLE 2.2

System Requirements Quick Reference (On-Premises and Outlook Deployments)

	Component	Minimum	Recommended
Dynamics CRM Application	Processor	1.5 GHz x64 CPU	Multi-core 2GHz or higher x64 CPU (Microsoft recommends the AMD Opteron or Intel Xeon processors)
	RAM	1GB RAM	2GB RAM or more
	Disk space	400MB available hard drive space[1]	400MB or more on RAID-5 array[1]
	Windows Server	Windows Server 2008 64-bit Standard, Enterprise, Datacenter, Web Server, SBS Standard or Premium; Indexing Service; IIS Admin service, World Wide Web Publishing service, MDAC 6.0; Microsoft ASP.NET	
	SQL Server	SQL Server 2008 editions: Standard (32-bit or 64-bit), Enterprise (32-bit or 64-bit); SQL Server Agent service; SQL Server Full Text Indexing; SQL word breakers for certain languages	
	IIS	IIS 7.0 in Native Mode with the MS URL Rewrite Module	
	Active Directory	The Dynamics CRM server must be a domain member in a domain with one of the following AD modes: 2000 (Mixed or Native), 2003 (Interim or Native), 2008 (Interim or Native). The Dynamics CRM server may not be a domain controller, unless it is installed on Small Business Server.	
Additional Dynamics CRM Server Components and Applications	SSRS Data Connector	SQL Server Reporting Services 2008. The Dynamics CRM server must be installed before installing the SSRS Data Connector.	
	E-mail Router	The E-mail router can be installed on most versions of Windows XP, Vista or 7; Windows Server 2003 or 2008. For Exchange Server integration, the Standard and Enterprise versions of Exchange 2003 SP2 and Exchange 2007 are supported.	
	SharePoint Integration (if desired)	All versions of Microsoft SharePoint 2010 are supported for integration with Dynamics CRM.	

continued

	Component	Minimum	Recommended
TABLE 2.2 *(continued)*			
Outlook client	Processor	750 MHz PIII (32-bit), or 1.5 GHz 64-bit CPU	Dual-core 1.8 GHz CPU or higher (32-bit), or Multi-core 2 GHz 64-bit CPU or higher
	RAM	1GB RAM	2GB RAM
	Disk space	Up to 500MB	Up to 500MB
	Display	S-VGA at 1024 x 768	Display with higher resolution than S-VGA at 1024 x 768
	Outlook versions	Outlook 2003 SP3, Outlook 2007, Outlook 2010[2]	
	Operating System	32-bit or 64-bit versions of Windows XP (SP2 or SP3), Vista or Windows 7; Indexing service; Internet Explorer 7/8+	
	Offline Access	SQL Server 2008 Express Edition (will be installed if missing)	
Web client	Browser versions	Internet Explorer 7/8+	
	Operating System	32-bit or 64-bit versions of Windows XP (SP2 or SP3), Vista or Windows 7; Indexing service; Internet Explorer 7/8+	

1 This does not include hard disk space for the SQL Server database, just the CRM application.

Accessing CRM

One of the most compelling reasons that Dynamics CRM has been so successful is because of its tight integration with a wide range of Microsoft products, especially Microsoft Outlook. Because it is familiar to many users, Outlook serves as a great entry point to users who are new to Dynamics CRM. Microsoft has also gone to great lengths to develop an approachable interface for Internet Explorer, providing similar visual elements and menus. And although Outlook and Internet Explorer are the two most common means of accessing Dynamics CRM, many organizations will wish to deploy either the included or third-party mobile clients.

There are many other ways that users could conceivably access CRM data and functionality. For example, many organizations are discovering the flexibility that SharePoint provides in not only displaying data from Dynamics CRM, but using Dynamics CRM data as SharePoint metadata to define lists and other SharePoint items. Similarly, rich clients can be built with just about any Web-enabled technology, such as Silverlight or non-Microsoft products. This chapter takes a look at the three most common scenarios for accessing Dynamics CRM: Internet Explorer, Outlook, and mobile clients.

Internet Explorer

The primary client that many users will use to access Dynamics CRM is the Web browser. For Microsoft Dynamics CRM 2011, Microsoft Internet Explorer (Figure 2.5) is the only supported browser, and only Version 7 or newer of the browser will work. Microsoft has designed Dynamics CRM to have the look and feel of an installed piece of software, to look more like a client application such as Outlook than a Web site.

FIGURE 2.5

The Dynamics CRM Web client in Internet Explorer

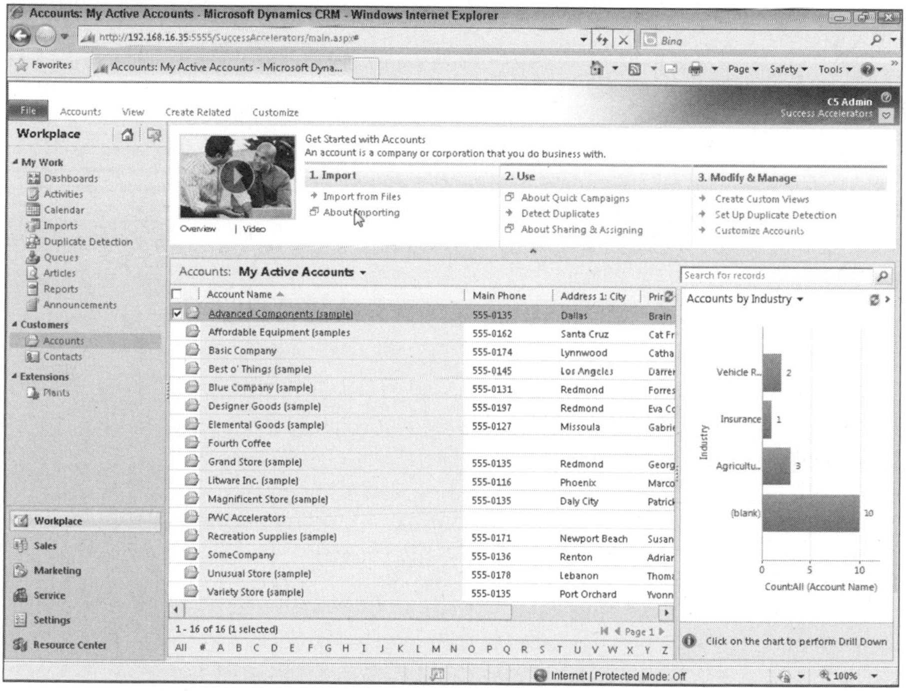

Dynamics CRM Online

When accessing Dynamics CRM Online, first-time users will need to create a Windows Live ID in order to log in through Internet Explorer. The standard URL for Dynamics CRM Online takes the form of `https://<orgname>.crm.dynamics.com`, where "orgname" is the Organization given to Microsoft at sign-up.

On-Premises

Users of properly configured on-premises Dynamics CRM will typically use an Active Directory domain logon to access Dynamics CRM, in which case Internet Explorer's support for Windows authorization will allow the user to log on without being prompted for credentials. The URL for an on-premises deployment is in one of the following forms, depending on the installation and configuration:

- Default Web site (port 80) installation: `http://<servername>/<orgname>/main.aspx` or `https://<servername>/<orgname>/main.aspx` if SSL is employed.
- For non-default Web site installation the Dynamics CRM install sets the port to 5555 (although this can be changed easily during installation): `http://<servername>:5555/<orgname>/main.aspx`.

Internet Facing Deployment

If Dynamics CRM has been configured for Internet Facing Deployment (IFD), the user will be presented with a sign-on page in which they must enter their username and password. The standard URL for Dynamics CRM IFD takes the form of `https://<orgname>.<domain>.com`, where "orgname" is the Organization name provided during installation or provisioning, and "domain" is a registered domain name.

Appreciating the power of Outlook integration

For the last few versions of Dynamics CRM, demonstrating integration with Outlook was a key part of a sales call, and one of the product's competitive value propositions. In other words, Outlook often sold Dynamics CRM. So while partners and customers have been asking for some improvements and feature-enhancements for the Outlook client, it's likely that very few anticipated the dramatic leap that comes with Microsoft Dynamics CRM 2011, especially when combined with Outlook 2010. It's a whole new game, and one that competitors will have a hard time playing.

Core functionality remains, and in many cases is much improved. Users can still perform daily tasks such as:

- Track an e-mail or Outlook activity into Dynamics CRM, including recurring appointments (but not custom activities, unfortunately)
- Set the "Regarding" field on an Outlook record that has been tracked into Dynamics CRM
- Create a new Dynamics CRM record
- Navigate through Dynamics CRM without leaving Outlook

On top of this core functionality, users are presented with an interface that may give them reason to forego the Web client altogether. Let's take a look at some of the more compelling changes in the Outlook client.

The Outlook interface

For starters, the Outlook client interface is dramatically changed from previous versions. Instead of Dynamics CRM list views merely being framed by Outlook, with Outlook 2007 and 2010 Dynamics CRM is fully part of the rich, interactive and user-tailored Outlook experience. (With Outlook 2003, the Dynamics CRM client still provides an improved integration, but the interface is much the same as it was with Version 4.0.)

Someone has said that where previous versions were good examples of Outlook *plus* Dynamics CRM, this version is Outlook *multiplied* by Dynamics CRM. Figure 2.6 shows many of the reasons for this observation. First, notice the Dynamics CRM "wunderbar" button that makes Dynamics CRM as integral to Outlook as e-mail and contacts. Outlook context menu (right-click) options, such as categories and follow-ups can now act on Dynamics CRM records. Contextual Dynamics CRM visualizations, already an impressive enhancement in the Web interface, are even more compelling when displayed in the Outlook client alongside the record list view, and the ability to preview selected records in the reading pane is a huge time-saver.

New features that have been incorporated into the Outlook client, include:

- Views are displayed in Outlook tabs, and are pinnable, meaning users can select their favorite views and have them always at hand in the Outlook interface.

- Views are automatically updated with new records that are created on the server, mimicking the Outlook experience of e-mail appearing in the user's Inbox without a manual refresh.

- In Outlook 2010, a new footer appears at the bottom of e-mails in the reading pane. E-mails tracked in Dynamics CRM show the Regarding button and link to the record, as well as additional details.

- An Import Contact Wizard guides users through importing Outlook contacts into Dynamics CRM, allowing them to select contacts by Outlook category, and helps users identify potential duplicates.

- Users can reorder the sections of a record form when previewing it in the reading pane, and these changes persist across the entity and across Outlook sessions, giving an unprecedented level of user-customizability to the Dynamics CRM interface.

FIGURE 2.6

The Dynamics CRM client for Outlook is tightly integrated with Outlook 2010's rich graphical user interface.

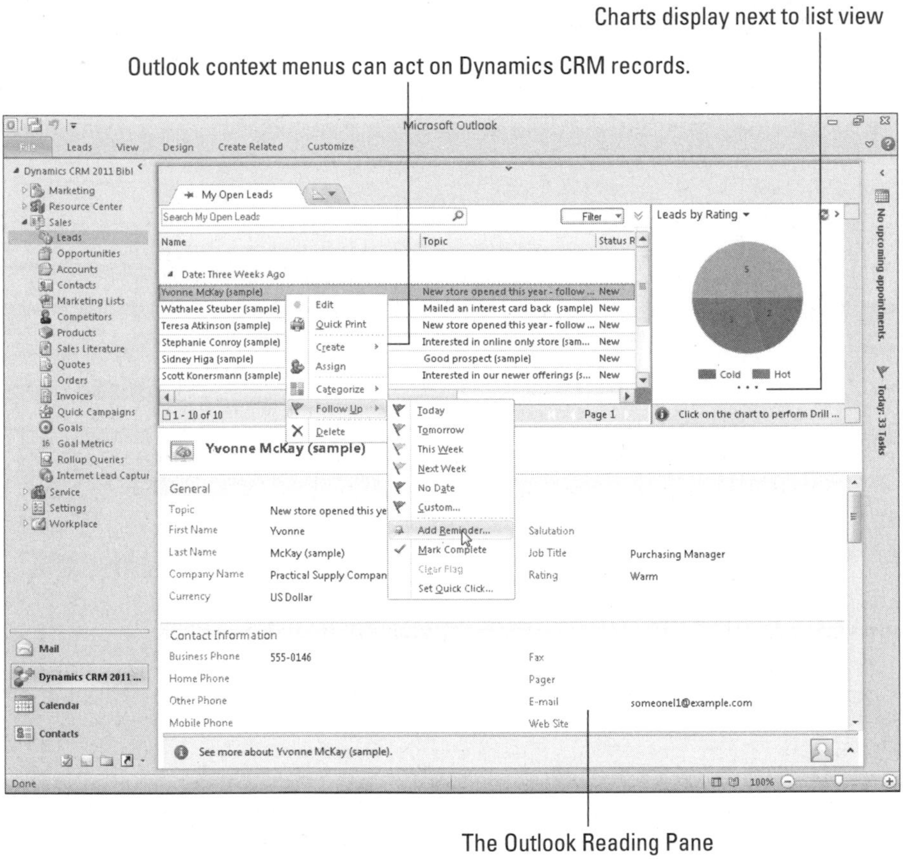

Charts display next to list view

Outlook context menus can act on Dynamics CRM records.

The Outlook Reading Pane

Going mobile

At this writing, Microsoft plans to release an updated version of Mobile Express for Dynamics CRM and Dynamics CRM Online. Mobile Express is a free and easy-to-configure mobile client that provides cross-browser support for online mobile access. No Dynamics CRM data is stored locally on the mobile device, and the Dynamics CRM server must be accessible from the Internet.

Mobile Express works on all HTML4 compliant mobile browsers and enforces Dynamics CRM security roles, allowing users full read/write capability of records that are published for the mobile client. In addition to selecting entities to publish to Mobile Express, administrators can configure the layout of mobile forms using a graphical interface in the Customizations area of Dynamics CRM.

Cross-Reference

Third-party options abound for mobile access that offer both online and offline access for a variety of mobile devices including iPhones, BlackBerries, Droids, and, of course, Microsoft Windows Phones. Two of the best-known providers of rich mobile clients for Dynamics CRM are CWR Mobility and Ten Digits. More information about these and other ISV solutions is available in Appendix B.

Summary

In this chapter, you learned that Microsoft Dynamics CRM 2011 introduces a host of new features that build on its capabilities for customization and user productivity. Among the most significant changes for this version are:

- The Dynamics CRM server is now offered exclusively as an x64 platform.

- The new Sandbox service and Azure integration make Dynamics CRM Online nearly as extensible as an on-premises implementation, though there are still some differences to consider such as custom reporting, full-trust plug-ins, and integration.

- Solutions are a new way to package up a set of customizations for easy import and export, as well as roll-back. Solutions include the customized entities, fields, charts, Web resources, and other components and dependencies.

- Dynamics CRM Online is increasingly available to a wide international market in many languages.

- The Ribbon menu system, visualizations, and enhanced navigation make for a dramatically improved user experience.

We also reviewed the deployment options and discussed the differences you should consider when comparing a hosted Dynamics CRM solution — whether Microsoft Dynamics CRM Online or a partner-hosted offering — and an on-premises implementation. Important factors to weigh in this decision are the total cost of ownership (TCO) and your company's long-term strategy for a CRM solution and cloud-based technologies.

This chapter also provided a quick reference for both hardware and software system requirements for the Dynamics CRM server, related components, and the Outlook client, as well as a discussion of the various ways users might access the system.

Part II

Installing Dynamics CRM

This part of the book introduces some of the core concepts you will need to understand when planning your implementation of Microsoft Dynamics CRM 2011, as well as key pointers for successfully installing the system's components.

Chapter 3 covers details to guide you through the decisions around the architectural design process, and the deployment options you should consider. It includes comprehensive coverage of server roles and how to configure Dynamics CRM under different deployment scenarios. In addition to server installation tips, Chapter 3 also covers the upgrade process and steps you'll go through when preparing your system for access from outside your firewall.

Chapter 4 covers the installation and configuration of the SQL Server Reporting and SharePoint integration extensions, setting up claims-based authentication, internet-facing deployment (IFD), and the E-mail Router. It also contains a discussion of the installation considerations for the Outlook add-in.

Architecting Your CRM System

Microsoft Dynamics CRM 2011 is unique in the CRM marketplace because it is just as likely to be deployed for a 5,000-user multinational corporation as for a local business with 20 employees. It is really quite remarkable that its architecture and extensibility make it affordable and flexible for both of these types of deployments, as well as the range of possible deployments in between.

Because addressing all of the potential architectural scenarios and considerations would be difficult, the goal of this chapter is to provide insight and guidance that will be important for the most common deployment scenarios. Whether you are deploying Dynamics CRM for a Microsoft hosting partner, a small non-profit organization, or a large enterprise, this chapter contains information that is important as you plan your implementation strategy.

Cross-Reference

This chapter covers planning and installing the Dynamics CRM server. Installation of additional components, such as the E-mail Router and the Outlook client are detailed in Chapter 4.

When starting your deployment, consider the analogy of building a house: before the first brick is laid an architect carefully drafts a blueprint, the building site is prepared, and appropriate tools and building materials are assembled. This process produces better, longer lasting results than simply showing up with some wood and nails and starting to hammer away. Similarly, although quickly scanning the installation guide, putting the DVD into your server, and starting to click through the setup can be a tempting approach, your organization will benefit dramatically from investing in some strategic planning and forethought.

Tip

Microsoft has provided an Implementation Guide that is freely available from their download site. The Implementation Guide, or IG, contains two sections: a planning section and an installing section. Available as Word documents or as a compiled help file, the IG is Microsoft's guide to supported deployment scenarios and methods.

Planning Your Installation Strategy

Dynamics CRM is more than a single piece of software. It is a system that relies on many components to work together. Installing and using Dynamics CRM requires proper configuration of Windows Server, Active Directory, SQL Server, the .NET 4.0 Framework, IIS, SQL Server Reporting Services, Outlook, Internet Explorer, and a number of other technologies.

Dynamics CRM is designed for scalability and ease of customization, with an architecture that provides many extensibility points. How your organization plans to use these APIs will impact how you deploy Dynamics CRM.

Considering your goals for Dynamics CRM

Before going any further, consider the immediate and long-term goals you have for deploying Dynamics CRM. The answers to the following questions will impact the decisions you make for your system architecture:

- What is the purpose of this deployment? Will it be used for a development, testing, or production environment?
- How many users will the deployment need to support?
- What are the plans for the future of the deployment? Will it have to accommodate more users or business units at some point?
- If you are deploying with a Professional or Enterprise license, how many servers will you be deploying on?
- How much data will the system contain in a year? Three years? Seven years?
- How complex will the system be? Will there be many business units, a lot of system jobs, or complex duplicate detection rules? Will there be a large number of processor-intensive workflow processes?
- What other systems will you need to integrate with? ERP, accounting, and other external applications can place a significant load on network and system resources.
- What will your organization's potential demand be on the SQL Server Reporting Services server?
- Will you be deploying Dynamics CRM for intranet usage or Internet-Facing Deployment? A combination of both?
- Does your organization require high availability, failover, or business continuity planning?

All of these objectives for your Dynamics CRM deployment serve as inputs into your architecture planning and should be well understood before installation. In addition to the IG, you may need to refer to your company's own policies and the guides for other systems as you prepare your implementation.

Cross-Reference
Microsoft occasionally provides guidance for different deployment scenarios. For example, for Dynamics CRM 4.0, Microsoft released a whitepaper that detailed the suggested hardware for a deployment with 500 concurrent users that may serve as an excellent starting point when architecting your deployment.

Other important considerations

In addition to the goals your organization has for deploying Dynamics CRM, a number of other important factors must be taken into consideration that may impact your deployment architecture.

- What is the current state of your network? Are there performance concerns that may be exacerbated by a new system? Do a thorough review and address any shortcomings or anomalies before introducing Dynamics CRM into the mix.

- Do you have the hardware and software needed, with the correct operating systems and versions of server and client applications? Do you have sufficient processing power, RAM, and storage? Sufficient RAM is especially important on the SQL Servers that will be used. RAM and processor capacity should also be reviewed for the server that will provide Dynamics CRM platform services, such as the asynchronous processing service and the sandbox service.

- Will you be deploying Dynamics CRM to a virtualized environment? Microsoft Dynamics CRM 2011 supports virtualization, but you should have a good understanding of the limitations of your organization's virtualization technology, as well as the impact on performance that virtualization may have on SQL Server databases.

- Has your SQL Server been tuned and optimized? See Chapter 9 for tuning steps that can help ensure you get the best performance out of your database server for Dynamics CRM.

- Do you have firewalls or other security appliances that will require configuration to permit Dynamics CRM to function properly?

- Will you be deploying Dynamics CRM to a new or an existing Web site? Will you use the standard or custom ports? When installing Dynamics CRM to a new Web site, the default port is set to 5555. However, if you will be using Internet-Facing Deployment, you will need to configure the site to use SSL. If using SSL, it is recommended to use the default port of 443 to eliminate the need for port forwarding or requiring users to type a port number to access the Dynamics CRM Web site. If you choose to install into an existing Web site, make sure that nothing is there that will be overwritten by the install routine.

Tip

Decide in advance which ports the Dynamics CRM Web site will use, as changing the port number after installation can be difficult, because they need to be properly configured within IIS, DNS, and the MSCRM_Config database. Changing the port numbers after installation can produce unexpected results and downtime.

- What authentication modes does your domain currently use — NTLM and/or Kerberos? Have you already implemented a claims-based authentication model with Active Directory Federation Services 2.0 (AD FS 2)? AD FS 2 is necessary for Service Provider License Agreement (SPLA) hosting partners and Internet-Facing Deployment (IFD) for Dynamics CRM 2011.

Cross-Reference

Chapter 9 covers tips for optimizing your network to get the best performance from Dynamics CRM.

Breaking Out Server Roles

Microsoft Dynamics CRM 2011 is designed using an n-tier architecture that separates the components of the user interface, the Web application, processing, and the databases into layers. Each of these components is referred to as a server role. Dynamics CRM is available in two basic licensing models: the Workgroup Edition is licensed for single tenants and the Enterprise Edition is the multi-tenant license.

Note

At the time of this writing, the final licensing model and product naming had not been announced. For clarity, this chapter refers to the Workgroup Edition when discussing the single-tenant licensing model, and the Enterprise Edition when discussing the full, multitenant licensing model.

With the Enterprise license of Dynamics CRM, server roles can be installed individually or in groups on different servers, enabling Dynamics CRM to be highly scalable and reliable. When installing with a Workgroup Edition license, all server roles are installed on each server where you run the setup program. This architecture provides a great deal of flexibility for customization and administration.

Cross-Reference

Chapter 7 provides details on how to use the Deployment Manager to manage servers and server roles within a deployment.

Understanding server roles and role groups

Dynamics CRM can be installed with all server roles on a single server, or with server roles broken out on multiple servers. Single-server deployments, referred to as Full Server deployments, are typically only seen in development or testing environments and are not recommended for production use.

In addition to Full Server deployments, server roles can also be grouped together as Front End servers, Back End servers, and Deployment Administration servers. Typically, Dynamics CRM is installed on a minimum of two servers: one that acts as the Front End and Deployment Administration role groups, hosting the Web application and services, and another Back End server to house the databases.

In general, server roles impact an entire deployment, not just individual organizations, so, for example, a server that provides the Front End server role group for a deployment will be the front end for all organizations in a multitenant deployment. An exception is the connector for SQL Server Reporting Services that can be installed for individual organizations within a deployment.

Caution

Dynamics CRM should not be installed on a domain controller, unless it is being installed on a Small Business Server. Installing Dynamics CRM on a non-SBS domain controller is not supported for production environments, though it is possible and is often done for self-contained development environments.

During the installation process, if you are using an Enterprise license, you will have the opportunity to select roles to install. Installing server roles in groups (Full Server, Front End Server, Back End Server, or Deployment Administration Server) to simplify administration is recommended to get the most out of the system (Figure 3.1). However, any individual role can be installed separately, if desired. If you are using a Workgroup Edition license, you can install all the server roles on multiple servers, pointing secondary installs to the existing database.

FIGURE 3.1

When installing Microsoft Dynamics CRM 2011 Enterprise on a server, you have the option of installing individual server roles or groups of roles.

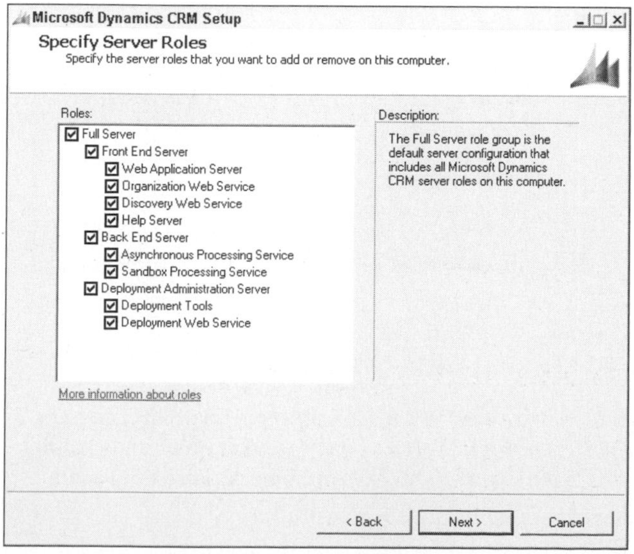

Front End Server

The Front End Server server role group consists of the following server roles:

- **Web Application Server.** A server with this role hosts the Dynamics CRM Web site. This role requires the Organization Web Service role.

- **Organization Web Service.** The Organization Web Service is specific to individual tenant organizations and is the primary API for interacting with the organization's system and custom entities, fields, and other elements via the SDK.

- **Discovery Web Service.** The Discovery Web Service is a front end API that helps discover which organization a Web service call is meant to interact with.

- **Help Server.** The Help Server role installs the Help Web site.

Back End Server

The Back End Server server role group consists of the following server roles:

- **Asynchronous Processing Service.** This role installs the service that handles asynchronous system jobs and workflow processing.

- **Sandbox Processing Service.** The installation of this role on a server provisions the sandbox processing service that enables custom server-side code to run securely in a multitenant environment, isolated based on organization.

Deployment Administration Server

The Deployment Administration Server server role group consists of the following server roles:

- **Deployment Tools.** The Deployment Tools role installs the Deployment Manager.

- **Deployment Web Service.** This role is a Web services API that developers can access by using the SDK to perform operations without accessing the Deployment Manager interface.

Other server roles

Other server roles are not part of a server role group. These are:

- **SQL Server role.** The SQL Server role is a logical role that is designated by default during installation of the MSCRM_Config database.

- **SQL Reporting Services (SRS) Data Connector role.** The SRS Data Connector can be installed per organization and must be installed on the reporting services server. It is installed separately from the Dynamics CRM server.

Server configurations

There are a variety of possible server configurations from single-server deployments to multi-site enterprise deployments. The three basic scenarios described here (single server, Small Business Server, and multiple server) cover the fundamentals that apply across a variety of deployment scenarios.

Single-server deployment

Installing Dynamics CRM (and all of its server roles) on a single server is not recommended for production environments but is commonly done to create a virtual demo or development environment.

When installing Dynamics CRM to one member server within a domain, the server needs all of the prerequisite software including SQL Server, SQL Server Reporting Services, and IIS. If you are creating a self-contained virtual environment for demonstration or development purposes, as depicted in Figure 3.2, you will also need Active Directory and DNS installed and configured. Keep in mind that to take full advantage of Microsoft Dynamics CRM 2011, you likely want to integrate Exchange Server and SharePoint, which can make for a very complex demonstration image. Installing Dynamics CRM on a domain controller is not supported unless it is a Small Business Server deployment. Because of the complexity of installing all of these components on a single server or virtual server, you may wish to consider using Dynamics CRM Online for demonstration or development purposes instead.

Cross-Reference

See Chapter 20 for more information on setting up a development environment. Development environments can consist of single-server or multi-server deployments, depending on your needs.

FIGURE 3.2

Dynamics CRM is frequently installed entirely on a single server to create a virtual development or demonstration machine. Single-server deployment is not recommended for production environments.

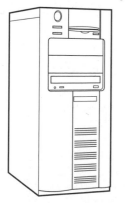

- Full Server
  - Front End Server
    - Web Application Server
    - Organization Web Service
    - Discovery Web Service
    - Help Server
  - Back End Server
    - Asynchronous Processing Service
    - Sandbox Processing Service
  - Deployment Administration Server
    - Deployment Tools
    - Deployment Web Service
  - SQL Server Role
  - SRS Data Connector Role

Small Business Server

Microsoft Dynamics CRM 2011 is supported on Microsoft Windows Small Business Server 2008 (SBS), a bundle of Windows Server 2008, Exchange Server, SharePoint, and other essential technologies. The Premium version of SBS includes licensing for a second Windows Server with SQL Server. If you have SBS Standard, it is recommended that you install SQL Server on a second server machine (whether physical or virtual), rather than on the single SBS server.

When installing Dynamics CRM in a two server configuration like SBS, shown in Figure 3.3, it is not necessary to run the setup routine on each server. During the installation process on SBS, the Front End, Back End, and Deployment Administration role groups will be installed on the primary SBS server (the one with IIS, Exchange, and SharePoint), and the MSCRM_ Config and organization databases will be installed on the second server with the SQL Server role. Immediately upon completing installation of the server, the SRS Data Connector install routine starts. This extension that enables integration between Dynamics CRM and SQL Server Reporting Services is installed on the report server.

Caution

You should install and configure SQL Server Reporting Services (SSRS) and SharePoint before running the Dynamics CRM server installation. However, make sure that you do not install SSRS in SharePoint integrated mode, as this will render it unusable for Dynamics CRM.

Multiple server deployment

There are many possible multi-server architecture models to take advantage of the Dynamics CRM n-tier architecture. A typical multiple server deployment of Dynamics CRM (Figure 3.4) will include a load-balanced Web farm for the Front End server role groups, a separate Help Server, a Back End server for processing, and a SQL cluster.

Microsoft recommends installing the Help Server on a server that is separate from the Front End server in order to reduce the system's exposure to denial-of-service attacks. Your deployment may also include integration with an Exchange server (not depicted in Figure 3.4) using the Microsoft Dynamics CRM E-mail Router. The E-mail Router can be installed on a server or workstation that has access to both Dynamics CRM and the mail server.

Note

One advantage of Microsoft Dynamics CRM 2011 that was not available in previous versions is that, in a multitenant deployment, tenant organizations can have their own base language, specified during organization creation from Deployment Manager. They do not need to inherit the deployment's base language as their own.

Setting up a Web farm with network load balancing (NLB)

When deploying Dynamics CRM to a Web farm with network load balancing, enable NLB before performing the Dynamics CRM server installation. Make sure that the servers in the Web farm all have proper trust with other servers in the deployment. This may require setting

Service Principal Names (SPNs) and trust for delegation in Active Directory. SPNs are typically created for servers when they join a domain that uses Kerberos, but additional SPNs may be required for Dynamics CRM. (Refer to Microsoft support documents for configuring NLB in your network.)

Small Business Server (SBS) is a popular option for organizations with fewer than 75 employees. Dynamics CRM is supported on Standard and Premium editions of SBS 2008, though it is recommended that you install SQL Server on a separate server for optimal performance.

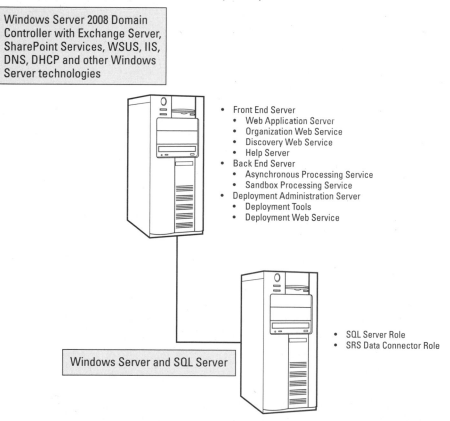

Windows Server 2008 Domain Controller with Exchange Server, SharePoint Services, WSUS, IIS, DNS, DHCP and other Windows Server technologies

- Front End Server
  - Web Application Server
  - Organization Web Service
  - Discovery Web Service
  - Help Server
- Back End Server
  - Asynchronous Processing Service
  - Sandbox Processing Service
- Deployment Administration Server
  - Deployment Tools
  - Deployment Web Service

- SQL Server Role
- SRS Data Connector Role

Windows Server and SQL Server

Install Dynamics CRM on the load balancing servers one at a time, and on each subsequent installation point to the existing databases. After installation, you must open the Dynamics CRM Deployment Manager and set that you are using NLB. For complete instructions on making this setting, see Chapter 7.

FIGURE 3.4

A typical multiple-server deployment of Dynamics CRM with six servers, some or all of which may be virtualized using Hyper-V or other virtualization technologies.

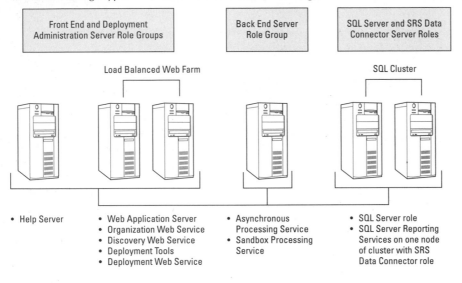

Cross-Reference

When using network load balancing (NLB) with Dynamics CRM, you must enable NLB in the deployment's properties by using the Deployment Manager. Complete instructions are in Chapter 7.

Deploying Dynamics CRM to a SQL Cluster

Dynamics CRM's databases can be deployed to a SQL Server cluster to provide failover protection for enterprises that demand high availability. When planning to deploy to a SQL cluster, configure the cluster first by following the instructions for your edition of SQL Server. Make sure that SQL Server is using Windows authentication.

SQL Server Reporting Services (SSRS) is not technically supported in a cluster (though it is possible). Therefore, you should install SSRS on a single node of the cluster. Keep in mind that, in this case, SSRS will not failover should its server have an outage. Alternately, you can install SSRS on a separate server. The best practice is to have SSRS installed and configured before starting your Dynamics CRM installation.

Installing the Dynamics CRM Server

With all of the prerequisite hardware and software in place, Dynamics CRM is relatively easy to install, with a friendly installation interface that guides you through the process with just a handful of clicks. The installation routine will perform a check of the environment to make sure that everything is in order before allowing you to proceed with the installation, helping to ensure successful installations.

Installations can be conducted from DVD installation media provided by Microsoft through your reseller or from a downloaded installation file. The installation generally takes under an hour to perform from inserting the media to the successful completion of the setup. Following this section are some post-installation steps you should follow as well.

Installing with installation media versus command line installs

Dynamics CRM can be installed manually or by using a command line install. Command line installs require certain parameters in the command line as well as a configuration file. The advantage of command line installs is that they can be carried out programmatically.

Both installation methods produce logs that you can inspect. Log files are located by default in the <SystemDrive>:\Documents and Settings\<User>\Application Data\Microsoft\ MSCRM\Logs folder, though you can specify a location for a command line install using the /L parameter.

To run the installation, you need to log onto the server with a domain account that has local administrator privileges on the server. The user account must also have administrative permissions on the SQL Server as well as privileges to create groups in Active Directory.

To run the installation from the command line, open the command prompt as an administrator and navigate to the folder containing the SetupServer.exe file in the Dynamics CRM install media.

A sample command line that runs a quiet installation and uses a custom installation configuration file is located in a folder call CRMtemp on the C: drive:

```
SetupServer.exe /Q /config C:\CRMtemp\installconfig.xml
```

An example of the contents of the installconfig.xml file for command line installation of the Dynamics CRM server with Internet-Facing Deployment (a copy of this is available on the Web site):

```
<CRMSetup>
  <Server>
    <Patch update="false"></Patch>
    <LicenseKey>XXXXX-XXXXX-XXXXX-XXXXX-XXXXX</LicenseKey>
    <SqlServer>SQLClusterName</SqlServer>
    <Database create="true"/>
    <Reporting URL="http://SsrsServer/ReportServer"/>
    <OrganizationCollation>Latin1_General_CI_AI</OrganizationCollation>
    <basecurrency isocurrencycode="USD" currencyname="US Dollar"
  currencysymbol="$" />
    <Organization>My Company Name</Organization>
    <OrganizationUniqueName>MyCompanyName</OrganizationUniqueName>
```

```
      <OU>OU=Users,DC=ADsubdomain,DC=ADsubdomain,DC=ADsubdomain,DC=com</OU>
      <WebsiteUrl create="true" port="5555"> </WebsiteUrl>
      <InstallDir>c:\Program Files\Microsoft Dynamics CRM</InstallDir>
      <CrmServiceAccount type="DomainUser">
        <ServiceAccountLogin>crmadmin</ServiceAccountLogin>
        <ServiceAccountPassword>password</ServiceAccountPassword>
      </CrmServiceAccount>
      <SQM optin="true"/>
      <Email>
        <IncomingExchangeServer name="EmailServer"/>
      </Email>
      <ifdsettings enabled="true">
        <internalnetworkaddress>10.10.0.0-255.255.0.0</internalnetworkaddress>
        <rootdomainscheme>https</rootdomainscheme>
        <sdkrootdomain>crm.mycompany.com</sdkrootdomain>
        <webapplicationrootdomain>crm.mycompany.com</webapplicationrootdomain>
        <discoveryrootdomain>crm.mycompany.com</discoveryrootdomain>
      </ifdsettings>
   <claimssettings enabled="true">
  <FederationMetadataUrl>
  https://stsauthserver.mycompany.com/FederationMetadata/2007-06/
     FederationMetadata.xml
  </FederationMetadataUrl>
  <EncryptionCertificate>
  cn=stsauthserver.mycompany.com
  </EncryptionCertificate>
        </claimssettings>
     </Server>
  </CRMSetup>
```

Note

Be sure to change the license key, server name, and other variables to match your environment when using the configuration XML above for an automated installation.

After running the installation, you must configure the "relying parties" in AD FS 2. The Implementation Guide contains detailed instructions for command line installs and configuring relying parties.

Running the setup

In addition to the required hardware and software detailed in Chapter 2, Dynamics CRM requires certain tools and components, which, if they are not previously installed, will be installed during the setup of the Dynamics CRM server. These include:

- The Windows Azure platform AppFabric SDK, which enables integration between Dynamics CRM and Azure's cloud-based service bus
- A report viewer control to render SSRS reports in the Dynamics CRM application
- The Native Client for SQL Server

- Microsoft's Application Error Reporting Tool
- The Visual C++ Runtime Library, which is required for the installation process
- MSXML 6
- Microsoft Identity Foundation
- The Web Server Roles for Windows Server 2008
- The .NET 4.0 Framework, which includes the Windows Workflow Foundation, Windows Presentation Foundation, Windows Communication Foundation, Chart Controls for .NET, and the .NET Services SDK

To install Dynamics CRM:

1. Navigate to the media or download location and double-click on SetupServer.exe. The Microsoft Dynamics CRM Setup screen appears.

   The first screen gives you the option to download updated installation files (Figure 3.5). Note that these updates are updates to the installation files only. You still need to download and install the latest updates after installation completes.

2. Select an option and click Next.

FIGURE 3.5

You can choose to download updates for the Dynamics CRM installation routine before proceeding.

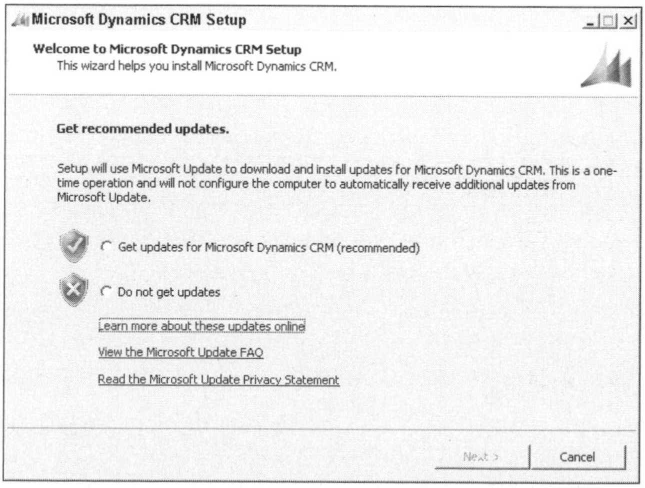

3. After downloading updates for the installation routine, enter your license key. The license key is a 25-character alphanumeric string. It is not case sensitive.

4. Accept the End User License Agreement (EULA). Accepting the EULA indicates your assent to abide by Microsoft's licensing terms for the software. The setup then

downloads and installs missing required software components such as the Azure AppFabric SDK or SQL Reports View Control (see Figure 3.6). When the components have been downloaded and installed, you will see a series of green check marks.

FIGURE 3.6

The setup routine downloads and installs missing software components that are required for Dynamics CRM to run.

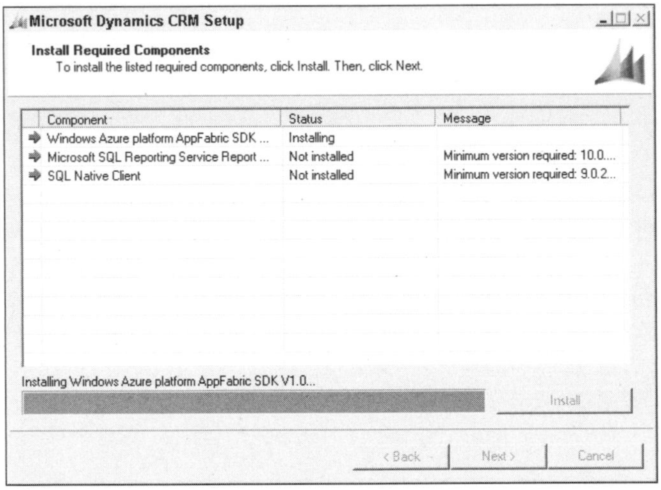

5. Select an installation location or accept the default location. If you entered an Enterprise Edition license key in Step 3, you are presented with the screen that allows you to specify the server roles to install (see Figure 3.1 toward the beginning of this chapter).

6. Select the SQL Server or SQL Server cluster to connect to. For a cluster, you must type the name you gave the cluster when configuring it. The cluster name does not appear in the drop-down menu.

7. Browse to the Active Directory Organizational Unit (OU) where you want the installation routine to create the security groups required by Dynamics CRM. The installation routine creates four security groups: the PrivReportingGroup, PrivUserGroup, ReportingGroup, and SQLAccessGroup.

8. Specify the security account under which the Dynamics CRM services will run (see Figure 3.7). If you use the Network Service account during installation and plan on using SharePoint integration with Dynamics CRM, you also need to add the SharePoint server to the list of site collection administrators in the format of computername$. However, it is recommended to use a low-privilege domain account with local user-level permissions on the server where you are installing Dynamics CRM. (See the IG for more information.)

FIGURE 3.7

You must specify a security account for the Dynamics CRM services. If you use the Network Service account and want to use SharePoint integration, you must grant the SharePoint server certain permissions within the site collection that Dynamics CRM will use.

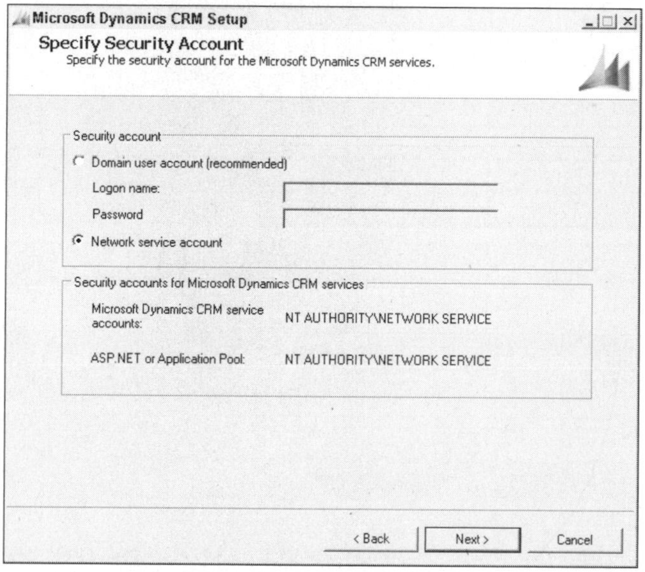

9. Select an existing Web site or create a new Web site. Using the default Web site simplifies user access and IFD configuration because it uses the default ports of 80 for HTTP traffic and 443 for HTTPS traffic, and users will not need to type a port number when browsing to the Dynamics CRM Web site.

10. You can optionally specify the server where you will install the E-mail Router. If you do not specify it now, you must manually add it to the PrivUserGroup later.

11. Enter the organization's friendly display name, the system name for the organization (Figure 3.8). The system organization name cannot contain any non-standard characters. This name will be used when creating the organization database, in the format of OrgName_MSCRM. You should also specify the currency settings and SQL collation if they differ from the prepopulated values, as these cannot be changed after the organization is created.

12. Enter the full address of the SQL Server Reporting Services report server Web site. This is the URL of the report server, not the report manager Web site. The best practice is to configure the report server before installing Dynamics CRM. Be sure to test out the URL to make sure you can access it.

13. Indicate whether you want to participate in the Customer Experience Improvement Program.

FIGURE 3.8

You cannot change the currency settings or SQL collation after the organization is created.

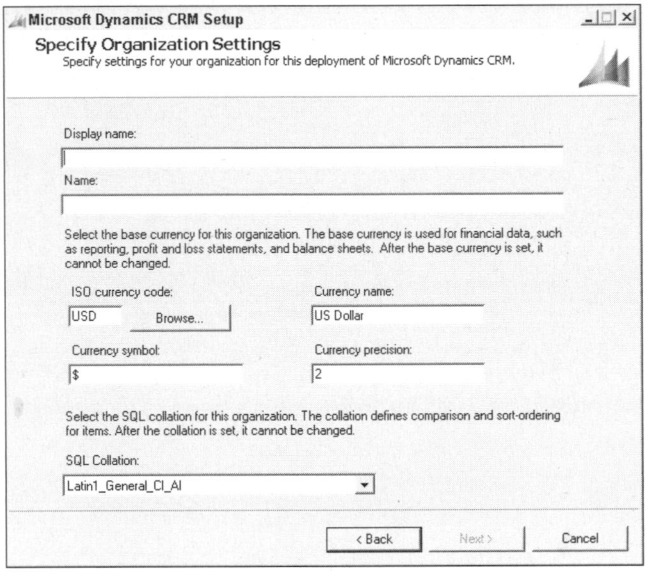

14. Select whether you want to use Microsoft Update to keep Dynamics CRM up-to-date. This new feature for Microsoft Dynamics CRM 2011 helps administrators keep the system updated in the same manner as most other Microsoft software.

    The setup program validates the settings you have selected and your server configuration, and alerts you if anything is amiss (Figure 3.9). The Help button launches the Environment Diagnostics Wizard help file that contains information on many common warnings and errors.

15. Fix any warnings or errors before proceeding.

16. The setup routine displays a summary of the options you have selected. If you are satisfied with your selections, proceed with the install. When the installation is complete, you will be presented with a screen indicating the success or failure of the installation, with a link to the installation logs (see Figure 3.10). If your installation was successful, you can also select whether to immediately launch the installation of the reporting services data connector extensions.

FIGURE 3.9

The setup routine will perform a series of verification checks to ensure that your selections and server configuration meet Dynamics CRM's system requirements.

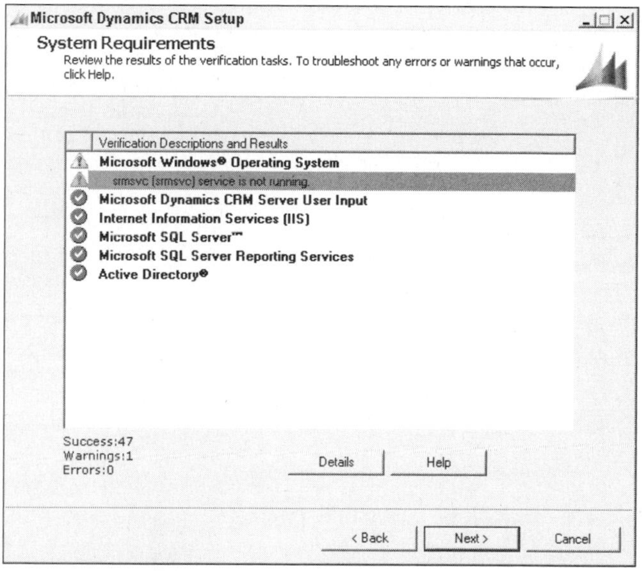

FIGURE 3.10

When the installation is complete, you can immediately launch the setup for the reporting services data connector extensions. The extensions should be installed on the server where SSRS is installed.

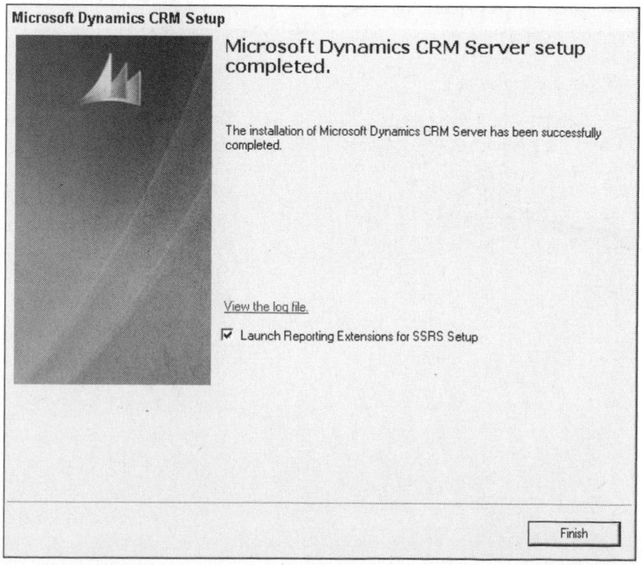

Completing the installation

After your installation is complete, there are several steps you may be required to complete in order for Dynamics CRM to function properly, depending on your deployment configuration.

Installing the SRS Data Connector Extensions

Dynamics CRM reports will not work until you have installed the SSRS connector. This extension enables client requests to be passed through the Dynamics CRM application server to the report server.

Configuring relying parties for claims-based authentication

Additionally, if you plan on allowing users to access the system from the Internet, you must configure Internet-Facing Deployment (IFD). In Microsoft Dynamics CRM 2011, IFD relies on the proper configuration of claims-based authentication (CBA). CBA is managed by Active Directory Federation Services 2.0 (AD FS 2). AD FS 2 must be configured to enable claims from Dynamics CRM users logging in from the Internet.

Cross-Reference

After completing the installation of the Dynamics CRM server, you must install the SQL Server Reporting Services connector. Without these extensions, reports will not function. You must also configure the relying parties for claims-based authentication if you plan on using Internet-Facing Deployment. See Chapter 4 for instructions on installing the SSRS connector and configuring relying parties with AD FS 2.

Installing other server roles

You can now proceed to install other server roles.

Using the Enterprise Edition license key, you can select individual roles or role groups as you progress from server to server. Make sure to test your installation and backup databases between each subsequent server roles installation.

Upgrading the Dynamics CRM Server

Microsoft Dynamics CRM 2011 has been designed to facilitate rapid and reliable upgrades via a variety of upgrade paths. Before conducting your upgrade, you should thoroughly document your upgrade plans and understand the possible upgrade paths available to your organization based on your current deployment.

Planning your upgrade

Microsoft Dynamics CRM 2011 supports upgrades only from Version 4.0. It is not possible to upgrade directly from a version earlier than 4.0 to Microsoft Dynamics CRM 2011. In that situation, you must first upgrade to Microsoft Dynamics CRM 4.0 and then upgrade to the current version.

Checking your current system

After upgrading a software system as integral to users' work as Dynamics CRM, some users may explore areas of the application that they did not use in previous versions, and mistakenly identify performance issues as appearing only after the upgrade. In order to avoid this, and to assist with providing your users with optimal performance, before conducting an upgrade of Dynamics CRM, test your current deployment to establish performance benchmarks and solicit input from your users to document existing problem areas. Fix any performance bottlenecks that you can identify, and plan on testing them after the upgrade as well.

If you have third-party add-ons for Dynamics CRM, or extensive custom code in the form of plug-ins, workflow extensions, client-side scripts, or custom Web applications in the ISV folder, be sure to clearly document them and review them with the vendor or your implementation partner to make sure they will work after the upgrade. If your third-party add-ons were built using the Version 4.0 SDK, they should upgrade without issue because Microsoft Dynamics CRM 2011 includes a backwards compatible Web services endpoint.

Moving to 64-bit hardware

Whereas Microsoft Dynamics CRM 4.0 ran on both 32-bit and 64-bit operating systems, Microsoft Dynamics CRM 2011 requires a 64-bit application server. This is because Microsoft and most major software companies are moving to 64-bit platforms, which provide greater performance and speed than their older 32-bit counterparts. However, many organizations are still running 32-bit hardware. In order to upgrade to Microsoft Dynamics CRM 2011, these organizations will need to purchase 64-bit hardware (or move to a Microsoft or partner-hosted deployment).

One potential upgrade path to move from a 32-bit environment to a 64-bit environment is to install Microsoft Dynamics CRM 2011 on a new 64-bit environment. Then, move the Version 4.0 database to the new environment and import the organization into the Version 2011 deployment. The import process will upgrade the Version 4.0 organization. This upgrade path is covered in more detail later in this chapter.

Going virtual

If your organization has not already done so, upgrading provides an excellent opportunity to incorporate today's virtualization technologies in your Dynamics CRM deployment. Virtualization provides numerous benefits for both production and non-production environments:

- Virtualizing some or all of the servers in your Dynamics CRM deployment can dramatically decrease hardware costs.
- Deploying to a virtual environment enables simpler administration, such as rapid backups and disaster recovery via snapshots.
- Upgrading to a virtual environment allows you to test your upgrades without disrupting your production environment.

Microsoft officially supports Dynamics CRM on their own Hyper-V virtualization technology, which is available with certain editions of Windows Server 2008. Other non-Microsoft virtualization technologies, such as VMWare's ESX are also suitable.

Upgrading Outlook clients

In previous versions of Dynamics CRM, upgrading large numbers of users' Outlook clients presented some significant logistical issues. After the server was upgraded, users were unable to use the Outlook client until it had also been upgraded. If they were in remote offices or traveling, this could mean extended downtime and reduced productivity.

With Microsoft Dynamics CRM 2011, Microsoft has taken a good step toward mitigating this issue. Users who have the Version 4.0 Outlook client and at least Update Rollup 7 will be able to connect to the Microsoft Dynamics CRM 2011 server from Outlook. If they use the online client, they will have the same functionality in Outlook and can then wait for an upgraded client to take full advantage of its expanded functionality. Offline users can also connect to the newly upgraded server, but they will not be able to go back offline until the Outlook client has been upgraded. Therefore, we recommend that after conducting the server upgrade, prioritize your Outlook client users by focusing first on the offline users.

Running the upgrade

Three main upgrade scenarios are used to move from Version 4.0 to Microsoft Dynamics CRM 2011: migration, in-place upgrades, and new installations that connect to an existing database. Read the following sections to determine which path is the best for your situation.

Migrating a Version 4.0 organization database

Many organizations need to make the switch from 32-bit architecture to 64-bit platforms. The good news for these organizations is that Microsoft has provided a relatively simple upgrade path via the ability to migrate a Version 4.0 organization database directly into a new Microsoft Dynamics CRM 2011 deployment (Figure 3.11). After standing up a new 64-bit server, and installing Dynamics CRM, you can import your Version 4.0 organizations with Deployment Manager.

SQL Server does not need to be 64-bit for Microsoft Dynamics CRM 2011, though it does need to be SQL Server 2008. Therefore, if your SQL Server already meets the minimum requirements for Microsoft Dynamics CRM 2011, you can still take advantage of the migration upgrade method by installing the Dynamics CRM application to a new 64-bit server and using the existing database hardware. An important caveat is that you cannot install Dynamics CRM to the same SQL instance as the Version 4.0 database. This is because the new MSCRM_Config database will create conflicts with the existing MSCRM_Config database for your Version 4.0 deployment.

The migration upgrade is the easiest — and therefore most highly recommended — upgrade path. The Version 4.0 organization database will be completely upgraded during the import process. If you have multiple organizations, you can import them and test them one at a time, minimizing downtime and disruptions to productivity.

FIGURE 3.11

Microsoft Dynamics CRM 4.0 organization database can be imported into Microsoft Dynamics CRM 2011 deployments. The import process will upgrade the database.

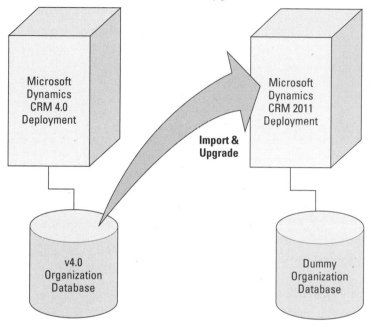

To upgrade a Microsoft Dynamics CRM 4.0 deployment using the migration upgrade path, follow these steps:

1. Install Microsoft Dynamics CRM 2011 on supported hardware or virtual servers. If you are using the Professional Edition license that allows only one organization, you will create a dummy organization during the installation process that you will later replace with your upgraded organization. Give the dummy organization a name that differs from the organization name you will be importing.

2. After the installation is complete and tested, make a backup of your 4.0 organization database. Open SQL Server Management Studio and right-click on the OrgName_ MSCRM database. Under Tasks, select Backup and run the backup, noting the location where the .bak file will be saved.

3. Copy the .bak file to the new SQL Server and restore it by launching SQL Server Management Studio and right-clicking on the Databases node and clicking Restore Database (Figure 3.12). In the Destination to restore box, enter the OrgName_ MSCRM name. Browse to the copy of the .bak file and run the restore.

4. On the new Dynamics CRM server, launch the Deployment Manager and right-click the Organizations node. Select Import Organization. As you work through the Import Organization Wizard and specify the organization database that you want to import, the wizard will detect that it is a Version 4.0 database (Figure 3.13).

Cross-Reference

The process of importing an organization database can vary slightly from scenario to scenario. For complete instructions on using the Deployment Manager to import an organization, see Chapter 7.

FIGURE 3.12

Restoring a Microsoft Dynamics CRM 4.0 organization database to SQL Server so it can be imported into Microsoft Dynamics CRM 2011

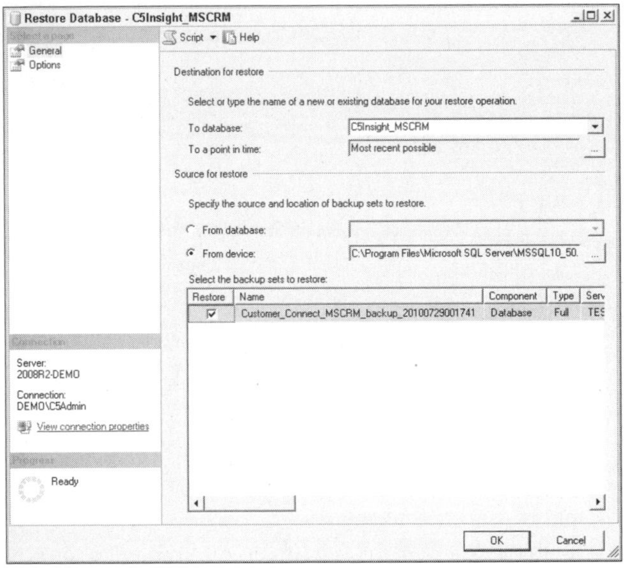

Note

When importing a Version 4.0 organization database and upgrading it, if you are moving your deployment to a new domain, make sure the active user accounts from the previous deployment have a matching user in the new deployment to which they can be mapped.

Performing an in-place upgrade

If your existing infrastructure meets the system requirements for Microsoft Dynamics CRM 2011, you may consider performing an in-place upgrade. When preparing for an in-place upgrade, it is important to test your capability to backup and restore both the Dynamics CRM application and the databases.

Backing up and restoring a SQL Server database is relatively straightforward and follows a consistent path. However, backing up and restoring an application server, with its attendant system files, Web site files, and dependent components (such as the .NET Framework) is quite a bit trickier. Recovering from a failed in-place upgrade can be very difficult, so plan and test your upgrade strategy thoroughly. A failed upgrade can leave your deployment in an unusable state.

FIGURE 3.13

The Microsoft Dynamics CRM 2011 Import Organization Wizard recognizes a Version 4.0 organization database and imports it, upgrading it along the way.

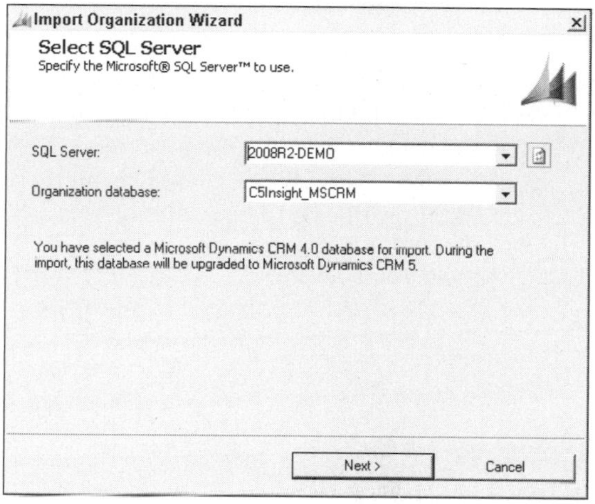

Performing an in-place upgrade on a multitenant deployment upgrades all organizations. Users must not be connected to Dynamics CRM during the upgrade.

Because of the level of difficulty attendant with this upgrade path, this method is the least recommended strategy.

To perform an in-place upgrade, follow the instructions in the Implementation Guide and these general steps:

1. Backup the MSCRM_Config and each organization (OrgName_MSCRM) database.

2. Perform a test restore of the databases to ensure that you can restore them to a functioning state.

3. Back up the application server and any other servers that are part of your Dynamics CRM deployment. Perform complete system backups including operating system, system state, and file-level backups. Again, test your ability to restore these servers to their working condition.

4. Be sure to back up the contents of the ISV folder and other custom files in the Dynamics CRM Web site. Best practice is also to make copies of your report RDL files and export the customizations XML from your organization. It would also be a good practice to export the solution XML for any plug-ins or workflow assemblies you have registered against Dynamics CRM. With these files and a backed up database, you can recover from a failed upgrade much more quickly if necessary.

5. Launch the Microsoft Dynamics CRM 2011 setup routine by navigating to the root folder of your installation media or download location and double-clicking the SetupServer.exe file.

6. Follow the steps outlined in the IG to complete the upgrade.

Installing a new deployment that connects to an existing database

This is a new upgrade path for Dynamics CRM. With Microsoft Dynamics CRM 2011, you can now install the application server components while pointing the installation routine to the existing Version 4.0 configuration and organization databases (see Figure 3.14). This method upgrades both the MSCRM_Config and organization databases during the installation process.

This is an excellent option if you have already migrated to SQL Server 2008 and merely want to upgrade your application and/or platform servers to 64-bit architecture. This option also helps to minimize downtime and provides a simpler recovery method than an in-place upgrade.

FIGURE 3.14

A new upgrade option is to install Microsoft Dynamics CRM 2011 on a new server while connecting to the existing Version 4.0 databases, which are automatically upgraded during the installation.

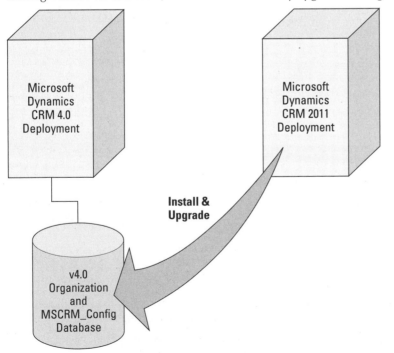

To conduct this type of upgrade, follow these steps:

1. Prepare the server or servers that will provide the Front End, Back End, and Deployment Administration server roles.

2. Back up the MSCRM_Config and each organization (OrgName_MSCRM) database.

3. Perform a test restore of the databases to ensure that you can restore them to a functioning state.

4. Launch the Microsoft Dynamics CRM 2011 setup routine on the new server by navigating to the root folder of your installation media or download location and double-clicking the SetupServer.exe file.

5. Follow the steps outlined in the IG to complete the upgrade.

Testing the upgrade

After the upgrade is complete, run through the following checklist to test that the upgrade process was successful and everything is functioning as expected.

Cross-Reference

In addition to installing or upgrading the Dynamics CRM server, a number of other components should be installed at this point. There are also many initial configuration tasks that you should perform to prepare the system for users. Chapter 4 covers the installation and configuration of other server components, and Chapter 5 goes into detail on post-installation system settings.

- Deployment functioning? Launch the Deployment Manager on the new Dynamics CRM server and expand the Organizations node.

- Organizations functioning? Right-click the new or upgraded organization name in Deployment Manager and click on Browse to open the organization in Internet Explorer.

- Authentication/IFD enabling seamless sign-on? Verify that you are not unexpectedly prompted to enter login credentials when accessing Dynamics CRM from both inside and outside of your network (depending on your configuration).

- Data and users properly mapped? Check that the data is intact and users have been properly mapped and enabled. Have several users log into the Web client to verify that they see the data they expect.

- Customizations working? Test forms with client-side script to see if they perform as anticipated. Run through your test scripts for any server-side extensions to validate their functionality.

- Migrated customizations? Go to the customizations area and open the default solution. Verify that all of your organization's customizations have been migrated.

- Reports Working? Test running several reports, including system reports and custom reports.

- Processing services running? Validate that the Asynchronous and Sandbox processing services are both running.

- Third-party add-ons working? Test third-party add-ons. You may need to upgrade add-ons that you have purchased and applied to a previous version of Dynamics CRM. Contact the vendors for instructions.

- Outlook client connecting? Configure a Version 4.0 Outlook client add-on to connect to the Microsoft Dynamics CRM 2011 server if the server address has changed. (Version 4.0 Outlook clients must have at least Update Rollup 7 for 4.0 applied to connect to Microsoft Dynamics CRM 2011.)

Cross-Reference

Chapter 9 provides useful tips to overcome common installation and upgrade errors as well as insight on how to optimize your new Dynamics CRM server for your users.

Summary

This chapter provided information to supplement Microsoft's Implementation Guide (IG). The IG is indispensable when planning your Dynamics CRM deployment and installing the server and related technologies.

Although Dynamics CRM is a valuable tool for organizations of many different sizes, with a nearly infinite variety of network architectures, it is also a complex system of technologies that rely on a deep stack of Microsoft products. Because of this complexity, your deployment or upgrade must be planned very carefully, with your organization's long-term needs for Dynamics CRM in mind.

This chapter also provided guidance on some of the ways you should prepare your network infrastructure for a new Dynamics CRM deployment.

Server roles and multi-server deployment provide a great deal of flexibility in matching your Dynamics CRM implementation with your organizations needs and infrastructure for a production deployment, and also enable a wide variety of options for the construction of test and development environments.

Installing Other Components for Dynamics CRM

Microsoft Dynamics CRM 2011 includes several components that are installed separately from the Dynamics CRM server, or which can only be configured after its successful installation. These components include:

- The Microsoft Dynamics CRM Reporting Extensions for SSRS
- The SharePoint grid
- Claims-Based Authentication and Internet-Facing Deployment
- The Microsoft Dynamics CRM E-mail Router and Rule Deployment Wizard
- The Microsoft Office Outlook client for Dynamics CRM

This chapter presents the concepts and instructions needed to successfully complete the installation and configuration of these components in your Dynamics CRM deployment.

Note

The Implementation Guide (IG) is a free resource from Microsoft that includes detailed instructions for installing and configuring the Dynamics CRM server and its related components. It is available from the Microsoft Downloads site (www.microsoft.com/downloads). This chapter provides the context for understanding these components' usage, as well as best practices and tips for each of them.

Installing Ancillary Server Components

Microsoft has designed Dynamics CRM to leverage the functionality of a broad range of other Microsoft technologies, such as SQL Server Reporting Services and SharePoint. When added to the capabilities of Dynamics CRM, these technologies empower users to access, analyze, and share business information and collaborate with one another in a variety of ways. To get the full value from Dynamics CRM, you must install and configure these components appropriately.

Connecting Dynamics CRM to SQL Reporting Services

When a user runs a report in Dynamics CRM, the request is passed from the user's machine (the "client") to the Dynamics CRM server, and from there to the report server. In order for the Dynamics CRM security rules to be enforced, the report is generated in the context of the user who requested it, meaning that the user's authentication credentials must accompany the request for the report (Figure 4.1). The user has authenticated to the Dynamics CRM server (either by using his or her Windows logon or by logging in via IFD). The Dynamics CRM server must be able to pass the credentials from the user to the report server, and the report server must "trust" that the Dynamics CRM server is authorized to pass credentials from users. This is sometimes referred to as a *double-hop*.

FIGURE 4.1

A user's request for a report passes the user credentials from the client machine to the Dynamics CRM server and on to the report server.

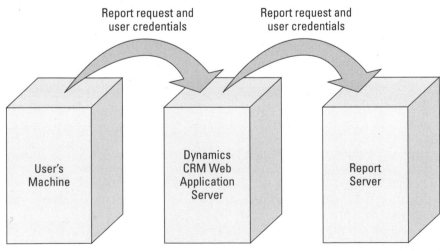

The Microsoft Dynamics CRM Reporting Extensions for SSRS are extensions to Dynamics CRM that enable user requests to be passed to the report server so that reports can be returned and security maintained. Without the Reporting Extensions for SSRS, reports will not run in Microsoft Dynamics CRM 2011. The extensions are also necessary in order to enable users to schedule reports from Dynamics CRM.

Caution

The Microsoft Dynamics CRM Reporting Extensions for SSRS are required for Microsoft Dynamics CRM 2011. Without it, reports will not function for any user, regardless of authentication mechanism or location. This is a change from previous versions of Dynamics CRM that only required the SRS Data Connector when the report server was on a different machine than the Dynamics CRM Web application.

The Reporting Extensions for SSRS can be installed any time after the Dynamics CRM server has been installed. (SQL Server Reporting Services should have been installed and configured before installing the Dynamics CRM server.) When you finish the installation of the Dynamics CRM server, you have the option of launching the installation of the Reporting Extensions for SSRS right away, as shown in Figure 4.2.

FIGURE 4.2

You have the option of launching the installation of the Reporting Extensions for SSRS immediately from the server setup when the server installation has completed.

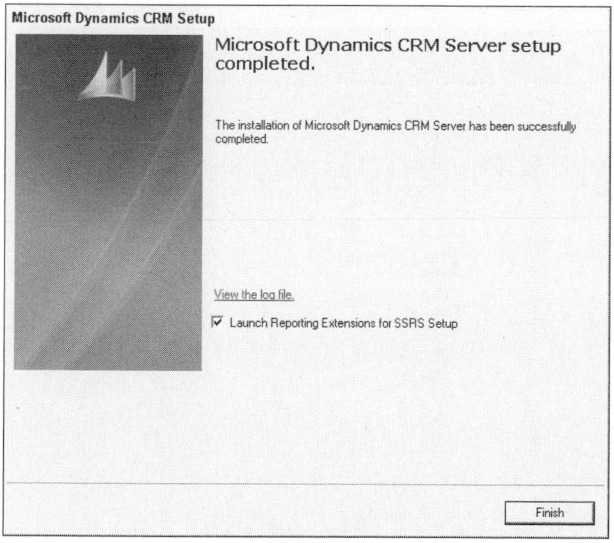

The Reporting Extensions for SSRS must be installed on the server where the SQL Reporting Services report server is installed.

To start the installation of the Reporting Extensions for SSRS, navigate to the Dynamics CRM server install media or download location. Open the "srsdataconnector" folder and double-click on setupsrsdataconnector.exe. The setup screen opens, as shown in Figure 4.3. Running the Reporting Extensions for SSRS setup publishes the reports that are included with Dynamics CRM to the report server (see Figure 4.4).

Cross-Reference

After installation, the Reporting Extensions for SSRS are displayed as the SRS Data Connector server role in the Deployment Manager, enabling you to see which servers the extensions have been installed on. The SRS Data Connector server role is the only organization-specific server role. All other server roles apply to the entire deployment. See Chapter 3 for more information about server roles and Chapter 5 for more information about the Deployment Manager.

FIGURE 4.3

When installing the Reporting Extensions for SSRS, you can select whether or not to update the installation files before proceeding.

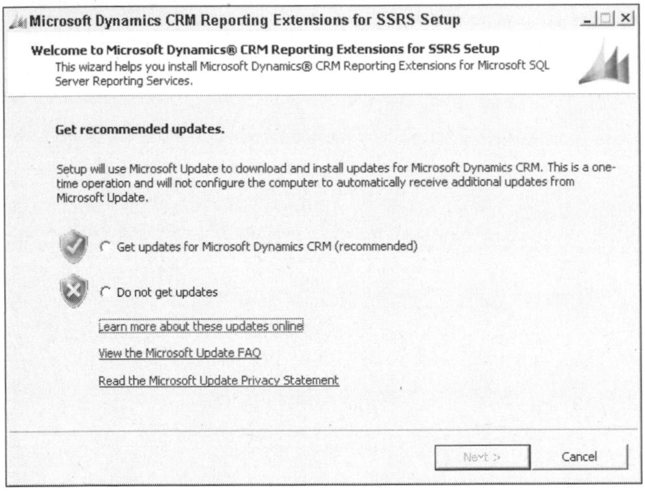

Installing and setting up the SharePoint Grid integration

Many users of previous versions of Dynamics CRM have recognized the natural complementary functions of Dynamics CRM and SharePoint. Where Dynamics CRM provides a platform for well-defined data capture and analysis to support business processes, SharePoint enables best-in-class collaboration and document management. Because of this natural fit, many partners and ISVs (Independent Software Vendors) have been building SharePoint integration for Dynamics CRM over the last several years. Now, with Microsoft Dynamics CRM 2011, SharePoint integration is built directly into the product, enabling dynamic creation of document libraries related to both system and custom entities in Dynamics CRM (see Figure 4.5).

Document libraries that are created through the built-in integration can also be nested so they roll up in the SharePoint site collection under a top-level customer Account site (see Figure 4.6).

FIGURE 4.4

Installing the Reporting Extensions for SSRS also publishes the out-of-the-box reports.

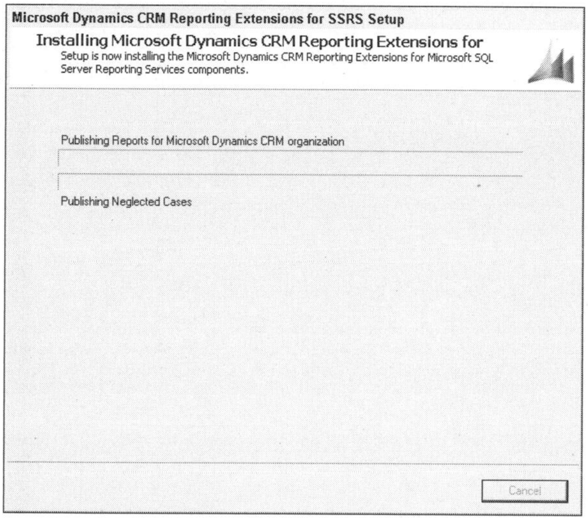

FIGURE 4.5

SharePoint integration is built into Microsoft Dynamics CRM 2011.

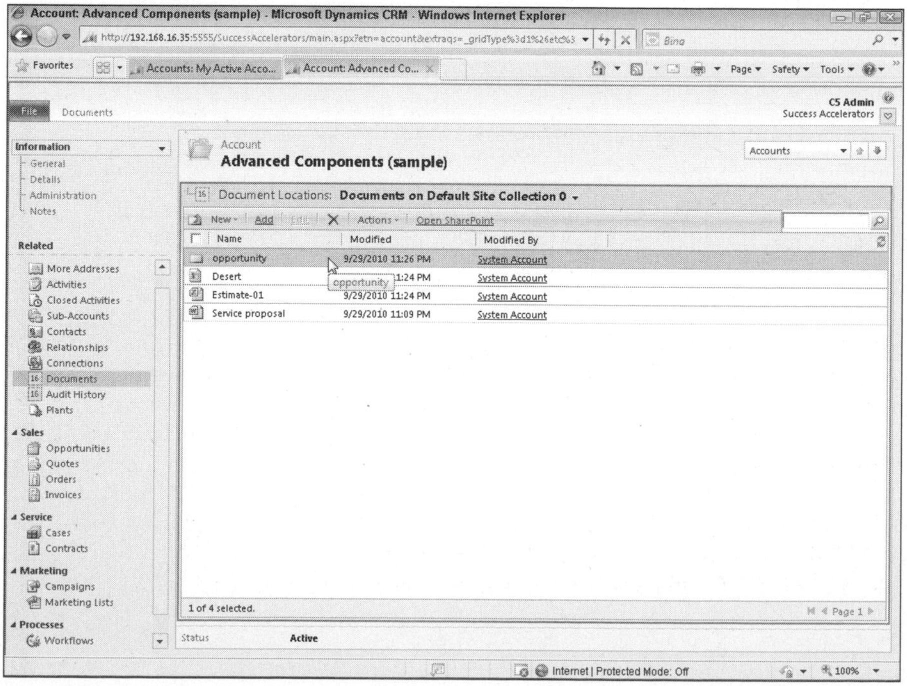

FIGURE 4.6

SharePoint integration can be configured to nest document libraries under a site for a record's parent Account.

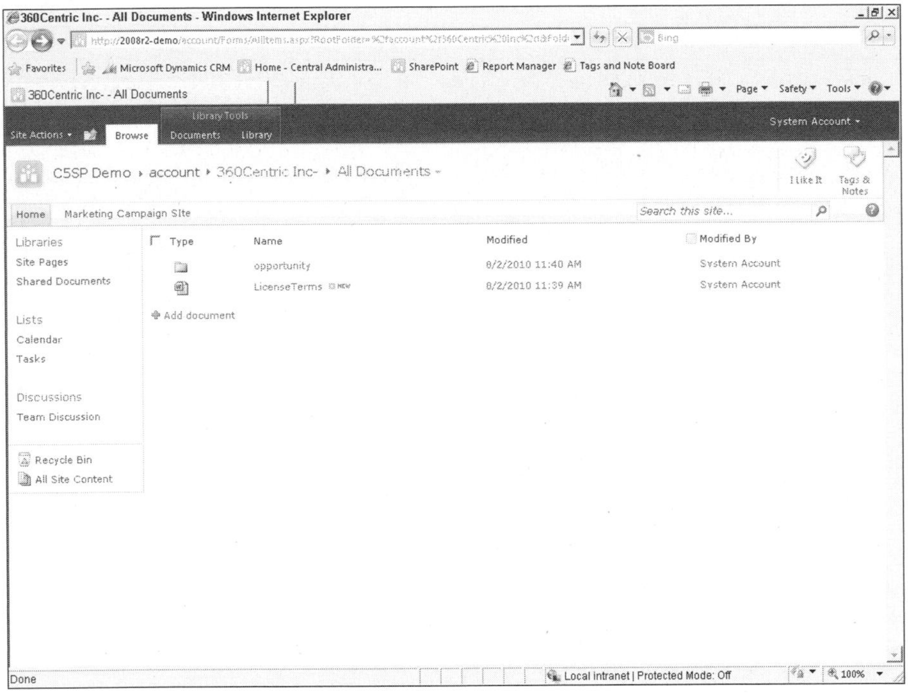

Preparing SharePoint for the Dynamics CRM integration

For the SharePoint Grid to function, SharePoint must be configured to permit Dynamics CRM to work with files in SharePoint. Follow these steps:

1. Open the SharePoint Central Administration Web site.

2. Click on the System Settings link.

3. On the System Settings page, click Manage services on server.

4. In the list of services, locate the Microsoft SharePoint Foundation Sandboxed Code Service and start the service if it is not already started.

5. Navigate to the Application Management page (Central Administration ⇨ Application Management), and click on the Manage Web Applications link.

6. Select the SharePoint site collection for which you want to enable Dynamics CRM integration by clicking on the site name.

7. On the Ribbon menu, click the General Settings button and click General Settings.

8. In the Web Application General Settings dialog, scroll down to the Browser File Handling section. Select the Permissive option. Scroll to the bottom of the dialog and click OK.

Installing the SharePoint Grid for Dynamics CRM

Microsoft Dynamics CRM 2011 integrates with all versions of SharePoint 2010 through a SharePoint Grid extension that must be installed on the Dynamics CRM server. The SharePoint Grid component can be installed on the Dynamics CRM server by using the install media, or it can be installed from the Dynamics CRM Web client interface by navigating to the Document Management page in the Settings area and clicking the appropriate link (see Figure 4.7).

FIGURE 4.7

The Grid Component for SharePoint integration can be installed from the Document Management page in the Settings area of Dynamics CRM.

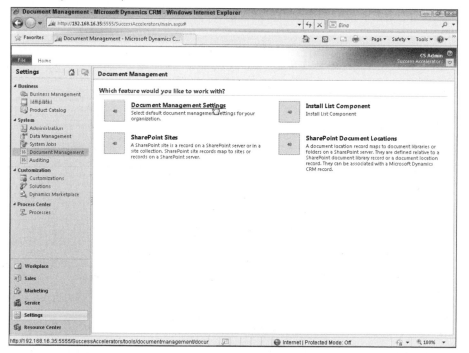

To install the SharePoint Grid component, you must have administrative permissions on the SharePoint site where documents will be stored. To install the grid, follow these steps.

To enable automatic integration with SharePoint 2010, you must first install the SharePoint grid component on your SharePoint site. The following steps assume that you are logged into the SharePoint server as a SharePoint site collection administrator. You must also be a farm administrator to change the file handling settings. The SharePoint User Code Host service must also be started as specified above, which in turn requires the Microsoft SharePoint Foundation Sandboxed Code Service to be enabled. With these prerequisites in place, follow the instructions below to upload and activate the SharePoint list component for Dynamics CRM:

1. Browse to the site collection where you wish to enable Dynamics CRM to create document libraries.

2. Click Site Actions ➪ Site Settings.

3. Under Galleries, click the Solutions link.

4. On the Solutions tab, in the New group, click the option Upload Solution.

5. Browse to and select the crmlistcomponent.wsp file that is included with the Dynamics CRM install media or download files and click OK.

6. On the Solutions tab, click the Activate button to activate the SharePoint list component.

Configuring Document Management Settings

After installing the SharePoint grid, you must specify which entities will be available for users to create document libraries.

1. Go to the Document Management page and click the Document Management Settings link.

2. In the Document Management Settings dialog, shown in Figure 4.8, select the entities for which document management should be enabled. Specify the URL of the SharePoint site collection and click Next.

3. Select the folder structure to use for organizing the document libraries. The Generic option creates a flat structure. The Account Centric option nests document libraries under a page created for a parent account, if one exists. Click the Finish button to apply the settings.

The sites used by the grid component and the document library locations created by Dynamics CRM can be viewed in list form and managed by an administrator from the links on the Document Management page.

FIGURE 4.8

Use the Document Management Settings dialog to specify the entities that will be enabled for document management, and the URL of the SharePoint site collection.

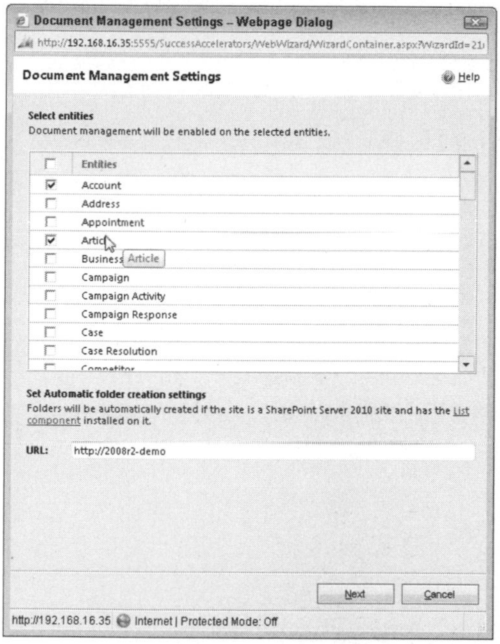

Configuring Dynamics CRM for External Access

Microsoft Dynamics CRM 2011 is designed to enable secure remote access from the Internet by using Internet Explorer, the Outlook client, and mobile devices using SSL encryption in what is called Internet-Facing Deployment, or IFD. Allowing users to log in to Dynamics CRM from outside of the LAN enables them to work with Dynamics CRM while traveling or while located in a remote or disconnected office. External access also makes it possible to set up users who may never otherwise connect to your network, such as a distributed workforce, partners, vendors, or contractors. Additionally, no VPN is required when using the Outlook client through IFD.

Because Microsoft has designed Dynamics CRM to be deployed in both hosted and on-premises installation models, it has incorporated a relatively new technology that federates different authentication sources like Active Directory and Microsoft's Live ID. This federation of authentication providers is referred to as claims-based authentication (CBA). A federation server, such as Active Directory Federation Services 2.0 (AD FS 2) manages which authentication providers are enabled for Dynamics CRM.

With Microsoft Dynamics CRM 2011, configuration of claims-based authentication is a prerequisite for external access via IFD. CBA is not required if users will only access Dynamics CRM within the intranet from a trusted domain.

Understanding claims-based authentication

When a user attempts to log in to Dynamics CRM, the federation server checks to see if the source of the user's credentials is one of the "identity providers" that has been configured for Dynamics CRM access. If the credentials are accepted, the user is granted a token which is used to access Dynamics CRM (Figure 4.9). In this way, Dynamics CRM can be configured to accept logon credentials that are managed in a variety of authentication providers, not just Microsoft's Active Directory.

Configuring IFD

To make Dynamics CRM accessible from the Internet, you need to configure several items:

- **Install a wildcard SSL certificate on the Dynamics CRM Front End (Web application) server.** This certificate should be for a URL in the format of `https://*.yourdomain.com`. Installing an SSL certificate involves generating the request from the server, acquiring the certificate using the information generated, and installing the certificate. For more information, refer to the article "Configuring Server Certificates in IIS 7" on Microsoft TechNet: `http://technet.microsoft.com/en-us/library/cc732230(WS.10).aspx`.

- **Configure DNS and firewalls so the internal and external URLs for your Dynamics CRM server are accessible.** You also need to request that your ISP configure the name servers for your domain name to direct traffic to the proper URL. For external access, you need a URL that points to the Dynamics CRM server (`https://crmserver.yourdomain.com`), as well as one that points to the organization (`https://orgname.crmserver.domain.com`). When users attempt to log in to the first URL, after authenticating they will be redirected to the URL containing their default organization name. Therefore, both URLs need to resolve correctly.

- **Configure the relying parties.** On the AD FS 2.0 server, you must configure the relying parties as specified in the Implementation Guide. This step identifies that your Dynamics CRM system accepts authentication claims from Active Directory.

- **Configure the Dynamics CRM server to use HTTPS in Deployment Manager.** Log in to the Deployment Manager and, in the Properties dialog for the deployment, click the Web Address tab. Select HTTPS for the Binding Type and click OK (see Figure 4.10).

- **Configure claims-based authentication in Deployment Manager.** Click the link in Deployment Manager to launch the Claims-Based Authentication configuration wizard. In the wizard, you need to enter the URL for the federation metadata XML file (see Figure 4.11). This file is located in the federation services Web site. After entering this file location, you need to specify an encryption certificate from the local server's certificate store.

FIGURE 4.9

Claims-based authentication (CBA) is a new authentication model that is required for Internet-Facing Deployments. When a user attempts to log in to Dynamics CRM, his credentials are redirected to the federation server (typically an AD FS 2.0 server) which checks his claim against the identity providers. If the claim is valid, a token is given to the user to provide access to Dynamics CRM.

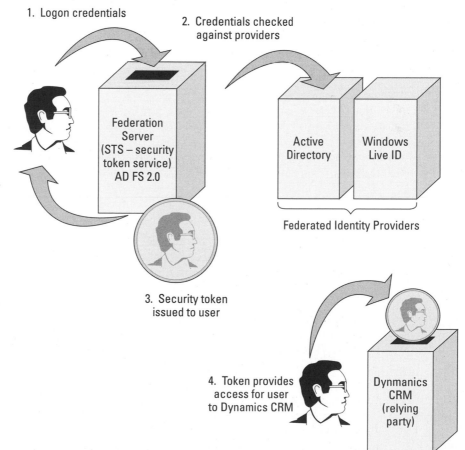

1. Logon credentials

2. Credentials checked against providers

Federation Server (STS – security token service) AD FS 2.0

Active Directory

Windows Live ID

Federated Identity Providers

3. Security token issued to user

4. Token provides access for user to Dynamics CRM

Dynmanics CRM (relying party)

- **Run the Internet-Facing Deployment Configuration Wizard.** This wizard can be launched from the Deployment Manager. You enter the external URL for your Dynamics CRM deployment in the format `https://crmserver.yourdomain.com`. Add the port number to the URL if it is not the default SSL port of 443.
- **Update the authentication method in the web.config.** After applying the changes, you must update the web.config file in the Dynamics CRM Web site root by changing the authentication strategy from OnPremise to ServiceProviderLicenseAgreement:

```
<authentication strategy="ServiceProviderLicenseAgreement" />
```

Cross-Reference

Chapter 7 contains details on using the Deployment Manager, where many of the steps are performed for configuring external access for Dynamics CRM.

FIGURE 4.10

Setting the Dynamics CRM deployment to use HTTPS. Do this before configuring external access.

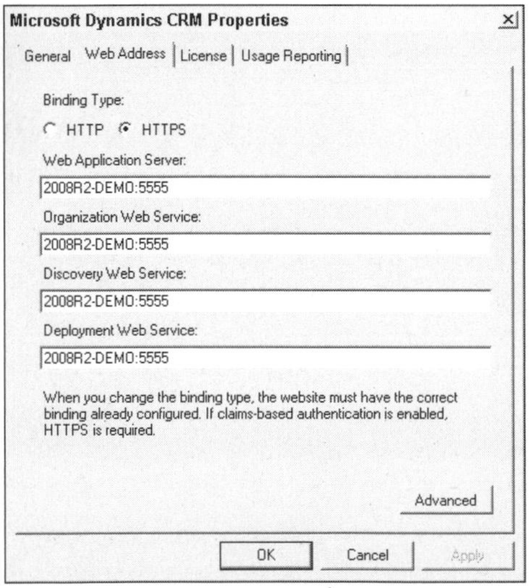

The Implementation Guide contains step-by-step instructions for configuring claims-based authentication and Internet-Facing Deployment. Refer to it and to Appendix B for more information about setting up the components required for external access for Dynamics CRM.

FIGURE 4.11

The Claims-Based Authentication (CBA) Wizard

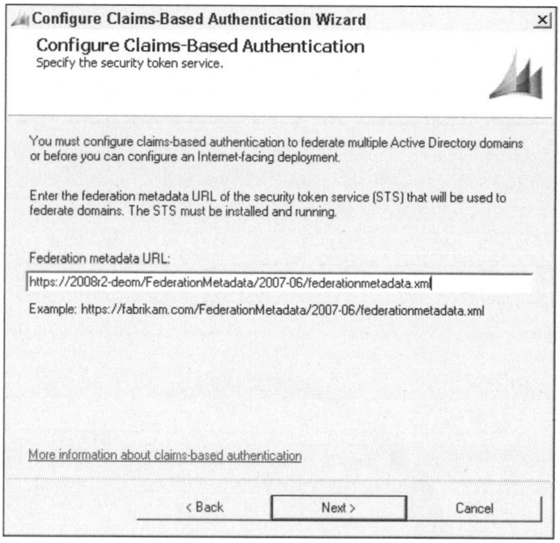

AD FS 2.0

Claims-based authentication requires a federation server like Active Directory Federation Services 2.0 (AD FS 2.0) to manage the relying parties and issue tokens. You can download and install AD FS 2.0 from the Microsoft Downloads Web site (www.microsoft.com/downloads) and run the AD FS configuration wizard (see figure) on a supported server.

AD FS 2.0 is the technology that enables Active Directory to be set up as a trusted identity provider. When the Active Directory user attempts to access an application that uses claims-based authentication, the user's request is routed through the AD FS 2.0 site, which checks the request against the identity providers and issues a token for the user to gain access to the resource.

AD FS 2.0 was formerly referred to by its codename of "Geneva" and is a relatively new technology that Microsoft has developed to assist enterprises with maintaining single sign-on (SSO) even when users access applications and servers that are in the cloud. As cloud services and applications such as Dynamics CRM Online become more prevalent, it will become increasingly important for administrators to understand technologies like AD FS 2.0.

AD FS 2.0 installs to the default Web site on a server so it may not be appropriate to install it on your Dynamics CRM server. The AD FS Web site must have a valid SSL certificate. The AD FS Web site URL is used when configuring claims-based authentication for Dynamics CRM. Read more about AD FS 2.0 at www.microsoft.com/adfs2.

Integrating E-mail with Dynamics CRM

E-mail is a critical part of any customer relationship management or line-of-business application. Microsoft has designed Dynamics CRM for tight e-mail integration, enabling incoming and outgoing messages to be tracked in the database and associated with the business. Dynamics CRM can integrate with Exchange Servers and POP3 mail servers through the use of the E-mail Router component.

The E-mail Router uses incoming profiles which are associated with the Dynamics CRM users or queues to connect to users' mailboxes to process incoming mail and identify which should be tracked in Dynamics CRM. Outgoing profiles are likewise used to permit the E-mail Router to connect to the mail provider to send outgoing messages. The E-mail Router runs asynchronously, meaning that messages are processed periodically. Three basic scenarios are supported by the E-mail Router (Figure 4.12):

- POP3 E-mail. When configured for POP3 e-mail, you must create an incoming profile for each POP provider within the Microsoft Dynamics CRM E-mail Router. Each user must enter his e-mail credentials in his personal options, accessible from the Outlook client, and indicate that the E-mail Router can send and receive e-mail on his behalf. You must also create a single outgoing profile for all outgoing mail per POP mail provider. Outgoing mail for POP providers uses SMTP.

- Exchange. Using a single incoming profile, the E-mail Router can check each user's inbox for messages that should be tracked in Dynamics CRM. An outgoing profile allows Dynamics CRM to route outgoing e-mail through the Exchange Server. This method requires the incoming profile to be configured with an account that has certain administrative privileges in Exchange so it can access each user's inbox.

- Exchange with a Forward Mailbox. With this method, a rule is deployed to each user's Exchange mailbox (using the Rule Deployment wizard or, optionally, the rule can be manually created by the user). The rule forwards a copy of every incoming e-mail message to a sink mailbox that is monitored by an incoming profile in the E-mail Router. An outgoing profile allows Dynamics CRM to route outgoing e-mail through the Exchange Server. This method allows the incoming profile to be configured with a user account that has access only to the sink mailbox. Another advantage of this method is that the forward mailbox is a single box that can be monitored, managed, and maintained, potentially reducing administrator overhead. With this method, however, the forwarding rule must be deployed every time a user account is added to Dynamics CRM.

Note

The Outlook client can also function as an e-mail router for Dynamics CRM. However, the Outlook client must be running in order for incoming and outgoing e-mail to be tracked into Dynamics CRM. One of the primary advantages of deploying the provided E-mail Router software component is that it is always running.

FIGURE 4.12

The E-mail Router supports three primary scenarios: POP3 E-mail, Exchange Server, and Forwarding Mailboxes.

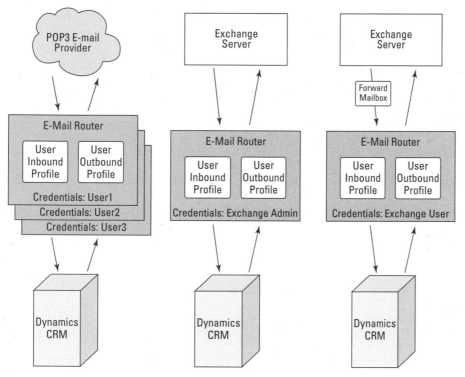

Installing the E-Mail Router

The E-mail Router can be installed on any computer that is running a supported operating system and which has access to both Dynamics CRM and the E-mail server. Supported operating systems include most versions of Windows XP, Vista, Windows Server 2003 and 2008, and Windows 7. For Exchange connectivity, the E-mail Router supports Exchange 2003, 2007, 2010, and Exchange Online.

The Rule Deployment Wizard requires the Exchange Server MAPI client runtime libraries in order to place rules in users' Exchange mailboxes. The MAPI Client and Collaboration Data Objects can be downloaded and installed from the Microsoft Downloads Web site. (See the Online Resources appendix for the full URL.)

Caution

The MAPI objects — and therefore the Rule Deployment Wizard — cannot be installed on a machine where Microsoft Office Outlook is installed. (It can be installed on the same machine as the E-mail Router, however.)

To install the Microsoft Dynamics CRM E-mail Router, follow these steps:

1. Navigate to the install media or download location and locate the Exchange folder. Double-click the setupemailrouter.exe file to launch the setup routine.

2. The first screen of the Microsoft Dynamics CRM E-mail Router Setup (see Figure 4.13) allows you to choose whether or not to get updates for the installation routine. Select an option and click Next. If you choose to download updates, when the download completes, click Next again.

FIGURE 4.13

Select whether you wish to download updates for the installation routine.

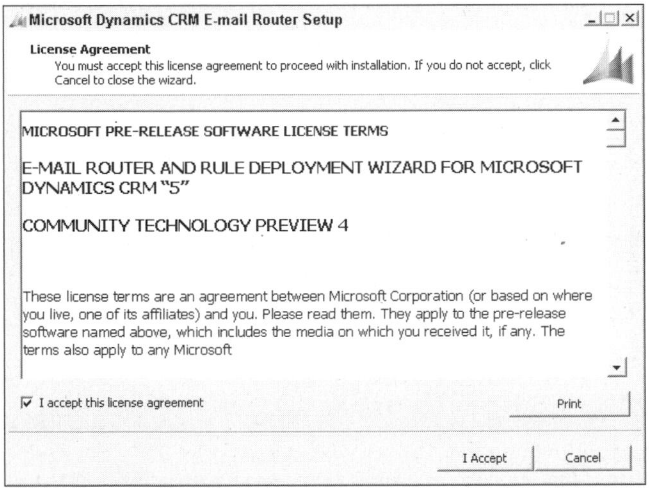

3. The E-mail Router setup checks for missing required components. If any are missing, click the Install button to download and install them, shown in Figure 4.14. When the missing components have been installed, click Next to proceed with the installation.

4. On the next screen, select which components to install. You can install the E-mail Router Service, the Rule Deployment Wizard, or both. After making your selection, click Next.

5. Select the directory where the E-mail Router components should be installed or accept the default location. Click Next.

6. The setup routine performs a series of checks to validate the settings you have input and the environmental variables. Fix any warnings or errors that the setup routine detects and, when all green check marks are displayed, click Next.

FIGURE 4.14

If any missing required components are detected, download and install them.

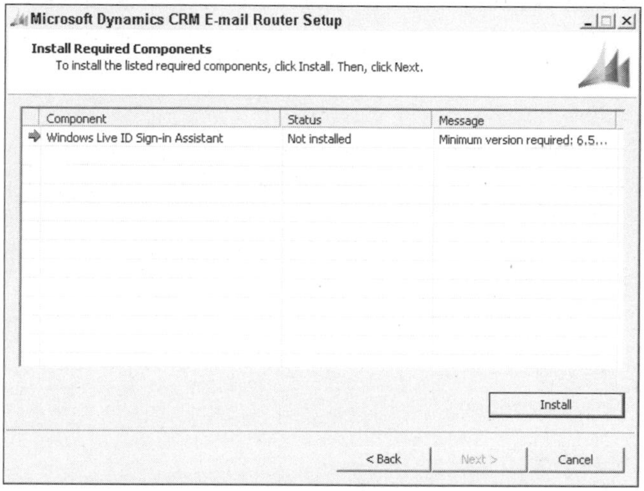

7. The setup program displays a summary of your selections. Click the Install button to begin the installation.

8. When the installation completes, click Finish to close the setup dialog, or click the link to immediately launch the E-mail Router Configuration Manager.

Configuring the E-mail Router

After the E-mail Router has been installed, you must configure the incoming and outgoing profiles that will handle E-mail authentication and processing for your users. Following are detailed instructions for configuring the E-mail Router for use with a POP3 E-mail Server. Similar steps can be followed for configuring the E-mail Router to work with various versions of Exchange Server and Exchange Online. See the Implementation Guide for complete instructions for these E-mail access methods.

From the Start menu, go to Programs and, under the Microsoft Dynamics CRM E-mail Router folder, click Microsoft Dynamics CRM E-mail Router Configuration Manager. The E-mail Router Configuration Manager program opens (see Figure 4.15). Then follow the steps below for the appropriate scenario.

Configuring incoming and outgoing profiles for use with POP3 e-mail accounts

Each user who uses POP3 e-mail must have both an incoming and an outgoing profile configured in the E-mail Router.

FIGURE 4.15

The E-mail Router Configuration Manager. To create a new incoming or outgoing profile, click the New button.

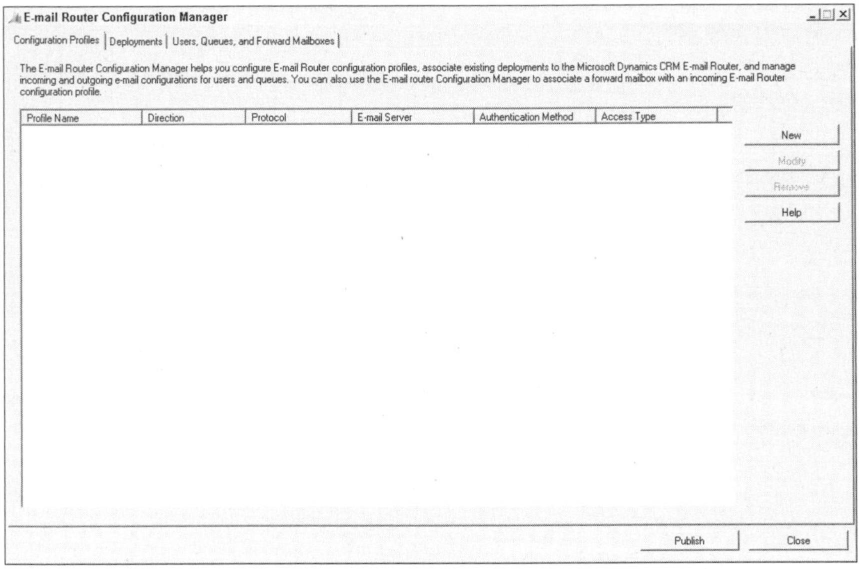

To configure the incoming profile for a POP3 e-mail account, do the following:

1. On the Configuration Profiles tab, click the New button.

2. In the E-mail Router Configuration Profile dialog (Figure 4.16) enter a name for the profile.

3. Select Incoming as the direction.

4. In the E-mail Server Type drop-down select POP3.

5. In the Authentication Type drop-down select Clear Text.

6. In the Location settings, enter the address of the E-mail server and indicate whether or not your POP server uses SSL.

7. Set the Access Credentials to be User Specified. (Users will need to enter their credentials in their personal options in the Outlook client.)

8. If your POP provider uses nonstandard ports, click the Advanced tab and enter the port number. Click OK.

9. Instruct users to enter and save their POP e-mail credentials in their Outlook client personal options.

FIGURE 4.16

Configuring an incoming profile for use with a POP3 e-mail account.

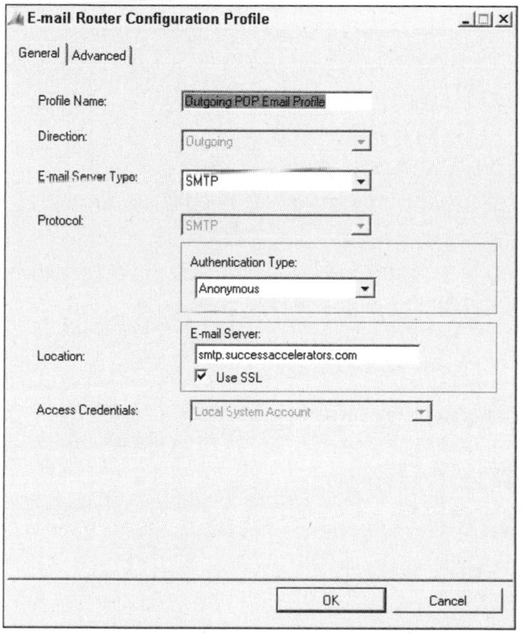

To configure the outgoing rule, repeat Steps 1 and 2 of the previous list and then complete the following steps:

1. For Direction, select Outgoing.

2. In the E-mail Server Type drop-down, select SMTP.

3. For Authentication Type, if your provider requires authentication for outbound e-mail, choose Clear Text. Otherwise, choose Anonymous.

4. Enter the name of the outbound SMTP server and select whether or not to use SSL.

5. Enter a username and password to authenticate to your POP provider's outbound SMTP server.

6. If your POP E-mail provider uses a nonstandard port for SMTP mail, click the Advanced tab and enter the port in the Network Port box.

Associating profiles with deployments

After your incoming and outgoing profiles are complete, you must associate them with the Dynamics CRM deployment and associate them with the users or queues for which they were created.

To associate the profiles with a deployment:

1. In the E-mail Router Configuration Manager click the Deployments tab and click New.

2. Select the deployment option for which you are configuring the E-mail Router (Figure 4.17).

3. Enter the address of the Microsoft Dynamics CRM server. Be sure to include the port number and organization name.

4. Select either Local System Account or Other Specified under Access Credentials. If you selected Other Specified, enter the username and password of a Dynamics CRM user who has access to the organization.

5. Choose the incoming and outgoing profiles you wish to use for this deployment and click OK.

Note

Each user's incoming and outgoing method is set on the user record in the Dynamics CRM application. For example, a user can be set to use Outlook for incoming e-mail, and the E-mail Router for outgoing e-mail. To set which method a user will use, open the Administration page in the Settings area of the Dynamics CRM Web site and click the User link. Open the user record and scroll down to the e-mail settings section. Outlook is the default incoming and outgoing method for new users. If the user will use the E-mail Router profile for either incoming or outgoing e-mail, you must set that option on the user record.

FIGURE 4.17

Associating the incoming and outgoing profiles with a deployment organization in the E-mail Router Configuration Manager

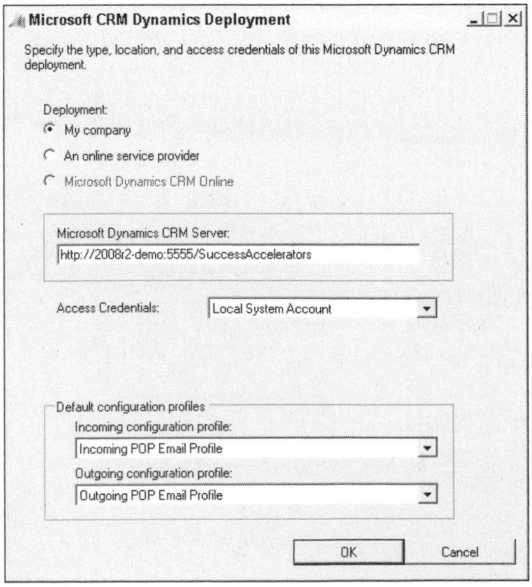

Specifying users for the deployed profiles

Next, you must specify which users and queues in the deployment will be using the incoming and outgoing profiles you have defined.

1. In the E-mail Router Configuration Manager, click the Users, Queues, and Forward Mailboxes tab.

2. From the drop-down list at the top, select the deployment for which you wish to configure users' E-mail Router profiles, and click the "Load Data" button. The users in the selected organization will be loaded and displayed.

3. Select a user or users, and click the Modify button on the right side of the window. In the dialog that opens, set the Incoming Configuration Profile and the Outgoing Configuration Profile you want the user to use. If a profile option is grayed out, this is because the user's e-mail access type in Dynamics CRM has been set to either Microsoft Dynamics CRM for Outlook, the Forward Mailbox, or None (see Figure 4.18). Click OK.

4. After configuring the profiles for each user and queue, click the Test Access button to run a test that will check whether the E-mail Router can access the incoming and outgoing mail servers for each profile. Fix any errors that the test detects.

5. When you are satisfied with the settings, click the Publish button at the bottom of the E-mail Router Configuration Manager window. After publishing is complete, click the Close button to close the window.

Note

If your organization opts to use the E-mail Router to handle the processing of inbound and outbound messages, you must run the E-mail Router Configuration Manager to set the incoming and outgoing profiles that will be associated with a user each time a user is added to Dynamics CRM. Because of this extra administrative overhead — a step that is frequently overlooked when setting up a new user — Microsoft has defaulted new users to use the Microsoft Dynamics CRM for Outlook client. This is the easiest setting for administrators because it requires no additional steps when creating new users. However, until a user has installed and configured the Outlook client, e-mail tracking will be unavailable for that user.

Configuring the E-mail Router for use with a forwarding mailbox

If you have elected to use a forwarding mailbox to process incoming e-mail messages, you must also specify the incoming profile the forwarding mailbox will use. To use a forward mailbox, you must first create the mailbox in the Exchange Server.

1. In the E-mail Router Configuration Manager, click the Users, Queues, and Forward Mailboxes tab.

2. Select the deployment and click the Load Data button.

3. When the data has loaded, switch to the Forward Mailboxes tab and click the New button.

4. In the Forward Mailbox dialog, enter a friendly name for the mailbox and its e-mail address.

FIGURE 4.18

A user record where one of the e-mail access types has been set to "None." To associate a profile for this user in the E-mail Router Configuration Manager, you must first set this user to use the E-mail Router for the specified access type.

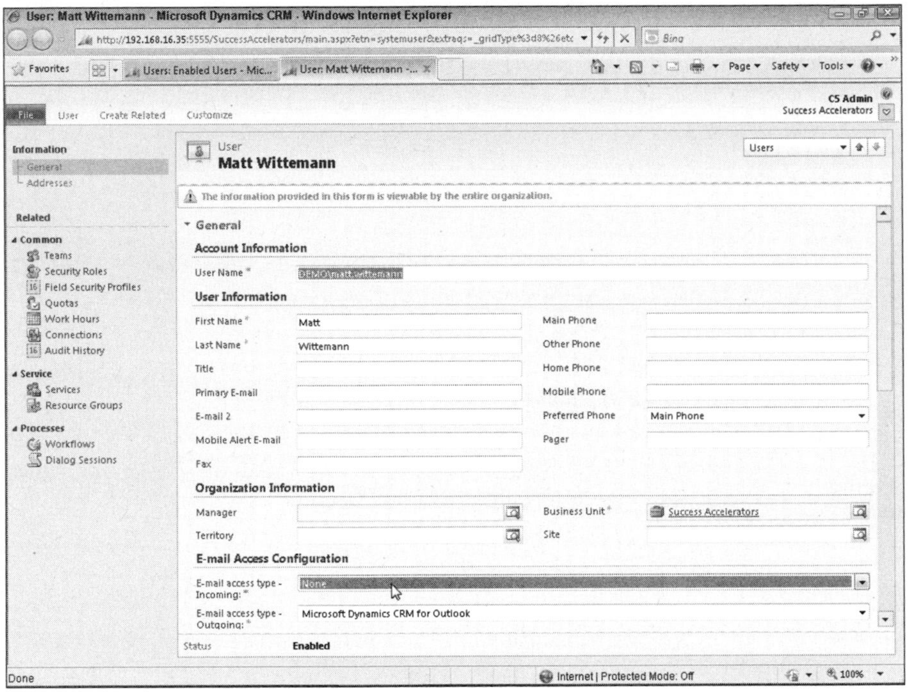

5. Select the incoming profile the forward mailbox should use.

6. Indicate whether messages should be deleted after being processed in the forward mailbox, and click OK.

7. Publish the configuration and close the program.

Tip

After creating a forward mailbox in the Exchange Server, log into the forward mailbox account and launch Outlook at least once before configuring it for use with the Microsoft Dynamics CRM E-mail Router. Depending on your version of Exchange, a mailbox may not be fully initiated until it has been logged into.

Using the Rule Deployment Wizard

When using a forwarding mailbox with the Dynamics CRM E-mail Router, you must publish a rule to users' Exchange profiles to forward a copy of all incoming e-mail to the forward mailbox. Microsoft provides a Rule Deployment Wizard for this purpose. The wizard can be installed when installing the E-mail Router. To use the wizard, you must have administrative permissions in Exchange to deploy rules to users' mailboxes.

The Outlook Client: New and Improved

Microsoft has supercharged the Outlook client for Microsoft Dynamics CRM 2011. No longer simply a way to track e-mail and frame the Dynamics CRM Web site, the new client makes Dynamics CRM as integral to Outlook as e-mail, the calendar, and the task list. Where previous versions of the Outlook client have been compared to Outlook plus Dynamics CRM, the current version has been likened to Outlook multiplied by Dynamics CRM. This is not just marketing hyperbole.

Dramatic improvements in the Outlook integration allow an unprecedented level of user control and interaction with Dynamics CRM records and data. Because Microsoft Dynamics CRM 2011 makes substantial use of the ribbon-style menus in Outlook 2007 and 2010, the user experience in Outlook 2003 is somewhat less dramatically improved from previous versions.

When used with Outlook 2007 and 2010, the new Dynamics CRM client for Outlook enables users to connect to multiple Dynamics CRM organizations, create their own record previews in the Outlook preview panes, and use features like inline charts, the "People Pane" for social media integration, and tabbed views directly within Outlook. These and other improvements to the Outlook integration are covered in more detail in Chapter 11, which includes a detailed guide to the new Outlook experience for Dynamics CRM users.

The significant changes to the Outlook client for Microsoft Dynamics CRM 2011 represent a dramatic leap beyond the capabilities of competitive software in the CRM market and a new dimension to the software's functionality that may compel many organizations to consider upgrading their versions of Outlook.

To use the Rule Deployment Wizard, follow these steps:

1. Click Start ⇨ Programs ⇨ Microsoft Dynamics CRM E-mail Router ⇨ Rule Deployment Wizard. A welcome screen appears.

2. Click Next. Specify whether you are using an on-premises deployment or a hosted deployment and enter the address of the Dynamics CRM server, including the organization name.

3. Click Next.

4. Enter the e-mail address of the forward mailbox and click Next. The users are loaded and displayed.

5. Select the users for which the rules should be deployed by highlighting them. Click Next.

6. The wizard displays its progress as rules are deployed, indicating any errors and successes. When the rules have finished deploying, click Close.

Installing the Outlook Client

The Microsoft Dynamics CRM for Outlook client has undergone significant improvements for this version of Dynamics CRM. From seamless integration of the full breadth of Dynamics

CRM functionality, to the native Outlook experience, the advantages of using Dynamics CRM within Outlook are among the top benefits of the application.

The Microsoft Dynamics CRM for Outlook client works with Outlook 2003, 2007, and 2010 and is available in two versions: the online client, which functions only with a connection to the Dynamics CRM server, and the offline client, which installs and synchronizes a local database copy of Dynamics CRM on the user's computer for full Dynamics CRM functionality while disconnected.

Additionally, Microsoft Dynamics CRM 2011 now allows users to configure the Outlook client to connect to multiple organizations. While only one organization can serve as the default synchronizing organization for tracked activities, users can navigate secondary organizations without leaving Outlook.

Before installing the Outlook client for a Dynamics CRM user, be aware of the following:

- The user must have a supported version of Outlook already installed, and the mailbox must have been logged into at least once.
- After installing the Outlook client, it must be configured to connect to the Dynamics CRM server.
- The Dynamics CRM client for Outlook only tracks items from the users' default data files. In recent versions of Outlook, IMAP mail cannot be set as the default data file. Therefore only POP3 or Exchange data files are supported.
- The Outlook offline client installs a local SQL Server Express 2008 database with an instance name of "CRM."
- If multiple users share a computer, the online client can be installed once on the machine and configured for each user. The offline client, however, can only be installed and configured for one user per machine.
- Updates to the Outlook client are now delivered via Microsoft Updates (or an update server if your organization is using one). This makes for a much more supportable application with less administrative overhead.
- If any required components are missing, such as the .NET 4.0 Framework, they will be downloaded and installed during the client setup. Installation of missing components may require a restart of the machine after setup completes.

Tip

Microsoft makes the Outlook client available as a download to users. If the Outlook client is not detected on a user's machine when the user accesses the Dynamics CRM web client, a message bar appears in the interface with a link to download the client. This message bar can be disabled for all users by creating a registry key on the Dynamics CRM server as follows: In the HKEY_LOCAL_MACHINE\SOFTWARE\Microsoft\MSCRM subkey, add a new DWORD value named DisableOutlookSetupLink with a value of 1.

An Overview of E-mail Settings

Four main components control how users' e-mail is integrated with Dynamics CRM. Each of these components must be properly configured to match the e-mail access policies and objectives for your deployment. The components that impact users' e-mail integration are:

- **The User record in Dynamics CRM.** The user record contains e-mail access settings for incoming and outgoing e-mail. The settings indicate if a user will have no e-mail access within Dynamics CRM or if the user will use the Outlook client or the E-mail Router. For incoming e-mail they may also use a forwarding mailbox. Users' primary e-mail addresses must also be approved by an administrator before e-mail messages can be sent.

- **The E-mail Router.** Incoming and outgoing profiles are configured and applied to users, queues, and forward mailboxes within a deployment. The E-mail Router enables server-side integration with Exchange and POP e-mail servers so users' e-mail can be sent and tracked from Dynamics CRM without user intervention.

- **The Dynamics CRM client for Outlook.** Even users whose user record is set for no e-mail access can use the Outlook client to track e-mail and synchronize activities, as well as use the full functionality of Dynamics CRM within Outlook. The user record e-mail access setting determines only whether the Outlook client or the E-mail Router checks inbound and outbound messages.

- **The users' personal options settings.** Users can set their personal options to specify which e-mail messages are tracked. If a user's user record has the E-mail Router set for either incoming or outgoing e-mail, the user must grant the router permission to process e-mail and enter his credentials in the Personal Options dialog. Note that the options available in a user's personal options settings depend on the access types specified in the user's user record. The default option is for only messages sent in response to a Dynamics CRM e-mail to be tracked.

The table below shows the possible configurations for Dynamics CRM users as well as the E-mail Router, Outlook client, and Personal Options settings that each configuration requires.

Possible E-mail Access Configuration Options on the User Record		Required Configuration in E-mail Router		Is the Outlook Client Required?	Must User Grant Permission for E-mail Router and Store Credentials in Their Personal Options on the E-mail Tab?
Incoming	Outgoing	Incoming Profile	Outgoing Profile	Yes/No	Yes/No
None	None	None	None	No	No

continued

continued

Possible E-mail Access Configuration Options on the User Record		Required Configuration in E-mail Router		Is the Outlook Client Required?	Must User Grant Permission for E-mail Router and Store Credentials in Their Personal Options on the E-mail Tab?
None	Dynamics CRM for Outlook	None	None	Yes	No
None	E-mail Router	None	SMTP or Exchange	No	Yes
Dynamics CRM for Outlook	None	None	None	Yes	No
Dynamics CRM for Outlook*	Dynamics CRM for Outlook*	None	None	Yes	No
Dynamics CRM for Outlook	E-mail Router	None	SMTP or Exchange	Yes	Yes
E-mail Router	None	POP3 or Exchange	None	No	Yes
E-mail Router	Dynamics CRM for Outlook	POP3 or Exchange	None	Yes	Yes
E-mail Router	E-mail Router	POP3 or Exchange	SMTP or Exchange	No	Yes
Forward Mailbox	None	Exchange	None	No	No
Forward Mailbox	Dynamics CRM for Outlook	Exchange	None	Yes	No
Forward Mailbox	E-mail Router	Exchange	SMTP or Exchange	No	Yes

*This is the default setting for newly created users.

In addition to the possible configurations listed above, security roles may also impact how users' e-mail interacts with Dynamics CRM.

Manually installing the Outlook client

The Outlook client can be installed by logging onto the user machine and navigating to the Dynamics CRM Web client in Internet Explorer. If it has not been disabled, a message bar appears in the Outlook client with a link to download the Outlook client setup files (see Figure 4.19). (These files can be downloaded from the Dynamics CRM server or from the Microsoft Downloads site. See the Implementation Guide for more information on how to configure the location of the Outlook client download.) Alternately, the Outlook client can be downloaded directly from the Microsoft Downloads Web site.

FIGURE 4.19

If a user has not installed the Dynamics CRM client for Outlook, a message bar will appear in the Internet Explorer client when the user accesses the Dynamics CRM Web site.

The CRM for Outlook message bar appears to users who have not installed the Outlook Client

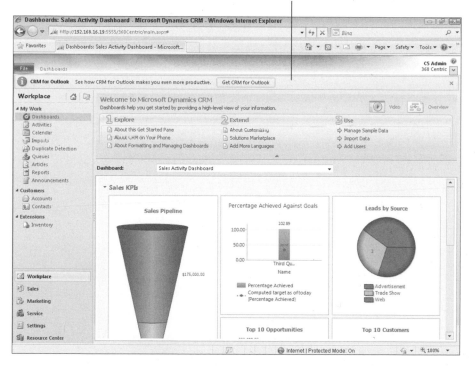

To install the Outlook client, follow these steps:

1. Click the Get CRM for Outlook button in the Web client or navigate to the location where you have extracted the downloaded setup files and double-click the setup client.exe file.

2. In the Microsoft Dynamics CRM for Outlook Setup dialog, accept the license terms and click Next.

3. Click the Install Now button to install the online client. To install the offline client, click the Advanced button (see Figure 4.20) and select it. Click Next. The installation runs.

4. When it completes, click the Close button to close the setup dialog.

FIGURE 4.20

By default the online client will be installed. If you wish to install the offline client, click the Advanced button and select it.

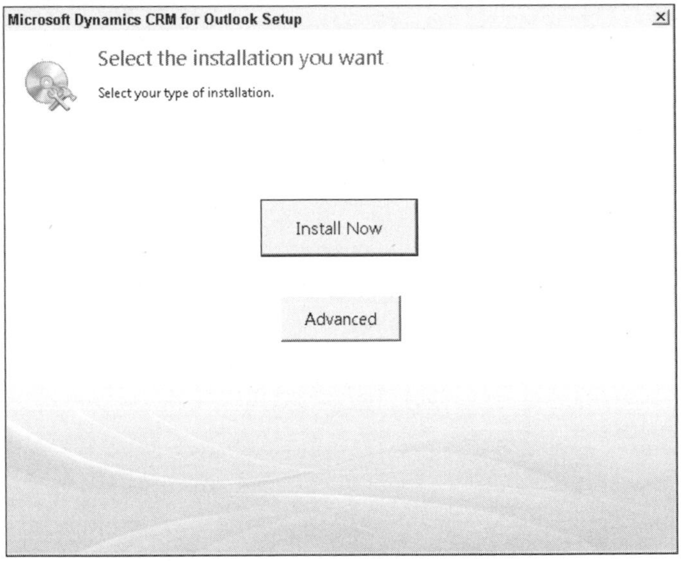

Configuring the Outlook client

After completing the installation of the Outlook client, it must be configured. To configure the Outlook client, follow these steps:

1. Open Outlook. The Microsoft Dynamics CRM for Outlook Configuration Wizard will open. Alternately, go to Start ➪ Programs ➪ Microsoft Dynamics CRM 2011 ➪ Configuration Wizard.

2. If no organizations have been defined, the Add Organization dialog will open automatically (see Figure 4.21). If you are defining a secondary organization, click the Add button.

3. In the Add Organization dialog, type the URL of the Discovery Web Services server and test the connection. Change the user credentials the user will be accessing this organization with different credentials.

4. The Add Organization dialog will display available organizations to which the authenticated user has access. Select the organization you wish to configure. If this is the first organization you are configuring, it will be set automatically as the default organization. This option can be changed later after other organizations have been configured for the user. Click OK. The configuration will be applied.

5. After the configuration is applied, repeat Steps 1–4 to add additional organizations that the user will access through Outlook. Click the Close button on the wizard and open Outlook to begin using Dynamics CRM.

FIGURE 4.21

The Microsoft Dynamics CRM for Outlook configuration wizard allows users to configure connections to multiple organizations.

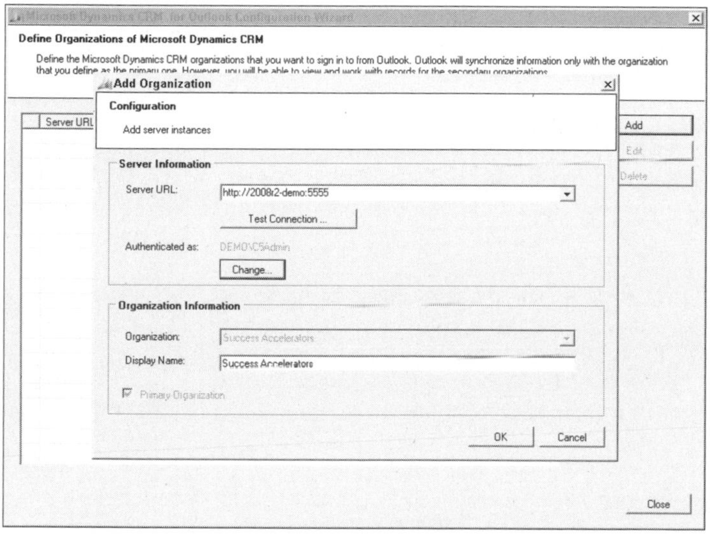

Installing and Configuring the Outlook client from the command line

The installation of the Outlook client can be scripted and performed from the command line by a user with local administration privileges. An example of a command line installation that quietly installs the online client to a specified directory and records a log of the installation to a text file:

```
Setupclient.exe /Q /l c:\clientinstalllog.txt INSTALLLEVEL=2
/targetdir "c:\Program Files\Microsoft Dynamics CRM Client"
```

After installation by command line, the client will need to be configured. This can also be scripted to use a configuration file that is referenced in a separate command line:

```
Microsoft.Crm.Client.Config.exe /Q /config C:\clientconfig.xml /l C:\configlog.
    txt
```

The contents of the example clientconfig.xml file for a user who will be accessing Dynamics CRM through IFD using the online client for Outlook:

```
<CRMConfiguration>
    <Client>
            <ServerUrl Type="SPLA" ShowUser="false">
https://orgname.crm.mydomain.com</ServerUrl>
<CEIP option="false" />
<Organization>OrgName</Organization>
<ExtranetServerUrl>
https://crm.mydomain.com</ExtranetServerUrl>
    </Client>
</CRMConfiguration>
```

In the example above, the ServerUrl type is set to use SPLA, an abbreviation for Service Provider License Agreement — an acronym for hosted Dynamics CRM providers. This same authentication method applies to on-premises deployments that are configured for external access.

The CEIP element opts the user in or out of Microsoft's Customer Experience Improvement Program. The Organization element specifies the system name of the organization, and the ExtranetServerUrl is the external address of the Discovery Web Services server.

The Implementation Guide contains information on all of the parameters available for use in command line installation and configuration.

You can use the examples above and in the Implementation Guide to script the installation and configuration of the Outlook client, or use a tool like Microsoft System Center Configuration Manager (SCCM). Using an automated deployment tool can help to efficiently manage installations of the Outlook client for large-scale deployments and deployments to users in multiple locations. Automated deployment is capable of installing both the online and offline client versions. Using automated software deployment tools, the setupclient.exe file can be pushed out to user machines along with the configuration file that inputs the required settings so users do not need to run the configuration wizard after the installation completes.

The Implementation Guide contains details on creating the configuration files and scripts necessary to package and distribute the Outlook client using an automated deployment tool.

Upgrading the Outlook client

The Microsoft Dynamics CRM 4.0 client for Outlook can be upgraded to the new Microsoft Dynamics CRM 2011 client by running the setupclient.exe program on the client machine. The client setup will detect the type of the existing installation of the Version 4.0 client and proceed with an upgrade to the new version of the same type. A 4.0 online client cannot be upgraded to the new offline client, and a 4.0 offline client cannot be upgraded to the new online client. To change the type of client, you must uninstall the Version 4.0 client completely and start a new installation of the Microsoft Dynamics CRM 2011 client.

Tip

If you have upgraded the Dynamics CRM server, it is not necessary to immediately upgrade all of the Outlook clients for your users. Microsoft Dynamics CRM 4.0 clients for Outlook that are on Update Rollup 7 or later will be able to connect to the Microsoft Dynamics CRM 2011 server. (If the server address or authentication method has changed, the Configuration Wizard may need to be rerun on the machines in order for them to connect.) If a user has the Version 4.0 offline client with Update Rollup 7 or later, and is offline during the server upgrade, the user will be able to go online and connect to the Microsoft Dynamics CRM 2011 server. The user will not be able to go offline again until the Outlook client has been upgraded. Use this information to prioritize your upgrade plans for your offline users first.

To upgrade the Outlook client, follow these steps:

1. Click the Get CRM for Outlook button in the Web client or navigate to the location where you have extracted the downloaded setup files and double-click the setup client.exe file.

2. In the Microsoft Dynamics CRM for Outlook Setup dialog, accept the license terms and click Next.

3. The installation program will detect the existing installation of the Version 4.0 client.

4. Confirm that you want to upgrade the client by clicking the Upgrade button.

5. Install any missing required components. When the installation is complete, click Next.

6. When the system requirements check completes, fix any warnings or errors. Click Next when all green check marks are displayed. The upgrade process will run.

7. When the upgrade process finishes click the Close button to close the setup dialog.

8. Start the Configuration Wizard to configure the client to connect to the Dynamics CRM server.

Summary

After the Dynamics CRM server has been installed, you must install and configure the other essential components of the Dynamics CRM system. This chapter covered the installation and configuration of the following items:

- **The Microsoft Dynamics CRM Reporting Extensions for SSRS.** Dynamics CRM uses Microsoft SQL Server Reporting Services (SSRS) as its report engine. The Reporting Extensions for SSRS are necessary to publish, run, and schedule reports.

- **The SharePoint Grid component.** The SharePoint Grid component enables tight integration between Dynamics CRM and SharePoint 2010 document libraries. The grid must be installed on the SharePoint server that hosts the site collection that Dynamics CRM documents will be stored in.

- **The configurations required for external access to Dynamics CRM.** In order to enable Microsoft Dynamics CRM 2011 for Internet-Facing Deployment, you must first enable claims-based authentication, which requires Active Directory Federation Services 2.0, a relatively new technology that enables multiple identity providers like Active Directory and Live ID to be federated together.

- **The E-mail Router and Rule Deployment Wizard.** How e-mail integration works for each user is a result of the union of settings in the user's e-mail access types on the user record in the Dynamics CRM application, the profiles in the E-mail Router, the Outlook client, and each user's personal options. The E-mail Router is a central location to create and manage the incoming and outgoing profiles that provide access to the E-mail server. The Rule Deployment Wizard deploys forwarding rules to users' Exchange mailboxes for deployments that make use of a forwarding mailbox for inbound E-mail processing.

- **The Dynamics CRM client for Outlook.** The Outlook client has been greatly enhanced for Microsoft Dynamics CRM 2011. This chapter covered the steps necessary for the installation and configuration of both the online and offline Outlook clients. In addition to the components and configurations already covered in this chapter, there are several other items which may optionally need to be installed or configured for your users. These include language packs, third-party applications, mobile clients, and reporting tools like Microsoft SQL Server Report Builder 2.0.

Part III

Administering Dynamics CRM

One of our primary goals in writing this book is to equip you to be a successful administrator of Microsoft Dynamics CRM 2011. This part of the book goes right to the heart of this goal with sweeping and in-depth coverage of everything you need to know after your system has been successfully installed and as you begin to prepare for your users.

In Chapters 5 and 6 we walk you through the steps you should take immediately after installing Dynamics CRM or setting up your online, Microsoft-hosted organization. From registering the software and taking steps to ensure your system is secure, to implementing your organization's IT policies and business structure, these chapters cover everything you need to know to get your shiny new system ready for users.

Chapter 7 provides in-depth instructions on creating and importing organizations, enabling claims-based authentication, and setting up internet-facing deployments.

Chapter 8 covers an administrator's guide to maintaining high-quality data using the tools at your disposal in Dynamics CRM, and Chapter 9 rounds out the administrative content by equipping you with the tools to keep Dynamics CRM humming along like a well-oiled machine.

Post-Installation System Settings

After completing a successful installation of Microsoft Dynamics CRM 2011 or signing up for Dynamics CRM Online, a number of tasks should be completed before you begin to tailor the system to your business processes or setting up users.

In some cases, the tasks require only simple configuration, but in other cases, you should take the time to understand how your organization will use Dynamics CRM, carefully plan the way you will set the system up, and document the decisions you make for later reference. If installing Dynamics CRM is analogous to building a house, then the post-installation steps detailed in this chapter are analogous to moving in and preparing for visitors.

This chapter covers three broad post-installation topics:

- Quick housekeeping steps
- Considerations regarding your corporate IT policies and planned usage of Dynamics CRM
- Planning and setting up your organization's structure and security

On the Web Site

We have included a helpful planning tool on the companion Web site (www. dynamicscrmbible.com): "Ch5_PlanningTool.xls" is a spreadsheet that will help you plan your business units, teams, users, security roles, and system settings. In addition, you can save this spreadsheet as documentation of your initial setup for future reference.

IN THIS CHAPTER

What to do after installing the Dynamics CRM Server and related components

Dynamics CRM and your organization's IT policies

Planning your organization's structure: Business units and security roles

Putting Your Dynamics CRM House in Order

Getting signed up for Dynamics CRM Online or completing your on-premises installation is a major milestone for your Dynamics CRM project — like finishing up the construction of a new home — and you are now ready to move in. This section details some of the recommended best practices for this stage of your project that will be important later as you begin to customize your system.

Creating a backup administrator

If you have installed Dynamics CRM on-premises, one of the first steps you should take is to create a backup administrator user. This simple safeguard is frequently overlooked but can save you and your company a great deal of grief down the road. Vacations, promotions, workplace turnover, and mistakenly deleted Active Directory accounts are among the most common reasons why creating a secondary system administrator user is a highly recommended best practice.

Note

If you are using Dynamics CRM Online or partner-hosted, it is not necessary to set up a backup administrator because the hosting provider should take care of these types of contingencies. However, Microsoft recommends that Dynamics CRM Online customers have at least two users who have access to the online billing and account management site. You can add account delegates on Microsoft's billing site.

When you install Dynamics CRM, you are automatically added to the Deployment Manager (an MMC snap-in on the Dynamics CRM server) as a Deployment Administrator. You are also automatically added as a user with the System Administrator security role in the default organization.

Deployment Administrators can create, import, and remove Dynamics CRM organizations from your installation. Users in Dynamics CRM who have the System Administrator role can create and disable other users, add entities, and set system-wide settings.

Cross-Reference

Chapter 7 contains a section that describes the function of a Deployment Administrator in detail.

To create a backup administrator, you add a new user record to Dynamics CRM, assign a security role to this user, and add the user as a Deployment Administrator in the Deployment Manager. Although Deployment Administrators do not need to be Dynamics CRM users, we recommend having a backup user who is both a Deployment Administrator and a user with the System Administrator security role within Dynamics CRM.

To create the user record and assign the System Administrator security role, follow these steps:

1. Verify that the selected user has an Active Directory account and has permissions to access the server where Dynamics CRM is installed.

2. Navigate to the User list view in the Dynamics CRM Web client by going to the Settings area and then clicking on Administration and then the Users link.

3. Click the New button at the top of the Users list view and select User.

4. In the User Name field enter the user's Active Directory log on in the form of DOMAIN\Username. When you tab out of the User Name field, Dynamics CRM attempts to query Active Directory and automatically populate the user's contact information from the Active Directory account. Add any other pertinent information to the user record and leave the Business Unit set to the default.

5. Choose an Access Mode (either Full or Administrative, not Read-only).

6. Click the Save button on the top of the User form. When the form completes saving, additional options will appear on the form toolbar.

7. Click Actions ⇨ Manage Roles to open the Confirm Security Role Assignment dialog.

8. Place a check mark next to the System Administrator role, and click OK to close the dialog. Save and close the User record. The user should now be enabled and capable of logging into Dynamics CRM and performing administration and customization functions.

Next, add the user to Deployment Manager as a Deployment Administrator:

1. Log onto the server where you installed Dynamics CRM, using the same account you used to install the software.

2. To launch the Deployment Manager snap-in, click on the Start button and go to All Programs ⇨ Microsoft Dynamics CRM ⇨ Deployment Manager.

3. In the Deployment Manager, right-click on the Deployment Administrators node and click on the New Deployment Administrator command.

4. Enter the user's logon name in the Select User dialog and click OK. The user is now a Deployment Administrator.

Running the Registration Wizard (on-premises installations only)

After completing an installation of Dynamics CRM, you must register the software with Microsoft by completing the Registration Wizard. You have 30 days to complete the registration before Dynamics CRM is put into read-only mode. To complete the registration, the server must have an Internet connection. The wizard asks you to furnish information such as your company name and industry, the number of users, contact details, licensing agreement method, and partner details. It takes only a few minutes to complete.

The Registration Wizard is available on the Dynamics CRM server by clicking Start>All Programs>Microsoft Dynamics CRM.

Designating a partner (Dynamics CRM Online customers)

If you have subscribed to Dynamics CRM Online with the help of a Microsoft partner, you may list them as the designated partner of record on CustomerSource. CustomerSource is a Microsoft Web site where you can log in with your Windows Live ID and manage account information and access benefits that come with being a licensed customer.

Benefits include access to training documents and online courses, access to support professionals, and a number of other resources that can help you get the most out of Dynamics CRM.

Cross-Reference
More information and links to CustomerSource are in Appendix B.

To designate a partner on CustomerSource, log in to your Dynamics CRM Online organization and go to the Resource Center area. Click on any of the links in the Resource Center left navigation (Highlights, Sales, Marketing, Service, or Settings) and find the box titled Get Started with CRM Online (see Figure 5.1). In the section labeled Connect with Us click the link to designate a partner.

Tip
Experience shows that CRM software projects can be fraught with unforeseen risks and obstacles. Engaging an experienced Microsoft partner with a good track record and excellent references can help mitigate these risks and improve your time-to-value. Microsoft has invested heavily in developing a well-trained partner network for Dynamics CRM. Appendix B contains links to help you locate a partner in your industry or geographic area.

You can find the link to designate a partner for your Dynamics CRM Online implementation in the Resource Center.

Downloading and installing the latest update rollup

Like any complex software system, Dynamics CRM requires the occasional bug fix, security patch, or performance improvement. To distribute these updates, Microsoft regularly releases software updates for Dynamics CRM through the Windows Update service. These updates include regression-tested fixes for the relevant version of Dynamics CRM, as well as occasional new features (for example, Mobile Express was released as part of an update rollup for Version 4.0).

Occasionally, updates may require manual changes to system settings or registry keys to take advantage of the included fixes. You should review the detailed documentation in the updates' associated knowledge base articles on the Microsoft support Web site to thoroughly understand these and other details.

Setting system settings

Dynamics CRM is designed to be tailored to your business requirements and therefore includes a large number of configurable settings that apply organization-wide. System settings affect only the organization for which you set them, so if you have installed a multitenant implementation (using Enterprise licensing), you will have to configure these settings on an organization-by-organization basis.

The System Settings dialog

Many settings are configured in the System Settings dialog, though a few are handled separately. Additionally, most of the system settings options can be exported as part of a solution and imported into a different organization. It is a recommended best practice to export the default solution in your new organization, including the default system settings, so you can restore your system to its original state if necessary. Also, because it is easy to change system settings, part of your change control and system governance plans should include documenting the settings you select. Simple screenshots can be an effective way to document these settings choices.

To open the System Settings dialog (see Figure 5.2), navigate to Settings ➪ Administration ➪ System Settings.

FIGURE 5.2

The System Settings dialog

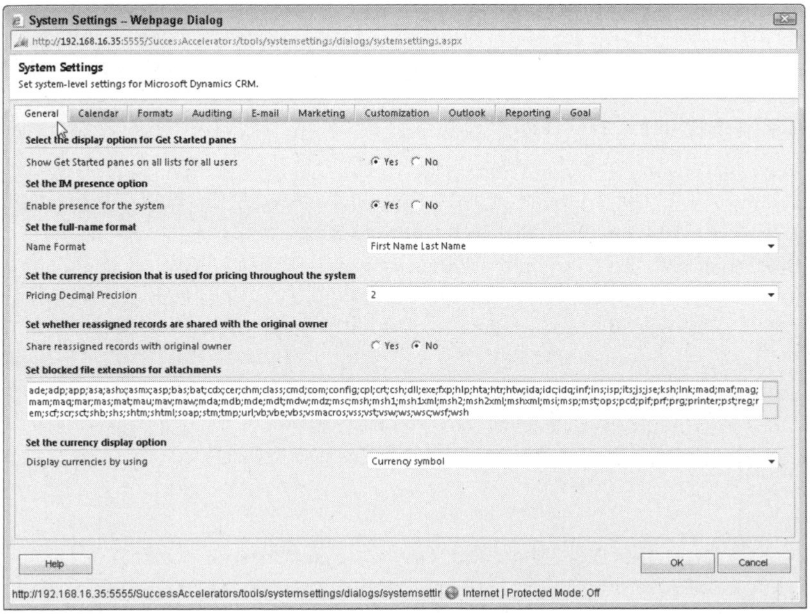

General tab

The settings you can configure on the General tab:

- **Select the display option for Get Started panes.** This organization-wide setting by default enables the Get Started panes to be displayed on many system entities. Leaving this set to Yes means that users will see the panes by default but can turn them off in their Personal Options. Setting this to No disables the panes for all users.

- **Set the full-name format.** Use this option to set how Contacts, Leads, and Users are displayed throughout Dynamics CRM. ***Note that any changes you make to this setting only apply to new Contacts, Leads, and Users.*** This is because the Full Name field on the Contact, Lead, and User entities is populated by concatenating the name fields when the record is created. (You can find numerous blog posts about a simple yet technically unsupported SQL script that will update the fullname field in the database, should you decide to change this setting after data has been loaded in these entities. The usual caveats about using technically unsupported techniques apply, of course: Be sure you are confident that you know what you are doing, what changes are taking place, and have backups!)

- **Set the currency precision that is used for pricing throughout the system.** This setting only impacts the pricing on products set up in the product catalog. Other currency (money) fields are not impacted.

- **Set whether reassigned records are shared with the original owner.** This is an important consideration when designing your security model for your organization. By default, when a user assigns a record he owns to another user, the record is not shared with the original owner. In some situations, it is helpful to allow the original user to retain certain privileges on the record that has been reassigned. However, this setting impacts *all entities in all situations*. It is recommended to leave this set at the default No option. If your organization has a specific requirement that differs from this default behavior on a particular entity, it is advisable to use custom code (in the form of a workflow assembly or plug-in) to handle this.

- **Set blocked file extensions for attachments.** Because file attachments are stored in the Dynamics CRM database, you need to leave the default settings for this option (and add any special cases that arise in your organization) intact to prevent dangerous files from being inserted into your SQL Server. In the Dynamics CRM UI, file attachments are visible as attachments to e-mail activities as well as files attached to Notes. This setting does not impact document management integration with SharePoint.

- **Set the currency display option.** Determines whether money fields display the currency symbol (such as the $ sign) or the currency code (such as USD).

Calendar tab

This tab is new to Microsoft Dynamics CRM 2011 and configures settings for the scheduling options. Use this option to configure the maximum duration of a Dynamics CRM appointment in days.

Formats tab

This tab determines the default formats for currency and date/time fields in your system. (If you set the currency precision option on the General tab, save your settings by clicking the OK button and reopening the System Settings dialog before changing the currency and number formats on this tab so the preview of your current settings is accurate.)

This tab shows a preview of your current settings. Click the Customize button to open a dialog to change the current settings. In the Customize Regional Options dialog, choose the number, currency, time, and date settings that reflect your organization's locale. The previews show you the default settings or those that have already been applied. To see your changes, click the Apply button. You can reset all these settings to their defaults by clicking the Reset button.

Auditing tab

The audit settings allow you to enable auditing for entities in the current organization. To use the auditing feature in Microsoft Dynamics CRM 2011, you must enable this feature and configure each entity, and each field on those entities, you wish to audit. This settings tab allows you to configure Dynamics CRM so the system creates an audit record each time a change is made to an audit-enabled entity, even if the change does not affect the fields you have specified as audit-enabled. In this way, you will always be able to determine that a change has been made. However, keep in mind that if you have a heavily used system with frequent changes to data, a high level of auditing may have a negative impact on system performance.

E-mail tab

When e-mail messages are sent from the Dynamics CRM application, whether by a user or through workflow, and when e-mail messages are tracked before being sent from Outlook, Dynamics CRM adds a tracking token to the subject line of the outbound e-mail. The tracking token is used by the E-mail Router in Dynamics CRM to identify with which record in the database the e-mail message should be associated. The token can be entirely disabled or configured to match your organization's requirements.

Cross-Reference

Integrating Dynamics CRM with Exchange Server or another e-mail provider is a complex topic that is impacted by numerous factors. Chapter 4 includes detailed instructions to manage the various components that play a role in tracking e-mail.

- **Prefix.** The e-mail tracking token can, in rare circumstances, cause e-mail messages to be caught by recipients' spam filters. Another way that the tracking token can be defeated is if two organizations that both use Dynamics CRM send e-mail messages to one another, and neither has changed the token prefix. To minimize this risk and give your recipients an indication of the purpose of the tracking token, using a prefix that relates to your organization is recommended. (For example, if your company is called ABC Enterprises, you might set the prefix to "ABCEnt.")

- **Deployment base tracking number.** If your organization uses multiple instances, or organizations, of Dynamics CRM, set this as a different number for each organization. (This not only helps the E-mail Router to track messages to the correct organization database but also helps users and administrators troubleshoot e-mail settings.)

- **Number of digits for user numbers** and **Number of digits for incremental message counter.** When the counter reaches its maximum number based on your configuration, it will roll over and begin tracking e-mail messages from the lowest number again. For example, if your tracking number is only three digits long after the prefix, it will reach 999 messages and then roll over and start at 001. The e-mail router uses the number in the token as well as other header information (date, subject, sender, recipient, and so on) to associate the e-mail correctly.

  If you have a large number of users, you can reach the maximum number very quickly. This is why the settings dialog allows you to set these options. If you have 1000 users, set the Number of digits for user numbers to 4 — the number of digits in 1000. Set the Number of digits for incremental message counter based on your estimation of the volume of e-mail your organization will send through Dynamics CRM. This is a subjective setting, but provides you with flexibility as an administrator should your organization find that e-mail messages are not being appropriately tracked.

- **Set tracking options for e-mails between CRM users.** If this option is disabled, only one activity record is created in Dynamics CRM when one user sends an e-mail message to another. This option was incorporated to address circumstances where the e-mail router may not capture e-mail messages that do not leave a domain.

- **Use secure frames to restrict e-mail message content.** When e-mail messages are tracked into the Dynamics CRM database, you may want to disable active content within the e-mail. This is the default setting. Users will see an information bar on the e-mail record denoting that active content has been disabled.

- **Allow messages with unresolved e-mail recipients to be sent.** Selecting Yes on this option allows users to type e-mail addresses into the recipient fields on Dynamics CRM e-mail activity records. By default, e-mail activities originating in Dynamics CRM and using the Dynamics CRM e-mail form can be sent only to Accounts, Contacts, or Leads using the primary e-mail address of these records.

- **Set file size limit for attachments.** When an e-mail message is tracked into Dynamics CRM, only attachments under this maximum file size will be stored in the database. By default, this setting is set to 5,120 kilobytes (5MB) and can be increased up to 8,192 kilobytes (8MB). (The maximum file size allowable for this option is controlled by values in the Dynamics CRM Web site's web.config file.)

Marketing tab

Dynamics CRM is often used to generate marketing messages through e-mail. This tab allows you to set certain options that impact e-mail marketing.

- **Set whether direct e-mail through mail merge is enabled in campaigns.**
  Campaigns and Quick Campaigns allow users with appropriate permissions to send mass e-mails to Dynamics CRM accounts, contacts, and leads. Some organizations may want to restrict this functionality as a large volume of outbound e-mail may have ramifications, such as getting your organization's domain blacklisted with spam filtering services.

Note

Dynamics CRM can be used to manage marketing campaigns that involve sending bulk e-mail messages, and, in many ways, this functionality can be helpful to professional marketers. However, because Dynamics CRM is not primarily designed to be a marketing execution platform, you should evaluate your organization's need for e-mail messaging and consider supplementing Dynamics CRM with a third-party tool that provides greater control over mass e-mail marketing. Companies like Eloqua, ExactTarget, Zoomio, and others provide sophisticated marketing tools that integrate with Dynamics CRM to provide powerful marketing solutions.

- **Set whether campaign responses are created for incoming campaign activity e-mail (available only if e-mail tracking is enabled).** When e-mail messages are sent from a Campaign or Quick Campaign, replies can be automatically logged as Campaign Responses under the Campaign. This is useful if your organization sends marketing communications through Dynamics CRM and wishes to track response rates. If this setting is disabled, e-mail replies must be manually converted to Campaign Responses by the users.

- **Set the auto-unsubscribe options (available only if e-mail tracking is enabled).** Enable this setting so that unsubscribe requests sent in response to campaign e-mail will automatically toggle the Do Not Send Marketing Material setting on the corresponding Leads, Accounts, and Contacts. You can also specify an acknowledgment e-mail to be sent when unsubscribe requests are received. In practice, this feature requires a number of things to work together in order to function as expected: E-mail messages sent from Campaigns and Quick Campaigns must have the Dynamics CRM Unsubscribe link embedded in the body of the message, and tracking tokens must be used in the outbound e-mail subject line. When the target of a campaign e-mail clicks the Unsubscribe link, his e-mail software will launch a reply with the word UNSUBSCRIBE: in the subject line, followed by the subject of the original campaign e-mail message and the tracking token. When the unsubscribe request is received and tracked into Dynamics CRM and auto-resolved to the correct Lead, Account, or Contact, the Do Not Send Marketing Material field will be appropriately toggled.

Customization tab

The Customization tab has one setting: whether to launch the Dynamics CRM Web site in Application mode or not. Application mode simply launches the Web client for Dynamics CRM without the address bar. This is a relic of earlier versions of Dynamics CRM where the emphasis of development was placed on creating a desktop-application experience.

Note

In previous versions of Dynamics CRM, the Customization tab controlled which clients ISV menu items would appear in (Outlook, Outlook offline, Web) and what prefix would be used for custom entities and fields. In Microsoft Dynamics CRM 2011, custom Ribbon menu items are individually set to display in appropriate clients, and prefixes for custom entities and fields are inherited from the solution publisher.

Outlook tab

The Outlook tab provides you with a great deal of control over how users' e-mail and local data is synchronized between Dynamics CRM and the Outlook client. The control that users have over their own personal settings in the Outlook client are limited by the settings you configure here.

- **Set e-mail promotion options for Microsoft Dynamics CRM for Outlook.** The Outlook client can automatically track e-mail messages into Dynamics CRM. These settings determine whether e-mail messages are checked for relevancy immediately upon receipt and how frequently the e-mails are promoted to the database. If a user's profile is set to use the Outlook client for outbound e-mail (as opposed to the E-mail Router) you can configure how frequently Dynamics CRM messages will be sent.

- **Set whether users can schedule synchronization in Microsoft Dynamics CRM for Outlook.** This setting allows you to restrict users from setting their own synchronizations of the Outlook client, and, if permitted, the minimum interval. This setting impacts users of both the offline and online-only Outlook clients.

- **Set whether users can update their local data in the background in Microsoft Dynamics CRM for Outlook.** Local data consists of records that users of the offline Outlook client synchronize to their computers for use when disconnected from the Internet or the Dynamics CRM server. This setting allows you to restrict background synchronization intervals. If you disable background synchronization for your offline users, they will need to synchronize all new data to Outlook each time they go offline. Background synchronization makes going offline a quicker process.

- **Set schedule for address book synchronization in Microsoft Dynamics CRM for Outlook.** Dynamics CRM automatically sets up an address book provider that is accessible in Outlook. This setting restricts synchronization of this address book and impacts only users of the offline client.

Reporting

The Reporting tab enables you to add, remove, set the sort order, and specify the default option for the labels used to categorize reports. Reports can be added to multiple categories.

Other administration settings

Before moving on to Business Units and Users, there are still several settings you should configure in the Administration page. We will address Business Units, Teams, Security Roles, and Users later in this chapter.

Auto-Numbering

Several built-in entities have fields that are automatically populated with numbers that make it easier for users to reference specific records. These entities are Contracts, Cases, Articles, Quotes, Orders, Invoices, and Campaigns. Use the Auto-Numbering dialog to set the prefixes for each of these entities and a suffix length that will be used by all auto-numbered entities. Prefixes can be up to three characters. Suffixes are used on entities that can be created while a user is offline in the Outlook client, thus avoiding clashes between two auto-numbered records that might otherwise have the same sequential number.

Languages

The Languages dialog displays the language packs that have been installed on your Dynamics CRM server. Language packs contain translations of menus, reports, messages, and other interface text. The base language in which Dynamics CRM was installed is not displayed (it is visible to users on the user Options dialog). You can enable and disable the languages that are available to the users in this organization. (Installation of language packs, or MUIs — multilingual user interfaces — is covered later in this chapter.)

Privacy preferences

Microsoft's Customer Experience Improvement Program (CEIP) is an automated program built into a variety of Microsoft products to help the software company collect anonymous data about the usage of its software and errors the system may encounter. By default this setting does not opt your Dynamics CRM system into participation in the CEIP.

Product updates

Clicking on this link opens a Web page where you can subscribe to e-mail updates and news about Dynamics CRM from Microsoft or partner companies.

Business management settings

The settings available from the Business Management page include settings and lists that are used throughout the system, but our focus in this section is on the items you should set up after installation and before adding users: Fiscal Year Settings, Sales Territories, and Currencies. The other lists on this page are related to service scheduling.

Fiscal year settings

This dialog allows you to set the start date for your organization's fiscal year as well as the formats for displaying fiscal periods, such as months or quarters. Fiscal year settings are primarily used when setting users' sales quotas.

Set the start date and choose the template that matches the way your organization divides the fiscal year. You can also set the way these periods are displayed. If your fiscal year does not coincide with the calendar year, use the "Name Based On" picklist to determine how the year should be referenced. (For example, if your fiscal year starts on June 1, 2011, should January 10, 2012 be displayed as belonging to fiscal year 2011 or 2012? If the former, set this option to Start Date.)

Caution

Fiscal year settings can only be set once and cannot be changed after they are set.

Sales territories

Sales territories are simple lists you can use to group users. When creating a territory you can set the user who is the manager of the territory, and add members to the territory.

Currencies

Dynamics CRM supports multiple currencies. When performing the installation or creating a new organization, a base currency is selected and set for the organization. Entities with money fields also have a Currency lookup that defaults to your organization's base currency but which can be set to other currencies that you add. When Opportunities or other transaction records are created from within an Account or Contact, they use the currency set on the customer record with which they are associated.

Money fields have two stored values in the database: a base value (in terms of the organization's base currency) and the display value (the amount entered by the user). The platform converts the numerical amount entered in the displayed money field using the exchange rate recorded in the currency record.

To add a new currency to your organization, click on the Currencies link in the Business Management area, and in the list view that opens, click the New button. In the Currency form, click the Currency Code lookup to select a system code, or change the Currency Type to Custom to enter your own (see Figure 5.3). When you select a system currency code, the currency name and symbol are automatically populated.

You must enter a conversion value manually. (If your organization utilizes multiple currencies, consider using custom code or a third-party add-on to update the exchange rate for your currency records.) The conversion value is used at the time the data is entered, and changes to the conversion value do not update amounts that have already been entered in money fields in other records.

For example, consider a scenario where your organization has a base currency of U.S. dollars and has added Euros as an additional currency with a conversion value, where USD 1.00 = EUR 0.79. If a user has selected Euros as his local currency and creates an Opportunity record with an estimated value of €7900.00, the value is stored in the database in two fields: the EstimatedValue field, which would have the number 7900.00, and the EstimatedValue_Base field which would have a value of 10000.00. The exchange rate at the time the Opportunity is created is also recorded. If you update the currency conversion value, the values on this Opportunity remain unchanged.

The base currency of an organization cannot be changed, and additional currencies that you have added cannot be deleted if they are used by a record in the system.

FIGURE 5.3

The Currency form. You must manually set and maintain the conversion value, or incorporate a custom solution to update this value for you.

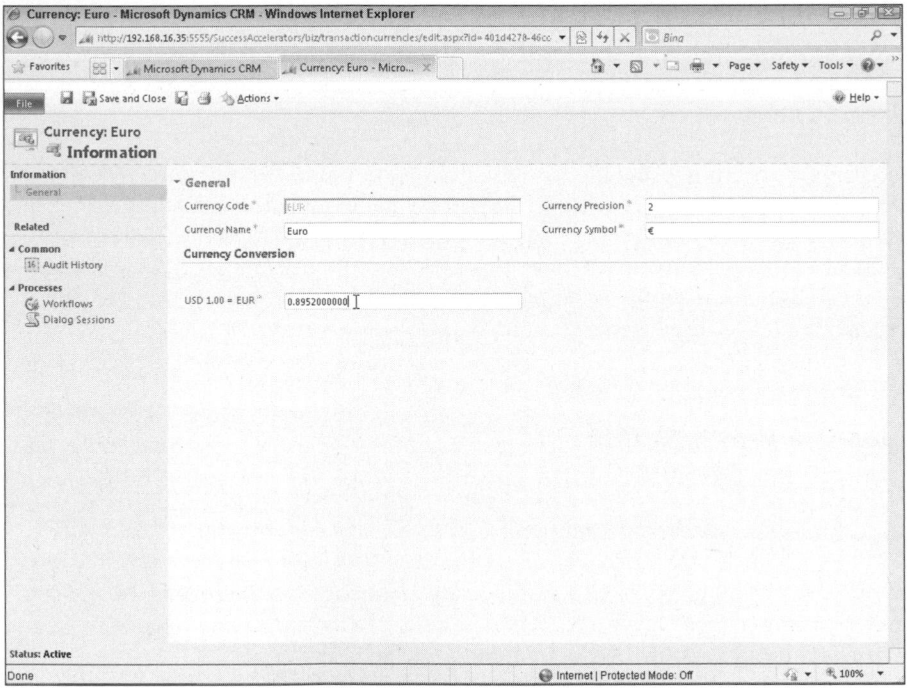

Business settings used for service scheduling

Lists that pertain to this functionality which are available on the Business Management page are:

- Facilities/Equipment
- Resource Groups
- Services
- Business Closures
- Sites

Service scheduling is covered in detail in Chapter 14.

Taking Your Network and Domain Policies into Consideration

As you prepare to add users to Dynamics CRM, consider your organization's security policies and technologies. This topic is broad and varies greatly from organization to organization, but some of the things you may need to consider as you roll out Dynamics CRM to users include:

- **Logon/authentication policies.** Depending on the deployment model you chose for your Dynamics CRM implementation, users may sign in to the application using Windows domain credentials (on-premises implementations), a Windows Live ID (Microsoft-hosted online), or a simple username and password combination (IFD-only or partner-hosted scenarios). Some organizations may require users to change passwords on a regular basis. Users who access Dynamics CRM using the Outlook client, or who permit the E-mail Router to send mail on their behalf, will have to update their passwords in Dynamics CRM when this occurs.

- **Firewall and virus protection settings.** In rare cases, you may need to adjust server or client firewall settings to allow users to access Dynamics CRM, or add Dynamics CRM to allowed application lists in firewall and antivirus settings. This is typically not a problem as users access Dynamics CRM through standard HTTP protocols on ports 80 (standard) or 443 (SSL), or port 5555 for an installation of Dynamics CRM to a new Web site. A complete list of ports for Dynamics CRM is in the Implementation Guide.

Depending on your organization's policies, there may be other security considerations that you must evaluate and respond to. Adequate testing should be performed after making any changes to security policies and roles to ensure a smooth rollout. To maximize adoption of Dynamics CRM, it's important that users' initial experiences with Dynamics CRM are favorable.

Tip
The Implementation Guide is an indispensable tool for every Dynamics CRM administrator and is available for free from the Microsoft Downloads Web site. The Implementation Guide, often referred to as the IG, is divided into two main sections: Planning and Installing. Both sections of the IG have important guidance and step-by-step instructions that relate to security configuration.

Settings for Internet Explorer

Microsoft Dynamics CRM 2011 relies heavily on Internet Explorer to deliver a rich, interactive experience to users. Therefore, Internet Explorer should be treated like any other business application in your organization. Following are some tips to make sure Internet Explorer is optimally configured for Dynamics CRM. Some of these settings can be controlled through Group Policy on your network domain.

- Based on your deployment option and organization's policies, add the Dynamics CRM Web site to the Intranet zone or Trusted Sites zone, and make sure that the zone is configured for automatic logon where applicable.

- Disable popup blockers for the zone in which you place the Dynamics CRM Web site.

- Remove or disable third-party toolbars from Internet Explorer. In some cases, third-party toolbars contain popup blockers or other features that may interfere with Dynamics CRM.

- Consider changing the tab settings in Internet Explorer so that popups always open in a new tab. This can streamline navigation through Dynamics CRM and minimize the confusion that having multiple open windows can cause. This may require retraining your users if they are unaccustomed to using Internet Explorer's tabs in this way.

Configuring Internet-Facing Deployment

If you did not configure Internet-Facing Deployment (IFD) during installation, you may decide to do so now. IFD allows users to access Dynamics CRM from outside of your network domain without using a VPN connection. IFD also allows remote users to configure the Dynamics CRM client for Outlook to access the application without a VPN connection. When IFD is configured, users can surf to the designated URL, where they will be directed to a sign-in page to authenticate to the Dynamics CRM Web site.

An IFD tool is available within the Deployment Manager on the Dynamics CRM server to assist with configuring Dynamics CRM for external access. The Implementation Guide includes detailed steps for configuring IFD. IFD requires a combination of manual steps and steps that can be automated by the IFD settings in the Deployment Manager, including:

- Configuring external (and internal, if necessary) DNS settings for the URL users and the Outlook client will use to connect to Dynamics CRM

- Setting the subnet zones that are internal to your network, and which should therefore use integrated Windows authentication and not present users with the IFD sign-in page

- Selecting the protocol for the Web site and Web services (HTTP or HTTPS)

- Testing that the IFD address properly resolves to the Dynamics CRM Web site and the correct organization

See the Implementation Guide for complete instructions on setting up IFD.

Tip

When configured for IFD, Dynamics CRM will be accessible at a URL in the following format: `https://org name.domain.com` where orgname is the Organization name for the configured instance of Dynamics CRM. You will need to have your ISP configure this subdomain to point to your Dynamics CRM server's external URL, ensure that the appropriate port is open on your corporate firewall, and deploy a wildcard SSL certificate on the Dynamics CRM Web site. (A wildcard SSL certificate enables the SSL protocol to encrypt traffic to sub-domains, such as the orgname in the URL above.)

Making a backup of Dynamics CRM

Before you add users, data, or customizations to Dynamics CRM, it is the recommended best practice to make a backup of your new implementation. Your backup should include the Dynamics CRM databases, SQL Reporting Services databases, Active Directory, and system state backups, directory backups of the Dynamics CRM Web site root and program folders, and the default solution XML and settings from the Dynamics CRM application.

Cross-Reference

Chapter 9 provides additional guidance on backing up your Dynamics CRM system.

Exporting the default solution XML after installation and before adding users provides you with an easy way to return to the baseline, uncustomized interface of a clean installation. The default solution XML contains the entities, forms, fields, charts, relationships, and settings that constitute the basic setup of Dynamics CRM after successful installation and configuring the system settings described earlier in this chapter.

Note

Importing customizations is an additive process. Restoring a backed-up version of your default solution by importing it back into Dynamics CRM will not remove any new custom entities or fields that you have added. Therefore, simply importing a backup customizations file will not restore your system to a true, clean baseline. To accomplish this, you must restore backups of the SQL Server databases.

To back up the default solution XML, follow these steps:

1. In the Settings area, open the Customizations page and click on the Solutions link.
2. Select the Default solution and click the Export button on the toolbar above the list view. The Export Solution dialog opens.
3. If you have configured any changes that have not been published, click the Publish All Customizations button. When the publish operation completes, click Next.
4. On the Export Settings page, place a check mark next to each of the settings in order to include them all in the backup of the default solution. Click Next.
5. On the Package Type screen, the Unmanaged option will be selected by default, and the Managed option will be grayed out (this is the Default solution, not a custom solution).
6. Click the Export button to begin the export operation. The export process may take a short time to complete. You are prompted with a File Download dialog that allows you to select where you want to save the exported XML.

The XML is exported in a compressed .zip file, and automatically provided with a name that reflects both the solution name and the version number. For a new installation of Dynamics CRM, this will be Default_1_0.zip.

Tip
In addition to a comprehensive backup plan for your system, you should regularly export the solution XML, including available settings, in order to undo any changes you or the users may make which are undesirable.

Planning and Implementing Your Organization's Structure

Dynamics CRM has a robust security model consisting of several components that work together to control the privileges and access levels to which users are entitled. The combination of these security controls also establishes an organizational structure within Dynamics CRM.

The hierarchy of security controls for Dynamics CRM:

- Access. How will users access the system? (HTTP/HTTPS, the Outlook client, mobile devices). Each of these gateways will have associated security protocols in place.

- Authentication. How are users recognized by Dynamics CRM? This can be established through Active Directory, Windows Live ID, or claims-based authentication.

- Organization. To which organization(s) does the user belong? Users have a default organization and may belong to multiple organizations.

- Business Unit. User will belong to a Business Unit (BU). BUs are also hierarchical and may have multiple child BUs. BUs establish the depth of the organization's structure in Dynamics CRM.

- Security Role. Users may have multiple security roles. Security roles establish the depth and breadth of access and privileges that users are granted.

- Team. Users may belong to one or more teams. Teams also have security roles and can own records in Dynamics CRM.

- Field Security Profiles. Field security profiles are used to enforce field-level security on Dynamics CRM objects.

As this list makes obvious, implementing a business structure for your organization can become a complex undertaking. The needs of your organization dictate the amount of time you should spend analyzing and planning the organizational structure and security model for your Dynamics CRM implementation.

Many administrators will start with an org chart depicting the different divisions, departments, and reporting structures in their organization. While an org chart can be helpful in visualizing the structure you want to implement in Dynamics CRM, remember that the combination of BUs, security roles, teams, and field security profiles that you implement should reflect the security and collaboration requirements of your organization and may differ substantially from the actual org structure.

Options for security model

CRM systems are intended to provide organizations with a quick and easy way to view and share information about customers. This collaboration and sharing of information can become a valuable asset and contribute to the return an organization realizes from its CRM investment. However, in many organizations, there are compelling business requirements, regulations, and other concerns that may require a more restrictive policy toward information sharing. Also, Dynamics CRM is increasingly being used to develop XRM solutions — solutions that are not focused on customer relationships, but rather on managing other line-of-business data. There are three basic approaches you can take as you plan and implement your organization's security model: open, balanced, or closed.

Open organization

In an open organization, every user can view and edit records throughout the system, regardless of who owns them.

Balanced organization

A balanced security model provides wide visibility of records to all users, but restricts the users to editing only their own records.

Closed organization

A closed organization restricts users to seeing and editing only their own records.

Custom sharing rules

Many organizations incorporate a hybrid of the open, balanced, and closed security models, perhaps granting open access to some records that are of common interest across the organization while restricting read/write privileges on entities that are pertinent to a specific division or department. The Dynamics CRM default security roles reflect a combination of the open and balanced models described above. If your organization requires custom sharing rules and a hybrid security model, you can use the default settings as a starting point, adjusting them to achieve your desired result.

Understanding business units

One of the greatest values of Dynamics CRM is its ability to increase knowledge-sharing and ease access to information for an organization. The real world, though, often requires a more structured approach to information access. Business Units are the fundamental building block that Dynamics CRM uses to establish the depth of a user's access.

Think of a typical org chart that consists of a hierarchical structure. At the top you have executives and headquarters departments. Each of these groups may have multiple divisions underneath them, branching out to the lowliest ranks of the organization. Business Units can be similarly structured. Each BU has one parent BU, but may have multiple child BUs. Each user (and team) must belong to one (and only one) BU. Security roles can be configured to provide users and teams with privileges (such as read, write, assign, and so on) limited to their own records, their own BUs, child BUs, or organization-wide. In other words, BUs represent the depth of a user's or team's privileges.

When designing and implementing the BU structure for your organization, expect it to change, and do your best to lay a solid foundation that you can modify as your business needs evolve. The best practice is to implement as flat a BU structure as possible, both to simplify administration and to minimize complexity.

Below are some simple rules to keep in mind when working with Business Units:

1. Business Units cannot be deleted or renamed, but they can be disabled or reparented. When disabling a BU, all users and teams within it are also disabled. When reparenting a BU, users' and teams' security roles are removed and must be reassigned manually.

2. When creating a new BU, security roles are automatically copied down from the parent to the child BU, where they cannot be edited. They must be edited in the parent BU, and changes will propagate down to the security roles in all child BUs.

Tip

Because you are likely to move business units around in the future, as your use of Dynamics CRM and business requirements evolve, it is a good practice after installation to create a new business unit to serve as the functional root BU. Leave the actual default root BU alone, and create a new child BU that you can easily reparent later if needed.

To create a new Business Unit, in the Settings area, open the Administration page and click the Business Units link. In the Business Units list view, click the New button and complete the form. Note that the root BU created during installation is automatically populated in the Parent Business field. Change this to the correct BU and save and close the form. Alternately, you can open an existing BU and create a new child BU from the left-hand link. Creating a BU from within a BU will automatically set the parent to the existing BU you started with.

Configuring security roles

If Business Units create the depth of your organization's structure in Dynamics CRM, security roles specify the breadth of a user's or team's privileges, and the depth to which they can employ them. Security roles use these two concepts — depth and privilege — to create a multidimensional set of permissions.

Privileges are the actions that a user may perform on a specific entity. The available privileges are:

- Create
- Read
- Write
- Delete
- Append (permits the user/team to attach an instance of the specified entity to another record as a child)
- Append To (permits the user/team to attach other records to the specified entity)
- Assign (not available for organization-owned entities)
- Share (not available for organization-owned entities)

The intersection of a security role's privileges on a given entity are referred to as access levels. Access levels determine the scope or range of records upon which a user may perform the privileges. Access levels (depths) are:

- None. The user cannot perform the privilege on any records.
- User. The granted privilege can only be performed on records the user owns.
- Business Unit. The granted privilege can be performed on records in the user's Business Unit, regardless of who owns the record.
- Parent: Child Business Units. The granted privilege can be performed on records in the user's Business Unit, or on any records in Business Units that are parented by the user's Business Unit.
- Organization. The granted privilege can be performed on any record throughout the organization.

Dynamics CRM's default security roles have more than 480 privileges, each of which can be assigned one of the access levels or depths (see Figure 5.4). Each new custom entity will add to this number.

Note
Microsoft Dynamics CRM 2011 introduces team ownership, the capability for records to be owned by teams rather than by users. Teams are assigned security roles just as users are. Users can be members of multiple teams.

FIGURE 5.4

A default security role showing the core system entities, privileges, and access levels that can be configured

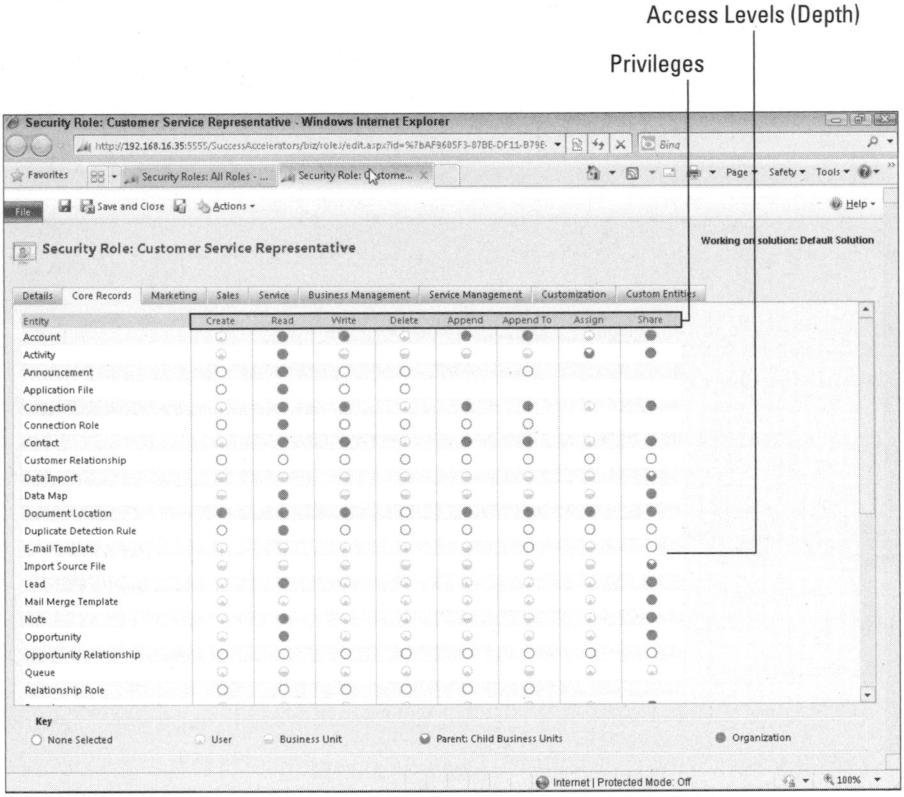

When users are assigned more than one security role, they receive the union of permissions from the security roles. In other words, they are given the least restrictive permissions. For example, if one security role has the User access level on the Write privilege for contacts, and a second role grants the Organization access level for the same privilege, a user with both security roles will have the greater permission — Organization-wide Write privileges on contacts.

Dynamics CRM ships with a number of default security roles. Among the default roles are two that have special behavior when it comes to custom entities. The System Administrator role and the System Customizer role are automatically granted privileges for new custom entities when the entities are added to the system. Other roles must be manually updated to accommodate new entities. (Alternately, since users can have multiple security roles, if you add a number of new entities as part of a solution, the solution may come packaged with security roles that you can add to users to grant them the privileges they need.)

Sharing Records with Users and Teams

Users can share certain records with other users or teams if they have the appropriate privileges. When sharing a record, users can specify the users or teams with which the record will be shared, as well as the privileges they are granting. Sharing grants access rights to a user or team only for the shared record and is a convenient way to handle collaboration when users wouldn't otherwise have permissions to the record in question due to access level restrictions.

If the user with whom the record is shared doesn't have the specified privilege (read, write, assign, delete) for that type of entity, sharing cannot grant them the ability. For example, if a user does not have write permissions on the Account entity, another user cannot grant write permissions on a shared account.

Tip

Do not modify the default roles. Instead, copy them and modify the copies to match your requirements. Also, when creating a new security role, start by copying one of the default roles. This will make sure that you don't leave out any necessary permissions that are required for minimal functionality and will make it easier to quickly customize the role to fit your organization's needs.

Security roles are also one of the ways you tailor Dynamics CRM's navigation to fit your users' requirements. Navigation throughout Dynamics CRM is always a combination of modifications to the Sitemap XML (the solution component that specifies the system's main navigational structure) and logged-in users' security role permissions.

To create a new security role, in the Settings area, navigate to the Administration page and click on the Security Roles link. Click the New button to create a new security role, or Copy Role on the More Actions menu.

Working with field security profiles

New to this version of Dynamics CRM is the ability to configure permissions on individual fields within an entity. Field-level security is enforced using a new type of role called a Field Security Profile.

Field security profiles behave similarly to sharing in that they cannot grant a user privileges that the user's security roles do not allow.

When a field is enabled for field security, Dynamics CRM starts with a restrictive default setting for the field. Users cannot read, update, or create the field until you specify roles that have these permissions. To create a field security profile and grant permissions for a field security–enabled field, follow these steps:

1. Open a solution in the settings area and navigate to the Field Security Profiles section. Alternatively, you can add field security profiles from Settings ➪ Administration ➪ Field Security Profiles. Click the New button and provide a name and description for the profile and save the record (Figure 5.5).

FIGURE 5.5

The field security profile screen is available in the Administration screen or from a solution.

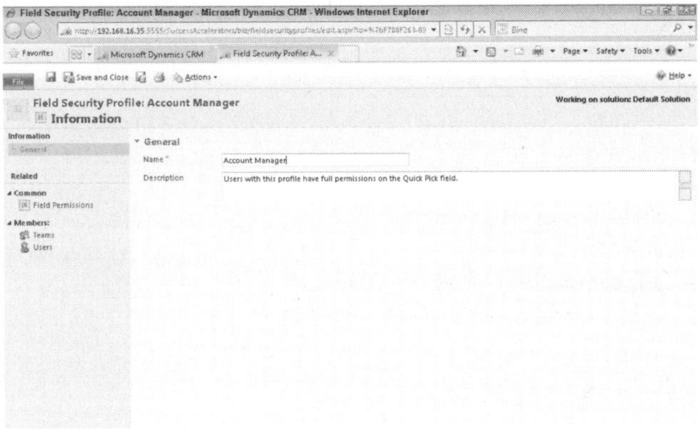

Any fields that have been enabled for field-level security within the solution appear on the profile's Field Permissions associated list.

2. Select the field, and click the Edit button. In the Edit Field Security dialog, shown in Figure 5.6, specify the permissions that users with this profile should have.

3. Save your changes and be sure to assign the profile to the correct users.

Note

Field security can only be enabled for custom fields. System fields cannot be enabled for field-level security in Microsoft Dynamics CRM 2011.

Setting up teams for your users

Teams are a convenient way to group users who work together on sets of records in Dynamics CRM. Teams can own records and are assigned security roles like users. Also, like users, teams must be parented by a single Business Unit.

To create a new team, click the Teams link from the Administration page in the Settings area. Give the team a name and make sure it is linked to the correct business unit.

The Edit Field Security dialog enables you to specify the permissions a user with the profile has on the selected field.

Preparing for Your First User

Now that the house is in order, and you have moved in, it is time to get it ready for guests. A good host anticipates the needs of his guests so they feel welcome and comfortable, and this section can help you prepare Dynamics CRM for its first users.

Installing sample data

If you are following an implementation methodology like Microsoft's Sure Step, before going live with the system, users will be provided with ample training. One of the best ways to train users is to allow them to work with Dynamics CRM hands-on, with sample data for practice. After training is complete, you will want to remove the sample data so your organization can begin using Dynamics CRM or import real production data from another system. Fortunately, Dynamics CRM has a quick way to install and uninstall a prepackaged set of sample data from the Data Management screen in the Settings area.

To install or uninstall the sample data, navigate to the Data Management screen in the Settings area and click the Sample Data link. Follow the steps in the Sample Data dialog.

Installing language packs

Microsoft Dynamics CRM 2011 is available in a number of languages for both on-premises and online use. The organization's base language is set during installation, and additional languages can be installed and enabled. MUI (multilingual user interface) language packs contain translations of labels, messages, the built-in reports, and other UI text and are available for download from the Microsoft download Web site.

To install a language pack, download the MUI file to the Dynamics CRM server and double-click it to launch the installer. Accept the license terms and click the Install button. (If you are using Dynamics CRM Online you can skip this step. If a partner is hosting Dynamics CRM for you, you may need to ask them to install language packs so they are available to your organization.)

To enable a new language for the Dynamics CRM interface, in the Settings area click the Languages link. In the Language Settings dialog (Figure 5.7), place a check mark next to the language you wish to enable, and click the Apply button. Close the dialog when it is complete.

FIGURE 5.7

Language packs must be installed on the Dynamics CRM server before they are available to be enabled in the Language Settings dialog.

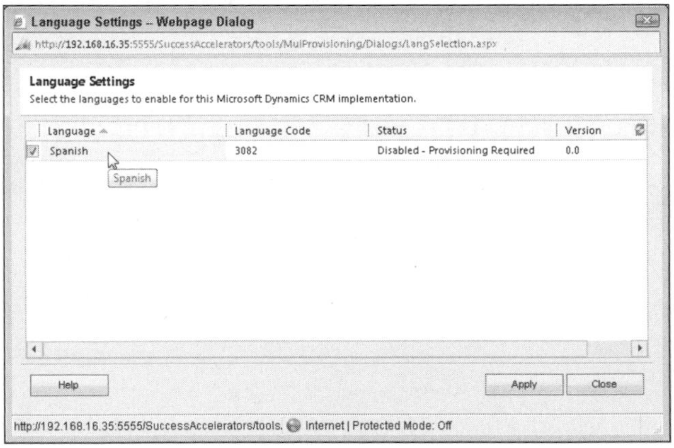

After a language is installed and enabled, users will be able to set their desired language in the Personal Options dialog.

Testing user connectivity and security

Finally, before creating your first users you should thoroughly test connectivity using the access and authentication methods your users will employ. (For on-premises installations, you can temporarily disable automatic logon in Internet Explorer so you are prompted for logon credentials, enabling you to log on as a test user to check the impact of any security role and sitemap changes.) You should verify all access methods, including through Outlook, mobile devices, and from the Internet if IFD is configured.

Summary

In this chapter, we covered many of the settings and initial configuration steps you should take to prepare the system for the way your organization will use it.

Among the most important steps you should take immediately after installing Dynamics CRM are:

- Set up a backup administrator user (or for Dynamics CRM Online, set up a second user who can access the billing and subscription management sites).
- Backup your system and export the base set of customizations in the Default solution.
- Install the latest updates for Dynamics CRM.
- Configure system-wide settings that impact e-mail and marketing communications, client synchronization, and the various formats and prefixes that system entities require.
- Implement the currencies and language packs needed by your organization.
- When planning your organization's security model, keep as flat of a business unit structure as possible and use copies of the default security roles to get up and running quickly and minimize administrative overhead.

If you invest some time to plan your organization and set it up well, you can smooth the transition users will experience as the begin using Dynamics CRM.

Managing Users in Dynamics CRM

P rior to beginning to use Dynamics CRM in a production environment, you need to purchase the appropriate licenses. Licensing options vary depending on the selected version (online or on-premise), required functionality, and if you will be using portals to allow access to external users. This chapter covers licensing options provided by Microsoft.

After you purchase the licenses and install the software, one of the first steps of setup is creating records for users. Creating user records includes adding the record to Dynamics CRM, adding a security role, and testing e-mail settings. As existing users are deactivated, records should be reassigned to new or existing Dynamics CRM users.

This chapter covers the basics of licensing and creating and managing users in Dynamics CRM.

Understanding Licensing Options

Dynamics CRM includes a number of different licensing components. The components required by your organization vary depending on the type of implementation (CRM Online or CRM On-Premise) and your goals for your Dynamics CRM project. In this section, we provide an overview of the various licenses and how to acquire them.

On the Web Site

At the time of this writing, Microsoft is still working out the details of licensing for Dynamics CRM 2011. The information in this chapter is based on the best currently available information. For up-to-date information on licensing Dynamics CRM 2011, check the site: www.dynamicscrmbible.com.

Understanding user licensing

Each Dynamics CRM user within your organization must have a license in order to legally use the software. Options for user licensing (also known as Client Access Licenses or CALs) vary depending on which version of Dynamics CRM your organization has selected.

Acquiring CRM Online licenses

If you are using Dynamics CRM Online, then each user requires an individual license. If you have not yet acquired CRM Online licenses, then you can visit the site for the book (www.dynamicscrmbible.com) to find a link to current Microsoft Dynamics CRM Online site where you can sign up for licenses.

If you are already using Dynamics CRM Online, you can acquire more licenses directly from within the user interface. Navigate to Settings ⇨ Subscription Management. From here, you can see a count of the total number of licenses as well as used and unused license counts. You can also purchase additional licenses if needed.

Dynamics CRM Online licenses are purchased through a leasing model. You pay a fee on a regular basis (for example: monthly or annually) for usage of the software. As long as you remain current in your payments, you continue to have access to the software.

Acquiring CRM On-Premise licenses

When using Dynamics CRM On-Premise, you need to purchase licenses through an authorized Microsoft Partner Network reseller or software advisor. You need to purchase licenses for the Dynamics CRM Server software (the software that runs on a computer server) and a client access license (CAL) for each user. CALs for CRM can be purchased either for the user (each individual user must have a license) or for a device (multiple users can share a single device, which can be helpful for organizations that have multiple shifts of employees that share a workstation). See Chapter 5 for more information on CALs.

Dynamics CRM On-Premise licenses are purchased through a traditional software model. After paying for the licenses, you own them indefinitely. If you want to have access to update rollups (containing bug fixes), new versions of the software, and support from Microsoft, then you must pay an annual fee for Software Assurance. Microsoft's Software Assurance is similar to what other software manufacturers refer to as maintenance. If your Software Assurance lapses and you wish to acquire the latest version of the software, you must purchase new licenses at the standard cost. Discuss the advantages of Software Assurance with a Microsoft partner prior to making a decision.

Understanding External Connector licensing

Individuals outside of your organization can access Dynamics CRM. For example, you may provide a Web-based customer portal where customers can submit and update cases and search your knowledge base (see Chapter 14). As another example, you may work with a network of distributors that update their leads and opportunities via a partner portal (see Chapter 12). In both of these cases, you will need to allow individuals outside of your organization to have some level of access to the data within Dynamics CRM.

Microsoft has created the External Connector license for this purpose. This license is a one-time purchase that covers an unlimited number of users. These users cannot be employees of your organization and they cannot directly access the Dynamics CRM user interface. They can, however, access Dynamics CRM by using Web portals. Microsoft has made a number of Web portals available freely on www.codeplex.com. You can also build your own custom Web portal for this purpose if desired.

On the Web Site

For information on the Web portals available for Dynamics CRM, check www.dynamicscrmbible.com.

Understanding other licensing components

Depending on how you have licensed CRM, licenses may also be required for one or more additional components. There are a large number of ways to license the software listed below. We recommend that you discuss licensing options with your Microsoft Partner Network partner to determine if you need any of the following, and the appropriate approach for licensing each.

- **Microsoft SQL Server:** This is the software that holds the data for Dynamics CRM. Think of SQL Server as a "warehouse" that holds all of your customer and prospect data, and think of Dynamics CRM as a trusty employee that fetches whatever data you request from the warehouse and delivers it to you. If you are using Dynamics CRM Online, then you will not require licenses for Microsoft SQL Server. If you are using Dynamics CRM On-Premise, then you will require a SQL Server license for each user (or a "processor" license for an unlimited number of users).

- **Microsoft Exchange:** This is the server software provided by Microsoft for handling e-mail. This is not required for using Dynamics CRM, but it does integrate with Dynamics CRM and can improve how your organization manages e-mail. You may also host your Exchange server with a partner or with Microsoft through their Business Productivity Online Services (BPOS) offering.

- **Windows Server:** This is the operating system that runs your server applications. It hosts other functions such as active directory (used to manage users) and internet information server (used to manage Web sites and Web applications, such as Dynamics CRM). If you are using Dynamics CRM On-Premise, then you will need to have a server running Windows Server. If you are using Dynamics CRM Online, then Windows Server will only be required if you plan to use Claims-Based Authentication (see the authentication section later in this chapter for more information).

- **Microsoft Office:** Dynamics CRM was built to run better when combined with Microsoft Office (and, in particular, with Microsoft Outlook). Dynamics CRM will integrate with Office 2003 or higher. For maximum productivity, we highly recommend using Office 2010.

- **SharePoint:** SharePoint is not a required component for Dynamics CRM. However, SharePoint offers functionality that significantly expands CRM's capabilities in a variety of areas including document management, collaboration, portals, and unstructured data management. SharePoint is available hosted or On-Premise (similar to Dynamics CRM). Because Microsoft has made a basic version of SharePoint available at no cost, every business that uses Dynamics CRM should have a copy installed to accelerate your performance.

Authenticating Users

When users attempt to log in to Dynamics CRM, their username and password go through a process called authentication. This process confirms who they are before they are allowed to complete the login and begin to access the Dynamics CRM system. The technology that supports the authentication process differs depending on your goals and which version of Dynamics CRM you have licensed. The following list provides a description of the options:

- **Dynamics CRM On-Premise:** If you have installed the Dynamics CRM server software On-Premise, then you will have two primary options for how to configure authentication:

  - **Active Directory:** Active Directory (or AD) is the technology used by Windows Server to store information about your users and equipment attached to your network. Think of AD as a "phone book" that your computer network uses to keep track of users, computers, and printers that access your network. AD stores the user ID and password for each of your users. When installing Dynamics CRM, the same credentials (user ID and password) that are used for your network are automatically assigned to CRM users. This enables users to sign into their computer only once, rather than having to also sign onto CRM every time that they open the application.

  - **Claims-Based Authentication:** If your organization wants to have Dynamics CRM configured as an Internet-Facing Deployment (so that users can log in without having to first log in to the network using a VPN, for instance) or if your organization wishes to set up portals that share some CRM information with the outside world, then you should plan to use Claims-Based Authentication. Microsoft has developed a technology called Active Directory Federation Services 2 (AD FS 2) to handle Claims-Based Authentication. In essence, AD FS 2 enables multiple different networks to "federate" to allow users to use only one set of credentials to log in across various different networks. AD FS 2 requires an additional server on your network and requires an experienced network administrator to fully configure. For more information on AD FS 2, see Chapter 7.

- **Online:** If you have purchased Dynamics CRM Online licenses, then the following two options will be available to your organization for authentication:

  - **Live ID:** Windows Live ID (or Live ID for short) is a Web-based technology that Microsoft has developed to allow individuals to use a single set of credentials to log in across multiple Web sites. Using this approach (which is the default for CRM Online), a user must create a Live ID before they can log in to Dynamics CRM Online. If users already have a Live ID, then they can use it with Dynamics CRM. CRM for Outlook remembers the user's Live ID, so when users open Outlook, they are not required to re-login to Dynamics CRM. This approach has the benefit of being easy to implement, but it does not give the organization control over password policies, location of access to CRM (any computer can be used), or permit single sign-on to Dynamics CRM.

  - **Claims-Based Authentication:** Claims-Based Authentication is described in more detail above. Organizations that wish to have more granular control over password and computer access policies to Dynamics CRM Online will need to set up an AD FS 2 server on their premises and can use this as their authentication method. AD FS 2 also supports a simplified single sign-on approach to signing into Dynamics CRM without having to enter (or store) Live ID information. See Chapter 7 for more information on AD FS 2.

Active Directory and Authentication

Active Directory (AD) is the default approach for authentication when installing Dynamics CRM On-Premise. When taking this approach, there are some important steps to take and pitfalls to be aware of.

- When the Dynamics CRM server software is installed, a number of Active Directory groups are created, including PrivReportingGroup, PrivUserGroup, SQLAccessGroup, ReportingGroup.

- When new users are added to Dynamics CRM, they are automatically made members of ReportingGroup. Removing users from ReportingGroup will disallow these users from running reports in Dynamics CRM. You should never remove CRM users from this group.

- Individuals who configure the Dynamics CRM Server should be added to PrivUserGroup.

- The other two groups are primarily for automation of internal processes and should not need to be assigned to users. For more information on these groups, download and review the CRM Implementation Guide (a link will be available on the site: www.dynamicscrmbible. com).

- Problems can occur if you rename an Active Directory account or if you try to create a CRM user who was removed from Active Directory. If a user changes names, the best practice is to create a new Active Directory account and a new user in CRM, then deactivate the old user and transfer all records to the new user.

Managing Users

Users in Dynamics CRM are managed in a list just like other lists, such as accounts and contacts. A record is created for each user from within Dynamics CRM. As your organization experiences turnover or reorganizations, user records need to be modified to reflect these changes. This section covers these fundamentals of user management.

Creating users

Before individuals can begin using Dynamics CRM, a user record must be created for them. This section outlines the process for creating user records, configuring their e-mail, and setting up their default queue and team.

Creating new users

Use the following steps to create new users in Dynamics CRM. Differences between Dynamics CRM Online and Dynamics CRM On-Premise have been noted.

1. Licensing. Begin by ensuring that you have sufficient licenses to create another user:

   - In CRM Online: Navigate to Settings ➪ Administration ➪ Subscription Management. Here you can see the total number of purchased licenses and the number that are still unused.

   - In CRM On-Premise: At the time of this writing, a method to check the number of licenses for CRM On-Premise is not available. You will either need to keep accurate records of license count or request a license count from your Microsoft CRM partner.

2. Authentication. If you are using Active Directory or Claims-Based Authentication (see the nearby sidebar), then you should ensure that the user has been added to your Active Directory prior to attempting to add them to Dynamics CRM. If you are using CRM Online and using Live ID, then you can skip this step.

3. Add the user. Navigate to Settings ➪ Administration ➪ Users. This presents a grid like other lists in Dynamics CRM. Click the New button on the Ribbon menu to add a new user. If you are using Dynamics CRM On-Premise, you also have the option of clicking New Multiple Users to add more than one user at a time.

   If you are using Dynamics CRM Online, or if you are using Dynamics CRM On-Premise and you clicked the New Multiple Users button, you are presented with a wizard that can walk you through the process of creating users. Follow the steps of the wizard to complete the entire process of creating a group of users. If you would like to edit individual user fields after completing the wizard, then click on an individual user name and follow the remainder of the process.

4. Create the user. If you are using Dynamics CRM On-Premise and you clicked New, you are presented with a data entry form, shown in Figure 6.1. Complete the form, paying particular attention to the following fields:

FIGURE 6.1

The user data entry form

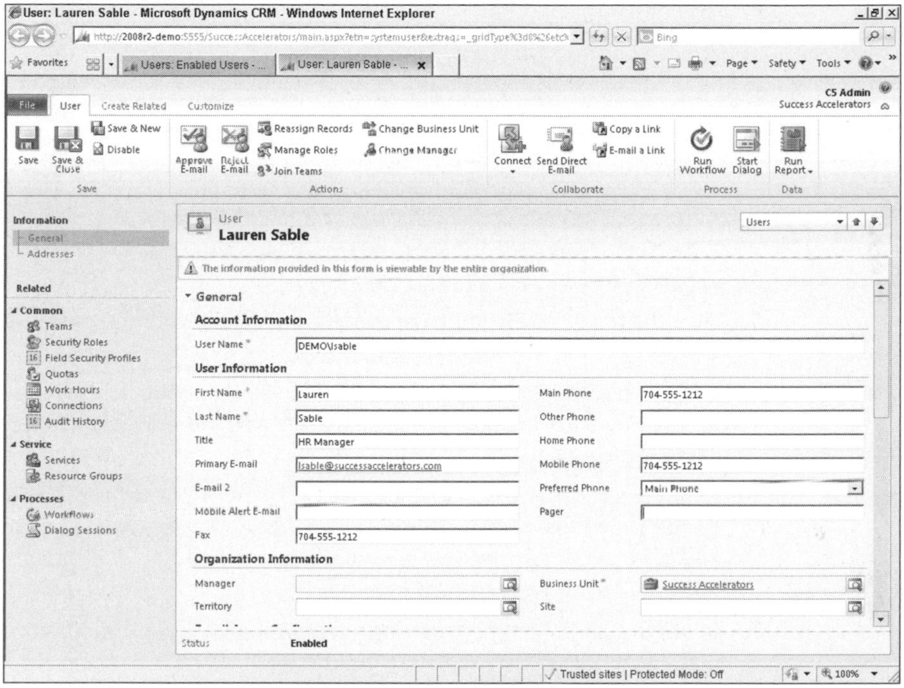

- **User Name:** This should be the same name assigned to the user in Active Directory or the user's Live ID. If using Active Directory, then after completing this field and tabbing out of it, other fields that were entered into Active Directory (such as first name and last name) will automatically populate. Note that this import from Active Directory is performed one time only — changes made to Dynamics CRM and to Active Directory after this point will not be kept in sync automatically.

- **Contact Information:** Be sure to enter (or have the user enter) complete contact information. This information may be used in templates and workflows to personalize communications.

- **Manager:** The manager field is not required. However, it may be used in workflows (to send alerts or assign escalations), reporting, and other areas. Note that the manager must also be a Dynamics CRM user in order to be available to add to this field. The manager must also either be in the same business unit as the user or in the chain of business units that parent the user's business unit.

- **Territory:** Although not required, this field can be useful for reporting, for assigning records to the user, or for generalized territory management.

- Business Unit: Be sure that the user is assigned to the correct Business Unit. This field is required and plays an important role in security and record visibility throughout the application.

- Site: If you plan to use the service scheduling functionality, then you should populate this field with the site that is the "home office" for this user.

- E-mail access configuration: Choose the appropriate values here depending upon how you have configured the e-mail router (see Chapter 4 for more information).

- Client access license information: See Chapter 5 for client access license information.

- Queue information: Whenever a new user is created, a queue is created for that user and is assigned to them as their default queue. You can change their default to a different queue if preferred.

5. **Save the form.** When you have completed your data entry, save the form (but do not close it).

6. **Add a security role.** Be sure to add a security role for the user. Users cannot log in unless they have at least one security role assigned. Security Roles are visible in the navigation pane to the left of the data entry form after you save the record.

7. **Configure the user in the E-mail Router and approve his e-mail.** If you are using the e-mail router, be sure to add the user to the router and then approve his e-mail address. Chapter 4 contains information on the router, and the following section of this chapter contains information on approving user e-mail addresses.

8. **Configure additional user settings.** Depending on additional functionality that you may want to use within Dynamics CRM, you will also need to take the time to configure Field Security Profiles, Quotas, Work Hours, and Resource Groups for this user.

On the Web Site

Dynamics CRM On-Premise does not include a facility for monitoring the number of licenses currently purchased and used. This can be problematic because organizations that use unlicensed software can be subject to significant financial penalties. The Web site contains a Dynamics CRM Solution called License Manager that provides a simple method for tracking not only your licenses for Dynamics CRM, but for other software your organization may own as well. Check the site www.dynamicscrmbible.com **for this solution.**

Approving e-mail

Dynamics CRM includes a security setting that can optionally require that all user e-mail addresses are approved before they can be processed by the e-mail router. To update this security setting, navigate to Settings ➪ Administration ➪ System Settings ➪ E-mail Tab and select or deselect the check box next to the Process e-mails only for approved users option.

Once the box in the above paragraph has been checked, you need to approve each individual user before e-mail can be processed by the router. To do this, navigate to the list of users (Settings ➪ Administration ➪ Users), select the user record(s) you want to approve, and click the Approve E-mail button on the Ribbon menu. On the dialog box that appears (see Figure 6.2) click the OK button. E-mail for these users will now be processed by the e-mail router.

FIGURE 6.2

Confirm approving user e-mail dialog box

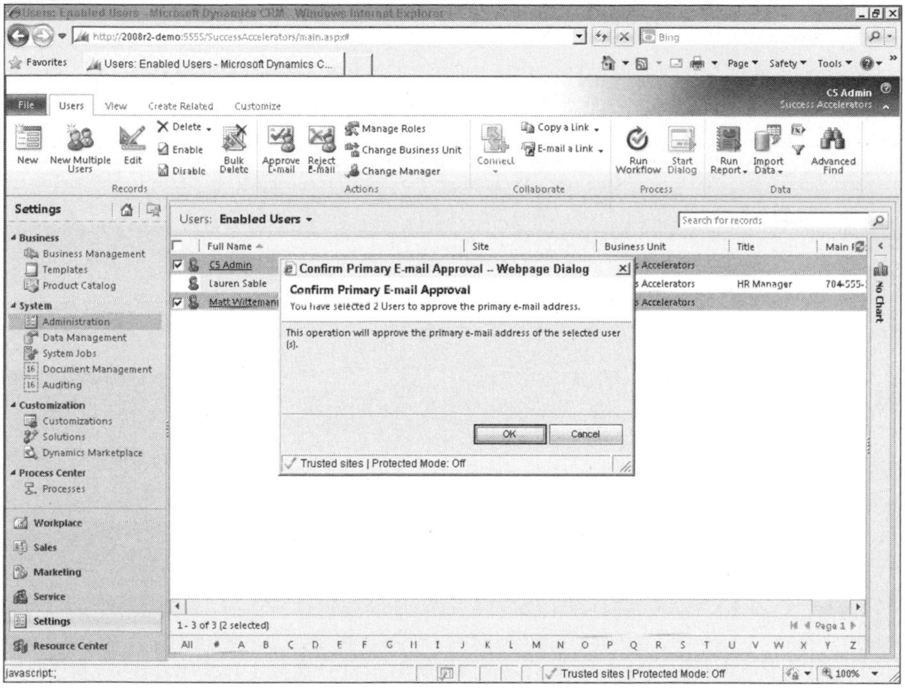

Cross-Reference

For more information on the e-mail router and other e-mail processing options, see Chapter 4.

Setting the default queue and team

In Dynamics CRM 2011, for every user you create, a default queue is created and the user is added to the default team for the business unit that you associate them with. You may change either (or both) of these defaults. Queues and teams can be deleted. However, you should take the time to understand queue and auto routing functionality before making changes to queues or teams.

Working with existing user records

After a user has been created, you can edit their information by navigating to Settings ➪ Administration ➪ Users and clicking on the user record you want to modify. From time to time you may need to make moderate changes to users (such as updating a phone number) or significant changes (such as disabling them when they leave the company or changing their manager). This section covers these items.

Bulk Manage Users

Large organizations may need to manage hundreds or even thousands of users.

Dynamics CRM includes some functionality to manage large groups of users. This includes the ability to select multiple users and reassign them to a new manager or business unit, deactivate them, or assign security roles to them. These options are in the ribbon menu above the listing of users.

Large organizations may also need to automate creating and removing users whenever a record is changed in their HR or employee management system. While this type of automation is not available through the user interface, you can use the SDK (software development kit) to integrate CRM with your HR system to fully automate the process of managing Dynamics CRM users. For more information on connecting to other systems, see Chapter 22.

Disabling users and reassigning records

When an employee leaves the company, or is reassigned to a business unit that does not have access to Dynamics CRM, you should plan to disable their user record and reassign records that they own to another user.

Caution

When an employee leaves the company, it may be tempting to delete their user record. However, you should never delete a user record. User records contain historical information about the activities, opportunities, cases, and other information that the user owned or contributed to. Deleting a user permanently erases potentially important history. Deactivating the user frees up a license, hides the user record, and retains important historical information. You can also re-enable disabled users later if the need arises.

To disable a user record, follow the procedure below.

1. Navigate to the list of users (Settings ⇨ Administration ⇨ Users).
2. Open the record for the user that you wish to disable by clicking on the user's name.
3. Reassign the records for this user to another user. The easiest way to do this is to click the Reassign Records button on the Ribbon menu on the user form.
4. In the dialog box, select to assign the records to yourself or to another user or team. If you choose the latter option, then select the user or team that you want to assign them to. When you have completed the dialog box, click the OK button. Dynamics CRM will take a few moments to reassign all of the records.
5. In the Ribbon menu, click the disable button and click OK on the dialog box that appears (see Figure 6.3). The user is disabled and has read-only access.

6. Close the form.

7. If you reassigned records to someone other than yourself, then any processes that were running for the disabled user have been suspended. To find and resume these processes for the new user navigate to Settings ➪ System Jobs and change the view to Suspended System Jobs. Select all of the relevant jobs in the list, and from the More Actions menu, select the Resume option (see Figure 6.4).

FIGURE 6.3

Disable users Ribbon menu and confirmation dialog box

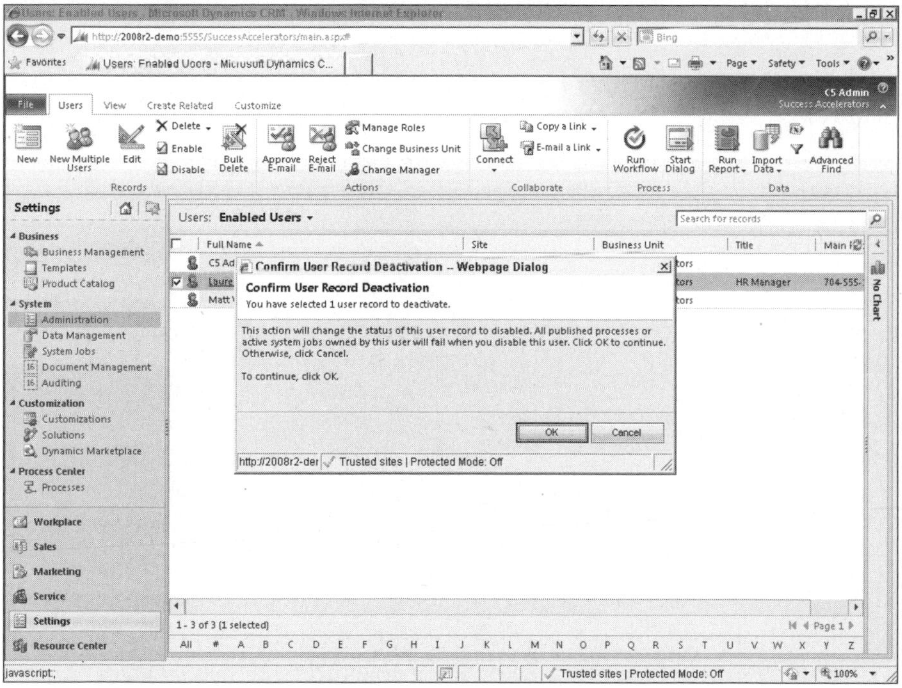

Tip

If you want to reassign records owned by the user to multiple users, then use the Advanced Find function to iteratively search for and reassign the user's records to other users until all records have been reassigned. If you use this approach, we still recommend that you use the Reassign Records button on the user form as a final step to ensure that any records that you may have missed with your Advanced Find filters will still get assigned to another user.

Resuming system jobs that were deactivated when a record was reassigned

Changing the manager or business unit

From time-to-time employees may be reassigned to new managers and/or to a new business unit. When this happens, use the steps below to reflect those changes in the user record in Dynamics CRM.

The process for changing a manager or business unit is very similar. There are, however, some differences in what happens behind the scenes and what must be done after completing the reassignment. In the case of assigning a new manager, the manager must be in the same business unit as the user, or in a business unit that is in the chain above the user's business unit. In the case of reassigning the business unit, all of the security roles assigned to a user will be removed after making the reassignment, so you need to re-add security roles to the user after making the reassignment.

Caution

After assigning a user to a different business unit, all security roles will be removed from the user record. The user will no longer be able to log in to Dynamics CRM until at least one security role has been assigned to their record.

Setting Up Outlook Synchronization for Users _____

Dynamics CRM synchronizes data with Outlook behind the scenes. Each user can configure exactly which records sync with Outlook by editing the local data groups within CRM for Outlook. This process is outlined in more detail in Chapter 11.

For some users, however, modifying local data groups can be an intimidating exercise. In those cases an administrator can work with each user to tailor their local data group settings. For larger organizations, there are tools in the software development kit (SDK) that can aid in automating the setup of local data groups. Check Appendix B for information on where to download the SDK.

To change the manager or business unit for a user, navigate to the list of users (Settings ⇨ Administration ⇨ Users) and select the user(s) that you wish to reassign. In the Ribbon menu, click either the Change Manager or the Change Business Unit link. Select the appropriate option from the dialog box and then click the OK button. Dynamics CRM makes the reassignment. Remember that if you changed the Business Unit, you need to add security roles back to the user record or the user will not be able to log in.

The user summary report

When working with large lists of users, it can be helpful to get a bird's-eye view of all of the users, their business unit, and their security role(s). Included with Dynamics CRM is a report called the User Summary Report that provides precisely this information. This report is easily accessible from the Ribbon menu while viewing the list of users (click Run Report ⇨ User Summary). You can also access the report from the reports area of Dynamics CRM.

Summary

Dynamics CRM offers a variety of options for licensing. Although selecting the correct hosting model and licensing approach can be a bit intimidating, a Microsoft partner can quickly guide you through the process. In addition, if you determine at some point in the future that you would like to switch to a different hosting approach, your data can be moved from one hosting arrangement to another fairly quickly.

Managing user records in Dynamics CRM is handled through the standard user interface. Users can be created and assigned to new business units or to a new manager. E-mail security settings enable you to approve or disapprove new user e-mail addresses before the E-mail Router can begin to use them. When users leave the company, they should be disabled rather than deleted.

Using the Deployment Manager

The Deployment Manager is a snap-in for the MMC (Microsoft Management Console) that is automatically installed during installation of the Dynamics CRM server. Administrators use the Deployment Manager to manage the organizations, licenses, servers, and authentication methods related to your Dynamics CRM implementation.

In essence, the Deployment Manager is the user interface for the MSCRM_CONFIG database that is created during installation to store information about the configuration of the Dynamics CRM server and its tenant organizations.

Note

The Deployment Manager is only used by organizations with on-premises installations of Dynamics CRM or by partners who are hosting Dynamics CRM. This feature is not available to users of Microsoft Dynamics CRM Online.

IN THIS CHAPTER

▶ **Product key changes**

▶ **Deployment administrators**

▶ **Creating, importing, and managing organizations**

▶ **Server roles**

▶ **Configuring Claims-Based Authentication and Internet-Facing Deployment**

Using the Deployment Manager Console

The Deployment Manager can be found on the server where Dynamics CRM is installed or on the server you specified for the Deployment Services role during installation.

To open the Deployment Manager, follow these steps:

1. From the Start menu on the Dynamics CRM server, choose Programs ➪ Microsoft Dynamics CRM.

2. Right-click Deployment Manager and choose Run as administrator (shown in Figure 7.1).

FIGURE 7.1

The Deployment Manager, which is installed as part of the Dynamics CRM server

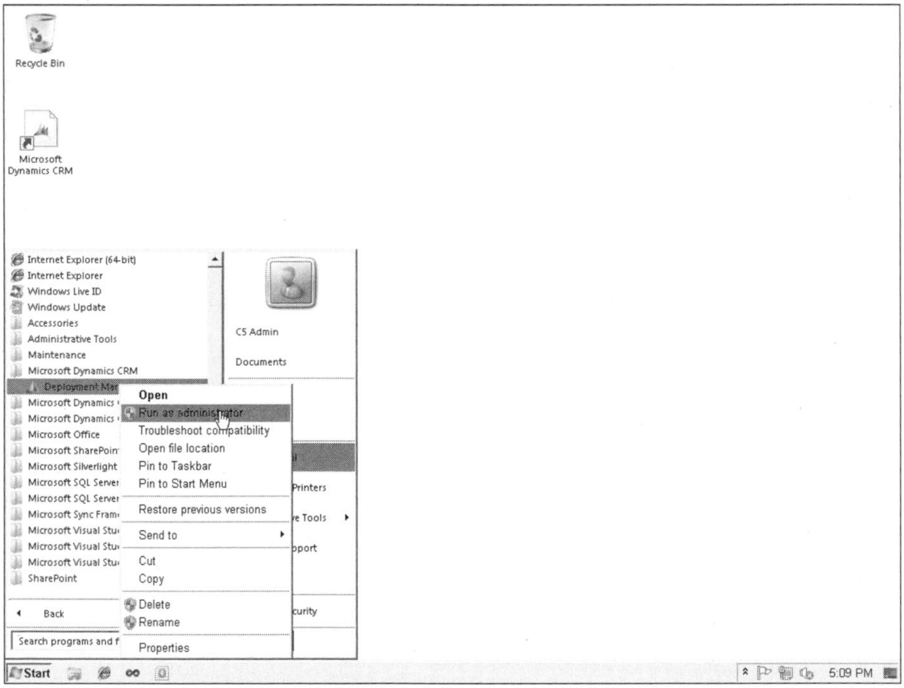

Managing your deployment product key

The main screen in the Deployment Manager provides a means to view a license summary that details the type of license and the product ID for your deployment. From this screen, you can also upgrade the product key.

To view your deployment's license type, open the Deployment Manager. This information is included in the Deployment Summary area of the main screen, shown in Figure 7.2.

FIGURE 7.2

View information in the Deployment Manager.

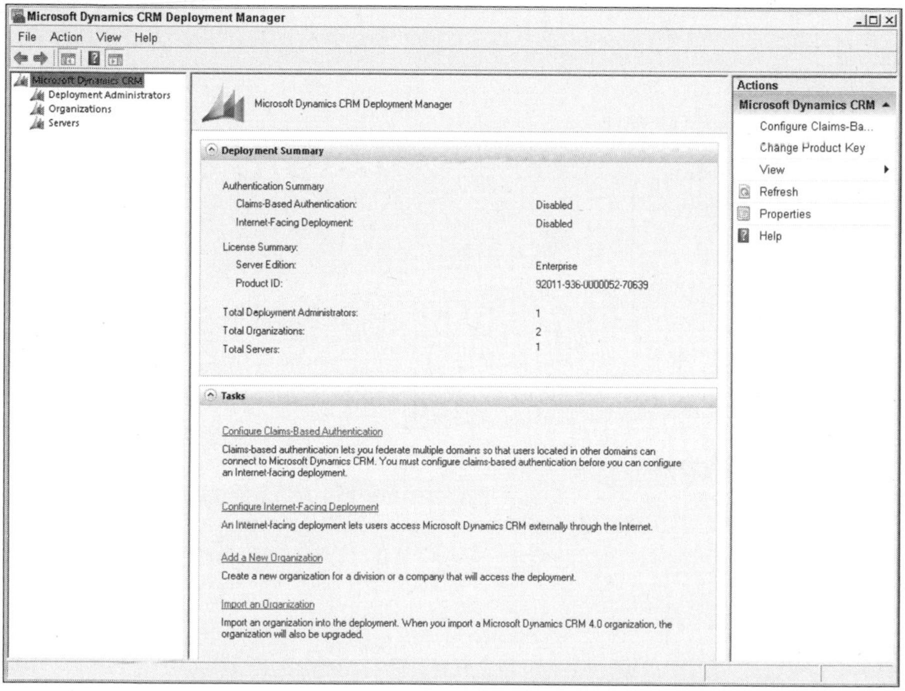

You can upgrade the product key for your on-premises deployment using the Deployment Manager. Product key downgrades are not available. The possible upgrade scenarios are detailed below:

- **Trial or MSDN license:** Can be upgraded to a full-use Workgroup or multitenant license.

- **Workgroup Edition license:** Can be upgraded to a multitenant license.

License keys are provided by Microsoft through your Microsoft partner or reseller.

To upgrade your license key, click the Change Product Key link on the Actions menu in Deployment Manager. Enter the alphanumeric license code, which is not case-sensitive, and click the Apply button (shown in Figure 7.3).

FIGURE 7.3

Use the Deployment Manager to upgrade trial and Workgroup Edition licenses.

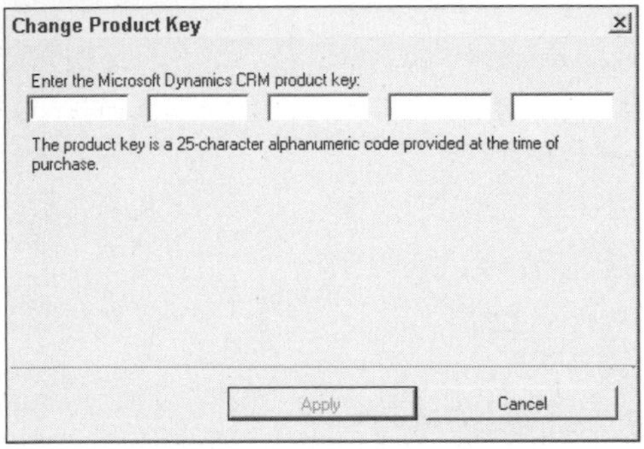

Changing deployment properties

The Deployment Manager provides a summary of deployment properties on the main screen (refer to Figure 7.2). Also, a Properties dialog box shows additional information about the deployment and allows several other properties to be managed. To open the Properties dialog box (see Figure 7.4), launch the Deployment Manager and choose Properties from the Action menu.

FIGURE 7.4

The Properties dialog box allows the configuration of the Web site binding and Web services addresses.

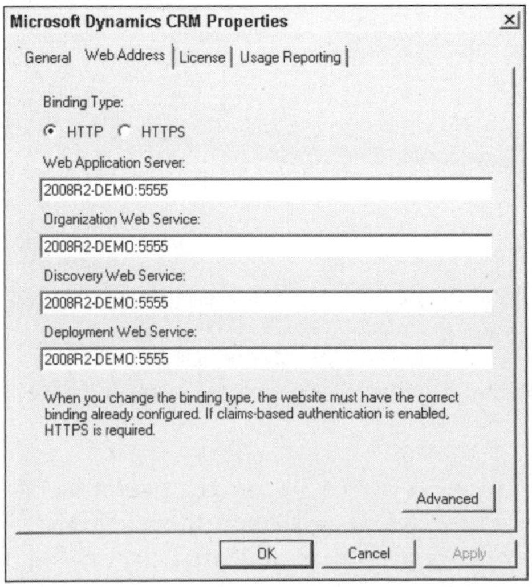

Deployment-wide properties that can be changed in this dialog box are:

- **Binding Type:** You can specify if your deployment should be available only through HTTPS. If you plan on using Claims-Based Authentication or Internet-Facing Deployment, you must set your deployment to use HTTPS. Note that in addition to changing this setting you may also need to make modifications to the Dynamics CRM Web site in IIS.

- **Web Application Server:** Use this setting to designate the Web front-end server for a multi-server deployment.

- **Web services Servers:** Organization Web Service, Discovery Web Service, and the Deployment Web Service.

Clicking the Advanced button on the Web Address tab of the Properties dialog box opens another dialog box, shown in Figure 7.5, where you can indicate if your deployment uses network load balancing and SSL offloading.

FIGURE 7.5

Specify if your deployment uses network load balancing or SSL offloading.

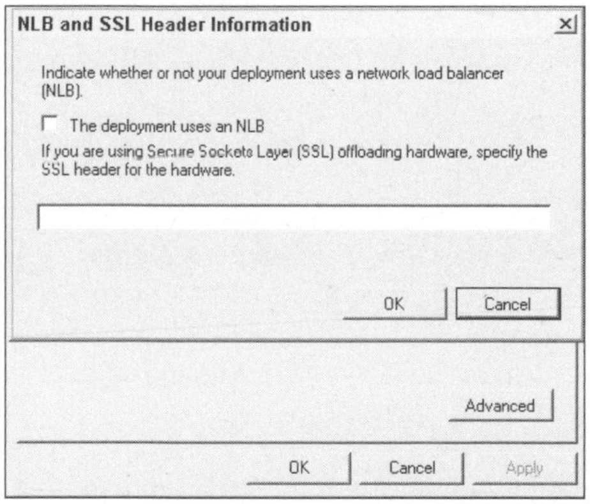

Adding Deployment Administrators

To use the Deployment Manager you must be a Deployment Administrator. Deployment Administrators can create or import organizations and have unrestricted access to disable all the organizations within the deployment.

By default, the user account that is used to install Dynamics CRM is set up as a Deployment Administrator. This user is also set up as a user with the System Administrator role in the default organization. Deployment Administrators who create new organizations are automatically set up as a user with the System Administrator role in the new organization.

Additional Deployment Administrators can be added, and it is not necessary that they be users in a Dynamics CRM organization. However, they must be local administrators on the Dynamics CRM server and members of the Microsoft SQL Server administrators group. (See the Microsoft KB article at `http://support.microsoft.com/kb/946686/` on the Microsoft support Web site for more information on the minimum privileges required for a user to be made a Deployment Administrator.)

To add a new Deployment Administrator:

1. Open the Deployment Manager on the Dynamics CRM server.
2. Right-click the Deployment Administrators node.
3. Click the New Deployment Administrator option to open the Select User dialog box.
4. Look up the user you want to add and click OK.

Cross-Reference

Deployment Administrator users are important even for organizations that make little use of the Deployment Manager. For example, Microsoft Dynamics CRM 2011 has a sandbox service that allows custom server-side code to operate in a secure, isolated fashion. However, for on-premises installations of Dynamics CRM, it is also possible to register plug-ins outside of the sandbox so they can operate with greater access to network resources. For these types of plug-ins to function, they must be registered to run under a user account that is also a Deployment Administrator. See Chapter 22 on server-side customization for more detail on registering plug-ins without using the sandbox service.

Managing organizations

In the context of the Deployment Manager, an organization is a single implementation of Dynamics CRM consisting of solutions, entities, fields, views, reports, users, data, and other items that together make up a comprehensive, fully functioning application. Each organization is a tenant on the Dynamics CRM server, and each tenant has its own organization database in SQL Server.

Microsoft sells Dynamics CRM under both single-tenant and multiple-tenant licensing models, so it is capable of hosting many organizations. If your deployment is under a single-tenant license, only one organization can be active at a time. If you have installed Dynamics CRM under a multitenant license, the Deployment Manager supports multiple active organizations at once.

Using the Deployment Manager, organizations can be created, enabled/disabled, imported, or set as the default organization. Organization settings can also be edited, such as changing an organization's name or report server.

Note

For single-tenant deployments using a Workgroup Edition license, you must first disable the default organization that was created during installation before creating or importing a new organization.

In the Organizations area of the Deployment Manager (see Figure 7.6), you can view the current organizations that are in your deployment, the status of each (Enabled or Disabled), the build version, and the update level that has been applied. Right-clicking on the organization name reveals an option that allows you to browse to the organization. Clicking Browse opens Internet Explorer and takes you to the home page for that organization.

Cross-Reference

In addition to the Deployment Manager console, Dynamics CRM also makes available a Deployment Web Service through which many of the functions detailed in the chapter can be accessed. The Deployment Web Service allows custom applications to access all of these functions programmatically. More details on how to use the Deployment Web Service is included in Chapter 22 which covers server-side customization.

FIGURE 7.6

To create a new organization in the Deployment Manager, click on the Organizations node and choose New Organization.

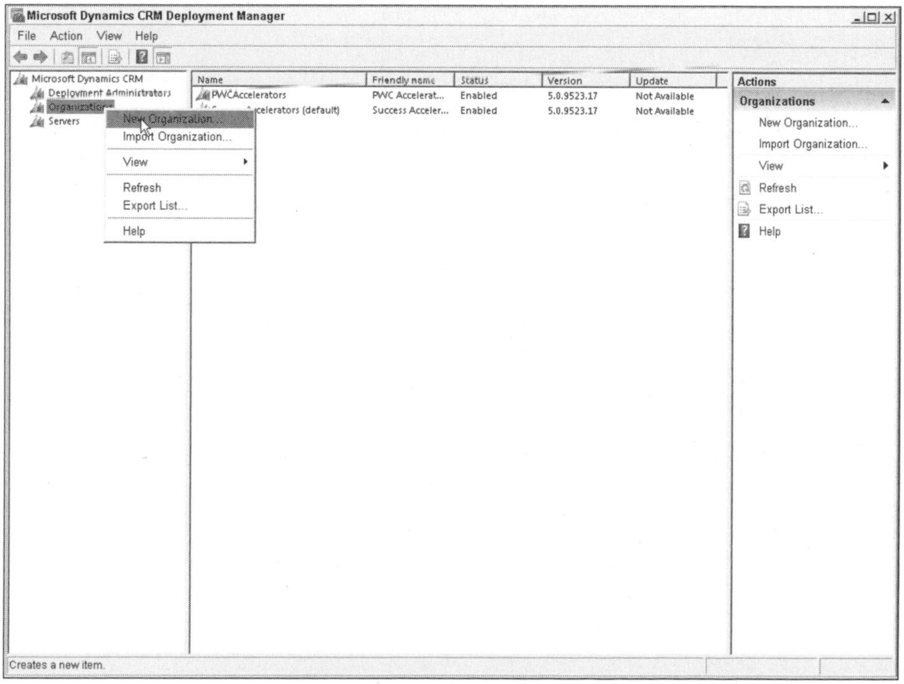

Creating a new organization

You can use the Deployment Manager to create new organizations in your Dynamics CRM implementation that contain the default customization solution and no data. The operation to create a new organization takes several minutes to run and is immediately usable when complete.

You can create a new organization in the Deployment Manager by right-clicking on the Organizations node (see Figure 7.6) and choosing "New Organization..." and then following these steps in the New Organization Wizard:

1. Enter the display name of the new organization. The wizard pre-populates the unique database name of the organization for you based on the display name you have entered. Organization names cannot contain extended characters such as spaces or semicolons. (A small list of reserved names cannot be used for an organization name. This list is maintained in the MSCRM_CONFIG database's ReservedNames table.)

2. Set the base currency, language, and SQL collation for the new organization and click Next. (Note that these cannot be changed after the organization is created.)

3. On the next screen, indicate whether you want to opt into Microsoft's Customer Experience Improvement Program, and click Next.

4. Select the SQL Server that will house the new organization database. (A new database will be created in the format Organizationame_MSCRM.) Click Next.

5. Specify the URL of the SQL Server Reporting Services report server, and click Next.

    The New Organization Wizard runs through a series of verification tasks to validate the options you have selected and determine if all of the system requirements have been met (Figure 7.7). Fix any warnings or errors that the wizard identifies, and, when all green checks are returned, click Next. The wizard displays a summary of your new organization's settings.

6. Click the Create button to create the organization.

Importing an organization

Importing organizations is one of the most powerful tasks that the Deployment Manager supports. Even administrators who plan on supporting only single-tenant deployments of Dynamics CRM should become familiar with the process of importing organizations, since this process is extremely helpful when performing routine administrative tasks such as:

- Creating and refreshing development and test environments
- Creating training environments
- Redeploying an organization from one server to another (such as when performing a hardware upgrade)
- Upgrading to Dynamics CRM 2011 from Dynamics CRM 4.0

The New Organization Wizard runs a number of verification tasks.

To import an organization, you must have a valid organization database that has already been restored and attached to the SQL Server where it will be housed. You can only import organization databases that are not deployed on another Dynamics CRM deployment. (For example, if you have an active organization deployed in a test environment, you cannot import that organization database to another Dynamics CRM deployment.) Additionally, you must have administrative rights on the SQL Server where the organization is being imported.

Depending on the size of the organization database you are importing and the performance characteristics of your environment, the import process can take several hours to complete.

To import an organization, open the Deployment Manager and follow these steps:

1. Right-click on the Organizations node and select Import Organizations. The Import Organization Wizard opens (shown in Figure 7.8).

2. Select the SQL Server and organization database you wish to import. Click Next. If you want to change the display or organization names, you may do so on the next screen. After you are satisfied with the display and organization names, click Next.

3. Input the SQL Reporting Services Report Server URL. Note that this URL is different from the Report Manager Web site's URL. Click Next. If you plan on using Dynamics CRM's SharePoint integration, input the URL of the site collection and click Next.

Generating and Editing a User Mapping File

When moving organizations between deployments via the Import Organization Wizard, you can use an XML mapping file to map users from the previous deployment to the users in the new deployment. You must first create the mapping file by following these steps:

1. Open the Deployment Manager and right-click on the Organizations node.

2. Click the Import Organization link to launch the Import Organization Wizard.

3. Specify the SQL Server and organization database that you will be importing and click Next.

4. Specify the organization names and click Next.

5. Specify the SQL Reporting Services server and click Next.

6. On the "Select Method for Mapping Users" screen, choose the "Select Custom Mapping Options" option (see figure below). In the resulting dialog, select the option to generate a new mapping file and browse to a location where you wish to save the XML file that will be created. Provide a name for the file and click Save.

7. Click Next to finish generating the mapping file. The import is canceled and a new mapping file is generated.

After the blank mapping file has been created, you must edit it to map the users from the previous deployment to the new users. Open the XML file in Visual Studio or another XML editor. The file contains a placeholder for the domain and for each user from the organization to be imported. It looks like this:

```
<MappingConfiguration>
<DomainMapping old="DEMO" new="" />
<UserMapping old="DEMO\C5Admin" new="" />
<UserMapping old="DEMO\asterling" new="" />
</MappingConfiguration>
```

Edit the XML by adding the new domain name in the DomainMapping node and the full domain logon for each user in the UserMapping node, as demonstrated below:

```
<DomainMapping old="DEMO" new="CONTOSO" />
<UserMapping old="DEMO\C5Admin" new="CONTOSO\JDoe" />
<UserMapping old="DEMO\asterling" new="CONTOSO\AJSterling" />
```

Save the XML file and return to the Deployment Manager. Restart the Import Organization Wizard, and when you reach the user mapping screen, choose the "Select Custom Mapping Options" option under auto-mapping to use an existing mapping file.

4. Select the method you want to use for mapping users. (See the Mapping Users section below for more information.) You can generate an XML mapping file and cancel the import at this point, edit the XML file to meet your needs, and use it during a second run of the Import Organization Wizard. See the "Generating and Editing a User Mapping File" sidebar.

5. On the Edit User Mappings screen, you can accept the mappings that the wizard displays or edit individual mappings. To edit a mapping, select the user and click the Browse button to locate the desired Active Directory user. When you are satisfied with the user mappings, click the Next button.

The wizard runs through a series of checks to verify that the organization can be successfully imported. Fix any errors or warnings before clicking Next.

The Ready to Import screen displays a summary of the settings you have selected. Click the Import button when you are ready to proceed.

FIGURE 7.8

The Import Organization Wizard helps when moving an existing Dynamics CRM organization database from one deployment to another, or when upgrading from Version 4.0 to Dynamics CRM 2011.

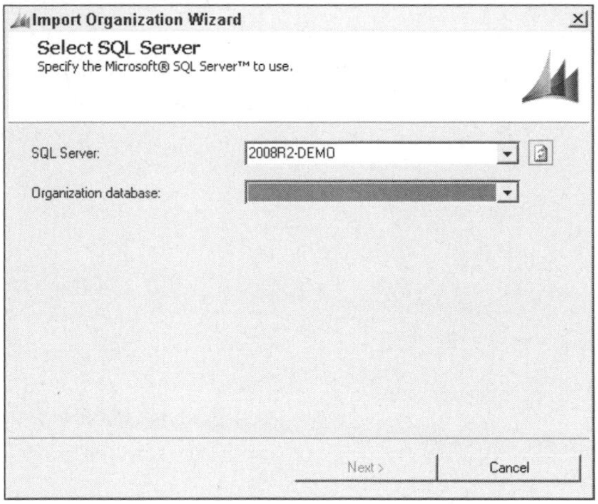

Mapping users

Dynamics CRM creates a unique ID for each user in the database. This ID is associated with the specific Active Directory user account for which it was created. Because many types of records are user-owned in Dynamics CRM, and the user ID is used to identify the user, Dynamics CRM must be able to associate users with an Active Directory account. Therefore, when importing an organization, the users in the organization will be relinked to Active Directory accounts. This is usually not an issue when the imported organization is within the same domain, and the users are remaining the same. However, when moving the organization from one domain to another, you need to make sure the user accounts are already in place before attempting the import process.

The Import Organization Wizard supports four different user mapping scenarios (see Figure 7.9):

- **Same Domain\Same Username.** The wizard automatically maps Dynamics CRM users by matching the Active Directory account name, assuming the domain and username for each user are not changing between deployments. This is often the scenario when upgrading the Dynamics CRM server hardware, for example. For this scenario, choose the Active Directory account name option as the method for mapping users in the Import Organization Wizard.

- **Different Domain\Same Username.** If you are moving the Dynamics CRM organization to a new domain, but the actual users will not be changing, select the Microsoft Dynamics CRM full name to Active Directory full name option in the wizard. An example of when this can be a helpful option is if you have one domain for training and another domain for production and wish to move a copy of your production database into the other domain so your users can train using real data without disturbing your production environment.

- **Different Domain\Sample Username.** Sometimes you may want to set up an environment to do development and testing work for Dynamics CRM, but there will be few actual users logging in. In this situation, you may pre-populate Active Directory with sample user accounts using a prefix of your choosing and an automatically incrementing number. In this situation, the Import Organization Wizard can map Dynamics CRM user records to the dummy Active Directory accounts. Select the third option on the user mapping screen and enter the prefix and starting number you have used for your dummy user accounts in Active Directory.

- **Different Domain\Different Username.** In some cases you may have to map user records to both a new domain and username altogether. For example, if your company's Active Directory domain name is changed and the format of user account names has also changed, or if you are importing an organization into a development or test environment that already has existing Active Directory user accounts. Or you may simply want to have complete control over how each user record is mapped. In these scenarios, you can create an XML map to specify precisely which users will be mapped to which Active Directory accounts and select the Use existing mapping file option.

FIGURE 7.9

The Import Organization Wizard has four different options for mapping users that allow a great deal of flexibility in moving organizations between deployments.

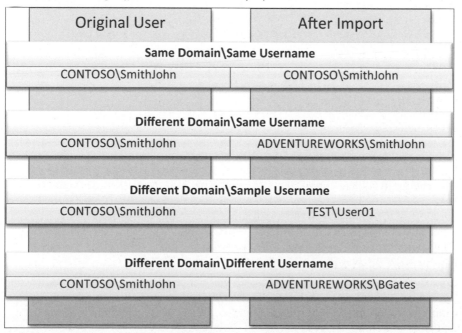

Original User	After Import
Same Domain\Same Username	
CONTOSO\SmithJohn	CONTOSO\SmithJohn
Different Domain\Same Username	
CONTOSO\SmithJohn	ADVENTUREWORKS\SmithJohn
Different Domain\Sample Username	
CONTOSO\SmithJohn	TEST\User01
Different Domain\Different Username	
CONTOSO\SmithJohn	ADVENTUREWORKS\BGates

Cross-Reference

Microsoft Dynamics CRM 4.0 organizations can be upgraded by being imported into a preinstalled Microsoft Dynamics CRM 2011 deployment through the Deployment Manager. The import process will automatically convert the organization database and perform the upgrade. See Chapter 3 for more information on upgrading from Version 4.0.

Logging into the newly imported organization

Each user has a default organization, which is the organization to which the user was first added. Users who have access to more than one organization have to specify the organization name in the URL in order to access an organization that is not their default organization. For example, if a deployment on a server named "crmserver" contains three organizations — Org1, Org2, and Org3 — a given user who was first created in Org1 can simply browse to `http://crmserver` in order to log into Org1. The user will automatically be redirected to `http://crmserver/Org1/main.aspx`. However, in order to log into Org2, the user must specify the organization name in the URL `http://crmserver/Org2/` in order to access the organization.

The same concept applies to newly created or newly imported organizations. In order to access the newly imported organization, you must specify the organization name (not the display name) in the URL.

Editing an organization

You can use the Deployment Manager to change the following settings for existing organizations:

- The organization's display name (Note that you cannot change the organization name, just the display name.)
- The SQL Server that the organization uses for its database
- The address of the organization's report server

Note

To edit an organization, you must first disable it. To disable an organization, right-click the organization name in the Deployment Manager and click the Disable item in the context menu.

Organizations have two names: one is a display name, such as *Company ABC Inc.*, and the other is the organization's unique database name with special characters removed, such as *CompanyABCInc*. After the unique database name is set, it cannot be changed. The display name can be changed in the Edit Organization Wizard. Changing an organization's display name does not change the URL for accessing the Dynamics CRM Web site for the organization. The URL will continue to use the system name for the organization.

If you have moved a copy of the organization database to another SQL Server, or set up a SQL Server cluster after installing Dynamics CRM, you can use the Edit Organization Wizard, shown in Figure 7.10, to change the SQL Server name.

If you have configured SQL Server Reporting Services (SSRS) to run at a different URL, you can also change those settings in the Edit Organization Wizard. Using the Edit Organization Wizard to point to a new SSRS URL will automatically republish the reports to the new report server.

Caution

If you have moved the database for an organization to a new SQL Server, you may need to adjust several registry keys, depending on your server configuration. Check the Microsoft support knowledge base article 952934 for more information.

To edit an organization, first back up your Dynamics CRM databases, including the organization database(s) and the MSCRM_Config database. Then follow these steps:

1. After disabling the organization, right-click the organization in the Deployment Manager and click Edit Organization.

2. In the Edit Organization Wizard, shown in Figure 7.10, change the display name, SQL Server, or the reporting services Web site URL, and click Next. The wizard performs a check of system requirements to validate the changes you have made.

3. When this check is complete, click Next.

4. Review the summary of the changes you wish to make, and click Apply. The wizard will update the system with your changes.

5. Click Finish when it completes. Re-enable the organization. (If you have changed the SQL Server, you may need to perform an IIS reset for the changes to take effect.)

FIGURE 7.10

The Edit Organization Wizard allows administrators to change an organization's properties.

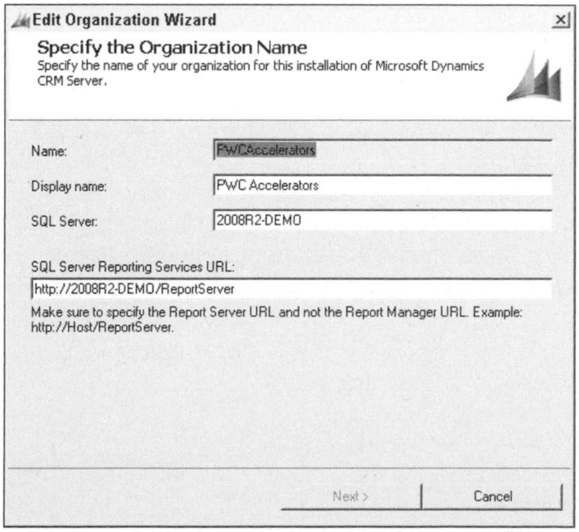

Deleting an organization

To delete a disabled organization from the Dynamics CRM deployment, right-click its name in the Deployment Manager and choose Delete. The organization is removed from the Deployment Manager, but the organization database is not affected. (To remove the database, you must use the SQL Server tools to manually remove it.) To delete the default organization, you must first make another organization the default organization.

To delete an active organization, you must first disable it and then right-click the organization name and click Delete.

Setting the default organization

You can specify which organization is the default organization in a multitenant (Enterprise) deployment. Changing the default organization in Deployment Manager does not affect users' default organization. A user's default organization is the organization to which the user was first added.

Initially, the default organization in a multiple organization deployment is the organization that was created during installation. Should you want to disable or remove this organization, you must specify another default organization.

Some client applications or custom code may stop functioning correctly if you change the default organization. Custom applications should be designed to use the Discovery Web Service to check the organization name against which the application is running. Therefore, if the custom application does not check the Discovery Web Service, it may expect the default organization to provide the data it needs to function.

To change the default organization, right-click the organization you want to make the new default organization, and click on Set as Default Organization. A dialog box opens, asking for confirmation to change the default organization. Click Yes.

Viewing servers and server roles in Deployment Manager

Microsoft Dynamics CRM 2011 is designed using a multi-tier — or n-tier — architecture. This means that the system spreads its presentation, application, and database components across several layers. This architecture enables Dynamics CRM to be highly scalable and also helps to provide additional interfaces for integration and extensibility. The Deployment Manager enables administrators to enable, disable, and remove servers from a deployment.

Understanding server roles

In Dynamics CRM, the tiers are further defined as server roles. Figure 7.11 depicts the server roles that make up Dynamics CRM.

Cross-Reference

Server roles can be configured during installation of Dynamics CRM under Enterprise licensing. See Chapter 3 for more information about the architecture of Dynamics CRM, planning your implementation for single or multiple servers, and how to distribute server roles.

Server roles in a deployment can be viewed in the Deployment Manager. Possible roles displayed here include the Full Server, Front End Server, Back End Server, and SQL Server role groups. Each of these role groups contains other roles as detailed in Table 7.1.

FIGURE 7.11

Microsoft Dynamics CRM 2011 is built on a n-tier architecture. Each tier is referred to as a server role. The roles for each server in a deployment can be viewed in the Deployment Manager.

Web Application & Web Services

Processing Services

Integration Services

Deployment Service

Database & Reporting Services

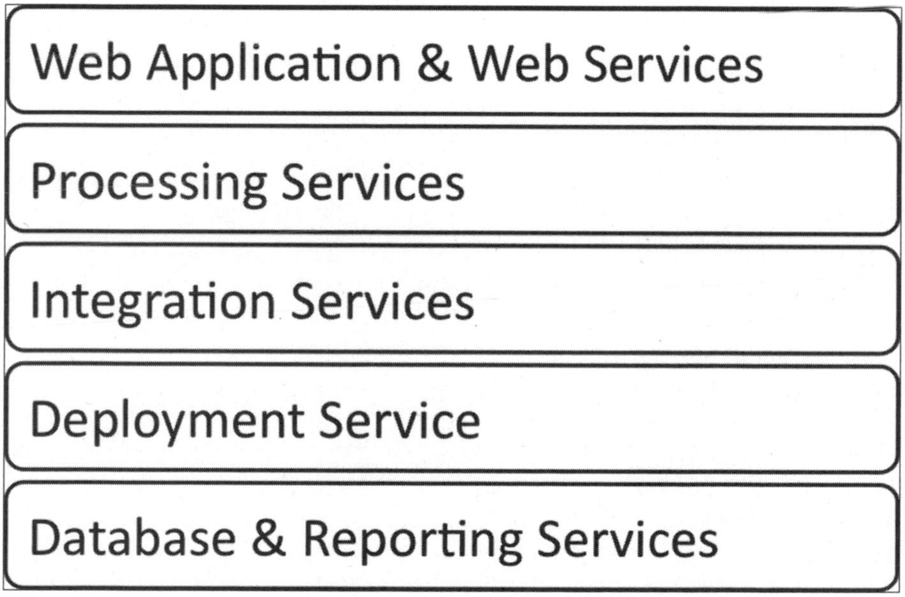

TABLE 7.1

Server Role Groups

Server Role Group	Server Roles
Front End Server	Web Application Server
	Discovery Web Service
	Organization Web Service
	Help Server
Back End Server	Asynchronous Service
	Sandbox Processing Service
	SharePoint Integration Service
Deployment Administration Server	Deployment Tools
	Deployment Web Service
Full Server	Includes the Front End Server, Back End Server, and Deployment Administration Server role groups
SQL Server	A logical role that is set during installation. Not part of a Server Role Group.
SRS Data Connector (for SQL Server Reporting Services)	Indicates a server with the data connector for SQL Reporting Services installed. Not part of a Server Role group.

In a single-server deployment, the Deployment Manager lists one server name with the Full Server and SQL Server roles, as shown in Figure 7.12. In multiple-server deployments, each server in the deployment is listed along with its corresponding role groups.

The SQL Server role is assigned by default to the server specified during installation. The Data Connector for SQL Server Reporting Services is installed on the report server, which may be a different server from the SQL Server. This server is displayed separately with the Data Connector role. (The Data Connector enables authentication to be passed from a client machine through the Dynamics CRM server to the report server.)

Disabling servers

You can also disable servers in your deployment from the Servers node in Deployment Manager. Disabling a server makes the server completely unavailable to end users. If the server's roles are not available on other servers, Dynamics CRM will be unavailable to users who attempt to access it. This is often necessary during deployment or server maintenance.

To disable a server, right-click the server name in the Servers area of the Deployment Manager and click on the Disable option.

FIGURE 7.12

Shown here is a single-server deployment with the Full Server role group and the SQL Server role on one server.

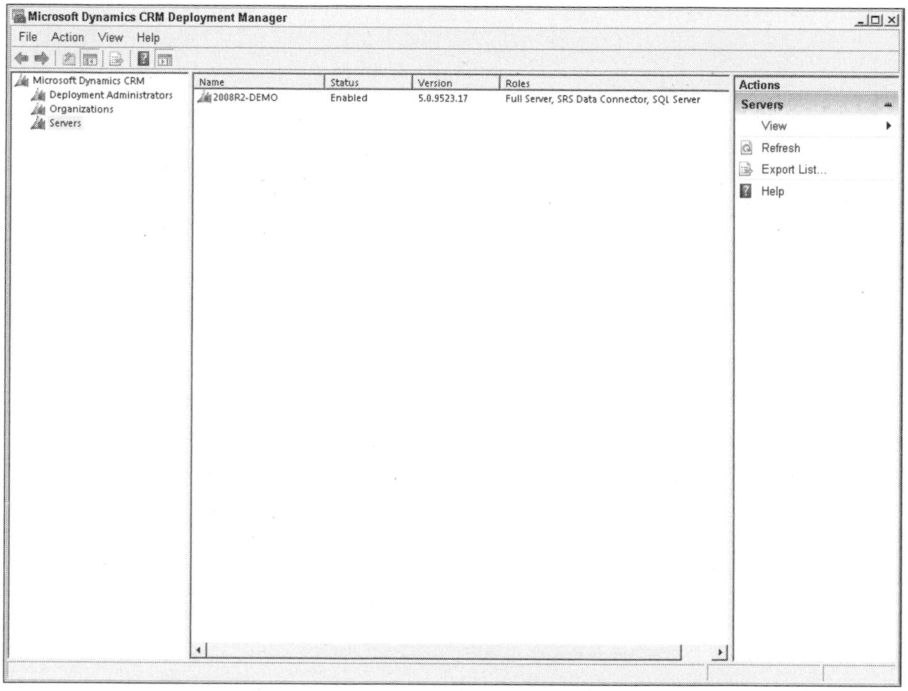

Deleting servers

Servers within a multiple-server deployment can be deleted once they have been disabled in order to remove them from the deployment. Deleting a server cannot be undone. To delete a server, first disable it, then right-click the server, and click the Delete option.

Reviewing Deployment Manager Logs

The Dynamics CRM server retains verbose logs by default to provide administrators with a way to review the actions that have been taken using the Deployment Manager. The default location where these logs can be found is C:\Users\%Username%\AppData\Roaming\Microsoft\MSCRM\Logs.

The logs detail all of the actions taken, as well as options that have been set during the creation, import, or renaming of organizations. In this way, they provide a useful tool for troubleshooting errors that may occur during changes to your deployment.

Configuring Claims-Based Authentication

Claims-Based Authentication allows users from different domains to access the same Dynamics CRM deployment. Claims-Based Authentication uses Microsoft Identity Foundation to enable Dynamics CRM to recognize and trust the identity providers that you specify. Claims-Based Authentication is also necessary for an Internet-Facing Deployment (IFD) of Dynamics CRM.

Note

To configure Claims-Based Authentication, you must first change the deployment to use only HTTPS. This setting affects all organizations within the deployment. (See the section on deployment properties at the beginning of this chapter for information on how to change the deployment from HTTP to HTTPS.) You must also have an available and configured Active Directory Federation Services 2.0 (AD FS 2) Web site. For more information about configuring Active Directory Federation Services, visit the following URL: `http://www.microsoft.com/forefront/en/us/identity-access-management.aspx`.

To configure Claims-Based Authentication, follow these steps:

1. Open the Deployment Manager, and on the Action menu, right-click Microsoft Dynamics CRM and select the option to Configure Claims-Based Authentication.

2. In the dialog that opens, enter the address of the federation metadata XML file on your AD FS Web site. Click Next.

3. Specify the encryption certificate by clicking Select to look up a local certificate. Click Next. The wizard verifies the settings you have entered.

4. Click Next. A summary of your settings is displayed.

5. Click the Apply button to apply the configuration changes.

Configuring Internet-Facing Deployment

Internet-Facing Deployment (IFD) allows users to access Dynamics CRM from the internet without using a VPN. This is especially helpful for users who will use the Outlook client for Dynamics CRM while disconnected from the network or outside of the domain.

To configure IFD, Claims-Based Authentication must first be configured, and you may need to also configure relying parties in Active Directory Federation Server 2.0 (AD FS 2). Once Claims-Based Authentication is configured, follow these steps to configure IFD:

1. In Deployment Manager, on the Action menu, select Configure Internet-Facing Deployment.

2. Enter the URL for external access to Dynamics CRM. The URL should be in the format: `https://<computername>.<domain>.com:<port>`. Click Next.

    The IFD dialog displays the paths for the Web application and Web services for Dynamics CRM. The paths do not need the computer name, just the domain name and port number. Additionally, the Discovery Web Service URL must start with "dev." as in `dev.<domain>.com:<port>`.

3. When these entries are complete, click Next. The IFD wizard performs a set of verification tasks to check the settings you have entered.

4. When this is complete and shows all green check marks, click Next. A summary of the settings to be applied is displayed. Click Apply to set the IFD.

5. After the changes are applied, you must also make manual changes to the web.config file in the root of the Dynamics CRM Web site. The web.config is usually located in the Web application server's Program Files directory, in the Microsoft Dynamics CRM\CRMWeb directory.

6. In the web.config file, find the authentication strategy element and change it from on-premise to `<authentication strategy="ServiceProviderLicense Agreement" />` .

7. Reset IIS and test access to Dynamics CRM.

Summary

This chapter described the functionality of the Deployment Manager, an administrative interface that manages deployment-wide and organization-level functions. Using the Deployment Manager, organizations can be created, imported, edited, disabled or deleted from a deployment. Organizations can be moved, or redeployed, from one deployment to another, and Dynamics CRM 4.0 organizations can be upgraded by using the import process in the Deployment Manager. The Deployment Manager also allows you to manage the licenses, servers, server roles, and other settings in your deployment.

We also covered the basic steps for configuring Claims-Based Authentication and Internet-Facing Deployment (IFD). These configurations are used to enable non-domain and/or non-local users to access Dynamics CRM. Claims-Based Authentication relies on Microsoft Identity Server and Active Directory Foundation Server, part of the Forefront group of products. IFD requires Claims-Based Authentication to be configured in order to function.

Managing Data

The single most critical function of any customer relationship management system is facilitating the creation and maintenance of useful, relevant data. No matter how well your system is designed or how enthusiastic your users are, your CRM system will be of little use if your data is incomplete, out-dated, or incorrect.

This is why Microsoft has put data management tools at the heart of Dynamics CRM. The Get Started pane at the top of system entity views includes links to tools and instructions for importing data and detecting duplicate records, and the Ribbon that is displayed when a user visits the Get Started screen or Settings area also includes links to data management tools (see Figure 8.1) — and it's available from the File menu throughout the application. There is also a feature that allows administrators to import and delete sample data, a feature that is very helpful for development, testing, and user training.

In this chapter, we provide step-by-step instructions for the three primary tools that are included in the Dynamics CRM user interface for data management: the Import Data Wizard, the Duplicate Detection Wizard, and the Bulk Delete Wizard.

Each of these wizards is designed to provide users of all levels with an easy way to maintain high-quality data in Dynamics CRM. Because there are several features common to these three tools, users who become familiar with one of them can more easily learn to use the other two. These common features are:

- The tools are all wizards — that is, they each use a simple dialog window to guide users one step at a time, with simple interfaces and links to helpful instructions.

- Each wizard works with most system entities as well as custom entities.

- Each tool creates a record, akin to a regular Dynamics CRM entity record, with list views that are sortable, searchable, and filterable, and forms that provide additional detail on the status of the jobs and links to related records (see Figure 8.1).

- The output of each wizard is treated as one or more asynchronous System Jobs that run in the background and can be monitored in the Settings area of the application.

FIGURE 8.1

The Imports page is visible in the My Work area of the Workplace.

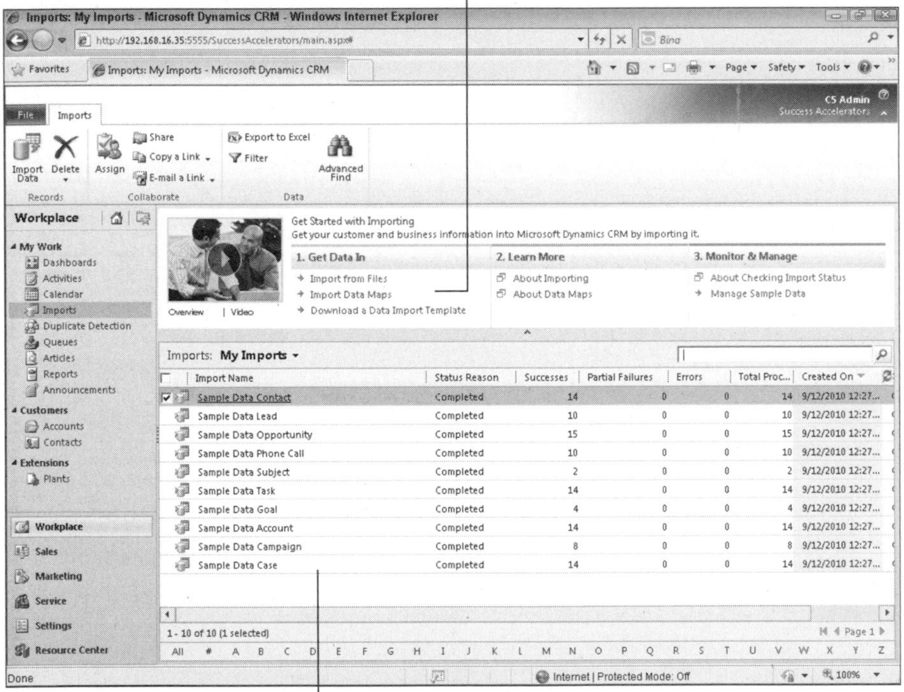

The Get Started panes have links to import data

Import jobs are visible in the imports list view

Importing Data with the Import Data Wizard

The Import Data Wizard is designed to make it quick and easy to get your data into Dynamics CRM, whether you need to import data into existing system or custom entities, or create a new entity or new fields on the fly.

The Import Data Wizard accepts four file types (see Figure 8.2):

- XML (in Excel's XML Spreadsheet 2003 file format)
- CSV
- TXT
- ZIP (a zipped file containing files of the other supported types)

Note
Each file can be as large as 8MB, though if they are zipped together you can import up to 32MB of data using this wizard. When zipping files together, all the files must be of the same type (.csv, .xml, or .txt).

Imported files can include lookup references that relate your source data to records already in the database. The Import Data Wizard automatically creates the relationship to the related record in Dynamics CRM. For example, if your source file includes an Owner column, the Import Data Wizard will assign the newly imported records to the appropriate owners — if the owner name in your source file exactly matches the username in Dynamics CRM. Similarly, if you import Contacts with a Parent Account column, the Parent Account must be an existing account record in Dynamics CRM with the exact spelling and case as the import file.

One limitation of the Import Data Wizard is the way it handles picklists, or drop-down items within a record. If the picklist contains a matching value, the record will be imported, but it will fail if there is no matching value, and the Import Data Wizard does not provide an option to add new picklist options to an existing picklist or option set.

Data maps

Data maps are XML files used by the import process to connect the data you are importing to the appropriate entities and fields in Dynamics CRM. If your source data is formatted with column headings and data that match the existing entity and field display names, the Import Data Wizard will automatically map your data when you select the target entity. If the wizard is unable to auto-map your data, you can select an existing map.

FIGURE 8.2

The Import Data Wizard allows users to import a variety of source file types.

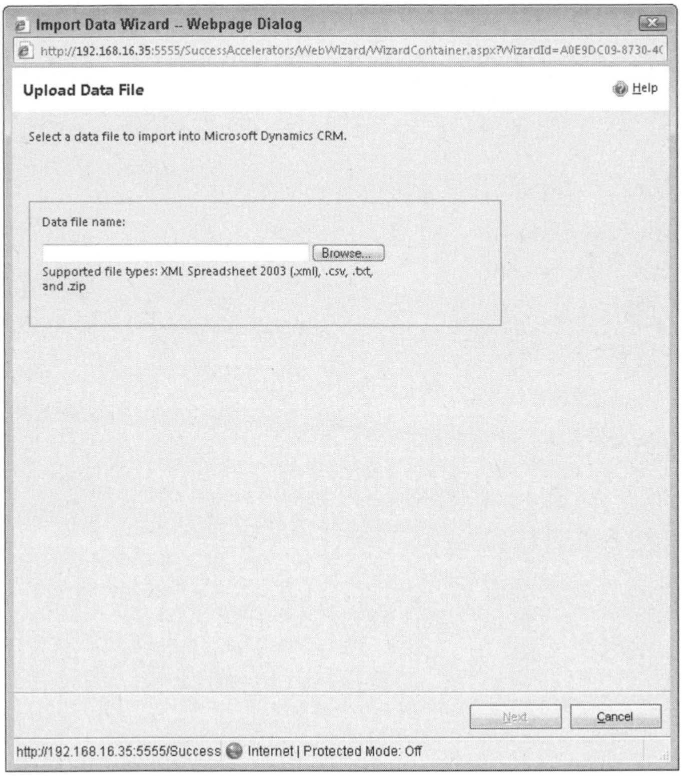

Dynamics CRM ships with several existing maps for Salesforce.com and Business Contact Manager data imports. You can modify these built-in maps or create your own and save them for later reuse.

If you are unable to take advantage of the auto-mapping feature or an existing data map, or you want to create a new Data Map for later reuse, the Import Data Wizard will present you with a mapping screen where you can match your source fields to the target fields in Dynamics CRM (see Figure 8.3). When you are done mapping and setting other options for the import, you can give the Data Map a name so it is easy to locate later. Data Maps can also be imported and exported in the Data Management area under Settings.

Tip

If you are going to import multiple files where there are relational references from one record type to another, start by importing the top-most records. For example, when importing Accounts and Contacts, where the Contacts have a Parent Account field, import the Accounts first. This way, the relationships can be automatically established when the Contacts are imported.

FIGURE 8.3

When you map source data fields to target data fields in the Import Data Wizard, you can save the results as a reusable data map.

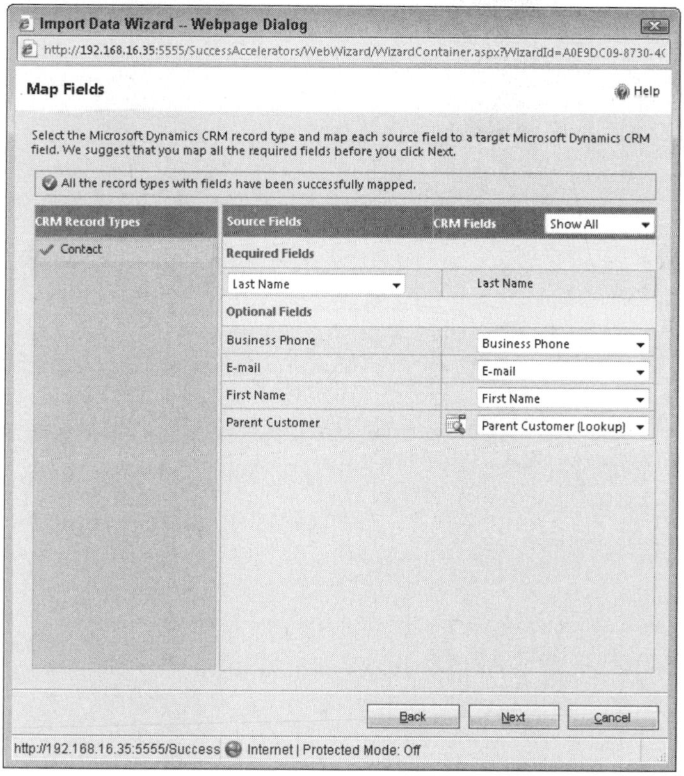

Preparing your source files

To smooth the process of importing data into Dynamics CRM, prepare your source files in advance and perform test imports with small samples of your data. Following are some tips on preparing your source data.

Use the data import templates

On the Data Management screen is a link to download templates for data import. This link opens a dialog that allows you to select the entity you are working with and export an Excel XML file that contains pre-formatted column headings for all of the entity's importable fields. You can use this template as a starting point to format the data you plan to import.

Note

The link to access data import templates is also available from the Ribbon menu above each entity's list view by clicking on the Import Data menu's drop-down and selecting the Download Template for Import option.

Make column headings match display names

If you do not want to use a template, rename the column headings in your source file so they match the display names in Dynamics CRM. For example, Main Phone is the default display label for an Account's primary phone number. In your source file, changing the column heading to match this *exactly* (spelling, capitalization, and spaces) will allow the Import Data Wizard to map the column automatically. A quick shortcut to see exactly what your column headings should be is to export a sample record to Excel from Dynamics CRM. Use the Advanced Find tool to create a query that includes the same columns as the data you want to import and copy the column headings to your source file.

Add necessary options to picklists

The Import Data Wizard will not add new options to existing picklists. Each row in your imported file that contains picklist values that do not exist in Dynamics CRM will fail to import. Make sure that you've added all picklist values and published the changes beforehand to avoid rejected rows.

Import lookup references first

If your import file contains references to related records, the related records must already exist. For example, if you are importing contacts with a parent account record, the parent account must be entered first or the row will fail to import.

Validate and format fields

If you're using client-side JavaScript on your entity forms to apply validation and formatting (such as is frequently used for phone number fields) this formatting won't be applied to your imported data since client-side script is not triggered during imports. You should format the data in your source file first.

Caution

Workflow rules and plug-ins that are configured to fire when a record is created will be triggered during data import. In some cases, this may be desirable, but it is always a good idea to review your workflow rules and plug-ins before importing data to avoid unexpected results. You can temporarily unpublish workflow rules during the import and re-publish them when you are done to avoid problems. Similarly, you can un-register plug-in steps and re-register them when your import is complete.

Dealing with floats and decimal precision

Float or decimal data may be imported even if the precision is different. For example, if your source file has a decimal value of 1.432 (a precision of three digits after the decimal point) and the target field only has a precision of two decimal places, your data will be imported as 1.43. The results of rounding are not always predictable and can produce unexpected results.

If your data requires a greater level of precision, make the change in Dynamics CRM first and publish it, before importing the data. There are two types of fields that allow decimals in Dynamics CRM: floating-point fields have up to five digits of precision, and decimal fields have up to ten digits after the decimal.

Remove carriage returns and line breaks

Carriage returns, line breaks, and other non-printable characters can cause failures during the import process. Remove extraneous non-printable characters before importing your data into Dynamics CRM.

Enriching (updating) existing data

The Import Data Wizard can also be used to update existing data in Dynamics CRM. It is designed to allow users to export data from Dynamics CRM to Excel, where it can be *enriched* or otherwise manipulated and reimported through the Import Data Wizard. Changes to the data will be updated to the existing records. In order to accomplish this, unique identifying data is included when exporting data from Dynamics CRM and must not be removed when manipulating the data in Excel. Users are given the opportunity to include these unique identifiers when exporting data (see Figure 8.4).

FIGURE 8.4

When you export data from Dynamics CRM, you have the option to include unique identifiers which will allow you to update the records using the Import Data Wizard.

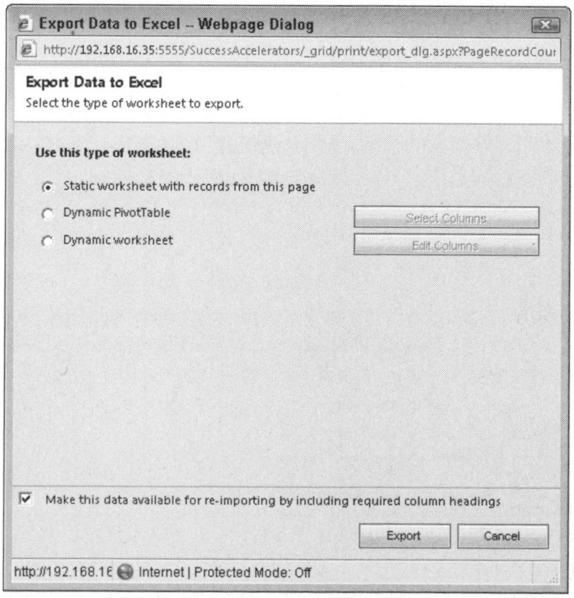

Reviewing the import job

You can monitor the progress of your import jobs in the Imports list view. Refreshing the view as the import is processed will allow you to watch the job as it moves from parsing your source file, through transforming it, and importing each record. The list view will show counts of the total rows in your source, as well as the number of successes and failures as the job progresses.

When the job is complete, you can open the Import record and view the results. If you are dissatisfied with the records that were imported, the Import record provides you with the option to bulk delete the imported records.

For each failed row, Dynamics CRM provides a description of the reason why the row failed to import. You can also export failed rows to Excel, where you can analyze them to determine the cause of the failure or modify them to attempt a re-import (see Figure 8.5).

FIGURE 8.5

Rows from your source file that fail to import are visible in the Failure associated view on the Import record. You can export them from here for further analysis or clean-up.

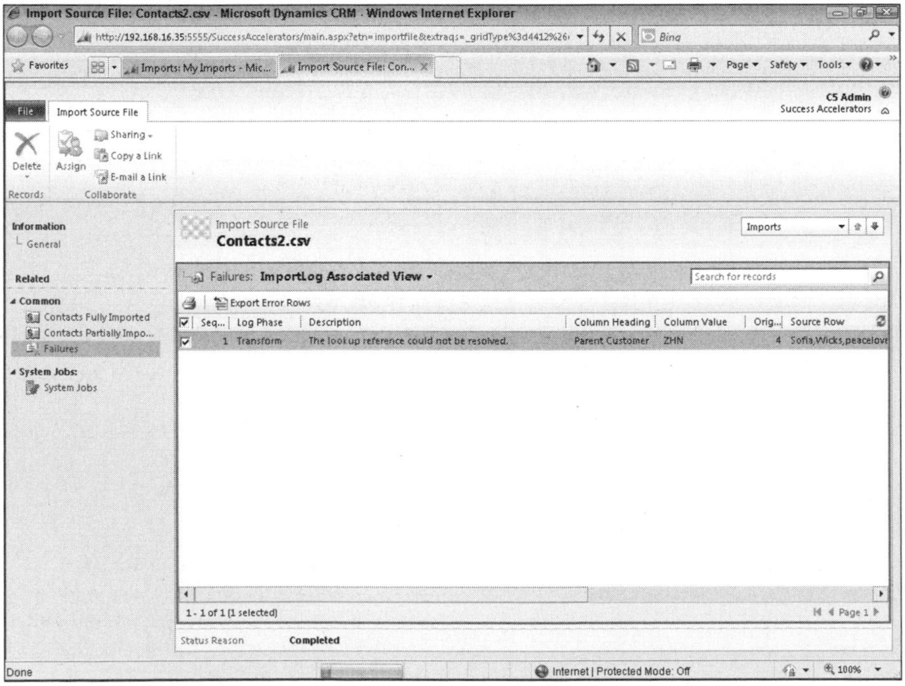

Using the Import Contacts Wizard from Outlook

Another common way data is imported into Dynamics CRM is by tracking contacts from Outlook using the Dynamics CRM Outlook Client. Contacts can be tracked individually or by using the Add Contacts Wizard in the Outlook add-in. You should consider the benefits and potential issues of allowing users, via security roles, to import large numbers of records — particularly if you do not have strong duplicate detection rules in place.

To use the Add Contacts Wizard in Outlook follow these steps:

1. Navigate to the Dynamics CRM options. In Outlook 2010, click File ⇨ CRM ⇨ Import Contacts ⇨ Add Contact Wizard.

2. The wizard dialog box opens and displays some introductory information. Click Next.

3. The wizard will analyze your Outlook contacts and group them by company names, domain names, and categories. Select the group type and the desired groupings, and click the Add Contacts button. The wizard imports the contacts according to your selections.

Detecting Duplicates

The Duplicate Detection wizard might better be called the Duplicate Detection Job Scheduling Wizard because it allows users to schedule a duplicate detection job. A number of configurations that must be completed before using the wizard to schedule a duplicate detection job, including defining the rules that determine duplicates and enabling entities for duplicate detection.

Dynamics CRM duplicate detection jobs scan the Dynamics CRM database tables for a selected entity, looking for records that appear to be copies of other records. Potential duplicates are identified and can then be managed within the duplicate detection job records. The duplicate detection jobs do not deactivate, delete, or otherwise modify potential duplicate records — the user or system administrator must manually deal with these records. Duplicate detection jobs can run against most system entities as well as custom entities and can be set to recur at regular intervals.

Note

Duplicate detection jobs are different from duplicate detection rules that can prevent duplicates from being created during an import job. Duplicate detection jobs use the same rules, but simply having the rules in place does not prevent users from creating duplicate records. It will still be necessary to run periodic jobs to detect duplicates and manually clean them up.

Tip

Before importing data for production use, it is best to have duplicate detection rules properly configured and tested. This way, when importing new data you can let the Import Data Wizard prevent duplicate records from entering the system.

Duplicate detection settings

Duplicate detection can be globally disabled or enabled in the Duplicate Detection Settings dialog available from the Duplicate Detection Settings link on the Data Management page. Disabling duplicate detection unpublishes all duplicate detection rules.

In addition to batch duplicate detection jobs, the Duplicate Detection Settings dialog enables you to configure when individual or a series of records are compared against the published rules:

- When a record is created or updated
- When Microsoft Dynamics CRM for Outlook goes from offline to online
- During data import

Creating duplicate detection rules

For the Duplicate Detection Wizard to function, Dynamics CRM must know what constitutes a duplicate of a given record type. For example, a common indication that two Contact records are duplicates is if they have the same e-mail address. Conversely, two Account records may share the same name but have different locations, such as is often the case with companies that have multiple offices. You can also compare one entity against another. In order for Dynamics CRM to know what your organization considers a duplicate record for a given entity, you must first configure and publish a duplicate detection rule.

Tip

Before you can create a duplicate detection rule, the entity must first be enabled for duplicate detection. Open the solution that contains the entity you want to manage, and on the entity's definition page, place a check next to Enable duplicate detection in the Mail Merge and Duplicate Detection section. Save and publish the solution. (Detailed instructions for customizing and publishing solutions are in Chapters 15 and 16.)

When a duplicate detection rule is published, Dynamics CRM uses the criteria you have specified in the rule to create a *matchcode*. A matchcode is then generated in the background for each record in Dynamics CRM and used to identify potential duplicates. For example, if you create a duplicate detection rule for Contacts that compares the entire last name and the same first three characters of the first name, the matchcode for a Contact named Franklin Smith as **SmithFra** (the exact last name plus the first three characters from the first name field). Another Contact with the name Francine Smith would also have a matchcode of **SmithFra** and would therefore be identified as a potential duplicate based on these criteria.

Matchcodes, and therefore duplicate detection rules, are limited to a maximum of 450 characters in order to preserve optimal performance while records are being created, imported, or scanned by duplicate detection jobs.

To configure a duplicate detection rule:

1. Navigate to the Data Management page in the Settings area of Dynamics CRM and click on the link for Duplicate Detection Rules.

2. Click the New button to create a new rule.

3. In the Duplicate Detection Rule form, enter a name and description to describe the rule you are configuring.

4. In the Base Record Type picklist, select the entity for which you want to create the duplicate detection rule. Only entities that have been enabled for duplicate detection are available from this picklist.

5. In the Matching Record Type picklist, select the entity against which you want to compare the base record type. If you want to be able to run duplicate detection against more than one record type, you will need to configure and publish multiple rules.

6. Indicate if you want your duplicate detection rule to be case sensitive. The default is to ignore case in the matching criteria.

7. Select the criteria that determine a matching record. If the duplicate detection rule will compare the entity against a different entity type, you need to select the fields you want to compare (see Figure 8.6). The options for comparing records include checking for an exact match or the same *n* number of first or last characters. You can create multiple matching criteria within a single rule. These criteria, or conditions, build a matchcode. The matchcode's length is shown below the selection criteria.

8. When you are done configuring the matching conditions, save the rule and then publish it by clicking the Publish button on the record toolbar. (You can also publish and unpublish rules from the list view's "More Actions" menu.)

Depending on the number of records in your system for which a matchcode must be generated, the publish action may take from a few seconds to several minutes to complete. You can monitor the progress of the publish action from the duplicate detection rules list view.

Scheduling duplicate detection jobs

Duplicate detection jobs can be run on a schedule, either on a one-time basis or as recurring jobs. When you schedule a duplicate detection job, it will use all published rules for the entity.

FIGURE 8.6

Duplicate detection rules can compare entities of different types and check for exact matches or matching first or last characters.

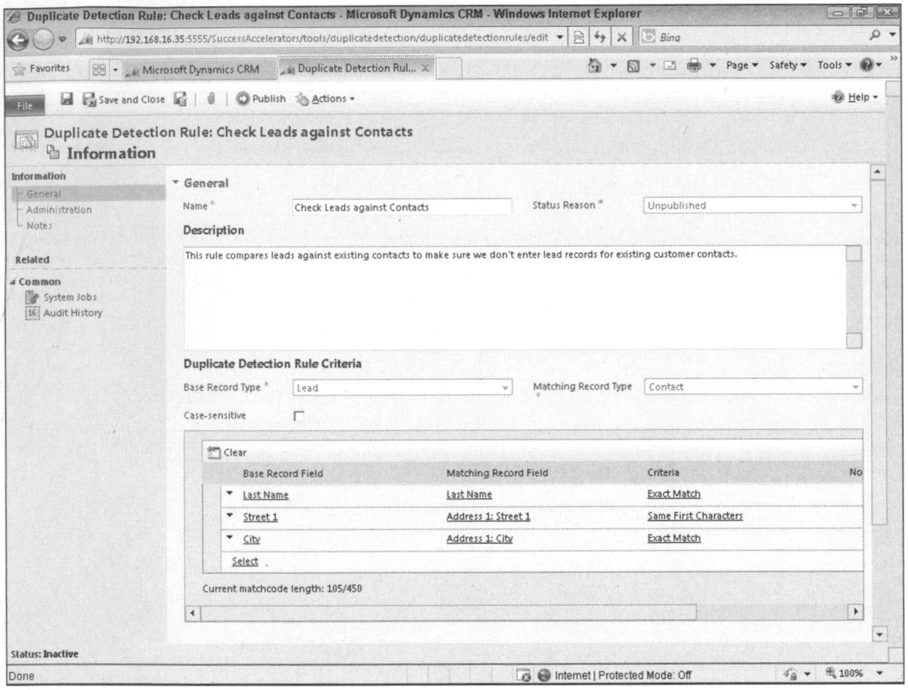

To schedule a duplicate detection job:

1. Launch the Duplicate Detection Wizard from the New button on the Duplicate Detection Jobs list view, accessible from the link on the Data Management page.

2. Click Next to proceed past the welcome screen.

3. On the Select Records page, select the entity you wish to scan for duplicates. This page is similar to the Advanced Find tool and allows you to limit the records to check based on filter criteria or saved views. To speed up the filtering process, you can start by selecting a saved view and then adding additional filtering criteria (see Figure 8.7). If you have a large number of records in your system, a minimal set of filter criteria is advisable in order to minimize the impact on performance and length of time the job will run. At a minimum, run the job only against active records.

4. Click the Preview Records button to check the results of your filtering criteria. If you want to run a duplicate detection job against all records of the selected entity, you can skip this filter. Click Next when you are satisfied with your filter criteria.

5. On the Select Options page of the wizard you can change the name the system has given the duplicate detection job.

6. Set the start date and time when you want the duplicate detection job to commence.

7. If you want to configure this job to run on a recurring basis, select the Run this job after every option and select the frequency in days that you wish the job to run.

8. By default, an e-mail will be sent to you when the duplicate detection job is completed. (This option is grayed out if your user record does not contain an e-mail address.) You can also choose to notify another user.

9. Click Next and then click Submit to complete the Duplicate Detection Wizard.

FIGURE 8.7

When scheduling a duplicate detection job, you can limit the records that the job will check for potential duplicates.

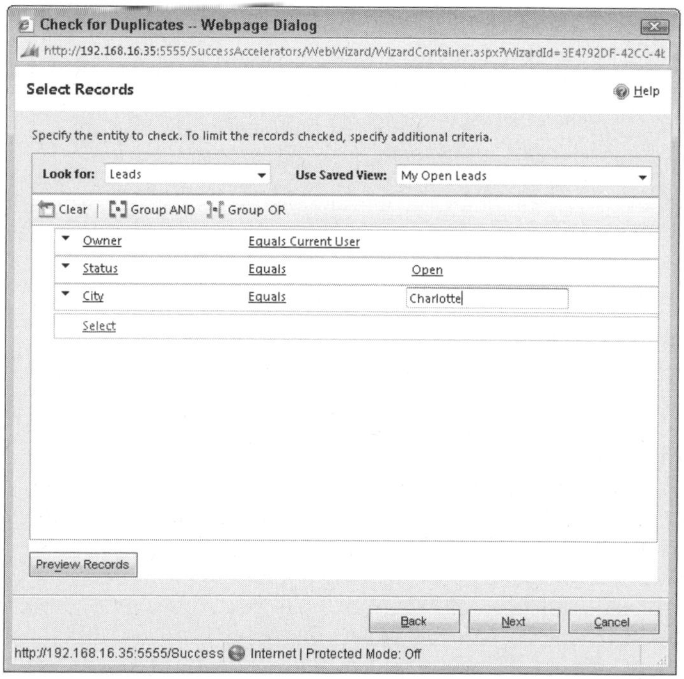

Handling duplicate records

When a duplicate detection job has finished identifying potential duplicate records, you must review the list of potential duplicates and decide what to do with each record. (This can be a very tedious process and underscores the importance of having well-defined and well-tested duplicate detection rules in place before data is loaded or users are allowed to begin creating records, so duplicates can be caught on the front end.) To view potential duplicates, click the link to go to the duplicate detection jobs list view on the Data Management page, and open the job you ran. On the left-hand side of the job, click the View Duplicates link (see Figure 8.8).

FIGURE 8.8

After a duplicate detection job runs, the potential duplicates must be manually merged or deactivated.

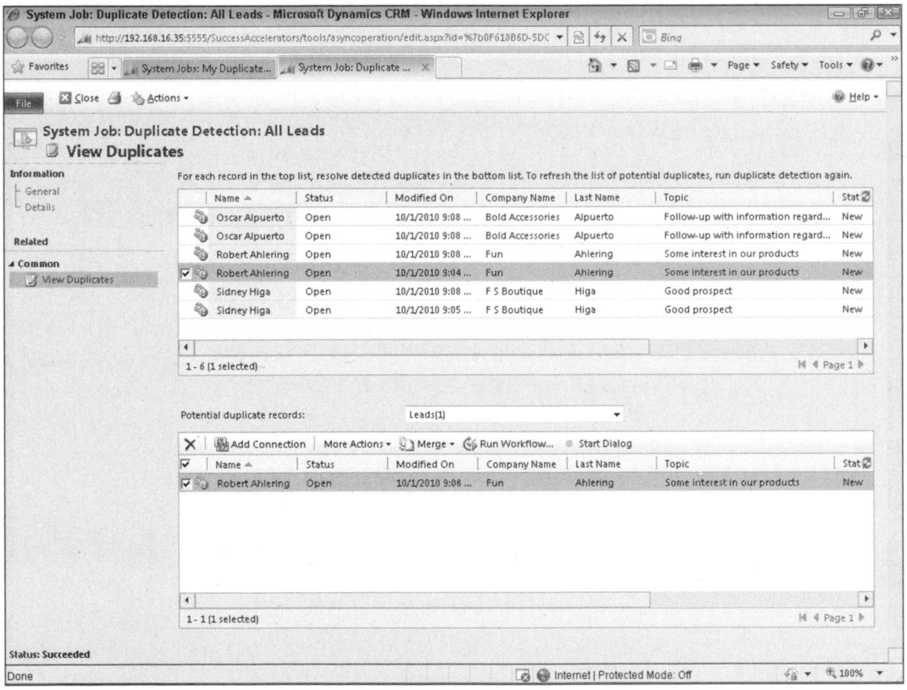

Potential duplicate records can be deleted, deactivated, merged, or ignored. When merging records, you have the option of selecting a master record that will survive and inherit all of the related records from the subordinate record, which will be deactivated. The Merge Records dialog also allows you to choose individual fields to move to the surviving record to help avoid data loss.

To manage and de-duplicate the records the duplicate detection job identified as potential duplicates, follow these steps:

1. Select a record from the top list. Potential duplicates for this record are displayed in the window below. The top list shows a maximum of 12 records at a time. The bottom list displays as many records as your individual user options allow.

2. Review the potential duplicates in the bottom list and decide whether to deactivate the potential duplicates or merge them with the record in the top list. If at the time the duplicate detection job ran your system had additional rules that compared the entity to another entity, you will be able to view all of the potential duplicates across the different entities by selecting the other entity from the drop-down option above the bottom list.

3. To deactivate a record in the bottom list, select the record(s) and click the More Actions toolbar button and choose Deactivate from the menu. You can deactivate multiple records at a time.

4. To merge records, click the Merge button. You can merge only two records at a time. Choosing to merge the two records automatically will set the record from the top list as the master record. If you are uncertain which record should be the master record, you can view the data in the two records side-by-side in the merge dialog by clicking the Merge button and choosing the Select Master option. You can also select individual fields to move to the master record.

Tip

After merging or deactivating a record from the bottom list, it helps to refresh the top list so you can see the status of the records and move on to deal with the next active record in the list.

Cleaning Up Your Data with the Bulk Deletion Wizard

The Bulk Deletion Wizard is the simplest to use and requires no prior configuration. This wizard is used to schedule and run a system job that deletes records of a given entity from Dynamics CRM.

1. To launch the Bulk Delete Wizard navigate to the Bulk Record Deletion list view under Data Management and click the New button.

2. Enter the search criteria you want to use to define the set of records you want to delete. You can start with a saved view and add additional filtering criteria. Each clause in the filtering criteria is treated as an "AND" statement, so if you have multiple criteria, the search will look for records that meet all of them.

3. Before continuing, preview the records that your search criteria have found, and when you are satisfied with the scope of the deletion job, click Next.

4. Provide a name for the job and set the start time and recurrence options. Click Next.

5. Click the Submit button to finish the wizard.

6. You can monitor the progress of the deletion job or check it for failures by going back to the Bulk Record Deletion list view.

Bulk deletion jobs can also be launched from a completed import job. Dynamics CRM keeps track of the records that were created by each import job, and this set of records can be targeted by a bulk record deletion job. This is very handy when performing test import jobs.

Caution

Dynamics CRM does not have any method of recovering deleted records. If you do not carefully limit the scope of the bulk deletion job, you can easily delete records that should not have been deleted. Depending on the entity's configuration, related records may also be automatically deleted if they are parented by a record in your bulk deletion job (and the relationship between the two entities contains a cascading delete setting).

Summary

Well-maintained data can become one of your organization's most valuable assets, which is why Microsoft has invested heavily in providing powerful, yet easy-to-use, data management tools right within the Dynamics CRM user interface. These wizard-based tools create system jobs that run in the background, performing critical tasks like importing data, detecting potential duplicate records, and deleting records in bulk.

Before importing data: Understand the structure of your Dynamics CRM data and the format it expects data to be in. Your source data will most likely need some clean-up, which you can do in Excel or another spreadsheet program, before importing it. Do a few test imports with a small number of records, saving and improving your data maps along the way, until you are confident you can launch a successful import job.

Having good duplicate detection rules in place is essential to keeping your system's data clean and useful, and you will have to spend less time managing potential duplicates if you can prevent them from making their way into Dynamics CRM in the first place. The Duplicate Detection Wizard requires that duplicate detection rules are defined and published before it will be able to launch duplicate detection jobs. By default, Dynamics CRM includes three duplicate detection rules, one each for Accounts, Contacts, and Leads. You can also create and publish multiple custom detection rules per entity. Like the Import Data Wizard, it can take some trial and error to get these rules and settings just right.

Maintaining, Optimizing, and Troubleshooting Dynamics CRM

The goal of this chapter is to equip you with the knowledge and resources needed to successfully administer Microsoft Dynamics CRM 2011 on a daily basis. Because of the many components that make up the infrastructure of Dynamics CRM — as well as the many possible deployment scenarios — the primary focus will be on familiarizing you with the tools at your disposal, providing references and links to external resources that will help you to maintain, optimize, and troubleshoot the system.

Throughout this book and this chapter, when speaking of the individuals responsible for maintaining Dynamics CRM, we frequently refer to them as administrators. We use the term administrator in a general sense, realizing that in some organizations one person may be responsible for all of the "administrative" functions, while in a large enterprise environment, there may be teams of specialized IT professionals with more narrowly defined responsibilities.

IN THIS CHAPTER

Backups and maintenance for Dynamics CRM

Measuring baseline performance

Optimizing Dynamics CRM Client, Application, Platform, and Data tiers

Troubleshooting and repairing errors

Maintaining Dynamics CRM

Maintaining Dynamics CRM requires familiarity with a broad range of server, Web, and network technologies and in many cases may call for highly specialized skills. Following is a partial list of the types of skills and knowledge that may be required in order to administer Dynamics CRM:

- **Database administration:** This skillset includes knowledge of how to install, configure, and maintain SQL Server, and how to write and use queries, stored procedures, and reports. Typical database administration for Dynamics CRM may require the ability to configure and restore backups of databases, use SQL Server Profiler, or troubleshoot database security and authentication.

- **Web server administration:** Skills required for administering the Dynamics CRM Web application include knowledge of IIS 7.0, the .NET framework, web services technologies, and DNS. (Chapter 20 contains a discussion of the many web technologies used to customize Dynamics CRM, knowledge of which may be helpful when troubleshooting certain issues.)

- **Network administration:** Dynamics CRM maintenance and troubleshooting may at times require knowledge about server hardware and operating systems, virtualization technologies, Active Directory, routing, and networking.

- **Workstation/client device administration:** Ultimately, it is the users of Dynamics CRM who are the administrator's "customers" and it is their machines and devices that sometimes are the locus of performance issues or system errors. Skills required for administering workstations and client devices may include desktop support, application support (such as Microsoft Office Outlook or Word), and mobile device support.

This summary of potential skill sets would not be complete without also including more "soft" skills, such as good troubleshooting instincts, knowing how to navigate Microsoft's support channels, or when to get outside help. There are also a host of related technologies such as Exchange Server that may play a critical role in your overall Dynamics CRM system. This chapter covers information that is specific to Dynamics CRM.

Cross-Reference

Many of the topics discussed in this chapter underscore the importance of properly planning your deployment and the design of your Dynamics CRM system architecture in order to simplify maintenance and prevent performance problems and errors before they occur. Refer to the System Requirements Quick Reference in Chapter 2 and the treatment of architecture and installation considerations in Chapters 3 and 4 for important recommendations to consider.

Simplifying updates

With the release of Microsoft Dynamics CRM 2011, Microsoft has improved the process of maintaining the Dynamics CRM server, server components, and the Outlook client add-in by designing them to leverage the Windows Update service. Windows Update is the method by which security patches and bug fixes are distributed to computers running Windows and other Microsoft products.

In previous versions of Dynamics CRM, updates were made available separately from other Microsoft products and often required manual processes to download, distribute, and install. Now, administrators can manage updates for Dynamics CRM in the same way as they manage other Microsoft products. In smaller organizations, this is often managed by individual users who set their preferences on their computers. Organizations that use update management software such as Windows Server Update Services (WSUS) can now leverage this technology to coordinate the distribution and installation of updates for the various components of Dynamics CRM.

With the simplification that Windows Update brings to Dynamics CRM, administrators can now focus their maintenance efforts on ensuring that the core components of the application — the databases and the application files — are properly secured and backed up, and use a variety of monitoring tools that are available to alert them of potential trouble spots.

Tip
The Dynamics CRM Offline Client for Outlook stores data locally in a SQL Server Express database. In addition to backing up this database, you should consider securing this data with Windows's BitLocker Drive Encryption. Without encryption, the offline data is more vulnerable to misuse or tampering should the user's laptop be lost or stolen. Microsoft has released a whitepaper on using BitLocker to encrypt the Dynamics CRM offline data. See the Online Resources in Appendix B for a link to this document.

Backing up the server and server components

Before beginning the configuration and customization of Dynamics CRM, and before rolling it out to users, you should put in place a comprehensive maintenance and backup plan to ensure that the system is providing consistent performance, and you can recover from system outages and user or developer-induced errors. Your backup plan should include the following elements:

- Database maintenance
- Database backups
- Web and application server backups
- Backup plans for other related components

The right approach for these maintenance tasks varies, depending on your deployment scenario and the availability of resources like professional database administrators. The following sections provide guidance for using built-in tools in Windows and SQL Server.

Setting up a database maintenance plan
Properly maintaining the Dynamics CRM data tier includes basic tasks such as updating indexes, checking database integrity, and backing up the databases. Fortunately, SQL Server Management Studio contains the SQL Server Maintenance Plan wizard that steps you through the configuration of a comprehensive maintenance plan. These wizard-based maintenance plans are often an excellent starting point for more customized plans and are a great way to ensure your Dynamics CRM databases are backed up and well-maintained. See the "Learning Key Concepts about SQL Server Databases" sidebar to get familiar with some of the terminology

and concepts used in the SQL Server Maintenance Plan Wizard. A properly configured maintenance plan can help to maintain optimal performance and assist you with disaster recovery and business continuity.

Databases that should be covered by your maintenance plan are:

- The MSCRM_CONFIG database
- Each *Organization*_MSCRM database (where *Organization* represents the system organization name in your Dynamics CRM deployment. If you have a multitenant deployment, there will be one *Organization*_MSCRM database per organization.)
- The SQL Reporting Services databases. There are two, called ReportServer and ReportServerTempDB.
- The master and msdb system databases.

To create a maintenance plan for Dynamics CRM, follow these steps:

1. Open SQL Server Management Studio and connect to the instance where your Dynamics CRM databases are housed. You can install Management Studio with SQL Server or on a separate machine. Choose Start ⇨ All Programs ⇨ Microsoft SQL Server 2008 R2 ⇨ SQL Server Management Studio.

2. After connecting to the SQL Server, expand the SQL Server instance name node, and then expand the Management node.

3. Right-click on Maintenance Plans and then click on Maintenance Plan Wizard, shown in Figure 9.1. The wizard opens. If this is the first time you have launched this wizard, an introductory screen appears.

4. Click Next to begin configuring the plan.

5. On the Select Plan Properties screen, give the maintenance plan a name and description. Choose whether to schedule each task in the maintenance plan separately. If you select a single schedule, the steps of the maintenance plan are carried out in the order that you select. A good practice is to schedule the plan to run when the system is not being heavily used, such as overnight during the weekend, for example. Click Next.

6. On the Select Maintenance Tasks page, select each of the options you want to include in your maintenance plan and click Next. Figure 9.2 shows the following options:
   - Check Database Integrity
   - Shrink Database
   - Reorganize Index
   - Rebuild Index
   - Update Statistics

- Back Up Database (Full)
- Maintenance Cleanup Task

FIGURE 9.1

To create a new maintenance plan, use the SQL Server Maintenance Plan Wizard.

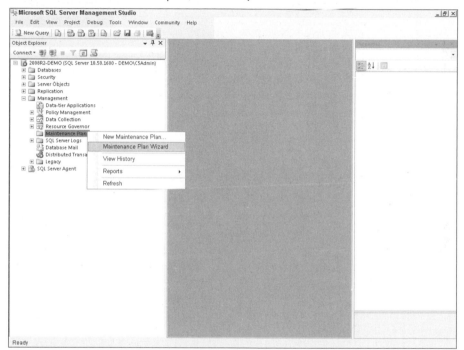

7. Accept the order that the wizard has set for the maintenance tasks and click Next.

8. For each maintenance task that you have selected, you must specify the databases that should be involved. Refer to the list of databases above to make sure that you have selected all of the appropriate databases for each task. Some tasks also have additional options. Consult SQL Server Books Online for more information on each of these optional settings. When you are finished selecting the options for each task, click Next.

9. Specify the location of the backups and the file extension to use (typically, bak). Consider using backup compression to reduce the size of the backed up databases, especially if you are performing full database backups or backing up transaction logs. Click Next.

10. Choose the options for the cleanup tasks and click Next. The wizard creates and schedules the tasks you have selected, and shows whether all of the tasks have been successfully created. When this process completes, click the Close button to exit the wizard.

The wizard allows you to select the most common maintenance tasks.

You can test the maintenance plan immediately, instead of waiting for it to execute, by expanding the Maintenance Plans node, right-clicking the maintenance plan you created, and selecting Execute. Keep in mind that the maintenance plan can impact performance, so you should only do this during off-peak usage hours.

The most important step of setting up your maintenance plan is to perform a test restore to ensure that your maintenance and backup plans function as expected in an emergency. Review the success and/or failure of the maintenance plan tasks in the log file viewer by right-clicking the plan name and selecting View History.

The maintenance plan that you created with the wizard can also be modified. Right-clicking the plan's name in SQL Server Management Studio and selecting Modify from the context menu opens a graphical maintenance plan design editor (see Figure 9.3). You can modify elements of the plan by double-clicking on them. You can also drag new maintenance tasks from the toolbox and position them in your plan.

FIGURE 9.3

Maintenance plans can be designed and edited in SQL Server Management Studio using a graphical, drag-and-drop interface.

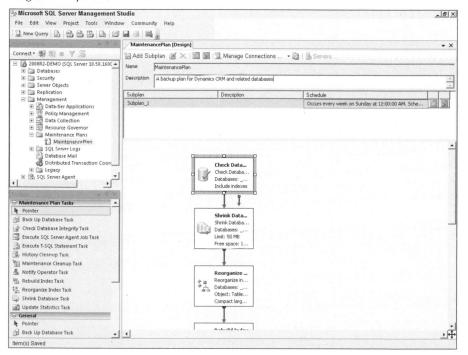

Backing up the Dynamics CRM application

In addition to backing up the Dynamics CRM databases, your disaster recovery and business continuity planning should incorporate a backup and recovery plan for the Dynamics CRM application server. This should include:

- The Dynamics CRM Web site
- The application files for the Dynamics CRM server and components (E-mail Router and Extensions for SSRS, for example)
- The registry

Though these files change infrequently, updates to the operating system or the application may cause them to change. For this reason, you should back them up regularly — especially before installing any updates — and test your ability to restore them.

Learning Key Concepts about SQL Server Databases

Many volumes have been written on the concepts and practices related to the proper care and feeding of SQL Server databases. One chapter, or even one book, cannot contain the best practices for every scenario. Indeed, even highly trained and experienced database administrators may prescribe different practices for different organizations with different needs. However, a few core concepts go a long way toward helping the novice administrator begin to grasp the inner workings of SQL Server and how they relate to the performance and stability of Dynamics CRM.

With a basic understanding of indexes, statistics, and database recovery models, you can make intelligent decisions about the configuration of your Dynamics CRM maintenance plan. (Note that in an enterprise environment, or when working with a SQL Server that houses the databases for numerous line-of-business applications, there may be important considerations that should be taken into account when designing a maintenance plan.)

- **Indexes.** Indexes are one of the ways that SQL Server quickly locates information stored in a database table. Without using an index, when a query is executed against a table, SQL Server must check the content of each row in the table to see if it matches the query. To speed this process, indexes can be used to help locate the rows more quickly.

  Indexes are similar to the idea of a phone book in which people are grouped by the first letter of their last names. If you are searching for someone whose name is Alex Smith, you can flip right to the group where the last names that start with S are located. Indexes in SQL Server serve a similar purpose. They are created using the columns that are used in common queries and provide the server with a quick way to jump to a specific group of records. In this way, instead of searching the whole table, SQL Server can search just the relevant subset of records.

  Indexes are import to a maintenance plan because they must be updated regularly to account for new records or records that have been removed or changed. Out-of-date indexes can result in slow performance when searching for a record.

- **Statistics.** SQL Server maintains statistics on each database to help it calculate the most efficient way to perform queries and other functions. Statistics include such things as the number of rows in a table, the amount of whitespace, size of the database tables, and so on. When statistics become outdated, SQL Server is not using the most recent data to improve its efficiency. Include an update of statistics in your maintenance plan to keep SQL Server performing optimally.

- **Recovery models.** A recovery model is a setting that allows you to specify how you want to attempt to restore a database should you need to. Three recovery models are available in SQL Server: full, bulk-logged, and simple. Each database's recovery model can be set on the options tab of its Properties dialog in SQL Server Management Studio. SQL Server maintains a running history of actions taken against each database. This history is called a transaction log. How transaction logs work depends on the recovery model you have selected.

  Simple: With a simple recovery model, you can recover your database only to the last time a backup was performed. Transaction log entries are not retained. This is the simplest method, as the name implies. Your maintenance plan only needs to account for the backup of the database.

Full: The full recovery model provides the opposite extreme from the simple model. With a full recovery model, you can restore a database back to a precise point in time. SQL Server will restore the last backup and then "replay" the transactions from the transaction log up to the point in time that you specify. If, for example, you have an error on Monday at 9:12 a.m., and your last backup was performed on Sunday at 12:00 a.m., the full recovery model will allow you to restore the database from your last backup and then replay the transactions up to 9:11:59 a.m. (if you select this time during the recovery). This method requires planning for the backup of both the database and the transaction logs.

Bulk-logged: The bulk-logged recovery model is typically used only during bulk operations such as a database load or bulk delete of records. This minimizes the amount of transactions stored in the transaction log, to improve performance during the bulk operation, and therefore prevents you from recovering to a specific point in time as with the full recovery model. It is recommended to only use this option temporarily during bulk operations.

This sidebar just scratches the surface on these topics, but hopefully provides some additional guidance on the concepts you will come across if you use the Maintenance Plan Wizard in SQL Server Management Studio. Consult SQL Server Books Online and other Microsoft documentation for more detailed information.

Tip

A variety of backup tools exist. The simplest of all methods is to manually copy the files to a mapped drive on another computer or a removable storage device. However, you should consider using a backup tool that allows you to schedule and automate this process. Microsoft has included the Windows Server Backup tool in all editions of Windows Server 2008 to provide an easy-to-use interface for scheduling and managing backups of applications, files, folders, and the system state. Full instructions for installing and using the Windows Server Backup tool are available on TechNet at `http://technet.microsoft.com/en-us/library/cc770266(WS.10).aspx`.

Cross-Reference

You should also make regular backups of the solutions XML and reports in your Dynamics CRM organizations. While this data is stored in the SQL Server database, it is much easier and less disruptive to import and publish customizations or a report than to perform a SQL Server restore. For instructions on exporting and importing customizations, see Chapter 16.

Backing up other server components

Numerous other server components may play an important role in your Dynamics CRM system. You should make a list of these components that are in use in your deployment and develop a disaster recovery plan that accounts for all of them. Your list might include the following components:

- Active Directory
- Exchange Server
- The IIS metabase
- Applications and databases that are integrated with Dynamics CRM
- SharePoint
- Custom development files (like code libraries or Visual Studio projects)

Monitoring Dynamics CRM

Maintaining the Dynamics CRM system and keeping it performing consistently requires an accurate understanding of the system's baseline performance when it is in a "healthy" state. Establishing this baseline will help to identify potential problem areas so you can take steps to mitigate them in advance. A baseline of various performance metrics is also helpful when troubleshooting errors or performance issues.

To help you establish this baseline, Microsoft has built hundreds of performance counters into Dynamics CRM that you can measure and analyze using Windows Reliability and Performance Monitor (PerfMon), an MMC snap-in included with Windows Server 2008. PerfMon can be used to show real-time performance and failure rates for server resources and software, perform on-demand or schedule monitoring of sets of counters, to view reports of completed monitoring jobs, and provide alerts when a counter deviates from a specified threshold.

Cross-Reference

Microsoft released a performance toolkit for Version 4.0 of Microsoft Dynamics CRM that assists with capturing and analyzing various performance metrics for Dynamics CRM. The toolkit includes tools to populate sample data into Dynamics CRM to simulate the data load of a production environment, and a performance benchmarking tool. To make full use of the toolkit, you must set up a test environment to simulate the environment you want to benchmark and use the testing infrastructure of Visual Studio to simulate workloads. This tool is available for download on CodePlex. See the link in Appendix B.

Monitoring a selected group of counters requires that you create a "data collector set" which can then be scheduled to run against the targeted Dynamics CRM servers. The data collector set contains the server and counters you wish to measure, as well as the format and target destination of the reports. Reports that are generated can be viewed in the PerfMon interface (see Figure 9.4).

Caution

Running performance monitoring utilities directly on the production server you want to monitor can have a significant impact on server performance. Windows Reliability and Performance Monitor can be run from a remote machine that connects to the various Dynamics CRM servers in order to minimize its impact on performance. Refer to the links to Microsoft TechNet in the Appendix B to learn more about using Windows Reliability and Performance Monitor.

FIGURE 9.4

Windows Reliability and Performance Monitor — known as PerfMon — provides a graphical interface to view and analyze the performance of various counters. Dynamics CRM exposes hundreds of counters to PerfMon.

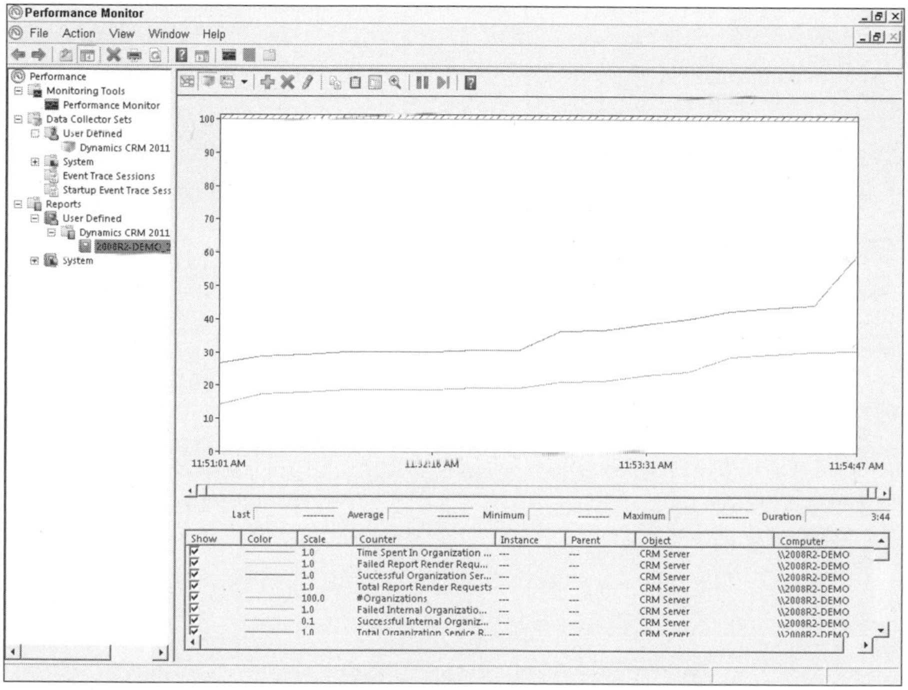

Creating a baseline report in Windows Reliability and Performance Monitor

To establish a baseline of your system performance, use the following steps to create a custom data collector set, run the data collector set, and view the resulting report.

1. Log onto a Windows Server 2008 computer that can connect to the Dynamics CRM servers. Go to the Start menu, and click on Run. In the Run dialog box, type **perfmon** and click OK.

2. In the PerfMon snap-in, expand the Data Collector Sets node, and then right-click on the User Defined node and select New ⇨ Data Collector Set.

3. Give the set a name, such as CRM Baseline. Select the Create manually (Advanced) option and click Next.

4. Under the Create data logs option, place a check mark next to the Performance Counter item to select it. Click Next.

5. The next screen allows you to select which counters you wish to monitor. Click the Add button to view the available counters. A selection dialog box opens (see Figure 9.5).

FIGURE 9.5

Microsoft provides hundreds of counters for Dynamics CRM. Add important counters to a data collector set in order to establish a baseline of your system's performance.

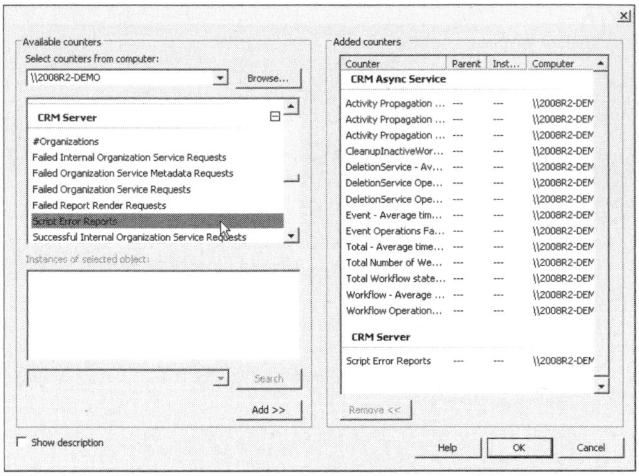

6. In the counter selection dialog, first specify which computer you wish to monitor. The dialog will display the available counters on that computer. In this example, we have selected several counters from the CRM Async Service group and the CRM Server group. The Async Service is responsible for workflows and bulk operations, and tends to be resource-intensive, which is why it bears close monitoring. See the list of counters below for help in determining which counters to include in your baseline. After adding the desired counters, click OK. Back in the data collector set dialog box, click Next.

7. Accept the default location for the performance data and click Next.

8. Keep the Run as user set to <Default>, select the option to save and close the set, and click Finish.

9. When you are ready to begin collecting counter data, right-click the data collector set you have just created and select Start. PerfMon will begin capturing data on the selected counters. Note that running PerfMon against a large number of counters can have a significant impact on server performance.

10. Allow the data to be collected for a meaningful amount of time, while the system is under normal usage. When you are done, right-click the data collector set and select Stop (Figure 9.6).

FIGURE 9.6

After you have collected performance counter data, stop the data collector set by right-clicking it and choosing Stop.

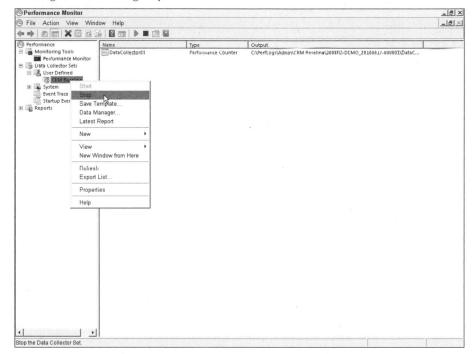

11. View the report in the Reports node of PerfMon. Expand Reports ⇨ User Defined ⇨ CRM Baseline. The data collector set reports will be listed. Choose one to open and analyze it. Running these reports on a schedule allows you to compare performance from one period against that of another.

Becoming familiar with the Dynamics CRM counters

Microsoft includes hundreds of counters with Dynamics CRM. The counters are grouped by function or server role. Depending on which server roles and components are installed, you may only have access to a subset of the performance counter groups listed below. See the Implementation Guide for complete descriptions of each counter in these groups.

- **CRM Async Service**. This group includes hundreds of counters for everything from system calculations to workflow operations, including database maintenance and bulk operations like duplicate detection jobs and the deletion service. The CRM Async Service performance counter group is one of the most comprehensive and useful for locating performance bottlenecks and reliability problems.

- **CRM Authentication.** Includes ten counters that measure access attempts and failures, as well as configuration of authentication methods.

- **CRM Client.** The CRM Client performance counter group contains a granular set of counters to track synchronization of the Outlook client add-in to the Dynamics CRM database, the number of requests and items tracked, error counts, and the cost of data syncs in terms of bandwidth and memory utilization. (The CRM OutlookSync group measures the performance of the Outlook client's attempts to go offline.)

- **CRM Discovery.** This counter group contains three counters to track the number of failed, successful, and total discovery service requests. This is helpful in identifying if your Dynamics CRM server is being targeted for DOS attacks or if there are misconfigured clients or custom applications making improper requests of the discovery server.

- **CRM Locator Service.** Two counters for the locator service, which may help to identify problems with the LocatorService cache or connections to the CONFIG database.

- **CRM OutlookSync.** Not to be confused with the CRM Client group of performance counters, the CRM OutlookSync counters track the sync requests for the address book provider (ABP) and offline synchronizations.

- **CRM Platform.** The CRM Platform group of performance counters measure cascading operations such as assign, delete, and share messages. This is helpful in diagnosing problems when users or workflows perform these actions against a record or set of records.

- **CRM Sandbox Client.** This group includes six counters that track the percentage of failures between the sandbox and Dynamics CRM, as well as the number and response times for execute and SDK messages.

- **CRM Sandbox Host.** Approximately 20 counters are included in this group to provide visibility into the sandbox host operations, such as the number of custom assemblies registered in the sandbox, the performance of worker processes, and memory usage.

- **CRM Server.** The CRM Server performance counter group includes 16 counters that track successful and failed service requests, script error reports, and report rendering requests.

- **MSCRMEmail.** Scrolling down through the list of performance counter groups will reveal the MSCRMEmail group, which contains approximately 24 counters that measure the number of messages the E-mail Router is processing inbound and outbound, how many unsuccessful attempts to process e-mail messages have occurred, and the rates of success or failure for access attempts to mailboxes.

Using System Center Operations Manager (SCOM) to Monitor Dynamics CRM

Microsoft's flagship monitoring and operations management tool, System Center Operations Manager 2007 R2 (SCOM) can be used to monitor Dynamics CRM servers and components. SCOM is used by large organizations and data centers to monitor servers, business-critical applications and Web sites, and to maintain service levels. To simplify enterprise monitoring of Microsoft Dynamics CRM 4.0, Microsoft released a Server Management Pack for SCOM. A management pack is a template that contains the best practices and knowledge for monitoring the target system.

As of this writing, Microsoft has not yet released a management pack for Microsoft Dynamics CRM 2011, though the Version 4.0 management pack can be modified for use with the 2011 version of the product by layering on an additional custom management pack for new features such as the Sandbox service. Although the Version 4.0 management pack is unsealed — meaning it can be customized — it is the recommended best practice to create a custom management pack to store these customizations rather than modifying the original template to simplify deployment.

Use the baseline performance created from the SCOM management pack or PerfMon reports as references to create performance threshold rules in SCOM. Performance thresholds allow SCOM to alert you to variances that can signal trouble with the system.

The Version 4.0 management pack for SCOM, available for download from the SCOM 2007 library at `http://go.microsoft.com/fwlink/?LinkId=82105`, includes templates for the most important Dynamics CRM performance counters and scripts to assist with discovering the Dynamics CRM server roles. The Operations Manager agent must be installed on each Dynamics CRM server you wish to manage, as the management pack does not support agentless monitoring. Check the accompanying guide for more information on how to use the management pack for Dynamics CRM.

Optimizing Dynamics CRM

Dynamics CRM can be a resource-intensive system. As a Web-based application with multiple client interfaces (Internet Explorer, Outlook, and mobile, as well as server-side APIs) a lot of network traffic can be generated by the system. Additionally, the rich, data-heavy and interactive user experience translates into a high-volume of round-trips between client and server. Optimizing the Dynamics CRM system to provide the best performance can be broken into four primary areas of focus for the administrator assigned this task:

- Database optimization
- Web server optimization
- Platform server optimization
- Client optimization

Cross-Reference

Appendix B contains a link to a whitepaper that Microsoft released for Version 4.0 of Dynamics CRM titled "Maintaining and Optimizing Microsoft Dynamics CRM 4.0." This whitepaper contains many valuable tips for improving the performance of the system that are just as applicable to Microsoft Dynamics CRM 2011.

Optimizing the database

Many deployments of Dynamics CRM perform well without any optimization beyond a standard maintenance plan that re-creates indexes, refreshes statistics, and backs up transaction logs and data files. The data tier of the application includes many built-in maintenance routines that clean up deleted records and process full-text indexing. However, a few simple optimization techniques and best practices can, in some situations, improve performance significantly.

Identifying performance problems in the database

As with any database, there are numerous potential points where the system can become inefficient over time, or where usage outstrips capacity. Common problem areas with the data layer that can impact Dynamics CRM performance include having too little memory or processor power allocated to SQL Server, disk I/O (input/output) that is too high for the hard disks' speed, poor physical data layout, and suboptimal indexes.

Using the SQL Server Activity Monitor

SQL Server 2008 provides many tools to identify and remedy potential performance bottlenecks. Activity Monitor (see Figure 9.7) is a feature that was added to SQL Server Management Studio with the 2008 version, and it is particularly useful in locating problem areas in the Dynamics CRM data layer (as well as any other line-of-business databases your SQL Server may house).

To use Activity Monitor to look for potential issues in the performance of your Dynamics CRM database, open SQL Server Management Studio and connect to the SQL Server instance where the Dynamics CRM databases are housed. Right-click on the SQL Server name in the Object Explorer and click on the Activity Monitor option.

The Activity Monitor displays an overview of the SQL Server's performance, lets you examine running processes, resource waits, data file I/O, and in the extremely useful Recent Expensive Queries pane shows resource-intensive queries. Each of the columns returned in the Recent Expensive Queries pane can be filtered, so you can drill into a specific database or sort by resource utilization levels. Hovering over a query displays a preview of the entire query (see Figure 9.7).

For more information on using the Activity Monitor, see SQL Server Books Online.

FIGURE 9.7

New in SQL Server 2008, the Activity Monitor is very easy to use to help identify performance bottlenecks. Especially useful is the Recent Expensive Queries pane.

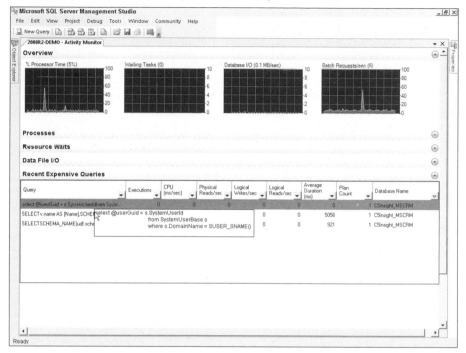

Using the SQL Server Database Engine Tuning Advisor

Another useful tool that assists with both identifying and correcting performance issues is the Database Engine Tuning Advisor (DETA). To make use of DETA, you must provide a SQL trace file for it to analyze. DETA will replay a workload from a trace file and analyze it for performance issues. Trace files can be created with SQL Server Profiler. Be sure to collect trace files when the SQL Server is being subject to typical usage so the tuning advisor has a realistic workload to analyze.

Both the Profiler and DETA are optional when installing SQL Server, so not all system administrators will have access to these tools.

The basic steps of examining the performance of your Dynamics CRM database with DETA are:

1. Collect a sample workload in a trace file. In SQL Server Management Studio, go to Tools ➪ SQL Server Profiler. Connect to the SQL Server where the Dynamics CRM databases are located. In the Trace Properties dialog, provide a name for the trace and select the Save to file option. Specify a location to save the output of the trace. Click the Run button to begin capturing the trace. After an interval, click the Stop icon to stop capturing trace information. The trace details are saved to the file you specified.

2. Process the trace file in the Database Engine Tuning Advisor. In SQL Server Management Studio's Tools menu, launch the Tuning Advisor. After connecting to the database, in the Workload section specify that you want to process a file and locate the trace file from the previous step. Select the database you wish to examine (typically the OrgName_MSCRM database), and click the Start Analysis button. Depending on the size of the trace file, DETA may take a long time to analyze the workload and generate recommendations. To implement the recommendations, consult the SQL Server documentation.

Caution

Before implementing any changes to the configuration of your SQL Server, be sure you understand the impact and dependencies that each change might have. Do not make any changes that are unsupported. Follow the instructions in the Implementation Guide as well as the documentation for Dynamics CRM and your version of SQL Server to ensure that your environment is properly configured. MSDN and SQL Server Books Online provide in-depth instructions for many optimization techniques. Back up your databases and verify that you can restore them to the previous condition if necessary, and, where possible, test each optimization technique in a non-production environment first.

Implementing basic SQL Server optimizations

You can make many possible optimizations in SQL Server to improve Dynamics CRM performance, and the particulars of your deployment scenario and the results of your analyses with the Activity Monitor and the Database Engine Tuning Advisor will help to identify which areas to focus on. Optimizing SQL Server's performance starts with the decisions about the hardware and operating system that SQL Server is installed on.

After establishing your baselines for system performance, try each of these performance optimization techniques, one at a time, to improve the performance of SQL Server. It is also recommended that you use PerfMon or Activity Monitor to test the impact of each configuration change before trying another.

The following optimization techniques have been shown to produce improvements for many deployment scenarios:

- **Keep data files and log files on separate physical disks.** Some of the most important optimization can take place before the first piece of data is written to your SQL Server. Configure the databases in SQL Server Management Studio to write the data files and log files to different physical disks (not just different partitions on the same disk). Doing this enables SQL Server to get the greatest level of I/O performance that the disks can provide for each of the files, especially during periods when there is a large amount of data being written to the database. To change the default location of the data and log files prior to installation, open SQL Server Management Studio, right-click on the server instance name, and select Properties. In the Server Properties dialog, on the Database Settings page (Figure 9.8) set the default locations of the data and log files.

FIGURE 9.8

Before installing Dynamics CRM, use the Server Properties dialog in SQL Server Management Studio to set the data and log files to use separate physical disks.

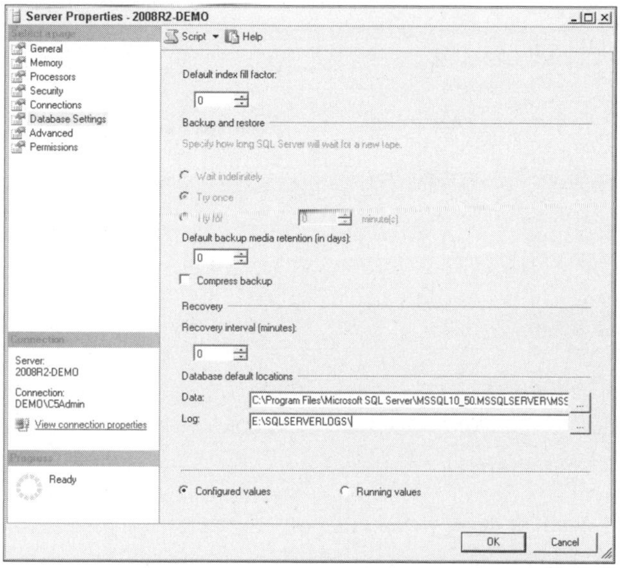

- **Create custom indexes to optimize query performance.** Dynamics CRM puts columns for custom fields in a secondary extension table, and the automatically built indexes may be improved with optimized indexes for queries (such as views) that make use of the custom fields. Analyze queries that have poor performance and create custom indexes where appropriate for frequently used views — especially those that use non-system columns.

- **Implement a regularly scheduled maintenance plan to rebuild indexes (see the section on the SQL Server Maintenance Plan wizard earlier in this chapter).** Indexes need to be refreshed regularly so they include new and changed data. Your database maintenance should update built-in and custom indexes.

- **Keep the system updated.** It should go without saying that one of the most important steps to keeping your database running at peak performance is to regularly download and install the latest updates for the operating system and applications, though this frequently is overlooked.

- **Allocate sufficient RAM to SQL Server.** The maximum amount of RAM available to your SQL Server depends on the edition of SQL Server and the operating system you are using in your deployment. By default, SQL Server 2008 dynamically adjusts the amount of memory it is using, up to the maximum available. This setting is controlled on the Memory page of the SQL Server properties. Dynamic allocation is preferred if no other applications are running on the same server (which, ideally, there shouldn't be).

- **Set the maximum degree of parallelism to 1.** SQL Server can run certain portions of T-SQL operations such as queries, updates, and inserts in parallel on multiprocessor computers. By default, SQL Server makes use of this functionality on machines with multiple processors. However, it has been shown that Dynamics CRM often performs better when operations are not carried out in parallel. Setting this option to 1 will restrict SQL Server to running these operations in series on a single processor. To change this option, open SQL Server Management Studio, right-click the server name, and click on Properties. In the Server Properties window, click on the Advanced page. Under the parallelism options, change the Max Degree of Parallelism to 1 (see Figure 9.9).

FIGURE 9.9

Set the Max Degree of Parallelism to 1 to see if this change improves your system's performance.

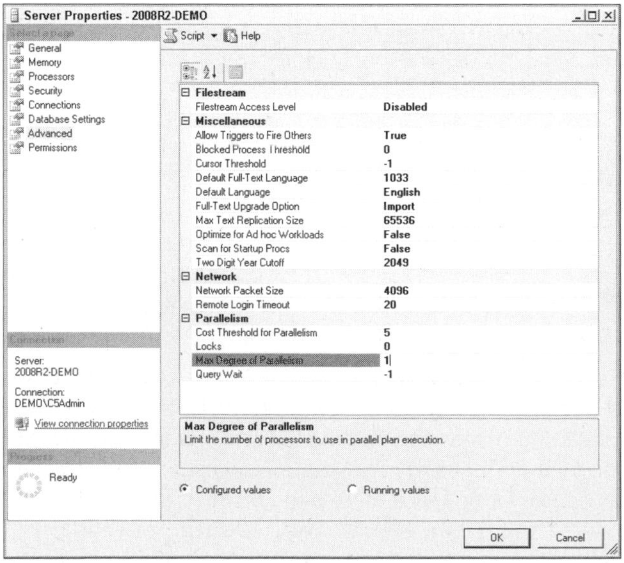

- **Adjust the size of the tempdb system database.** The tempdb database is used by SQL Server during normal server operations, and it grows incrementally as the server is used. Each time the server or the SQL Server service is restarted, the tempdb is reset to its initial size, which by default is 8MB. There is a slight increase in overhead on the SQL Server each time the size of the tempdb is automatically increased. To minimize this overhead, set the tempdb's initial size to a value sufficient for normal operations on your SQL Server. You can gauge this by reviewing the database's size after the server has been running under normal conditions for a time. To change this setting in SQL Server Management Studio, right-click the tempdb (located under System Databases) and open the database's Properties window. The General page displays the current size of the database. On the Files page, locate the initial size column for the tempdev database file, and set it to a value that is more than 10 percent larger than the current actual size of the database. (For example, if the current size of the tempdb database is 20MB, set the initial size to 25MB.) Restart the SQL Server service.

- **Increase the OrgName_MSCRM database data file size.** Similar to the preceding recommendation for the tempdb, the OrgName_MSCRM database data file size will be increased incrementally as the amount of data grows. By setting the data file size to a reasonable amount in advance, SQL Server does not have to perform this increase. Having available space in the database beforehand is especially helpful during periods when a large amount of new data is expected, such as during bulk data loads and migrations. To change the size of the .mdf file, open the Properties windows for the OrgName_MSCRM database, and on the Files page, set the initial size to a value that matches your anticipated needs. Restart the SQL Server service. (Remember to perform these types of operations during off-peak hours and only after performing complete backups.)

- **Consider using the data compression features of SQL Server 2008.** SQL Server 2008 introduced new data compression features that can have a significant impact not only on the size of the data stored in a database, but also on the performance of queries. Though data compression can increase CPU utilization, the gains in I/O performance may offset this and provide a net boost to database performance. SQL Server 2008 has two types of data compression: page and row. Data compression can be configured using the Data Compression Wizard, which can be launched by selecting a table, right-clicking, and choosing the Manage Compression option from the Storage menu, as shown in Figure 9.10. Read SQL Server Books Online and the documentation available in the help files for more information on using data compression and the Data Compression Wizard.

- **Configure search views in the Dynamics CRM application to use a small number of indexed fields.** In the Dynamics CRM application there are special views that can be used to look up records. These are the Lookup view and the Quick Find view. Customizers can designate which columns will be used in evaluating the search criteria that users enter when looking for matching records. By default, Dynamics CRM indexes system fields. If your search criteria include custom fields, the performance of these queries can be negatively impacted. Further, the more "find columns" that these views use, the slower the query. As a general rule of thumb, when possible use three or fewer system fields as the find columns in these views in order to provide the fastest performance. Alternately, you can mitigate the performance impact of using custom fields in these views by adding a custom non-clustered index that includes these fields. In general, the performance of views can be improved if the filter criteria use only fields from a single table (either the entity base table or the entity extension table), though with properly built indexes query performance may be acceptable even if the find columns span multiple tables.

FIGURE 9.10

In SQL Server 2008, data compression is managed using the Data Compression Wizard.

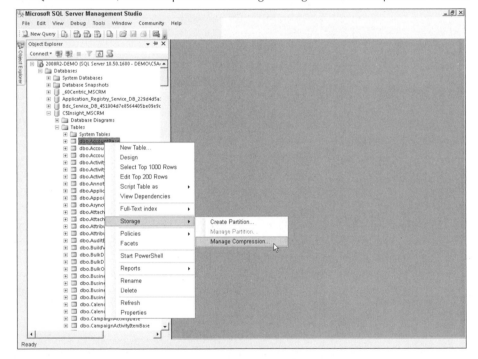

Optimizing the Web server

In many deployments, the Dynamics CRM Web server has the front end server roles, including the Web application server, the organization and discovery Web services, and the help server. Front end servers also frequently serve as the deployment administration servers, hosting the Deployment Manager MMC snap-in and the deployment Web service. These functions can be subject to the same performance challenges as any Web-based application.

Identifying potential problem areas with the Web server

Common challenges with the Dynamics CRM Web server include latency, bandwidth constraints, and caching issues. Performance issues with the web application server can be difficult to diagnose. However, tools like the Windows Reliability and Performance Monitor (PerfMon) can be helpful in surfacing the root causes of performance issues through the monitoring of the performance counters for IIS.

Making recommended changes to the Web server

Following are several recommended optimization methods that can be implemented to improve the performance of the Dynamics CRM Web server:

- **Consider a federated architecture.** If your users are scattered across the country or around the globe, they may experience significant latency when accessing a centralized Dynamics CRM application. Latency is the amount of time a Web request requires to travel between the client and the server and back again. Even in high-bandwidth networks, latency can be an issue. Generally speaking, the farther away a user is from the Web server, the longer it takes for data to make the round-trip. Because the Dynamics CRM application requires many round-trips, latency can cause significant problems for distant users. One way of heading this off is to consider deploying a federated Web architecture. A federated architecture places multiple Web application servers in locations where they will be in greater proximity to the end users, potentially reducing latency. One drawback of this method is that it is more complex. Federated architectures will often distribute not only Web servers but also database servers that must then be replicated to one another to keep data synchronized. Typically this is only an option for very large enterprises that already support multiple data centers for a large user base. (This is another reason why Dynamics CRM Online is increasingly becoming a desirable option for larger organizations, since the hosting provider, Microsoft, manages a highly distributed and high-performing architecture.)

- **Utilize compression techniques.** IIS 7.0 provides compression methods that reduce latency and boost performance. By default, IIS 7.0 uses compression of both dynamic and static content. To verify this, open IIS and navigate to the Microsoft Dynamics CRM Web site. In the Features view in IIS, double-click the Compression icon and verify that check marks are in place for both options. Compression applications and appliances are available from third-party vendors, such as WAN accelerators, that can provide even greater compression and speed.

- **Implement output caching.** Another optimization technique available in IIS 7.0 is output caching, which retains frequently used objects in memory so they can be quickly delivered in response to client requests. Output caching is configured based on file extension. Common file types that can be cached include image and script files such as those with the following extensions: .gif, .jpg, .tif, .png, .js, and .css. To configure output caching for each of these file types, click the Output Caching icon in the IIS snap-in. Click the Add link in the Actions panel and add user-mode caching rules for each extension (see Figure 9.11).

Configuring IIS 7.0's output caching feature to cache .gif image files for the Dynamics CRM Web site

- **Optimize client-side scripts.** If your deployment customizations make heavy use of extensive client-side JavaScript, users can experience slow page load times, as well as delays in client-side functionality while scripts are being interpreted by the browser. Significant performance improvements can be gained by optimizing the scripts by removing white space, refactoring the scripts to minimize redundancy, and compressing the script files. You can find a variety of free tools and resources on the Web to help reduce the size and improve the speed of your client-side scripts.

Optimizing the platform server

The platform server — also referred to as the back end server — houses Dynamics CRM's asynchronous service and the sandbox processing service. Both of these services can be resource-intensive, consuming memory and processing power while they carry out their functions.

Identifying potential problems with the platform server

Problem areas that can arise on the platform server include high utilization of RAM and CPU cycles, which can be caused by heavy usage, as well as inefficient custom server-side code and highly nested workflow processes. Administrators must analyze custom-code such as plug-ins and workflow extensions; workflow processes; hardware configuration; and operating system configuration to identify the source of performance issues.

Making recommended improvements to the platform server

The remedies for performance issues on the platform server can be relatively straightforward (although sometimes costly as well), depending on the source of the problem. Additional RAM is relatively inexpensive and easy to install if your server can accommodate it. But increasing processor power typical means replacing the server altogether.

Identifying opportunities for improving custom server-side code can also be difficult, requiring a high level of expertise and a variety of analysis methods.

Tip

If your platform server has a modest amount of RAM, you might consider an unsupported technique to throttle the number of active workflow rules that the server will process at a given time, queuing up other workflows until it has resources available to process them. The minimum and maximum thresholds for active workflow and system jobs are controlled by settings in the Deployment Properties table in the MSCRM_CONFIG database. The IntColumn values in the AsyncItemsInMemoryLow and AsyncItemsInMemoryHigh settings are set to 1000 and 2000, respectively, by default. You can adjust these lower to reduce the number of operations the asynchronous service will process at a given time. Keep in mind that modifying the Dynamics CRM databases is strictly unsupported, and you should only attempt this change in a test environment where you have proven backups.

Optimizing the client

Two primary client applications are used for accessing the Dynamics CRM application: Internet Explorer and Microsoft Office Outlook. Other clients can include mobile device browsers or third-party mobile applications, as well as custom applications. This section focuses on a handful of optimization techniques for Internet Explorer and the Outlook client.

Identifying potential problem areas with the client

There are a number of potential problem areas that can have a negative impact on client performance. These can be as fundamental as underpowered or misconfigured client machines, and as esoteric as mysteriously incompatible applications. Identifying the source of performance bottlenecks on client machines can involve a wide variety of tools and techniques. Start with simple observation, and move on to event logs, diagnostic tools, and deductive reasoning to narrow down the source.

Implementing recommended changes to improve client performance

Regardless of the large number of potential issues, you can take several basic steps to improve the performance of both the Internet Explorer and Outlook clients.

Optimizing settings in Internet Explorer

Test the following Internet Explorer (IE) settings in your environment to see if they provide an appreciable improvement in performance:

- **Remove third-party toolbars.** Dynamics CRM makes heavy use of the core features and functionality of IE, transforming the browser into a business application. This is sometimes at odds with users who see their Web browser as the gateway to social media, file sharing, shopping, and other uses. Unfortunately, if not controlled by network policies, third-party add-ons and toolbars often find their way into the Internet Explorer browser. These add-ons often collect information from the stream of data being downloaded through the browser or cause other unexpected behavior in IE that can negatively impact the performance of the Dynamics CRM Web application. If a comprehensive group policy or Web monitoring tool is not a suitable solution, encourage users to keep Internet Explorer in its default condition and consider allowing them to use another browser for personal use.

- **Optimize IE caching.** Configure IE to check for newer versions of Web pages automatically only when the cache has reached its maximum size. In Version 8 of IE, go to Safety ➪ Delete Browsing History and delete temporary internet files and cookies. Next, in the Tools menu, click on the Internet Options item. In the Internet Options dialog, on the General tab, click the Settings button in the Browsing History section. In the Temporary Internet Files and History Settings dialog, select the Automatically option for when IE should check for new versions of Web pages and set the disk space to use to 250MB.

Optimizing settings in the Outlook client

The Outlook client, with its two versions (online and offline clients) and greater complexity, presents additional opportunities to improve performance:

- **Use adequate hardware.** Make sure to deploy hardware that is up to the job, particularly for users who will employ the offline client, with its local database and built-in local Web server. RAM is especially important. Even though the official guidance may prescribe less, use at least 2GB of RAM in client machines.

- **Use the Diagnostics Wizard.** The Outlook client for Dynamics CRM includes a Diagnostics Wizard that not only identifies potential performance issues, but, in many cases, can automatically fix them.

- **Tune synchronization settings based on user needs.** Based on the individual user's needs, consider the following tuning suggestions for the Outlook client: 1) Deactivate unused local data groups; 2) In the add-in's options dialog, select only relevant record types for synchronization; 3) Limit the e-mail matching to only those records owned by the user; 4) For offline users, set offline synchronization to run in the background every 15 minutes to minimize the time it takes them to go offline, and select the synchronization option that prevents the add-in from creating duplicate records.

Keep in mind that even after optimizing Internet Explorer and the Outlook client, performance can still be significantly impacted by the condition of the computer and its configuration, such as whether it is using a wired or wireless connection, running on a low battery, or using an encrypted hard drive. Impediments to a machine's performance can mean the difference between sub-second and multi-second page load times.

Troubleshooting Errors and Performance Problems

As with any software, Dynamics CRM will occasionally experience errors or unexpected behavior. Successfully addressing these issues begins with good troubleshooting practices to quickly identify the source of the problem and implement the correct fix.

Follow these troubleshooting tips when attempting to resolve system errors with Dynamics CRM:

1. Identify the part of the application that is having a problem. Between error messages and user descriptions of problems, you should be able to isolate whether the issue is with the Dynamics CRM Web or platform server, the Outlook client, the report server, or another component. When you're not able to look over a user's shoulder, screenshots can be very helpful when attempting to reproduce the problem.

2. Use the process of elimination to identify the source of the issue. Start with the simplest possible causes and work your way through to the more complex. Ask questions that will eliminate certain possibilities. Is the issue being experienced by one user or all users? If one user, what is peculiar about that user? Do they have a different machine configuration or security role? If all users are experiencing a problem, what changed in your environment? Can you reproduce the problem when logged onto the local Dynamics CRM server?

3. Error messages in Dynamics CRM may often be generic. Use the tools and methods described later in this section to identify the underlying error message from the appropriate source.

4. Don't overlook common problems that may be technically unrelated. Dynamics CRM uses many different technologies and can reveal weaknesses in your network. Failing network cards or faulty cables can look like performance problems.

5. Know when to get outside help. Many administrators enjoy the investigative work involved in troubleshooting, but it's helpful to have a threshold established beforehand so you know when you've spent more time trying to fix a problem than it's worth, and when an outside resource like a partner or Microsoft support may be able to fix the problem and return your users to productivity faster.

Using built-in, free, and included resources

Numerous free or included tools and resources can assist you with maintaining Dynamics CRM and troubleshooting errors.

Cross-Reference

This section references many resources available on the Internet. See Appendix B for links to the listed resources.

- **System documentation.** The Implementation Guide, SDK, release notes, and Users Guide all contain helpful guidance and address common known issues.

- **Built-in resources.** Every page of the Dynamics CRM application has a link to a contextual help file with detailed instructions for using the system and administrative instructions. The main navigation also includes a link to the Resource Center, which is an extensive online Web site with articles, videos, and links to updates. The Resource Center is also accessible directly on the Web.

- **Microsoft support resources.** Microsoft has many support channels. Administrators often leverage a combination of them, including KB articles on the Microsoft support Web site and a help desk that can be reached via phone or Web to open support incidents. If your company has access to it, CustomerSource, Microsoft's extranet site for Dynamics customers, also contains a variety of support tools.

- **Server diagnostic tools.** A free tool Microsoft released for Version 4.0, called the CRMDiagTool, enables tracing and dev errors and works with the Dynamics CRM server, E-mail Router, and SQL Server Reporting Services. Enabling dev errors causes in-depth information to be displayed in the interface when an error is encountered, rather than simply the friendly but less informative error messages a user would typically encounter. Though designed for a previous version, the CRMDiagTool also works with Microsoft Dynamics CRM 2011. SQL Server's Profiler and other performance tools are also extremely helpful in locating the source of application bottlenecks.

- **Client diagnostic tools.** In addition to the built-in Diagnostics tool (Figure 9.12) that is installed with the Outlook client add-in (available on the client machine from Start ⇨ Programs ⇨ Microsoft Dynamics CRM 2011), there are other tools that can be helpful in diagnosing errors on the client or Web application. Dynamics CRM administrators often leverage tools like the Internet Explorer Developer Toolbar (press F12 in IE) or the Fiddler Web Debugger (see the link in Appendix B). These tools can be helpful in troubleshooting script and Web page errors.

Getting good information from Dynamics CRM errors

When working through Dynamics CRM errors, there are a number of places to find detailed error descriptions, depending on the source of the error and the circumstances under which it occurred. Some error logs are generated automatically, and others require configuration steps and should only be enabled temporarily.

FIGURE 9.12

The Dynamics CRM for Outlook client includes a built-in diagnostic tool that can identify problems that slow performance or decrease functionality

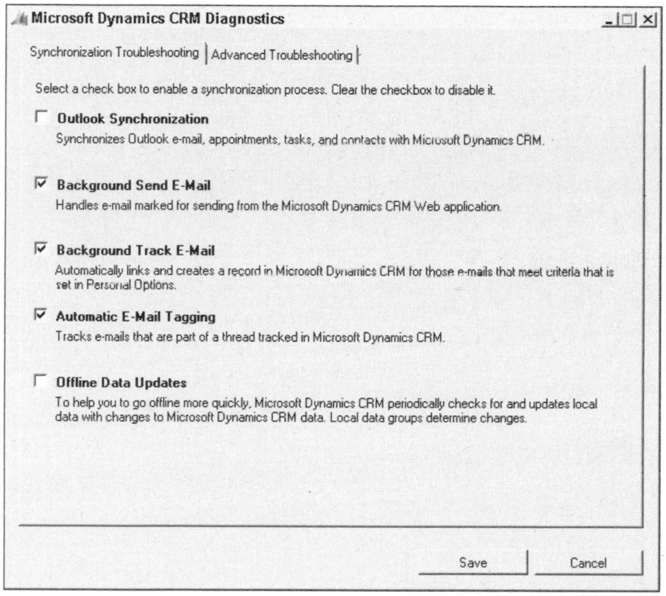

Examining event logs

Windows application event logs can provide helpful information, warnings, and detailed error messages for Dynamics CRM client and server components. To view the application event logs, from the Start menu, right-click on Computer and then click on Manage. In the Server Manager, expand the Diagnostics node to reveal the Event Viewer. The Application log is located under Windows Logs. Application event logs can be filtered by source, time of the error, and a number of other parameters (Figure 9.13).

The following source categories can be used to filter the application event log to locate information specific to Dynamics CRM. Note that some sources may be available only on client computers or on servers with the relevant server roles:

- MSCRMAddin
- MSCRMAddressBook
- MSCRMAsyncService
- MSCRMAsyncService$client

- MSCRMAsyncService$maintenance
- MSCRMCallout
- MSCRMDeletionService
- MSCRMDeployment
- MSCRMEmail
- MSCRMKeyArchiveManager
- MSCRMKeyGenerator
- MSCRMLocatorService
- MSCRMOfflineSync
- MSCRMPerfCounters
- MSCRMPlatform
- MSCRMReporting
- MSCRMReportingDataConnector
- MSCRMSandboxClient
- MSCRMSandboxService
- MSCRMSandboxWorker
- MSCRMSyncQueue
- MSCRMTracing
- MSCRMUnzipService
- MSCRMWebService

On the Web Site

The book's companion Web site contains a link to download an XML configuration file that can be imported into the custom views area of the Event Viewer on the Dynamics CRM server. It contains the definitions to create a custom view that pre-filters the application event log by components of the Dynamics CRM server and E-mail Router, and displays only critical, error, and warning messages. Remove filters that are unused in your deployment.

Turning on developer errors

Sometimes users report generic Dynamics CRM error messages that they receive in Internet Explorer or the Outlook client. Although Microsoft has attempted to provide friendly, informative error messages, in many cases these error messages will direct the user to contact the System Administrator for assistance. When these types of errors crop up, you can temporarily enable more detailed developer errors, or DevErrors, on the Dynamics CRM Web server.

To enable DevErrors, log onto the Dynamics CRM Web server and navigate to the folder containing the Web site root for the Dynamics CRM Web site. This is typically either the <drive>:\inetpub\wwwroot folder, or the <drive>:\Program Files\Microsoft Dynamics CRM\ CRMWeb folder. Then follow these instructions:

FIGURE 9.13

The application event log on Windows computers can be filtered to locate specific error messages.

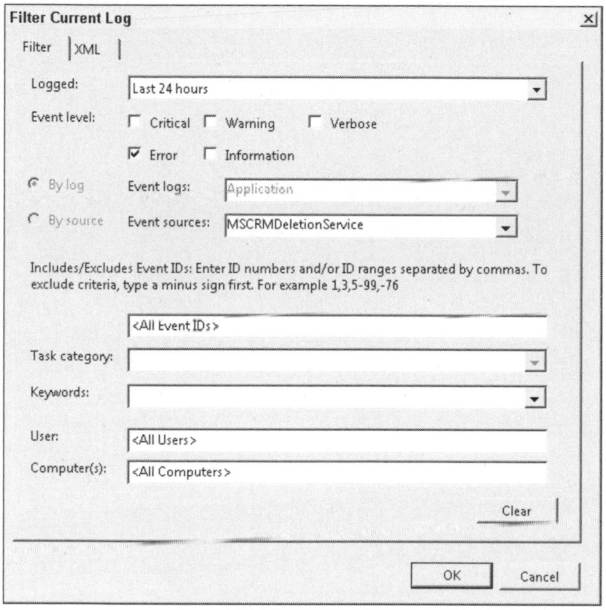

1. Locate the web.config file in the root of the Dynamics CRM Web site. Make a copy of this file so you can restore it if necessary. Then open the web.config file in a text editor like Notepad or Visual Studio.

2. Find the DevErrors key and change the value from Off to On:

```
<add key="DevErrors" value="On" />
```

3. Save the web.config file and repeat these steps on each Dynamics CRM Web server in your deployment.

4. Reproduce the behavior that caused the original error message.

Error messages with DevErrors turned on display four different views of the error details: one with detailed error information (Figure 9.14), a standard ASP.NET error page with stack details (Figure 9.15), a debug page that provides details about the server environment and client (Figure 9.16), and a page that displays what the user would have seen (what the error would look like with DevErrors turned off), as shown in Figure 9.17. The DevErrors page also provides a button to copy all of the error details to the clipboard.

FIGURE 9.14

With DevErrors enabled in the Dynamics CRM Web site, the administrator can view detailed error information.

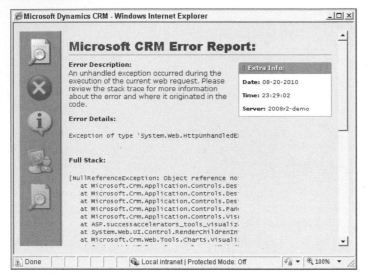

FIGURE 9.15

DevErrors also provide standard ASP.NET error text and stack trace details.

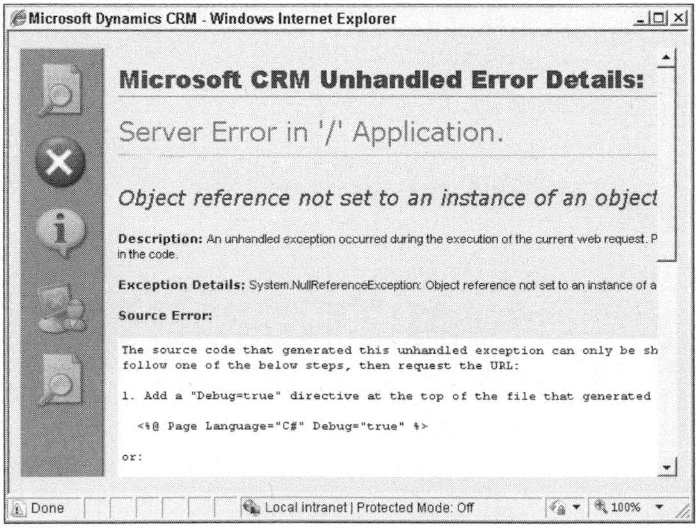

FIGURE 9.16

The DevErrors screen also includes a page with environmental information that can be helpful in debugging an error, such as the server OS version and browser version.

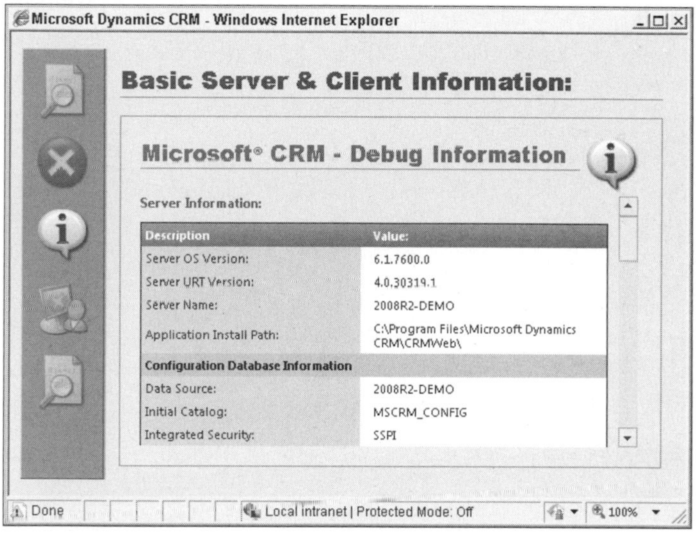

FIGURE 9.17

Be sure to view the original error message, just as the user would have seen when DevErrors were disabled, in order to verify that you are troubleshooting the same error that the user reported.

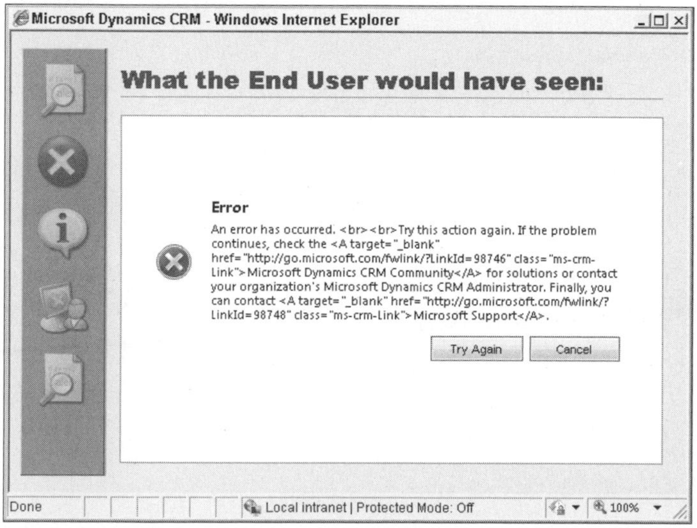

Tip

When investigating an error with the Dynamics CRM Web application, Web server logs from IIS can also be helpful in analyzing what was happening on the Dynamics CRM Web site when the error occurred. If logging has been enabled for the Dynamics CRM Web site in IIS, the logs are stored in the <systemdrive>:\inetpub\ logs\LogFiles folder. Logs are stored in folders with the naming format of W3SVCx, where x is the Web site ID. To determine the ID of the Dynamics CRM Web site, open IIS and click on the Sites node. The sites will be listed along with the ID, status, and other information.

Enabling tracing

Tracing is a way to capture the stream of messages passing between the components of a system like Dynamics CRM. This stream of messages contains records of user actions and system operations in a (mostly) human-readable, chronological format.

When tracing is enabled for Dynamics CRM, a text log file is created that contains all of these messages, including records of thrown errors that can be useful when troubleshooting problems. Tracing is helpful when errors are not caused by user interaction with Dynamics CRM and turning on DevErrors doesn't provide useful information.

Tracing can be enabled for the Dynamics CRM server or the Dynamics CRM client for Outlook.

Cross-Reference

A free tool that makes it easier to read and understand Dynamics CRM trace files is available from an independent software vendor called Stunnware.

Caution

Because tracing captures so much information from the various components of Dynamics CRM, it is extremely resource-intensive and will cause a significant slowdown in performance. In some situations, trace logs can also include sensitive data, so be sure to handle them appropriately. Only enable tracing when troubleshooting critical errors or during development debugging, and immediately disable it when you are done.

Enabling tracing for Dynamics CRM

To enable tracing, you must modify the registry on the Dynamics CRM computer (see Figure 9.18). As with any registry modification, make sure to back up the registry first to ensure that you can restore it if necessary.

Follow these steps to turn tracing on:

1. On the Dynamics CRM computer, open the registry editor by clicking on Start ⇨ Run. In the Open: box, type **regedit** and click OK. If prompted by UAC to allow the program to launch, click Yes.

2. Locate the appropriate node in the registry as indicated below and create the following registry keys if they do not already exist:

- **TraceEnabled**. Create the TraceEnabled key as a DWORD with a decimal value of 1. A value of 1 enables tracing. A value of 0 disables it.

- **TraceRefresh.** Create the TraceRefresh key as a DWORD with a decimal value between 1 and 99. The act of changing the value of this registry key causes the trace settings to be recognized by the platform. The actual value is irrelevant.

3. Close the registry editor.

Tracing can be enabled by adding certain registry keys on the Dynamics CRM computer. Optional keys can modify the behavior of tracing.

You can also add optional registry keys to modify how the trace capture behaves:

- **TraceCallStack**. A decimal value of 1 in this DWORD key causes tracing to include the call stack in the trace file. By default the call stack is not captured.

- **TraceFileSizeLimit**. A DWORD key with a decimal value between 1 and 100, used to indicate the maximum size of the trace logs in megabytes. The default maximum size is 5MB.

- **TraceCategories**. TraceCategories are string or multi-string registry keys, with values in a specific format that can be used to limit the data captured in a trace. The key values are in the format *Category.Feature:Level*. A multi-string key can contain multiple TraceCategories values separated by semicolons. Some examples of possible values:

  - *Application.*:Error*. This captures only error messages in the trace log for all application features.

  - *Application.Outlook:Error*. This value captures errors only for the Outlook client application.

  - *Platform.Sql:Verbose*. Adding this value (see Figure 9.18) to the TraceCategories key will capture verbose logs of interactions with SQL Server.

Cross-Reference

More possible values for the TraceCategories key are available in the Version 4.0 knowledge base article #907490 on Microsoft's support Web site. You can also use the CRMDiagTool to capture trace information. See the links in Appendix B.

Location of the Dynamics CRM server tracing registry keys and log files

The Dynamics CRM server tracing registry entries are located in the following registry subkey:

    HKEY_LOCAL_MACHINE\SOFTWARE\MICROSOFT\MSCRM

The trace logs will be located in the <drive>:\Program Files\Microsoft Dynamics CRM\ Trace folder. Enabling trace logs for the Dynamics CRM server will create trace logs for the Dynamics CRM Web site (in the format *servername-w3wp-CRMWeb-yyyymmdd-1.log*), SQL Server Reporting Services, the sandbox processing service, and the unzip service.

Note

The unzip service processes the decompressing of zipped files that are imported using the Import Data Wizard or the import API.

Location of the Dynamics CRM Outlook client tracing registry keys and log files

The Dynamics CRM server tracing registry entries are located on the computer with the Outlook client installed, in the following registry subkey:

    HKEY_CURRENT_USER\SOFTWARE\MICROSOFT\MSCRMClient

The trace logs will be located in this folder: <drive>:\Users\InstallingUser\ AppData\Local\Microsoft\MSCRM\Traces.

Enabling logging for the Microsoft Dynamics E-mail Router

The Microsoft Dynamics CRM E-mail Router is an optional component that can be installed on any computer that has access to both the Dynamics CRM server and the e-mail server. As a stand-alone application, it has its own logging capabilities. It records informational, warning, and error messages in the Windows application event log, with the logged events having the source of MSCRMEmail. You can also enable more in-depth logging for the E-mail Router as follows:

1. Locate the E-mail Router configuration file Microsoft.Crm.Tools.EmailAgent.xml located in the `<drive>:\Program Files\Microsoft CRM Email\Service directory` and open it in a text or XML editor.

2. In the `<LogLevel>` element, change the value from 1 (the default, which enables logging standard events to the Windows application event log) to 3.

3. Add a `<LogFile>` element below the `<LogLevel>` element to specify the location of the output log file. Specify a location of your choosing. In this example we have created a folder on the C: drive called TempEmailRouter. The two elements should then look like this:

```
<LogLevel>3</LogLevel>
<LogFile>C:\TempEmailRouter\EmailRouterTrace.txt</LogFile>
```

Be sure to change the XML file back afterwards by switching the LogLevel value back to 1, and removing the LogFile element.

Enabling logging and finding logs for other components

There are other components of Dynamics CRM that produce log files that can be helpful when troubleshooting errors.

Deployment Manager logs capture messages about the creation or import of new organizations, addition of Deployment Administrators, changes to Claims-Based Authentication or Internet-Facing Deployment configuration, and other deployment service operations.

The Deployment Manager logs are located in the following directory: `<drive>:\Users\<InstallUsername>\AppData\Roaming\Microsoft\MSCRM\Logs`

Tracing can also be enabled for SQL Server Reporting Services. While this is a separate component from Dynamics CRM, it can be the source of issues with report performance or malfunction. To enable tracing, set the RSTrace element to a value of 1 (it is set to 1, and tracing is enabled by default) in the configuration file ReportingServicesService.exe.config located in the following directory: `<drive>:\Program Files\Microsoft SQL Server\MSRS10_50.MSSQLSERVER\Reporting Services\ReportServer\bin`.

SQL Server 2008 R2 Reporting Services consolidates trace logs into a single file in format of ReportServerService_mm_dd_hh_mm_ss.log, which can be found in the `<drive>:\Program Files\Microsoft SQL Server\MSRS10_50.MSSQLSERVER\Reporting Services\LogFiles` folder.

Repairing and Uninstalling Dynamics CRM

In some instances, it may be necessary to repair or uninstall the server or client components of Dynamics CRM. To repair or remove a component, on the computer where it is installed, open the Control Panel and locate the application in the Programs dialog. Follow these tips when repairing or uninstalling these applications.

- **Repairing the server and server components.** Log in as the user who installed Dynamics CRM and back up the MSCRM_CONFIG and OrgName_MSCRM databases, as well as the report and system databases. It is also helpful to make sure you have copies of the exported customization solution XML and custom reports from your deployed organizations.

- **Repairing the Outlook client.** Before using the Programs panel in the Control Panel to repair the Outlook client, try using the built-in Diagnostics tool to fix any problems you are experiencing with the client. If you must run a repair routine and you are using the offline client, attempt to go online first and synchronize the client to the Dynamics CRM server, if possible.

- **Uninstalling the server and server components.** Using the Control Panel Programs window to launch and run the uninstall routine for the Dynamics CRM server will not remove the Dynamics CRM databases or detach them from the SQL Server. We recommend backing up the databases first. To totally remove the server components and databases requires manual processes to delete the database and application files. To remove the databases, in SQL Server Management Studio delete the databases and select the option to close existing connections.

- **Uninstalling the Outlook client.** Similar to the server, running the uninstall routine on the Outlook client add-in may not completely remove all components of the application. You may need to manually remove application files from the Program Files directory, as well as local data files if using the offline client.

Additional information on repairing and removing the Dynamics CRM components can be found in the Implementation Guide.

Summary

Reliable and consistent performance starts with a good implementation plan and the proper system architecture, but there are a number of best practices that you can follow to maintain and optimize Dynamics CRM:

- Implement and test a comprehensive backup strategy to ensure that you can recover your system from unexpected outages. Your backup strategy should include a maintenance plan for your SQL Server databases and should also include backing up the application files and Web site root, as well as any other related components such as Active Directory and Exchange Server.

- Use the counters in the Windows Reliability and Performance Monitor (PerfMon) or an application like System Center Operations Manager (SCOM) to monitor system performance.

- Optimize performance by tuning SQL Server, the Web server, and the platform servers to make the best use of system resources like RAM and processor power.

- Use diagnostic tools like DevErrors and tracing to reveal deeper error information regarding platform operations. DevErrors and tracing can have an impact on performance and should only be used while troubleshooting. There are also numerous other log files available for each of the components of the Dynamics CRM system, each of which can be helpful to administrators.

Part IV

Using Microsoft Dynamics CRM

So assuming you have mastered the skills required to implement and administer Microsoft Dynamics CRM 2011, it's probably important that you be able to support the end users of the system. There's no better way to tackle that job than by familiarizing yourself with Dynamics CRM's out-of-the-box functionality.

Now in its fifth release, Dynamics CRM offers a very mature toolset to handle marketing, sales, and customer service functions.

Part IV focuses on the features and functionality that are included with Dynamics CRM, with a thorough treatment of topics like finding your way around the interface, to using the built-in customer relationship management processes.

Chapters 10 through 14 take you on a guided tour of the built-in functionality of Dynamics CRM, the types of things you'd want to know if you were a brand new user to the system and turned loose to start managing your customers with it.

Getting to Know the CRM Application

The Dynamics CRM application provides a powerful set of tools and concepts that work across the entire application. Once you understand the core concepts, you will be ready to begin using the application for automating sales, marketing, customer service, call center, and XRM operations. Taking the time to understand the basics laid out within this chapter will shorten your learning curve with all of the other areas of Dynamics CRM.

In this chapter you, learn how to navigate the Dynamics CRM using interface including using the Ribbon menu and navigation pane and how to navigate lists and forms. You will also learn about record ownership, the role ownership plays in managing security, and how to share records with other users. Activities play a central role in Dynamics CRM; you learn how to work with activities to manage the details of your day. You learn how to use queues to manage individual workloads and for collaborating to share work across a team. Duplicate records are always an issue with CRM systems — in this chapter you will learn how to merge duplicate records without losing data. Lastly, you will learn about the options for using your mobile device to access Dynamics CRM.

IN THIS CHAPTER

Navigating the CRM interface

Record ownership

Connections and customer relationships

Managing activities

Creating custom queries and views with Advanced Find

Using queues

Creating and using templates

Merging duplicate records

Cross-Reference

This chapter focuses on components of Dynamics CRM that are available in both the Web version and in Dynamics CRM for Outlook. The Outlook version, however, includes some important additional functionality as well as some variations in how some functions work. See Chapter 11 for a complete overview of Dynamics CRM for Outlook.

Navigating the Dynamics CRM Interface

Dynamics CRM delivers a tremendous amount of functionality to the user. This section outlines the four most significant areas of the user interface. Once you understand these four components, you will shorten your learning curve with all of the remaining features. Figure 10.1 illustrates three of the four areas of the user interface (the Ribbon menu, navigation pane, and lists). Double-clicking on an item in a list opens the underlying fourth area of the user interface (the form), which is illustrated in Figure 10.2.

FIGURE 10.1

Ribbon menu, navigation pane, and lists

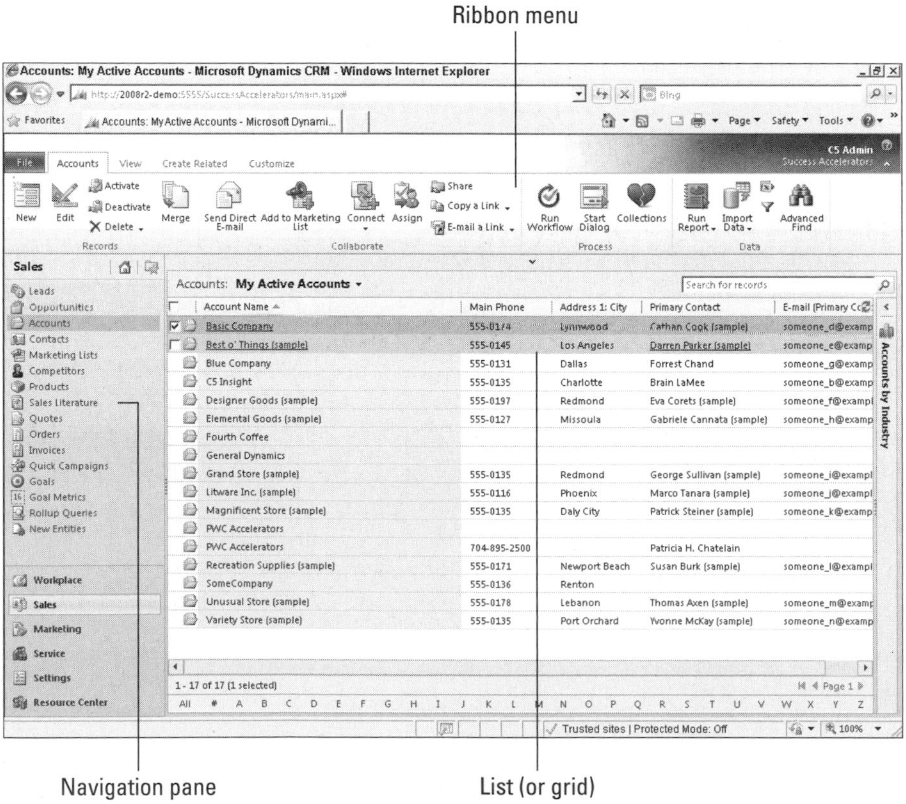

FIGURE 10.2

Dynamics CRM forms

Understanding the Ribbon menu

The Ribbon menu will look familiar to you if you have been using Office 2007, 2010, or SharePoint 2010. Microsoft has been building this new component into the user interface of all their applications, and Microsoft Dynamics CRM 2011 marks the first version of CRM that includes the Ribbon menu. This new feature consolidates functionality previously found in menus, toolbars, and buttons in earlier versions of Dynamics CRM. As illustrated in Figure 10.3, the Ribbon menu includes tabs that are context-sensitive based on which area of CRM you are currently using.

Ribbon menu tabs

If Ribbon menus are new to you, you can think of ribbon menu tabs as the top level menu in applications that you may be more familiar with. You can click on the tabs to see different functions (or submenus) available within those areas.

Standard and context-sensitive Ribbon menu tabs

The file tab is visible in all areas of Dynamics CRM.

Active menu based on context of currently selected all of screen

Context sensitive tabs based on user role and location in Dynamics CRM.

Areas of the currently selected tab.

Every menu Ribbon includes the File tab. This tab, however, behaves a bit differently from other tabs. When clicking File, a drop-down menu appears, as shown in Figure 10.4, that contains standard options for creating, saving, or printing records. The specific options that appear are context sensitive based upon which portion of the application you are currently viewing.

File tab with options

Context-sensitive Ribbon menu tabs and buttons

As you navigate through the Dynamics CRM user interface, the tabs available within the Ribbon menu change. Microsoft has built intelligence into the menu to provide options that are related directly to the task that the user is currently working on. As noted in Figure 10.3, most of the tabs on the Ribbon menu are context sensitive.

A bit more subtle is the fact that the available options also change based upon Security Role assigned to the user. For example, if you are the system administrator, you often see a tab titled Customize that enables you to make changes to the configuration of the area of CRM that you are currently viewing — most other users will not see that option in their Ribbon menu. The same is true for individual buttons within a tab.

Cross-Reference

For more information on how to set up Security Roles to govern what users can see in the Ribbon menu, see Chapter 6.

Collapsing the Ribbon menu

Although the Ribbon menu can be a helpful time-saver, it can limit the amount of space available on your monitor to work with information in Dynamics CRM. To remove the Ribbon menu from view, double-click on any tab on the Ribbon menu. The buttons on the menu then collapse, leaving only the tabs and providing more real estate on your screen. When you're ready to work with the Ribbon menu again, a single-click on a tab returns the menu to its normal state.

Cross-Reference

The Ribbon menu can be customized to add or remove tabs and buttons within the tabs. This level of customization enables you to create entire new functions to improve the productivity of those using Dynamics CRM. For more information on customizing the Ribbon menu, see Chapter 21.

We refer back to the Ribbon menu throughout the book to point out context-sensitive items available to you in each area.

Using the navigation pane

The Dynamics CRM application menu is found along the left-hand side of the user interface and is called the navigation pane. It is available in most of the application (except on forms and in certain portions of the settings area). As illustrated in Figure 10.5, the navigation pane includes a number of tools to rapidly navigate the CRM interface.

Areas, groups, and subareas

The navigation pane consists of areas, groups, and subareas. Areas encompass each of the primary functional areas of Dynamics CRM (in another applications, these are often referred to as modules). The following list describes each of the default areas:

- **Workplace:** The workplace delivers a list of the most frequently used Dynamics CRM functions and consolidates some functions that appear in the other areas of CRM. The workplace can also be customized by each user to show just the information that they want to see.

Cross-Reference

Each user can make changes to what is displayed in the Workplace to suit their preferences. For more information on how to customize the workplace, see Chapter 6.

- **Sales, Marketing, Service:** These three areas contain the functionality to support each of the three primary functions built into Dynamics CRM. More information on each of these functional areas is discussed in subsequent chapters.

FIGURE 10.5

The Dynamics CRM navigation pane

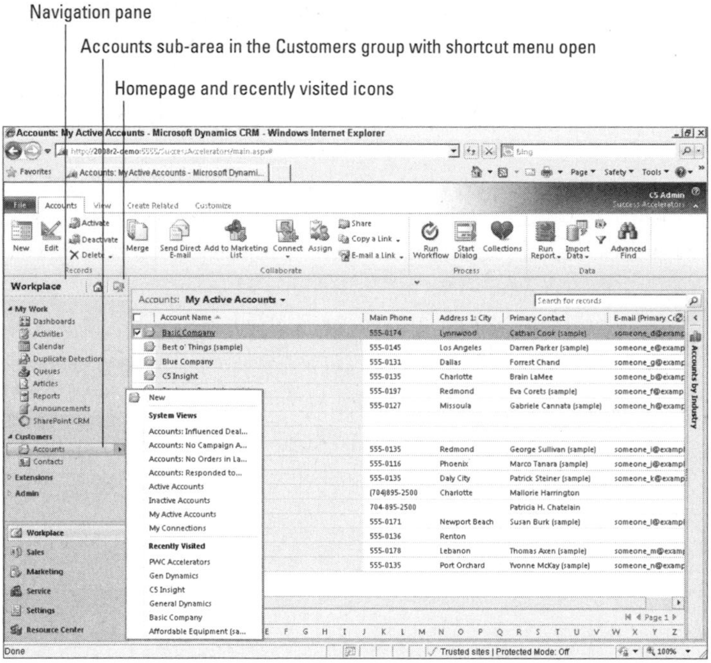

Navigation pane

Accounts sub-area in the Customers group with shortcut menu open

Homepage and recently visited icons

- **Settings:** The settings area provides the tools to customize how Dynamics CRM works. This includes basic setup (such as Security Roles), customization (such as changing the fields on forms), workflows, and other administrative features. Much of the settings area will not be visible to most users — but as the administrator you will be able to access all the functionality in this area.

- **Resource Center:** The resource center contains a number of links to helpful information to aid you in learning more about Dynamics CRM. The information in this section is brought in from the Internet, so it often features new tips and help for getting the most out of Dynamics CRM.

Some areas contain groups, which provide a way of organizing similar functions together. For example, the Workplace contains groups for My Work and Customers by default (Figure 10.5). Groups can be collapsed and expanded again by clicking on the group name.

Subareas represent the actual menu items that you can click on to navigate to a specific functional portion of Dynamics CRM. Most subarea links bring up a list of records (described below). Most subarea links in the navigation pane include shortcut menus to save you a few clicks in navigating to particular portions of a subarea (as illustrated in Figure 10.5).

Shortcut menus

As you hover over subareas with your mouse, you notice that some of them have a shortcut menu as indicated by a small triangle in the right-hand portion of the subarea link. Clicking on the shortcut menu brings up a link to create a new record, a list of available views, and recently visited records within the subarea. Although subtle, this navigation feature can be a real time-saver as you move around Dynamics CRM.

Homepage

Each user can set up an individual homepage within Dynamics CRM. Some users want to see dashboards while others want to see their list of daily activities and so forth. To navigate to your homepage, simply click on the home icon at the top of the navigation pane. Changing your home page can be done from within the personal options described in Chapter 6.

Recently visited and favorites

Next to the homepage icon is the recently viewed icon. This is another great time-saving item built into the Dynamics CRM UI. Click the icon to retrieve a list of places that you have recently visited in Dynamics CRM. If you would like to make any of these items a favorite that always shows up in the list, simple click the pushpin icon to the right of it, and it will always be available in this menu.

Cross-Reference

The areas, groups and subareas of the Dynamics CRM navigation pane can be customized a number of different ways. See Chapter 17 for information on how to update which entities are available within which areas and groups of the navigation pane. See Chapter 21 for information on how to update the sitemap to deliver custom functionality.

Navigating CRM lists

At the core of Dynamics CRM is the ability to manage lists of information. Lists can take the form of information that is built into CRM (such as activities, opportunities, or contacts) or custom information that you configure (such as expenses, projects, or assets). List views in Dynamics CRM include a number of features and context-sensitive Ribbon bar items to help you quickly sort, search, find, and process records within the lists (see Figure 10.6).

FIGURE 10.6

Dynamics CRM list view

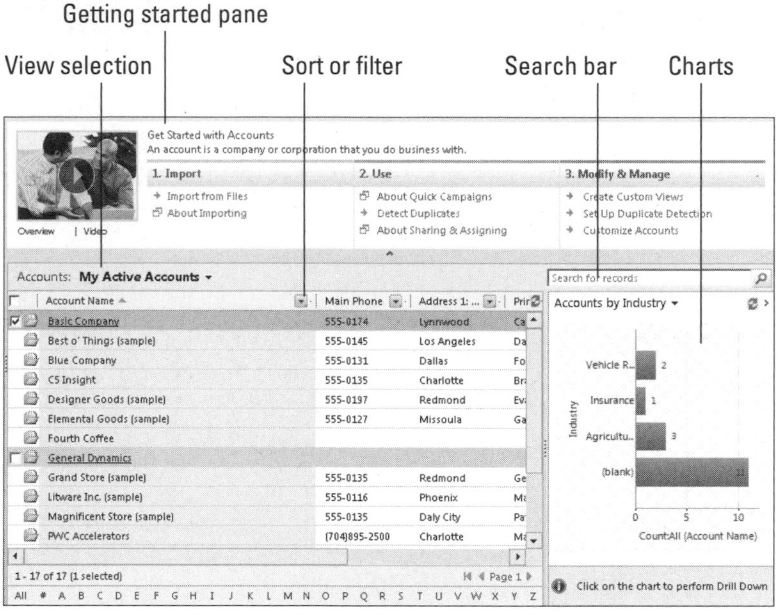

Views

Views are predefined filters and columns that can be applied against a given list view. The list of predefined views is visible above and to the left side of the list. You can see which view is currently applied next to the name of the list (in Figure 10.6 the active filter is named Active Accounts). You can click the small triangle to the right of the current view to see a list of all available views.

For each list, you can define the default view that you would like to see when you initially view that list. To set the default view, first select the view that you would like to have as your default, then click the Views tab in the Ribbon menu and click the Set as Default View button. The next time you load Dynamics CRM and visit the list, the selected view will be loaded by default.

Tip

If a view returns a long list of records, only a subset of the full list will be returned. To move through the entire list, you will need to click on the arrows to the left and right of the page number in the lower right-hand corner of the list.

Creating Personal Views with Advanced Find

In addition to the views that are included with Dynamics CRM, you can create your own personal views. Here's how to create a personal view:

1. Navigate to the list that you wish to create a personal view for and select a view that is close to what you want. For example, if you want to create a view of Accounts that you own that are in the state of North Carolina, then navigate to the accounts list and choose the My Active Accounts view.

2. In the Ribbon bar, click the Advanced Find button. The advanced find builder will appear and the view you had selected will be visible.

3. Make desired changes to the query (you may need to click the Show Details button to be able to edit the query).

4. To add or remove columns to the view and to change the sort order, click the Edit Columns button.

5. You can run your view immediately by clicking the Results button.

6. You can save your view as a personal view by clicking the Save As button.

7. Once saved, your personal view will appear in the list of views for the selected list (you may need to refresh the Web page after initially creating the personal view for it to be added to the list).

Tip

Personal views can also be created by either clicking the list of views and choosing Create Personal View or by clicking the View tab in the Ribbon menu and clicking the Create Personal View button.

Cross-Reference

See Chapter 17 to learn about creating system views that are visible across the organization and for more details on how to use the advanced find functionality.

Using the search bar

A variety of methods are available to search for specific records within Dynamics CRM. In addition to views, you can use the search bar, which is located above and to the right of every list.

- Users can type the first few letters of what they're searching for into the search bar, press the Enter key, and Dynamics CRM returns a list of results.

- If you are searching for something and you do not remember the first few words, you can precede your search with the wildcard character (an asterisk, *) and search again. For instance, if you search for *appliance in the account list, Dynamics CRM will return a list of all accounts that have the word appliance anywhere in the company name.

- Dynamics CRM can be configured to allow you to search virtually any field available in a list. However, not all fields are included in the search criteria to start with. The administrator can change the search settings to enable you to search for other records (for more information, see Chapter 17).

Sorting

Lists in Dynamics CRM can be easily sorted by clicking the column head that you want to sort by. Click the header once and the list is sorted in ascending order. Click it again and the list is sorted in descending order.

Tip

You can sort a list by more than one column. Begin by clicking on the first column that you want to sort by. Next, hold the Shift key down and click on each of the remaining columns that you want to sort by.

Filtering

Dynamics CRM also includes the ability to interactively sort and filter lists. If you have ever used AutoFilter in Microsoft Excel, then this functionality will be very familiar to you. While on a list, click the Filter button on the View tab in the Ribbon menu. Notice that a drop-down button appears on each header on the list. Click the drop-down to bring up filtering options. You can set filtering and sorting options for every column that is visible in the view.

Tip

If you use filtering to create a list view in Dynamics CRM that you would like to use frequently, you can save the filter as a new view. Click the Views tab in the Ribbon menu and select Save Filters as New View. You can name the view and, once saved, it will be in your list of personal views for that list.

Caution

Filters work on top of the view that you are currently using prior to creating the filter. For example, if you are currently using a view titled "Accounts in zip code 90210" and you add a filter to display only records that do not have data in the city field, then you will get a list of accounts with a zip code of 90210 but that do not have a city. If you save this filter as a view, be sure to give it an understandable name such as "Zip Code 90210 without a City".

Charts

Charts provide a way to visualize information presented within a view. They also allow interactive drill-down to dig deeper into the data. This tool is great for giving managers a snapshot of what is going on with their group or for giving users an overview of their pipeline or workload.

To turn on charts for an existing view, navigate to the view for which you want to see charts. On the Ribbon bar tab for that list, click on the Charts button. After clicking this button, the default chart for that view is visible. In addition, a context-sensitive tab is added to the Ribbon bar for managing charts.

You can select different charts by clicking the drop-down menu just above the displayed chart. You can drill into the chart by clicking on the chart, selecting which field you wish to drill down into, and then selecting the chart type to display.

The Chart Tools Ribbon menu provides a number of options for customizing and creating new charts. Creating new charts uses a wizard-like process to prompt you through the process of creating and saving a new chart. Similar to views, users can create "personal charts" that are visible only to them, and administrators can create system charts that are available to all users.

Cross-Reference
To learn more about creating custom charts, see Chapter 24.

Getting Started pane
Most lists in Dynamics CRM include a Getting Started pane. This pane provides guidance to new users on how to use the various lists and other functions available. Most Getting Started panes include access to help files as well as videos and overviews. After you are familiar with how to use an area of Dynamics CRM, you can hide the getting started pane by clicking the small up arrow that is just between the Getting Started pane and the list you are viewing. The pane slides away; you can access it later by clicking the arrow again.

Using CRM forms to view and update records

In Dynamics CRM, forms are used to view, create, and update information. To open a form for an existing record, click on the primary field for the record in the list. To create a new record, click the New button on the far left of the Ribbon bar.

Microsoft has also built functionality into forms that enable the user to more rapidly update data, navigate records, and connect with clients, prospects, and colleagues. Forms appear in their own window and use their own navigation pane. Figure 10.7 represents a typical Dynamics CRM form and related components.

Navigating forms
Forms contain a number of elements that are important to understand as you learn to find your way around the interface. Each form may be laid out differently, but the main elements are the same:

- **Tabs:** Tabs are displayed as blue section dividers on the main form, and as the first items in the Navigation pane. Tabs are the only items in the navigation pane that do not include any icons. You can navigate between tabs by clicking on the tab names in the Navigation pane, or by using the scroll bar. Tabbed sections can be collapsed by clicking on the tab heading in the data entry area of the form.

- **Status Bar:** At the bottom of every form is a footer that generally contains the status bar (unless your administrator has removed it from your view). The status bar indicates the status of the record. The list of possible status values varies depending upon the type of record you are viewing. Most records are either active (and can be edited) or inactive (and cannot be edited).

FIGURE 10.7

Dynamics CRM form

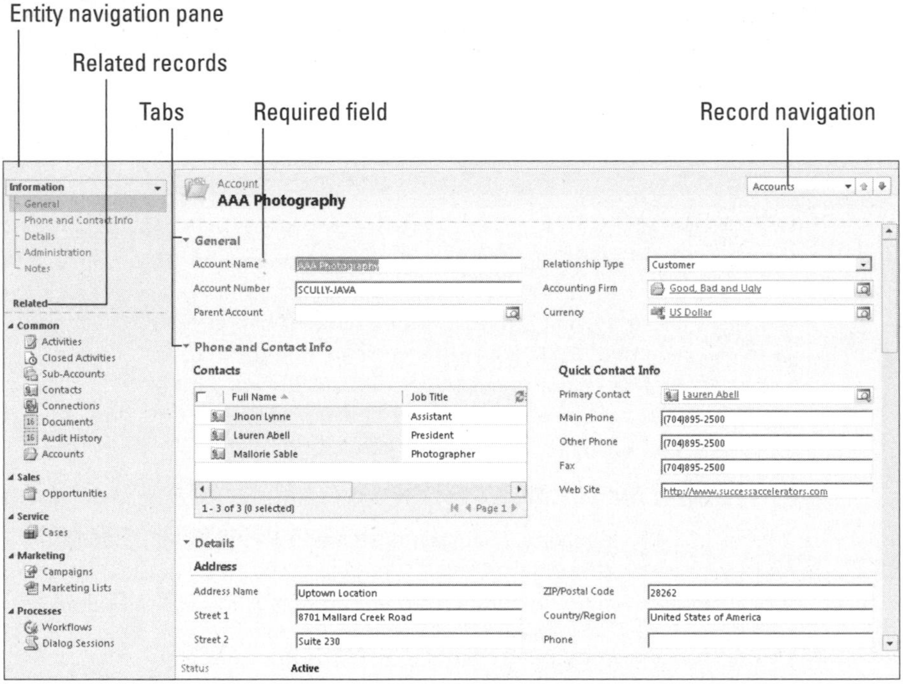

Entity navigation pane

Related records

Tabs   Required field   Record navigation

- **Sub-Lists:** Records in Dynamics CRM are almost always linked to many other records. These related lists of records can also be called sub-lists. Sub-lists can appear in-line within the data entry form — which can be a very nice time-saver when entering data. They also appear in the navigation pane to the left of the form. You can click on sub-list links in the navigation pane to bring up a view of a specific sub-list. When viewing a sub-list, you have much of the same functionality available as you do when looking at lists in the main area of Dynamics CRM. When creating new records in sub-lists, Dynamics CRM pre-fills many of the fields for you automatically based on the parent record you were viewing when you created the sub-record.

Tip

Dynamics CRM will pre-fill many fields in records for you when you create the records from a parent. For example, if you are on an account record, and you create a new contact, Dynamics CRM will pre-fill in the name of the account, phone number, and address fields. You can change these values on the contact if you wish. On the other hand, if you create a new contact without first viewing the account, then the fields will not be pre-filled and it will take extra time to enter the record. Navigating to the parent record before creating a subrecord is a best practice because it will improve the speed and accuracy of your data entry.

Navigating records

You can navigate to different records without having to close the form and go back to the List view. To navigate to another record, you can use the up and down arrows just above and to the right of the form. You can also use the drop-down list of records. You can only navigate through the records that were in the view that you used to open the current form. This is useful functionality for quickly processing a list of records without having to open and close each one.

Entering data

After you have opened a form in Dynamics CRM, data entry is a fairly simple process. Understanding a few key items saves you some time and frustration.

- **Required fields:** Fields marked with a red asterisk are required. You will not be allowed to save changes if any of these fields are blank.

- **Saving changes:** You have several options for saving your work. These are available from the Ribbon bar from the tab named for the record type you are currently editing.

  - **Save:** Allows you to save changes to your record and continue working.

  - **Save and Close:** Saves your changes and closes the form; you are returned to the view you were on prior to opening the form.

  - **Save and New:** Saves your changes and opens a new, blank record. This feature is useful if you are adding a series of records.

  - **Other Save Options:** Depending on the type of record you are editing, you may also be able to send (for e-mail) or mark complete (for activities) as other save options for your record.

Caution

Always remember to save your changes before you close a form. Because Dynamics CRM is a Web application, your data is not being automatically saved as you enter it into a form. If you close a form without saving your data, any changes you have made will be lost. The good news is that Dynamics CRM prompts you to save your record if you attempt to close a form without saving.

Editing multiple records

Bulk edit is a powerful feature that is included in Dynamics CRM. It provides users with the ability to rapidly update multiple records at the same time. This can be useful if, for example, a customer moves to a new location and you want to update the address on all of their contacts. To edit multiple records:

1. Navigate to the view containing the records that you want to update. This can be a list in the main area of Dynamics CRM or it can be a sub-list under an existing record. For example, you can go to an account and then navigate to the sub-list of all the contacts for that account.

2. Select which records you want to update. To select all records on a page, click the check box just above the list. To select multiple records, click the check box to the left of each record that you want to edit.

3. In the Ribbon menu, click the Edit button.

4. You will see a popup screen with a blank form. Enter data into only the fields that you want to update (do not enter any information in the fields that you do not wish to update).

5. Click the Save button.

Record Ownership

In Dynamics CRM, most records must be assigned to an owner. Record ownership is a convenient tool for ensuring that you know who has responsibility for winning an opportunity, who a task has been assigned to, or who needs to respond to a customer service request.

Record ownership is also used for views. Whenever you see a view preceded by the word "My" (such as "My Open Leads") it implies that this view will return only records that are owned by you. This makes it simple and convenient to limit the list view to only those records for which you are responsible.

Tip
"My" views, as referenced above, only show records in which the current user is the sole owner of the record. Records which are owned by a team that the current user is a member of are not displayed in "My" views. New views can be created to show team-owned records if preferred.

Record ownership also plays an important part in security. Security settings determine which records each user is able to create, view, update, or delete. Security is driven largely by record ownership. For example, I may be able to create and update records that are owned by me but only view records that are owned by my peers. My manager, on the other hand, may be able to view, create, update, and delete records that are owned by anyone that reports to her.

Cross-Reference
For more information on security and related concepts, see Chapter 5.

Organization ownership

Not all records types will have an owner assigned to them. These records are said to have organization ownership (meaning that the organization is responsible for maintaining these records). Some examples of organization-owned records include competitors, products, and articles.

In general, you know that a record requires an owner when you see the field labeled Owner on the form.

User or team ownership

Records that must be assigned to an owner can be assigned to either an individual user or to a team.

Team ownership is a useful concept when a record may be managed by multiple users. For example, one business may have account management teams that are assigned to customers to handle inside sales, outside sales, and customer service.

Team ownership can also be helpful when a record may need to temporarily be visible to an entire team until it is claimed by a single user. For example, a new service case may be assigned to a team until the first available person can work it. After that person opens the record, it can be automatically assigned to that person as the exclusive record owner. This can be combined with the Queue functionality described later in this chapter.

Tip

When a record is created, the owner is set to the user that created the record by default. The record can be reassigned to another team or user at any time.

Sharing records

Records in Dynamics CRM can also be shared with other users. By sharing records with your colleagues, you can expand some or all of your permissions to view, edit, and update records to other individuals within your organization. In Figure 10.8, read only access has been shared to the record Access MediQuip, LLC with David Jaffe and Don Funk. To share a record with other users:

1. Navigate to the record you wish to share and click on the record in the list.
2. In the toolbar, click the Sharing button.
3. Click Add User/Team.
4. Select the user or team that you want to share the record with.
5. Click the OK button.
6. Now select the permissions that you wish to assign to the user.
7. Click the OK button.

FIGURE 10.8

Sharing records with other users

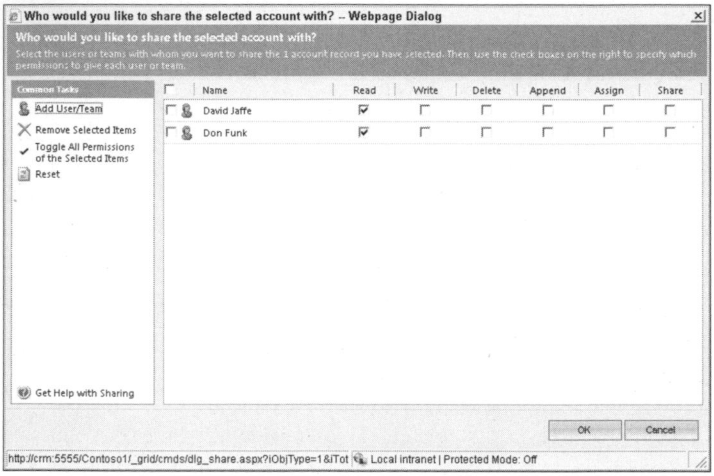

Connections and Customer Relationships

Connections provide a flexible way of relating records in Dynamics CRM to other records in Dynamics CRM. Connections go beyond the standard sub-list type connections (such as linking all contacts to the account that they work for), to support any kind of connection. Here are some examples of how you can use connections:

- Connect a partner (tracked in Dynamics CRM as an account) to opportunities that they have referred to you.
- Connect two contacts to each other as spouses.
- Connect a quote to all the individuals that must approve it before it can be accepted.
- Connect a distributor account to all of their customer accounts.

Cross-Reference

Connections can be setup to work with any entity in Dynamics CRM — for information on setting up entities, see Chapter 17.

Use the process below to add connections to an existing record in Dynamics CRM:

1. Navigate to the record you wish to create a connection to and click on the record in the list.

Connections versus Relationships

Previous versions of Dynamics CRM contained a function similar to connections called relationships. Relationships contain a subset of the functionality that is available in connections. Microsoft left relationships in Dynamics CRM 2011 in order to remain compatible with previous versions. However, having both connections and relationships available in CRM can be confusing for users.

If you are new to Dynamics CRM, then you should use the connections functionality and not the relationships functionality. As the administrator, you can simplify this process for your users by eliminating visibility into relationships by setting up security roles.

If you are upgrading from a previous version of Dynamics CRM and your users made use of relationships before, then you should leave this functionality visible. You may, however, want to either train your users to begin to migrate their old relationships information over to connections or use automation to migrate the data on behalf of users.

2. In the toolbar, click the Connect button (if the button is not visible, then you will need to configure the entity to allow connections). The new connection form appears.

3. In the Connect To area, select the name of the record that you want to connect this record to.

4. Now choose the role for each of the records (note that you can create new roles on the fly if desired).

5. You can enter other notes and a start/end date for the connection if you like (this can be very helpful for time-based connections, such as referral fees that are owed to partners if a transaction is completed within a specific time frame).

Managing Activities with Dynamics CRM

Activities are one of the central concepts to Dynamics CRM. If you're using Microsoft Outlook, you're already familiar with activities such as e-mails, appointments, and tasks. In the next chapter, we discuss how Outlook and Dynamics CRM activities are synchronized with each other.

Activities in Dynamics CRM have a field titled "regarding" that allows you to link an activity to almost any other record. For example, you can regard an e-mail to an opportunity, case, account, quote, or just about any other record in CRM. The regarding tool is a useful field for organizing all of your activities and communications so you can find them easily if they are needed later.

In addition to the regarding field, most activities can be linked to other records in CRM using additional fields. For example, you may send an e-mail to a contact, thanking them for referring an opportunity to you. The "to" field would link to the contact that you are sending the e-mail to, and the regarding field would link to the opportunity that the contact referred to you. In this case the e-mail activity would be visible under both the contact record and the opportunity record. This ability to track multiple links is a great way to ensure that activities are visible under every record that an activity is associated with, making it easier for you to find the information you need wherever you are in CRM.

In addition to the above links, Dynamics CRM also rolls up activity views so that they are available on parent records. For example, if you record an activity on a contact record it is also visible on the account that is the parent of the contact. This is a convenient way to view everything that is going on with an account without having to go to each individual record to view the underlying activities. Figure 10.9 illustrates rolled-up activities.

FIGURE 10.9

Account record with activities from related contacts and opportunities

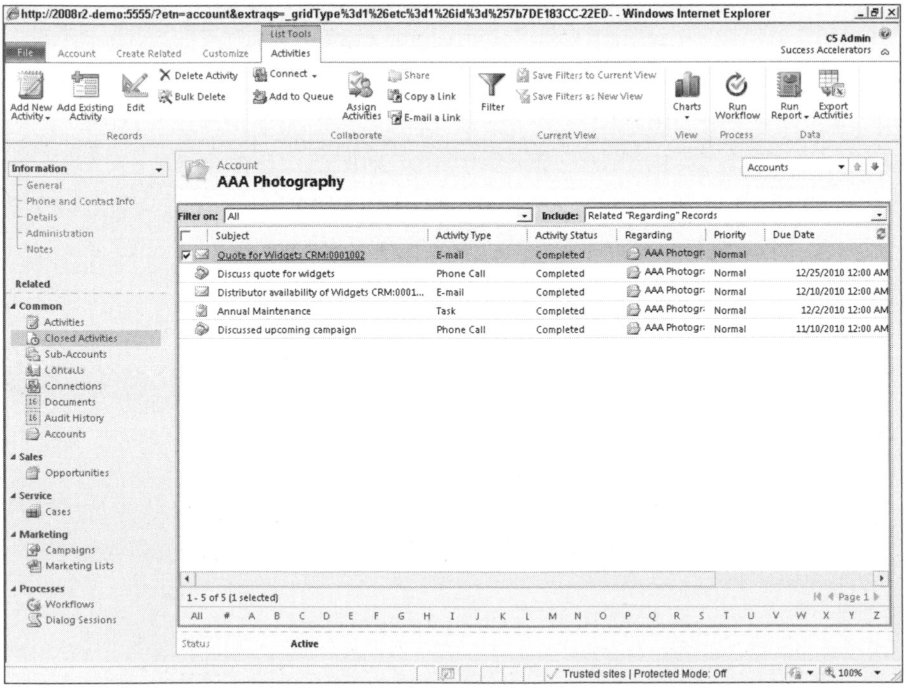

To summarize how all of these activity links work, let's say you call a prospect to check the status of a quote. You enter the name of the contact in the recipient field of the phone call activity and your name in the sender field. You then enter the name of the quote into the regarding field. When you look at the quote in the future, you will see the completed phone call in the closed activity list for the quote (because you entered that in the regarding field), for the contact (because you entered that contact as the recipient), under your own record (because you entered yourself as the sender), and under the account that the contact belongs to. Figure 10.10 illustrates entering a phone call activity with these links.

FIGURE 10.10

Phone call activity and associated linking fields

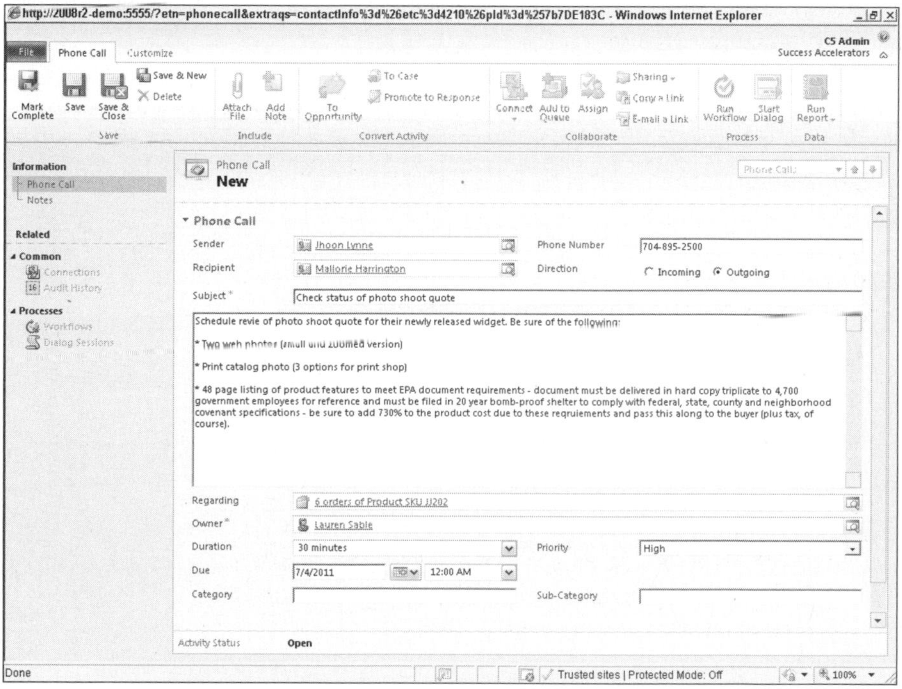

Understanding activity types

Dynamics CRM includes a large number of different activity types including phone calls, e-mails, tasks, appointments, and a number of others. There are several benefits to using different activity types:

- Using different activity types is a convenient way to get at-a-glance information about which types of interaction you have had with an individual. Figure 10.9 illustrates different icons that represent the different activity types.

- Activity types also enable organizations to track different types of information that may be relevant for different types of activities. For example, an e-mail activity includes a rich text field to track the specific content of the e-mail that was sent — this kind of information is not necessary in a phone call activity.

The Hidden Complexities of Activity Reporting ———

Each activity type in Dynamics CRM is managed by a different table. Microsoft has done an outstanding job of making these different tables seamless to the end user by creating custom views that merge all the different activity types into a single list that is available in Dynamics CRM. Beneath the surface, however, it can be quite complex to work with these different activity types if you are developing custom activity reports.

When Microsoft created their custom views for activities they included fields that are common across all activity types. So in these views you will see fields like subject, activity status, and regarding. On the other hand, you won't see fields like category or any custom fields you may have created.

You have the option of building reports and views for individual activity types. Using this approach you could create a report of all phone calls by category. However, if management wants a report of all activities by category you won't be able to do this with the report wizard or with advanced find. To develop a complex report like this you would need to develop custom queries using SQL Server Reporting Services (SSRS).

Similarly, many sales managers want to see a list of everyone on their team with a breakdown of the different activity types for each user in a grid. This seemingly simple report introduces a need to understand how to develop custom reports and queries to provide the required data.

Activities are an area of Dynamics CRM that management often wants quite a bit of custom reporting from in order to understand if their teams are engaging in the right activities. Keep this in mind as you work with activities to ensure that you are tracking data in a way that you can easily report on.

On the Web site

See the Web site for an example report (built in SSRS) that includes links to multiple activity types. This will provide you with an understanding of the complexities of wrapping multiple activities into a single report — and may also provide you with a helpful management report for your team.

- Many organizations have key performance indicators (KPIs) associated with activity types. For instance, some sales people are required to make a certain number of calls and face-to-face visits on a weekly basis. Using activity types makes reporting easier on these activities to ensure that KPI goals are being met.

In addition to the standard activities above, Dynamics CRM also includes a number of specialized activities such as campaign responses, service activities, and opportunity close. These types of activities are associated with specific functionality within Dynamics CRM and will be described in more detail in other portions of this documentation.

With Dynamics CRM 2011, Microsoft introduced the concept of custom activities. These are activity types that an administrator (or third party) can create to extend the functionality of Dynamics CRM. These may include new communication activities (such as Facebook messages) or possibly internal activities (such as approvals or research notes).

Cross-Reference

For more information on creating custom activity types, see Chapter 17.

Working with activities

Most Dynamics CRM users spend more time creating, tracking, and completing activities than just about anything else. In fact, a quick analysis of most Dynamics CRM databases shows that organizations have more activity records than all other types of records combined — by a fairly wide margin. Microsoft recognized this and built a number of tools into the Dynamics CRM interface to make it simple and fast to manage activities.

Creating activities

There are many places in the user interface where you can create activities. The best place to go to create an activity will be a matter of personal preference, or a function of what you're currently doing in Dynamics CRM when you decide to create an activity. Here are some of the most frequently used places to go to create an activity:

- **File menu:** In the Ribbon menu, the File tab is always visible, and you can click on it and then on New Activity to create an activity.

- **Activities list:** While viewing the list of all activities in Dynamics CRM, you can use the Ribbon menu to add new activities by clicking the button for the appropriate activity type.

- **Toolbar on parent record:** While viewing the parent record that you want to create an activity for, you can use the Ribbon menu to create a new activity and link it directly to that record. To do this:

  1. Navigate to the record on a list and either click once to select it, or double-click to open the form.

  2. On the Ribbon menu, click the Create Related tab and then select the record type that you want to link to this record, as illustrated in Figure 10.11.

- **In Outlook:** You can create Dynamics CRM activities directly inside of Microsoft Outlook. See the following chapter for more information.

Cross-Reference

For more detailed ideas on managing activities in Dynamics CRM, see the blog entry "11 Habits of Effective Activity Management" on http://blogs.c5insight.com.

Tip

When creating activities, you'll save some time if you first navigate to the parent record and create the activity from there because Dynamics CRM fills in some of the fields for you. For example, if you navigate to a contact and create a phone call, the recipient and phone number will be auto-filled for you. This not only saves time, but also reduces the chance of data entry errors.

FIGURE 10.11

Creating an activity from the Ribbon menu

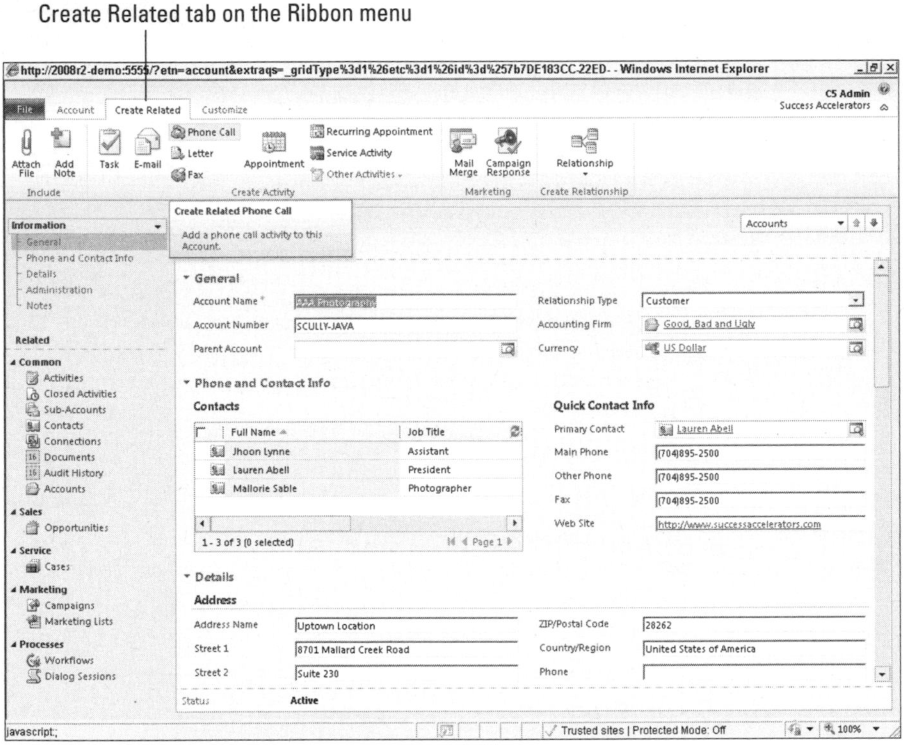

Create Related tab on the Ribbon menu

Viewing activities

Users need to be able to quickly find activities on their "to do" list. On the other hand, it is also important that users be able to quickly view just the activities associated with customers or other records. For this reason, Microsoft delivered two primary ways to view activities within Dynamics CRM.

Activities list sub-area

The activities list in Dynamics CRM provides a list of all activities that are visible to the user. In general, this list is used by individual users to work through the activities that they are responsible for. It can, however, also be used to view completed activities or even activities assigned to other users.

Activity Management and User Adoption

If you've done much reading about any CRM system, you know that user adoption can be a major problem with any CRM system. User adoption refers to the success rate of getting users to integrate the CRM tool into their everyday business activities.

The inability to fully and properly leverage activity management is one of the biggest drivers of user adoption (or lack thereof) with any CRM system. As you begin to use CRM, you should pay special attention to how you are working with activity management. If you get frustrated, it may very well be that you are not aware of some of the options open to you for activity management or you may be struggling with how relational activity records link up to their parent records.

The biggest two tools available to you are experimentation and persistence. Experiment and find the best way to create activities for you. Persist with investing time in creating, completing, and finding activities until you get comfortable with exactly how this works.

Dynamics CRM makes a number of additional tools available to you. Consider using UI scripts, workflows, queues, Outlook integration, and other tools described within this book to simplify the process and automate some of the steps in activity management.

Activities and Closed Activities related lists

As we noted earlier in this chapter, activities can be linked to a variety of different records in Dynamics CRM and it is important that individuals within your organization have visibility to see the activities that are either scheduled or completed for each record. To view the activities for a specific record, use the steps below:

1. Navigate to the form for the record that you wish to see related activities.

2. Click on the Activities item in the navigation pane to see activities that have not yet been completed, or click on the Closed Activities item in the navigation pane to view activities that are closed (either completed or cancelled).

Figure 10.9 is an example of a Closed Activity list for an account record; note that immediately above the Closed Activity link is a link to Activities (meaning open activities) for that account.

On the Web Site

Users often find it helpful to have a view of activities that are assigned to them and are due today or that are past due. This view, however, is not available by default in Dynamics CRM. On the Web site, you will find a view that you can load called My Today's Activities. For information on how to create this type of view see the section related to Advanced Find later in this chapter. For information on how to load this custom view to Dynamics CRM see Chapter 16.

Activity alerts

When it comes to managing activities, it is always helpful to be able to receive alerts when you need to be in an appointment, make a call or complete any of a variety of activities. Dynamics CRM does not include a popup reminder or similar feature. Instead, Microsoft has tightly integrated Dynamics CRM with Outlook with the expectation that you will use Outlook to generate your reminders. More information on Outlook is in Chapter 11.

Completing activities

Every activity that you create in Dynamics CRM must be completed — otherwise it will continue to be listed as a "to do." To complete an activity, open the form and click the Save as Completed button in the Ribbon menu.

Using Queues

Queues are a useful way to track records that need to be placed into a "holding tank" until someone is available to "claim" them and take some action. They are particularly helpful if you have records or activities that should be assigned to the first available qualified individual from a team. Think of a queue as an inbox that multiple individuals can see and can take items out of that they want to take responsibility for.

As an example, many organizations have a support team. Individuals on this team would like to be able to view a list of all recent customer service inquiries and accept items to add to their list of activities to handle. Simply assigning cases to these individuals in round-robin fashion would not work well because some cases take far longer to handle than others — so this could lead to having some customers wait too long for a response to their inquiry. This problem could be solved by placing these cases into a queue so a new case is not assigned to a service rep until they have completed cases currently assigned to them.

Queues can be used for any work process that requires a team of individuals to claim items from a list. This can include lead qualification, quote approvals, job candidate resume reviews, or bank property appraisals in addition to the cases we described in the preceding paragraph.

By default activities and cases can be assigned to queues, but your administrator can configure Dynamics CRM to allow almost any type of record to be in a queue. You can tell if a record can be added to a queue by navigating the record in a list and checking to see if the Add to Queue button appears in the Ribbon menu next to the Sharing button.

Cross-Reference

Queues are set up by the Dynamics CRM administrator. For more information on setting up queues, see Chapter 19.

Sending records to queues

Records can be sent to queues in a variety of ways. Your organization may use one or more of these approaches to aid with automating your business processes:

1. A user can navigate to a record and click the Add to Queue button in the Ribbon menu. For example, an Outside Sales Rep may put a quote into a queue called Validate Product Configuration that can then be claimed by an Inside Sales Rep to be sure the quote is valid before it is shared with a client.

2. You may set up an e-mail address dedicated to capturing items into a queue. For example, all e-mail messages sent to support@yourdomain.com may get added to your support queue.

3. You can use workflow to place items into a queue under certain conditions. For example, all leads that are more than 24 hours old may go to a queue called Shark Tank and the first available rep can claim them.

Viewing queues

To view a list of queues, navigate to the queues item in the workplace area in the navigation panel. From here, you have two filtering options. The first is the standard view that you see in other lists. The second is a selection of which queues you wish to view. To see the items in all queues that are open for someone to work on, select the view titled Items available to work on and the queue named All Queues. Figure 10.12 is an example of how this view may appear.

Keep in mind that queues honor the security roles assigned to each user. If a lead is in your queue and your security role does not allow you to view the lead record, then although you will see the item in your queue, you will not be able to open the lead to look at it until it has been assigned to you. This can be a useful feature of Dynamics CRM because you may not want users to be able to see the details of a record until it has been assigned to a specific user.

Working items in a queue

Items stay in a queue until they have been assigned to an individual's queue as part of their workload. There are a variety of methods that can be used to move an item from a public queue to an individual's queue.

To view the options for working items in a queue, navigate to the queue list and click an item in a queue. Options for working items in the queue will be displayed in the Ribbon menu.

Routing queue items

Your organization may require a manager to "triage" items in a queue to determine how they should be handled. Or, an individual may view an item in a queue and determine that they cannot work it, but they can route it to another queue to be worked. Items can be routed to a specific individual or to another, more specific, queue.

FIGURE 10.12

Viewing items that have not yet been claimed in all queues

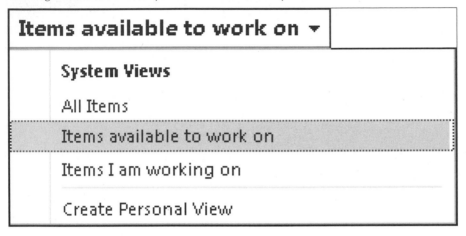

To route items, click the Routing button in the Ribbon menu. You have two routing options:

1. You are required to select a queue to add the item to. If you do not wish to add it to a new queue, you can enter the name of the current queue. You may assign it to an individual user's queue or to a general queue.

2. You can optionally choose to keep the current user that the queue item is assigned to, or you can reassign the record to someone else.

Tip

Adding a record to a queue is different from assigning the record to a user. For example, a case may be assigned to a service rep but may also be in the Level 1 Support queue. It can then be added to the Level 2 Support queue while remaining assigned to the same service rep. This is a useful feature because you may still want one user to own the record while another user performs some work on it (such as a sales person owning an opportunity record, but assigning it to a queue visible to sales assistants to do research before proceeding with calling the prospect).

A Typical Queue Process

Queues are powerful tools for automating workflow steps that can be accepted by one of many potential individuals on the same team. Moreover, queues are flexible enough to be adapted to fit different work processes. Here is an example of a workflow that uses a queue.

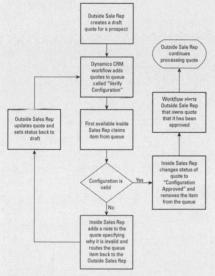

Typical queue workflow

Keep in mind that this is only an example. You can use queues for cases, leads, quotes, outbound calling, or virtually any other business process. Before implementing a queue, you should take the time to map out your own unique process.

Working on items

Individual users can monitor queues and can quickly claim items that they are available to work on. To accept an item to work on, navigate to the item you wish to accept from a queue list and then click the Work On button in the Ribbon menu. A dialog box appears. You may accept the item or you may assign it to another user to work on. The Worked By column will then be updated with the name of the user that the item is assigned to.

Releasing items you are working on

There may come a time when you are not able to work some of the items listed as being worked by you in a queue. To release items back to the general queue to be worked by the first available person who has visibility into a queue, click the Release button in the menu Ribbon. You will be removed as the person that the item is being Worked By, and the item will again be visible in the Items available to work on view.

271

Removing items from a queue

Once you are done working an item in the queue, you may remove it from the queue. Removing an item from a queue does not delete the underlying record; it simply removes it from being visible in the queue.

Deleting queue records

You can delete records that are in the queue. However, unlike removing items from a queue, deleting a record from a queue will delete the underlying Dynamics CRM record. So, for example, if you delete a queue item for a new lead, then the lead record will also be deleted.

Working with E-mail Templates

Templates can be used to quickly create documents that include information from records in Dynamics CRM. Many organizations expend a tremendous amount of time rekeying data into documents that already exists in their customer databases — templates can play an important role in eliminating this redundant data entry.

You can find the list of templates in the Settings area of Dynamics CRM. Four different types of templates are available. We will discuss e-mail templates here.

Cross-Reference

For information on creating article and contract templates, see Chapter 14. For information on creating Microsoft Word mail merge templates, see Chapter 15.

Creating e-mail templates

Follow these steps to create an e-mail template:

1. In Dynamics CRM, navigate to Settings ⇨ Templates and then click on E-Mail Templates.

2. Click New in the menu. The E-mail Template Type dialog box in Figure 10.13 enables you to select a global template type or a specific entity. Select global if your template will need to be available across all entities and will not include data from an entity. If your template will include data from a specific entity (such as from a lead) then be sure to select that entity as the template type.

3. Fill out the form using the following information:
   - Title is the title that will appear in the list of e-mail templates; it will not appear in e-mails that are sent.
   - Description is also strictly for internal usage.
   - Subject is the subject line that will appear in the e-mail.

4. Now fill in the body of the e-mail. Note that you can insert merge fields into the e-mail body and into the subject line by clicking on the Insert/Update button in the menu.

5. If desired, you can also add attachments to the e-mail. To do this, you will first need to save the e-mail (without closing it) and the New E-mail Attachment button will become available. These attachments can be PDFs or any other file (but they cannot contain mail merge fields within them).

6. Once complete, click the Save and Close button in the menu.

FIGURE 10.13

The E-mail Template Type dialog box

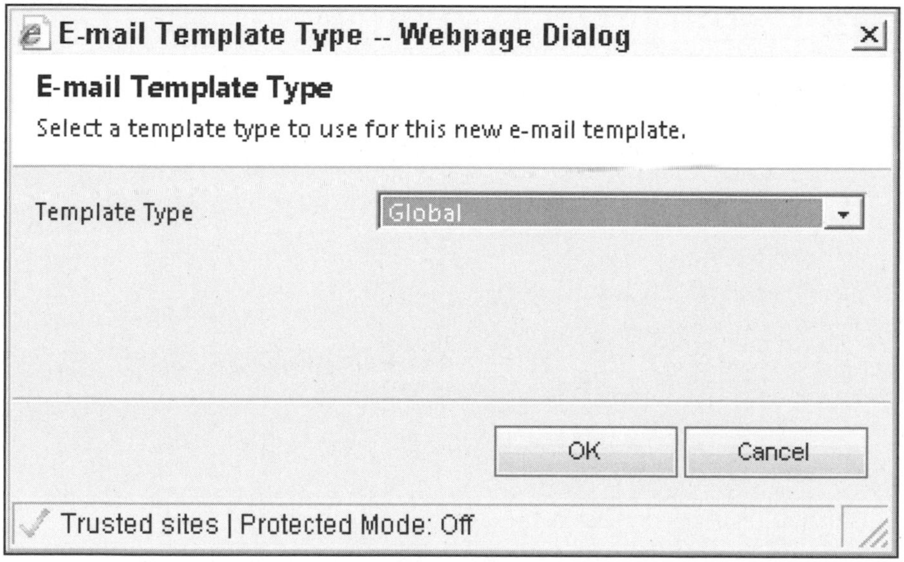

Using e-mail templates

Follow these steps to use the e-mail template that you created above:

1. Navigate to the record that you wish to use with the e-mail and open the form for the record.

2. In the Ribbon menu, click on the Create Related tab and then click E-mail.

3. Fill in the address and regarding fields for the e-mail.

4. Click Insert Template in the Ribbon menu. Depending on which fields you completed in Step 3, you may be prompted to select the target record associated with the template; if so, select the appropriate record from the list.

5. Select the preferred template from the Insert Template dialog box in Figure 10.14.

6. Fill out the remaining fields on the form.

7. Click the Send button in the Ribbon menu.

If you want to send a bulk e-mail merge to multiple individuals at once, you can use the Send Direct E-mail button on the Ribbon bar above the contact list.

FIGURE 10.14

Insert Template dialog box

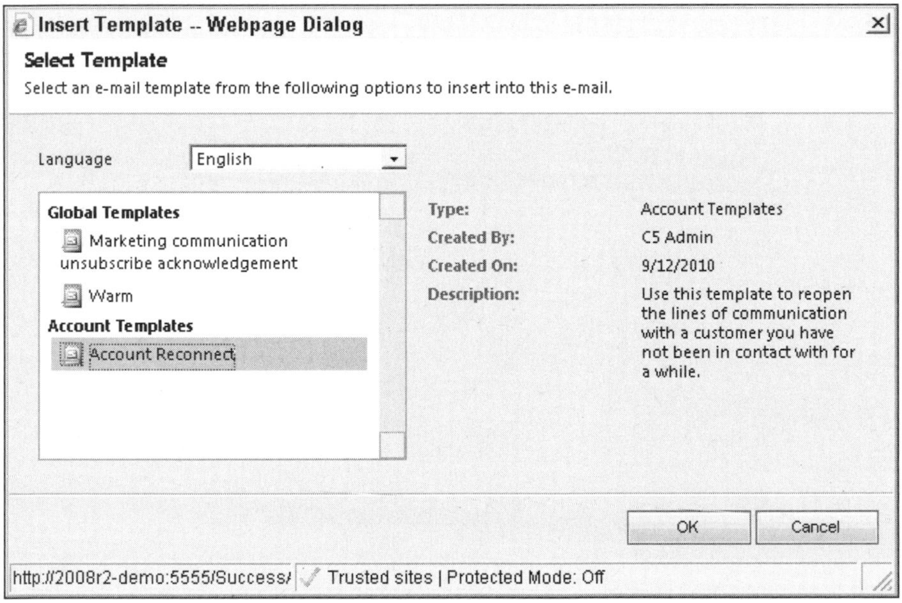

Tip

If you click the Save button in the Ribbon menu for an e-mail, the e-mail will not be sent but will be saved with a pending status. To be certain that your e-mails are being sent, click the Send button and not the Save button on the Ribbon menu.

Cross-Reference

E-mail templates can also be sent directly from Microsoft Outlook. For more information see Chapter 11.

Merging Duplicate Records

In every CRM system, occasional duplicate records are a fact of life. Although Dynamics CRM includes built in duplicate detection, users will still occasionally find duplicate records that they will want to eliminate.

Cross-Reference

For more information about auto-detecting duplicate records, see Chapter 8.

While working with Dynamics CRM, if you notice some records that should be merged, use the procedure below to merge the records.

1. Make sure both records are visible in the current view (you may need to use the Advanced Find button to create a custom view) and select both records (click the check box on the left side of each record as illustrated in Figure 10.15).

FIGURE 10.15

Contact view with two records selected

2. In the Ribbon menu, click the Merge button located in the first tab after the file tab (generally this tab is named after the list you are viewing) and in the Records section. Figure 10.16 illustrates the Merge Records dialog box.

3. Select the fields you wish to keep from each record and then click the OK button.

Dynamics CRM merges the two records together, including the related lists of information, and deactivates the record that was not primary. Deactivation means that the record that was not the master is kept, but it is hidden from view so that no historical information is lost.

FIGURE 10.16

Record merge dialog box

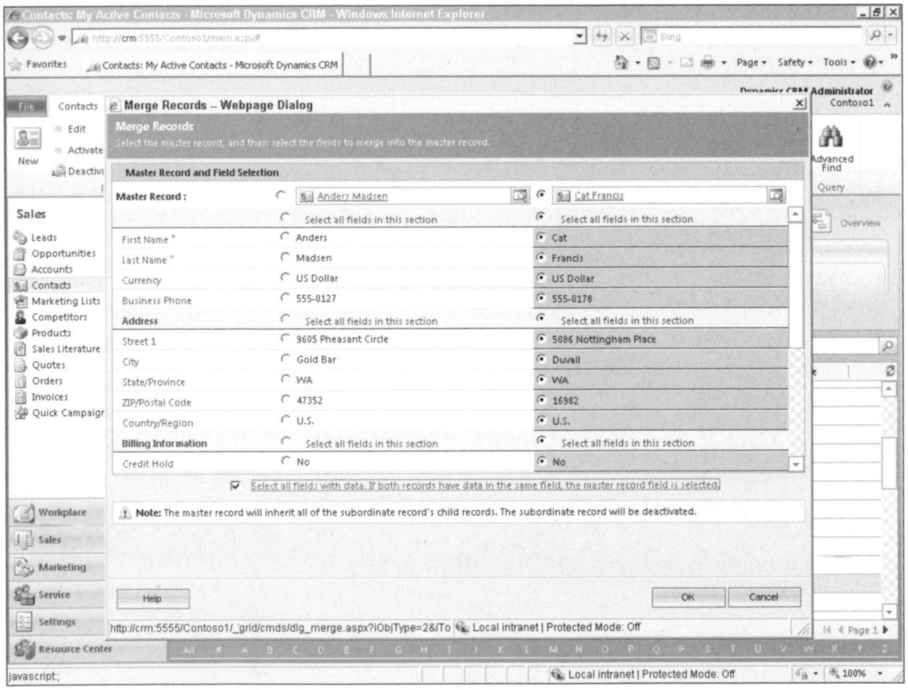

Using Your Mobile Device with Dynamics CRM

Microsoft and their partners have provided three ways to access your Dynamics CRM data using your mobile device. There are pros and cons to using Outlook synchronization, Dynamics CRM Mobile Express, and third-party tools to access CRM data via your mobile phone. We walk through each of these below.

Outlook synchronization

Most of the data in Outlook synchronizes with Dynamics CRM. This includes contacts, tasks, appointments, and e-mails. This information also synchronizes with your mobile device. When you create new records in Dynamics CRM, they automatically sync with Outlook, which then syncs with your mobile device. So, for example, if you create a contact in Dynamics CRM, it will sync with Outlook and will then sync with your mobile device. If you update that contact in any of those three locations, it will automatically sync with the copies in the other two areas. Of course, you must have Microsoft Outlook running in order for this sync to take place.

Cross-Reference
For more information on synchronizing Dynamics CRM with Outlook see Chapter 11.

Mobile Express

Sometimes the data available in Outlook is not everything that you will want to see on your mobile device. For example, you may want to have a list of leads, opportunities, or cases available. Microsoft provides Dynamics CRM Mobile Express for this reason. An administrator can set up Mobile Express to provide access to virtually any data that is in Dynamics CRM. The configuration tools also enable the administrator to minimize the data that is visible on the tiny mobile phone display to make it easier for users to see just their critical data.

Third-party options

Mobile Express does have a few significant downsides. It is only available while you are connected to the Internet — your data won't be available if you cannot browse the Internet on your mobile phone. It also does not integrate with the mobile phone functionality so you won't be able to automatically capture incoming calls and e-mails as activities. There are, however, some third-party mobile tools available to provide access to Dynamics CRM. One of the more popular tools is CWR Mobility, which includes versions for most of the popular mobile phone operating systems. Of course third-party options do require additional fees.

Summary

The Dynamics CRM Web interface includes four basic elements used throughout the application. The navigation pane is used as a menu to launch different areas of functionality. Lists provide a way to manage the data in the various areas of the application — views and the search bar make it easy to sort, search, and filter data in lists. Forms enable you to create and update data and display related lists of data relevant to the record you are currently viewing. The Ribbon menu interacts with data in lists and forms.

Most records in Dynamics CRM are owned by a user or a team. Record ownership plays an important role in determining who can create, read, update, or delete records within Dynamics CRM. Record ownership also makes it easier for users to find the tasks and customers for whom they are responsible.

Managing activities is a central concept to Dynamics CRM. There are a wide variety of activity records including phone calls, tasks, appointments and e-mails. Activity records can be related to almost any other record in the application. You can view activities related to records by opening the form for those records and looking at the related lists titled Activities and Closed Activities. You can manage your individual activities by viewing the activities area in Dynamics CRM.

Connections are a simple way to link otherwise unrelated records together (such as a quote and the list of contacts that must approve the quote). Queues can be used to manage tasks that can be "claimed" by anyone on a team. You can use templates to automate regular communications with customers, prospects, and others in Dynamics CRM. Record merging allows you to remove duplicate records from the application.

The concepts discussed in this chapter are fundamental to using all other areas of Dynamics CRM. Understanding these concepts results in a shorter learning curve when working with other areas of the application.

Using Dynamics CRM for Outlook

Microsoft Outlook has become the communications, scheduling, and contact management hub for most business people. With the introduction of Outlook 2010, even social networking connections have become visible in Outlook. As a result, every CRM solution provider makes integration with Outlook a high priority for their product. As you may expect, Microsoft has done an exemplary job of integrating Dynamics CRM with Outlook. Businesses that are using Dynamics CRM report that this integration has played a significant role in reducing the learning curve for their users and getting the business to realize a return on their investment faster.

Microsoft Dynamics CRM 2011 for Outlook (also referred to as the Outlook Client) takes the already outstanding integration with Microsoft Outlook and ratchets it up a level of magnitude. As you work with Dynamics CRM for Outlook you will find that much of the Dynamics CRM functionality is available in the Outlook forms that you use every day (such as e-mail, appointments, tasks, and contacts). All of the Dynamics CRM views and forms can also be accessed directly within Outlook. When accessing Dynamics CRM views within Outlook, you have access to many of the same functions that you already use with Outlook views (such as filtering, grouping, sorting, segmenting, and setting follow-ups). Dynamics CRM for Outlook provides functionality in two areas:

IN THIS CHAPTER

Comparing the Outlook and Web versions of Dynamics CRM

Navigating the Outlook interface

Sharing data between Microsoft Outlook and Dynamics CRM

Taking Dynamics CRM offline

Using Outlook only functionality

Dynamics CRM for Outlook versus Outlook Synchronization

Synchronizing Outlook with Dynamics CRM and using Dynamics CRM for Outlook are two different things. This can be a bit confusing to understand initially. Here is a quick overview of the differences:

- Outlook synchronization means linking data that is already in Outlook (contacts, tasks, activities, and e-mails) to records in Dynamics CRM. Once this data is synced, it can be updated in either location and it will be kept in sync. Furthermore, because Outlook syncs with your mobile phone, data can also be updated there and kept in sync. But this only applies to data that Outlook tracks (such as contacts) — not the unique data that Dynamics CRM tracks (such as leads, accounts, and opportunities).

- Dynamics CRM for Outlook allows you to access all of the Dynamics CRM data and functionality directly within Microsoft Outlook. If you are taking Dynamics CRM for Outlook offline, then selected data from Dynamics CRM (such as leads, opportunities, and cases) will sync with Outlook so you can access all of the Dynamics CRM functionality even while offline.

- Core CRM Functionality: All of the functionality available within the Web version of Dynamics CRM is available directly within the Outlook user interface. This functionality is described in the section "Using Dynamics CRM within Outlook."

- Extended CRM and Outlook Functionality: Dynamics CRM for Outlook also adds functionality to Outlook that is not available directly within Dynamics CRM. This functionality enables users to quickly track their Outlook e-mails, contacts, tasks, and appointments in Dynamics CRM. It also enables direct access to Dynamics CRM templates, sales literature, and articles from within Outlook E-mail. This functionality is described in the section "Using the Outlook Extensions."

Tip

If you've used previous versions of Dynamics CRM and preferred to use the Web version, we strongly urge you to give the Outlook client another try. Microsoft has made numerous changes, and many users will find that they now prefer Dynamics CRM for Outlook.

Caution

Dynamics CRM for Outlook can be used with Microsoft Outlook versions 2003, 2007, or 2010. The instructions in this chapter assume that you are using Microsoft Outlook 2010.

Comparing the Outlook and Web Versions of Dynamics CRM

There are more similarities between the Outlook and Web interfaces of Dynamics CRM than there are differences. In fact, after you are comfortable with using either version, you may find learning the other version is an almost completely intuitive process. With that said, there are also some important differences. Which version your individual users work with is purely a matter of personal preference, so encourage your team to work with each version for a while and then decide which version is best for them.

Caution

In previous versions of Dynamics CRM, the Outlook version and the Web version functioned very similarly. In Microsoft Dynamics CRM 2011, however, Microsoft has focused a significant amount of attention on leveraging the native Outlook functionality in the Outlook version. While this has resulted in a more powerful Outlook version, it has also resulted in some differences in the user interface. Although they are still very similar, your users may experience a slight learning curve if they shift from using the Web version of Dynamics CRM to the Outlook version.

Understanding the differences: Outlook extensions and views

Even if you prefer to use the Web version of Dynamics CRM, you can still notice some helpful updates to Outlook after installing Dynamics CRM for Outlook. One of the most powerful differences is the extensions built into the Outlook forms that you use every day. For example, you will now be able to use Dynamics CRM sales literature and templates from the e-mail form whenever you send an e-mail from Outlook. You will also be able to "push" your Outlook records (including contacts, e-mails, appointments, and tasks) into CRM.

When viewing lists in Dynamics CRM for Outlook (such as leads, contacts, or opportunities), the view will look quite a bit different in the Outlook version than in the Web version. You will be able to use many native Outlook functions with these lists (such as sorting, grouping, adding fields, categorizing, and preview panes). In the Outlook version views appear in a tabbed format, whereas in the Web version they use a drop-down format. Figure 11.1 illustrates the difference between a list in Dynamics CRM for Outlook and a list in the Web version.

Understanding the similarities: Navigation, forms and data entry

The core concepts of navigating remain the same. This includes a navigation pane, Ribbon menu, forms, and related lists. Although a few of these items look slightly different or include some additional functionality, the basic concepts are the same.

After you open a Dynamics CRM form in Outlook, the form view and the data entry process are almost identical to the process you follow in the Web version. The form may look somewhat different, depending upon your Internet Explorer settings.

FIGURE 11.1

Views in the Outlook and Web versions of Dynamics CRM

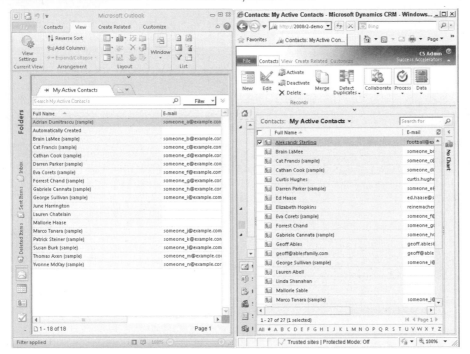

Using Dynamics CRM within Outlook

Using the Dynamics CRM interface from within Outlook is particularly helpful to users who have been using Outlook for many years. These individuals are comfortable moving around within the Outlook interface and find that the new functionality delivered by Dynamics CRM is intuitive for them to adopt. Figure 11.2 illustrates the Dynamics CRM for Outlook interface.

Caution

Microsoft Outlook has gone through some significant upgrades from version 2003 to 2007 to 2010. While it may be tempting to upgrade to a new version of Outlook at the same time that you implement Dynamics CRM, we have found that this can be detrimental. Learning two things at once (even though they are integrated) makes the learning curve steeper. Our advice is to allow at least three months after implementing Dynamics CRM before upgrading Outlook (or vice-versa).

FIGURE 11.2

The Dynamics CRM for Outlook interface including navigation pane, contacts view, tabs, and reading pane

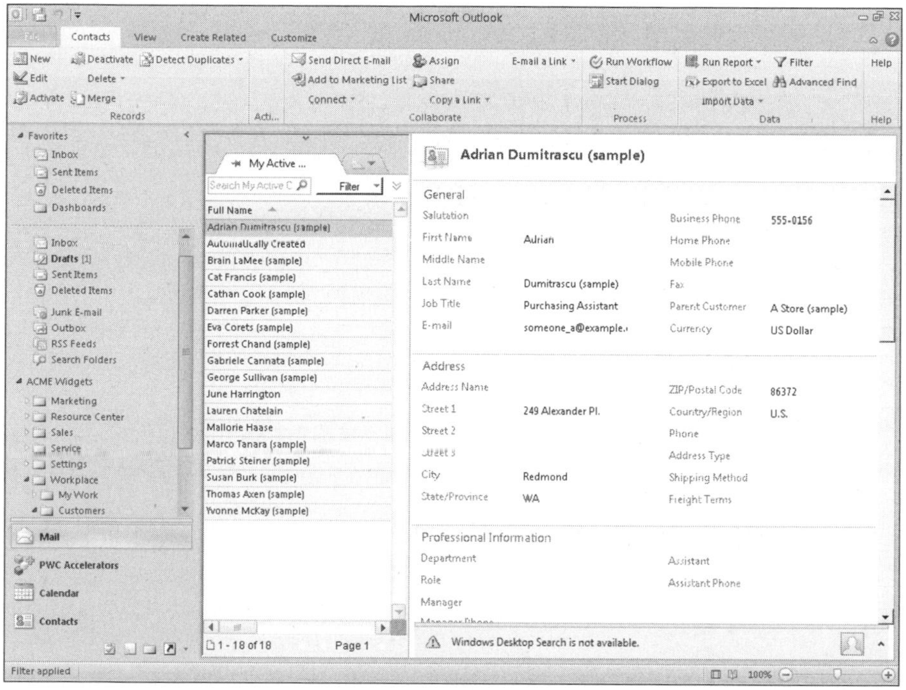

Using Outlook with Multiple CRM Organizations

Because Dynamics CRM is such a powerful application development framework, many organizations run multiple instances for different lines of business. For example, the Research and Development department may be using an instance of Dynamics CRM to track their projects. Sales may also be using CRM to manage prospects and customers.

In Outlook, you can see both instances of Dynamics CRM as a separate set of folders. This capability allows users to visit the R&D instance to check the status of a project and then go right back to the Sales instance to communicate with a customer.

When you set up multiple Dynamics CRM instances (also referred to as organizations or orgs) in Outlook, only the instance designated as your main organization will synchronize.

Using the Outlook navigation pane

Dynamics CRM installs as another area inside of Outlook just like your mail and contacts. To start using Dynamics CRM in Outlook, click on the menu item in the Outlook navigation pane labeled Solutions. You see a new set of folders that is very similar to what you see in the Web version of the navigation pane. Click on an item to see the list for that particular Dynamics CRM area.

Working with Dynamics CRM views in Outlook

When working with views in Dynamics CRM for Outlook, you have access to all of the same functionality that you use when working with other Outlook views (such as contacts, tasks, and calendar appointments). Having access to native Outlook functionality is helpful because it enables each user to configure their lists and views to work in the manner that is the most comfortable for them. The stronger your skills are with Outlook views, the more quickly you adapt to working with CRM views within Outlook.

The fundamentals of the view functionality remain the same in Outlook. Views present a list of all records in a Dynamics CRM entity. You select different views to filter your lists, and you can use the Ribbon menu to interact with records in a view. But the similarities end there.

The look and feel of views in Outlook are quite different from what you see in the Web. In addition, views in Outlook add some exciting and useful functionality that is not available in the Web version of Dynamics CRM. Outlook also includes a number of ways that you can personalize views to match your specific preferences.

Using tabs as views

Views in Outlook are presented as tabs. To open a view, click on the right-most tab and select the view that you want to open. You will notice that your old view stays open as a tab and your new view is visible as a new tab. Tabs give you several new capabilities in Outlook that are not available in the Web version:

- Full views: Unlike the Web version, which displays only 50 to 250 records at a time, tabs view in Outlook displays an unlimited number of records at a time.

- Default views: Tabs that have their pushpin selected (facing up and down rather than left-to-right) will remain visible by default the next time you open Outlook and navigate to the selected view.

Filtering views

You can change the filtering settings for a view by clicking the Filter button just below the tabs. Use the Add Filter option to add a new filter. To display a list of filters that are currently applied to a view, click the "double arrow" button to the right of the Filter button. You can interactively change the list of current filters by hovering over each line of the filter and using the buttons that appear next to the filter.

Tip

If you make changes to a filter, and you want these changes to be remembered the next time you open the filter, then be sure to save the changes. To update a personal view, click the Filter button below the tabs and choose Save Filters to Current View. To create a new view, click the Filter button and choose Save Filters as New View.

Formatting views

Dynamics CRM views can be sorted, filtered, categorized, grouped, and formatted in exactly the manner that you prefer using the view management features built into Outlook. The features that allow you to configure a view are available through a number of different parts of the user interface. You can left-click on a view to access some features, you can select the filter drop-down below the tabs to filter a view, and you can click column headings to interactively sort a view. To access all of the view formatting features in one place, navigate to the view that you wish to format and from the View tab on the Ribbon menu, click the View Settings button. These settings are automatically remembered when you navigate back to the view. Figure 11.3 is an example of the view settings dialog box; below the image is a brief description of how each of the buttons can be used.

- **Columns:** Use this button to add new columns to the existing view or to reorganize the existing columns. After clicking this button, select User-defined fields in folder in order to display fields from Dynamics CRM to add to the view. You can also select Frequently-used field to put common outlook fields such as categories and flag status on the form.

- **Group By:** Use this button to display a view in groups. For example, you can group opportunities by parent company, contacts by state, and activities by due date. Grouping a view, as illustrated in Figure 11.4, creates a "twisty" above each group that can be used to quickly drill down into a set of records.

FIGURE 11.3

The Advanced View Settings dialog box

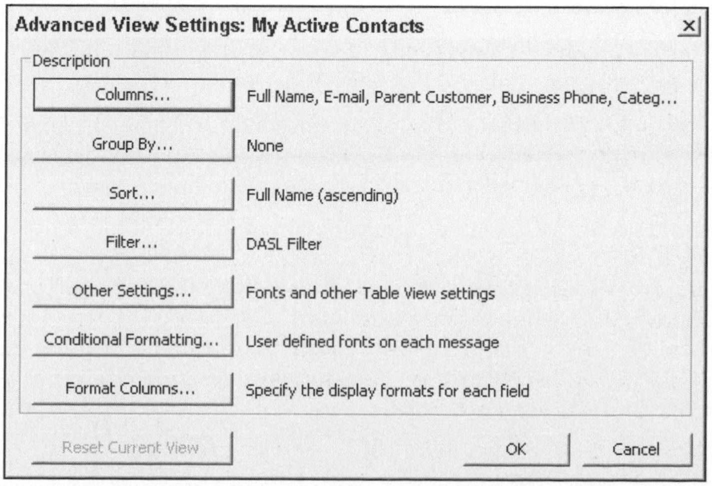

FIGURE 11.4

Contacts grouped by parent customer and using conditional formatting

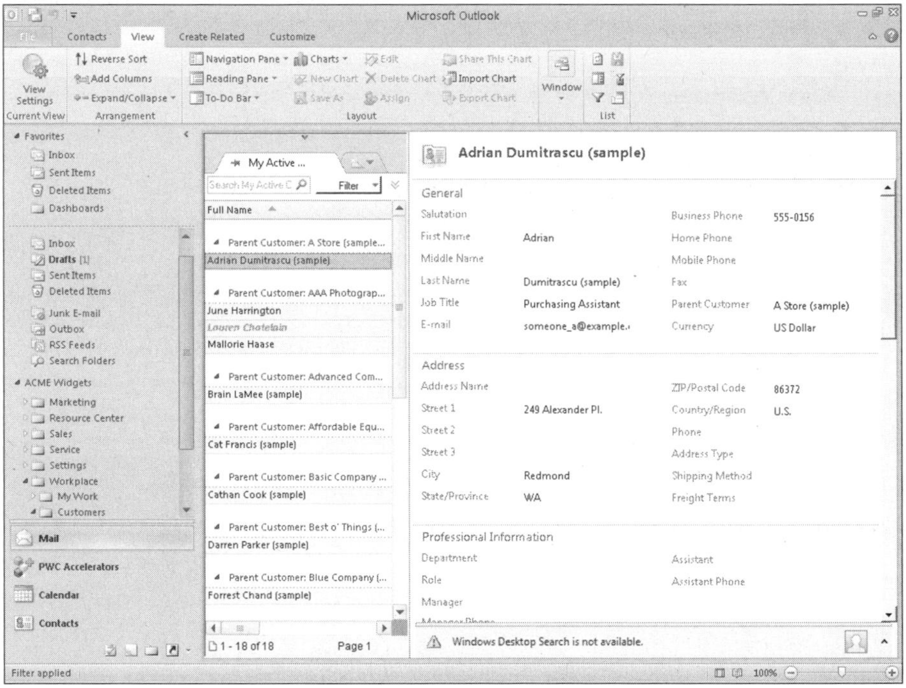

- **Sort:** This button enables you to sort your list by a broad range of criteria.

- **Filter:** The filter button allows some limited functionality. However, we recommend that you use the filter button below the tab if you wish to change the filter criteria for a view.

- **Other Settings:** This button provides control over fonts and some other formatting settings.

- **Conditional Formatting:** This button provides the capability to format records in the view differently depending on the underlying data. For example, in Figure 11.4, we have configured one name to show up in bold italics based on their state.

- **Format Columns:** This last button allows you to format the width and format of individual columns. For the most part, the settings behind this button can be accessed by interactively clicking a column divider and dragging it to change the width.

Setting up Outlook categories, follow-ups, and reminders on Dynamics CRM records

Microsoft Outlook includes tools for categorizing (or tagging) records, scheduling follow-ups, and setting up reminders.

To set,up a category, follow-up, or reminder, right-click on the record in a view that you want to mark. Make your selection from the popup menu (select either Catcgorize or Follow Up). If you want to schedule a reminder, then under the Follow Up option, select Add Reminder. Note that you can also select the Create option from the popup menu to create a related Dynamics CRM activity if you prefer.

To view records grouped by category, right-click on any column header and choose Arrange By and then Categories. As illustrated in Figure 11.5, you can expand and collapse category groups interactively when using this view.

FIGURE 11.5

Outlook categories and follow-ups in a Dynamics CRM for Outlook view

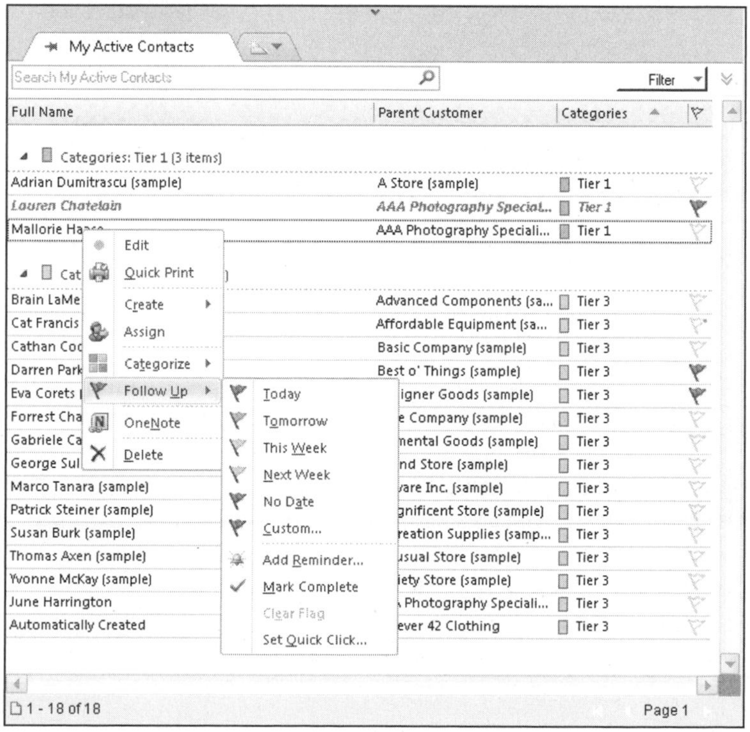

The reading pane

The familiar Outlook reading pane is available as you navigate through the records in a view. The reading pane provides a read-only view of the complete form for the record that is currently selected in the view.

You can customize where the reading pane appears by clicking on the View tab on the Ribbon menu and then clicking the Reading Pane button. You can display the pane on the right, bottom, or hide it completely. Outlook remembers your setting the next time you open the view.

You can also customize how sections are shown in the reading pane by clicking the title of a section and dragging it to a different section in the pane. Sections can be hidden completely by clicking the View tab in the Ribbon menu and then clicking the Customize Reading Pane button.

The people pane

When using Dynamics CRM within Outlook, you also have access to the Outlook people pane. The people pane provides a list of communications, tasks, and social contacts you have had with the individual you are currently viewing as shown in Figure 11.6. The people pane can be made visible, minimized, or completely hidden using the view tab on the Ribbon menu. Note that only e-mails and activities stored in Outlook will be visible in the people pane (items that are stored in Dynamics CRM are not visible in the people pane).

FIGURE 11.6

The people pane

Taking Dynamics CRM offline

Because Outlook can be accessed even when you're not connected to your business network, you can view and create e-mails, contacts, and activities when you are away from the office. When you connect to the network again, all of your changes synchronize and e-mails are sent and received.

Taking Dynamics CRM for Outlook offline works in a similar manner. You can still access most of your information while offline and make updates. When you go back online, all of your changes are synchronized. This only applies to Dynamics CRM for Outlook (not the Web version of Dynamics CRM); and the offline capability must be installed prior to going offline for the first time.

Cross-Reference
For more information on the versions of Dynamics CRM for Outlook and how to install them, see Chapter 4.

Going offline and online

Before going offline, go to the CRM tab of the Ribbon menu and click the Go Offline button. If you have not already installed the offline capability, then you will be prompted for this installation. Dynamics CRM will then synchronize your data to your local computer. Once this process has been completed, you can safely disconnect your computer from the network and shut down.

Tip
If you forget to click the Go Offline button before leaving the office, Dynamics CRM will automatically use data from the most recently available synchronization.

To go back online, begin by making sure that you are connected to your network. Then navigate to the Ribbon menu in Outlook, choose the CRM tab, and select Go Online. Dynamics CRM synchronizes all the data from your local computer to the CRM server, so you can get right back to work!

Tip
Like Outlook, Dynamics CRM can usually automatically detect when you are online. In these cases, it will automatically reconnect to your network and sync your data.

Choosing data for offline usage

By default Dynamics CRM does a pretty good job of synchronizing the data you're most likely to use while offline. You can fine-tune these settings by using local data groups. To access local data groups:

1. Make sure you are currently working online.
2. In the Outlook Ribbon menu, choose File ⇨ CRM.

3. If you are working with multiple organizations, then choose the organization you want to configure near the top of the screen.

4. Select the Synchronize button and then click on Outlook Filters. You are presented with the Local Data dialog box. In the upper-right side of the dialog, make sure that you have selected the Offline Synchronization Filters option from the picklist, as shown in Figure 11.7. Each item that appears in the User Filters tab is a data group and represents data that will synchronize to be available offline. You can add and change the filters or you can deactivate filters that you no longer wish to use. Changing filter criteria is similar to creating personal views with advanced find in Dynamics CRM (see Chapter 10 for more information).

5. After you finish editing the filters, click OK.

Troubleshooting Dynamics CRM for Outlook

If you run into unexpected difficulties using Dynamics CRM for Outlook, run the included diagnostics program. From the Windows Start menu, navigate to Microsoft Dynamics CRM 2011 ⇨ Diagnostics. Select the appropriate options on each tab and click the Save button.

FIGURE 11.7

The Local Data dialog box with Offline Synchronization Filters selected

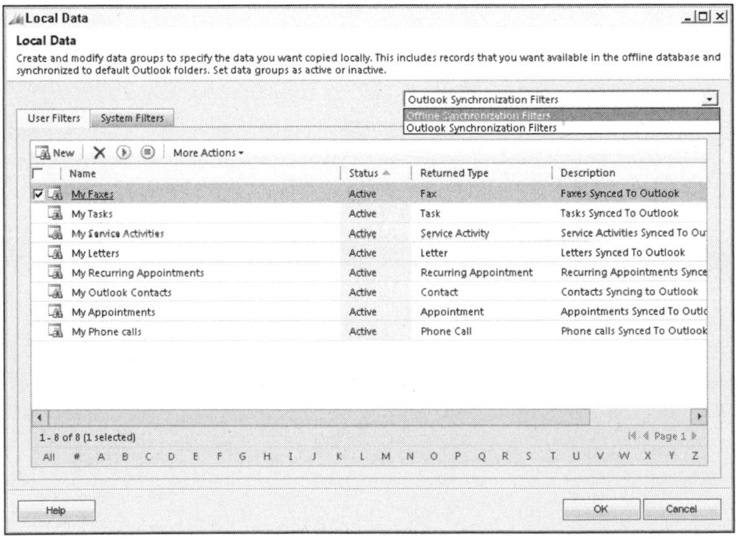

Using the Outlook Extensions

In addition to using Dynamics CRM within Outlook, as described in the preceding section, the Outlook client also adds a number of new extensions to Outlook. These extensions embed CRM capabilities directly into the parts of Microsoft Outlook that you use every day. As you become familiar with these extensions, you will quickly realize a boost to productivity.

With most competitive CRM solutions, even those that include Outlook integration, users are forced to constantly toggle back and forth between their CRM software and Microsoft Outlook to get their jobs done. With Dynamics CRM for Outlook, the most important parts of CRM functionality will be available at your fingertips while you are sending e-mail, working through your to-do list, setting appointments, or interacting with clients and prospects.

Tracking Outlook records in Dynamics CRM

Records from Outlook can be pushed into Dynamics CRM to create a link; once the link is made, the records will automatically be kept in sync. This "push" is generally a simple, but manual process that users go through for each record that they want to track. This is by design because many individuals track personal information in Outlook such as e-mail and contact records for family members — and they don't want this information automatically visible to their colleagues in Dynamics CRM.

Cross-Reference

If would like to bulk import your Outlook contacts or Outlook of Business Contact Manager information, see Chapter 8.

Tracking in CRM and setting regarding

Regardless of which type of Outlook record you are tracking (contact, task, e-mail, or appointment), the process is similar:

1. Navigate to the record in Outlook that you want to sync with CRM.

2. Click on the record to select it in Outlook (this also works if you open the record).

3. Using the Ribbon menu, click on the first tab to the right of the File tab (in most cases, this tab will already be selected). Using the CRM section of the tab, take one of the following actions:

   - If you want to sync the record without setting a regarding field, then click the Track button.

   - If you want to sync the record and regard it to another record (recommended) then click the Set Regarding button (or, in the case of a contact, if you want to link it to a parent record, then click the Set Parent button) and select the record that it should be regarding.

Outlook and Dynamics CRM: Better Together

We have run into a number of organizations that use Dynamics CRM without connecting it to Microsoft Outlook. Dynamics CRM is not a complete CRM solution without making the connection to Microsoft Outlook. Consider some of the advantages of using Dynamics CRM and Outlook together before you opt out of using it with Outlook:

- **Alerts:** Dynamics CRM does not include popup alerts. If you want to get an alert when you have an upcoming appointment, you need to sync with Outlook.

- **Calendars:** The calendar view in Outlook is much more powerful than the calendar view built into Dynamics CRM. If you want drag-and-drop calendaring and visibility into colleague's calendars, you need to sync Dynamics CRM with Outlook.

- **E-mail Tracking:** For most businesses, the majority of the communication that they have with clients and prospects takes place via e-mail. Without the link to Outlook, you won't be able to track all of these e-mail communications in Dynamics CRM.

These items are only the simple everyday items that can improve user productivity and adoption of Dynamics CRM. In addition to these, Dynamics CRM for Outlook delivers dozens of other features and extensions to further boost productivity, improve the customer experience, and aid your users in getting up to speed faster.

4. If the record that you tracked was an e-mail, then Dynamics CRM will link it to the correct contact in CRM (by matching the e-mail address). Depending on your personal settings, Dynamics CRM will also create a contact and/or account in Dynamics CRM if a matching one does not exist.

Cross-Reference

Your personal settings play an important role in determining how Outlook information will be used to create new records in Dynamics CRM. For more information on changing your personal settings, see Chapter 6.

Tracking e-mail threads

After you track an e-mail, Dynamics CRM for Outlook will automatically track all subsequent e-mails in the thread. This means that whenever you or one of the other recipients replies to a tracked e-mail, the reply is automatically tracked and visible in Dynamics CRM. This can save quite a bit of time in situations where you have a long trail of e-mail communications that you wish to track.

Tip

You can configure Dynamics CRM for Outlook to automatically track some (or all) e-mails without having to click the Track or Set Regarding buttons. This setting can be found within Outlook by navigating to File ⇨ CRM ⇨ Options ⇨ E-mail tab. We recommend taking care with these settings as they may result in personal or confidential e-mail getting tracked in Dynamics CRM.

Untracking and re-regarding Outlook records

Outlook items that are being tracked in Dynamics CRM can be untracked by clicking the Untrack button. The behavior associated with clicking the Untrack button varies depending on which type of record you select when clicking the button and is summarized in Table 11.1.

TABLE 11.1

Untrack Behavior

Record Type	Untrack Results
Contact	The link between the Outlook contact and the Dynamics CRM contact is broken. The record is not deleted in Outlook or in Dynamics CRM. If you click Track on the contact in Outlook again, a duplicate contact will be created in Dynamics CRM.
E-mail, Task, or Appointment	The selected Outlook record is deleted from Dynamics CRM.

Set Regarding versus Track

When you begin using Dynamics CRM for Outlook, it may be a bit confusing deciding between clicking the Track button or the Set Regarding button. For many users, the natural inclination is to use Track because it is a single-button click, whereas Set Regarding takes a few more clicks. Our recommendation, however, is to use Set Regarding in almost all cases. The extra few clicks will pay off with information that is easier to find in Dynamics CRM.

Using the track button, the record will be pushed from Outlook into Dynamics CRM with only a single-button click. However, the record will only be linked to e-mail addresses that have already been associated with it in Outlook.

For example, clicking Track on an e-mail record will link the e-mail to any contact that is listed in the from, to, cc, or bcc fields. However, most e-mails are "regarding" a certain record (such as an opportunity, quote or case) — clicking Track will not link to these items. If, however, you click the Set Regarding button, then you can pick the opportunity, quote, case, or other record to link the item to. After choosing a record using the Set Regarding button, you will be able to find the e-mail in the closed activities list under the selected record in Dynamics CRM.

In the case of Outlook contacts, if you click only the Track button, the contact will be pushed into Dynamics CRM but it will not be listed under a parent customer. For most businesses (and particularly for businesses that sell to other businesses) it is important to have all contacts listed under an account record. Using the Set Parent button enables you to immediately link the contact to the correct parent customer in Dynamics CRM.

When using Set Regarding, records in Outlook are associated not only with the record that you manually select, they are also still associated with the contact e-mail addresses associated with the record. Dynamics CRM, in turn, "rolls up" these contact associations to the parent customer record. So, when you use Set Regarding, you will be able to view the closed activity history on the record that was manually selected, all associated contacts, and all parent customers above those contacts.

If you mistakenly regard an Outlook record to the wrong Dynamics CRM record, just navigate to the record in Outlook again, click the Set Regarding button, and choose the new record to regard it to.

Setting connections

After an Outlook record is being tracked in Dynamics CRM, you can set a connection between the record and any Dynamics CRM record that is capable of tracking connections. For example, you can set a connection between an e-mail and an opportunity. To set a connection, begin by tracking the record, then click the Add Connection button in the Ribbon menu, and choose the record to connect to.

Connecting Outlook records to other Dynamics CRM records can be useful for a number of reasons. You may wish to connect an e-mail to a case in the event that a client sends you an e-mail related to two cases. Making this connection allows you to create a link between all the cases that the e-mail is related to.

You may also wish to connect to a Dynamics CRM record to support a specific business process. For example, you may want to be able to easily find an e-mail that contains a final signed version of a contract for each opportunity. Using the standard set regarding functionality may not be sufficient because a user may have to wade through hundreds of e-mails to find the one with the proposal attached. Using connections, the user can connect the e-mail to the opportunity with a role of Signed Proposal to make it easy to find in the future.

Navigating to Dynamics CRM records from Outlook

Once a record in Outlook is tracked in Dynamics CRM, there are a number of ways to navigate to the record or to other related records. These are shown in Figure 11.8.

In the Ribbon menu, you can navigate to the record by clicking the View in CRM button. On contact records, you can view the parent customer record by clicking the View Parent button in the Ribbon menu.

At the bottom of Outlook records that are tracked in Dynamics CRM is a CRM information pane. In this pane, you can update the record that it is regarding. You can also navigate to any of the records that it is linked to. For example, you can navigate to every contact that an e-mail or appointment is related to by using the information pane.

Converting an Outlook record to a Dynamics CRM opportunity, lead or case

Oftentimes, an Outlook activity will lead directly to a follow-up action that needs to be recorded in Dynamics CRM. The Outlook client includes the capability to convert an e-mail, appointment, or task directly into an opportunity, lead. or case in Dynamics CRM. To convert an item, start by tracking it in Dynamics CRM; then click the Convert button in the Ribbon menu and select the desired action.

FIGURE 11.8

Navigating to records using the Ribbon menu or information pane

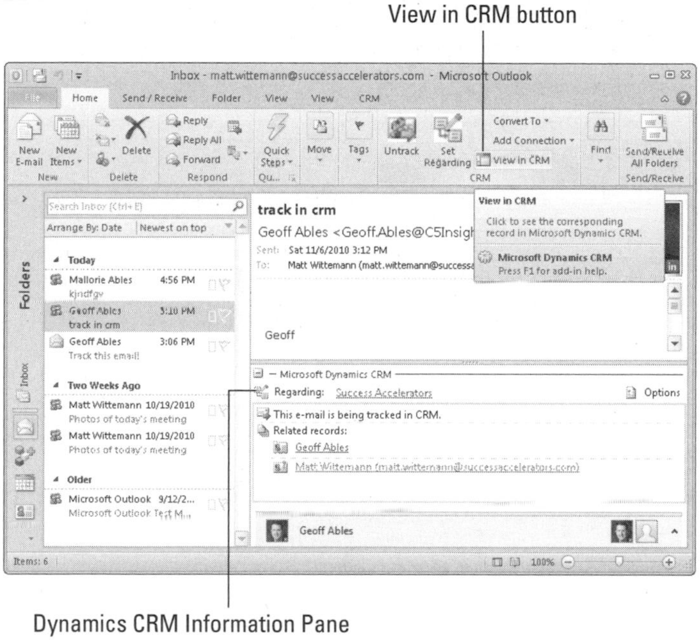

View in CRM button

Dynamics CRM Information Pane

Synchronizing from Dynamics CRM to Outlook

When you enter contacts or some types of activities (tasks, appointments, phone calls) into Dynamics CRM, they are automatically synchronized with your Microsoft Outlook. For example, when you add a contact or a task in Dynamics CRM, these records will automatically become available in Outlook after the next synchronization. If you have Outlook syncing with your mobile device, then all of your contacts and activities will flow from Dynamics CRM to Outlook and then to your mobile device with almost no effort on your part.

Note that not all activities are synchronized between Dynamics CRM and Outlook. Figure 11.9 illustrates which records are synchronized between Outlook and Dynamics CRM.

Tip

In order to have data sync between Microsoft Outlook and Dynamics CRM, you need to be sure that you have the Dynamics CRM for Outlook installed on your computer.

FIGURE 11.9

Data that is synchronized between Outlook and Dynamics CRM

Microsoft Outlook (manual sync)		Dynamics CRM (auto sync)
Contacts	⟺	Contacts
Appointments	⟺	Appointments
Tasks	⟺	Tasks
		Phone Calls
		Faxes
		Letters
E-mail	⟹	E-mail

Choosing records for automatic synchronization

Oftentimes you will want to synchronize more than just the Dynamics CRM records that you own with Microsoft Outlook. For example, a Sales Manager may want to synchronize all of the contacts owned by all of the Sales Reps on his team. Changing which records automatically sync between Outlook and Dynamics CRM is almost exactly the same as changing the records that are available when taking Dynamics CRM for Outlook offline. For more information on this process, see the "Choosing data for offline usage" section earlier in this chapter. When following the instructions, be sure to choose Outlook Synchronization Filters from the picklist in Step 4.

Updating synchronized records

After a record has been synchronized between Outlook and Dynamics CRM, it can be updated in either place and the changes will be synchronized. If Outlook is synchronized with a mobile device, then you can make changes there and they will flow back to Outlook and then into Dynamics CRM too. So you can make changes to your records wherever it is most convenient for you, and the changes will be reflected everywhere else automatically.

Manual and automatic synchronization

Depending on your personal settings, the automatic synchronization between Dynamics CRM and Outlook occurs as frequently as every 15 minutes. If you want to synchronize data right away, you can navigate to the Ribbon menu in Outlook, click the CRM tab, and click the Synchronize button. To change synchronization preferences, from Outlook navigate to File ➪ CRM ➪ Options ➪ Synchronization tab.

Using Dynamics CRM e-mail features within Outlook

Microsoft Outlook is the most popular e-mail management tool in the world, yet CRM tools (including earlier versions of Dynamics CRM) force users to work within their own watered-down e-mail tool to leverage important CRM functionality. Dynamics CRM 2011 adds subtle, but powerful features directly into Outlook. These new features result in better user performance and more powerful CRM e-mail management capabilities.

Cross-Reference

In addition to the functions outlined within this section, e-mail in Microsoft Outlook can be synchronized with Dynamics CRM. For more information on this, see the section "Tracking Outlook records in Dynamics CRM" elsewhere in this chapter.

Tip

Dynamics CRM is not intended to be used as your e-mail inbox. Outlook is a much more powerful tool for reading and composing e-mails. You should plan to continue to use Outlook as your e-mail communication tool.

Sending Dynamics CRM templates, articles, and sales literature from Outlook

In the past, users needed to send e-mail from Dynamics CRM if they wanted to use templates, sales literature, or articles from the Dynamics CRM knowledge base. While this can still be done within the Dynamics CRM Web client, these resources can also be accessed directly within Microsoft Outlook. This can save time, drive higher quality and consistently formatted communications, and enable users to leverage the built-in Outlook e-mail capabilities that are not available within Dynamics CRM (such as managing signatures, visual editing, and adding images). To use these capabilities:

1. Make sure that you have a template, sales literature item, or article available in Dynamics CRM.

2. Create a new e-mail message in Microsoft Outlook.

3. In the Ribbon menu, click the Set Regarding button in the CRM section and choose the record that the e-mail will be regarding. The three buttons on the right-hand side of the CRM section of the Ribbon menu will become active.

4. Click the button that describes the item that you wish to attach (Insert Template, Insert Article, or Attach Sales Literature) and follow the instructions to use the item that you want. Note that you can attach multiple pieces of sales literature.

5. Make any changes that you want to the e-mail.

6. Send the e-mail as you normally would.

Creating new leads and contacts

If you receive an e-mail from an e-mail address that is not already in Dynamics CRM, the individual can quickly be added to Dynamics CRM as a new lead or a new contact. This can be done automatically or manually, depending upon your preferences.

To have all new e-mail addresses automatically added to Dynamics CRM, within Outlook navigate to File ➪ CRM ➪ Options ➪ E-mail tab. From this tab you can select to automatically create records and, if so, which type of record (lead or contact) to automatically create. If you prefer, you can deactivate this capability and manually create leads or contacts only when you want to.

To manually create a new lead or contact from an e-mail, open the CRM information pane at the bottom of the e-mail and click on any e-mail address that is highlighted in red. From the popup menu, choose to create either a lead or a contact. Follow the prompts to enter the basic information about the record. We recommend that you immediately open the record after creating it so you can enter the relevant details right away.

Summary

Integration with Microsoft Outlook is not an "add on" for Dynamics CRM; it is a core part of the application. In fact, using Dynamics CRM for Outlook doesn't just give you access to Dynamics CRM functions within Outlook; it delivers an entirely new set of functions, including some of the most important portions of the product. To extract the greatest possible value from Dynamics CRM, you need to understand and leverage the Outlook integration.

Dynamics CRM 2011 includes many improvements to the Outlook version. Individuals who have used only the Web version of Dynamics CRM in earlier versions should reconsider the Outlook version in order to leverage these new features.

Dynamics CRM also synchronizes with data from Outlook (such as contacts, tasks, activities, and e-mails). This synchronization allows you to update these records either in Outlook or in Dynamics CRM, and they will be updated in both places. Because Outlook also synchronizes with your mobile device, you may also update records there. Records created in Dynamics CRM auto-sync with Outlook. Records created in Outlook or on your mobile device must be manually synced with Dynamics CRM.

Using the Sales Functions

The sales functionality in Dynamics CRM improves sales productivity through all stages of the business development lifecycle. Your organization can ensure that leads are followed up and qualified in a timely manner, opportunities follow consistent best practices, territories are aligned, and existing accounts receive regular contact. Sales reps can be more productive and efficient by keying less data, shortening sales cycles, and ensuring that no opportunities slip between the cracks. The reporting functions give management visibility into the pipeline to forecast sales revenue and analyze trends to uncover threats and opportunities.

In addition to the sales functions available out of the box, Dynamics CRM also includes customization tools so you can configure and extend this functionality to work the way that your business does. In fact, Dynamics CRM was built with the intention that it be tailored to follow your unique business process. In this chapter, we focus on the sales functionality available out of the box, but be aware that customization (discussed throughout this book) is critical if you want to maximize the value in your Dynamics CRM investment.

IN THIS CHAPTER

Creating and qualifying leads

Opportunity and pipeline management

Product catalog fundamentals

Quotes, orders, and invoices

Cross-Reference

Keep in mind that you need to learn some prerequisites before reading this chapter. In Chapter 1, we define a number of terms and concepts that are important to understand before jumping into sales with Dynamics CRM. In Chapter 10, we review many core functions that you should understand before using the specific sales functions.

Understanding the Sales Lifecycle

In our experience, most sales processes fall into one of four broad areas. Shown in Figure 12.1, these areas include:

- **Lead Management:** Lead records contain information about individuals that you do not yet have any relationship with, and you have not yet determined if you are interested in pursuing a relationship with them.

- **Opportunity Management:** Opportunities are potential sales deals that you are actively working on with a prospect or customer with a goal of eventually converting them into revenue for your business. Records in the opportunity funnel typically go through several stages before being won or lost.

- **Sales Transactions:** Sales transactions may consist of quotes, orders, and/or invoices. These interrelated steps of the process are sometimes handled in accounting systems and sometimes in Dynamics CRM.

- **Account Management:** Managing existing client accounts is the most frequently overlooked part of the sales process. The best source of new business is your existing or past customer base — but many organizations stop following up with customers after their first transaction. This topic is not specifically covered in this chapter, but some concepts around it are discussed in Chapter 10.

FIGURE 12.1

Overview of a sales process

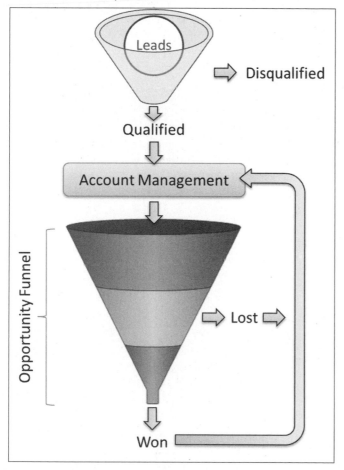

Managing Leads

Lead records represent a person or company that you may be interested in doing business with. In some cases, a lead may not even yet know about you and your company. Leads have a specific lifetime. They start life when you initially learn of the lead through your Web site, acquiring a list, by referral, or any other channel. They reach the end of their life when you determine that they are (or are not) qualified to do business with you and you qualify them. The duration of a lead's lifetime varies greatly for different organizations. In all cases, the objective is to minimize the time between generating a lead and (dis)qualifying it.

Cross-Reference

For information on lead reports that you can use to track the effectiveness of you lead management campaigns and processes, see Chapter 26.

Creating leads

Organizations typically use a broad range of tools to generate leads. For this reason, there are usually a variety of different ways that new leads can enter your system:

- **Data entry:** Sales reps may enter the contact information of people that they met through networking into Dynamics CRM as individual leads.

- **Web-to-Lead:** Many businesses generate a large volume of leads through their Web site. Your Web site can be set up to automatically convert information entered into a Web form into a Dynamics CRM lead. Having this process automated reduces data entry time, improves quality, and can ensure a rapid follow-up (see the nearby sidebar"Lead Automation").

- **Social Networking Accelerator:** Social networks are becoming just as important in generating leads as are corporate Web sites. Microsoft offers a free add-in (on www.codeplex.com) to convert social network contacts into leads.

- **Import:** Leads can be imported into Dynamics CRM in bulk. This may include purchased lists, conference attendees, or scanned business cards.

- **Marketing campaigns:** Marketing campaigns can result in the generation of new leads that are added to Dynamics CRM. See the next chapter for more information on marketing campaigns.

Tip

Many organizations train their teams to always create a lead first — even if you know that you will immediately convert it to a qualified account, contact, and opportunity. This ensures a consistent record creation process and can also save some time with data entry. Experiment with creating a lead first or creating an account, contact, and opportunity separately to see which process works best for you.

Working leads

A variety of functionality can be applied against leads to ensure that they receive appropriate follow up. Below is a brief overview of the functionality to consider (see the nearby sidebar "Lead Automation" for other ideas):

- **Views:** You can use views to see which leads have been added to your list of leads recently.

- **Activities:** Schedule activities for your leads to ensure that none of them slip through the cracks.

- **Queues:** Assign leads to queues to be certain that the first available person can follow up with each lead.

- **Dialogs:** Use Dialogs to ensure that your lead qualification team is gathering consistent information and is following a consistent process to qualify leads.

- **Workflows:** Use workflows to automate the usage of the above items.

- **Reports:** Use the neglected leads report to see if any leads have not received follow-up in a timely manner.

Lead Automation

Lead management is an area of the sales process that often lends itself to automation to improve the efficiency, effectiveness, and consistency of the process. Here are seven ideas to consider implementing to speed your lead management process:

1. **Web-to-Lead:** In many businesses, Web leads often sit in an e-mail inbox until someone can determine who to forward them to, at which point they sit in another inbox until they're worked. Worse still, there is no way to see which leads have been worked and which have been dropped. Invest the time to connect your Web site to Dynamics CRM to automatically convert Web contacts to leads and use the other items recommended here to streamline follow-up.

2. **Auto-Assign Leads:** Use workflows to automatically assign leads to the appropriate person, team, or queue. Workflows will allow you to assign leads based on location, product interest, or any other field. You can also have leads temporarily assigned to marketing who can then manually assign them to the right person for follow-up.

3. **New Lead Alert:** Whenever a new lead is assigned to an individual, use a workflow to send them an e-mail with the phone number and the e-mail address of the lead. Also assign a phone call follow-up task to the person. This helps to ensure the reps can follow up with their leads right away — even when they're out of the office. The follow-up phone activity enables you to track how quickly the leads have been followed up.

4. **Lead Auto-Responder:** In some cases (Web leads in particular), you can set up an auto-response rule to e-mail the lead after the record has been created. Ideally, do this after the lead has been assigned to someone so you can send them a personalized e-mail such as, "Hi, my name is Geoff and I have been assigned to work with you." This creates a personal link between the lead and their representative within minutes of the time that they have hit your Web site.

5. **Unworked Lead Escalation:** Chances are, you've made a pretty big marketing investment in generating leads and you don't want that investment to go to waste. Using workflow, escalate leads to a manager or to a queue if they are not followed up promptly.

6. **Nurture:** Set up a series of automated communications that you can apply to dormant leads to ensure that they continue to be nurtured even if you do not have enough resources to follow up with all of them.

7. **Reporting:** Set up reports so you can determine which programs and which individuals are doing the best job of generating leads and converting them into new business.

Cross-Reference

To learn more about setting up these automation techniques, see Chapter 10 to learn about activities, Chapter 18 to learn about Dialogs and workflows, and Chapter 19 to learn about queues.

Qualifying Leads

When you make contact with a lead, your purpose will be to determine if they are qualified (your organization would like to establish a relationship with them) or unqualified (you cannot engage in a mutually beneficial relationship with them). The criteria used to determine qualification varies widely for each organization, but the end result is the same — you will need to qualify the lead.

Cross-Reference

See Chapter 1 to learn more about the difference between a lead and an opportunity and when to qualify a lead into an opportunity.

Tip

In most organizations, it is important that consistent lead qualification criteria are met. You can add qualification criteria as required fields (see Chapter 18) and even set up a scoring system to rank your leads using JavaScript (discussed in Chapter 21).

To qualify a lead, open the lead record in Dynamics CRM and click the Qualify button in the Ribbon menu. You will then see the dialog box in Figure 12.2, which provides two primary options for qualifying the lead. Choose the appropriate option and, if appropriate, move forward with managing the opportunity:

- **Qualify:** When you qualify a lead, Dynamics CRM creates at least one of the following: an account, a contact, and/or an opportunity. It sets the lead status to qualified and deactivates the lead record (so that you cannot edit it, but it can still be used for reporting). Figure 12.3 illustrates this process and the options.

Tip

When qualifying a lead, you can check the Open newly created records check box to open the records created by Dynamics CRM immediately after they are created. This can be a time-saver when you need to modify the records immediately after they are qualified.

- **Disqualify:** When using this option, you can choose a reason why the lead has been disqualified. Dynamics CRM then sets the status to disqualified and deactivates the lead. This removes the lead from the list of leads you are working.

FIGURE 12.2

The lead conversion dialog box

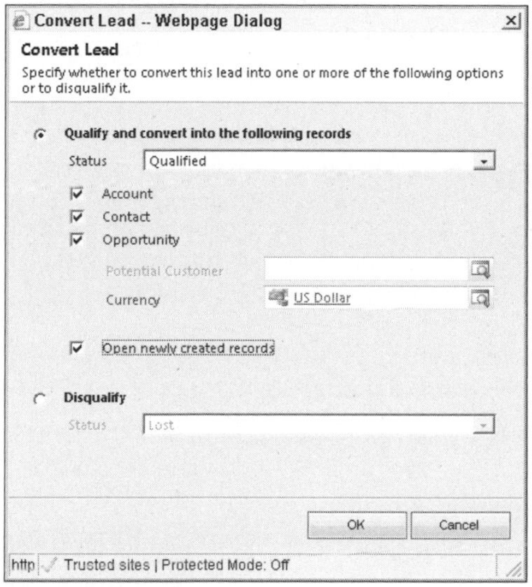

Convert Lead -- Webpage Dialog
Convert Lead
Specify whether to convert this lead into one or more of the following options or to disqualify it.
Qualify and convert into the following records
Status
Qualified
Account
Contact
Opportunity
Potential Customer
Currency
US Dollar
Open newly created records
Disqualify
Status
Lost
OK
Cancel
http Trusted sites | Protected Mode: Off

FIGURE 12.3

The lead conversion process

Company Information
Contact Information
Convert
Qualified
Disqualified
Account
Contact
Opportunity

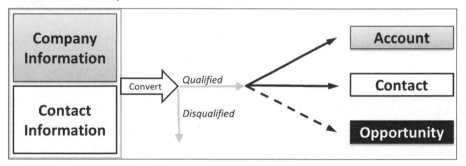

Managing Opportunities

Opportunities are the centerpiece of sales functionality in Dynamics CRM. An opportunity is a potential sales deal. Using opportunities, an organization can forecast revenues by assigning a probability and an expected amount to each opportunity. Conventional forecasts take sales from the previous year and project how much an organization will improve upon those figures. Opportunity management enables an organization to gauge likely sales based on what is actually in the pipeline now and how successful the organization has previously been in closing sales deals.

Opportunities are similar to leads in that they have a limited lifetime. In highly transactional organizations, an opportunity can be discovered, won, and closed all in a single telephone call. In organizations that pursue large contracts over a long period of time, an opportunity may remain open for months or even years. Most organizations have a combination of opportunity types, and it is important to define different sales processes for each of these different opportunity types.

Important opportunity fields

The opportunity form includes a large number of fields, possibly including custom fields that your organization has added. Among these are some important fields that you need to understand to make effective use of opportunity records, including:

- **Topic:** This is a description of the opportunity and generally includes the product or service that the potential customer is interested in.

- **Potential Customer:** This links to either an account or a contact. Generally this is an account for B2B organizations, and for B2C organizations this is a contact. Many B2B organizations add the primary contact as a second field on the opportunity.

- **Owner:** This is the individual (or team) that is responsible for this opportunity.

- **Est. Close Date:** This is the date that the rep expects this opportunity will be won or lost. We recommend making this field required and using this for reporting purposes to make sure that no reps have past due opportunities in their pipeline.

- **Price List:** If you are planning to use a list of products for this opportunity, then you should plug a value into this field. See the product catalog section later in this chapter for more information.

- **Revenue:** If this field is set to System Calculated, then the estimated revenue (below) will be calculated automatically by aggregating the revenue on each of the products for this opportunity. If this field is set to User Provided, then the estimated revenue will be keyed in by the user.

- **Estimated Revenue:** This is the total estimated value of this opportunity. See the description of the Revenue field for information on how this value is calculated.

- **Probability:** This is the percentage likelihood that this opportunity will be won (a value between 0–100). Many organizations customize Dynamics CRM to auto-calculate this field based upon the Pipeline Phase. This field plays a role in calculating the forecast amount (see the "Sales forecasting" section below).

- **Pipeline Phase or Stage:** By default, the pipeline phase field is in the footer of the form and cannot be edited by the user. See the "Custom opportunity processes" section later in this chapter for more information on this field.

- **Originating Lead and Source Campaign:** These fields are generally automatically populated either by qualifying a lead or converting a campaign response. These fields are an important part of tracking the return on investment for your lead generation efforts and marketing campaigns.

Cross-Reference

Currency fields are used throughout the application to support different international currencies. You can generally leave the default value in the currency field. To learn more about the currency field, see Chapter 5.

Adding products to an opportunity

You can track a list of products that are associated with an opportunity (called Line items). Products tracked under an opportunity are automatically used to calculate the estimated revenue for an opportunity. These products are also automatically added to quotes, orders, or invoices tracked under the opportunity. By tracking products under an opportunity, you can improve the accuracy of your sales forecasts and capture more intelligence about your sales processes.

Businesses that use a fixed product catalog usually track products under their opportunities. Organizations that have highly complex product configurations or that focus primarily on providing business services often do not use products at all. Note that to fully use the line items list, you need to first configure the product catalog, described in the section "Working with the Product Catalog," later in this chapter.

Write-in and existing products

When adding products to an opportunity, you can choose from existing products that are in the Dynamics CRM product catalog, or you can create write-in products. Existing products auto-populate many other fields on the product form, while write-in products allow you to enter most of the fields manually. Even if you use the product catalog, write-in products can come in handy when you need to include something in an opportunity that is not in your current catalog.

Units

Units can be set up on individual products in your catalog to provide different pricing for different units. For example, a customer may buy a single item, a box, a crate, or a truckload of a product. Each different unit type can use different pricing.

Recalculating opportunities

As you add products to an opportunity, the estimated revenue and other related fields are recalculated in the database — but they are not made available on the opportunity form until it has been reloaded. To quickly recalculate these fields and display them on the opportunity form, click the button titled Recalculate Opportunity on the Ribbon menu.

Adding competitors to an opportunity

Tracking competitors in order to learn how you perform in specific products and services relative to your competition is important. You can add any number of competitors to an opportunity. To add a competitor, click on the competitors list on an opportunity and then click the Add Existing Competitor button in the Ribbon menu. Choose a competitor from the list or click the New button to create a new competitor.

You can link competitors to opportunities, products, and sales literature. In addition, you can enter analytical information about each competitor in their record. By keeping track of all of this information, your business can have a dynamic source of intelligence about each of your competitors. When a sales representative runs into a competitor for the first time, he or she can consult this competitive profile to improve their odds of winning an opportunity against the competitor.

Closing opportunities

When an opportunity has been either won or lost, it is time to close it. To do this, open the opportunity form and click either the Close as Won or Close as Lost button. Doing either opens the Close Opportunity dialog box shown in Figure 12.4. Complete the information in the form and click the OK button.

When recording a lost opportunity, capture the reason the opportunity was lost and the competitor that it was lost to. This information is an important part of your competitive intelligence-gathering process. If the client did not provide this information when he informed you of his decision, then a best practice is to call the prospect and ask them if they would provide this information to help you improve your sales process. The more information you can gather and store in Dynamics CRM, the greater your chances will be of winning future opportunities.

Tip

Whenever an opportunity is closed, a custom activity record called an Opportunity Close is created. This record captures some basic information about the opportunity. If a closed opportunity is reactivated and then closed again, then a second Opportunity Close activity is created.

Don't Let Opportunities Go Stale

Sales reps are optimists. They are reluctant to close an opportunity when they think there is even a small chance that it may yet be won. As a result, many organizations have a large number of stale opportunities in their pipeline.

This practice is actually counterproductive. Wasting time with opportunities that are unlikely to be won can be far more time-consuming and costly than finding new opportunities. After a prospect has delayed a decision indefinitely or has stopped returning calls, it is time to close the deal. This keeps your pipeline clean and easier to manage. It also has the added benefit of getting your Sales Manager to stop asking you about that deal!

You can always schedule follow-up phone calls periodically to see if they get serious about pursuing a relationship again.

FIGURE 12.4

The Close Opportunity dialog box

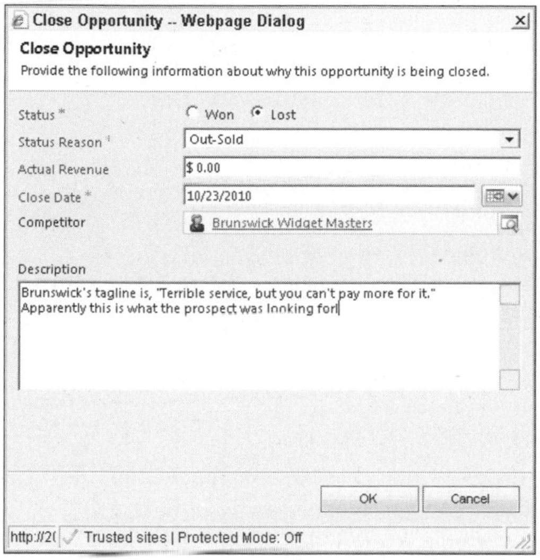

Setting goals

Dynamics CRM includes functionality that allows anyone in the organization to track goals. To set goals, navigate to the Sales area and use the Goals, Goal Metrics, and Rollup Queries sub-areas to set and monitor goals. Goals can be set for actual performance (for example, total revenues generated per quarter) and for performance indicators (for instance, number of calls made per day or number of new account records created). Although goals are located in the Sales area, they can be used to set goals for any Dynamics CRM user.

Forecasting sales

The sales forecasting and pipeline management reports included with Dynamics CRM use the information you populate on the opportunity form to calculate the forecast. The probability assigned to each opportunity is multiplied by the estimated revenue to calculate a field called weighted revenue. For example, if you have an opportunity with $100,000 in estimated revenue and a 50 percent probability, then the weighted revenue for that opportunity will be $50,000.

Forecast revenue is not intended to predict the likely revenue of a particular opportunity. In most cases you will either win or lose an opportunity — you won't win 50 percent of an opportunity. However, when you take the weighted revenue across all opportunities in aggregate, you can start to get a sense of what your current pipeline is worth and forecast what revenues may be over the next month, quarter, year, or more.

Cross-Reference

For information on sales forecasting reports, see Chapter 26.

Custom opportunity processes

Your organization can change the opportunity form and configure custom workflow processes to streamline the opportunity management process. How you configure opportunities will depend upon your unique sales processes, but here are a few suggestions to help you consider the options:

- **Plan your processes:** In Chapter 1, we go over how to define your sales process. This is a critical step for leveraging Dynamics CRM to accelerate the success of your sales process in terms of more opportunities, with faster sales cycles and higher close rates.

- **Add a stage pick list:** You can add a pick list to the opportunity form to enable users to choose which stage a sales opportunity is currently in.

- **Automate probabilities:** Using JavaScript (see Chapter 21), you can change the probability field automatically whenever the user changes the stage of an opportunity.

- **Enforce consistent sales steps:** Using workflows (see Chapter 18) you can automatically assign tasks to a user when an opportunity reaches a specific stage. Similarly, you can automatically advance an opportunity to another stage when specific tasks are completed.

- **Use stages in your workflow:** The default sales pipeline report requires using stages in your opportunity workflows in order to properly report on different sales processes. Take advantage of this functionality to report on different sales processes within your organization.

- **Get smarter:** Most businesses make educated guesses at the probability of winning a sale. After you have been using Dynamics CRM and following a consistent sales process for a number of months, you can remove the guesswork. Run audit reports to determine exactly what your close probabilities are and update your processes accordingly.

Working with the Product Catalog

If you plan to work with line items, quotes, orders, or invoices, then your organization needs to first configure a product catalog in Dynamics CRM. The product catalog enables you to track all of the products, price lists, discount lists, and units that products are sold in. After the product catalog has been configured, the data will be used to automatically calculate prices on products that you enter in quotes, orders, invoices, and on line items. Many organizations choose to use integration (see Chapter 26) to sync their accounting or ERP product catalog with the Dynamics CRM product catalog to minimize double-entry of product data.

To begin configuring the product catalog, open Dynamics CRM and navigate to Settings and then to Product Catalog. The product catalog consists of five different lists, the first four of which are available on the screen Product Catalog that you just navigated to.

- **Discount lists:** This list allows you to apply discounts to products based on the volume that is purchased. You can track different discount lists for different product types.

- **Unit groups:** This list enables you to determine different sets of unit groups which can then be associated with different prices. For example, you can set up a unit group for selling shoes that can have a base unit of a pair and can have additional units for crate, palette, or truck. You can set up a software license list with a base unit of license and additional units for team (5 licenses), corporate (25 licenses), and enterprise (500 licenses). Each of those units can be sold at different prices.

- **Price lists:** This list allows you to establish different price lists. Price lists can be assigned to different customers (such as consumer pricing, business pricing, and distributor pricing). You can also establish limited-time price lists (such as a Christmas price list).

- **Products:** This list contains a list of every product that you want to have available for sale within your product catalog.

- **Price list items:** You can only get to the price list items by either first going into a price list record or a product record. Price list items contain the specific entries for products in a price book and contain links to any related discount list or unit group. For example, you can have a price list item that links to your wholesaler price list, for the widget product, purchased by the crate, with its own discount list. Note that one product may have multiple price list item entries.

Working with Quotes, Orders, and Invoices

Quotes, orders, and invoices all share similar functionality. Each of these lists enables you to manage a list of products and each maintains a total for all the line items in the parent record. Users can create a quote from an opportunity, convert a quote into an order, and convert an order into an invoice (see Figure 12.5).

Not all organizations use the quote, order, and invoice records in Dynamics CRM. In fact, these types of records are a gray area between what your CRM system should do and your ERP system should do. You can use them in the following ways:

- You can completely disregard these lists, setting security roles to hide these from the view of users.

- You can integrate these lists with your ERP or accounting system. Exactly where and how you integrate depend on your specific business need. One typical example is to push quotes into your ERP system once they are accepted by the client, and when orders and invoices are created in your ERP system, they would then push back into Dynamics CRM.

- You can utilize some or all of these lists directly inside of CRM. This is not, however, a replacement for an accounting or ERP system.

FIGURE 12.5

The relationship between opportunities, quotes, orders, and invoices

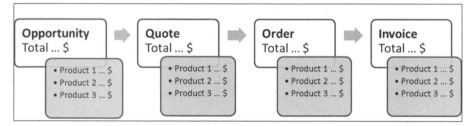

Although quotes, orders, and invoices can all be associated with opportunities, this is not required. This can be useful for handling transactional sales versus long-term sales. For example, you might have an outside sales group that spends many months winning relationships with new clients. Once those new relationships are established, you may have an inside sales group that takes phone orders from these customers. The outside sales group may use opportunities to manage their pipeline while the inside sales group may enter orders directly into Dynamics CRM without using opportunities.

Cross-Reference

Quotes, orders, and invoices share many traits with opportunities and line items. For more information on adding product line items to quotes, orders, and invoices, see the "Adding products to an opportunity" section, earlier in this chapter.

Managing quotes

The quoting functionality in Dynamics CRM enables you to create a quote, print it, obtain approval on it, and convert it into an order. As a quote is revised, new versions are created to provide an audit trail of all the versions that a quote passed through prior to receiving final approval from the client. Figure 12.6 represents the process that is used to manage quotes using Dynamics CRM.

FIGURE 12.6

The quote management process

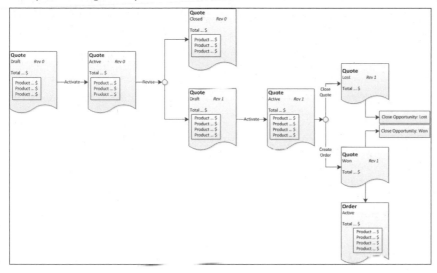

Creating a quote

There are two methods for creating a quote in Dynamics CRM. You can create a quote directly, without associating it with an opportunity, or you can add a quote to an existing opportunity. The latter approach can save a significant amount of time by rekeying opportunity data into the quote. Follow these steps:

1. Navigate to the opportunity you wish to add the quote to, navigate to the sub-list of quotes, and then click Add New Quote in the Ribbon menu. The quote record will open up and you'll notice that a great deal of information from the opportunity has been carried over into the quote. This includes the customer name, price list, and the list of products (assuming you added line items to the opportunity).

2. You can add an address to the quote manually or by clicking Look Up Address in the Ribbon menu. Addresses available in the lookup will only include addresses assigned to the parent customer that you named (if you did not type a name for an address, then it will not appear in this list).

3. You can add products to the quote by clicking on the products sub-list and adding products one at a time. You can also click the Get Products button in the Ribbon menu and fetch the list of products from any opportunity (including the original parent opportunity in the event that you updated the list of products from there). Note that you can also add addresses to individual quote line items — this is helpful if you have a quote that has products that ship to different addresses.

4. After you have finished creating the quote, you can click the Print Quote for Customer in the Ribbon menu to run a Word mail merge to generate a hard copy quote that you can then deliver to the customer. Alternatively, you can click the Run Report button in the Ribbon menu and choose the quote report. Either the mail merge document (Chapter 10) or the report (Chapter 25) can be customized to your business.

5. When you click the Activate Quote button in the Ribbon menu, the quote will be locked down and will not allow any additional changes without creating a revision. Depending on your business process, you may choose to activate a quote upon internal approval or upon client approval.

Revising a quote

After a quote has been activated, you cannot update it unless you create a revision. When you create a revision, the status of the existing quote will be set to closed and an exact copy of the quote will be created with a new revision ID number and a status set to draft. You can then edit this new draft quote and reactivate it by following the procedures under "Creating a quote."

To revise a quote, navigate to the active quote that you want to revise. Open the quote form and click the Revise button in the Ribbon menu. After a few moments the new quote opens, and you can begin editing it.

Converting a quote

Every quote should eventually be closed out. Each quote ends its life by either converting into an order or closing as lost.

- To close out a quote as lost, click the Close Quote button in the Ribbon menu. Complete the dialog box and click the OK button.

- To close a quote by converting it to an order, click the Create Order button in the Ribbon menu. Fill out the appropriate information in the dialog box (note that this also gives you the ability to close out the opportunity at the same time) and click the OK button. After a moment, the quote form closes and the order form opens with all of the products and other information transitioned to the order.

Understanding orders and invoices

Orders and invoices function in a manner very similar to quotes. Just like quotes, you can retrieve products from other opportunities for an order, and add addresses to individual line items or to the parent record. Products on orders and invoices can be changed before closing them out to reflect changes that were made in the latter stages of the sales process. The differences are mostly related to how you close out orders and invoices and are described below.

Closing orders

Orders can be closed using a combination of three different options. These options allow you to cancel an order (losing the revenue), fulfill an order (lock it down to prohibit further changes), or invoice an order (convert it into an invoice record).

- **Cancel an order:** Click the Cancel Order button in the Ribbon menu and fill in the dialog box. This closes out the order as lost. Note, however, that this will not change the status of the opportunity that the order is related to (if the opportunity is marked as won, it will remain marked as won). If this is not the desired behavior for your organization, then you will need to configure Dynamics CRM accordingly.

- **Fulfill an order:** Click the Fulfill Order button in the Ribbon menu and fill in the dialog box. This will lock the order, disallowing further updates. You can still, however, create an invoice from this order.

- **Invoice for an order:** You can invoice an order by clicking the Create Invoice button in the Ribbon menu for each invoice that you want to create. Doing this creates a separate invoice record that you must the complete.

Closing invoices

There are two methods available for closing out invoices. If you cancel an invoice, it will set the status to Canceled and will disallow additional editing. If you set an invoice to paid, then the invoice status will be set to paid and it cannot be updated further (although you can still cancel it). Use the appropriate button on the Ribbon menu to either cancel the invoice or record that the invoice has been paid.

Summary

Managing the sales process is one of the chief reasons that most organizations invest in Dynamics CRM. Sales representatives benefit by reducing data entry, improving their close rates, and accelerating their pipeline. The visibility that Dynamics CRM provides into the sales process enables the organization to better manage and improve sales performance, predict cash flow, identify gaps in the pipeline, and quickly engage new sales reps with minimal downtime. Within larger organizations, Dynamics CRM enables sales teams to collaborate with others — sales teams for different business units can refer leads to each other, marketing can quickly and easily assign leads to sales, and sales and support can have visibility into each other's activities for the same customers.

Not all of the sales functionality outlined within this chapter is right for all businesses. Virtually all businesses that use Dynamics CRM for sales choose to utilize opportunities. However, not all businesses use leads, quotes, orders, and invoices. Assess your sales process and your other internal systems to determine which functionality is right for your business.

The sales functionality included in Dynamics CRM is powerful. However, you should avoid the temptation to jump in and use it right out of the box. The full benefits of a customer relationship management process will not be realized without adequate planning, customization, and training. Take the time to understand and document your sales process (Chapter 1). Configure Dynamics CRM to work the way your business does — including reconfiguring Dynamics CRM and integrating it with other technologies such as accounting and your Web site. Schedule time to train and retrain and reinforce your training with users until it has been fully adopted.

Using the Marketing Functions

I n many organizations there is a disconnect between the Sales and Marketing functions. Marketing develops sales collateral, but Sales complains that the right collateral is never available. Sales asks for better leads, and Marketing complains that the leads they provide are never worked. Marketing asks for feedback on their campaigns from Sales, but Sales doesn't have the tools to quantify the results.

The marketing functionality available in Dynamics CRM not only closes the gap between Sales and Marketing but can also bring new efficiencies to the marketing function. Using Dynamics CRM, marketers can:

- Build and manage dynamic marketing lists

- Execute complex multistep and event-driven campaigns

- Generate and qualify business leads, assign them to sales, and monitor follow-up

- Deliver sales literature to reps in a format that is easy to pass along to prospects

- Track marketing projects and analyze the bottom-line impact

Beyond the already strong marketing functionality built into Dynamics CRM, a number of add-on products further enhance this functionality (some freely distributed by Microsoft). Using these tools, marketers can fully automate campaigns, conduct large e-mail projects directly out of Dynamics CRM, and integrate their Web site with the marketing campaigns in real time.

Cross-Reference

In addition to the topics in this chapter, marketing often uses functions described in other chapters. For more information on e-mail templates and mail merge documents, see Chapter 10. For more information on leads and the lead management process, see Chapter 12.

Managing Campaigns

In Dynamics CRM, campaigns are used to manage all of the information and action items for your marketing projects. Using campaigns, you can track each of the steps in a marketing project plan and assign them to yourself or others within your organization. Specific campaign actions can be planned, budgeted, and executed, including phone calls, e-mails, and letters. Campaigns can also be associated with items in your product and sales literature lists so you can easily find all the relevant campaigns for these items. Figure 13.1 illustrates the campaign management process.

FIGURE 13.1

The campaign management process

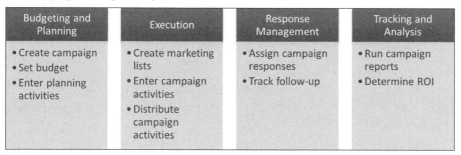

Budgeting and Planning	Execution	Response Management	Tracking and Analysis
• Create campaign • Set budget • Enter planning activities	• Create marketing lists • Enter campaign activities • Distribute campaign activities	• Assign campaign responses • Track follow-up	• Run campaign reports • Determine ROI

Creating campaigns

You can create a new campaign by clicking the New button in the Ribbon menu, or you can use an existing campaign or campaign template to create a new campaign. Using past campaigns or campaign templates provides a time-saving shortcut to reuse complex campaign plans.

Creating your first campaign

To create your first campaign, navigate to the campaign list in Dynamics CRM and click the New button on the Ribbon menu. Keep in mind that most of the fields described below can be changed to work with your specific business process. You need to understand and use the following fields to utilize the campaign functionality.

- **Status Reason:** Use this field as an indicator of the current stage of the campaign.
- **Campaign Type:** Designate the type of campaign using this field. This is an area where you may want to customize campaigns by adding some other options in this list (see Chapter 17).
- **Total Cost of Campaign Activities:** This field tracks a running total of the costs for all of the campaign activities associated with a campaign.
- **Miscellaneous Costs:** If there are other miscellaneous costs for this campaign not tracked in campaign activities, then enter that amount here.
- **Total Cost of Campaign:** This field is the total of the two fields listed above. It is calculated whenever the record is saved.
- **Budget Allocated:** Enter the total allocated budget here. Reports are available that compare your budget to your actual costs for each campaign.
- **Estimated Revenue:** Enter the estimated amount of revenue that the campaign will generate. Reports are available that will compare the estimated revenues to actual revenues in the campaign. For more information on campaign revenues, see the "Working with campaign response records" section.

When Should I Use a Campaign?

The campaign functionality in Dynamics CRM is most frequently used for direct marketing campaigns such as e-mail marketing, direct mail, or telesales. These types of campaigns readily lend themselves to a CRM tool because they target a specific list, with a specific message, and drive a specific response.

However, Dynamics CRM can be used to handle virtually any marketing campaign at all. Types of campaigns can include the grand opening of a new location, a new product launch, a press release, search engine marketing, and so on. Some campaigns can be complex, with multiple customer contacts (for example, a new product launch may include developing new literature, a press release, and sending e-mails). By using Dynamics CRM to manage all of your marketing campaigns, you can track the full marketing budget in one place. You can also associate new leads and opportunities directly to campaigns to measure the ROI of every campaign.

One-off direct marketing campaigns are a great way to start using the campaign functionality, but you should plan to fully leverage campaigns to manage all of your marketing projects.

Working with campaign templates

Campaign templates can be created as a way to ensure that a consistent process is followed in similar campaigns and to save time keying campaign data. You have the same functionality available when creating a campaign template as you did when creating a standard campaign.

- **Creating a campaign template:** To create a new blank campaign template, navigate to the list of campaigns and click the New Template button in the Ribbon menu. If you want to create a new template based on a previous campaign or template, then open the campaign form and click the Copy as Template button in the Ribbon menu. Fill out all the desired information in the campaign template and add any planning activities and campaign activities that you would like to include in the template.

- **Using a campaign template:** To use a campaign template, double-click on the record in the campaign list and then click the Copy as Campaign button in the Ribbon menu. A copy of the template is created, including all of the planning activities and campaign activities.

Working with planning activities

Use the list of planning activities as the project plan for your campaign. Activities in this list can be assigned to yourself or to other Dynamics CRM users within your organization. As activities are completed, this view is updated so you can track what is completed and what remains to be done.

Working with campaign activities

Campaign activities are either paid steps in the campaign management process (such as professional copywriting) or direct contacts made with members of your marketing list (such as e-mail campaigns). The costs that you associate with individual campaign activities are aggregated and totaled in the Total Cost of Campaign Activities field on the campaign form. In addition, you can distribute your campaign activities across the records on your marketing lists for the campaign to automate direct communications to leads, contacts, and accounts.

Using campaign activities

You can create campaign activities for a campaign by navigating to the campaign activity list for a campaign and clicking the Add New Campaign Activity button. Use the following fields to get the most out of campaign activities:

- **Channel:** If your campaign activity will not be distributed to a target marketing list, then select the Other value for this field (or leave it blank).

- **Outsource Vendors:** If you are working with an outside vendor on this activity, then you can use this field to select the vendor from among your list of accounts in Dynamics CRM.

- **Budget Allocated:** This is an optional field that does not total back to the campaign.

- **Actual Cost:** This budget field that totals back to the campaign record. If you want to track the actual costs for your campaign, then be sure to enter a cost here.

Distributing campaign activities

Distributing campaign activities is the process of assigning an activity to each record in a target marketing list in Dynamics CRM. For example, if you create a campaign activity and assign it a channel of "e-mail" and you assign a target marketing list to the campaign activity called "Leads in Liverpool," then distributing the campaign activity will send an e-mail to each lead in Liverpool. To distribute a campaign activity:

1. Create your campaign and assign at least one marketing list to it.

2. Create a campaign activity record.

3. Populate the Channel field with anything except Other or blank.

4. Assign at least one target marketing list to the campaign activity.

5. Save the campaign activity record.

6. Click the Distribute Campaign Activity button in the Ribbon menu.

7. A form pops up for the activity (such as an e-mail form). Complete this form and click the Distribute button.

8. A second dialog box (see Figure 13.2) is displayed to determine who the activity should be assigned to and (if this is an e-mail activity) whether it should be sent immediately. Complete this form and click OK.

9. Dynamics CRM automatically assigns an activity to every record in the selected target marketing lists.

Note that you do not need to distribute all of your campaign activities. If, for example, you have a campaign activity titled "Have agency write e-mail copy," then you should not distribute this activity. Instead, after the activity has been completed and the actual cost invoiced, you should use the Close Campaign Activity button on the Ribbon menu to close the activity without distributing it.

Working with campaign responses

Campaign responses are activity records that track responses that you have received to your campaigns. Campaign responses are listed under a campaign and also appear in the standard list of activities in Dynamics CRM. These records include additional functionality to ensure that the proper follow-up takes place and that campaign results can be tracked.

FIGURE 13.2

The activity owner assignment dialog box

Creating campaign responses

Campaign response records can be created in one of four ways. The method of creation varies depending on the type of campaign and the campaign activity.

- **Manually created:** Campaign responses can be created just like any other activity record in Dynamics CRM. This method can be helpful for untargeted campaigns — such as foot traffic to the opening of a new location.

- **Convert an activity:** An activity record that was generated as a distributed campaign activity can be converted into a campaign response. This method can be helpful, for example, if you receive a phone call or an e-mail and later determine that this was received as the result of a campaign. To do this, click the Convert Activity button on the Ribbon menu for the activity record and select To Opportunity. In the dialog box, make sure to select to Record a closed campaign response.

- **Auto created:** Dynamics CRM can automatically create a campaign response for a variety of reasons. You can set it to record a campaign response when a customer responds to a campaign e-mail, you can set up Web forms to generate responses, or you can integrate other tools, such as the Event Management Accelerator (www. codeplex.com), which generate campaign responses.

- **Import:** Campaign responses can be imported directly into Dynamics CRM. This can be helpful, for example, when importing event attendees. See Chapter 8 for information on importing.

Planning Activities versus Campaign Activities

Trying to decide if an activity should be a planning activity or a campaign activity may seem a little bit confusing at first, but if you understand the differences between these two types of records, the best practices become clear.

Planning activities are standard Dynamics CRM activities. As such, they cannot have costs associated with them. In addition, planning activities cannot be distributed against a target list. You can, however, track the amount of time that was spent on planning activities. Planning activities, therefore, are well suited for tracking internal steps that do not have an associated cost.

If you want to track activities that will have an associated cost, enter them as campaign activities. This may include paid copywriting and direct mail print production, for example. If you want to distribute activities against a target list then these, too, should be entered as campaign activities. This may include outbound phone calls, e-mails, or letters.

The best practice is to track internal activities as planning activities and to track both external activities (such as paid copywriting) and customer contacts (such as outbound calls) as campaign activities.

Working with campaign response records

Campaign response records are treated like other activity records by Dynamics CRM. This ensures that campaign responses appear on the assigned user's activity list until they are converted or closed. To ensure that marketing can properly track the return on investment for each campaign, users must receive training in the proper steps to convert their campaign responses.

Depending upon how campaign response records are initially created, they may not be assigned to the correct user to receive required follow-up. As part of your campaign planning process, you should ensure that appropriate manual steps or workflows are created that will result in all campaign responses getting assigned to a user.

To convert a campaign response record, follow the procedure below:

1. Open the record and click on Convert Campaign Response in the Ribbon menu.

2. On the convert campaign response form (see Figure 13.3), select the appropriate action from the following:

    *   **Create new lead:** This action uses information from the campaign response to create a new lead in Dynamics CRM. Only use this option if a lead or customer record does not already exist for this campaign response.

    *   **Convert an existing lead:** If a lead already exists for this record, and the campaign has resulted in qualifying the lead, then select this option.

    *   **Create new record for a customer:** If a customer record already exists for the campaign response, then select this option and then choose the customer record and the type of record to create for the customer (such an opportunity).

- **Close response:** If you do not want to create any record for this campaign response (for example, the campaign response did not result in a new lead or new business opportunity), then select this option.

3. Click OK.

Adding products and sales literature to campaigns

In addition to the above information, you can also track target products and sales literature for a campaign. Entering this information for a campaign builds links between your product list, your sales literature, and your campaigns. These links enhance your marketing intelligence. For example, you can navigate to a product and see the competitors, sales literature, and marketing campaigns associated with the product. This can be used to improve on your marketing planning, sales literature, and your competitive positioning in the future.

Cross-Reference

For more information on the campaign reports provided with Dynamics CRM, see Chapter 23.

FIGURE 13.3

Convert campaign response form

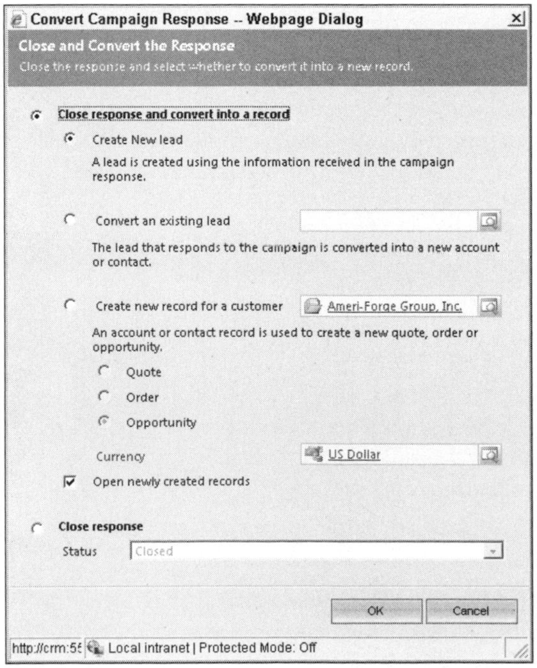

Using Quick Campaigns

Quick campaigns are simplified marketing campaigns. Quick campaigns use a wizard interface to enable users to rapidly roll out campaigns and require very little learning curve. They forego some of the more complex functionality and tracking features found in marketing campaigns in favor of an easier to use interface. Use the following process to execute a quick campaign:

1. Navigate to a list of leads, accounts, or contacts that you want to target with the campaign.

2. Select the records you want to target by using one or more of the steps below (usually the first option is all that is needed):

   - Use a view or an advanced find to select the records you want to target.

   - If necessary, navigate to the page that contains the specific records you want to target.

   - If necessary, Ctrl+Click on records to select the specific records you want to target.

3. In the Ribbon menu, choose the Create Related tab and then select Quick Campaign. Select the option for the list targeting that your quick campaign requires.

4. Follow the prompts through the Quick Campaign Wizard (see Figure 13.4). Note your options for assigning ownership of records and (if applicable) auto-sending the e-mail.

FIGURE 13.4

The Quick Campaign Wizard

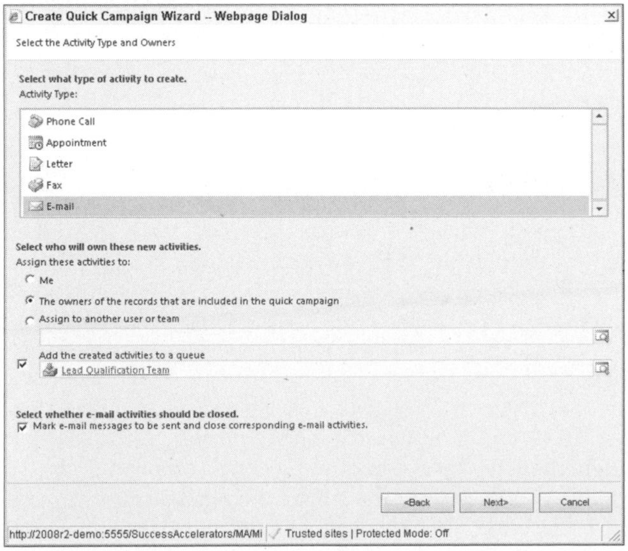

Campaigns Respect Customer Wishes _____

Wondering what all those fields about contact methods do on the lead, account, and contact records? Marketing campaigns (including quick campaigns) make use of these fields to ensure that you are respecting the wishes of your customers and prospects.

For example, if run a campaign that attempts to send an e-mail to a lead that has "Do Not Allow" selected in the Bulk E-Mail field, then the e-mail will not be sent to this individual. You will be able to check the activity history for this individual as well as the contacts excluded list for the campaign activity to see who did not receive the e-mail.

5. Finish the wizard and approve the quick campaign.

6. Dynamics CRM automatically creates activities for your campaign.

Working with Marketing Lists

Marketing lists provide a flexible way to manage lists of accounts, contacts, or leads. Marketing lists can be used as a part of campaigns (as noted above), but marketing lists can also be used independently of campaigns if desired. You can create marketing lists for a variety of purposes, including:

- For use with campaigns
- To run mail merges (without campaigns)
- To track subscribers to newsletters
- To quick create opportunities (such as for all customers that have expiring service agreements)
- To manage a Christmas mailing list

Managing list members manually

You can add members to your marketing lists directly from the lead, contact, or account forms. This can be useful if you want to have a group of individuals collaborate on creating a marketing list. For example, you may ask everyone on the team to add members to a Christmas list, or you may allow everyone to add individuals to a newsletter list. To do this, navigate to the record you wish to add to a list and then click the Add to Marketing List button in the Ribbon menu.

Dynamics CRM provides a rich set of tools for adding members to a list in bulk. To bulk add members to a list, open the form for the marketing list you wish to update, click on the Marketing List Members sub-list, and then click on the Manage Members button on the Ribbon menu. You are presented with the dialog box in shown in Figure 13.5. By using the options presented within this dialog box, you can add and remove members to your list until it contains exactly who you want to target.

FIGURE 13.5

Manage Members dialog box

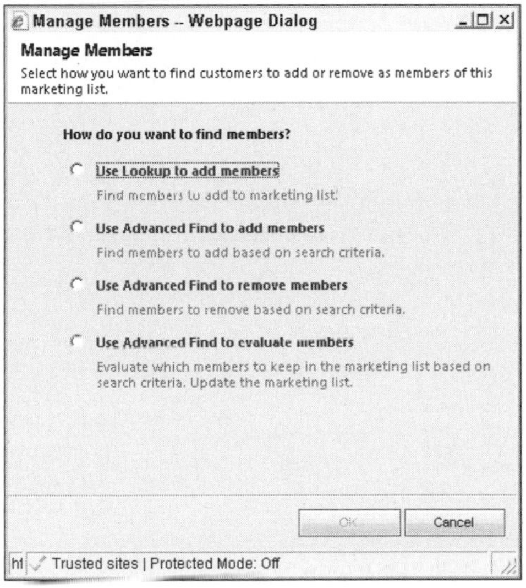

Managing list members dynamically

Dynamics CRM 2011 includes the ability to create marketing lists that update themselves automatically. This capability gives marketing administrators the ability to create event-driven campaigns with lists that automatically adjust based on changing information about a lead, contact, or company.

As an example, a dynamic marketing list can be created, titled Expiring Contracts. A query can be used to create this marketing list that includes all customers that have a contract set to expire within the next 90 days. Phone call activities can then be assigned to members of this list to ensure that the account executive gets the contract renewed.

To create a dynamic list, create a new marketing list and select a type of "Dynamic" on the marketing list form. After saving the list, click the Manage Members button in the Ribbon menu. Create a list by defining an advanced find filter. Whenever the list is used, the filter will be reprocessed to dynamically generate the desired list.

Using mail merge documents with marketing lists

Marketing lists can be used to create a targeted list for mail merge documents. To do this, create a mail merge document by using the instructions in Chapter 10. Build your marketing list by using the instructions in the preceding section. While on the list form, click the Create Related tab in the Ribbon menu and then click Mail Merge on List Members. Follow the instructions in Chapter 10 for running a mail merge document.

Other Marketing Functions

Marketing can leverage a number of other functions available in Dynamics CRM. In addition, Marketing can enhance its productivity with various add-on tools that integrate with Dynamics CRM.

Sales literature

The sales literature list enables marketing to create and catalog all collateral and other materials utilized by the sales force. This can include PDFs of product collateral, scanned images of competitive materials, product catalogs, newsletters, and so on. Use the sales literature list to create records for each piece of sales literature. After these records have been created, sales reps can access them to attach directly to outgoing e-mails that they create using Dynamics CRM.

Sales literature can also be linked to products and campaigns. These links provide sales and marketing with a dynamic source of intelligence that can be used to improve your marketing campaigns, your brand positioning, and your competitive sales pitches.

Internet marketing

Because Dynamics CRM is a Web application, it can be integrated with your Internet marketing initiatives to make them more effective and measurable than ever before. Integrating Dynamics CRM with your Internet marketing can be accomplished through custom programming, through freely distributed accelerators from Microsoft, and through third-party applications (some of these options are mentioned in the section "Third-party add-ons."

If you are working with Dynamics CRM Online, then you also have the option of using built-in Internet marketing capabilities. To activate Internet marketing, navigate to Settings ➪ Business Management and then click on the Internet Marketing item. After setting up Internet marketing, navigate to Marketing ➪ Internet Lead Capture to configure Dynamics CRM to capture leads from your Web site.

Third party add-ons

Marketing groups often require capabilities outside of the core Dynamics CRM functionality. Many free as well as paid add-ons are available to further enhance the capabilities of marketing groups that use Dynamics CRM. Here are a few of the ones for which we see demand:

- **Event Management:** Microsoft has made a free event management add-on available via www.codeplex.com. This add-on integrates event campaigns with your Web site to automatically generate new event listings on your Web site, accept registrations and log them as campaign responses, and track event performance. Because it is open source, it can be expanded to integrate with social media sites, publish RSS feeds, accept credit cards for paid events, and track viral marketing referrals.

- **Social Networking:** Another free option from Microsoft is the social networking solution accelerator. This is designed to integrate Dynamics CRM with popular social networking sites to generate leads, push out social content on a scheduled basis, and monitor marketplace feedback on your business.

- **Capturing Web Leads:** The ability to capture and process Web leads in Dynamics CRM can be a daunting issue for nondevelopers. Even if using Dynamics CRM Online, you will find that the lead capture functionality falls short of the needs of most organizations. Web2CRM, from CRM Innovation, provides a cost-effective solution that most CRM administrators will be able to use to set up Internet lead capture,

- **E-Mail Management:** E-mail management is another area where marketers often want to go beyond the built-in capabilities of Dynamics CRM. With third party e-mail integration tools from Exact Target, Eloqua, and Vertical Response, you can develop highly personalized e-mails, deliver detailed response reports and build workflows that are triggered when e-mails are opened or bounced.

Summary

Campaigns in Dynamics CRM can be used to track a variety of marketing projects. Because marketing campaigns are connected to sales results, organizations can do a better job of aligning the efforts of sales and marketing groups. Proper planning and usage of campaign functionality will deliver detailed campaign project planning, contact history, budget tracking, and return on investment reporting. Quick campaigns provide a simplified user interface into marketing campaigns and can be used by sales managers as well as by marketing.

Marketing lists are an important component of campaigns but can also be used independently of campaigns. Marketing lists provide a means of organizing accounts, contacts, and leads for direct contact via phone call, e-mail, or other direct communication channel. Marketing lists are also a good tool for tracking subscriber lists.

Sales literature provides a library for managing all of the sales and marketing collateral and other materials utilized by your organization. Documents in this library can be linked to products, competitors, and campaigns to form a cross-reference to improve marketing intelligence. Sales literature documents can also be attached to outgoing e-mails to enable sales to more rapidly follow up on opportunities.

Using the Service Functions

The service functionality available in Dynamics CRM enables businesses to track customer service issues to resolution, reduce handling time for service calls, ensure a consistent customer service experience, and to rapidly schedule service appointments based on complex rules.

Data tracked in the service area can be made visible to other personnel across the organization. Management can view customer service and satisfaction trends using dashboards and visualizations. Sales representatives can view customer support incidents for individual customers. Visibility into support information leads to continuously improved customer service processes and enhanced customer profitability through better collaboration between sales and service.

Managing Cases

In Dynamics CRM, cases are used to manage the information and action items for individual service incidents with customers. A service incident may be a maintenance issue on a piece of equipment, a software bug report, or a request for instructions on how to use a product sold by your organization. Many organizations refer to cases as "service incidents" or "trouble tickets." Articles in the knowledge base in Dynamics CRM can be used to build up a library of information that is used to resolve cases — rapidly resolving customer issues while maintaining corporate branding standards.

What Else Can Cases Do for You?

Cases can be used to manage a variety of activities beyond trouble tickets. Some organizations deploy Dynamics CRM as a human resources information system (HRIS) and use cases to manage employee requests for support. Others use cases as a method to manage simple projects for their clients. Some professional services firms make use of cases to manage their client engagements.

As you think about how else you might use cases, keep in mind that Dynamics CRM provides a flexible framework that you can create entirely new lists with. Weigh the option of repurposing cases versus creating a new list for your project carefully before making a decision.

Creating and tracking cases

To create a case, navigate to the Service area of Dynamics CRM and then to the Cases sub-area. Click on the New button to create a new case. When you create a case, knowing about the following fields can help:

- **Subject:** Dynamics CRM includes a "subject tree" to categorize items such as cases and products. For more information on setting up the subject tree, see the appropriate section later in this chapter.

- **Contract and Contract Line:** When creating a case, you have the option of linking it to a service contract. For more information on contracts, see the appropriate section later in this chapter.

- **Product:** You can link a case to a product. Doing so enables your organization to track the performance history of each product line. In addition, this can reduce the amount of time to find a relevant article to resolve frequent issues with the specified product.

- **Article:** If you used an article from the knowledge base to resolve this issue, the article can be selected and viewed within the case record. For more information on knowledge base articles, see the appropriate section later in this chapter. When clicking on the article field to select an article, the Form Assistant (on the right side of the form) will display a list of likely articles based on articles related to the subject and product — saving your service reps time finding the appropriate solution to the case.

Cross-Reference

The new dialog functionality introduced with Dynamics CRM 2011 can be a powerful extension to case management. For example, a dialog can be used to prompt a customer through a specific set of questions to understand and resolve a specific type of case. For more information on dialogs, see Chapter 18.

Tracking time

Cases allow you to track the time it takes to resolve a case. As users create activities associated with a case, they can enter the amount of time associated with each individual activity into the duration field. When the activities are closed, they are added to the total hours for the case. Tracking hours by case can be important for businesses that charge by the hour for customer service or that provide service contracts that include a specific number of hours of service. Figure 14.1 is an example of a customized case form displaying a visualization of the number of hours recorded against the case to date.

Closing cases

Every case in CRM should eventually be closed as either resolved or cancelled. To close a case, click on the appropriate button in the Ribbon menu with the case form open. You are presented with a dialog box to confirm your choice and provide some more information on the status of the case resolution.

FIGURE 14.1

Case form with total number of hours visualization displayed

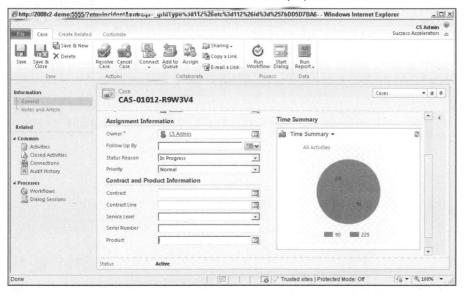

If you choose to resolve the case, then you will be asked to provide some more information before saving the resolution. Dynamics CRM automatically calculates the total time spent on the case by adding up the duration of all the completed activities associated with the case. You have the option of changing the billable time if you like (for example, if you decide to provide service for free or if you bill a minimum amount of time for each service incident). Figure 14.2 illustrates what the resolve case form looks like.

FIGURE 14.2

Resolve case dialog box

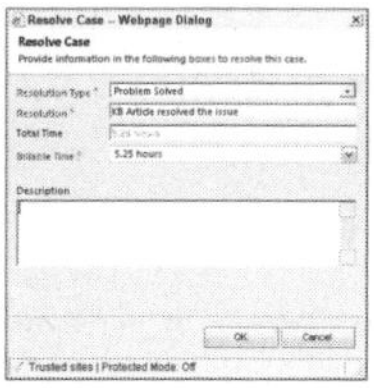

After a case is closed you can no longer edit the case record. However, if needed, you can click the Reactivate Case button in the Ribbon menu. Doing this changes the status of the case back to active and allows you to continue to edit the case. Every time you close a case, a case resolution activity record is created in CRM to track the closure of the case.

Caution

Every time you close a case, a case resolution activity record is created in CRM to track the closure of the case. This record includes the billable time for the case resolution. If you reactivate a case record and close it again, then two case resolution activity records will be created. While this may be helpful, it may also cause some reporting issues if you add up all the hours on your case resolution records at the end of the month because you may be double-counting some of the billable hours for these cases.

Setting up subjects

Dynamics CRM includes a subject hierarchy (or "tree") to enable you to tag and categorize products, sales literature, knowledge base articles, and service cases. By using the subject tree, you can speed the process of servicing customers and providing relevant sales literature. In addition, you can improve reporting on product performance, understand gaps in your sales literature, and analyze service quality by subject area.

To set up your subject tree, navigate to Settings, then to Business Management and select Subjects. Subjects can be "nested" into parent and child categories to create a treelike hierarchy.

Best Practices in Subject Trees

After your subject tree is in place, it can be time-consuming if you decide to make significant changes (every product, knowledge base article, and sales literature item may need to be re-categorized). So it is a good idea to put some time and planning into the development of your subject tree.

A typical subject tree

A variety of different approaches are available to you in the design of your subject tree. The idea is to create a tree that is granular enough to provide meaningful details without having so many items that it is difficult to find what you're looking for. You should also avoid creating ambiguous items that make it unclear what subject an item should be related to. Below are some ideas to help you get started:

- **Product hierarchy:** Many businesses already have a product hierarchy that can readily be used as a starting point for your subject tree. Keep in mind that your subject tree doesn't need to include a node for every product (that's what your Dynamics CRM product catalog will be used for), but you may have a lists of product categories and subcategories.

- **Service areas:** Similarly, your service areas may fit nicely into categories and sub-categories in your subject tree. For a law firm, subjects may be practice areas. For an advertising agency, subjects may include different media channels.

Some good places to get more ideas for subject trees are your financial reports and your corporate organization chart. These items often categorize your organization into lines of business that will be familiar categories that everyone in the business will recognize.

Using knowledge base articles

Articles (also called knowledge base articles) can be used to solve customer problems, document processes, and store frequently asked questions for rapid response. Articles are integrated with cases, e-mail, and the Dynamics CRM Workplace to make it easy to find articles for individual research and to forward articles to customers and colleagues to help them resolve their issues. Articles are built by using article templates that enable your organization to use a consistent layout and branding approach for each of your articles. Figure 14.3 is an example article.

FIGURE 14.3

An example article

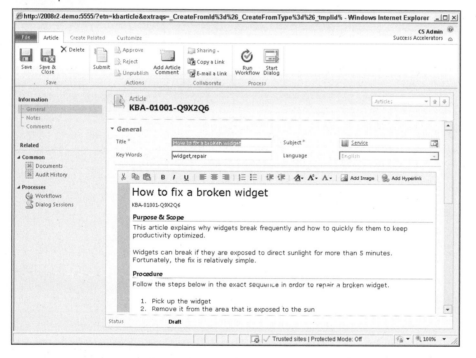

Creating article templates

A number of article templates are included right out of the box with Dynamics CRM. If these suit your needs, then you may never need to create an article template. Most organizations require some customizations to the article templates to support business processes or branding requirements.

You can create (or modify) article templates by navigating to Settings and then to Templates within Dynamics CRM. When you are in the templates sub-area you can click on the Article

Templates heading to display the list of article templates. You can name your template, add images, create sections, and set up default fonts. Once complete, save your template and close the form. The template will be available in the list of templates whenever you create a new article in Dynamics CRM.

Creating and approving articles

New knowledge base articles can be created by navigating to the Service area and then to the Knowledge Base sub-area of Dynamics CRM. Articles also include an approval and publication process. This process can be helpful if you want anyone to be able to create new articles, but you want to ensure that they pass a technical and/or marketing review prior to being available to send to customers.

- **Create a new article.** Click the New button in the Ribbon menu above the list of knowledge base articles and complete the form to create a new article. When you save this article, it will be saved as a draft article.

- **Submit an article for approval.** Select the Draft Articles view in the knowledge base sub-area. Click on the article you want to submit for approval and then click on the Submit button on the Ribbon menu. The status of the article will be changed to unapproved and it will be visible in the Unapproved folder. This view serves as a queue for the appropriate individual to review and approve.

- **Publish an article.** Select the Unapproved view from the knowledge base sub-area. Double-click an article to open it and review it before approving. Click the Approve button on the Ribbon menu. The article status is changed to published, and it is now visible in the Published Articles view and is available to share with customers or attach to e-mails.

Using articles

You can use articles in a number of areas throughout Dynamics CRM. Using articles makes it fast and easy to get the correct information to the right person to quickly solve his problems. The following list is a summary of the places where you can use articles:

- **Cases.** As noted in an earlier section of this chapter, articles can be associated with cases. Not only does this help to quickly solve cases, but it enables Dynamics CRM to track which articles are being used most frequently to solve which types of problems. The more you use this function, the smarter Dynamics CRM will be in recommending articles to solve customer issues.

- **Email.** When sending e-mail from Dynamics CRM or from Outlook, you can click Insert KB Article in the Ribbon menu to select an article and insert it into the body of the e-mail message.

- **Workplace.** In the Workplace area of Dynamics CRM is a sub-area called Articles. This sub-area enables you to search or browse through articles. This functionality makes it easy to find an article to solve a problem you may be working on without having to first open a case or an e-mail.

Tip

Articles do not need to be limited to solving problems for customers. Your organization can create articles that solve internal facing issues, too. This can range from standard procedures for new employees, to troubleshooting printer problems, to explaining how to set up your product for a new customer.

Working with contracts

Using contracts in Dynamics CRM, an organization can set up service level and maintenance agreements with their clients and ensure that their contractual requirements are met. If the client requests services outside the scope of the contract, Dynamics CRM can alert your support team.

Contracts are linked to cases in Dynamics CRM. You can choose a contract and a contract line item to associate each case with. As cases are closed, the number of cases and total hours are summed up for the individual contract line. If you exceed the total number of hours or case incidents allowed on a contract line and you attempt to create a new case using that same line, you will receive a message informing you that the case cannot be created for this contract. This information can be used to ensure that service commitments are met, but not exceeded.

Caution

Contracts provide more rigid functionality than do many other areas of Dynamics CRM. Be sure to fully understand contracts in CRM and ensure that they adhere to your business process before deploying this functionality to users.

Contract templates

Each contract is based on a contract template. Contract templates include information that is used to track the service level agreement for contracts. To create or update a contract template, open CRM and navigate to Settings ⇨ Templates ⇨ Contract Templates (Figure 14.4 is an example contract template). Key information includes:

- **Billing Frequency:** Indicates how often the customer should be invoiced.

- **Contract Service Level:** Dynamics CRM includes gold, silver, and bronze service levels. These distinctions can be used to create workflows to ensure that response time service level agreements are met on individual contracts.

- **Allotment Type:** This enables you to enforce a contractual agreement based on the units of service that have been agreed upon (unlimited service during a specified period of time, a specific number of hours per billing cycle, or a specific number of cases per billing cycle are examples).

- **Calendar / Service Hours:** Use this area to define the hours during which service will be available on this type of contract. Some contracts may include 24x7 support hours and others may provide 8x5 support, still others may be for special weekend only support. Note that these service hours are enforced when scheduling service management (see below) for a case that is associated with a contract using the selected template. This ensures that your business only provides services during the agreed upon hours.

FIGURE 14.4

The contract template screen

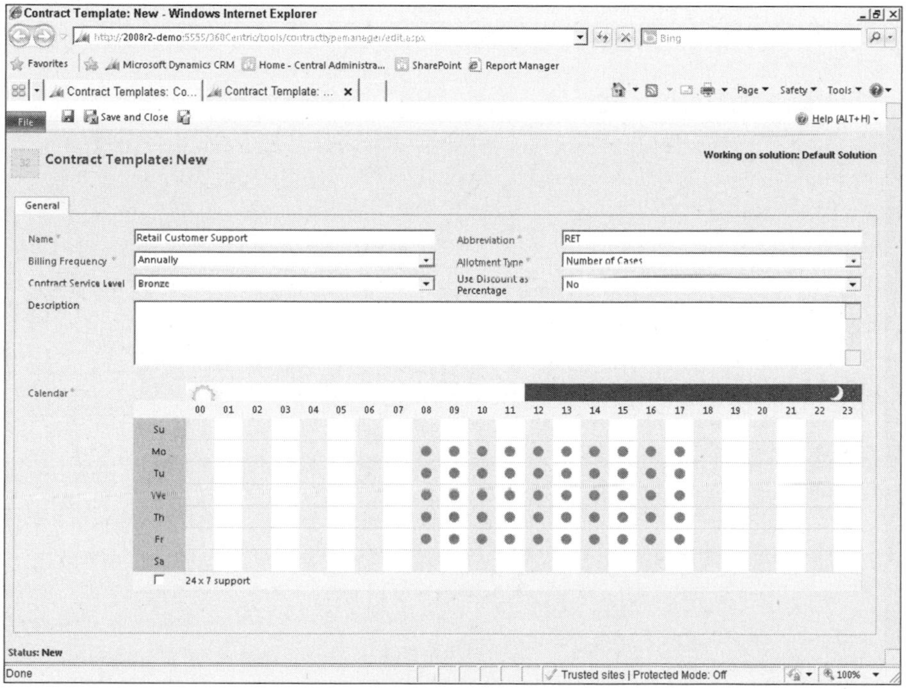

Caution

Although contracts contain fields such as billing frequency, price, and discount, these fields do not include any automation to create invoices. If you want to trigger invoicing from contracts, it will require the development of custom workflows or integration with your accounting system.

Contracts

Every contract must be based on a contract template. To enforce this, when you click the New button to create a contract, CRM opens a dialog box and requires that you first choose a template before creating a contract. Important fields to consider when completing the contract form:

- **Start Date / End Date.** These fields are the beginning and ending dates of service for the contract.

- **Contract Address.** This field is the specific address that the service contract is related to. You can use the lookup button to select the address (note, however, that only addresses that have a name assigned to them for this customer will appear in the list).

- **Billing Information and Pricing.** These sections contain financial information. This information does not automatically create invoices — this type of functionality is usually set up by integrating Dynamics CRM with your accounting system.
- **Originating Contract.** If this contract is a renewal of an existing contract, the original contract is here.

After you have completed entering a contract, and all of the contract lines, you can click the Invoice Contract button in the Ribbon menu to go from draft to invoiced status. Activated contracts are available to use for managing your cases.

Contract lines

Contracts contain the summary information about service contracts. Contract lines contain the details about the products covered, the total provided service allotment (number of cases or minutes), and pricing. Each contract line can relate to a different product. As cases are recorded against these contract lines, allotments are recorded against them so you can quickly see exactly how much service is left on an existing contract.

You can add additional lines to contracts that are already active. This can be helpful if a customer purchases new equipment that they want to cover under the same contract. However, these contract lines are immediately locked as read-only when you save them, so be sure that your line has been entered correctly before saving it.

The contract process

The diagram in Figure 14.5 represents the functions included in Dynamics CRM to enable your business to manage contracts. The contract (including contract lines) is locked from data entry during many stages of the contract management process. Only when a contract has a status of Invoiced will you be able to link it to cases for tracking contractual allocations. If you select to copy a contract then an exact copy (including the same contract lines) is made, but with a new Contract ID.

On the Web Site

Revenue from service or maintenance contracts is an important part of the bottom line for many businesses. If you're using contracts in Dynamics CRM, you can help your business to improve contract renewal dates with a simple workflow that alerts account owners of expiring contracts 90 days ahead of time and creates a new opportunity to renew the contract. We have created this workflow for you and included it on the CD. You can use it as a starting point and modify it to suit your needs.

Caution

After a contract has been activated, no data on the contract can be changed and the contract can never be deleted. If you need to alter a contract after it has been invoiced, you must cancel the contract and create a new one. Active contracts cannot be deleted (but they can be cancelled). Although you can add lines to an active contract, these new lines are immediately locked from editing upon saving them.

FIGURE 14.5

The contract management process

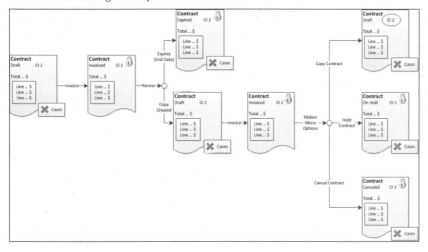

Scheduling Service

Dynamics CRM enables you to set up services with related resources and facilities to increase the speed and accuracy of service scheduling. Using the scheduling functionality and the visual schedule area, your team can have a centralized view of service workers' calendars as well as other business resources. Services include "rules" for how resources are allocated to a specific service. For example, you may provide on-site installation of equipment that requires individuals with specific skills, specific company vehicles, and certain replacement parts. All of these rules can be set up in the services area. After the rules are set up, Dynamics CRM can be used to schedule service delivery based on the availability of all the appropriate people, resources, and equipment. As noted in the preceding section, contracts can also be used to ensure that services are only provided during the hours that the customer has agreed upon in their service contract.

Setting up CRM for service management

To take full advantage of service management and service scheduling in Dynamics CRM, you need to set up a number of areas in the application. Taking the time to understand and properly set up the service management areas results in a more efficient process for your service scheduling users.

Setting up sites

Sites are locations where service operations take place or where service resources are located. When service is scheduled, you can choose which site the resources will be selected from in order to deliver the service. If multiple resources will be required for service, the user will be able to select if the resources must all come from the same site or if they can come from multiple sites. After you create sites, you will be able to assign resources (including users and facilities/equipment) to them.

To access the Sites list, navigate to the Settings area, then to Business Management, and click on Sites. Use the new button in the Ribbon menu to add an item.

Setting up facilities/equipment

Facilities and equipment are corporate resources that your organization uses to fulfill service requests. This can include service bays, LCD projectors, conference rooms, or specialized tools. By entering your inventory of these items, you can more rapidly schedule them for usage and ensure that there are no scheduling conflicts.

To add an item to Facilities/Equipment, navigate to the Settings area, then to Business Management and click on Facilities/Equipment. Use the new button in the Ribbon menu to add an item. Note that you can use the Work Hours related list to set up scheduled downtime for facilities and equipment.

Setting up resource groups

Resources include users or facilities/equipment. Resource Groups enable you to create collections of resources. When creating Resource Groups, the scheduling engine in Dynamics CRM will evaluate everything in a Resource Group as equal. Therefore, you should not mix different resource types in a resource group. Table 14.1 illustrates some good and bad examples of resource groups. For examples of how these resource groups are used in rules, see the "Setting up services" section.

TABLE 14.1

Resource Group Examples

Best Practice Resource Groups	Not Recommended Resource Groups
Senior Lift Installation Technicians	All Lift Repair Personnel and Equipment
Lift Installation Equipment	Lift Installation, Inspection, and Repair Tools
Lift Inspection Trucks	Company Vehicles for Installation, Inspection, and Executive Shuttling

To view the Resource Groups list, navigate to the Settings area, then to Business Management, and click on Resource Groups. Use the buttons on the Ribbon menu to add or update your resource groups.

Setting up business closures

Keeping your list of business closures up to date helps you avoid scheduling resources for service work during holidays or other business closures.

To update Business Closures, navigate to Settings ⇨ Business Management and click on Business Closures.

Setting up working hours for users

Daily working hours and time off can be scheduled for each user to ensure that they are scheduled only when they are available. This task can be performed by the user, a manager, or a system administrator.

To set up work hours for a user, navigate to Settings ⇨ Administration and then click on Users. Open the user record you want to set work hours for and then click on the Work Hours related list. Use the Ribbon menu to set up working hours, monthly availability, weekly work schedule, time off, schedule for a specific day, service restrictions (a specific time that a specific service cannot be performed), and to set capacity (the number of simultaneous tasks that can be performed by this individual — the default value of 1 is usually desired).

Setting up services

After you have set up all of the preceding areas that your organization will use in order to schedule service resources, you are ready to set up a list of services. These Services include rules that determine how resources are allocated for each service. To configure Services, navigate to Service ⇨ Services. The Service form contains a set of data entry fields and a Required Resources section for defining resource selection rules for the service. When completing the Service form, the following fields are important to consider:

- **Initial Status Reason:** Depending on your business process, you may want to change this field from the default value ("Reserved") to one of the other available values. This can be changed when service is being scheduled, but getting the default value right can save your users some time.

- **Default Duration:** This field is the standard amount of time scheduled for this service.

- **Start Activities Every:** This field is the incremental time unit that CRM will use for starting activities. If your organization wants service delivery to always start at the top of an hour, then use the 1 hour setting.

- **Beginning At:** This field designates the first activity start time for each work day.

The Required Resources section of the form is where you will set up the rules (also referred to as *selection rules*) for scheduling your service. These rules determine how many resources, of which types, from what locations, and for what period of time are required to fulfill a need for this type of service. These rules can be simple or highly complex. Figure 14.6 illustrates a simple rule that describes a specific set of personnel and equipment required for inspecting a site to see if it is suitable for an installation. Figure 14.7 illustrates a complex rule that contains nested rules and sub-rules to assign two different teams to each installation project; each team sub-rule includes assignments for the appropriate people, equipment, and trucks.

A simple service selection rule

To define a rule, select the default rule and either click the Edit Selected Item (to the left of the rule) or click on one of the hyperlinks in the rule. You will initially edit the "root" rule, and you can then add nested rules and sub-rules if desired. Defining rules is an open-ended process, but here are some best practices to consider as you develop your rules:

- **Defining the root rule:**
  - Each rule can have only a single root rule.
  - If you will be defining a simple rule (with no nested rules) then use a specific quantity of resources to apply; if you will be defining a complex rule (that includes nested rules and sub-rules) then select the quantity of All to allow your nested rules to define the individual quantities.
  - The site field in the root will affect all nested rules: Same Site will require that resources from all nested rules come from the same site; Any Site allows resources for nested rules to come from any site.

- **Creating nested rules:** To create a nested rule, click on the parent rule and select the Add Selection Rule item to the left of the rules.

- **Adding more resources to a rule:** You can add multiple different resources and resource groups to a single rule. However, these are treated as one large resource group for scheduling purposes.

- **Test your rules:** Create service activities to thoroughly test your rules prior to putting them into production. Rules can become quite complex so make sure to check your work.

Tip

Whenever you add a group of resources to a rule, Dynamics CRM asks if you want to save the selection as a new resource group. Although this is not required, you will find it easier to maintain your resource groups if you always create a named resource group.

FIGURE 14.7

A complex service selection rule

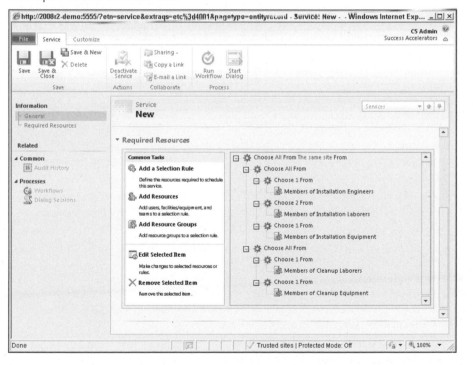

Scheduling services

Dynamics CRM includes a powerful scheduling engine that combines your rules, resources, and calendars to quickly find available time slots to schedule service appointments with customers. A specialized activity called a *service activity* enables you to tap into the scheduling engine. Service activities use the scheduling engine to automate finding available time for service delivery.

You can create service activities directly, or you can create them associated with cases. If you associate a service activity with a case, and the case is associated with a contract, then the hours of service in the contract will also be considered in the scheduling engine. Use the following process to schedule services:

1. Create a new service activity. Typically you do this within a case or from the service calendar.

2. Complete the service activity form. Figure 14.8 is an example of the service activity form; important fields are summarized below:

   - **Service:** Prior to scheduling a service activity, you must define at least one service. See the preceding section of this chapter for information on setting up services.

   - **Site:** If the resources come from a specific site for this activity, then enter the site here (otherwise the scheduling engine selects a site for you).

   - **Resources:** Leaving this field blank allows the Dynamics CRM scheduling engine to dynamically select resources for this appointment based on the rules that your organization has defined. If you want to handpick which resources should be used for this service, then you may enter them here (you can use the form assistant to use the service rules to select resources).

   - **Location:** A free-form field you can use to enter more information about the location at which the service will be delivered. Using this field can be a convenient way to provide additional information about the location to your field service team.

   - **Show Time As:** The scheduling engine uses the information from this field to determine if this time should be blocked out as unavailable or if it can remain available until the appointment is confirmed.

   - **Scheduling Information:** This information can be dynamically populated by the scheduling engine, or you can manually enter it.

3. Save the record. If you entered all of the scheduling and resource information manually, then you can save and close the record. However, if you want to use the scheduling engine (recommended for service activities), then just save the record (without closing it) and proceed to the next step in the process.

4. Click the Schedule button on the Ribbon menu. This opens up a dialog box titled Schedule Service Activity (Figure 14.9 includes an example of this form). This dialog box contains much of the same information that you just entered into the service activity form. You can change these fields while using the scheduling engine to see various scheduling options. Important fields include:

- **Start Date / Start Time:** Using this set of fields, you can limit the scheduling engine to only those times that are best for the customer.

- **Duration:** You can use the default duration that is included with the service definition or you can override this with a new duration.

5. Click the Find Available Times button. This activates the scheduling engine, which will find times that all selected resources are available to deliver this service. The list is displayed in the Available Times section of the dialog box. If none of the times are convenient for the customer, then you can change some of items on the form and click the button again.

6. Select a time and click the Schedule button. After you find a time that works for the customer, select the check box next to the desired time and click the Schedule button. You are returned to the service activity form, the time will be filled in, and any resources selected by the scheduling engine will also be filled in.

7. Save and close the service activity. The scheduled time is reserved and is visible on the service calendar.

FIGURE 14.8

Service activity form

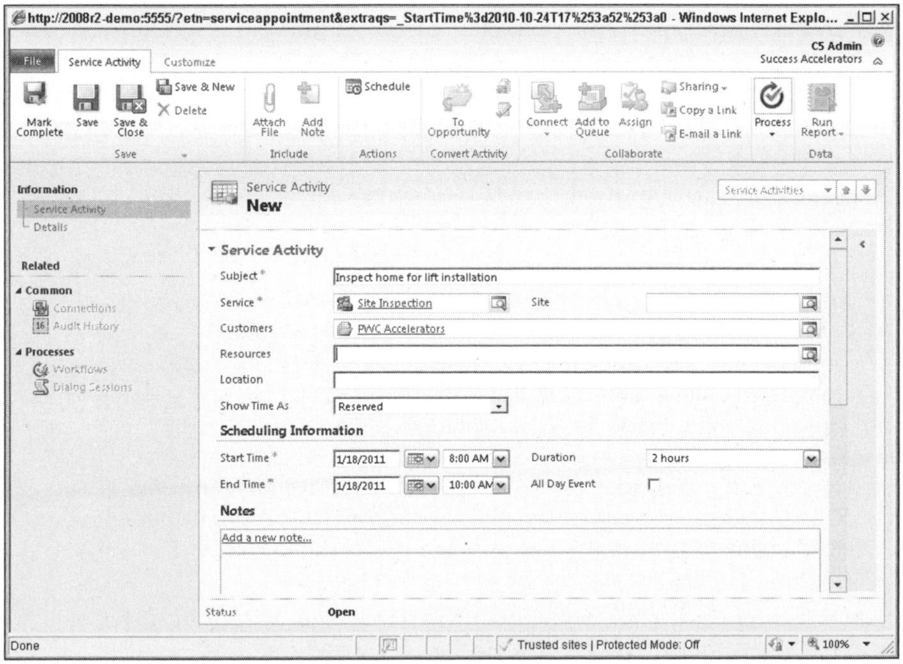

FIGURE 14.9

Schedule Service Activity dialog box

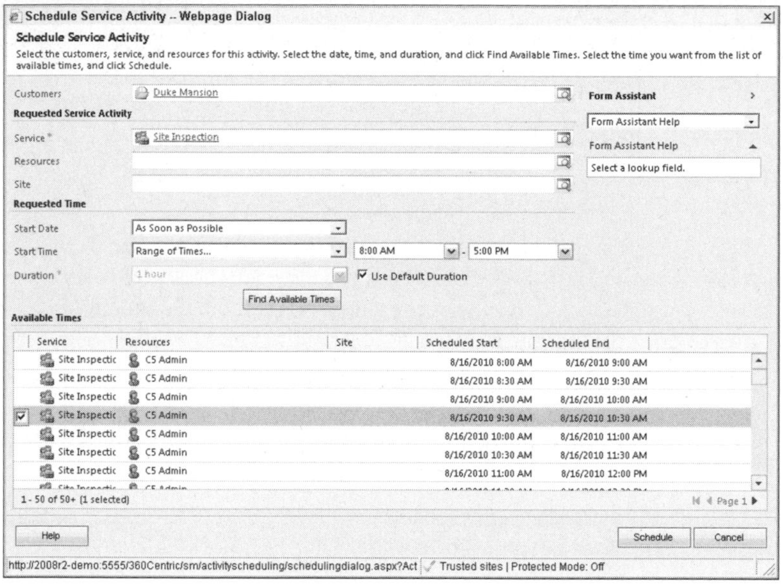

Tip

When viewing the service activity calendar, it can often be helpful to zoom in or out of the calendar to see more detail. You can do this by changing the From and To dates below the service activity calendar, by using the zoom slider (also below the service activity calendar), or by selecting the day, week, or month view to the right of the service activity calendar.

Summary

Case management in Dynamics CRM enables organizations to manage service incidents with individual customers. Cases allow service representatives to ensure that every service incident is followed up until a final solution has been delivered. Workflow rules can be set up to escalate cases to managers or more seasoned service representatives if cases are not resolved quickly enough. Articles are a library of solutions to issues that customers frequently experience. Articles can be applied to cases to resolve them quickly. Contracts allow organizations to track contractual service agreements with their customers and ensure that service level commitments are met.

Service management uses a powerful scheduling engine to set service appointments based on rules defined by your organization. Scheduling takes the availability of personnel, equipment, and facilities into account. When properly configured, service and service activities can result in reducing the number of steps that it takes to schedule appointments to deliver service to customers.

Part V

Customizing Dynamics CRM Through the User Interface

I f you've been using previous versions of Dynamics CRM you're probably already familiar with the powerful tools that are available directly in the application that allow you to configure the software to meet your business needs. If you've worked with the software going back several versions, you're probably also familiar with some of the earlier versions' frustrating limitations.

Microsoft Dynamics CRM 2011 brings a whole new level of flexibility to the game. While no software will ever be "frustration-free," this version of Dynamics CRM has some truly incredible UI tools that can often get you ninety percent of the way to where you want to take your system.

Realizing the Benefits of Office and SharePoint Integration

Microsoft has steadily improved the integration between Dynamics CRM and Office with each release. The integration is so strong at this point that talking about Dynamics CRM without also talking about Word, Excel, and Outlook is sometimes difficult.

With the release of Dynamics CRM 2011 Microsoft has also included direct integration with SharePoint. SharePoint is a framework used for collaborative employee and customer Web sites, business intelligence reporting, document management, and a variety of other functions. Using Dynamics CRM along with SharePoint results in a significant boost to an organization's ability to streamline processes, collaborate with colleagues, and make data visible across the organization.

Organizations that use Dynamics CRM without fully understanding the integration with Office and SharePoint are not realizing the full value of the product.

Exporting and Importing Data with Microsoft Excel

The most popular program in the world for managing data is Microsoft Excel. Excel provides an easy way to rapidly update data, analyze trends, and share information with others. Dynamics CRM includes tools to quickly export data to Excel, update existing records from changes you make in Excel, and insert new records by importing data from Excel.

Cross-Reference

Microsoft Excel can also be used to create custom reports in Dynamics CRM. For information on how to use Excel as a reporting tool, see Chapter 23.

Exporting data to Microsoft Excel

Exporting data to Microsoft Excel is a relatively straightforward process. After exporting data, you can share it with others or update it and import it back into Dynamics CRM. Use the procedure below to export data to Microsoft Excel:

1. Navigate to the list that you want to export data from in Dynamics CRM.

2. Select the view that contains the filters and columns that you want to apply to the list before exporting the data.

3. If the proper view does not exist, you can go to the View tab in the Ribbon menu and select Create Personal View (or Advanced Find). See Chapter 17 for information on working with Advanced Find. After you are done designing the specific view that you need, you can either:

   - Save the view if you expect to reuse it frequently and return to the first step of this process to use the view.

   - Click Results in the Ribbon menu, if you don't expect to need to reuse the view, and continue with the remainder of this process below.

4. In the Ribbon menu, click the Export to Excel button.

5. You are presented with the Export Data to Excel dialog box, shown in Figure 15.1. You have several options from which to choose:

   - Use this type of worksheet: For purposes of this chapter, always select the Static worksheet with records from this page option. The other options are used for creating dynamic reports and are covered in Chapter 23.

   - Make this data available for reimporting by including required column headings: If you plan to make changes to the data and then update the records in Dynamics CRM (covered in a section later in this chapter), then select this option.

6. Click the Export button.

7. When prompted, click the Open button and then click the Yes button in the dialog box. Note that you also have the option of clicking the Save button, but not all computers can read the resulting file, so we recommend using the Open button at this point as a best practice.

8. From Excel, go to File and select Save As.

9. From the Save As dialog box select the appropriate file type based on how you intend to use the file. Here are some pointers:

- Save as Type Excel Workbook if you plan to share the file with non-CRM users inside or outside of your organization.

- Save as Type CSV (Comma delimited) if you plan to import the file into another system. Comma delimited is a file format that virtually all systems will recognize for import purposes — but verify this with the owner of the system you wish to import data into to be certain.

- Save as Type XML Spreadsheet 2003 if you plan to make changes to the data and reimport it (note that you should have selected the appropriate option under Step 5 for this to work).

FIGURE 15.1

Export data to Excel dialog box

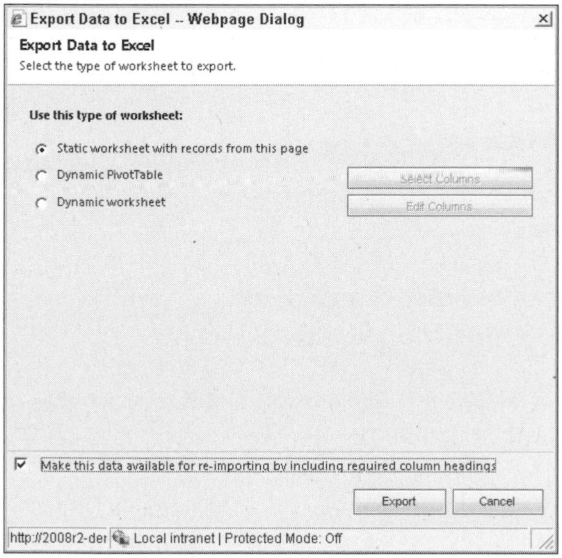

Cross-Reference

For security reasons, many organizations do not want to allow their users to export data in Microsoft Excel format. Security roles allow you to limit the availability of this function to only select users. See Chapter 5 for more information on setting security roles.

Now that you have completed exporting your data, you can update it in Excel, share it with others, import it into other systems, or otherwise freely manipulate the data using Microsoft Excel. If you would like to make revisions to your data and then reimport those changes into Dynamics CRM from Excel, then proceed to the next section.

Updating existing records from Microsoft Excel

Dynamics CRM is a powerful tool for tracking and updating records. However, there are times when you may want to update a large number of records very quickly. For example, you may add a new column on the account form, and you would like to populate it for all of your accounts very quickly. Opening each form in Dynamics CRM to make this type of change can be time-consuming. In Microsoft Excel you can make these updates very quickly and then import them back into Dynamics CRM.

Cross-Reference

If you would like to import only new records into Dynamics CRM (rather than reimporting updates to existing records as we describe here), see Chapter 8.

Use the procedure below to update records in Dynamics CRM by importing them from Microsoft Excel. This procedure assumes that you will export your records from Dynamics CRM for reimport. Follow the steps in the preceding section to ensure that your data is exported in the correct format. In the final step of the procedure, you should save your Excel file as type XML Spreadsheet 2003.

1. Open the file in Microsoft Excel. This Excel file has some unique characteristics that simplify the data entry and reimport process:

    - The initial columns are hidden. When exporting data for reimport, Dynamics CRM exports additional information about each record so it will know which records to update (in the event, for example, that two accounts have the same name) and the time of the last update of each record (see the nearby Caution for more information on this).

    - As you click on each cell, you will notice a popup that tells you the format of the data in the cell and whether the field is required or not. This can aid you in being certain that you are keeping data in the correct format for reimport.

2. Update the data in the spreadsheet to meet your needs. There are some special field types that you should be aware of as you go through this process that will help you with the speed and validation of your data entry:

    - **Option Sets (picklists), Boolean, Status:** These field types include a drop-down selection so you don't have to remember the valid values for your picklists (see Figure 15.2).

    - **Lookup:** You can enter values for these fields, but the values you enter must have a unique match back to an existing record in Dynamics CRM or the record will not be updated on reimport. For example, if you want to enter a primary contact on an account, the full name you enter must exactly match to one (and only one) contact record in Dynamics CRM or none of the changes you made to the account record in Excel will be updated when you import it into Dynamics CRM.

    - **Date, Date/Time:** These field types include functionality to ensure that values are entered correctly for import. If you are not sure how to format a date/time field, you may enter a date without the time and the time will be updated for you (you can then update the time using the correct formatting).

- **Numbers (decimal, integer, money, etc.):** These field types include functionality to ensure that values are within the appropriate ranges.

- **Text:** Text fields do not incorporate formatting for URL, e-mail, and other values. Use caution when entering these fields as you could potentially enter information that is in a format that will not be imported into Dynamics CRM.

- **Mandatory:** Required fields are not enforced in Excel, so it is possible to delete a required field. If a record is missing a required field, it will not be updated in Dynamics CRM when you import it.

- **Related Fields:** Fields from related tables cannot be updated in Excel. For example, if you have the e-mail of the primary contact in a list of all accounts, you should not attempt to update the field in Excel.

FIGURE 15.2

Entering option set values in Microsoft Excel

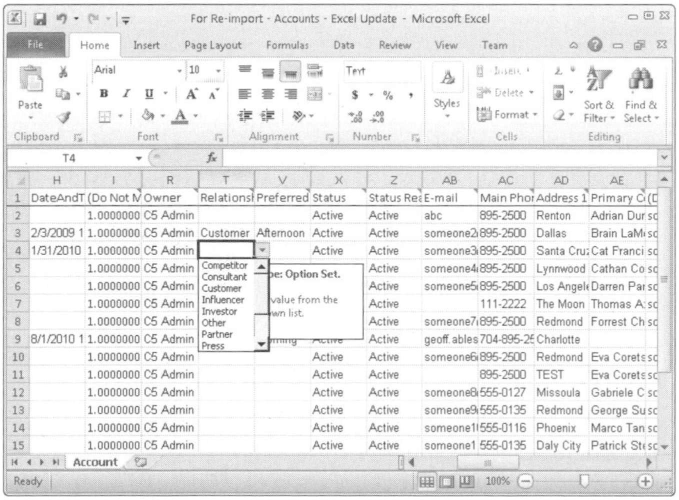

3. Add any new records you want to create. You can create new records by entering them at the bottom of the exported list. These records will be added as new records when you re-import the list. Be sure to fill in any required fields and that all data is formatted correctly.

4. When you have completed making your changes, save the Excel file. You may receive a warning that not all features are supported in this format — you may safely ignore this warning and continue with saving the file.

5. In Dynamics CRM, click on the File tab in the Ribbon menu, select Tools, and then Import Data. You are presented with the Upload Data File page of the Import Data Wizard (Figure 15.3).

6. Browse to the XML file that you saved from Excel and then click next.

FIGURE 15.3

The Import Data Wizard Upload Data File page

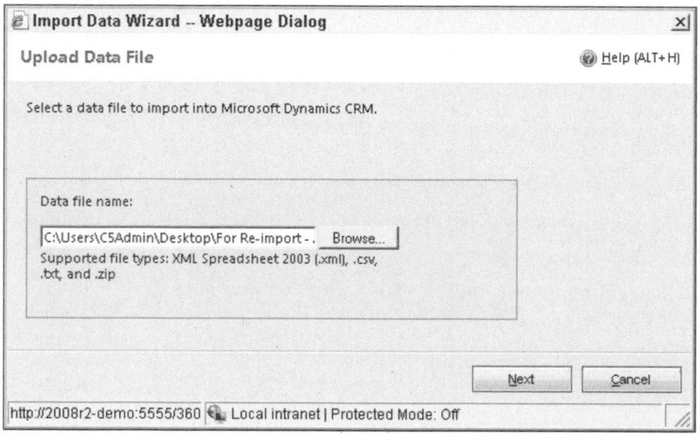

7. Enter the desired values on the Review Settings and Import Data page and then click the Submit button.

8. The final page of the Import Data Wizard appears, confirming that your data has been submitted to import into Dynamics CRM.

Tip

Wondering if your import finished or if there were any problems with it? Go to Settings ➪ Data Management ➪ Imports and you can check the status of your import job, which includes viewing a list of all records that did and did not import.

Caution

Dynamics CRM will not import records that were updated after the time that you exported them. For example, if you export data on Tuesday morning and a colleague updates one of the records that afternoon, and you attempt to reimport on Wednesday, the record your colleague updated will not be updated with the changes you made in Excel. See the nearby tip for information on how to check to see if there were any errors with your import job.

Integrating Line Item Data Entry

Importing data from Excel is a great way to quickly update a large quantity of records. Many organizations, however, need the capability to rapidly update records built directly into Dynamics CRM. For example, you may want to be able to rapidly enter (or update) products under an opportunity without having to open the form for each individual product line item. Fortunately there are a number of options for integrating line item data entry directly into Dynamics CRM. At the time of this writing, no solutions had been announced for Dynamics CRM 2011, but you can check the Web site for the book (www.microsoftcrmbible.com) for available options.

Importing Contacts for Existing Accounts

Many organizations need to regularly import contacts for existing accounts. To do this, follow the instructions for standard importing (see Chapter 8). When creating the contact records in the Excel worksheet, enter the name of the account exactly as it is spelled in Dynamics CRM. When you import the contacts, Dynamics CRM will automatically associate them with the name of the matching account. Prior to importing, make sure that the account has a unique name to ensure that the contacts will import and associate with the correct account. This method works for importing any "child" record (such as products related to opportunities).

Mail Merging with Microsoft Word

Templates can be used to quickly create documents that include information from records in Dynamics CRM. Many organizations expend a tremendous amount of time keying data into a database and then rekeying data into documents. Templates can play an important role in eliminating wasteful data entry while improving accuracy. You can find the list of templates in the Settings area of Dynamics CRM. Four different types of templates are available. We discuss Word mail merge templates here.

Cross-Reference

For information on creating article and contract templates, see Chapter 14. For information on creating e-mail merge templates, see Chapter 10.

Creating a Word mail merge template

If you have ever performed a mail merge using Microsoft Word, then the process of creating a mail merge document for Dynamics CRM will be familiar to you. Mail merges can be used to create individual documents such as proposals and fax cover sheets or to create a large number of documents such as direct mailings.

Mail Merge in Outlook or the Web?

The mail merge functionality has a number of improvements when accessed using Dynamics CRM inside of Outlook (also referred to as the "Outlook client") rather than from the Web. In our instructions in this section, we have pointed out some of the strengths of using the Outlook client for your mail merge projects. Also notice that, if you use Outlook, you can skip some of the steps that are required when running a merge using the Web version of Dynamics CRM.

Our recommendation is to use the Outlook client when designing or running mail merges to make the process smoother and leverage the extra functionality.

To create a new mail merge document, use the procedure below:

1. Navigate to Settings ⇨ Templates and then click on Mail Merge Templates.

2. Click the New button in the menu.

3. Fill in the fields on the form including the following:

   - **Name:** This is the name that will appear in the list of word mail merge templates in Dynamics CRM. Be sure to use a descriptive name that is easy to understand.

   - **Associated Entity:** This will be the list that your mail merge fields will come from. It is typically a contact or a lead, but it can be any entity that supports mail merge in Dynamics CRM.

4. Click on the save button in the menu. After the record is saved, some additional options will be made available.

5. Click the Data Fields button. Choose the fields that you want to have available for your merge document. Only the fields that you choose are going to be available to merge into your document, so, if in doubt, select a field. Note that you can also choose fields from other records related to the list you are using. This allows you to include information about the record owner or other information related to the entity that you are building the merge for.

6. In the menu, click Save again, then click the button labeled Create Template in Word.

7. If prompted by Word, accept any security questions to allow macros and document editing in Word.

8. In the Word ribbon menu, click the Add-Ins tab and then click the Dynamics CRM button.

9. Click the OK button if prompted to confirm the list of recipients.

10. You should now be on a blank Word document, with the Mailings tab selected in the Ribbon menu and the Mail Merge task pane on the right-hand side of the screen as seen in Figure 15.4.

11. Create your mail merge document. Here are some pointers to help you in developing the body of the document:

    - Use Insert Merge Field in the Mailings tab on the Ribbon menu to insert fields from Dynamics CRM into the document.

    - You can use the Address Block and Greeting Line buttons in the Ribbon menu as well. If you do this, be sure to click the Match Fields button (also in the Ribbon menu) first in order to choose the correct fields from Dynamics CRM to include.

    - Be careful when choosing fields. Some field names actually contain a unique ID number though they may appear to contain text based on the field name. For example, if you wish to put the account name in a document, choose the Account_ Name field and NOT the Account field.

- You can also merge in data for the user that is running the merge OR for the owner of the record that the merge is being run for. Be sure to select the right fields depending on what you want displayed on your merge document. See Step 5, above.

Creating a Word mail merge

12. When complete, save the Word template to your computer desktop and close Word.

13. Back in Dynamics CRM, click the Browse button on the template form and navigate to the document you just saved and then click the Attach button. Your Word mail merge form should look something like the image in Figure 15.5.

14. Save and close the template record in Dynamics CRM.

You've just created your first mail merge document using Dynamics CRM! You can leave this as a personal template so that it is only available to you, or you can set it as an organizational template so anyone else in the company can have access to it.

FIGURE 15.5

The Word mail merge form in Dynamics CRM

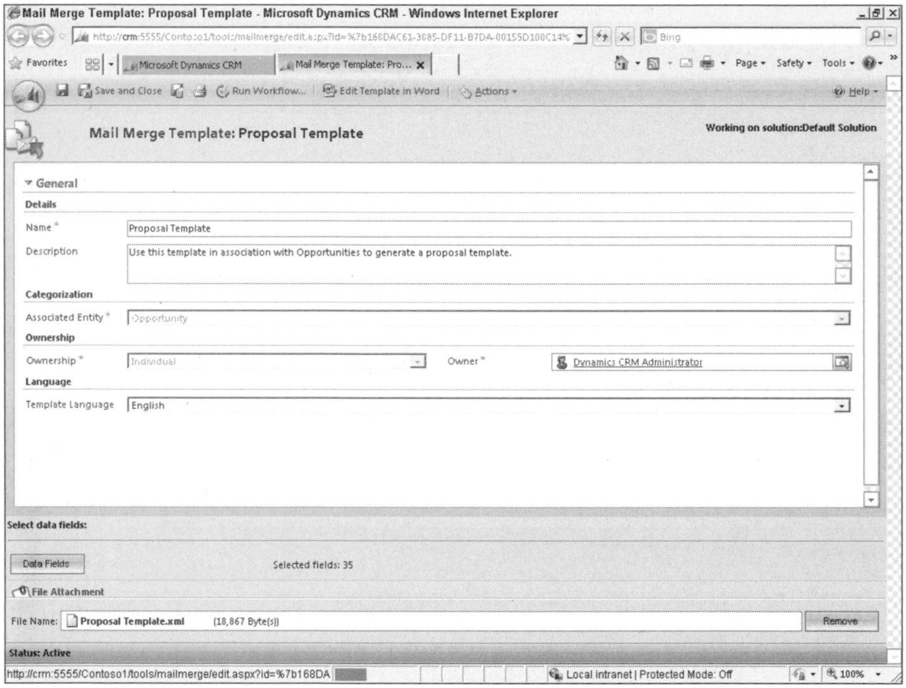

Using a Word mail merge template

After you create your Word mail merge template, you want to be able to use it to quickly create new documents. In our example above, we created a mail merge for opportunities, so I continue to use that in the instructions below — but you can use this with any mail merge–enabled entity in Dynamics CRM.

1. Navigate to the list that you wish to run a mail merge for.

2. Select the records you want to run your merge on using views, filters, advanced find, or selecting the check box next to individual records (or some combination of all of these).

3. In the Ribbon bar, click the Create Related tab and then click the Mail Merge button. You are presented with the dialog box in Figure 15.6.

4. Complete the form and click the OK button. Note that you need to select a Personal or Organization mail merge template depending on the visibility settings for the mail merge template you want to use.

5. Click Open to open the Word document.

FIGURE 15.6

Mail merge dialog box

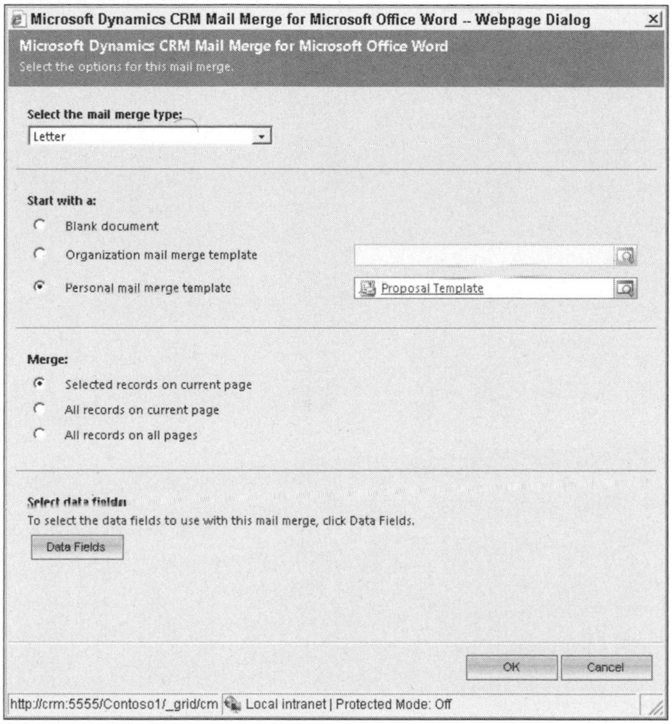

6. If you see a security warning, you will need to click Enable Content (the exact warning may vary depending on the version of Word you are using). To avoid this warning in the future, you can revise your Office trust settings to trust content from Dynamics CRM. You may also need to enable macros in word (these are disabled by default).

7. Click the Add-Ins tab in Word and then click the Dynamics CRM logo. You will be presented with a list of all the records you selected for merging.

8. Click OK to close this dialog box.

9. In the Ribbon menu in Word, make sure you are on the Mailings tab and click the Preview Results button. Use the arrows near Preview Results button to move through the records.

10. After you are satisfied that the merge is ready to run, click the Finish and Merge button and follow the instructions to complete the merge. If you are using Outlook for the merge, you are now presented with the option to update records in Dynamics CRM with an activity indicating that they were targeted with the mail merge (Figure 15.7).

11. Fill out the dialog box with the appropriate information to create an activity of the desired type, assign it to the appropriate individual, set the desired completion status, and run a quick campaign if desired.

FIGURE 15.7

Create activities dialog box

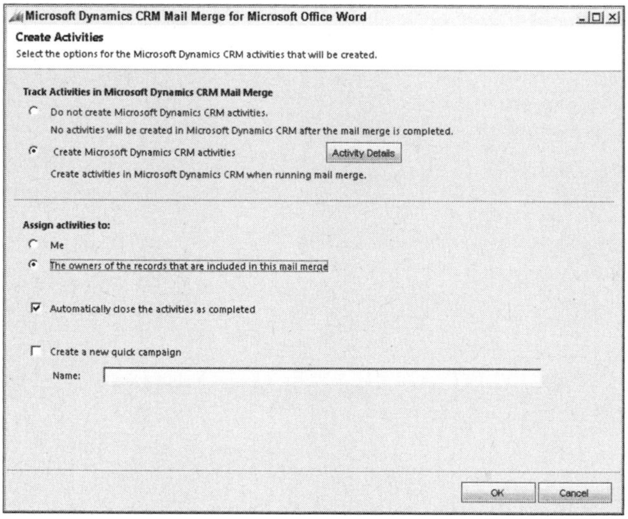

You can reuse the merge document as frequently as you like to create documents that use data from Dynamics CRM. Note that mail merges run with Word can be used for printed documents, bulk e-mail campaigns, envelopes, and other mail merge activities.

Advanced Mail Merge: Quotes

Using Dynamics CRM and Microsoft Word, it is possible to create mail merge documents that include both "header" and "product line item" information for quotes. Developing this type of mail merge document requires some in-depth knowledge about Word mail merge functions. Here are a few tips to get you started:

- **Start with the included template:** Dynamics CRM includes a mail merge template for quotes. This includes much of the functionality that will be required to create your own mail merge quote. Find this template and edit it as a starting point. As a safeguard, save your edits as a new template so you can always go back to the original once you've made changes. After opening the template in Word, press Alt+F9 to edit the full template.

- **Use a directory merge:** Microsoft Word includes a specialized type of merge called a directory that enables you to list multiple records on a single page.

- **Mail merge may not be the answer:** Keep in mind that Dynamics CRM also includes a powerful reporting tool for creating custom reports called SQL Server Reporting Services (SSRS). If the capabilities available in mail merge are not sufficient for creating quotes (or other advanced mail merges) then consider using SSRS for this. This is discussed in Chapter 25.

Working with SharePoint Integration

Increasingly, organizations are finding that marrying SharePoint and Dynamics CRM provides them with a flexible framework for collaborating, managing documents, automating processes, and developing custom applications. This section provides an overview of SharePoint integration that is either built into Dynamics CRM or is easy to create.

Cross-Reference

This section assumes you have properly set up SharePoint integration and installed the SharePoint CRM Grid Component. For information on setting up Sharepoint integration, see Chapter 4. For information on advanced SharePoint integration, see Appendix A.

Storing documents in SharePoint

Dynamics CRM has long included the ability to attach documents to records. However, it was never a very good solution for document management. Document versions could not be maintained, documents could not be searched, and it took a lot of manual effort to find exactly the document that you were looking for. Integrating Dynamics CRM 2011 with SharePoint changes all of that. Integration works with SharePoint 2007 or SharePoint 2010, though this chapter assumes you are working with the stronger capabilities found in SharePoint 2010.

Activating document management for a CRM entity

Dynamics CRM allows you to manage documents for most of the different entities in the system. However, before you can begin to use document management for an entity, you need to activate document management for it. Use the process below to activate document management for an entity:

1. Navigate to Settings ➪ Document Management and click on Document Management Settings.

2. If the entity that you wish to manage documents for has not yet been selected, click the check box next to it and click the Next button (this assumes the SharePoint URL has already been configured correctly).

3. In Chapter 4 you should have already selected an appropriate folder structure for your SharePoint configuration. So you can click Finish on this page to complete the setup process.

The next time you open a record for the entity that you just selected, you will see a new related list in the navigation pane titled "Documents." This area will allow you to manage documents, in SharePoint, for these records. By default each record is given a separate subdirectory in SharePoint.

Associating a SharePoint location to a Dynamics CRM record

Every record in Dynamics CRM that you want to manage documents for will need to be associated with a SharePoint document location. A document location is a folder within a SharePoint library. There are two methods you can use to make this association, described below.

Auto-creating a location

The first time you navigate to the Documents related list in a record, you will be prompted with a popup message that a new folder will be created. You can click the OK button to create a folder automatically. After a few moments, the folder will be created, and you will see it in Dynamics CRM (Figure 15.8).

FIGURE 15.8

A SharePoint document location in Dynamics CRM

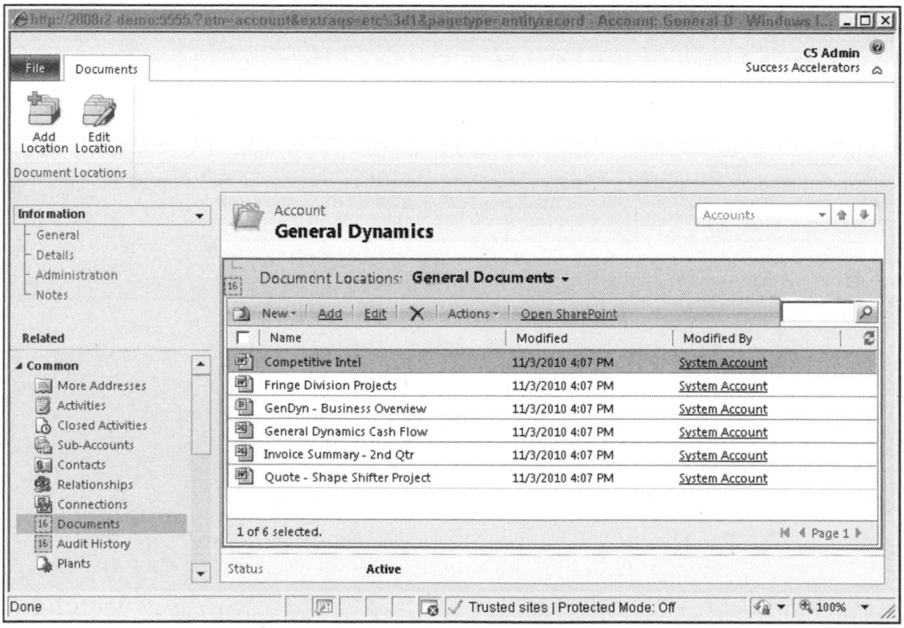

Other SharePoint Document Integration Options

Auto-creating document locations in SharePoint is limited to adding folders into a specific document library for each new record. In some cases, you may want to create an entire site in SharePoint for each record. For example, you may wish to create a customer site that has several document libraries, a wiki for sharing knowledge, and a discussion group for resolving issues for each account in Dynamics CRM. If this is how your SharePoint site is structured, then you have a couple of options for SharePoint integration.

1. You can manually associate document locations with each Dynamics CRM record (described below).

2. If you would like to use a SharePoint site template to auto-create a complete site every time a record is created in Dynamics CRM, then you should consider developing some code to automate this process. Appendix A has some ideas for advanced SharePoint integration.

Auto-created locations don't always have understandable location names. To change the name of the location, click the Edit Location button in the Ribbon menu. In the dialog box, change the name of the location to something easier to understand and then click the Save button. The next time you open the record, you will see the new name for the document location.

Manually associating a location

You can also manually associate a location with a Dynamics CRM record. This can be handy if you have created custom sites and document libraries for records in SharePoint. For example, you may create a site for every marketing campaign so you can collaborate on the campaign by sharing ideas, meeting agendas, and documents. Using the automatic approach to creating document locations won't work well in this case because the documents for your campaign will not be kept in the same Sharepoint site as all of your other campaign information. Use this method to manually associate a SharePoint document location to a Dynamics CRM record:

1. Navigate to the SharePoint document library that you want to associate with the record in Dynamics CRM. Copy the URL to the clipboard. Note: If you set up a parent URL for this location already, then you can bypass this step.

2. Navigate to the record in Dynamics CRM that you want to associate with the SharePoint document location and then click on Documents related list.

   - If this is the first time you have come to the Documents area, then click the Cancel button when prompted to bypass creating a new document location automatically.

   - If you already auto-created a document location, you can still continue with the instructions below to associate this record with a second location.

3. In the Ribbon menu, click on the Add Location button.

4. In the dialog box (see Figure 15.9) enter the name of the location and then specify the location as follows:

- If you copied an existing location in Step 1, above, then you can paste it into the existing location field.

- If you set up a parent URL for this type of Dynamics CRM entity, then you can choose the Create a Location option, select the appropriate Parent URL, and name the location.

Add Location dialog box

5. Click the Save button, and your association is made and the document library is displayed.

Tip

You can associate a record in Dynamics CRM with multiple document locations. This can come in handy if, for example, you work with distributors who sell into the accounts that you track in Dynamics CRM. Under the distributor record, you may want to be able to browse to the document locations for all of the accounts that they serve. To set up multiple document locations for a single record, follow the instructions for manually associating a location for each document location you want to add.

Working with SharePoint documents

If you're already familiar with SharePoint, then many of the functions available in Dynamics CRM for working with documents will be familiar to you. Because all of the documents from Dynamics CRM are stored directly inside of SharePoint, you can access them from either SharePoint or from Dynamics CRM. Here are some of the things you can do with SharePoint documents from within Dynamics CRM:

- **Create new documents.** You can click the New button to create a new document directly within Dynamics CRM. When you save the document, it will be saved to the document library.

- **Add existing documents.** You can click the Add button to add new documents. From the dialog box you can choose to add a single document or multiple documents. If you select multiple documents you can drag multiple documents from your desktop and drop them directly into the document location.

- **Edit documents in the library.** You can double-click a document to edit it.

- **Work in SharePoint.** You can click the Open SharePoint button to open the SharePoint site that contains the document library. This can be handy if there are other SharePoint features that you want to use on the site.

- **Other options.** The actions menu contains a number of familiar SharePoint functions that you can also access directly within Dynamics CRM. One of the most useful ones is the Copy Shortcut option — this allows you to send a link to a selected document to your colleagues via e-mail without having to attach the document. Tracking your documents in SharePoint keeps you from having to reconcile different versions that may be in multiple e-mail boxes and keeps the size of your e-mail folders smaller.

Sharing Documents Outside of Your Organization

SharePoint is a great tool for collaborating and managing documents within your business. But the native SharePoint integration with Dynamics CRM doesn't facilitate sharing documents with individuals outside of your organization. For example, if you were to embed a link to a SharePoint document into an e-mail that went to a client, they would not be able to open that document unless you had configured SharePoint correctly.

Many options are available for configuring SharePoint to collaborate with others outside of your organization. A few of the more widely implemented approaches are:

- Create a document sharing portal. This can be a single document library that is open to outside access without requiring any authentication. Any individual inside or outside of your organization can download documents from this library without a login. This has the advantage of being a very fast way to delivery documents. But, of course, it also has the disadvantage of leaving itself totally open to anyone (including competitors) accessing the documents.

- Set up individual customer portals. Although this takes a bit more time and effort, customer portals can provide secure access to unique SharePoint sites and document libraries to each customer. This provides a strong foundation for collaborating with those inside and outside of your organization.

See Appendix A for more information on integrating SharePoint with Dynamics CRM to create a collaboration portal to connect people inside and outside of your organization.

Publishing Excel pivot tables as SharePoint dashboards

In Chapter 23, you will learn how to create dynamic reports and charts from Dynamics CRM data using Microsoft Excel. These reports (dynamic pivot tables) can be published into SharePoint using the Microsoft Excel Web part. Because these reports have a live connection to data in Dynamics CRM, the dashboards are refreshed every time the SharePoint page is updated. The following list provides an overview of the steps you need to take to publish Excel pivot tables as SharePoint dashboards:

- **Make sure you have the correct version of SharePoint.** You need to be sure that you are using the Enterprise version of SharePoint to take advantage of Excel services.

- **Create a dashboard page in SharePoint using the Excel Web part.** This is the page that you use to display your report. You can include reports from sources other than Dynamics CRM on this page as well to provide a complete corporate dashboard.

- **Create an Excel pivot table.** Using the information provided in Chapter 23, create an Excel pivot table and any accompanying charts.

- **Load the pivot table to a SharePoint document library.** Most SharePoint dashboards include a library dedicated to holding the files needed to render the dashboard pages. Load your Excel file to the appropriate SharePoint document library.

- **Add the Excel Web part.** On the SharePoint dashboard page, add an Excel Web part and configure it to use the file that you loaded to the SharePoint document library. SharePoint includes a number of settings you can change to configure exactly how the report will work.

Using SharePoint 2010 tags and notes

SharePoint 2010 includes a number of new collaboration tools including tags and notes.

Tags enable you to associate terms with any Web page or SharePoint document in a free-form manner. For example, you can tag a document as good quote template. Similarly, you can tag Web pages with items such as "competitor." Because every record in Dynamics CRM is assigned a unique URL, you can use tags to associate terms with any Dynamics CRM record. For example, you can tag an account as "at risk" or "hot." You can then view a list of your tags in a "tag cloud" and can click on the tag "hot" to see a list of all of the Dynamics CRM records that were tagged with this value.

Notes are similar to tags in that they can be used on any Web page. Notes, however, allow you to publish more information (think of them as "taking notes") about the specific page. For instance, you can post a note entry to an opportunity in Dynamics CRM that says, "Excellent demo with this prospect, they seem interested in a proof of concept project." Notes are visible in the SharePoint noteboard to all users who have subscribed to view them (similar to Facebook or LinkedIN social media posts).

SharePoint 2010 includes a simple-to-use tool for taking advantage of tags and notes. Depending on how your organization has set up SharePoint 2010, the ways to access this tool may vary. With a typical setup you will:

1. Visit your My Site in SharePoint.

2. Navigate to My Profile and then to Tags and Notes.

3. On the bottom left-hand side of the screen you will see a section titled Add SharePoint Tags and Notes Tool. Follow the instructions in this section to add this tool to your favorites in Internet Explorer.

4. After the link has been added to your favorites bar, you can click it from any page (including a Dynamics CRM record) to add tags or notes to the record.

After a record has been tagged or had notes posted to it, anyone who navigates to the same page can see the notes and tags. Figure 15.10 is an example of a tags and notes popup for a Dynamics CRM record.

FIGURE 15.10

SharePoint tags and notes on a Dynamics CRM record

Summary

When combined with Office and SharePoint, you can significantly expand on the breadth, depth, and speed of what you can accomplish with Dynamics CRM. Microsoft Excel integration enables you to export records and to rapidly update existing records. Microsoft Word integration provides the ability to quickly create and access mail merge documents and update Dynamics CRM with activities whenever a mail merge is run. SharePoint enhances the document management capabilities of Dynamics CRM and provides social networking tools.

CHAPTER 16

Tailoring CRM to Your Organization

Dynamics CRM 2011 was built from the ground up to be customized. In fact, if your organization is using only the functionality available directly out of the box, then you are tapping into only a small fraction of the power available to you. Moreover, much of the customization available in Dynamics CRM can be accessed without writing any code — bringing customization within reach of nondevelopers. This chapter provides an overview of the concept of developing applications without coding (also referred to as "model driven development") by customizing Dynamics CRM.

With the release of Dynamics CRM 2011, Microsoft has introduced the solution framework. Solutions serve as "containers" that contain multiple customized components in an easy-to-manage package. Solutions provide a way to more easily manage the process of deploying customizations within your organization or from third-party organizations. For individuals who will be making customizations to Dynamics CRM, it is important to understand the solution framework explained in this chapter in order to ensure that your customizations are easy to manage and take advantage of best practices in working within the solution framework.

The purpose of this chapter is to cover customization concepts and how to work with the solution framework. Subsequent chapters will focus on how to make specific customizations to Dynamics CRM.

Caution

The ease-of-customization available to organizations in Dynamics CRM is a double-edged sword. On the one hand, organizations can adapt to a changing environment faster than ever before. On the other hand, it means that the application can quickly become over-complicated and difficult to use. It is important that organizations develop a governance process to ensure that all changes are reviewed and prioritized before implementation — and that ongoing training is provided.

Understanding Customization and Configuration

Customization and configuration in Dynamics CRM brings custom application development within reach of nondevelopers. This is a great advantage to businesses of all sizes. Smaller businesses can develop customizations that deliver a competitive advantage without requiring full-time developers. Larger businesses can have business analysts perform core customization tasks and can free their developers to focus on only the portions of application development that require their skills.

However, this also presents a range of new terminology and concepts that are important to understand. This section provides an overview of some of the terminology that may be new to you as well as some of the core concepts related to developing solutions using a model driven development (MDD) approach.

Understanding customization terminology

The terms in Table 16.1 are used throughout the remainder of this section to describe concepts related to the customization and configuration of Dynamics CRM.

TABLE 16.1

Customization Terminology

Term	Definition
Code	Computer code (such as jscript, HTML, Visual Basic, C#, or Silverlight) can be included in custom Dynamics CRM solutions. Options for coding are discussed in section VI.
Component	Components are portions of a Dynamics CRM solution. A partial list of components includes entities, reports, processes, security roles, and dashboards.
Configure	Configuration is a broad term that has become somewhat diluted. In general, we refer to configuration as the process of setting up the basic portions of Dynamics CRM (such as security roles, business units, and other settings). However, configuration is also often used in connection with making customizations to the user interface.
Customize	Customization is the process of making changes to the Dynamics CRM user interface. This can include making changes though the user interface (as we discuss throughout this section) or through writing custom code (discussed in the next section).
Declarative design	Declarative design (or declarative programming) is an approach to developing computer applications where the application is controlled by a set of rules and properties rather than through writing custom code. Dynamics CRM incorporates declarative design concepts to make many customization features available to non-programmers.

Term	Definition
Dependencies	Dependencies in Dynamics CRM are components which are dependent upon other components. For example, if a field is included on a form and in a view, then the form and view are both dependent upon that field. If the field were deleted, it would create a situation in which the view and form could not be displayed properly.
Entity	Entities in Dynamics CRM are similar to tables in database applications or to Excel spreadsheets. In Dynamics CRM, however, entities include not only fields but also data entry forms, views, and charts related to the entity. Entities are discussed in detail in Chapter 17.
Field	Fields are the individual data elements that are stored in an entity. For example, First Name and Last Name are both fields on the contact entity. Fields are discussed in detail in Chapter 17.
Instance	An instance of Dynamics CRM can be thought of as an "installation." The difference, however, is that many instances can be a part of a single installation. For example, some organizations will have a "sandbox" instance of Dynamics CRM just for testing and development purposes, and a "production" instance that they use to run their business. Others may have an instance for one business unit (such as Human Resources) and another for a different business unit (such as Research and Development).
Managed solutions	Managed solutions allow Dynamics CRM solution publishers to control the ability of others to make modifications to some or all of the components in a solution. Managed properties and managed solutions are discussed within this chapter.
Model driven development	Model driven development (MDD) is similar in concept to declarative design (above). The concept behind model driven development is that individuals can create parts of a software application while still in the design stage that can be incorporated directly into the final product (blending together the process of documenting application requirements and developing the final solution — thus reducing the amount of time required to produce a final solution). The Dynamics CRM solution framework incorporates an MDD approach to development.
Publisher	Publishers in Dynamics CRM are organizations that develop custom solutions. A publisher can include an organization that makes their own solutions for internal usage or third-party developers who re-sell their solutions. Publishers are discussed in more detail later in this chapter.
Relational database	Relational databases link multiple tables (or entities in the case of Dynamics CRM) together in different types of relationships. For example, the account entity is related to the opportunity entity so that when you view one account you can see many opportunities that are related to it. Relational databases are discussed in more detail in Chapter 17.
Solution	Solutions in Dynamics CRM are "containers" that hold a set of components and associated customizations. Solutions make it easier to manage, share, and control customizations that have been made to Dynamics CRM. Solutions are discussed in more detail later in this chapter.
Solution layering	Solution layering describes the process of creating a solution that incorporates components of an existing solution in a new solution.

Understanding model driven development

Dynamics CRM 2011 incorporates model driven development (MDD) approaches designed to make it faster and easier for organizations to customize and expand upon the core CRM functionality. As the name implies, MDD enables application development that requires relatively little custom coding. Using MDD, portions of a software application can be modeled during the earliest stages of a project. Those portions can then be incorporated directly into the application without requiring additional development in later stages.

Traditional software application development, in contrast to MDD, typically launches with a requirements stage in which the needs of the project are thoroughly assessed and documented. This is usually followed by design and coding phases in which the application is built primarily by writing custom computer code.

MDD offers an approach that delivers results much faster than traditional development, at a lower cost, and with a reduced need for developer expertise. Furthermore, using the MDD approach, individuals who understand the business needs can be directly involved with modeling the application — delivering a result that is much more closely aligned with the needs of the business.

While knowledge of MDD is not a requirement for working with Dynamics CRM, it is helpful to understand the MDD concepts outlined below.

Documenting and designing

MDD can reduce the time required to develop and extend software applications. However, it is still important to develop proper design documentation for any software application project — particularly for complex projects that will support a large number of users. The strength of MDD is that portions of the application can be created as a part of the documentation phase. Thus, the documentation process can be completed faster and with a higher quality outcome because users can review a model that is closer to the actual end product. Furthermore, the model can be reused during the development phase to shorten that portion of the project lifecycle as well. For example, a form can be laid out very close to what will be presented to the user in the final product, and users can approve the form design far earlier in the project lifecycle. The model elements (such as forms, reports, and charts) can then be reused later in the project lifecycle to reduce the amount of time required to develop the application.

Design and code: Identifying the gaps

MDD also enables a nondeveloper to focus on modeling the core set of customizations for a solution. Gaps that require custom coding can be noted in the project requirements documentation and can be addressed during the development phase. For example, while creating a form for a pilot project, the design team may note that custom code is required to provide a set of sales tips to users based on the phase of the sales process. This code can later be written by a developer and added to the application.

Working with a development sandbox

Because the MDD approach to customizing Dynamics CRM can involve a fair amount of trial and error, most organizations will find it beneficial to set up a separate environment for development. This will allow the design team to publish and test changes without impacting the individuals who are currently using Dynamics CRM in production. The concept of a development environment is discussed in Chapter 20.

Accessing the customizations area

The functionality we discuss in this chapter is found in the customization group in the settings area of Dynamics CRM, as illustrated in Figure 16.1. This area includes sub-areas for customizations and solutions, as described in the following list:

- **Customizations:** This sub-area includes access to all components associated with customizing Dynamics CRM. Typically, you navigate to this area when:

  - You want to customize Dynamics CRM without storing the changing in a solution. For more information, see the "Using the default solution" section.

  - You need to add a new publisher or update the default publisher. In most cases, organizations will need to update the default publisher once after going live with Dynamics CRM.

  - You need to download the Web services description files (WSDL). If you are developing custom code that works with Dynamics CRM, you may need to download the WSDL file to integrate into your programming code.

- **Solutions:** This sub-area takes you directly to a list of all available solutions in your instance of Dynamics CRM. You navigate to this area when:

  - You want to make changes to existing customizations. You can access any solution directly from this sub-area. After you have opened a solution, you can make any desired changes to it.

  - You want to create a new solution. From this sub-area, you can create new solutions to extend your instance of Dynamics CRM or to share with other Dynamics CRM instances.

- **Dynamics Marketplace:** Navigate to this area when you want to browse the Solutions Marketplace. Microsoft has developed a marketplace where third parties can make their solutions available for sale and download directly into Dynamics CRM. This marketplace is integrated directly into Dynamics CRM.

FIGURE 16.1

The customizations group in Dynamics CRM

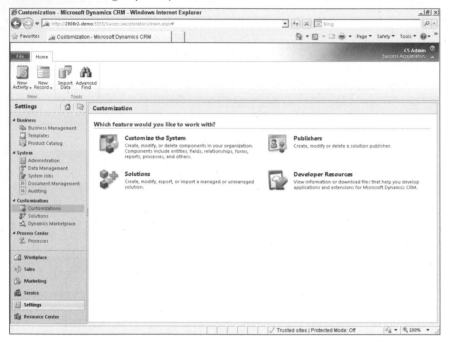

Working with Solutions

New in Dynamics CRM 2011 is the concept of solutions. Solutions not only make it easier to acquire third-party add-ons for Dynamics CRM, they also give you an excellent tool for managing the customizations that your own organization makes to the application. By using customizations you can improve:

- **Solution manageability:** Solutions are containers that bundle sets of customizations together. In previous versions of Dynamics CRM, customizations were not grouped into solutions, and it was often difficult to differentiate the components of one solution from another.

- **Solution portability:** Entire solutions can be exported from one instance of Dynamics CRM and imported into another. This means that you can develop customizations in a test environment and easily redeploy them into a production environment. In addition, it means that third-party customizations can be readily installed into other instances of Dynamics CRM.

- **Team development:** Different individuals can work on different solutions using different instances of Dynamics CRM at the same time. These different solutions can be imported into the same production instance of Dynamics CRM. This can speed the development process by allowing different individuals to work on development at the same time (so long as they are not working on the same solution).

- **Control your customizations:** Customizations can be controlled. Properties for individual components can be "managed" to disallow others from making changes. This enables your organization to lock down certain portions of the functionality, while allowing some power users to make some of their own customizations.

- **Merge (or layer) solutions:** Functionality delivered in one solution can be expanded by "layering" other solutions that reuse components from the first solution.

Understanding the steps of solution management

This section provides an overview of the solution management process. Although the process for working with solutions is fairly open ended, we will present it in the typical sequence of steps that most individuals use when getting started. Figure 16.2 is a diagram of the typical process for creating and managing solutions. Below the figure is a brief explanation of each step with cross-references to other sections in this chapter or subsequent chapters.

FIGURE 16.2

The solution management process

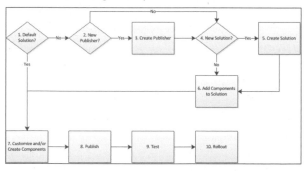

1. **Default Solution?:** Determine if you will be making changes to the default solution or to a custom solution. We do not recommend making changes to the default solution. See the "Using the default solution" section for more information.

2. **New Publisher?:** If this is the first solution that your organization has developed, then you should either update the default publisher or create a publisher. Most organizations will only need to update the default publisher once.

3. **Create Publisher:** See the section later in this chapter, "Creating a new publisher" for information on how to create a publisher.

4. **New Solution?:** If the customizations you want to make are associated with an existing solution, then you should use that solution if possible. If you wish to modify a solution that is managed (such as a third-party solution) then you will need to create a new solution and reuse components from the existing solution. If your customizations are not related to any existing solutions, then you should create a new stand-alone solution.

5. **Create Solution:** See the section later in this chapter, "Creating a solution," for more information.

6. **Add Components to Solution:** Any components required by your solution should be added at this time. This can include system components (such as the account entity) or components that are part of other solutions. For more information see the "Adding components to a solution" and "Layering: Building on existing solutions" sections.

7. **Customize or Create Components:** Within the selected solution, customize or create the components required to complete your solution. How to create and customize solution components is covered in subsequent chapters of this book.

8. **Publish:** After you have completed the solution, publish it to Dynamics CRM. Publishing is explained in Chapter 17.

9. **Test:** As always, it is important that you test your changes prior to rolling them out for others in your organization. If your tests fail, you may need to go back to Step 6 or 7 until your solution passes all tests.

10. **Rollout:** Depending on the size and complexity of your business, the rollout step may take on one of many different forms:

    - Smaller organizations may move directly into user training.

    - Mid-sized organizations may export changes and import them into their production environment.

    - Large organizations may export changes and import them into a testing environment that exactly mirrors their production environment. After completing testing, they may then import the changes into their production environment.

Understanding solutions and publishers

Publishers are organizations or individuals that make customizations to Dynamics CRM. Prior to making changes to Dynamics CRM for the first time, you should edit the default publisher. For most organizations, this one-time edit of the default publisher is all that should be required. If, however, you plan to republish your customizations and provide them to other organizations, then you may want to create a publisher specifically for that purpose. Some larger organizations may wish to create publishers based on different business units or even different individual developers.

When Should I Create a Solution?

The framework for creating new solutions is flexible and will allow your organization to develop their own set of business practices for solution creation and management. Use the examples below to help you along in the process of deciding when you should and should not create new solutions.

Create a new solution

- To manage a customized sales process that includes forms, fields, Web resources, processes and reports.

- To manage a single solution containing all of the general configurations that you wish to make to Dynamics CRM (see the section "Using the default solution" below, for more information).

- To manage a significant new piece of functionality that may involve custom entities, charts, processes, and reports. This may include items such as expense reporting, inventory tracking, or distributor management.

Do not create a new solution

- To manage each miscellaneous customization that you make (for this, we recommend using a "base solution" which is explained in the section below, "Using the default solution").

- To manage customizations on an entity-by-entity basis. Many organizations manage large projects by scheduling milestones on an entity-by-entity basis. While this is perfectly acceptable from a project management perspective, most entities are interrelated with other entities so solutions should focus on functionality rather than data structures.

Solutions are containers that hold a set of customizations. Any publisher may create any number of solutions to manage customizations that are being made to Dynamics CRM. A solution can be owned by only one publisher and, as a rule, should only be managed by that publisher. You may also import solutions from third-party publishers. See the nearby sidebar for tips on when you should (and should not) create solutions.

Using the default solution

When you install Dynamics CRM 2011, it creates a solution with the name "Default Solution" for your organization. This default solution contains all of the components available in Dynamics CRM, including any new components that have been imported as part of another solution. Rather than creating a solution for your customizations, you are free to make changes directly to the default solution.

However, as a best practice, we recommend that you avoid making changes to the default solution. Keeping all of your customizations compartmentalized into named solutions gives you an easier way to roll customizations back if needed. We recommend the following approach for solution management:

- Create a new solution called Base Customizations to manage all of the general customizations that you make to Dynamics CRM that may not fall into a specific solution. This may include changes to fields, forms, and views for accounts, contacts, leads, and so forth.

- Create additional solutions for new functionality that can be clearly bundled together (see the nearby sidebar, "When Should I Create a Solution?"

With the above recommendation in mind, there are also some good reasons why you may want to use the default solution. To help you decide on the best approach for your organization, consider the list of pros and cons in Table 16.2.

TABLE 16.2

Pros and Cons of Using the Default Solution

Pros	Cons
Simplicity: For nontechnical system customizers, it is easier to work with a single default solution rather than to create multiple solutions for different functionality. This is particularly true for small businesses that mostly use the core functions that are included with Dynamics CRM	**Solution tracking:** If all customizations are made to the default solution, then it can be difficult and time consuming to identify discrete customizations that have been made.
Ease of access: The Dynamics CRM user interface includes Ribbon menu shortcuts that provide fast access to the default solution to make quick changes. If you do not use the default solution, then it will require a few extra clicks to access the solution that you wish to modify.	**Solution documentation and management:** If all customizations are maintained within the default solution, then it can be very difficult to determine the purpose of each individual customization.
	Team development: On larger teams, multiple individuals can concurrently work on different solutions. However, if only the default solution is being utilized, then merging customizations from different sources can introduce a number of quality issues.
	Portability: Exporting and importing a solution is a fairly straightforward process. Customizations that are made to the default solution, however, introduce some time-consuming issues for exporting and importing.

Creating a publisher and editing the default publisher

When you initially install Dynamics CRM, you should edit the default publisher with your organization's settings. You may also want to create a new publisher at that time. To navigate to the list of publishers in Dynamics CRM, go to Settings ⇨ Customizations and then click on Publishers.

Editing the default publisher

The default publisher contains settings that describe your organization. You want to change these settings prior to making any customizations. To edit the default publisher:

1. Navigate to the list of publishers and click on the value in the Name column of the default publisher (this will usually be something like "DefaultPublisher[Your Company Name]"). You will be presented with the data entry form in Figure 16.3.

2. Update the fields on the form as follows:

   - **Display Name:** Change this to a name that describes your organization (in most cases this will be the name of your organization, but in large organizations it may be the name of your business unit).

   - **Name:** This value cannot be changed. For most organizations this will not present a problem. However, if you plan to make your solutions available to others and you want to create a unique name that aligns better with your company branding, then you will want to create a new publisher for this purpose (see below).

   - **Description:** Entering good, descriptive information for the description is always a best practice — particularly if you plan to create multiple publishers. A good description might be, "We use this publisher to make internal-facing solutions and customizations to Dynamics CRM; do not use this publisher for solutions that you plan to share with others inside or outside of our organization."

   - **Prefix:** This small field is the most important one on the form. It permanently impacts every customization you make to Dynamics CRM using this publisher. Every component (entity, field, and so on) that you create in Dynamics CRM will be prefixed with this value. The value will only show up in views available to administrators and developers. Although this value can be changed later, components created with this value permanently retain it — so select a value that you don't plan to change. This is usually a three- to five-letter acronym that your organization may be known for. The prefix makes it fairly easy to identify customizations that your team made to Dynamics CRM versus changes that may have been made by others.

   - **Option Value Prefix:** These are the first numbers that will be assigned to any new option set values that you create with this publisher. These numbers reduce the chance that duplicate values are created when importing solutions from this publisher that contain option sets. In general, you can leave this number unchanged.

   - **Contact Details:** Fill in the contact information for your organization in this section.

Creating a new publisher

Most organizations will never need to create a new publisher. However, if your organization will share their solutions with other organizations (internally or externally), then you may want to create an additional publisher to identify the source of each solution.

To create a new publisher, navigate to the list of publishers and click the New button. Follow the instructions in the preceding section to fill out the publisher form.

FIGURE 16.3

Publisher data entry form

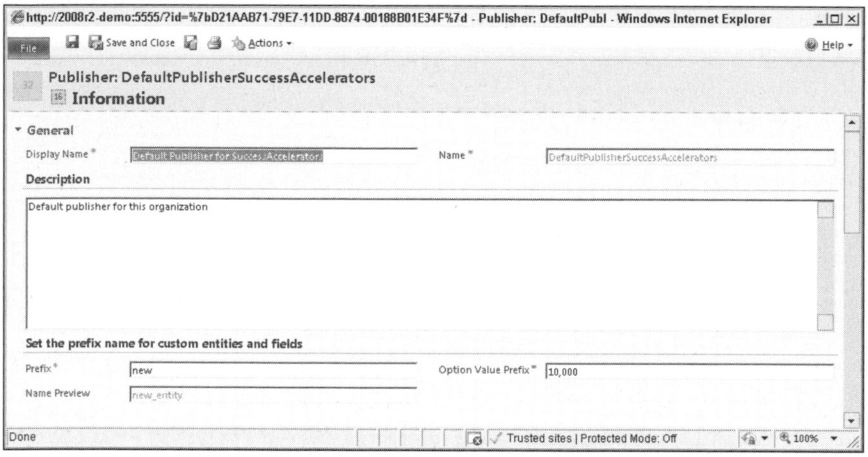

Other publishers

Note that other publishers may also be visible in the list of publishers in Dynamics CRM. These are other organizations that have provided solutions which have been imported into your instance of Dynamics CRM. These publishers cannot be edited. The publishers cannot be deleted unless you first delete any solutions that were provided by the publisher.

Creating a solution

Use the steps below to create a new solution:

1. Navigate to Settings ➪ Solutions and click the New button. You are presented with the data entry form in Figure 16.4.

2. Fill out the form using the list below as a guideline:

   - **Display Name:** Enter a name that describes your solution.

   - **Name:** Dynamics CRM also suggests a unique name after you enter the friendly name, but you can change this to another value. Note that after the form has been saved, this value cannot be changed.

   - **Publisher:** Select the publisher that this solution should be associated with. Note that the prefix set for the publisher will be used for all customizations in the solution.

- **Configuration Page:** This value allows you to create a page that can be used to provide more information on your solution and that can provide configuration controls. The field can initially be left blank and a Web resource can be created as a part of the solution that serves as the configuration page.

- **Version:** Enter a version number for this solution, such as 0.0.0.1. The convention for this numbering is major.minor.build.revision — though you can use whatever numbering convention your organization agrees upon. You can also choose to enter only the first two to three portions of the version if you prefer. Version numbers should be manually updated as you go through the development process.

- **Description:** As always, it is a best practice to provide a thorough description of the solution using this space. Good descriptions make solutions easier to maintain.

- **Package Type:** This field cannot be edited until the solution is exported. See the section "Working with managed properties" later in this chapter for more information.

3. After you have completed the form, click the Save button to save the solution without closing the form. The solution is saved, and you can begin adding components to the new solution.

FIGURE 16.4

Solutions data entry form

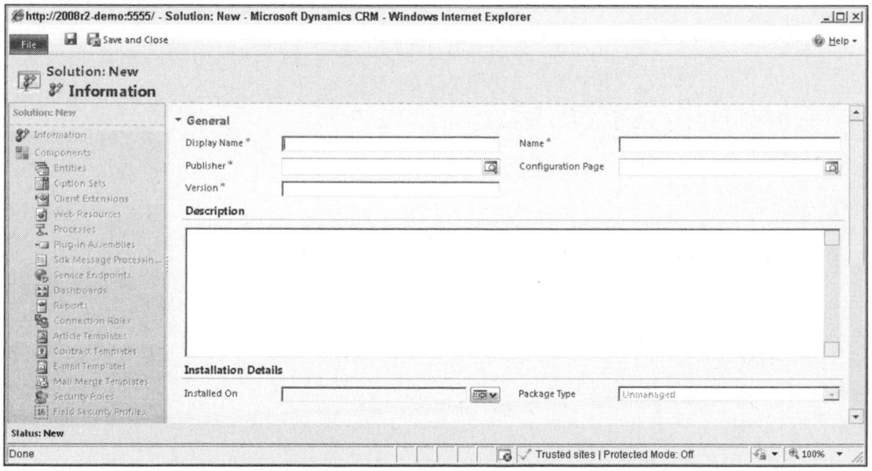

Adding components to a solution

After you have created a solution, add the components to it that you wish to customize. Solution components may include new components (for example, create a new entity called "Project" for a project management solution), existing system components that you wish to customize (for example, add the account entity if you wish to add fields to the account data entry form), or components that are part of other solutions that you wish to extend (see the section on Layering later in this chapter for more information on extending other solutions). Components can include entities (and their associated fields, forms, views, and charts), option sets, security roles, dashboards, templates, Web resources, and a number of other items. Figure 16.5 is an example solution; the navigation pane includes a list of the various different components available for a solution.

Use the steps below to add new components to a solution.

1. Open the solution (Settings ⇨ Solutions and click on the name of the selected solution).

2. In the Navigation pane, click on the type of component that you want to add, such as Entities or Dashboards.

3. Do one of the following based on the type of component that you wish to add:

   • If you plan to modify an existing component as part of your solution, then click the Add Existing button. Browse to the component that you wish to add (or select multiple components) and click the OK button.

   • If you need to create a new component, then click on the New button. Fill out the appropriate forms to create the component (see the relevant chapters of this book for more information on how to create the various different types of components).

4. Repeat Steps 2 and 3 for every component that you wish to add to the solution.

Layering: Building on existing solutions

There may be times when you want to expand on a solution that was created by another publisher. To accomplish this, you can include components from other solutions in your solution. Depending on the managed property settings for the component you can then make additional modifications to the selected components. The process for layering solutions is fairly open-ended, but the steps below provide a general framework for layering:

1. Import (or create) an initial solution (we will call this "solution A").

2. Create a new solution (we will call this "solution B") and choose to add existing components to it.

3. Browse to the components in "solution A" that you want to extend using "solution B."

   - If you do not see the component available in the list, then it is because the publisher has set the managed properties for this solution to prohibit customizations.

   - When you import a component, Dynamics CRM is aware of dependencies that require other components to also be included in the solution and will prompt you to add those components as well (as shown in Figure 16.6).

4. Modify the components however you like. You can make any modifications that the publisher has allowed in the managed properties. Dynamics CRM will merge changes you make in solution B with solution A.

Solutions can be created in any number of layers. Figure 16.7 is a conceptual illustration of a candidate recruiting solution that was then modified with a candidate communication process and was further modified to include a reporting dashboard.

FIGURE 16.5

A custom solution and the component navigation pane

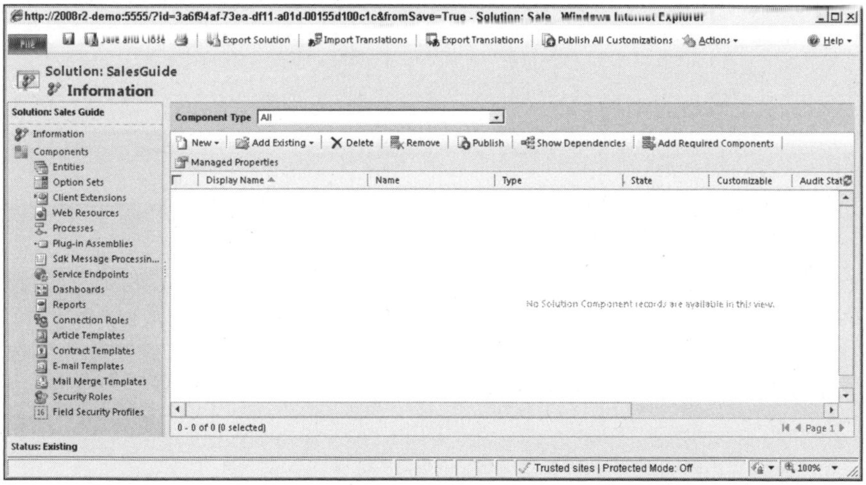

Add dependent components dialog box

Missing Required Components -- Webpage Dialog

Missing Required Components

The system detected that the selected components require other components currently not included in the solution. Do you want to add those components?

○ Yes, include required components.
○ No, do not include required components.

Missing Required Components

Display Name ▲	Name/Id	Component Type	Parent Entity	Managed Solution
Inventory	c5_contractlineinventory	Entity		Active Solution

Help   OK   Cancel

http://2008r2-demo:5555/360Centric/_grid/cmds/dlg_addsolut   Local intranet | Protected Mode: Off

---

Conceptual overview of a layered solution

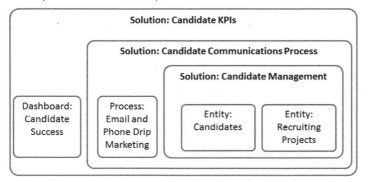

Solution: Candidate KPIs

Solution: Candidate Communications Process

Solution: Candidate Management

| Dashboard: Candidate Success | Process: Email and Phone Drip Marketing | Entity: Candidates | Entity: Recruiting Projects |

Working with managed properties

Managed properties allow you to lock down some or all of the custom components in a solution. You can create solutions that limit the ability of others to make further customizations.

To Layer or Not to Layer

If your organization is the sole publisher of a solution, then in most cases you will not need to layer in multiple solutions. One reason why you may want to layer an internally developed solution is if you want to maintain different versions for different instances of Dynamics CRM. For example, you may create a project management solution that will be deployed into two different instances of Dynamics CRM within your organization. One business group may require a simple base level version, while another one may require a complex set of additions. By maintaining a layered solution, you can modify the base customization and make those improvements available to both business units while making the complex additions available only to the second business unit.

If you obtained a solution from a third party, and it is a managed solution, then your only option to extend the solution will be to layer it into another solution. This assumes that the managed properties for the third-party solution allow you to reuse it.

Each component has its own set of managed properties that control how it can be customized. Note that system components (such as the account and contact entities) cannot be assigned managed properties — this prevents other publishers from locking you out of the components that were included with Dynamics CRM. Follow these steps to manage components of a solution:

1. Open the solution containing components that you want to manage.

2. Navigate to a component that you would like to set the managed properties for, such as an entity, field, form, or security role.

3. In the menu bar, look for the button titled Managed Properties (Figure 16.8 is an illustration of the Managed Properties button for a custom entity) and click it.

4. You are presented with a dialog box containing all of the managed properties for the selected component as illustrated in Figure 16.9. Select the desired options from the dialog box and click OK.

5. Repeat Steps 2 through 4 for each component that you wish to manage.

6. Export the solution as a managed solution and import it into the targeted instance of Dynamics CRM. Managed properties are only in effect on managed solutions, and solutions cannot be set to managed until they have been exported. So although you can set managed properties in a solution, those properties are not active until the solution has been exported as a managed solution and reimported.

Caution

It is possible to lose the ability to update your solution! If you are using a single instance of Dynamics CRM and you want to set up a managed solution, then you could potentially export the solution as managed, delete the original solution from Dynamics CRM, and then reimport the managed solution. Because the solution is managed, you can no longer make changes, and because you deleted the original, unmanaged version, you cannot go back. If you want to create managed solutions, we recommend that you maintain a development environment for Dynamics CRM where you can keep original, unmanaged copies of all of your solutions.

The Managed Properties button in the menu bar for an entity

FIGURE 16.9

Managed properties dialog box for an entity

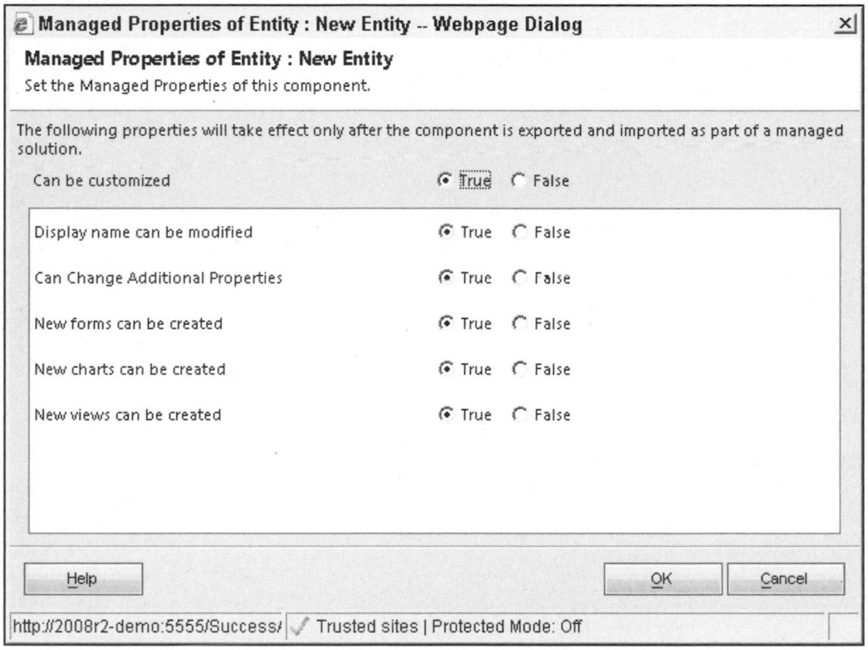

Understanding dependencies

Dependencies are created when components depend upon each other in order to function properly. A simple example of a dependency is a field on a form. The form is dependent upon the field in order to function properly. If you were to delete the field without first removing it from the form, then the form would not work properly.

Dynamics CRM automatically tracks most dependencies for you and prevents you from removing dependent components. In the example in the preceding paragraph, if I attempt to delete a field from the list of fields, and that field is still on a published form, Dynamics CRM will not allow me to make a deletion.

In some cases, Dynamics CRM is unaware of dependencies that may exist. For example, some external scripts may use fields on a form. Because Dynamics CRM does not know about these dependencies, it is possible that a field could be removed from a form that results in an error when a script is run that requires that field. Dynamics CRM allows you to manually declare these dependencies so that fields can be locked on a form. To manually declare a dependency on a form, open the form, click Form Properties in the Ribbon menu, click the Non-Event Dependencies tab, and add fields to the dependent fields list as appropriate (Figure 16.10). Iframes and Web resources also allow you to manually create dependencies.

FIGURE 16.10

Dependent fields list for forms

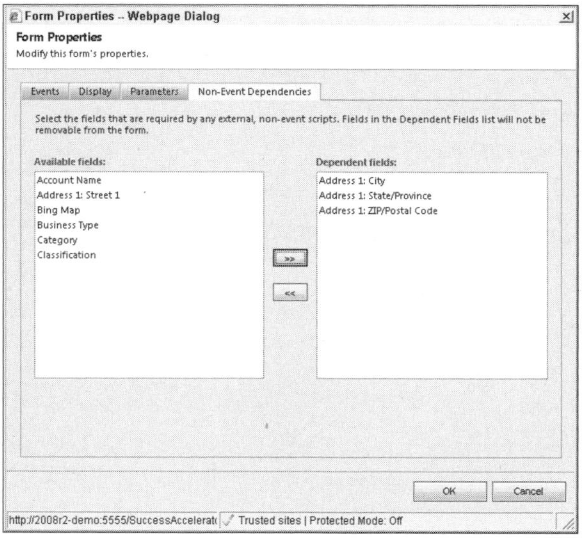

While working on a solution, you may want to know what the dependencies are on a specific component. For example, if you plan to add the component to another solution or if you are considering deleting a component, you may find it helpful to produce a list of all the dependencies for that component. In those cases, you can use the "Show Dependencies" in the menu bar to view the list of dependencies. When you click this button, you will be presented with the list of dependencies (Figure 16.11). From the list, you can double-click on each item to manually remove the dependency if desired.

Sharing solutions with import and export

One of the biggest benefits of using solutions to manage customizations is that solutions can be readily exported from one instance of Dynamics CRM and imported into another. This portability makes it easy to create and redistribute customized solutions either internally within a business or externally through third-party developers.

FIGURE 16.11

Show dependencies dialog box for a field

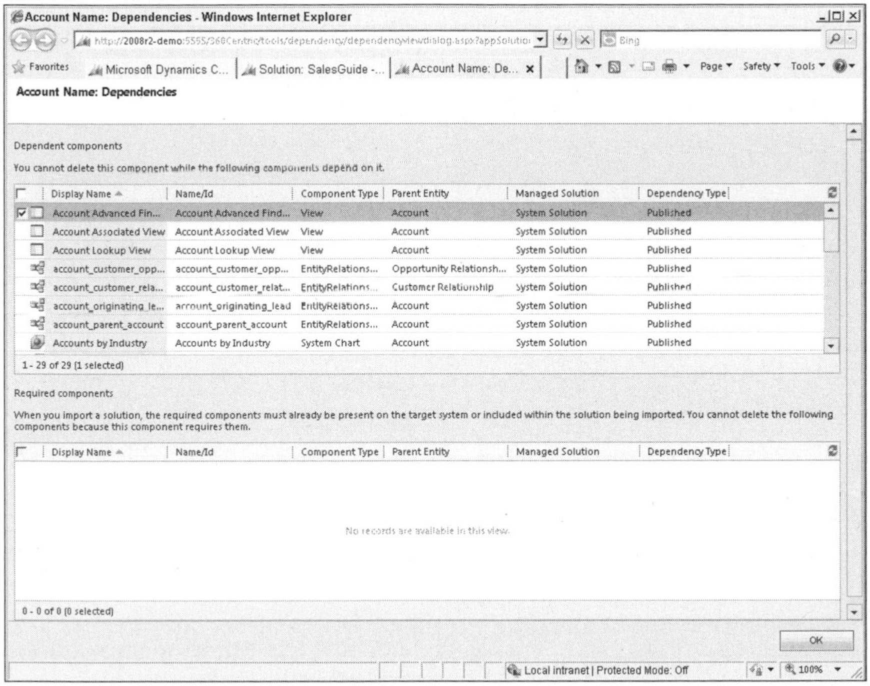

Exporting a solution

To export a solution, follow these steps:

1. Navigate to the list of solutions and select the solution that you want to export.

2. In the menu bar, click the Export button.

3. If you have not yet published all of your customizations, then click the Publish All Customizations button to be sure that your entire solution is exported.

4. Click the Next button.

5. At this point, you may be presented with a list of components that your solution will require that are not included with the export. You can either choose to export the solution without the components or you can cancel the export, add the components to the solution, and re-export it. Note that components that are a part of the System Solution can be assumed to be a part of other instances of Dynamics CRM and do not need to be included in your solution. Click the Next button to move to the next screen.

6. On the Export Settings dialog box, choose any settings that your solution relies upon to export. In most cases, you will be able to leave these boxes unchecked.

7. Choose the type of package that you would like to export this solution as. Options include:

   - Unmanaged: Choose this option if you would like to allow others to have unrestricted access to make changes to the solution after it is imported.

   - Managed: Choose this option if you set up managed properties for this solution and you want to keep others from making customizations to it.

8. Click the Export button.

Tip

You may want to export customizations that are not in a solution, or when you may want to export only a portion of the customizations from a given solution. To do this, create a new solution, add the customizations you want to export to the solution, and then export the solution. You may want to consider keeping a solution called "Quick Export" available for just this purpose.

Importing a solution

Solutions can be imported using the following procedure:

1. Navigate to the solutions area and click the Import button in the menu bar.

2. Click the Browse button and find the solution that you want to import. Click the Next button.

3. On the Solution Information page, you may want to click the check box to activate workflows and other steps that may be required to fully activate the solution. Click the Next button. The solution begins to import, and when completed, a list of imported components is displayed.

4. Click the Publish All Customizations button to make the solution available to users or click the Close button if you would like to review the solution prior to publishing it.

Deleting a solution

Solutions can be deleted by navigating to the list of solutions, selecting a solution, and clicking the delete button (which appears as an X) in the menu bar. Depending on which type of solution you are deleting, the results are as follows:

- Unmanaged solution: If you delete an unmanaged solution, then you are presented with the confirm deletion dialog box in Figure 16.12. When deleting an unmanaged solution, all of the customizations become a part of the default solution. If you want to delete the entire solution, then you should first open the solution and delete all of the customizations from within the solution. Once you have completed this step, you can then delete the solution.

- Managed solution: If you delete a managed solution, then all of the components for the solution will be permanently deleted from Dynamics CRM.

FIGURE 16.12

Delete unmanaged solution dialog box

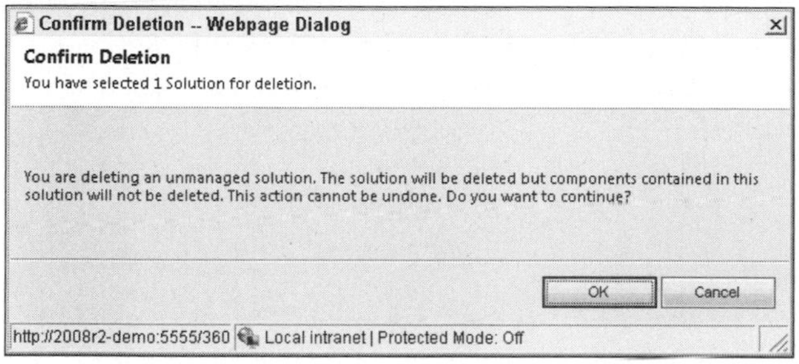

The Solutions Marketplace

Microsoft launched the Microsoft Dynamics Marketplace along with Dynamics CRM 2011. The marketplace provides a way to quickly find, test, purchase, and install solutions for Dynamics CRM. For example, if you are searching for an expense reporting add-on for Dynamics CRM, you can visit the marketplace, search for "expense reporting," and download a test solution, all within a few minutes. The marketplace saves time, lowers costs, and provides a competitive distribution channel for extending the Dynamics CRM 2011 platform.

To access the solutions marketplace, navigate to Settings ⇨ Dynamics Marketplace.

Summary

Dynamics CRM was developed with the intention that organizations customize it to work the way that their business does. To aid in the process of developing, sharing, and extending customizations, Microsoft introduced the solutions framework in Dynamics CRM 2011. Solutions are containers that hold groups of customizations, which can then be exported and imported. Managed properties allow solution publishers to lock down individual components within a solution to prevent them from being changed.

Taking the time to understand how the solutions framework is designed is an important first step prior to making customizations. Although it is possible to make customizations without first understanding solutions, this runs the risk of creating customizations that are more difficult and time-consuming for your organization to maintain.

Working with CRM Entities

Entities are the heart of Microsoft Dynamics CRM. The ability to customize entities and create new entities plays an important role in fine-tuning Dynamics CRM to work the way your sales, marketing and service organizations work. Moreover, this functionality enables you to create entirely new applications in Dynamics CRM. Because entities can be customized without having to write code, your organization can develop applications and automate processes more quickly and inexpensively than ever before.

By customizing entities, you can format forms to include exactly the fields and functionality that your users need. Views can be developed to enable your users to see only the information that they need in order to quickly connect with the right customers and prospects. Charts can be delivered to users to help them quickly make business decisions. And your organizational terminology can be incorporated into Dynamics CRM to provide a comfortable and familiar experience.

The information in this chapter provides an important foundation for upcoming chapters. Although an understanding of the configuration tools in Dynamics CRM is important, a successful CRM project relies upon a clear CRM strategy and a proven methodology for implementation (these concepts are covered in Chapter 1). Familiarity with the user interface (Chapters 10 to 15) and the solution framework (Chapter 16) are also necessary. An understanding of relational database concepts is also critical (covered early within this chapter). With those concepts in mind, this chapter has been designed to deliver a comprehensive guide to working with entities for non-programmers.

Caution

Before jumping into the concepts presented in this chapter, you should take the time to fully understand the concept of solutions as described in Chapter 16. While it is possible to begin customizing entities without understanding solutions, you will find that your customizations are simpler to maintain if they are properly integrated into a solution.

Cross-Reference

The concept of developing new applications in Dynamics CRM is often referred to as XRM (or eXtended Relationship Management). For more information on creating XRM applications, including some example applications, see Chapter 27.

Cross-Reference

Only Dynamics CRM Users with the appropriate security settings are able to create or edit entities. For more information on security settings, see Chapter 6.

Understanding Entities

In Dynamics CRM, entities are the containers that hold all of the data, forms, views, charts, and other information associated with managing and presenting information to users. Examples of entities included with Dynamics CRM are leads, accounts, contacts, opportunities, cases, campaigns, and marketing lists. As you'll note, the primary entities associated with Dynamics CRM are accessible directly through the navigation pane for the application. You can also create new custom entities that can also be made available directly through the site navigation.

If you are familiar with databases or Excel spreadsheets, then entities can be considered to be similar to tables or to the rows and columns of data you might manage in a spreadsheet. In fact, many organizations convert their existing database and spreadsheet applications into Dynamics CRM entities. One difference between an entity and a table is that entities include not only the data (the rows and columns) but also the presentation (forms and charts, for example) and metadata (validation rules, code, and so on) that is used in connection with your data.

Cross-Reference

Entities include a number of terms that may be new to you. If you are not yet familiar with terms such as view, advanced find, field, user, record ownership, account, contact, activity, history, security roles, or queues then we recommend you review Chapters 1 and 10 to get grounded in these concepts before continuing.

Understanding entity types

Several different types of entities are included (or can be created) with Dynamics CRM and are described below. Note that any given entity can belong to one or more of the entity types — depending upon the settings you select when creating the entity.

- **System entities:** These are the entities that are included with Dynamics CRM. You are probably already familiar with (accounts, contacts, and so on) and some secondary entities that are less obvious (quote products, price list items, and addresses, to name a few).

- **Custom entities:** These are entities that were not included with Dynamics CRM. They may have been created by you, others in your organization, or by third parties. Custom entities are often included in third-party add-on products that extend the functionality of Dynamics CRM.

- **Customizable entities:** These are entities that you are allowed to customize. Some system entities do not allow customizations. Also note that although most system entities are customizable, there are some limits to how you can customize certain entities (this is done to ensure that the base functionality of Dynamics CRM remains intact).

- **Customer composite entity:** The concept of a "customer" in Dynamics CRM includes either the account entity or the contact entity. This is also referred to as a *composite entity* because it allows records from either of these two different entities to be used in the customer field. This feature of Dynamics CRM enables your organization to treat either accounts (other organizations) or contacts (individual people) as customers. Note, however, that only system entities can include a link to the composite customer entity within them. If you create your own custom entities, you can create a single link to either accounts or contacts, or you can create two links (one to accounts and one to contacts), but you cannot create a single composite link to either an account or a contact.

- **Activity entities:** Activity entities include tasks, phone calls, e-mails, and a number of other entities for tracking user activities. Activities are special entities because of how they synchronize with Outlook and in how they can be linked to a large number of different entities via the "regarding" field. New in Dynamics CRM 2011 is the ability to create custom activity entities.

Understanding relational databases

When customizing entities in Dynamics CRM, you set up relationships between entities that link them. A basic understanding of relational databases is important to ensure that you are properly setting up these links. This section provides a very brief overview of relational database concepts.

Creating a relationship in a database means linking the records in one table (or entity) to the records in another. If you have been working with Dynamics CRM for a while, then you probably know that the account table is linked to the contact table. When you create an account, you can link it to one or more contacts that work within that organization through the contacts related list in the Navigation pane. Likewise, when you create a contact record, you can link it to one (and only one) account through the parent customer field. In this example, the account can be thought of as the parent entity and the contact can be thought of as the child entity. Figure 17.1 illustrates the relationship between an account (Success Accelerators) and its associated contacts (Ed, Linda, and Will). This relationship can also be said to be "one-to-many" because one account can have many contacts. Looking at it from the contact perspective, it can be said to be "many-to-one" because many contact records relate back to one account record. Table 17.1 outlines some of the common terms used when discussing relational databases.

FIGURE 17.1

An account record and the related contact records (parent/child or one-to-many relationship)

TABLE 17.1

Common Relational Database Terms

Terms	Meaning
Parent/Child One-to-many 1:N Primary entity	One record in this "parent" table can be related to many records in a "child" table. For example, one account may have many contacts. Note that the parent entity is also often referred to as the "primary" entity.
Many-to-one N:1 Related entity	Many records in this table can be related back to a single parent. For example, many contacts may be related to the same account. Note that the child entity is also often referred to as the "related" entity.
Many-to-many N:N	Many records in this table may be related to many records in an associated table. For example, an organization may track the associations that contacts are members of. One association can have many related contacts; one contact can belong to many associations.

When you see relational data in reports, the relationships may be less obvious to you than when you see them on data entry forms. For example, many organizations produce quotes as a part of their sales process. Quote documents are made up of data from the customer, the quote, and the products (or line items) associated with that quote. Figure 17. 2 illustrates a quote that contains relational information from three different entities.

IT professionals who work with databases on a regular basis have developed a number of shorthand ways to illustrate the relationships between entities in a database. Figure 17.3 is an example of a relational database diagram. The figure can be read as, one customer can have many quotes and one quote can have many quote products. This type of diagram, produced with Microsoft Visio, can be a helpful tool when designing complex customizations within Dynamics CRM.

Cross-Reference

If the concept of relational databases is new to you, and you expect to spend a lot of time making customizations to entities in Dynamics CRM, then we recommend that you spend some time reviewing other Wiley books that ground you in relational database concepts. You may want to consider SQL For Dummies by Allen G. Taylor, which includes not only an excellent introduction to relational databases but also material on SQL concepts (which may help you in going deeper working with SQL — used behind the scenes by Dynamics CRM).

A printed quote with information from the customer, quote, and quote products (or line items)

Information for the Quote entity

Information from the Customer (Account) entity

Information from the Quote Products entity

Relational database diagram

Understanding the steps of entity customization

This section provides an overview of the entity creation and customization process. Although the process for working with entities is fairly open-ended, we will present it in the typical sequence of steps that most individuals use when getting started. Figure 17.4 is a diagram of the typical process for creating and customizing entities. Below the figure is a brief explanation of each step. Note that this figure fits into the overall solution design figure in the previous chapter. The remainder of this chapter describes each step in much more detail.

FIGURE 17.4

An overview of the entity customization process

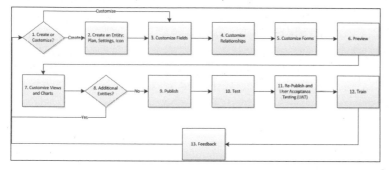

1. **Create or Customize:** Before getting started you will have to decide if you will be creating an entirely new entity or if you will be modifying an existing entity.

2. **Create an Entity:** If you determine that you need to create a new entity, then there are several steps that you will need to take including:

   - **Plan:** Take the time to plan out your new entity. How will it relate to other entities? What fields will you need? What visualizations and reports do your users expect from it?

   - **General Settings:** Some general settings will need to be made when you initially create an entity. It is important that you get these right the first time because many of them cannot be changed later. These settings are highlighted when you create a new entity and are documented in the section "General entity settings and the primary field."

   - **Custom Icon:** You can create a custom icon for your custom entities. Although this is not required, it does give your custom entities a more professional and polished look.

3. **Customize Fields:** Set up the fields in your entity to support your users. Although this can be done from the form designer, we recommend that you set up most of your fields at once and only update them from the form designer when you need to make small changes.

4. **Customize Relationships:** Relationships result in the creation of new items to add to the form. These, too, can be created and updated from the form designer, but we recommend starting out by setting these up in the relationships area of the entity.

5. **Customize Forms:** After your fields and relationships have been customized, you will have everything you need in order to create your forms.

6. **Preview:** Dynamics CRM allows you to preview your form prior to publishing it. This enables you to be comfortable that your form customizations behave as expected prior to rolling them out to your users.

7. **Customize Views and Charts:** Set up views and charts that users will need in order to quickly find the information that they will need to get their jobs done.

8. **Additional Entities:** Many customization projects will require that you make changes to multiple existing entities or create multiple new entities.

9. **Publish:** Once you have completed creating and testing your customizations, publish them to Dynamics CRM.

10. **Test:** Although you previewed your forms while you were customizing them, you should always test your customizations at least one more time prior to training users on them to ensure that they are behaving as expected.

11. **Re-Publish and UAT:** For larger businesses, you should be making your customizations and thoroughly testing them in separate instances of Dynamics CRM made specifically for development and testing. After you have completed testing them in that environment, you are ready to publish them into your production environment and to perform user acceptance testing (UAT) with your user group.

12. **Train:** Always include time in your plan to train your users. For simple changes, this may just be an e-mail announcing an update. For extensive changes, you may schedule a full day (or more) for training for each user.

13. **Feedback:** Assume up front that some modifications will be required. Take the time to develop a plan to solicit feedback from users and to make improvements thereafter.

Caution

The decision to create a new entity or customize an existing one is pretty straightforward in most cases. However, there are some instances where it may require some thought and planning. An example of this may be if you want to track a list of distributors. You could use the account entity to track this list (in addition to tracking customer records). Alternatively you could create an entirely new entity just for tracking distributors. Both approaches have pros and cons and should be weighed carefully before jumping in.

Accessing the entity customization area

The functionality we will be discussing in this chapter is all found within the entity customization area of Dynamics CRM as illustrated in Figure 17.5. There are a number of ways that you can navigate to this area depending on exactly how you want to manage your customizations and what type of customizations you expect to make (see Chapter 16 before deciding how you want to handle making changes to customizations). Here is an overview of the methods for accessing the entities area:

- **Customize the Default Solution:** You can customize the default solution by navigating to Settings ➪ Customizations ➪ Customize the System.

- **Customize a Named Solution (recommended approach):** Solutions you develop internally, and many third-party solutions, will allow you to make customizations within the named solution. This is the preferred method for maintaining your customizations wherever possible. To customize a named solution navigate to: Settings ➪ Customizations ➪ Solutions. In the grid, click on the name of the solution you want to modify.

- **Customize the Default Solution from the Ribbon Menu:** New in Dynamics CRM 2011 is the ability to quickly navigate from a form or grid directly into the entity customization area. This can be done by clicking the Customize tab of the Ribbon menu and then selecting the appropriate option. This can be very convenient for rapidly updating Dynamics CRM without having to go through the extra clicks to navigate to the customizations area. However, you can only customize the default solution using this method — so use care when using this approach.

Caution

The way that you navigate to the customizations area will have consequences in terms of how your customizations can be managed in the future. Please take the time to thoroughly understand solutions, in Chapter 16, prior to making decisions about how you will access the entity customizations area.

FIGURE 17.5

The entity customization area of Dynamics CRM

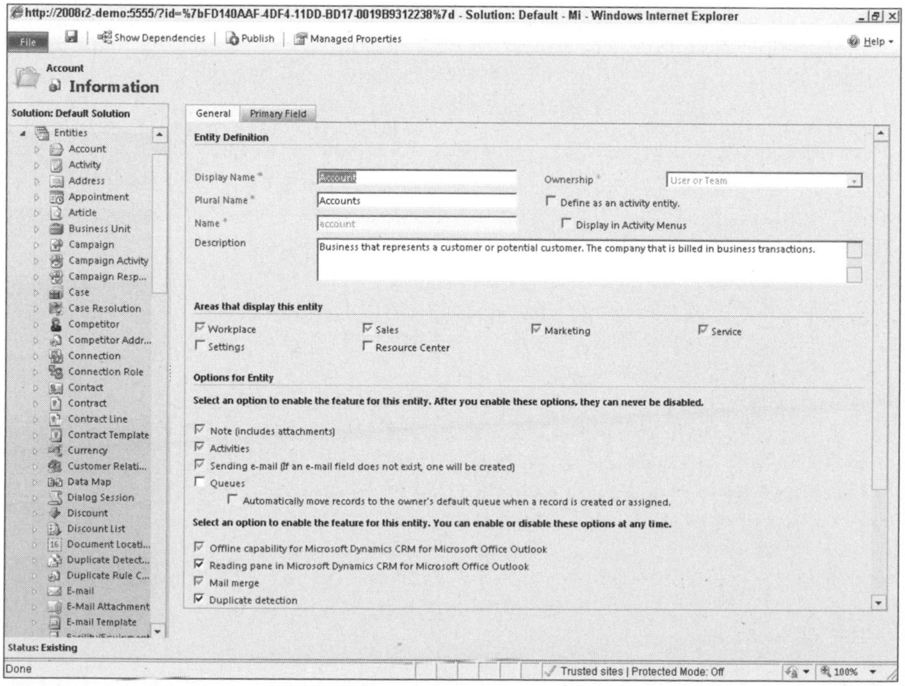

Once you are in the customizations area, your navigation will vary slightly depending upon which solution you are modifying. If you are modifying the default solution, then when you expand the entities view (by clicking the triangle to the left of entities) you will see a listing of every entity in Dynamics CRM. If you are modifying a named solution, then under the entities listing you will only see the entities that are a part of that solution (you can add existing entities to the solution by clicking the Add Existing button in the menu).

Regardless of which type of solution you are viewing, you will see a list of all the other solution components below the list of entities.

Publishing customizations

While making changes to entities in Dynamics CRM, your changes are not visible to users until you publish them. This feature allows you to set up and preview all of your changes without affecting the user experience. You can still save your customizations without publishing them — so you can work for multiple days on a single set of customizations without having to publish them.

As illustrated in Figure 17.6, there are two buttons for publishing customizations in Dynamics CRM: Publish or Publish All Customizations. The button you select will depend upon what you want to accomplish:

- **Publish All Customizations:** This button will publish all customizations that have been made to the solution that you are currently working on. If you are currently working on the default solution and have pending changes on both the default solution and on a solution named "Distributor Management," then when you click the Publish All Customizations button, only the changes on the default solution will be published. You will need to navigate to any other solutions and publish those changes separately.

- **Publish:** The publish button only publishes changes for the specific entity or component that you are currently viewing (or that is highlighted in the grid). For example, if you are currently on the account entity in the grid and you click the Publish button, then any pending customizations to the account entity in the current solution will be published. You can select multiple entities in the grid if you want to publish multiple entity customizations. Similar to the Publish All Customizations button, the Publish button only publishes changes to the currently selected solution.

Importing and exporting customizations

Customizations made to entities can be exported from Dynamics CRM. You can use your exported files to reimport into other instances of Dynamics CRM or as a way to back up your customizations. Note that customizations must be added to a solution and published before they can be exported.

Cross-Reference

Importing and exporting customizations is a part of the solution management functionality in Dynamics CRM. For more detailed information on solution management and importing/exporting, see Chapter 16.

FIGURE 17.6

Buttons for publishing some or all customizations

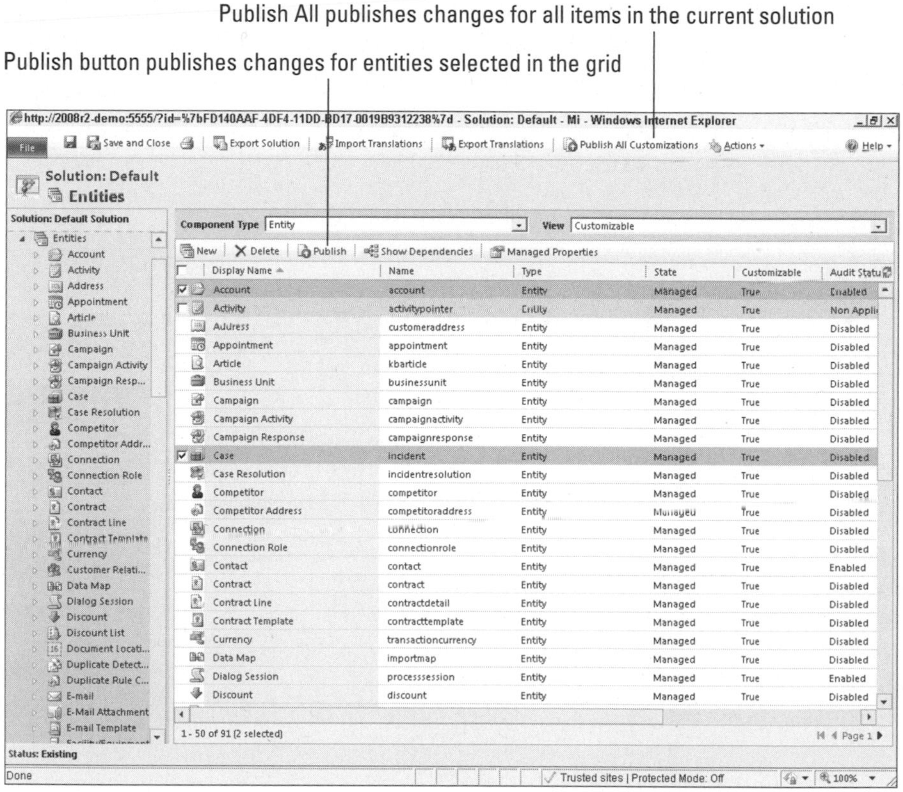

Publish All publishes changes for all items in the current solution

Publish button publishes changes for entities selected in the grid

Creating Custom Entities

In this section we will walk through the process of creating a new, custom, entity. Once a custom entity has been created, the steps required to customize it are the same as they are for modifying any other entity. So we will focus on creating entities in this section and on customizing entities in the next section.

To create a custom entity:

1. Navigate to Settings ⇨ Solutions. From here, select the appropriate solution you want to add your entity to. You can also create a new solution for your entity if you prefer. See Chapter 16 for more information on solutions.

2. Inside of the selected solution, make sure you have selected Components in the Navigation menu, click the New button, and then select Entity (Figure 17.7). You are presented with the information form in Figure 17.8 for entering general entity settings.

FIGURE 17.7

Creating a new entity from the components list

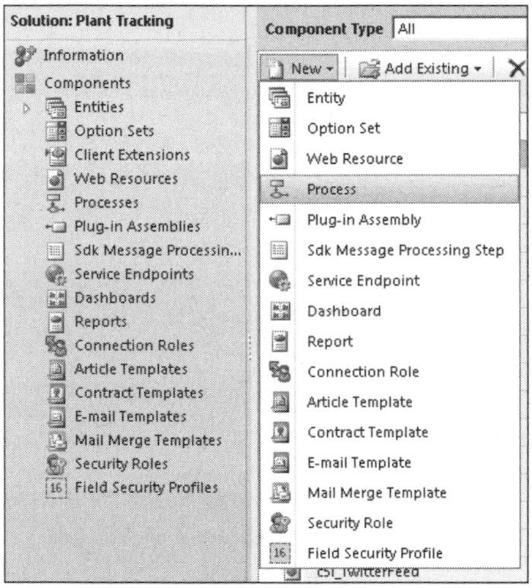

FIGURE 17.8

The information form for entering general entity settings

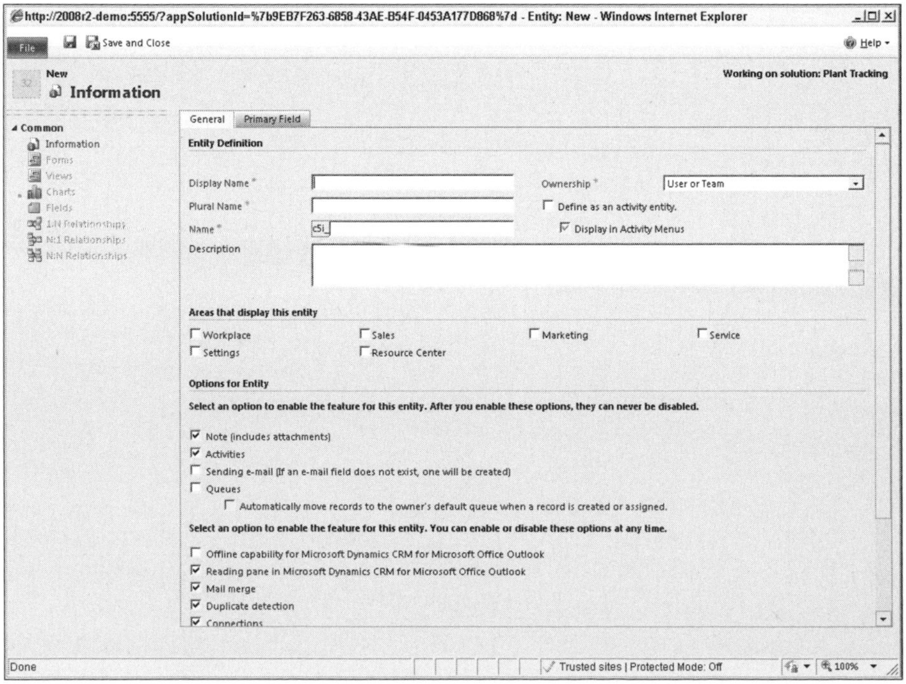

3. Follow the instructions in the next section, "General entity settings and the primary field."

4. When you have completed entering your settings, click the Save button. You can continue to customize the entity.

General entity settings and the primary field

The first thing you need to do when creating an entity is to enter some general settings. Many of these settings can be changed later, but some can only be made when you initially create the entity, and others can be set after the initial entity creation but cannot be changed again after that. Before creating an entity, you should understand these limitations so you can plan an entity that will meet your long-term needs. This section describes each of the settings and your ability to modify the setting. Table 17.2 provides an overview of the various settings and when you can/cannot change them.

TABLE 17.2

General Settings and Primary Field for Entities

Setting General Tab	Must Be Set When Entity Is Created	Cannot Be Changed After Entity Creation	Can Be Enabled Only Once and Never Disabled	Can Be Changed Any Time
Display Name	✔			✔
Plural Name	✔			✔
Name	✔	✔		
Description				✔
Ownership	✔	✔		
Define as an activity entity	✔	✔		
Display in activity menus	✔	✔		
Areas that display this entity				✔
Notes (includes attachments)			✔	
Activities	✔	✔		
Sending e-mail			✔	
Queues			✔	
Offline capability in Outlook				✔
Reading pane in Outlook				✔
Mail merge				✔
Duplicate detection				✔
Connections			✔	

continued

TABLE 17.2 *(continued)*

Setting	Must Be Set When Entity Is Created	Cannot Be Changed After Entity Creation	Can Be Enabled Only Once and Never Disabled	Can Be Changed Any Time
Document management				✔
Mobile Express				✔
Auditing				✔
Primary Field Tab				

Note that some of these items cannot be changed from the Primary Field tab after the entity is created. However, many of them can be changed by navigating to the list of fields for the entity and editing the primary field. Items have been marked below based upon being able to change them in either the Primary Field tab or from the list of fields in Dynamics CRM.

Setting	Must Be Set When Entity Is Created	Cannot Be Changed After Entity Creation	Can Be Enabled Only Once and Never Disabled	Can Be Changed Any Time
Display Name	✔			✔
Name	✔			✔
Requirement Level	✔			✔
Type	✔	✔		
Format	✔	✔		
Maximum Length	✔			✔
Description	✔			✔

Entity definition

The entity definition area includes a number of different important settings as follows:

- **Display Name / Plural Name.** These two fields represent the name of the entity as it will appear in Dynamics CRM. In some contexts the plural name will be used, and in others the display name will be used. These values can be changed later if desired.

- **Name.** This field is the name that the entity will be referred to if it is referenced within custom code including custom reports, JScript, or other programming code. This field cannot be changed after the entity has been saved for the first time.

- **Description.** This field is an optional field with more information on how the entity will be used within Dynamics CRM. It is a best practice to enter text into description fields that documents how the entity will be used. By entering this documentation, you will make it easier to support your instance of Dynamics CRM in the future.

- **Ownership.** This field determines who will own each record in the entity. Another way to think about ownership is to ask, "Who will be responsible for maintaining this record in Dynamics CRM?" This field plays an important part in defining security roles and in establishing views and charts of data. After you select a value for this setting and save the entity, you cannot change it. Options for this field are as follows:

- **User or Team:** Select this option if every record in this entity will be "owned" by a user or by a team of users. For example, if you create an entity to track projects, then you will most likely want to use this setting because your projects will be assigned to an owner who is responsible for making sure that his or her projects are managed properly.

- **Organization:** Select this option if records won't be owned by any particular individual or team. For example, if you create an entity to track customer inventory, then you will most likely want to use this setting because this inventory will not be owned by a particular user (or team) in your business.

Cross-Reference
You may notice that a prefix that cannot be edited is automatically added to the name field. This prefix is set in the solution. See Chapter 16 for information on setting the prefix in the solution.

Activity entity types

An activity entity is a special entity type that appears in the list of activities in Dynamics CRM and in your activities and closed activities for other entities. So, for example, if you have integrated Dynamics CRM with your customer Web portal and you want to track every time someone updates their profile on the portal, you could create an activity entity called Web Portal Update.

Activity entities have a number of unique features. Activity entities include a Customers field (enabling you to link it to one or more account and/or contact records) and a regarding field (enabling you to link it to any entity enabled for tracking activities). Activity entities show up in the activity area of Dynamics CRM and cannot be included in other areas. Activity entities can be included in reports and dashboards that include other activities. When creating an activity entity, many of the other settings are automatically set and locked from changing.

When creating an activity entity, you also have the option of displaying it in the list of activities that users can create when they selected to create a new activity. If this is an activity you want users to be able to create, you should select this option. If this is an activity you only want to be created on an automated basis (such as the "Web Portal Update" mentioned above), then you should not select this option. Note that this option cannot be changed once the entity has been created.

Tip
Custom activity entities will not synchronize with Microsoft Outlook.

Caution
If you create a custom activity entity and you uncheck the option "Display in Activity Menus," then the activity will not be visible in views for open activities. For example, if you create a custom activity type called Request for Quote and you only want to create new records of this type from workflow, but you also want users to see all open requests under their Opportunities, then you will need to manually update the default views to add this activity type to the list.

On the Web Site

We have created a solution using an activity entity on the CD for you. This solution, called Approvals, uses an activity entity to request and track approvals associated with processes you may want to automate in Dynamics CRM.

Notes

Notes (and attachments) allow you to track a date and time-stamped list of either individual notes or attached documents on the entity (such as the illustration in Figure 17.9). You can leave this option blank when you initially create a new entity, but once you check it and save the entity, you can no longer remove the option. Keep in mind that you can also track related documents in SharePoint, which is a much more powerful document management tool than Dynamics CRM. In addition, tracking notes for an entity is often counterproductive because they are not easy to search and may conflict with notes that you are tracking on associated activities.

FIGURE 17.9

A list of notes and attachments associated with an entity

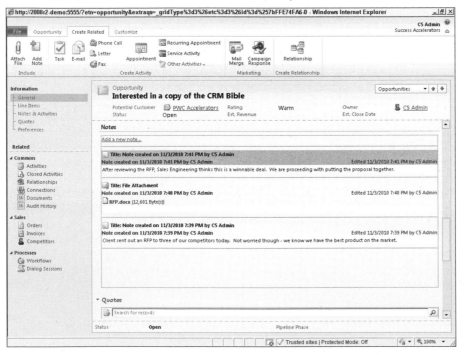

Best Practice: Be Strategic About Related Activities

Many system customizers assume that it is safe to enable tracking activities for new entities just in case users might ask for this in the future. However, enabling this type of tracking on too many entities can make it confusing for users to wade through a large list of different related entities every time they want to track something from Outlook or set the regarding field on an activity. Having such a long list of options can create a time-consuming process for users. The best practice is to be strategic about selecting entities that can have related activities.

Activities

Activities enable you to track activities associated with this entity by selecting a record from this entity in the activity's regarding field. You will need to decide if you want to track activities for this entity before you save it. After a new entity has been saved, you can no longer enable or disable activity tracking for it, so you will need to be careful to make the correct choice during your initial design.

Sending E-mail

If this entity will have any e-mail addresses in it, then you can enable it for e-mailing. You do not have to enable this option when you initially create an entity, but once enabled you can no longer disable it. This option allows you to send and track e-mails to the addresses tracked on these records. You can use this option, for example, if you are creating an entity to track competitors' contacts.

Queues

Select this option if you want to be able to add records in this entity to a queue. You can leave this blank when you initially create a new entity, but once you check it and save the entity, you can no longer remove the option. The option to move records automatically to the owner's default queue can be a helpful way to streamline processes.

Cross-Reference

For more information on working with queues, see Chapter 10.

Auditing

Auditing allows you to track the change history for an entity. This feature allows you to track fields that have been updated on a selected entity. For example, if you want to track whenever someone changes a date field on an entity that you are designing, you can activate auditing for the entity using this option. Once you have activated auditing for the entity, you should then activate it for the individual fields that you want to audit. Figure 17.10 is an image of audit records on the opportunity entity.

FIGURE 17.10

Audit history on an opportunity record

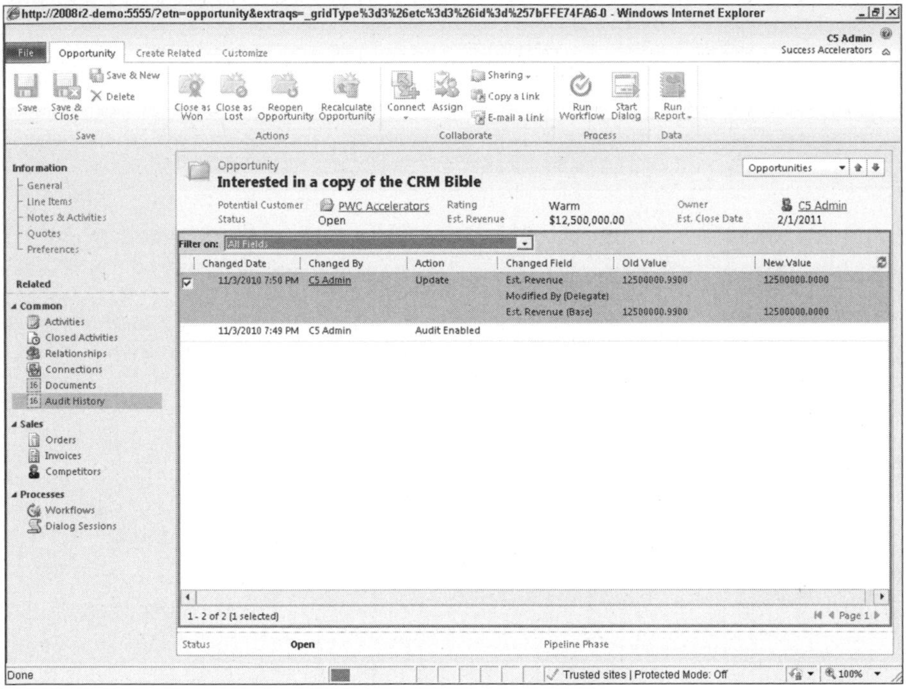

Note

Before auditing becomes active in Dynamics CRM, you need to activate it for your organization. To do this, navigate to Settings ⇨ Auditing and click on Audit Global Settings. From the popup form select Start Auditing and then click OK.

Other settings on the general tab

The general tab contains a number of other settings that you can also work with to configure your entity exactly the way that you like. These remaining settings, which can be changed at any time, are summarized below:

- **Offline capability in Outlook:** Enable this option if you want users to be able to access data in this entity from Outlook even when they are offline and away from the office.

- **Reading pane in Outlook:** If you want to allow users to set up Outlook to show a preview of records in their Outlook reading pane, select this option. In most cases you can leave this option selected and allow users to individually choose if they will use their reading pane or not.

- **Mail merge:** If you want to use this entity to generate a mail merge document in Microsoft Word, then select this option.

- **Duplicate detection:** If you want to use automated duplicate detection to find potential duplicate records entered into this entity, then select this option. For more information on duplicate detection, see Chapter 8.

- **Connections:** This setting allows you to connect records in this entity to records in other entities using the connections functionality in Dynamics CRM. For information on using connections, see Chapter 10. For information on configuring connections, see Chapter 19. Once enabled, the connections option can no longer be disabled.

- **Document management:** This setting enables SharePoint document management for the entity. For information on configuring and using SharePoint document management, see Chapters 4 and 15.

- **Mobile Express:** If you want users to be able to access data in this entity with their mobile device, enable this option. Dynamics CRM includes custom forms for mobile devices, so you can deliver a mobile experience that delivers only the data needed on smaller mobile device screens (for more information, see the section "Customizing forms," later in this chapter).

Primary field

The second tab of the entity settings is used to define the primary field for the entity. Every entity must have a primary field that is used to name the individual records within the entity. You can enter whatever display name that you like and set the requirement level. Primary fields are always a single line of text, but you can change the number of characters in the field.

After you save a newly created entity, the fields on the Primary Field tab cannot be changed from the Primary field tab. However, you can navigate to the list of fields for the entity and open the primary field from that list, where you can then make changes to the display name, length, and requirement level.

Understanding the default fields

When you create a new entity in Dynamics CRM, a number of fields are automatically created as a part of the entity. The specific list of fields varies depending upon the settings you selected when you initially created the entity. You will be able to see a view of all the fields by navigating to the fields section of the entity designer. Table 17.3 summarizes the fields.

TABLE 17.3

Default Entity Fields

Display name	Appears when...	Description
[Variable] (primary key)	Always	This field is unique identifier for each record.
[Variable] (Single Line of Text)	Always	This is the Primary Field that was created in the general settings area when the entity was initially created.
Activity Type	Activity entities	The type of activity that this is (i.e., e-mail, phone call, etc.)
Actual End	Activity entities	The date that the activity was marked as completed.
Actual Start	Activity entities	The date selected as the start date of the activity by the user.
Created By	Always	See detailed description, below.
Created By (Delegate)	Always	See detailed description, below.
Created On	Always	See detailed description, below.
Currency	Activity entities	The financial currency associated with the activity (if any).
Description	Activity entities	The description of the activity.
Due Date	Activity entities	The scheduled end date for the activity.
Exchange Rate	Activity entities	The exchange rate for the currency (used for multi-currency implementations).
Import Sequence Number	Always	This field is used behind the scenes by Dynamics CRM. Whenever records are imported, the import job is assigned a unique number, which is stored in this field.
Is Billed	Activity entities	Indicates if the activity was billed as part of closing a case.
Is Regular Activity	Activity entities	Indicates if this is a standard type of activity if it is exclusively arranged with events.
Is Workflow Created	Activity entities	Indicates if this activity was created by a workflow rule or not (i.e., by a user).
Modified By	Always	See detailed description, below.
Modified By (Delegate)	Always	See detailed description, below.
Modified On (or Last Updated)	Always	See detailed description, below.
Organization ID	Organization owned entities	The ID of the organization that owns this record. This is tracked by Dynamics CRM and cannot be updated by the user.

Display name	Appears when...	Description
Organizer, Customers, Resources, Outsource Vendors, Optional Attendees, From, BCC, CC, To	Activity entities	These fields can all be used to track optional "party lists" which contain one or more customer or other records.
Owner	User or team owned entities	See detailed description, below.
Owning Business Unit	User or team owned entities	See detailed description, below.
Owning Team	User or team owned entities	See detailed description, below.
Owning User	User or team owned entities	See detailed description, below.
Priority	Activity entities	The priority of this activity for completion.
Record Created On	Always	Can be used to track a separate created on date based on the date the record was migrated into Dynamics CRM.
Recurring Instance Type	Activity entities	Used for recurring activities.
Regarding	Activity entities	The record that this activity is regarding (i.e., a link to a record that supports activity relationships).
Scheduled Duration	Activity entities	The scheduled duration of the activity.
Series ID	Activity entities	Used for recurring events.
Service	Activity entities	ID of an associated service record.
Start Date	Activity entities	The scheduled start date of the activity as defined by the user.
Status (or Activity Status)	Always	See detailed description, below.
Status Reason	Always	See detailed description, below.
Subject	Activity entities	The subject of the activity.
Tome Zone Rule Version Number	Always	Used internally by Dynamics CRM for time zone calculations.
UTC Conversion Time Zone	Always	Time zone code that was in use when the record was created. Used to convert to local times.
Version Number	Always	Used to track the version of the record.

Status (or activity status) and status reason

Every entity in Dynamics CRM has a status field and a status reason field. These two fields operate in combination with each other. You can think of the status field as answering the question, "What is the status of this record?" The status reason field answers the question, "Why is this the status of the record?"

Other than changing the display name, you cannot customize the status field on any entity in Dynamics CRM. Custom entities all have only two choices for status: active and inactive. System records in Dynamics CRM often have other available values in their status field depending upon the usage of the entity. Active records are available when using the quick find (search bar) to find records. Inactive records (also referred to as deactivated records) are not available when using quick find but they can still be located using advanced find. Records should be deactivated if they are no longer needed for day-to-day operations but are still useful for reporting purposes. Deactivated records can be reactivated if necessary.

Note

Deactivating records is often the preferable best practice rather than deleting records. Because Dynamics CRM does not have a recycle bin, it can be difficult to recover deleted records. Deactivated records, on the other hand, are only hidden from view and can fairly easily be found and reactivated if needed.

The values available in the status reason field vary depending upon the value in the status field. This is what is also called a dependent picklist (the values available in one picklist change depending upon the currently selected value in another picklist). You can edit the status reason field and change the available values in the field by selecting a status and then editing the values for the status reason for that particular item. Figure 17.11 illustrates editing the status reasons for inactive records. See Chapter 10 for more information on activating and deactivating records.

FIGURE 17.11

Editing the status reason values for records that have an inactive status

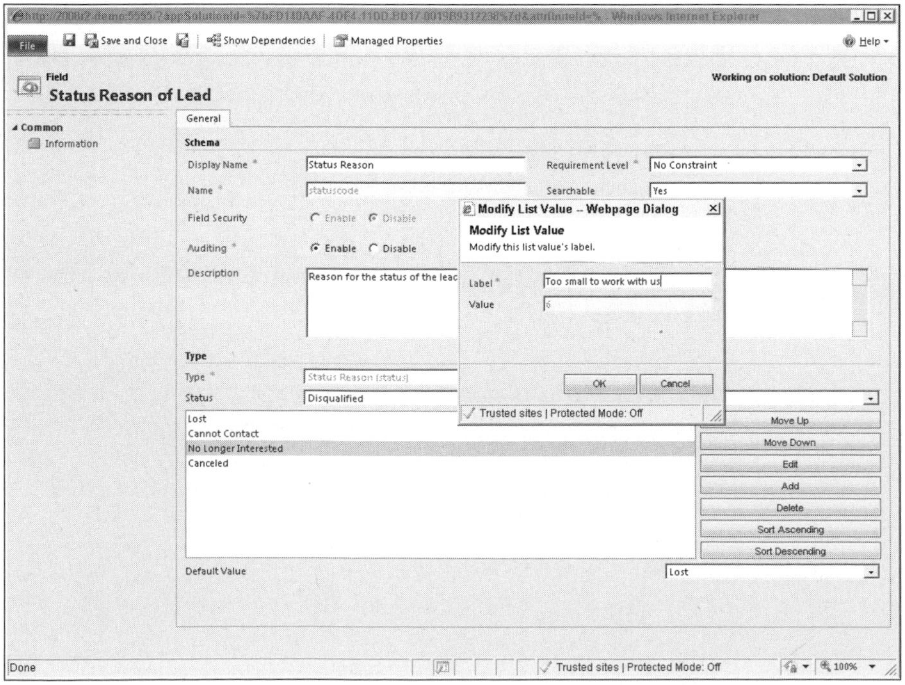

Created and modified fields

Dynamics CRM automatically tracks a number of fields to keep up with who has created and modified records, and at what times that they did this. These fields can be useful to use in reports, workflows, and personalized e-mails. None of these fields can be updated directly by users — they are updated only by Dynamics CRM on an automated basis. These fields include:

- **Created By / Created On:** The individual who created the record and the date that they created it.

- **Modified By / Modified On:** The individual who last modified the record and the date that they modified it.

- **Created By (Delegate) / Modified By (Delegate):** This field is used behind the scenes by Dynamics CRM to track when the system automatically makes updates to records.

Owner, Owning Team

If you selected to have records owned by users or teams, then the entity will have an owner field. The owner field can be changed if the record is ever reassigned.

Other default elements

After saving an entity, you can begin customizing the elements of the entity. The elements include the fields, views, charts, forms, and relationships. More information on customizing the entity is found in the "Customizing Entities" section of this chapter. When you initially create a new entity, Dynamics CRM automatically creates a number of default elements outlined in Table 17.4.

TABLE 17.4

Default Elements on New Entities

Element Type	Element Name	Description
Form	Information ⇨ Main	This is the main form that will be used for data entry by users.
Form	Information ⇨ Mobile	This is the form that will be visible on a mobile device (assuming you have made this entity available for mobile access).
Form	Information ⇨ Preview	This is the preview form that will appear when users click the triangle next to a record in a grid.
View	All [Entity name]	This view shows all records.

continued

TABLE 17.4 *(continued)*

Element Type	Element Name	Description
View	[Entity name] Advanced Find View	This view is the default view that is used when a user creates an advanced find.
View	[Entity name] Associated View	This is the default view that is used for related lists. For example, when you are on accounts and you click the contacts link in the navigation pane, you will see the Contacts Associated View.
View	[Entity name] Lookup View	This is the default view that is used when the user is completing a lookup field that references this entity. A number of other options are available for this functionality from the form.
View	Closed [Entity name]	This view returns all records in the entity with a status of inactive.
View	My Open [Entity name]	This view is only created for user or team-owned records. It returns all records owned by the individual currently using the view.
View	Quick Find Active [Entity name]	This is the view that is returned when the user enters a value into the search box to search for a record in the entity.

Updating icons

Custom entities are automatically assigned a default icon. Creating a custom icon for each entity can improve the overall quality of your customizations while also giving users an easy-to-recognize symbol to help them remember the associated functionality and reduce their learning curve. There are a number of paid and free icon libraries available for download on the Internet.

Note
You cannot update system entity icons.

Because Dynamics CRM uses icons of different sizes for different parts of the application, you will need to prepare and load three different sized icons to update the icons. Specifically, you need to prepare icons in the following formats and sizes (none of the icons can be over 10KB):

- Web application icon: 16x16 pixel icon
- Microsoft Outlook icon: 32x32 pixel icon
- Entity form icon: 66x48 pixel icon

On the Web Site
Microsoft has developed an application that can convert a single icon into all three sizes and then load it as the icon for a selected Dynamics CRM entity. At the time of this writing, the application is only available for Dynamics CRM 4.0, but it will likely be rolled out for Dynamics CRM 2011 as well. We provide a link to download this tool on the Web site.

After you have prepared your three icons, use the steps below to load them into Dynamics CRM:

1. Navigate to the entity customization area of Dynamics CRM, within the appropriate solution.

2. Click the entity that you want to modify the icon for. Ensure that you are on the name of the entity in the navigation bar (clicking on the sub-items in the navigation bar will change which buttons are available in the menu).

3. Click the Update Icons button in the menu.

4. Follow the prompts in the dialog box (see Figure 17.12) to upload your custom icons.

5. Publish the entity for icons to become available.

FIGURE 17.12

The update icons dialog box

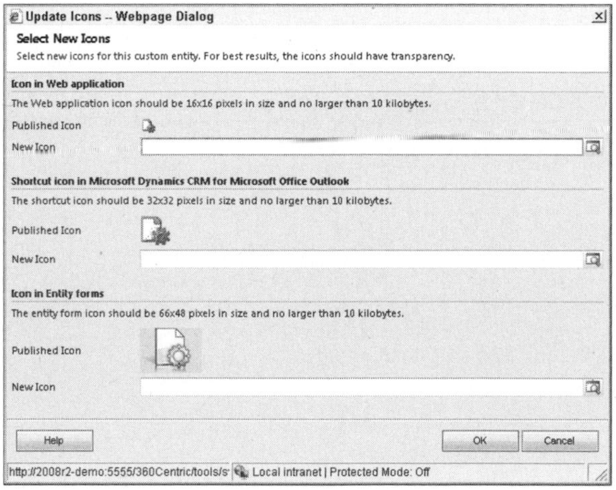

Customizing Entities

You can customize any entity that you have created as well as the customizable system entities that are included with Dynamics CRM. This section describes the customizations you can make using the Dynamics CRM user interface without requiring any programming knowledge. Deeper customizations can also be made using custom code and are referenced in other sections of this book.

Cross-Reference

The previous section included some general settings that you can modify when creating a new entity. Many of these settings can be changed when you are modifying entities as well. For more information about working with the general settings for an entity, see the earlier section "General entity settings and the primary field."

Use the steps below to customize existing entities:

1. Navigate to Settings ⇨ Solutions and select the solution you want to make your changes to. See Chapter 16 for information on working with solutions.

2. Navigate to the entity that you want to update. You can do this by either double-clicking the entity in the grid or by expanding the list of entities in the navigation pane and clicking on the entity that you want to customize.

3. Use the navigation pane to move to the various different components of the selected entity. Figure 17.13 shows the navigation pane with the fields area selected.

4. Using the instructions in this section, make whatever customizations you like to the entity.

5. If your customizations included changes to fields or to the form, preview the changes before publishing them.

6. When you are satisfied with your customizations, publish them. See the preceding section of this chapter for instructions on publishing customizations.

FIGURE 17.13

Entity customization area navigation pane with Fields selected

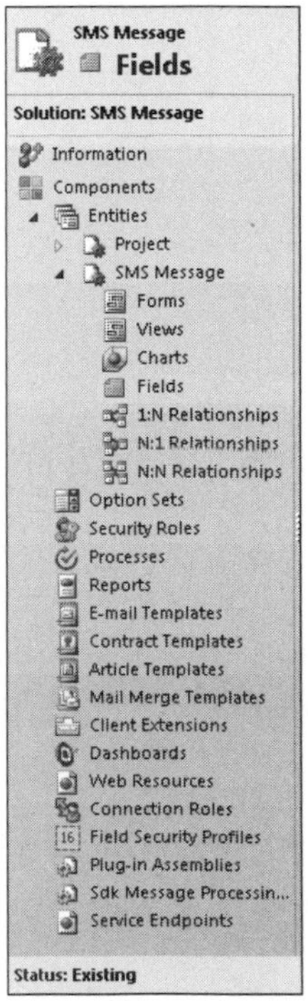

Customizing fields

You can add and update fields for an entity by clicking on the Fields item in the Navigation pane under an entity. Click the new button to create new fields or double-click existing fields to make changes. Figure 17.14 is the data entry form that is used to create or customize fields. The sections below the figure provide details on the available options.

Display name

This is the name that will be displayed on forms, views, and reports by default. You can change this field later, if desired.

Name

This is the name that the field is given in the Dynamics CRM database. After you enter the display name, Dynamics CRM auto-fills the name field for you. You can change the name that Dynamics CRM creates if you would prefer something else. This name refers to this field in programming code and custom reports. After you save the form, the name field can no longer be changed.

The field customization form

Cross-Reference

You may notice that a prefix that cannot be edited is automatically added to the name field. This prefix is set in the list of solution publishers. See Chapter 16 for information on setting the prefix for a publisher.

Note

You may want to develop some naming conventions for your Dynamics CRM application. Naming conventions improve the ease-of-use of the application as well as the ease-of-maintenance. In addition, if you have a large number of fields with similar names, using a consistent naming convention for both the display name and for the database name is even more important.

Field security

Field level security enables you to define privileges for users to view or update individual fields. If all users will have the same access to this field, then leave this value as "Disable." If different users will have different levels of access to this field, then set the value to "Enable." See Chapter 6 to understand the other settings that control field level security.

Auditing

If you want Dynamics CRM to automatically track every time a change is made to this field, then select Enable for this option, otherwise select Disable. For more information on auditing, see the Auditing heading of the previous section of this chapter.

Requirement level

This setting enables you to determine how important a field is and controls some of the behavior for how the field is presented on forms. Settings are:

- **Business Required:** The field has a red asterisk next to it on the form. The form cannot be saved if the field has not been populated. The field cannot be removed from the form.

- **Business Recommended:** The field has a blue plus sign next to it on the form. The field does not need to be populated to save the record and does not need to be on the form.

- **No Constraint:** The field is optional and is not flagged with any special symbol.

Searchable

Set this value to "Yes" if you want this field to appear in the list of available fields for advanced find, quick find views and lookup views. Otherwise select "No." This can be a useful feature for controlling user access to fields and for simplifying the interface for users by hiding irrelevant fields from view.

Description

Enter a description for how the field should be used here. It is always a best practice to enter a description in this area. By taking the time to carefully track this kind of information, you will make maintaining Dynamics CRM easier in the future.

Type and format

The type and format settings allow you to determine what kind of data will be accepted in the field, as well as the formatting options for the field data. Options for these two fields are in Table 17.5.

TABLE 17.5

Type and Format Options

Type	Format	Notes
Single Line of Text (nvarchar)	E-mail	Ensures that the field will only allow a properly formatted e-mail address as input. Once populated, clicking on the field will open an e-mail to the specified address.
	Text	Allows the entry of any text in the field. Allows up to 4,000 characters of text.
	Text Area	Similar to text, but allows you to set up the field to accept multiple lines of text on the form.
	URL	Ensures that the field will only allow a properly formatted Web URL as input. Once populated, clicking on the field will automatically open the underlying Web site.
	Ticker Symbol	Converts the value entered into a hyperlink. Clicking the hyperlink opens Microsoft money central with details on the value of the stock and latest news.
Option Set (picklist)		See below for more information on working with option sets.
Two Options (bit)		This allows you to create a simple yes/no type field. On the form, it can be displayed as a check box, a picklist, or as radio buttons.
Whole Number (int)	None	Accepts a whole integer number within the specified range.
	Duration	Accepts duration in the field using a pick list.
	Time Zone	Accepts a time zone in the field. Uses a pick list to present a user-friendly format for the time zone.
	Language	Accepts a language in the field. Uses a picklist to present a user-friendly format for this field. Only languages that have been installed with Dynamics CRM will appear in the picklist.
Floating Point Number (float)		Accepts a floating-point number in the selected precision (up to five digits) and range.
Decimal Number (decimal)		Accepts a floating point number in the selected precision (up to ten digits) and range.

continued

TABLE 17.5 *(continued)*

Type	Format	Notes
Currency (money)		Accepts a money field (with optional levels of precision) within the specified range. NOTE: When adding currency fields, a second field is automatically added with the same name and a prefix of "(Base)" which is used for tracking multi-currency configurations.
Multiple Lines of Text (ntext)		Allows up to 100,000 characters of text.
Date and Time (datetime)	Date Only	Accepts a date value.
	Date and Time	Accepts a date and time value.
Lookup		Looks up a record from another entity. Using this field creates a relationship to the other entity. You can use this field type to create a simple relationship to another entity. For more information and advanced relationship settings, see the "Viewing, creating, and customizing relationships" section.

Cross-Reference

Type and format aid with getting data entered into Dynamics CRM in the right format. There are a number of other methods for validating that data is being entered correctly. See the forms section (below) for some other validation concepts. See Chapter 21 for some advanced validation methods (such as auto-formatting phone numbers) that use JScript code.

Creating new option sets (picklists)

Option sets are fields that allow the user select from a predefined range of values (also known as a picklist) to populate the field. You can create option sets that are related to only one entity, or you can create option sets that can be used in any entities in Dynamics CRM.

Caution

The instructions below are for creating an option set that will be used on a single entity. If there is any likelihood that you will want to reuse the same option set on multiple entities, then you should select Yes for the option to use an existing option set. For information on using options sets that can be reused across multiple entities, see Chapter 19.

To create an option set that is associated with only one entity, follow these steps:

1. Choose a type of Option Set (picklist).
2. Select No next to Use Existing Option Set. You are presented with the option set data entry form in Figure 17.15.
3. Click the "+" button in the button bar to add a new option to the list.
4. Change the label for the option.

5. If desired, you can also change the value. The value is a unique numeric ID assigned to each option in an option set. For the most part, this value is only used in programming code. Optionally, enter a description.

6. Repeat Steps 3 through 7 until you have completed your list.

7. If you want to make changes to an item, click on the item in the list and change the fields to the right of the list.

FIGURE 17.15

The option set area of the field data entry form

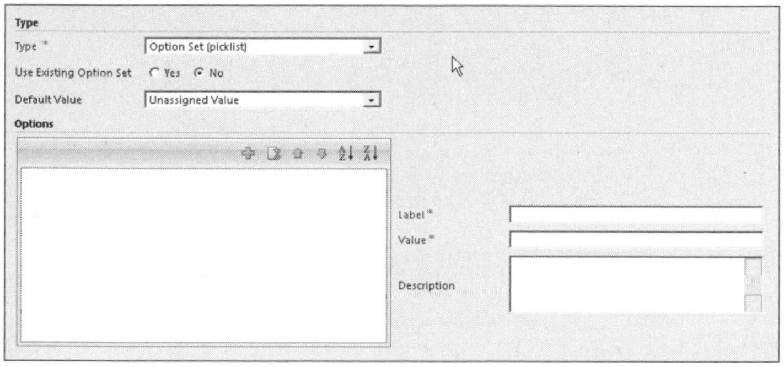

IME mode

IME (Input Method Editor) allows Dynamics CRM to work with Japanese, Korean, and Chinese characters. If you do not plan to use any of these character sets in your Dynamics CRM solution, then you can safely leave the default option selected. Because these writing systems have more characters than other keyboards, IME allows a sequence of characters to represent a single character in these languages. Using the IME mode, you can enter these characters into text boxes. Options for this value include:

- **Auto:** The IME mode is not changed.
- **Active:** All characters are entered in IME mode, but the mode can be deactivated.
- **Inactive:** Characters are entered without IME mode, but the mode can be activated.
- **Disabled:** IME mode is disabled and cannot be activated.

Working with relationships

One of the more important steps in planning and setting up a custom entity (or customizing an existing entity) is to determine how the entity relates to the other entities in Dynamics CRM. Relationships define the connection between entities. For example, you may create a custom entity called Customer Inventory, and you may want it related to cases so that for every case, you can see the inventory item that it was related to.

In this section, we will cover an overview of the types of relationships available in Dynamics CRM, how to setup relationship behaviors and how to map fields from a parent entity to its children. If the concept of relational databases is new to you, then we recommend that you review the section "Understanding relational databases," earlier in this chapter.

Understanding relationship types

Dynamics CRM supports two basic relationships between entities. These two relationships can be configured in a variety of ways in order to relate almost any two entities to each other. Figure 17.16 represents the available relationship types and how they can be configured. We will refer to it throughout this section.

FIGURE 17.16

All available relationship types

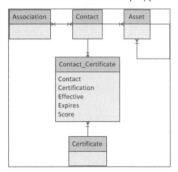

One-to-many (1:N) and many-to-one (N:1) relationships

Figure 17.16 includes a number of 1:N and N:1 relationships. These are the types of relationships that you will be creating most frequently in Dynamics CRM. Some of the options when creating these relationships, as illustrated in the figure, are:

- **1:N:** In Figure 17.16, the relationship between Contact and Asset is a typical 1:N relationship. Each contact may have many different assets associated to them.

- **N:1:** If viewing the same relationship from the Asset entity, then the relationship back to Contacts can be said to be N:1. In other words, many assets are related back to a single contact.

- **1:N Self-Referencing:** Note that the asset entity has a 1:N relationship back to itself. An organization may want to set this up if one asset could be the parent to one or more child assets. This type of relationship is very helpful, for example, if an organization tracks a piece of equipment and, within that, they also track all the subcomponents of that individual piece of equipment. Another example is a company organization chart — making the contact entity self-referencing enables a limitless range of parent/child relationships between managers and their subordinates.

Many-to-many (N:N) relationships

Many-to-many relationships enable you to link many records in one entity to many records in another entity. There are two ways to create many-to-many relationships in Dynamics CRM:

- **N:N Direct:** In Figure 17.16, the relationship between contact and association is an N:N direct relationship. This means that from an individual contact, you can see the multiple associations that the contact belongs to; and that from an individual association, you can see the multiple contacts who are members of the association.

- **N:N Connector Entity:** In the figure, the relationship between contact and certificate is an N:N relationship — but it is actually created by first creating a custom entity (called Contact_Certificate) and using it as a "connector" entity (also often referred to as a cross-reference entity or intersection entity). A connector entity has an N:1 relationship back to the two parent entities — thus creating an N:N relationship between them. The connector entity can also be used to track additional information about each relationship. In our example, the connector entity tracks the effective date, expiration date, and testing score for each certificate held by each contact. Connector entities can create a powerful way to manage data — but they can also create some drawbacks for the ease-of-use of your solution, because users will be required to use three different forms for data entry.

Unsupported relationships

There are some relationships types that are not supported by Dynamics CRM at this time. The listing below includes unsupported relationship types and some concepts for work-arounds:

- **Composite Customer Relationships:** Some system entities (such as accounts, contacts, opportunities, and cases) are associated with a parent customer. The parent customer can be either an account or a contact. The idea of a customer in Dynamics CRM is called a composite customer entity, that is, it is a "virtual" entity called customer that can be either an account or a contact (but not both at the same time). This concept enables organizations to easily handle business-to-business relationships or direct-to-consumer relationships within Dynamics CRM. However, new relationships to the composite customer entity cannot be created by the user. In other words, you cannot create a new entity called asset and have it related to a parent customer. In most cases, this is not necessary. In situations where you do need to define this relationship, you can either link an entity to both the account and contact (creating two relationships); you can use the Connection entity type (see nearby sidebar) to link to either of these, or you may be able to use a custom activity entity if it suits your purposes.

- **Any-to-Any Relationships:** In some cases, you may want to allow a user to establish a relationship between a custom entity and any other entity in Dynamics CRM. This is not supported. You can, however, use the Connection entity type (see nearby sidebar) to support a similar behavior. Depending on exactly what you want to accomplish, you may also be able to create a custom activity type entity and use the regarding field to link to any entity that allows relationships to activities.

- **1:1 Relationships:** A one-to-one relationship allows tables to have one (and only one) record linked to another table. These are not supported in Dynamics CRM at this time.

Cross-Reference

If you think the Connection entity may be suitable for a relationship that you are trying to define, you can learn more about it in Chapter 19.

Understanding relationship behavior

In addition to defining relationships between entities, you will also need to define how those relationships will behave. Relationship behaviors have to do with how changes made to a parent record will "cascade" to child records. As such, relationship behaviors only apply to 1:N and N:1 relationships and do not apply to N:N relationships at all.

Relationship behaviors are triggered based on six different behavior actions that can be taken by a user. For each of those six actions, a cascading behavior rule can be assigned to determine how this action will be cascaded to child records. In addition, Dynamics CRM predefined behavior types that can be applied to a relationship to automatically select appropriate rules for each action. The diagram in Figure 17.17 explains the relationship between behavior actions, cascading behavior rules, and behavior types. Below the diagram is a more detailed discussion of these items.

FIGURE 17.17

Understanding behavior actions, cascading behavior rules, and behavior types

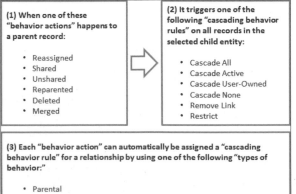

(1) When one of these "behavior actions" happens to a parent record:

- Reassigned
- Shared
- Unshared
- Reparented
- Deleted
- Merged

(2) It triggers one of the following "cascading behavior rules" on all records in the selected child entity:

- Cascade All
- Cascade Active
- Cascade User-Owned
- Cascade None
- Remove Link
- Restrict

(3) Each "behavior action" can automatically be assigned a "cascading behavior rule" for a relationship by using one of the following "types of behavior:"

- Parental
- Referential
- Referential, Restrict Delete
- Configurable Cascading

Behavior actions

Behavior actions are the six different actions that are taken on related (child) records after those same actions are taken on a parent (primary) record. Table 17.6 summarizes the six available behavior actions.

TABLE 17.6

Behavior actions

Action	Description
Assign	When the record in the parent (primary) entity is reassigned to a different owner, how will this affect the ownership of records in the child (related) entity?
Share	When the parent record is shared with other users, how will this affect sharing in the child records?
Unshare	When sharing is removed from the parent record, how will this affect sharing in the child records?
Reparent	When the parent record is re-parented, how will this affect the child records?
Delete	When the parent record is deleted, should child records also be deleted?
Merge	When the parent record is merged with another record, should child records be re-parented to the surviving parent record?

Cascading behavior rules

Different cascading behavior rules can be applied to each of the above behavior actions. Cascading behavior rules answer the question in the description column of Table 17.6. The available rules change depending upon the action taken and the type of relationship. Table 17.7 provides an overview of the different behavior rules and which behavior actions they can be set to work with.

TABLE 17.7

Cascading Behavior Rules

		Works with					
Rule	**Description**	Assign	Share	Unshare	Reparent	Delete	Merge
Cascade All	Cascade the change made to the parent record to all child records.	X	X	X	X	X	X
Cascade Active	Cascade the change made to the parent record to active child records. This can be useful, for example, for reassigning active opportunities to a new owner while retaining the owner of inactive opportunities for historical reporting purposes.	X	X	X	X		
Cascade User-Owned	Cascade the change made to the parent records to all child records that have the same original owner as the parent.	X	X	X	X		
Cascade None	Do not cascade the changes to any of the child records.	X	X	X	X		

continued

TABLE 17.7 *(continued)*

		Works with					
Rule	Description	Assign	Share	Unshare	Reparent	Delete	Merge
Remove Link	When the parent record is deleted, do not delete the child records, but remove the link to the parent record from the child.					X	
Restrict	Do not allow the parent record to be deleted if it contains any associated child records.					X	

Type of behavior

When defining the relationship behavior between entities, Dynamics CRM includes a picklist of types of behavior. The function of this list is to automatically set a cascading behavior rule for each of the six behavior actions. Using the type of behavior picklist simplifies the process of defining behaviors. Table 17.8 describes each of the four types of behaviors.

TABLE 17.8

Types of Behavior

Type of Behavior	Description
Parental	This setting cascades all changes from the parent entity to child records.
Referential	This is the default behavior for new relationships created between entities. It does not cascade any changes from the parent entity to child entities.
Referential, Restrict Delete	This setting does not cascade any changes from the parent entity to child records. However, it does prohibit parent records from being deleted if there are associated child records.
Configurable Cascading	This setting enables the administrator to manually set a behavior rule for each of the six behavior actions.

Viewing, creating, and customizing relationships

To view, update, or create relationships, you will need to navigate to the customizations area of Dynamics CRM and then to the entity that you want to use. Relationships are available as a series of three items in the navigation pane. Follow the procedure below to navigate to this area:

1. Navigate to Settings ➪ Solutions and select the solution that you want to view relationships for.

2. Within the solution, navigate to the desired entity in the Navigation pane and click the triangle next to the entity name to expand the list of items for that entity.

3. In the Navigation pane, click on the type of relationships that you want to work with (1:N Relationships, N:1 Relationships, or N:N Relationships as illustrated in Figure 17.18).

Relationships area of an entity

4. From here, you have several options as follows:

   • Create a relationship. You can click the New button in the menu bar to create a new relationship.

   • Edit a relationship. Double-click any relationship to open it and make changes (this includes changing relationship behavior or mappings).

   • Delete a relationship: If you want to remove a relationship, you can click on the relationship and click the X button in the button bar. Note that many relationships that are set up out of the box in Dynamics CRM cannot be deleted.

Dynamics CRM provides a relationship form (Figure 17.19) for creating or updating relationships. Important fields and sections on this form include:

   • **Primary Entity:** This is the name of the parent entity in the relationship. If you created a new 1:N relationship, then this field is populated with the name of the current entity. If you created an N:1 relationship, then this field is a drop-down from which you should choose the desired primary entity.

   • **Related Entity:** This is the name of the child entity in the relationship. If you created a new N:1 relationship, then this field is populated with the name of the current entity. If you created a 1:N relationship, then this field is a picklist from which you should choose the desired child entity.

   • **Name:** This field is a unique name that describes the relationship. Dynamics CRM auto-populates this field, but you can change it to a more descriptive name if you like.

   • **Display Name:** This is the name of the lookup field that appears on child records that link the record to a parent. For example, if you create a 1:N relationship between account and inventory, this value could be set to Account or Parent Account as the field that will show up on the inventory form to link back to the account record.

- **Requirement Level:** This determines if the link to a parent record will be required on the child record form or not.

- **Name:** This unique name is assigned to the lookup field on the child record.

- **Navigation Pane Item for Primary Entity Section:** This section enables you to define where (or if) a link to the list of child records will be displayed on the parent entity and, if displayed, what the label on the list should be.

- **Relationship Behavior Section:** This section contains the settings that define the relationship actions, rules, and behaviors. For more information on the settings in this section, see the earlier section in this chapter, "Understanding relationship behavior."

FIGURE 17.19

The relationship form

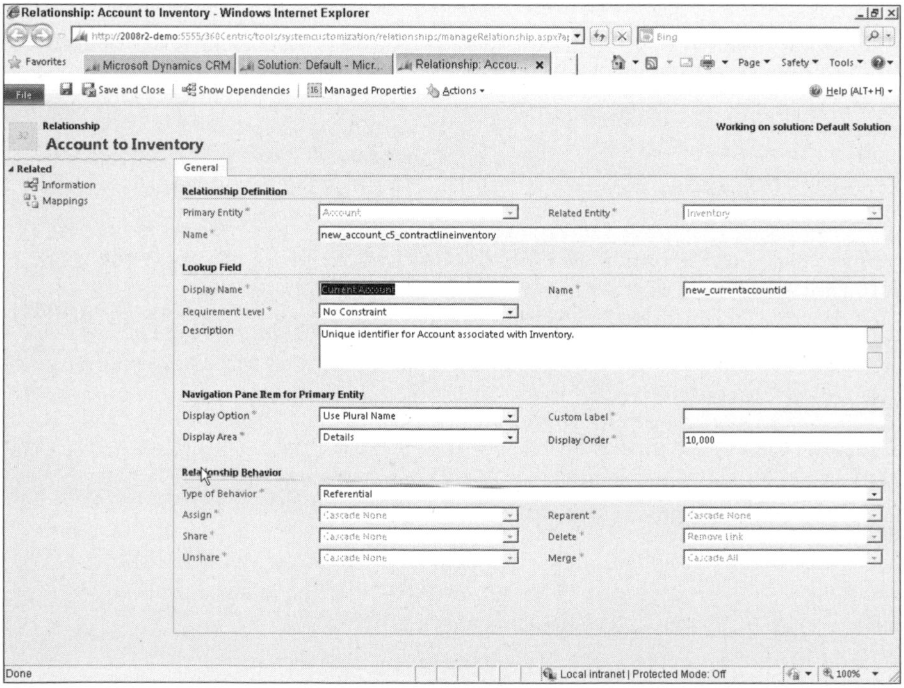

Note

The relationship form for an N:N entity looks a bit different from a 1:N or N:1 entity and the setup for N:N entities is simpler (not requiring setting up behaviors or mappings).

Mapping fields between relationships

Mapping fields between related entities allows you to save users time by automatically copying certain information from a parent record to a child record whenever a new child record is created. An example of this is the information, such as address and phone number that is copied from an account to a contact whenever a new contact is added to an existing account. Follow these steps to map a field from a parent record to a child:

1. Create fields on both the parent and child entities that should be mapped. Ensure that these fields are formatted in exactly the same manner.

2. Create the relationship between the parent and child entities (follow the instructions earlier in this chapter if you need assistance with this).

3. Click the mappings link in the Navigation pane of the relationship form. You are presented with a listing of all existing mappings between the parent and child entities.

4. Click the new button in the button bar to create a new mapping. You are presented with the Create mapping dialog (Figure 17.20).

5. In the left portion of the dialog, click the field from the parent entity that you want to map. On the right portion, click the field to which you want to map. When you have selected both fields, click the OK button.

6. Repeat Steps 4 and 5 for each field that you want to map.

Tip

If there are a number of fields that you want to map, you can click on More Actions ⇨ Generate Mappings to auto-create mappings between fields with similar names and formats. However, you should only do this on new relationships because this will reset any existing mappings that you have already set up (including deleting mappings that may not have similar names or formats).

FIGURE 17.20

Field mapping dialog box

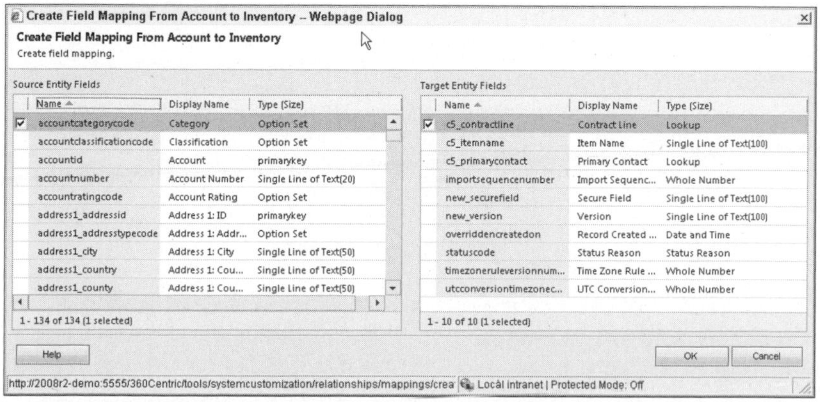

Working with forms

Forms are a central portion of the interface that users will access daily to enter and find information in Dynamics CRM. As a result, forms are also an area where users most frequently request changes. To successfully administer Dynamics CRM, it is important to understand the options and best practices for form management.

To navigate to the list of forms for an entity, use the process below:

1. Navigate to Settings ➪ Solutions and select the solution that contains the form you want to view.

2. Within the solution, navigate to the desired entity in the Navigation pane and click the triangle next to the entity name to expand the list of items for that entity.

3. Click the Forms link in the Navigation pane. You are presented with a list of all of the forms available for the entity.

Understanding form types

Dynamics CRM 2011 includes three different types of forms which are used in the application for different purposes:

- **Main:** The main form type is the data entry form that is used in the application (Outlook or the Web). Each entity has one form of this type by default, but more can be created if needed. Creating more than one main form enables *role-based forms*, which are discussed later in this section.

- **Mobile:** The mobile form is used when accessing dynamics CRM using a mobile device. Having a separate form for mobile devices makes it easy to manage a custom view of data on the limited screen space of mobile devices. Only one form of this type can be created for each entity.

For the remainder of this section, we will focus on the form types of "main." However, the process for managing mobile and preview forms is the same as it is for main forms (though there are fewer options for mobile and preview forms).

Understanding form layout

Dynamics CRM includes a flexible framework for laying out forms. This allows you to deliver an experience to the user that is efficient in terms of both data entry and presenting the information that they are looking for. Figure 17.21 is an illustration of a Dynamics CRM form. Below the figure is a description of each of the components of the form.

- **Fields:** Fields are added to the header, body, and footer of forms.

- **Controls:** Controls can also be added to forms in the header, body, footer, and navigation areas. These include navigation links, Web resources, Iframes, and spacers.

- **Navigation Pane:** The Navigation pane is on the left-hand side of the form. This area can be customized by moving and renaming sections, by moving navigation links between sections, and by creating custom navigation links.

FIGURE 17.21

Layout of a Dynamics CRM form as seen in the form designer

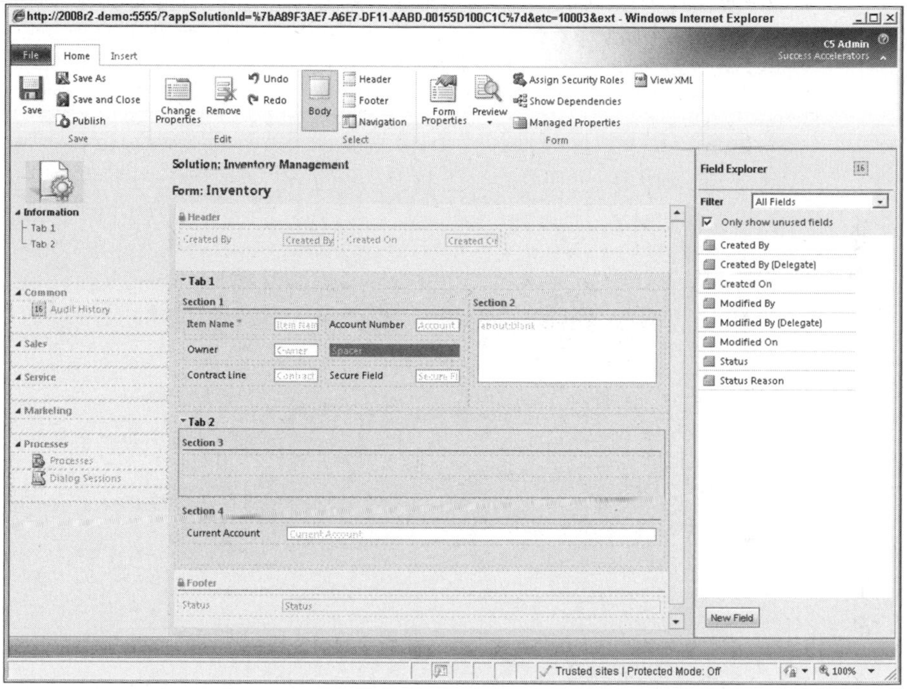

- **Header and Footer:** The header and footer are available on every form. These areas can be customized with fields and components that are always visible on the form regardless of which tab or related list is being shown.

- **Body:** The body of a form is where all of the data entry is performed. Fields and components can be added to the body. The body of the form can configured to be further subdivided as follows:

  - **Tabs:** Tabs enable users to rapidly navigate within a form. For every tab that is added to a form, a link is added to the Navigation pane to allow users to rapidly navigate to the tab. Note that Figure 17.21 contains two tabs and that, for each tab, a navigation link appears in the information section of the Navigation pane.

  - **Sections:** Tabs are made up of one or more sections. If a tab has two columns, then sections can be placed in each of the two columns. Sections can have from one to four columns to further control how information is presented on the form.

In Figure 17.21, the form is made up of two tabs. Tab 1 has two columns, each column containing one section. Section 1 has two columns. Tab 2 has a single column with two sections.

Using the form designer

To access the form designer, navigate to the list of forms for a selected entity and click the name of the form that you want to open. The form designer enables you to add new tabs, sections, navigation links, and components to forms. The designer provides a drag-and-drop interface, making it easy to move items around on a form to try out different layouts quickly. In addition, you can quickly create new fields and relationships without having to leave the form designer — saving time on rapidly creating new forms in Dynamics CRM.

Moving around the form

Forms are composed of four areas (the body, header, footer, and navigation as outlined in the preceding section). To make changes to any of these areas, go to the Home tab of the Ribbon menu and then click on the area that you want to update in the Select portion of the Ribbon menu.

Changing the form layout

Changing the layout of a form can include adding, deleting, moving, or updating tabs and sections on a form. The form designer provides several tools to make this process fast and flexible.

- **Adding tabs and sections:** Click the Insert tab in the Ribbon menu. Click the appropriate button in either the Section or Tab area of the Ribbon to insert an item with the selected number of columns into the form.

- **Moving tabs and sections:** Tabs and sections can be moved using drag-and-drop. Click and hold on the item you want to move and drag it to a new location. A red bar will highlight the place that the item will be dropped as you move around the screen. Release the mouse button and the item will be dropped into the selected area of the form.

- **Updating tab and section settings:** Tabs and sections have a number of formatting settings that you can change to alter how they look to the end user. To make changes to these settings, double-click on the name of the tab or section. You are presented with a dialog box of settings. Look at the Display and Formatting tabs for options on what can be controlled.

- **Deleting tabs and sections:** To delete a tab or a section, click on the item that you want to delete so that it is outlined with a green box. In the Ribbon menu, on the Home tab, click the Remove button. Select OK on the confirmation dialog box to delete the selected item.

Working with fields

Most of your work on forms will focus on setting up fields for viewing and for data entry. The form designer includes drag-and-drop features and in-place editing that speeds and simplifies the process of working with fields on your forms. Use the processes described below to work with fields on your forms:

- **Adding fields:** On the right-hand side of the form designer is the Field Explorer pane. Fields can be dragged directly off of this pane onto your form. You can change the filter of the Field Explorer to view only fields that are not already on the form, only custom fields, or all available fields. Note that the same field can be added to the form in multiple locations if desired.

- **Creating new fields:** If, while working on a form, you realize that a field needs to be created, you can click the New Field button at the bottom of the Field Explorer. Using the dialog box, you can create a new field for the entity on the fly and add it to the form.

- **Moving fields:** Fields can be moved within a form by clicking on them and dragging them to their new location, and releasing the mouse button to drop them there.

- **Updating field properties:** Double-click a field to update properties about the display and formatting of the field. Use the tabs in the dialog box to make changes. Note that lookup fields contain special record filtering properties (see the nearby sidebar).

- **Removing fields:** Field can be removed from a form by clicking on the form and then clicking the Remove button on the Home tab of the Ribbon menu. Note that this action removes the field from the form but does not delete the field from the entity.

Working with form controls

In addition to fields, there are a variety of other components that can be added to forms, called controls. To add a control to a form, click the Insert tab in the Ribbon menu and click the button for the appropriate control in the Control section of the Ribbon menu. To change the properties for a control after you add it to your form, double-click on it. To remove a control, click the control on the form and then click the Remove button on the Home tab of the Ribbon menu.

Using additional form controls, you can provide deep customization to your forms that deliver an unlimited range of functional enhancements to make your users productive. Figure 17.22 illustrates some of the customizations that can be available using form controls. The following controls are available to add to forms:

- **Iframe:** An Iframe control allows you to insert a "window" into another Web site or Web application directly within your page. Information can be passed into an Iframe from Dynamics CRM and back to Dynamics CRM from the Iframe. Using Iframes you can integrate with mapping and other applications by creating "mash-ups" with Dynamics CRM. Iframes are described in more detail in Chapter 21.

- **Navigation Link:** Navigation links are available only for use within the Navigation pane of the form. Adding a navigation link enables you to add a new item to the Navigation pane. This item can be a Web resource or an external URL (similar to an Iframe). This enables you to quickly enhance Dynamics CRM with integration to other systems, Web reports, or sites. See the Iframe and Web Resource bullet points in this list for more information.

- **Notes:** If your entity uses notes and attachments, you can add the notes control to provide an interface for this functionality to your form.

- **Spacer:** Spacers are used to provide extra space between fields and controls on your form. They do not provide any functionality other than to create gaps on the form where needed.

- **Sub-Grid:** A sub-grid control allows you to place a grid for a child entity on the parent form. For example, you can add a grid of related activities to a case. Sub-grids also provide you with control over how the grid works, including chart and view settings.

- **Web Resource:** Web resources are Web files (HTML files, images, Silverlight applications, etc.) that are managed on the Dynamics CRM server. You can think of them as similar to Iframes, except that the content within a Web resource is hosted in Dynamics CRM. Using Web resources you can create highly customized functionality embedded directly within your Dynamics CRM forms. See Chapter 21 for more information on Web resources.

FIGURE 17.22

A form with a number of additional controls

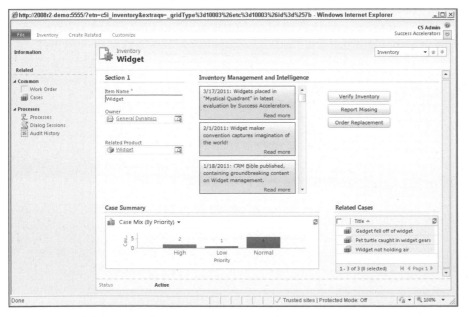

Working with Lookup Field Properties

Lookup fields allow users to look up a value from a related parent table. Properties for lookup fields can be set to save users time finding the appropriate parent record — or to restrict users to selecting from among a subset of records in the parent entity. To bring up the properties for a lookup field, double-click on the field in the form designer. The figure illustrates the properties available for a lookup field.

Properties for a lookup field.

Special properties for lookup fields include the following:

- **Turn off automatic resolutions in this field**. When entering values into lookup fields, Dynamics CRM will auto-populate fields if a user enters a partial value and then tabs away. This can be a helpful time-saver, but there may be cases where you do not want this functionality. Check this option to turn this functionality off.

- **Disable most recently used items for this field**. Lookup fields also provide a list of recently selected values for end users to choose from — another potential time-saver that may not always be desirable. Select this option to deactivate this function.

continued

continued

- **Only show records where**. This option provides a way to limit the list of records that the user can choose from. When combined with the Allow users to turn off filter option, this option can either be a guideline or a rule for which records should be used in this field. This can be useful for setting up a "sub-lookup." For example, one lookup field can be titled Law Firm to capture the name of the firm that provides legal services to this account (see "Additional Properties" section). In that case, a second field called Primary Attorney could limit the list of contacts to only individuals who work for the selected law firm.

- **Additional properties**. This gives you control over how much search flexibility the end user will have in terms of typing in search terms and using views to find records. You can also use this area to restrict the user to a predefined view when selecting a record. For example, you can setup a lookup field for Law Firm that uses an account view which restricts the user to only accounts where "Category=Law Firm."

Using these functions, you can have tight granular control over exactly how individual lookup fields function on a given form.

Previewing your form

Dynamics CRM includes the ability to preview and test your form prior to publishing it for end users. It is a best practice to always preview changes to a form prior to publishing them in order to mitigate the risk that changes you publish will cause problems on the form for users.

To preview the form, select the Home tab on the Ribbon menu and click the Preview button. There are options for previewing the form when a record is created, updated, or read only. While in preview mode, interact with the form by filling out fields to ensure that all works as expected. Click the "Simulate Form Save" button to see if desired actions during the save are taken.

Saving and publishing customizations

Changes to your form are not saved until you explicitly save them. Once you are satisfied with your changes to a form (or if you're leaving your computer for a while), click one of the Save buttons in the Ribbon menu to save your changes. In the event that you make changes to a form and you want to discard them, you can close the form without saving it.

Saved changes to forms are not published until you explicitly publish them. This allows you to make all of your desired changes to a form without publishing them until you have had an opportunity to notify users of the changes (and/or provide training if necessary). Once you are ready to publish your changes to a form, you can click the Publish button in the Ribbon menu.

Cross-Reference

In addition to the properties described in this chapter, there are a number of advanced customizations that can be made to forms to expand their functionality even further. These are covered in Section VI and include form events, field events, Web resources, Iframes, client-side scripting, and related concepts. Using these tools you can streamline data validation and formatting (for example, consistently format phone numbers), integrate with other Web sites (for example, show a map of a client location), provide user shortcuts (for example, display custom buttons to trigger workflows or dialogs), and integrate with your other internal systems (display reports or screens with information from other related internal systems).

Working with role-based forms

Dynamics CRM 2011 includes the capability to develop multiple different forms for the same entity. These different forms can then be assigned to be the default form for users based on their role within the organization. This can be very useful functionality for showing users only the data that they need to see for their job function. For example, a service technician may want to see a very different view of a case than would a sales representative. Use these pointers and best practices to configure multiple role-based forms for a specific entity:

- **Creating forms:** Create as many forms as you want to handle the different roles that need to interact with an entity. Keep in mind that the more forms you create, the more difficult it will be to manage changes to the entity in the future. For example, if you add a new field that should be visible on all forms, you will need to manually add it to all forms.

- **Assigning roles:** To assign roles to specific forms, navigate to the form view for the desired entity, select the desired form from the grid, and click the Assign Roles button in the menu bar. Select the desired roles from the assign roles dialog box (Figure 17.23) for the selected form and click the OK button. Individuals with the selected role will see the selected form by default.

FIGURE 17.23

Assign roles dialog box

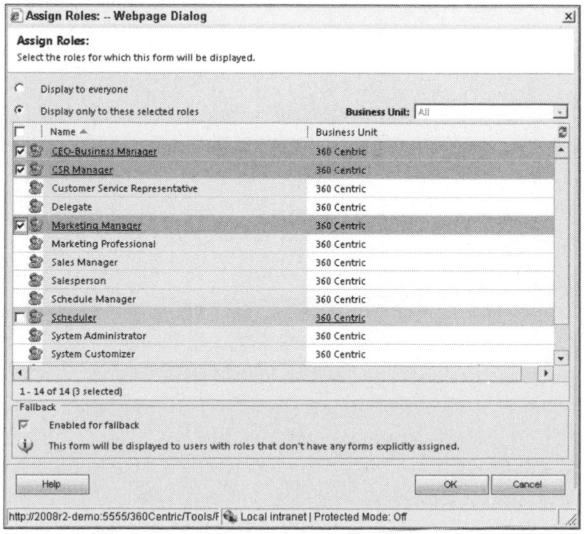

- **Form order and multiple forms:** Some users may have permission to view multiple different forms. In those cases, the default form will be the first form on the list of forms for the entity. To change the default form, use the Form Order button on the menu bar above the list of forms. If a user has permission to see multiple forms, they will see a drop-down indicator at the top of the form navigation pane. By clicking the indicator (Figure 17.24), they can choose which form they would like to view.

Cross-Reference

Note that-role based forms are not the same as field level security. Role-based forms are designed to improve the design and efficiency of the application for users, but they are not designed to hide secure fields from specific users. Chapter 6 provides more information on security roles and field security.

Deleting fields

In some cases, you may find that you create a field that you later want to delete. This can happen when business processes change or you realize that a field on a Dynamics CRM form is no longer capturing valuable information. Use the steps below to delete an unwanted field.

1. Remove dependencies on this field. The field you want to delete needs to be removed from items that depend upon it. This may include forms, views, workflows, and reports. Use the steps below to find the dependencies and then remove the field:

   1. Navigate to Settings ⇨ Solutions and select the solution that contains the field you want to delete.

   2. Within the solution, navigate to the entity containing the field you want to delete and then to the list of fields.

   3. Click on the field you want to delete.

   4. Note that this step is optional but is a recommended best practice. By following this step, you can temporarily hide fields until a later date to be absolutely certain that fields can be deleted prior to removing them from the Dynamics CRM database. Double-click to open the field configuration form. At the beginning of the Display Name, add the prefix "DEL_" and add the following text to the Description, "This field may be removed as of xx/xx/xx" (replacing "xx" with the date on which the field can be deleted). Save and close the form.

   5. You should now be back on the list of fields for the entity. Make sure you have clicked on the field you want to delete and then select More Actions ⇨ Show Dependencies. This list (Figure 17.25) shows you the views, forms, workflows, and other areas where the field is currently being used.

   6. Double-click on each item in the list to open the underlying item. Remove the field from the dependent item and save your changes. Repeat this step for each item in the list of dependencies.

   7. Publish all customizations for the entity. See Chapter 16 for more information on publishing customizations.

FIGURE 17.24

Form toggle drop-down list

Drop down indicator and two alternate forms that this user has permission to view

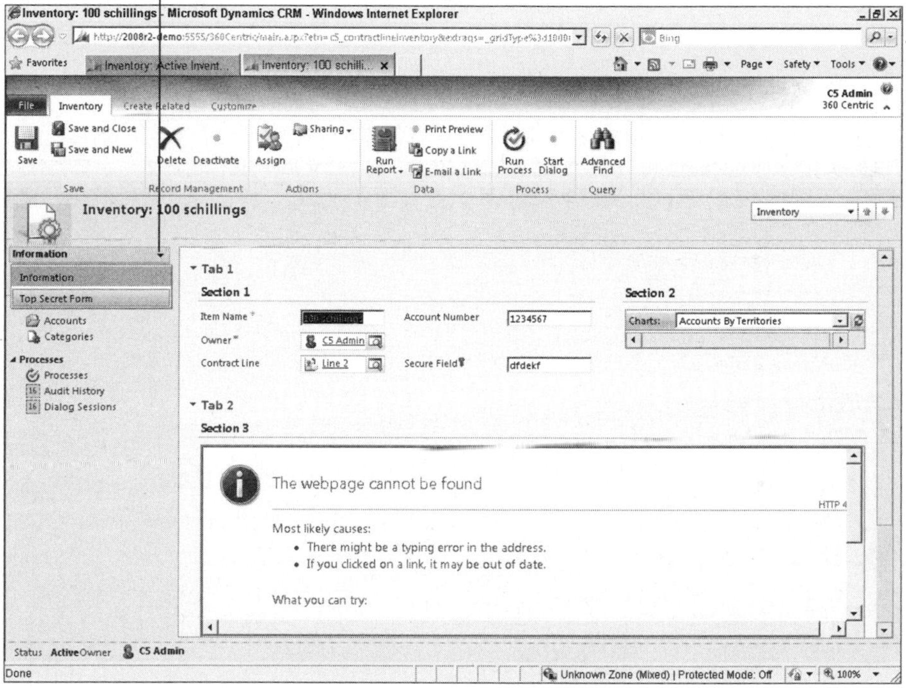

2. Delete the field. If you followed all of the steps above, then the field should now be completely removed from the view of your users. You may now either delete the field immediately (Step 2, below) or wait until an appropriate time in the future to clean up any extraneous fields (start with Step 1, below).

1. Navigate to the list of fields of the entity containing one or more fields that you want to delete and click the column heading labeled "Display Name" to sort the list by name. Scroll down the fields that have a prefix of "DEL_."

2. Select each field that you want to delete and then click the delete button (this is the button that appears to be a handwritten X above the list of fields).

3. You are prompted to confirm prior to proceeding. After you click the OK button, the field (and all data within it) will be deleted from the database and will not be able to be recovered. Click the OK button to proceed.

Caution

Deleting a field is permanent. All data contained within the field will also be deleted. Use extreme caution when deleting fields. Note that the above process includes some best practice precautions to help you avoid deleting data that you may need at a later time.

FIGURE 17.25

The dependencies list for a field

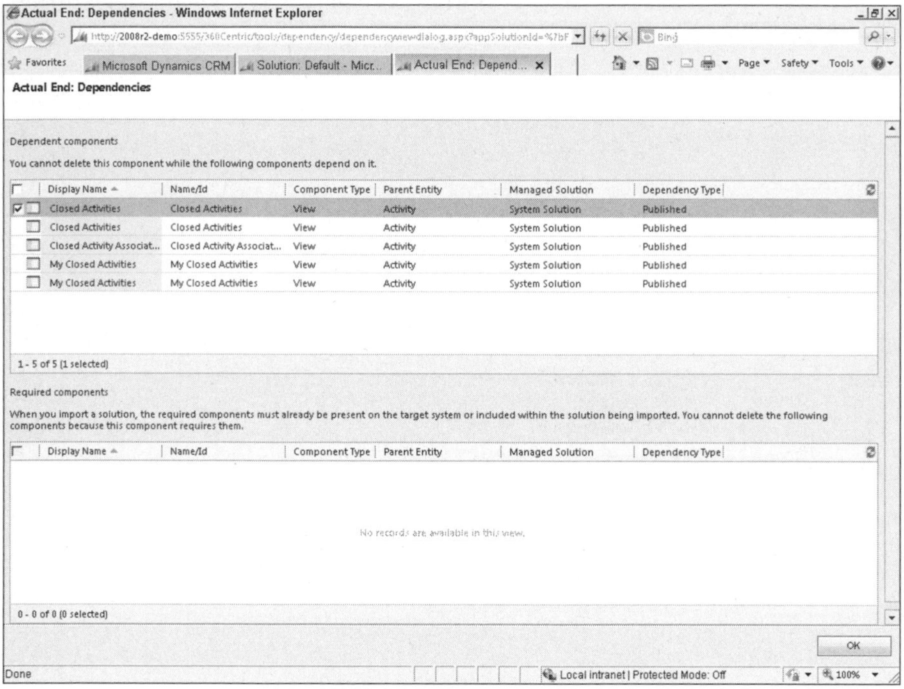

Tip

Do not delete system fields that are included with Dynamics CRM. Most of these fields were created by Microsoft with a specific purpose in mind. Although you may not initially use the fields, it is possible that you may find them helpful in the future. Also, system fields are kept in separate tables from user-created fields, so these fields do not reduce the total number of fields that you can create. You can safely remove the fields from forms and views without also deleting them.

Customizing views

Views are a predefined set of filters, sorting sequence, and columns that can be applied to data grids (or lists). Users can select the desired view for a given entity by clicking the drop-down above the grid. For every entity, you should maintain a list of the most useful views for all users to access.

Cross-Reference

Users can create their own "personal views" by using advanced find, filters, and personal view functionality. A general overview of views is covered in Chapter 10. The process for configuring personal views and public views is identical in most respects.

Understanding view types

Six types of views are available for each entity in Dynamics CRM. Any number of public views can be created for an entity. Only one of each of the remaining types of views is allowed, and each of these types of views is required. Table 17.9 explains the various types of views.

TABLE 17.9

View Types

View Type	Usage	Number Required
Public View	Available to all users. The filter, columns, and sorting for these views can all be customized.	0–unlimited
Default Public View	This is a public view that is the default for all users when they initially navigate to the entity. Any public view can be made the default public view by selecting it in the entity customization area and then navigating to More Actions ⇨ Set Default.	1
Advanced Find View	This is the view used by default when creating a new advanced find. A filter cannot be created for this view, but default columns and sorting can be selected.	1
Associated View	This is the view that is used on related lists when a sub-grid of items from this entity is visible on a parent entity (or on the navigation pane). Because the parent entity automatically sets the filtering, this view does not allow customization of the filter. You can, however, manage the columns and the sorting for this view.	1
Lookup View	This is the default view that is used on lookup fields on entities that are children of this entity. The filter for this entity cannot be edited, but the columns and sorting can be edited. Note that the filter can be edited from the form of the child entity.	1
Quick Find View	This view controls the quick find settings for the entity (when a search is conducted using the quick find bar above a grid). The view includes the columns that are displayed as well as the fields that are searched.	1

Creating and modifying views

To create a new view, navigate to the list of views for the desired entity and click the new button on the menu bar. To update an existing view, navigate to the list of views for the desired entity and double-click on the view that you want to update. Whether you are creating a new view or modifying an existing view, you will see the view designer (Figure 17.26) with the following options:

- **View Properties:** This option allows you to change the name and description for the view.

- **Edit Filter Criteria:** This option is available only on public views. Using this option, you can configure exactly which records are visible in this view. A more detailed discussion on configuring filter criteria is in the next section of this chapter.

- **Configure Sorting:** This option allows you to sort the view by one or two columns.

- **Add Columns:** This option allows you to add columns to the grid returned by the view. On the quick find view, this option reads, "Add View Columns." Note that your columns can include columns from other entities that are parents of the entity that you are creating the view for (for example, you can display the parent customer in an opportunity view).

- **Add Find Columns:** This option is available only on the quick find view and allows you to select which columns will be searched when a user conducts a quick find or when a user populates a lookup field.

- **Change Properties:** This option allows you to select the width of the selected column. You must first click on a column before selecting this option.

- **Remove:** This option allows you to remove the selected column from the view. You must first click on a column before selecting this option.

Editing filter criteria

Filter criteria is used throughout the Dynamics CRM application including public views, personal views, advanced find, reports, and processes. Filter criteria delivers quite a bit of precision and control over what users can see and do. Figure 17.27 is an example of a view that uses advanced filter criteria.

Filter criteria basics

Filter criteria contains one or more rows of filter conditions. Each row consists of three columns that define an individual filter. The first column is the name of a field for a filter (such as the last name of a contact). The second column is the operator (such as "equals" or "contains"); note that the available operators change depending upon the selected field. The third column is the filtering criteria. Depending upon the type of field, you may be able to select the third column from a picklist, a lookup, or you may need to key it in manually.

Grouping with and/or

When a filter contains multiple lines, it is assumed that all of the criteria must be true for the record to be selected. For example, in the filter in Figure 17.27, the owner must be the current user *and* the date the record was created must be within the past three months.

If you want to select a record if any of multiple criteria are true, then you should use the "group or" function. To select multiple rows that can be true, select each of the targeted rows (use the drop-down to the left of each row and choose "select row") and then click the "Group OR" button in the Ribbon menu. In figure 17.27, selected records can be from the state of NC, WA, CA, or MA.

FIGURE 17.26

The view designer

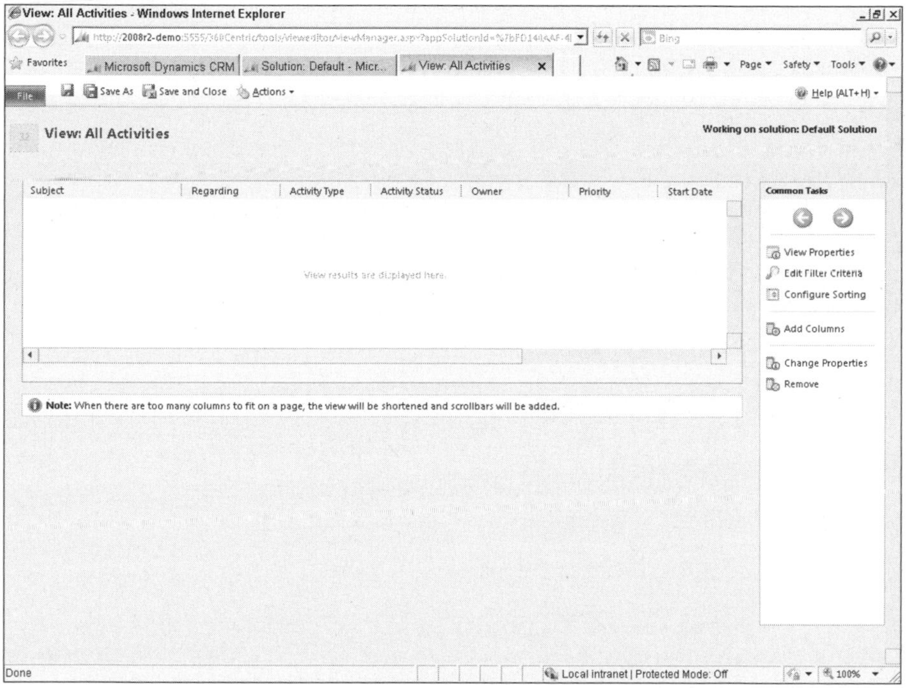

Within your "or" criteria, you may sometimes want to set some subcriteria to be "and." In figure 17.27 we want to select records in any of four states, but within the state of NC we want to also limit the list to only businesses with over $500 million annual revenue. Setting up an "and" group is accomplished in exactly the same way that we set up the "or" in the previous paragraph.

Referencing other entities

Your filters can also reference other entities that are related to the primary entity used for your view. A simple example is a contact filter that requires that the parent account have an industry of financial services. A more complex example appears in Figure 17.27, which requires that the individual have responded to a specific event campaign by registering for an event.

Limitations of filter criteria

With all of the flexibility included in the filter criteria function, there are also some limitations. Workarounds for these limitations can include adding new fields to entities to capture this information, using reports rather than views, and writing code to generate calculated fields. Table 17.10 lists some of the limitations and suggested workarounds.

FIGURE 17.27

Edit filter criteria dialog box with an advanced filter

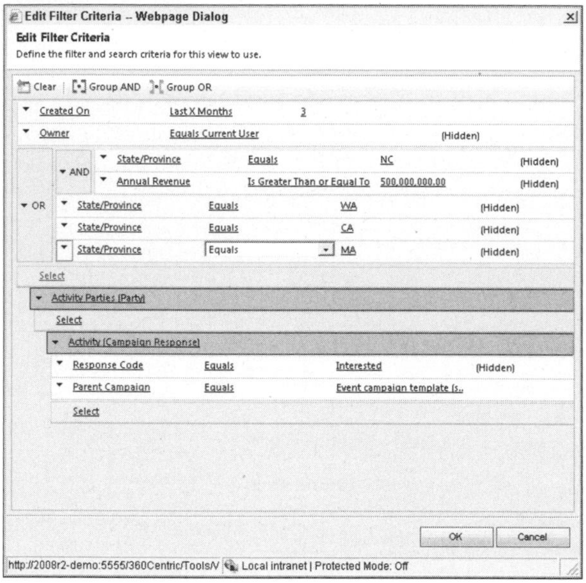

TABLE 17.10

Limitations of Filter Criteria

Limitation	Example	Suggested Workaround
Process filters do not allow the "group and" and "group or" options.	When developing a process (such as a workflow or a dialog), you want to develop a filter that includes multiple and/or criteria, but this option is not available.	You can create conditional branches in your process to check all conditions. For example, Step 1 can check if value 1 is true, and, if not, it can run a conditional branch to check to see if an alternative value is true.
Related tables do not allow aggregation.	You want to develop a filter to show all accounts with no associated activities that are open (in other words, there are no future activities scheduled for them). Or you want to create a filter showing all accounts where the total value of won opportunities is greater than $250,000. Neither of these is possible.	Calculated fields can be created on entities to automatically aggregate targeted values for filtering (search for "CRM Solution Accelerators" on www.codeplex.com for a free workflow add-on to handle this task). Alternatively, you can create reports with complex filtering criteria to meet this need.

Limitation	Example	Suggested Workaround
Relative field values are not flexible enough — dates are particularly problematic.	You want to create a filter of "aging leads" that were created between 15 and 45 days ago without having to "hard code" specific dates into the filter that need to be updated daily.	You can create a report for this purpose. If having a view is critical, you can write code to store the number of days on the lead entity or to return a custom view.
Lists are not supported in some field types.	You want to develop a filter that returns all leads with a rating of hot or warm and within the states of VA, MD, DC, NC, SC. You have been able to create a list of the selected ratings in a single line of your filter, but when you try to create a list of states, the filter does not work.	You can create a separate list row for each item in your list (using the "group or" function). You can create a field to summarize multiple values (such as using a "region" field to cluster multiple states together).

Customizing charts

Entities in Dynamics CRM can also have associated public charts. To create a public chart, navigate to the settings area and select the solution and the entity that you want to add a chart for. Under the entity, click the Charts link in the navigation pane and then click the New button above the charts grid. Design your chart and publish it to make it available to users.

Cross-Reference
For detailed information on chart design, see Chapter 24.

Renaming entities

Any customizable entity in Dynamics CRM can be renamed (this includes customizable entities that are included with Dynamics CRM such as accounts, contacts, and opportunities). Renaming entities can be helpful if you are fine-tuning entities that you created internally or if you want to rename entities that shipped with Dynamics CRM to align better with your internal. Table 17.11 includes the step-by-step process for renaming an entity and some of the considerations you should make before you begin the process.

Quick Tips for Managing Views

Creating and managing views can be a tedious and time-consuming process. Here are four quick tips on how to get the most out of views and how to manage them efficiently.

1. **Copying views:** You can quickly copy an existing view to use as a starting point for a new view. This can be a big time-saver if you have a complex view that you need to create a small variation of. To do this, just navigate to the list of views for an entity, open the view you want to copy, and click the Save As button in the menu bar. Enter a new name for the view and it will be saved as a copy of the original.

continued

continued

2. **Sharing views:** Use this tip if you want only a small group of users to have access to a view, or a user has created a personal view that other users may find helpful (and you don't want to re-create it as a public view). Assign the view to yourself (you can do this by logging in as the user who created the view, opening the view in advanced find, selecting Saved Views in the Ribbon menu, selecting the view, and then clicking Assign Saved Views in the Ribbon menu. Once the view is assigned to you, you can navigate back to the Saved Views area and use the share button to share it with targeted users.

3. **Creating view templates:** Sometimes your users will have a need for a view that can be altered in small ways to suit their needs. For example, they may need a view of individuals who have responded to a campaign — but the name of the campaign may need to be changed. You can create a "template view" that contains all of the needed filters, but leave the specific campaign name blank and save it (using a prefix of "TEMPLATE" in the view name to make it clear that it is a template). Users can then modify this view using advanced find to plug in the last bits of information that they need. You can even use the "hide in simple mode" option to hide fields that the user should not be able to change to keep the filter simple for them to update.

4. **Hiding unused views without deleting them:** Dynamics CRM includes a number of views out of the box that your users may not want to use initially. You can remove these from the list of views, while leaving them available to use later, by deactivating them. Navigate to the list of views for an entity in the configuration area, select the view you want to hide, and then choose More Actions ⇨ Deactivate.

Caution

You should carefully consider the pros and cons of renaming existing entities before continuing. Retaining original naming conventions can reduce user learning curve because new employees are more likely to already be familiar with conventional CRM terminology. In addition, the name of an entity cannot be changed in every place, and some areas where the name is used may require ongoing updates to keep the new name in sync. We've noted some of these considerations in the table below.

TABLE 17.11

Instructions for Renaming an Entity

Step	Instructions	Considerations
Alert users	If you are going to change the name of an entity that is already in production within your organization, be sure to let your users know about the upcoming change.	If users have created personal views, charts, reports, or dashboards, then they may want to update these to reflect the new name.

Step	Instructions	Considerations
Change the entity name	Navigate to the entity that you want to change the name of in the customizations area. Change the display name and the plural name to the desired value.	Note that you cannot change the name field. This field is used when writing code and developing some reports.
Change entity field display names	Navigate down to the list of fields for the entity. If the display name for any field uses the old entity name, then update those.	This will change how field names appear in a number of other places throughout the application.
Change form information	Navigate to the forms list for the entity in the customizations area and open each form. If the form name or description includes the entity name, then edit the form properties to change those. If any fields have a label on the form that uses the old entity name, then change those (in most cases this will not be necessary, but it is possible to use a different label on the form than the display name in the field list). Change any tabs or section headers that use the old name.	Names on some system forms and dialog boxes cannot be changed.
Change entity view names	Navigate to the list of views for the entity and update the names of each view with the new name for the entity.	Users may have personal views that they also want to update.
Change entity chart names	Navigate to the list of charts for the entity. If any of the charts use the entity name in their name, then rename these accordingly.	Users may have personal charts that they also want to update.
Change system messages	If this is a built-in entity (not an entity that was created by your organization or a third party) then there are some built-in messages that need to be updated. In the customization area for the entity, click on the Messages link in the navigation pane. Update each message, changing out the old entity name with the new.	Some error messages and messages tracked in log files cannot be changed. Note that messages can include substitution parameters (think of these as mail merge fields). When updating messages, the new message must include the same number of these fields as the original message did.
Publish changes	Publish all of the changes that you have made to the entity.	
Change dashboards	Navigate to the dashboards area and change the names of any dashboards that include the entity name.	
Change reports	Edit report names and formatting to update with the new entity name.	In some cases, this may mean manually editing reports in Excel, SQL Server Reporting Services, or other report writing tools.

continued

TABLE 17.11	*(continued)*	
Step	**Instructions**	**Considerations**
Change help content	Edit help files to replace the name of the entity within these.	Consult the Microsoft Dynamics CRM 2011 software development kit (SDK) for more information. The SDK can be downloaded freely from the Microsoft Web site.
		NOTE: Microsoft updates the help files from time to time, so your changes may be overwritten.
Change user documentation	If you have any online or offline user documentation or training materials, be sure to update those with the revised naming as well.	

Summary

Customizing entities, creating new entities, and managing all of the associated components are some of the areas that CRM administrators can expect to spend most of their time. Leveraging this functionality enables organizations to initially configure Dynamics CRM to work the way they do (rather than forcing them to change their processes to work with the software). The easy-to-use framework for configuring entities also enables businesses to rapidly adapt to the ever-changing needs of their customers and other stakeholders.

Custom entities and customizing existing entities can be used to extend the functionality available in Dynamics CRM. In fact, a growing number of businesses have found that Dynamics CRM is a development framework that can be used to create entirely new applications through entity creation and customization. The chapter included details on the many components of entities that can be customized.

Automating Your Organization with Processes

Organizations constantly struggle with streamlining, standardizing, and automating their processes. Although organizational leaders understand that process automation results in lowering costs, improving service, and accelerating workplace productivity, they lack the appropriate tools to make this a reality. This is particularly true of large enterprises with many employees and complex processes. As a result, processes are often managed in Excel spreadsheets, documents shared through e-mail, sticky notes, or, in some cases, are passed along only through word-of-mouth. Process automation is a struggle because it typically involves writing computer code. Because processes are complex and change frequently, computer code can become time-consuming and expensive to maintain.

Dynamics CRM includes a flexible set of process automation tools and an engine to constantly monitor and run processes in the background. Dynamics CRM processes support the concept of "programming without coding." As you work with processes in Dynamics CRM, you'll be surprised at the rules, alerts, scripts, and other automation that can be created by nondevelopers. On those occasions where the available process tools do not fully support your needs, you still have the option of using computer code for just the steps of the process that require this extra flexibility.

Understanding Processes in Dynamics CRM

Customizing software applications is partly about capturing and presenting data and partly about automating processes. As you have seen in preceding chapters, Dynamics CRM includes a customizable approach to gathering and visualizing data that even non-programmers can work with. This chapter focuses on the tools available within Dynamics CRM for automating processes. Tools for automating processes in Dynamics CRM are so powerful that many organizations are beginning to use it as a business process automation (BPA) tool that streamlines and standardizes tasks across their entire organization (not just customer relationship-oriented processes).

Programming without coding

If you have ever created a macro in Microsoft Excel, then you are familiar with the concept of developing a computer program without writing code. Processes in Dynamics CRM can be thought of in a similar manner. From the user interface, you can create a series of steps that include decision rules, user interaction, database updates, and automated e-mails. These steps can automate routine business processes, ensure a greater level of standardization, aid in training new employees, and ensure that enterprise policies are followed.

If you have never developed code, created a macro, or written a script, then workflows may take some getting used to. Plan to carefully work through this chapter and experiment with different processes to get the hang of it.

Understanding business process automation

Business process automation (or BPA) is a growing segment of the software marketplace. BPA applications are built to automate rules, processes, policies, and human interactions within an organization. Business processes evolve quickly, making it costly and time-consuming to use custom code to automate them. As a result, BPA applications have evolved with a focus on interfaces that can be quickly customized without requiring development (similar to Dynamics CRM). The advantages of BPA are clear: leaner businesses, following more consistent processes, leading to greater efficiency, higher quality, and improved customer satisfaction.

The primary disadvantage of BPA is not quite as easy to identify. BPA systems have evolved largely as "siloed" systems. This means that these systems operate separately from other business systems (such as accounting, project management, human resources, customer relationship management, document management, and other systems). Integrating BPA systems with other systems can be just as costly as writing custom code to automate processes. With Dynamics CRM, Microsoft has addressed this issue with a three-step approach:

1. The Microsoft Windows Workflow Foundation (WWF) is a pair of tools built into the .NET development platform. The first tool is the workflow designer, which can be used to create processes using a visual design environment. The second tool is a workflow engine that can be used to run processes either interactively with a user or in the background. Applications developed using the .NET platform can tap into WWF to deliver BPA.

2. Dynamics CRM processes use the WWF tools to aid in the design and execution of processes. Because Dynamics CRM also includes the ability to easily extend the database with new business functions, many organizations are finding that it is the only platform that they need for most of their BPA projects.

3. SharePoint also uses the WWF as its foundation for managing workflows. Because both SharePoint and Dynamics CRM share the same foundational layer for managing workflows, the two applications can share workflow processes and data. SharePoint functionality is complementary to CRM (see Chapter 1, Chapter 15, and Appendix A for more information). So combining these two tools delivers the only platform that most businesses need for complete business process automation.

Okay, so that was a lot of TLAs (three-letter acronyms) to get through. Simply put, Dynamics CRM brings the power of business process automation within easy reach of customer relationship management processes. When combined with the ability to customize entities and reports — and when further combined with SharePoint — organizations are finding that they can automate, monitor, and improve on all of their processes within a fraction of the time and effort that this type of automation required in the past.

Designing and diagramming processes

With all of this talk about how easy it is to create processes in Dynamics CRM, you're probably tempted to jump right in and start automating some of your organization's processes right away. Like anything else, however, creating *useful* processes takes thoughtful planning on the front end. Think of creating processes as something like giving a speech. It is easy to stand up and start speaking — almost everyone has the necessary "tools" to do this (a voice). But if the goal is to deliver a memorable and engaging speech, then time needs to be invested up front on structuring, planning, and rehearsing. To prepare for process automation, you need to do the following:

- Determine which processes you are trying to automate. This step sounds simple, but if you ask three different people how something is done around your business, you are likely to receive three different responses. Take the time to fully understand what is needed and work with the subject matter experts within your business to validate that what you are designing is what they want.

- Create a workflow diagram of your process. A picture is worth a thousand words, and taking some extra time up front to diagram your process almost always saves a tremendous amount of time later. Figure 18.1 is an example of a swim lane diagram that maps out not only the process steps, but also the stages that the record goes through as the steps are executed. You can use a tool like Visio or you can handwrite your process. After you define an initial process, you should focus on breaking it down into smaller steps that translate into individual steps in your Dynamics CRM process. Whatever you do, don't make the first step of designing your process be to click the New button in the processes area of Dynamics CRM.

FIGURE 18.1

An example swim lane diagram

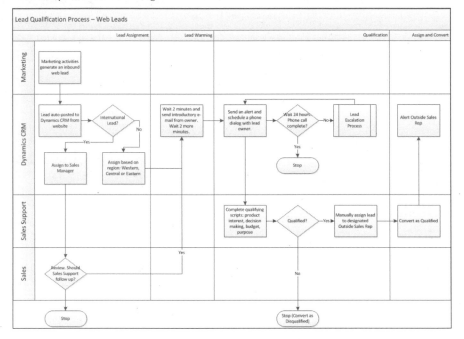

- Plan up front to take the time to test and tweak your process. Although processes are fairly easy to develop in Dynamics CRM, it is still possible to introduce bugs. Your testing plan should include a checklist that ensures you execute every single step of the process at least once during testing to see if it works as expected. If you have to make changes to the process, you should start from the top of your checklist again and work through every possible outcome before putting it into production. Doing this may seem like a tedious exercise — but taking this step now is less painful than it is to deal with angry users and data that has been transformed into garbage by bad processes. See the section "Monitoring processes" later in this chapter for information on looking at processes as they are running for testing purposes.

Process Brainstorming

Are you anxious to put processes to work, but not sure where to get started with your business? Here are some questions you can ask yourself or others in your business to begin the brainstorming process.

- How do we know who to assign leads to?
- How do we know if we want to do business with a prospective client? How do we qualify and prioritize them?

- What are the steps of our sales process? What actions need to be taken during each step?

- What steps are taken to resolve issues that customers raise? How are these tracked?

Ask others in the organization to think up four or five ways to end each of the following statements:

- We waste a lot of time on

- I would like to know whenever

- Whenever someone changes . . ., we need to make sure that . . .

- I would like to have a magic button that . . .

These questions come from a much larger list of questions that we frequently use as part of our assessment process on new projects. Use it as a starting point to develop your own list of questions.

On the Web Site

Check the Web site for the Process Planning Worksheet to aid you in defining your processes.

Processes and solutions

Processes developed in Dynamics CRM can be incorporated into solutions. This capability allows you to bundle together the data elements, reports, and automated processes required to deliver a complete solution and transfer them to other instances of Dynamics CRM. Perhaps more importantly, it means that third parties can develop solutions and provide them to you as a package that you can then install into your instance of Dynamics CRM. For more information on working with solutions, see Chapter 16.

Working with Workflows

Workflows are a predefined set of rules and steps that can be used to update records, send e-mail alerts, assign tasks, and perform other automation. They can be triggered to run automatically when a value on a form is changed, on demand by a user, or from another workflow. Workflows run in the background so their actions are not immediately visible to users. Once workflow rules are created, they continuously run — but they do not update existing records until a trigger event occurs. Workflows can be used to automate an unlimited range of activities; some examples include:

- Sending an e-mail alert to a manager when a sales opportunity for over $100,000 is created

- Escalating a case to a senior service rep queue when it is not resolved within 24 hours (see Chapter 14 for information on cases; see Chapter 10 for information on queues)

- Auto-assigning a lead to a user based on the product interest entered into the lead form, scheduling a follow-up phone call from the assigned user, and reassigning the phone call to another user if it is not completed within 30 minutes

- Inserting contact information into the description field of phone call activities so that the information will be available to reps on their mobile devices when they are away from the office

Tip

Workflows run in the background. After a workflow is executed, it may take anywhere from a few seconds to a few minutes to complete. Plan to use workflows for actions that can take a few minutes to complete (such as sending an e-mail to a user). Avoid using workflows for actions that need to be completed immediately (such as updating data on a form).

There are seven basic steps to creating a workflow in Dynamics CRM. Figure 18.2 provides an overview of the steps with a summary of each step below the diagram. The remainder of this section provides the details for each step of the process. Here are the steps:

FIGURE 18.2

The seven-step process for creating workflows

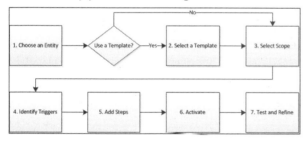

1. **Choose an entity:** Workflows are applied to records within an entity. When you make a selection, choose the entity that will trigger the workflow and the primary entity that the workflow will act on. For example, if you want to send an e-mail when a large opportunity is created, then use the opportunity entity.

2. **Select a template:** If you are using a template to develop your workflow, then select one from the list. See the section on creating and using process templates later in this chapter for more information.

3. **Set scope:** The scope of a workflow governs the records that the workflow is allowed to take action on.

4. **Identify triggers:** Triggers are used to determine which actions can cause the workflow to execute. Workflows can start automatically when a field is changed, can be run by users on demand, or can be started by other workflows.

5. **Add steps:** Workflows contain a set of logical steps including conditions and actions. Workflows can contain just a few steps or dozens of steps.

6. **Activate:** When you are satisfied that your workflow is complete, activate it to put it into production.

7. **Test and refine:** Remember that workflows are computer programs that are developed without code. This means that they are capable of automating processes and saving time; but they are also capable of creating some unintended consequences such as updating the wrong records. Take the time to carefully and fully test each step of your workflow prior to putting it into production.

Creating workflows

To begin creating a workflow, navigate to the Settings area of Dynamics CRM and click on Processes. Click the New button to create a new workflow. The dialog box in Figure 18.3 opens. Give your workflow a name in the Process name field, select an entity, and be sure to select a category of Workflow.

FIGURE 18.3

New process dialog box

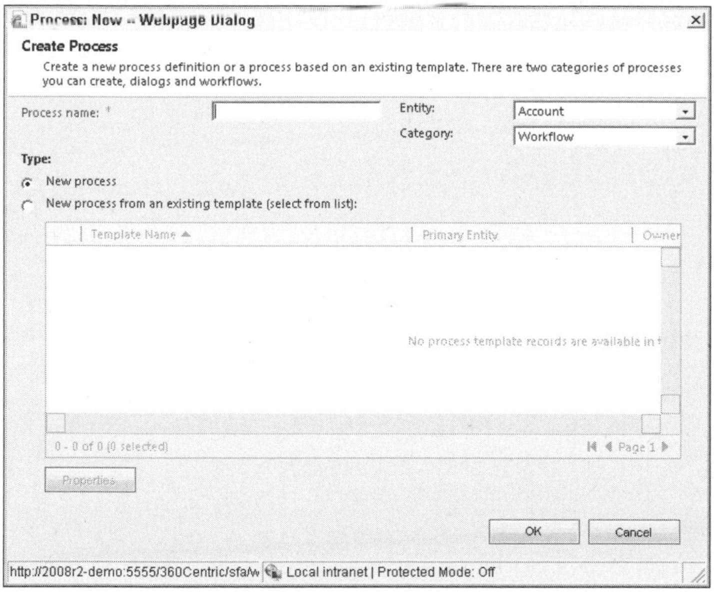

When choosing an entity, be sure to select the correct entity. Workflows are triggered by, and act upon, individual records. If, for example, you want to create a phone call activity whenever a case is more than 24 hours old, you choose the case entity.

Click the OK button to proceed to the next step of creating your workflow. You are presented with the process data entry form in Figure 18.4. Follow the instructions in the remainder of this section to complete the workflow form.

The process data entry form for a workflow

Workflow scope

The workflow scope determines which records your workflow will be allowed to act upon. The scope of a workflow is limited based upon the permissions and security roles assigned to the owner of the workflow and based on the workflow scope that is selected. The options for workflow scope are the same options available for security role privileges:

- **User:** The workflow only acts upon records owned by the user that owns the workflow.
- **Business unit:** The workflow acts upon records owned by the user or by anyone else in the user's business unit.
- **Parent-child business units:** The workflow acts upon records owned by the user, by anyone else in the user's business unit, or sub-units.
- **Organization:** The workflow acts upon all records for the entire organization.

For small companies, the scope setting is usually either User for personal workflows (workflows designed by a user and intended to be used only by that user) or Organization for company-wide workflows. Larger enterprises use the other categories to support variations on business processes for different business units.

Workflow triggers

Workflow triggers are the actions that can cause a workflow to begin to execute. The various triggers are listed under the sections titled Available to Run and Options for Automatic Processes on the form. Options for workflow triggers include:

- **On demand:** The workflow can be manually started by a user. If this option is selected, the user can navigate to a record for the selected entity type and manually start the workflow by clicking the Run Workflow button on the Ribbon menu. See the section "Running on demand processes" later in this chapter for more information.

- **As a child process:** Select this option if you want to be able to launch this workflow from another workflow or from a dialog.

- **Start when:** Select from among these options to automatically trigger the workflow based on a change to a record. This section gives you a great deal of flexibility in choosing how your workflow will be triggered.

Cross-Reference

Workflows can also be started from JScript Web resources. For more information on JScript and Web resources, see Chapter 21.

Trigger Troubles: Avoiding Problems with Automatic Triggers

Automatic workflow triggers deliver a great deal of control over how and when workflows are executed. However, care should be taken in how you select from among the options in this list and in how you structure the steps of your workflow. Here are some examples of the issues that can arise:

- Sales reps want to be alerted whenever an opportunity is assigned to them. The administrator creates a workflow with an automatic trigger to start when the record is assigned. Sales reps soon start to complain that they are not receiving alerts on some of their opportunities. This is because the alerts are only being sent when the record is reassigned — not when it is initially being created. The administrator should have selected both the Record is created and the Record is assigned options.

- The service group wants to receive an e-mail alert 90 days before maintenance agreements are due to expire so they can renew them if the customer has not already submitted a renewal. The administrator sets up a workflow that starts when a maintenance agreement is created and waits until 90 days before the agreement (a custom entity) is set to renew to send the service rep an alert. Service reps complain that they receive alerts on agreements that customers have already renewed, and they don't receive alerts after the first renewal. The administrator should have set up the workflow to run on creation of a maintenance agreement or a change in the maintenance agreement expiration date. The administrator should have also inserted a conditional check prior to sending the alert to see if the agreement was still due within 90 days or if the customer had already renewed it.

continued

continued

- Marketing sets up one workflow to send campaign responders an e-mail reminding them of an event one week in advance; the workflow also updates their attendance status to Confirmed after the e-mail is sent. They set up a second workflow to send the customer an e-mail if their attendance status changes to acknowledge the change in status. Customers complain that they consistently receive two e-mails in one day. This is because the first workflow is triggering the second workflow.

These are just a few examples of how even simple workflow triggers and associated logic can lead to problems. Although Dynamics CRM processes enable you to develop without coding, they still require careful design and testing to avoid these potential pitfalls.

Caution

Workflows can trigger themselves. For example, you may set a workflow to start when the status changes. One of the workflow actions may be to change the status again — which would trigger the workflow to start again. In programming, this is what is called an endless loop, and it can cause significant problems. Dynamics CRM will stop workflows that call themselves a number of times within a short period — but you should still take precautions to avoid this situation.

Adding workflow steps

To add steps to a workflow, click the Add Steps button in the menu bar about halfway down the workflow data entry form and select the step you want to add. Figure 18.5 is an illustration of the add steps menu with the different types of steps available.

Workflow conditions

Conditions are used to control the flow of a workflow. They can include an initial condition, conditional branches, and default actions. For example, conditions can be used to take one action for high-priority cases (check condition) and a different action for normal cases (conditional branch) and yet another action for low-priority cases (default action). Figure 18.6 shows how this might look in a flowchart diagram, and Figure 18.7 shows how it would look in a Dynamics CRM workflow.

Workflow conditions can be used throughout a workflow. For example, the first step in a workflow may test to see if an opportunity has a value of more than $100,000. Later in the workflow, another condition may test to see if the opportunity still has a status of open 90 days after it was created.

FIGURE 18.5

The Add Step menu on the workflow process data entry form

Workflow conditions   Stage

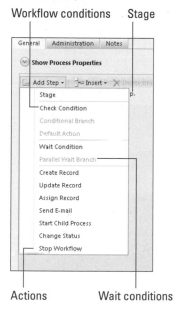

Actions   Wait conditions

FIGURE 18.6

Flowchart for a workflow condition

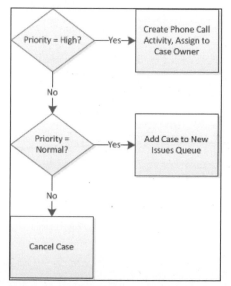

Cross-Reference

Conditions in workflows are similar to advanced find filters or views. Chapter 17 contains detailed information on how to work with filters.

FIGURE 18.7

The workflow steps that match Figure 18.6

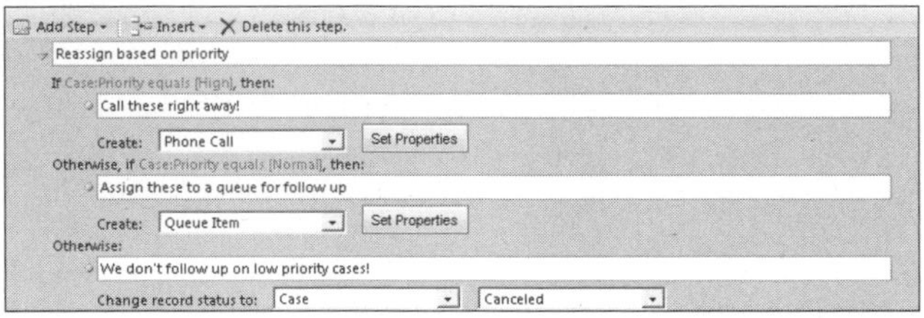

Wait conditions

The wait condition and parallel wait branch steps can be used in combination with one another. These steps cause a workflow to pause and wait for a condition to be met before proceeding. They can also wait for a certain amount of time to pass (called a timeout) before continuing with the workflow. Parallel wait branch steps allow you to monitor several possible conditions at once and branch to the appropriate sequence of steps when any one of the conditions is met. These wait conditions can be used in a variety of ways as described below.

- A workflow could begin by assigning a follow-up phone call to a new lead. An initial wait condition will wait until the phone call is completed and assign a task to the sales rep to qualify the lead. A parallel wait condition will wait until the lead status is changed to Qualified.

- Another example is a workflow that waits 24 hours after a case is created (using a timeout). It then tests to see if the case is still open and, if so, sends an e-mail alert to the case owner. Figure 18.8 illustrates this example.

FIGURE 18.8

A workflow with a wait condition that uses a timeout

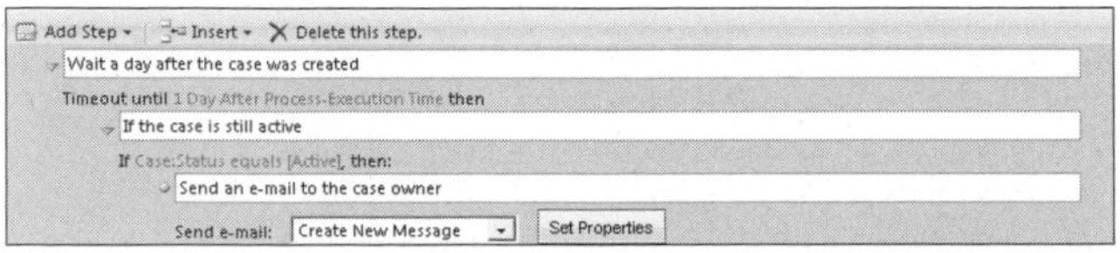

- Wait conditions are often used in combination with stages to automate a sales process (see the "Workflow stages" section). For example, in the first stage of a sales process the workflow may assign three tasks to the owner of an opportunity. A wait condition then monitors those tasks. After all three tasks are complete, the workflow then advances to the next stage of the sales process where a number of additional conditions may need to be met before proceeding.

On the Web Site

It takes a little more time to understand and work with timeouts in workflows. To help you along, we have included a sample lead follow-up workflow on the site that you can use to better understand timeouts.

Workflow actions

Workflow actions are steps that update the Dynamics CRM database or otherwise automate steps that a user may typically perform manually. Actions include sending e-mails, creating activities, updating existing records, and starting additional workflows. Workflow actions include:

- **Create Record:** This action creates new records in Dynamics CRM. This is typically used to create new activity records. For example, when a new lead is entered, the create record action can be used to create a new phone call activity and assign it to a user for follow-up. Another example may be to create an opportunity whenever a contract is within 90 days of expiration.

- **Update Record:** This action updates records that already exist. This may include simple updates, such as changing the probability of an opportunity when it reaches a certain stage. Any record related to the record that triggered the workflow can be updated. For example, when an opportunity is changed to "won" you can switch a field on the parent account from "prospect" to "customer."

- **Assign Record:** This action allows you to reassign a record to another team or user. For example, after an initial evaluation of a case it may be set to have a category of "bug report." A workflow can then reassign all cases of this type to the development team for follow-up.

- **Send E-mail:** The e-mail sent by this action can be directed to any address that is associated with the record that triggered the workflow. For example, if the workflow is triggered by creating a new lead, then the e-mail can be sent to the e-mail address for the lead, or it can be sent to the owner of the lead. This step can be used to automate routine communications with prospects and customers. It is also frequently used to send alerts to Dynamics CRM users when certain conditions are met.

- **Start Child Process:** Complex workflows may trigger other workflows when certain conditions are met. This action allows you to start another workflow that has been defined for the same entity and that is set to be available to run as a child process. Child workflows can be very helpful when you have some steps that need to get executed by multiple different workflows.

- **Change Status:** This action changes the status (and status reason) for a record associated with the workflow. Figure 18.9 is an example of updating the status of a case using a workflow.

- **Stop Workflow:** This action can be used to stop a workflow from running when certain conditions are met. This can be helpful if there is a reason why a workflow should stop running rather than continuing to wait or process other steps. An example may be a workflow running on a case that waits 24 hours before escalating; a parallel wait branch can be set up to stop the workflow if the status is set to resolved or canceled before the 24 hours have elapsed.

FIGURE 18.9

Changing a case status using a workflow

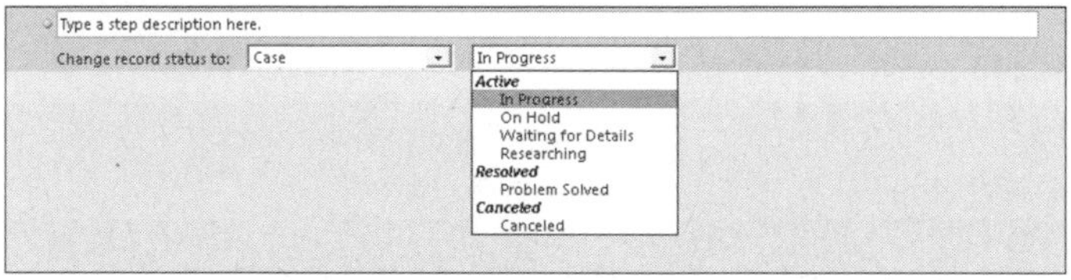

Working with dynamic values

Most workflow conditions and actions can include dynamic values. These values bring a great deal of flexibility to your workflows. Using dynamic values, you can insert variables directly into your conditions and into records created or modified by Dynamics CRM. Use the form assistant to create and insert dynamic values into your workflows. Figure 18.10 is an example of setting dynamic values for an e-mail.

Organizations use dynamic values in a number of ways in their workflows. Some examples include:

- **Mail/merge:** When creating activities or sending e-mails, dynamic values can be used to incorporate mail/merge like functionality into the workflow. Figure 18.10 is an example of using dynamic values to control not only who an e-mail is sent to, but also the content of the e-mail.

- **Record updates:** Field can be updated with values generated by the workflow. For example, an opportunity can be reassigned to the user listed as the sales support specialist on the account once the opportunity reaches a specific stage.

- **Calculated fields:** Simple calculations can be made to fields. For example, a field called Counter can be incremented by a value of 1 whenever the workflow runs — so subsequent workflows will be aware that other workflows have already run on this record (see the nearby sidebar "Getting Loopy: Creating Recursive Workflows" for more information on using counters).

- **Timeouts:** A timeout workflow is a workflow that uses a wait condition to pause for a specified amount of time prior to resuming. Dynamic values can be used to set the duration of the timeout for these workflows. (Figure 18.8 is an illustration of this type of wait condition.)

- **Relative conditions:** Dynamic values can be used in conditions, too. For example, if the creator of an opportunity is not equal to the owner of the parent account, you may want to send the account owner an alert about the opportunity.

FIGURE 18.10

FIGURE 18.10

The form assistant with dynamic values for an e-mail

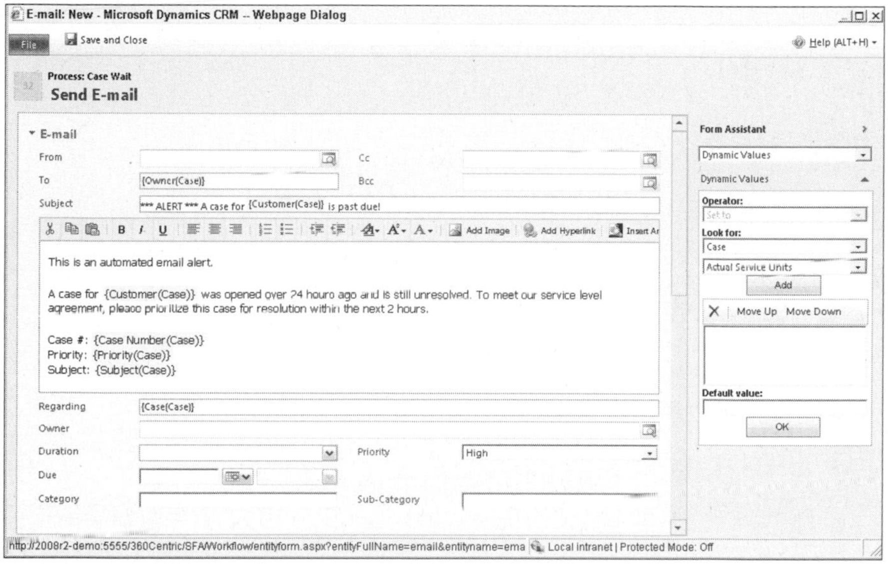

Workflow stages

Stages are a way of grouping sets of steps in a workflow together. Stages can be very useful for managing complex workflow processes. Workflows can contain any number of stages. If you decide to use stages in your workflow, then every step in your workflow must fall within a stage. Stages should only be used in workflows that will run over a period of time and that will involve wait conditions. For example, if you have a case management process or an opportunity process that involves waiting until certain actions have been completed before proceeding to a next step, these are good candidates for using stages.

As you design your staged workflows, you will usually insert a wait condition at the conclusion of each stage. This wait condition monitors the requirements for completing a stage prior to advancing to the next stage. Completion requirements may include completing tasks created during the stage, updating fields on the entity, or a certain period of time passing. Wait conditions on tasks do not necessarily need to have action steps below them. (See Figure 18.11 for an example of a wait condition at the conclusion of a stage.)

In general, you want to use stages if you create a sales process using workflow (as illustrated in Figure 18.11). This is particularly true if you plan to use built-in sales pipeline reporting. The built-in sales pipeline report allows users to group reports by sales processes. Sales process stages for this report are directly tied to the stages defined in workflows. This report is powerful because it supports reporting on multiple different processes. So, for example, if you have a large account sales process and a rapid sales process, you can view the report grouped by each of the different sales processes.

FIGURE 18.11

A sales process using stages

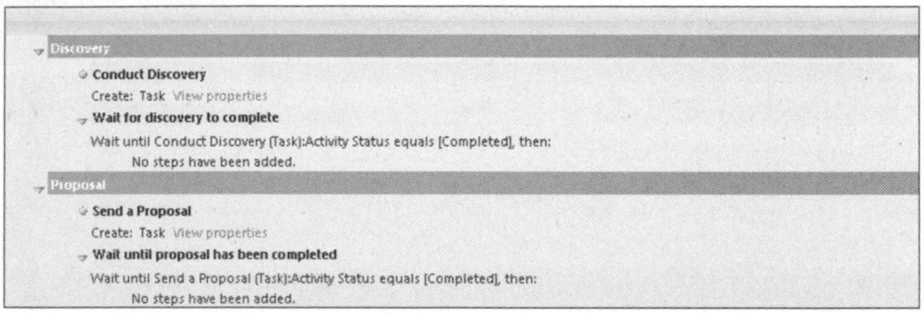

Getting Loopy: Creating Recursive Workflows

For those of you familiar with development, you may have noticed that workflows do not include the ability to "loop" — that is, workflows run from the top down and cannot circle back and rerun earlier steps. Someone might want to have a loop in their workflow if they are developing a sales process that has to roll back to an earlier stage if certain conditions are met. Another example may be that a case must be iteratively escalated to higher levels of management if it is not resolved in a timely manner. In both cases, you may want to go back to a prior step of your workflow to reuse some of the same steps. Without looping, this is not possible.

Fortunately, child processes can be used for this purpose. If a workflow is set to be available to run as a child process, then it can be set up to call itself as that child process. In development, creating a process that calls itself is referred to as recursion. The figure is an illustration of a simple workflow process that calls itself.

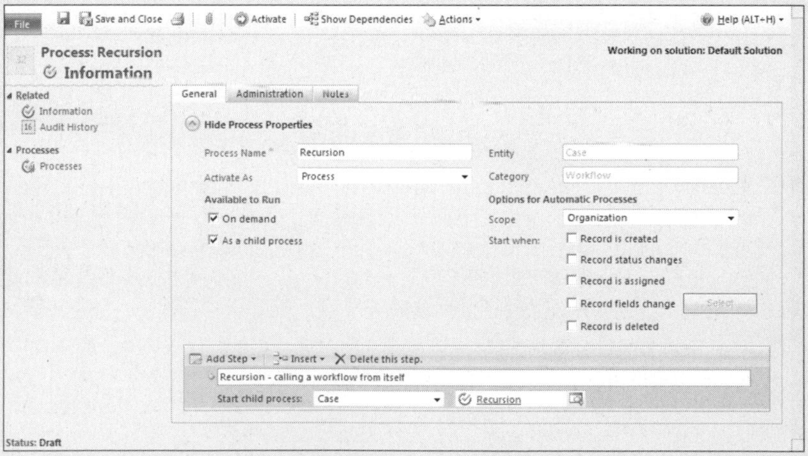

A recursive workflow process

Using recursive workflows, you can effectively rerun portions of your workflow multiple times. There are, however, some risks and techniques you'll need to be aware of to effectively use recursion in your workflows.

The primary risk is that you can create workflows that endlessly call themselves again and again. This can result in incorrect updates to the database or an avalanche of e-mails. Dynamics CRM includes automated workflow monitoring that causes workflows to fail if they appear to be running in an infinite loop to help to reduce this risk.

As you design recursive workflows, you need to consider some different techniques than you use in standard workflows because recursive workflows need to respond differently on successive runs.

- For example, if you want to escalate a hot lead to a different sales queue, how will your workflow know that it needs to go to a new queue the next time it runs? One technique that can work is maintaining a "counter" on the record that triggered the workflow. For example, you can have a field called "Follow Up Attempt" that has 1 added to it (using dynamic values) with each successive iteration of the workflow. Your workflow would then start by checking the value of this field and trigger different actions based on the value.

- Another example is an opportunity process with multiple sales stages. The early stages of an opportunity may focus on gathering data about the opportunity. When the workflow initially launches, it can check to see if certain data exists in the opportunity and, if so, it can skip the first stages. Your workflow can also use a custom opportunity field called Restart Stage, which can be set by the workflow before it calls itself — when the workflow restarts it can use the value in this field to determine which stage it should jump to.

As you can see, recursive workflows are powerful tools — but they also introduce some risks and complexities. When using recursive workflows, a good process for diagramming your workflow up front and testing your workflow before production is more important than ever.

Updating existing workflows

To update an existing workflow, navigate to it, deactivate it, make your changes, and then reactivate it. There are a few issues to be aware of when updating existing workflows:

- **Deactivated workflows:** Although workflows are deactivated, they no longer run when trigger conditions are met. If a workflow is used heavily, and you deactivate it for a short period, it will not be executed for any records that are created or modified during that period. For critical workflows, you should either work on them in a "sandbox" instance of Dynamics CRM, wait until off-hours to make updates. or make a copy of them to perform edits on a separate workflow (copies can be made by deactivating the workflow, saving it as a template, and creating a new workflow using the template).

- **Workflows in progress:** Workflow jobs that have already started running prior to making updates will continue to run without change. So, for example, if you edit an e-mail that is being sent by a workflow, all the workflows that were already running before you made the revision will send the same e-mail as before.

- **Moving complex steps:** As you work through testing and refining your workflow, you may find that a complex step should be moved to another location within the workflow. Unfortunately, Dynamics CRM does not include the ability to move steps within a workflow. Options for managing this include careful up-front planning to avoid having to move steps later, updating conditions to leave the step where it is, or completely re-writing the step.

Working with Dialogs

Dialog processes share many common traits with workflow processes. As a result, we will frequently refer back to the preceding section of this chapter for more information. We recommend that you thoroughly understand the workflows section of this chapter prior to beginning to work with dialogs.

Unlike workflows, dialogs run immediately. Therefore, when you start a dialog, it immediately begins executing the steps of the dialog. Dialogs also have the ability to interact directly with the user (Dynamics CRM is having a "dialog" with the user). Dialogs can ask the user a question, and branch to ask different questions or take different actions depending upon the response. Custom forms, prompts, and scripts can be integrated into dialogs to automate process steps. These features can be linked together to create a series of forms that work like a wizard to prompt a user through a process. Some examples of dialogs include:

- Prompting a call center rep through triaging a service issue so that it can be resolved in the first call or so that it can be promptly and consistently assigned to the appropriate queue for follow-up.

- Setting up a new user on a partner portal by interactively prompting a Dynamics CRM user to choose the level of access, username, and password for the partner. The dialog can launch workflows that e-mail the partner their portal access information.

- Providing a sales discovery script to a sales support rep so that leads can be properly qualified and assigned to the appropriate outside sales rep for additional follow-up.

Replacing a Dynamics CRM Dialog with a Dialog Process

We are frequently asked by our clients if dialog boxes built into Dynamics CRM (such as the lead conversion form, case resolution form, or opportunity close form) can be customized with new fields and processes. Until Dynamics CRM 2011 was released, the only way to accomplish this was by developing custom code. Dialog processes, however, can be used to fairly quickly replace many of the dialogs that are built into Dynamics CRM.

On the Web Site

Many businesses struggle with the lead conversion dialog box because, in many cases, the account already exists in Dynamics CRM and they want to just convert the contact and attach it to the account. These businesses relied on training users to make the conversion and to then update the contact with the account after the conversion — but this training was rarely retained, so many orphan contacts were created. The solution called "Lead Conversion 2" on the site provides a dialog process to address this issue.

Note that most dialogs that are built into Dynamics CRM are activated from a button in the Ribbon menu. To fully replace an existing dialog, you need to remove the existing button and replace it with a new button that calls your dialog. This process is included in the solution on the site and is discussed in Chapter 21.

Creating dialogs

To begin creating a dialog, navigate to the Settings area of Dynamics CRM and click on Processes. Click the new button. Give your dialog a name in the Process name field, select an entity, and be sure to use a category of Dialog.

When choosing an entity, be sure to select the correct entity. Dialogs are run from, and act upon, individual records. If, for example, you want to start a dialog during a phone call, then choose the phone call entity.

Click the OK button to proceed to the next step of creating your dialog. You are presented with the dialog process data entry form in Figure 18.12. Follow the instructions in the remainder of this section to complete the dialog.

FIGURE 18.12

The dialog process data entry form

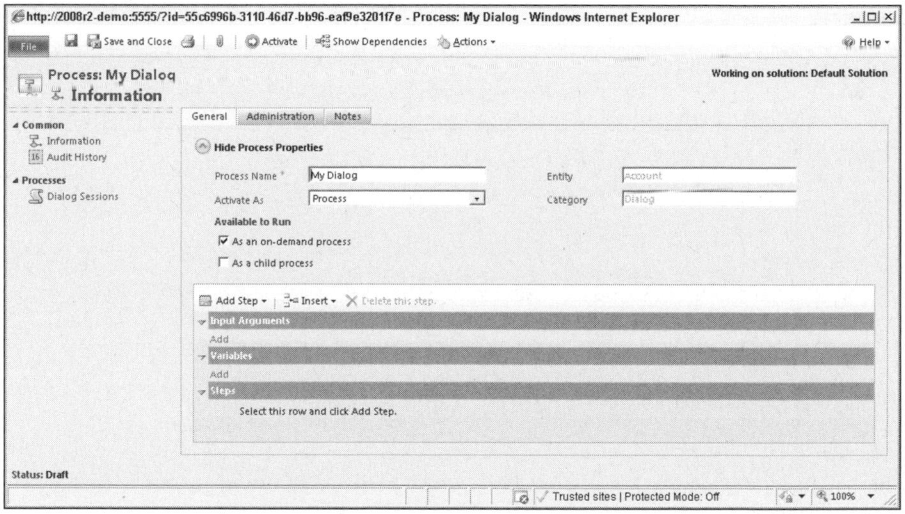

Dialog triggers

Dialogs can be triggered either on demand (the user selects to start the dialog by clicking a button) or they can be launched by other dialogs. Check the appropriate boxes on the process data entry form to indicate how you want your dialog to be available to run.

Cross-Reference

Note that dialogs can also be called from custom code. This concept is covered in Chapter 21.

Input arguments and variables

Before adding steps to a dialog, you may need to create input arguments and/or variables. The process for creating these items is fairly similar: just click the Add link below these sections and you are presented with a dialog box shown in Figure 18.13. You will name the field, choose a data type, and select a default value. Although creating input arguments and variables is similar, they serve different purposes:

- **Input arguments:** If you are creating a child dialog, then you can include input arguments if the child will need to be passed an argument from the parent. For information on passing an input argument to a child dialog, see the "Link child dialog" topic in the "Dialog actions" section.

- **Variables:** These items allow you to store and pass data within the dialog. Variables can be modified and used anywhere within the dialog. They can be embedded into prompts and e-mails and can be used to update records in Dynamics CRM. Variables can be used to hold calculations that are updated throughout the lifecycle of the dialog. As an example, you can use variables to calculate a lead score. Responses to various questions in the dialog can be assigned different weights which can then be calculated into the score to present a final value at the conclusion of the dialog.

FIGURE 18.13

The input argument dialog box

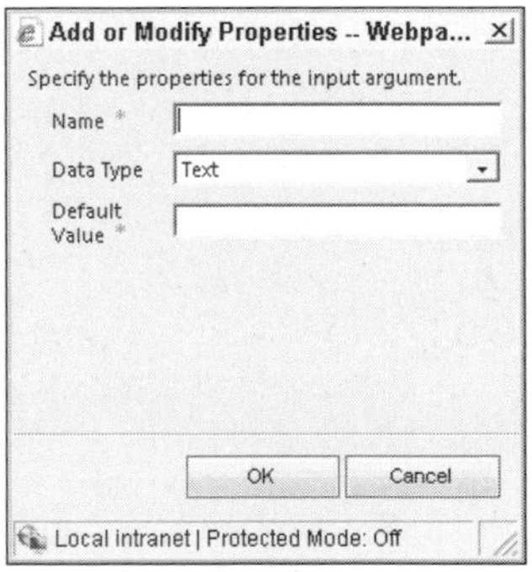

Adding dialog steps

To add steps to a dialog, click the Add Steps button in the menu bar about halfway down the dialog data entry form and select the step you wish to add. Figure 18.14 is an illustration of the add steps menu with the different types of steps available.

Stages, conditions, and dynamic values

These steps work in exactly the same manner as they do with workflow processes. For more information on working with these types of steps, see the section earlier in this chapter, "Working with Workflows."

FIGURE 18.14

The Add Step menu on the dialog process data entry form

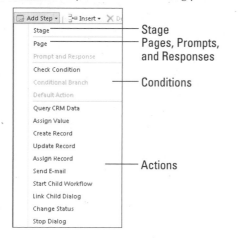

Stage — Stage

Page — Pages, Prompts, and Responses

Prompt and Response

Check Condition

Conditional Branch — Conditions

Default Action

Query CRM Data

Assign Value

Create Record

Update Record

Assign Record

Send E-mail — Actions

Start Child Workflow

Link Child Dialog

Change Status

Stop Dialog

Pages, prompts, and responses

Pages are the tool used by dialogs to interact with the users. Pages can include any number of prompts and responses. Prompts are used to share information with users, and responses are used to gather information from users. Responses can be used to update records, look up Dynamics CRM records to use in the dialog, branch to different pages, or customize the prompts presented on subsequent pages.

To add a page to a dialog, click the Add Step button and select Page. Be sure to enter a descriptive name for your page. A page only serves as a container to hold one or more prompts and responses. So as soon as you add a page, you should add a prompt and response to it by selecting Add Step again and clicking Prompt and Response. You can add as many Prompts and Responses to a page as you like.

To configure a prompt and response step, click the Set Properties button next to it. You will be presented with the properties form for the prompt and response (Figure 18.15 is an example of the properties for a prompt and response that queries CRM data to get the name of an account from the user). Use the guidelines below to set the properties for the prompt and response:

- **General:** This is not displayed to the user. It is used only to describe the prompt and response within the dialog. Use a good descriptive name that identifies the purpose of the prompt and response.

- **Prompt Details:** This section contains the information that will be shared with the user and is required.

  - **Prompt Text:** This is the text that the user will see for this prompt. You can think of this as the name of a field. Prompt text can also be used to simply share information with a user. It could be a welcome message that requires no input from the user, for example. Prompt text can include dynamic values, so you can prompt users with information such as "Thank you for your call today [Contact Name]. What kind of issue are you experiencing?"

- **Tip Text:** This text is used to provide additional help to the user. This can include more detailed information about the prompt. As the user moves from one prompt to another on the same page, the tip text changes accordingly. Tip text can also include dynamic values.

- **Response Details:** This section contains the response that the user will be required to enter to the prompt. Note that this section is not required — some prompts will only share information with the user and will not require a response.

  - **Response Type:** Choose the type of field that the user will see on the form. If you want to allow the user to pick a value that is in a Dynamics CRM entity, then choose Picklist here. For more information on using values from Dynamics CRM, see the "Query CRM Data" topic under the section "Dialog actions."

  - **Data Type:** This field provides some validation of the data entered by the user and determines how the data will be represented in subsequent steps.

    For example, you may define a prompt of "Case Type," with a response type of radio button containing values for Problem, Suggestion, Request. You may then define the data type as integer (if you want to map it to a CRM option set) or text (if you are mapping to a CRM text field or if you are only using the field for branching later in the dialog). Note that if you map a dialog field to a CRM option set, then you must ensure that the integer values for the dialog exactly match the values for the option set.

  - **Log Response:** Choose yes if you want the response to be captured into the history log for this dialog; choose no if the response does not need to be retained. In general, it is a good idea to retain responses. However, for privacy reasons, it is sometimes desirable to omit some responses from the log.

  - **Default Value:** If you want to assign a default value to this response, then enter it here.

  - **Provide Values:** If you selected radio or picklist as your response type, then this field and others in this section will be available for input. Choose Define Values if you want to manually create a set of radio options or a picklist for this field. Choose Query CRM Data if you want to allow the user to look up a record from a Dynamics CRM entity. (See Figure 18.15 and the section, "Dialog actions" for information on creating a CRM query.)

  - **Response Values, Value, and Label:** If you choose to build your own radio list or picklist, then you will need to click the green "plus" button above the response values list to add values to the list. For each value, you will need to set a value and a label. The label is what the user will see. The value is the numeric representation of the label that is stored in the database.

Each prompt and response can collect only one field of data from the user. So repeat the above process for every response that you need to gather from the user on a single page. After you are done with the page, you can add steps to update records or that ask the user for more pages of input, depending upon what they entered on the first page.

FIGURE 18.15

Prompt and response properties using Dynamics CRM data as the response

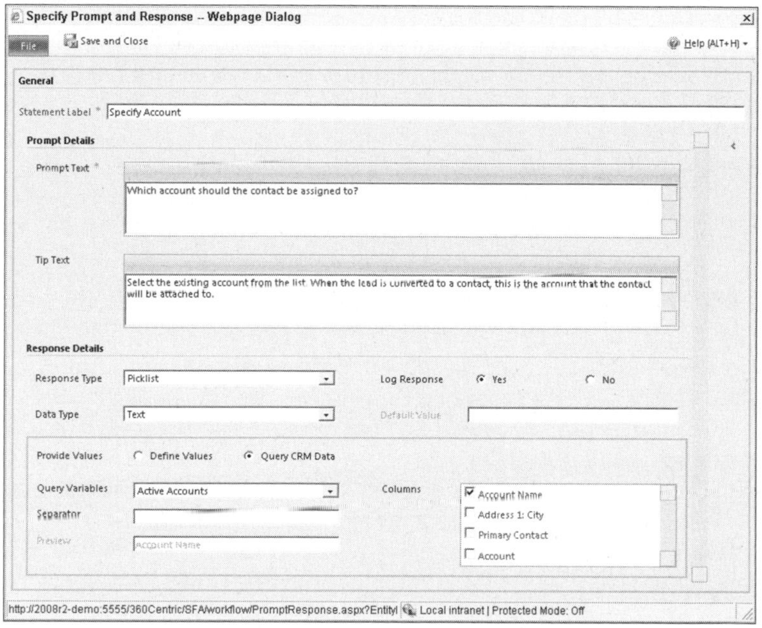

Note that pages can only contain prompts and responses. They cannot hold steps of any other kind. While you are adding steps "inside" of a page, you can only add new prompts and responses. To add other steps (such as conditions and record updates, for example) make sure to click on a step outside of the page step.

Dialog actions

Dialog actions are steps that update the Dynamics CRM database or automate steps that a user may otherwise have to perform manually. Actions include retrieving data from CRM, sending e-mails, creating activities, updating existing records, and starting additional processes. Dialog actions include:

- **Query CRM Data:** Add this action as a step if you want to make Dynamics CRM data available for a lookup within a dialog page. Click the Set Properties button after adding this step to configure the lookup. The lookup can be configured like any other view or advanced find (see Chapter 17 for details). Advanced users can click on the "Define fetch XML query text" tab to create custom filters (including parameters) that are not possible with the standard advanced find features available in Dynamics CRM.

Tip

The functionality behind the "Define fetch XML query text" tab can be a bit intimidating, but it is powerful and worth taking the time to experiment with so you can use it in your dialogs. When you initially click the tab,

Fetch XML code will be generated based on what you have entered into the Design New tab. So begin by using the "Design New" tab to take your query as far as you can without writing code. You can then click the "Define fetch XML query text" tab to add parameters to your query. Parameters are available using the Form Assistant (on the right-hand side of the screen); all of the responses from preceding steps of the dialog are available as parameters for your query. At the end of your query, add "QueryStep.Records != 0" to ensure that the query returns a record. One example of using this feature is to look up a contact based on their phone number and present detailed contact information in the next step of the dialog.

- **Assign Value:** Use this action to assign a value to a variable or input argument that you added at the top of the list of steps. This field can use dynamic values that include fields from the entity that the dialog is based on, entities related to the dialog entity, responses to dialog prompts, and custom fields used by the process.

- **Start Child Workflow:** Use this action to start a workflow. Keep in mind that workflows do not run immediately, so the workflow will not interact directly with the dialog.

- **Link Child Dialog:** Use this action to start another dialog linked to this one. After adding this step, you can choose which entity it should be related to (it must be the same entity as the parent dialog, or an entity that has a relationship to the parent dialog), and then choose the specific dialog (only dialogs that are available to run as child processes will be available). After making these selections, click the Set Properties button. You will be presented with a list of input variables for the child dialog. You can dynamically pass values from the parent dialog to the child by placing them into the value fields. Figure 18.16 is an example of the input properties for a child dialog.

FIGURE 18.16

Input properties for a child dialog

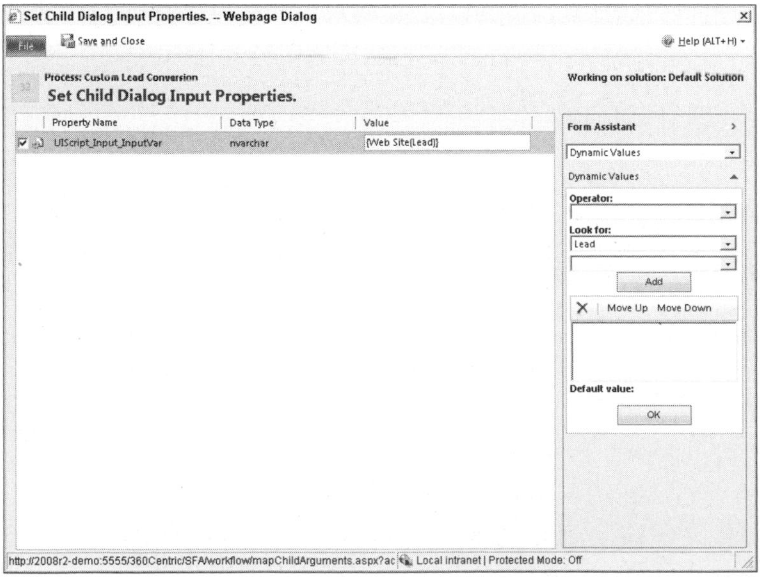

- **Create Record, Update Record, Assign Record, Send E-mail, Change Status:** Each of these actions works in the same manner as the actions by the same name in workflow processes. See the "Working with Workflows" section of this chapter for more information on these actions.

- **Stop Dialog:** This action can be used to stop a dialog from running when certain conditions are met. This can be helpful if there is a reason why a dialog should stop running rather than continuing to process subsequent steps. An example may be when a user has an option to provide a response that either continues the dialog or completes it. If they choose the response that completes it, then a stop dialog action can be inserted based on meeting that condition.

Understanding Other Process Concepts

Processes include a broad range of functions that can be used to streamline the process of creating processes, improve process management, assist users in accessing processes, and to extend processes. This section describes some of the other features, including some advanced process options, available to you in Dynamics CRM.

Running on demand processes

To run an on demand process, navigate to the record that you wish to run the process on and select it from a grid view. In the Ribbon menu, you will see buttons for Run Workflow and Start Dialog. Click the appropriate button depending on which type of process that you want to run, and the process will run. Note that you can select multiple records and run a workflow against all of them at once. Dialogs, on the other hand, can only be run against a single record at a time.

Administration, notes, and attachments

Dynamics CRM includes some helpful tools for documenting your processes and for "cleaning up" your processes after they complete. When creating or updating a process, these items are available in the Administration and Notes tabs.

Documenting your processes

It is always a best practice to maintain a description and any ongoing notes about your processes. This becomes more important over time as your Dynamics CRM implementation becomes increasingly complex and handles a broader range of processes. Use the Administration and Notes tabs on the process data entry form to provide a detailed description of your processes and to record ongoing notes about the changes you make on various dates. You can also attach documents to a process — so if you took the time to diagram your process using Visio or a similar tool, then attach the document to the process so you can refer back to it in the future.

Deleting completed workflow jobs

Each time a workflow runs, Dynamics CRM creates a "workflow job" to track the progress of the workflow. This can be a useful tool for monitoring the status of your workflows and for debugging. Each of these saved workflow jobs, however, consumes disk space and can slow down the performance of Dynamics CRM. To avoid this issue, you can click on the Administration tab while creating or editing a workflow, and select the check box titled, "Automatically delete completed workflow jobs." You can also manually delete older workflow jobs manually if you prefer.

Creating and using process templates

Process templates allow you to create a process, save it as a template, and then reuse it to create similar processes. To create a template follow the steps for creating a process, but on the process data entry form, change the Activate As field to Process Template and then activate the process. The next time you create a new process for the same entity, you can select the template as a starting point and modify it from there.

Process templates can also be a handy way to make a copy of existing processes. Just deactivate the process, switch it to a process template, and activate it. Now you can create a new process that is an exact copy of the original. You can also use this method to create a "version" of a process to save while you make modifications. If you ever need to revert back to the earlier version, you can just go back to the template.

Monitoring processes

When a process is applied to records, it creates an individual process job for each record. Each of these jobs performs the actions specified in the steps. Each job can be monitored to see which step is currently running if there are any problems with the process. There are a number of places you can go to monitor processes:

- From the process: You can open the process and click the Processes link (for workflows) or the Dialog Sessions link (for dialogs) in the navigation pane. This brings up a list of all the jobs that have been run for this process.

- From the targeted record: If a process has been run against an individual record (such as a lead or contact) you can open that record in Dynamics CRM and click the appropriate link in the navigation pane to bring up a list of processes.

- From the system jobs list: In the settings area, there is a link in the navigation pane to System Jobs. Clicking this link will bring up a list of all workflow jobs (as well as other types of jobs) that you can work with.

Once you are viewing the list of processes, you can click on the name of any of them to open it and see the specific details (including any error messages) associated with that job. You can also cancel, resume, postpone, or pause a job if desired. Completed or canceled jobs can be deleted.

Tip

Keeping a record of each completed workflow job can take quite a bit of storage space and slow down system performance. To minimize this issue, you can automatically delete completed workflow jobs. See the section "Administration, notes, and attachments" for more information.

Running processes using JScript

You can run processes by calling them from JScript. This means that you can trigger processes (both dialogs and workflows) directly from your forms. This can be done by adding buttons to the Ribbon menu, adding custom Web resources with buttons, or by calling them when a field value changes. This adds more control over how and when processes are executed — delivering more standardization and automation to your business. For more information on JScript, see Chapter 21.

Process extensions

Process extensions allow you to add more actions to the list of steps available for a process. For example, process extensions can aggregate values from subentities (so when you run a workflow on an account, it can return the total value of all active opportunities). Process extensions use custom code, usually developed in .NET, to extend the functionality available in processes. For more information on process extensions, see Chapter 22.

Custom workflow actions can be created by using programming code or can be acquired from third parties. Custom workflows can perform actions such as calculating fields, making complex related record updates, or capturing the URL of Dynamics CRM records that can be used to provide a link directly to the record to an end user (for example, a link to a record can be embedded in an e-mail to make it easier for the user to navigate to the record). For more information on custom workflows, see Chapter 22.

Using .NET and the Windows Workflow Foundation to extend your processes

The Dynamics CRM process engine is built using the Microsoft Windows Workflow Foundation. This is the same toolset that is used to manage processes in SharePoint and to build processes using the .NET development platform. Because processes use this foundation, you can export them into a file (called a XAML file) and import them into .NET. See Chapter 21 for more information.

Plug-ins: Using custom code for added process flexibility

Plug-ins are similar to workflows, but they are developed using custom code. Plug-ins allows an even broader range of possibilities for process automation. For more information on developing plug-ins, see Chapter 22.

Process examples

We have included several sample processes on the CD that you can use as a starting point to learn more about processes. Here is a summary of each:

- **Big deal alert:** This is a very simple workflow process that sends an alert to a user's manager whenever the user creates or updates an opportunity with an estimated value of greater than $100,000. You can edit the workflow to use whatever value you like.

- **Case triage:** Large organizations often have to triage a case before they can assign it to a user or a group for resolution. The case triage dialog process is an example of a process that identifies the needs associated with an issue and assigns it to different users based on feedback gathered from the customer.

- **Lead conversion replacement:** See the section "Replacing a Dialog" earlier in the chapter for more information on this dialog process.

Summary

Processes are one of the most powerful and useful customization features available in Dynamics CRM. Using processes, organizations of all sizes can automate customer-facing processes immediately. When combined with the other customization features available in Dynamics CRM, processes can deliver a complete business process automation platform to streamline and standardize practices across any organization.

Although processes are easy to use and enable you to develop computer programs without writing code, you should resist the temptation to create complex processes without a well thought-out plan. Take the time to map out your processes and think through the implications. In your project plans, include adequate time for testing.

Workflows are processes that run in the background. They can be triggered automatically or can be run on demand by users. Workflows can be used to update records, schedule activities, send e-mails, and ensure consistent actions are taken by users. Because workflows run in the background, however, they do not interact with users and may take a few minutes to run.

Dialogs are processes that run in the foreground. They include forms, prompts, and responses that can interact with users. Dialogs can include complex decision rules and branching so they can change how they interact with users based on user input and based on data stored in Dynamics CRM.

Part VI

Customizing Dynamics CRM with Custom Code

T hough this book is not aimed at developers, every administrator should have a thorough understanding of the terminology, concepts, and methods that can be used to customize Microsoft Dynamics CRM 2011.

Indeed, there are many customization methods described in this next part of the book that a non-developer can begin implementing. We've included a lot of practical examples to get you started. Who knows? By the end of this part of the book, you may decide you want to dive deeper into the development arena for Dynamics CRM!

With that in mind, we start this part of the book off by providing an overview of the options available to you and to developers.

Understanding the Other Customization Options

A s you have seen in preceding chapters, Dynamics CRM 2011 provides a broad range of options for customizing the application without having to write any code. In addition to the concepts presented in other chapters of this section, a number of other options are available for customization from the user interface. This chapter covers these additional customization options.

Customizing Option Sets

In Chapter 17, we briefly covered using option sets when customizing fields and forms within entities. Option sets are picklists that can be reused across multiple entities in Dynamics CRM. Use option sets if you expect to use the same picklist on multiple forms.

Creating new option sets and customizing existing option sets can be performed within the customizations area.

Use the steps below to create or customize an option set.

1. In Dynamics CRM, navigate to the Settings area.
2. Select which solution you want to add option sets to:
   - For the default solution, navigate to Customizations and select Customize the System.
   - For a custom solution, navigate to Solutions and then open the solution that you wish to modify.
3. In the list of solution components, choose the Option Sets item.
4. Click New to add a new option set (or click an existing option set if you wish to make changes).

5. Complete the form, illustrated in Figure 19.1, using the information below:

- **Display Name:** Enter the name that will appear on the Dynamics CRM form.

- **Name:** This name will be used to refer to the field in code. This is auto-populated for you, but you can change it if you wish.

- **Description:** It is always a good idea to include a detailed description of your option set so you will know exactly what it should be used for when you reference it later.

- **Options:** This is the area you use to create and update the list of options that appear in the option set. Use the buttons above the list to add, delete, or sort items.

- **Label:** This is the label that is presented to the user within the picklist.

- **Value:** A numeric value must be assigned to each label. This number is auto-assigned based on settings that have been made in Dynamics CRM, and it generally does not need to be changed.

- **Description:** This field is optional.

6. Once complete, click the appropriate option in the menu bar to either save your changes or publish your changes so that they will be immediately available on forms (assuming you were modifying an existing option set).

FIGURE 19.1

The option set data entry form

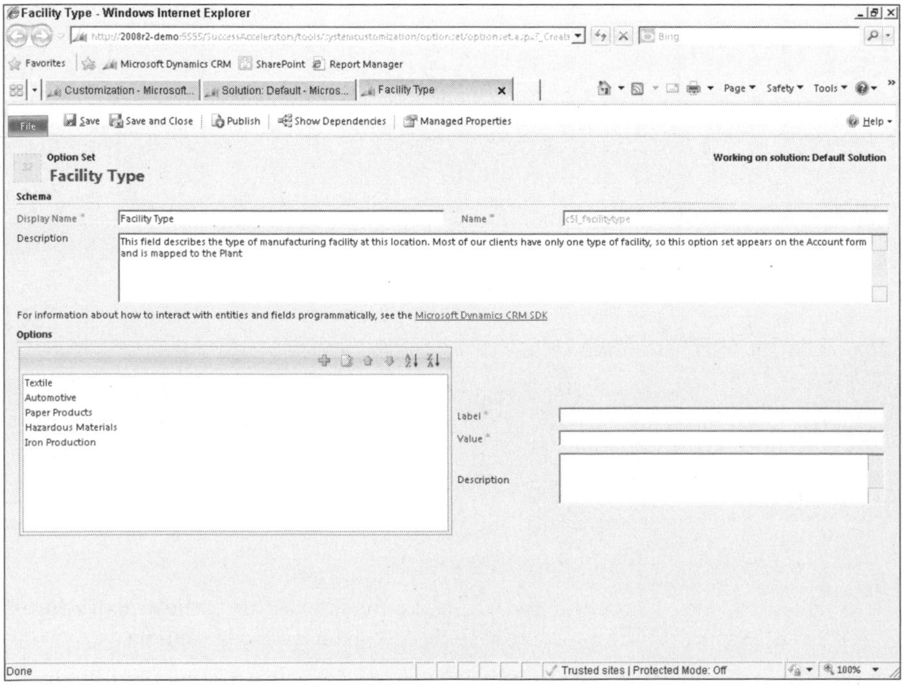

After you have completed setting up option sets, you can add them as fields on an entity just like any other field.

Setting Up Queues

Queues are containers that hold actions that need to be completed by an individual or a team. Think of a queue as an inbox containing work that needs to be processed. Almost any record can be shared with a queue. Some examples of queues include:

- During the sales process, a prospective customer needs to undergo credit approval. To accomplish this, Dynamics CRM assigns accounts to a queue named Credit Approval The accounting department monitors this queue and processes items as they are added.

- The HR department is using Dynamics CRM for their hiring process. After initial interviews, if the business wants to extend an offer, the candidate must go through a background check and a reference check. These contacts are assigned to two different queues at the same time (one called Background Check and the other called Reference Check). Two different business units monitor the two queues and process items as they come in.

Queues can also be associated with e-mail addresses. This can be useful for sending and receiving e-mails associated with a work process. For example, you may set up an e-mail address for service with the address service@yourcompany.com. Whenever an e-mail comes into that address, it can automatically be added to a service queue for processing. Similarly, outbound e-mails can come from the same address in order to provide customers with assistance in resolving issues (when users respond to these e-mails, the response can automatically be tracked to the queue). By using this single address, the e-mail can be "worked" by the first available person who checks the queue.

Cross-Reference
This chapter deals with setting up queues. To learn more about using queues, see Chapter 10.

Creating and customizing a queue

To create a new queue, or customize an existing queue, navigate to the Settings area, click on Business Management in the Navigation pane, and then select Queues in the main window. You will be presented with a grid listing queues. Click New to create a new queue or click on the name of the queue that you want to modify. You are presented with the form illustrated in Figure 19.2. Complete the form as follows:

- **Queue Name:** Give the queue a descriptive name.
- **E-mail:** If your queue will receive and/or send e-mails, then enter the e-mail address assigned to the queue. This e-mail address should be unique to the queue.
- **Owner:** Assign the queue to an individual or a team. Security roles work with queues in the same manner as other records.

- **Convert to e-mail activities:** Use this setting to determine which e-mails will get added to the queue.

- **E-mail Access Configuration:** Configure this section based on the settings you have made in your e-mail router (see Chapter 4 for more information). If you plan to send outgoing e-mails from the queue, then you may also want to check the box for "Allow credentials for the E-mail Router" and fill in the username and password.

The queue data entry form

Automating queues

Using processes, you can create routing rules to automatically assign records to queues and route records into escalation queues. By combining queues with processes, you can create complex business processes that can assign records to different queues throughout the lifecycle of a process. For example a new lead may be assigned to a Pre-Qualification queue where one of several Sales Support personnel may process leads. Once a lead has been prequalified, the Sales Support employee working it may then convert it and create an opportunity. From there a Sales Rep may make contact and, eventually, develop a quote. The quote may then be added to a queue for approval by a manager before it can be delivered to the customer. If the quote is not approved within four hours, it may be escalated to a senior manager queue for rapid approval. Once approved, it may then be added to a credit check queue, and so on.

Because e-mail addresses can be assigned to queues, your queue automation processes can send and receive e-mails. For example, a customer may send an e-mail to a general e-mail address your company has created and assigned to a queue (support@yourcompany.com). Incoming e-mails to this address can automatically be assigned to the queue. When an employee selects to work on an item in the queue, a workflow can send a message from the assigned e-mail address (support@yourcompany.com in this example) to the customer that submitted the case, informing them that their case is being reviewed. E-mail communications can continue to be sent as the case status is updated in order to keep the customer informed about the status of their case.

Queue automation makes it possible to improve the efficiency, quality, and consistency of business processes. Perhaps more importantly, it also enables multiple individuals to collaborate throughout the lifecycle of a lead, opportunity, case, project, or any other type of record that you may be tracking in Dynamics CRM.

Caution

The term "assign to a queue" is a bit misleading. In Dynamics CRM, the term "assign" usually refers to record ownership. If you assign an account to a queue, you won't see that the name of the owner has been changed to the name of the queue. Rather, when you assign a record to a queue, it means that you are creating a new record in the queue that is linked to the record that has been assigned to it.

Caution

Assigning a record to a queue allows all users who have access to the queue to see the record in the queue. However, if any of those users do not have a security role that allows them to view the linked record, then they won't be able to open the record form. For example, a user may see an item in the support queue, but the user may not have permission to see cases unless they own them. Take care when assigning records to queues to ensure that users with access to the queue will be able to work with the underlying records.

Approving queue e-mail

If you create a queue that uses an e-mail address, then e-mails can be sent directly into the queue as long as the e-mail address has been configured in the router. You can activate a security model for queues by navigating to Settings ➪ Administration ➪ System Settings ➪ Email Tab and checking the Process e-mails only for approved queues. Once the security model is active, you will need to click the Approve E-mail button on the queue data entry form before the queue can send and receive e-mails. If you deactivate the security model, then queues will be able to send and receive e-mails without requiring approvals.

Caution

If you have activated the security model for queues, then only users with the appropriate privileges can approve a queue e-mail address. To set the appropriate privilege, navigate to Settings ➪ Administration ➪ Security Roles ➪ select the role you want to update ➪ Business Management Tab ➪ under "Miscellaneous Privileges," select "Approve E-mail Addresses for Users or Queues."

Customizing Mobile Express

Mobile Express is a "light" version of Dynamics CRM that can be accessed from any mobile device that has an Internet connection and does not require any additional licensing fees. With Mobile Express, you can give your users access to virtually any of the data in Dynamics CRM from their mobile phone. You can also tailor exactly which data is visible in Mobile Express — making the most of the limited real estate available on the screen of mobile devices. Figure 19.3 illustrates the opening menu of Mobile Express and a form in Mobile Express.

FIGURE 19.3

Mobile Express menu and a Mobile Express form

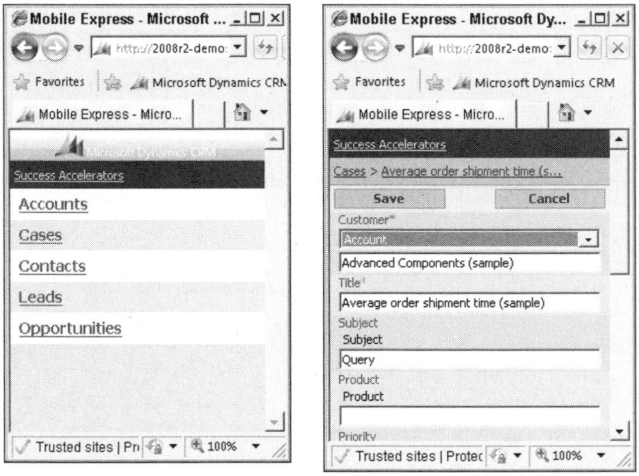

Microsoft Outlook synchronizes with some of the most frequently used data in Dynamics CRM (such as contacts, tasks, and appointments). Outlook, in turn, synchronizes with most mobile devices. For many organizations, this is all of the information that users will need to access from their mobile device. There are many cases, however, where your users will want to access data that is not available in Outlook while they are away from the office (such as leads, accounts, opportunities, and cases). In those cases, you will find that Mobile Express is an excellent option.

Caution

Mobile Express does not support all of the functionality that is found in the desktop version of Dynamics CRM. For example, if you are using script (such as JScript) on a form to format phone numbers, this functionality will not be available in Mobile Express.

Mobile Express is automatically installed with Dynamics CRM. To access Mobile Express, go to the same URL that you use to access Dynamics CRM, but add "/m" to the end (for example:

`http://yourcompany.crm.dynamics.com/m`). If your Dynamics CRM is installed on-premise, then you will need to either set it up to be accessible from the Internet or you will need to install VPN software on your mobile devices in order to use Mobile Express (see Chapter 7 for more information).

Use the following steps to customize Mobile Express. These instructions assume you are customizing the Campaign entity — but you can apply these to almost any entity in Dynamics CRM.

1. In the settings area, either open the default solution (Settings ⇨ Customizations ⇨ Customize the System) or select the solution you wish to modify (Settings ⇨ Customizations ⇨ Solutions ⇨ select the appropriate solution).

2. In the navigation bar, open the list of Entities and then click on the Campaign entity (or whichever entity that you want to customize).

3. On the General tab for the entity, scroll down to the check box for Mobile Express for Microsoft Dynamics CRM and ensure that it is checked. Save the change.

4. Click on the Forms component under the entity in the navigation pane. Click on the name of the mobile form. You are presented with the mobile form editor (see Figure 19.4).

FIGURE 19.4

The mobile form editor

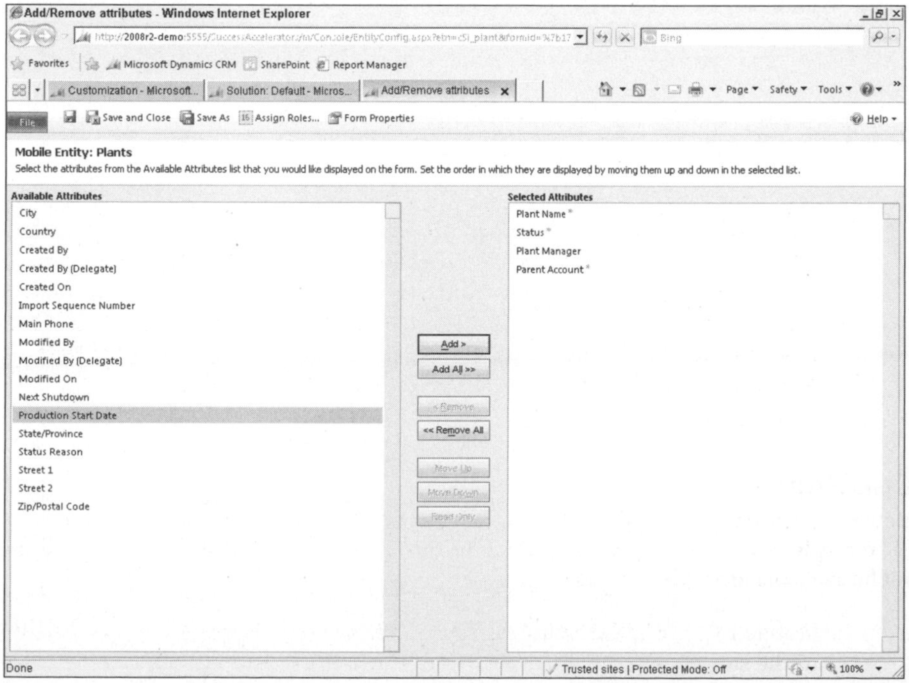

---

5. Change the form as appropriate. Note that you can have multiple forms for Mobile Express just like you can for the desktop. See Chapter 17 for more information on working with multiple forms.

6. When you are satisfied with your changes to the form, save them.

7. Note that you may want to create a custom view with just a few columns of information at this time and name it something like "Mobile View."

8. Publish the entity.

The next time you open Mobile Express, the changes that you have made will be published and available. If you added an entity to Mobile Express, it will appear on the home page. The form will be configured according to your specifications.

On the Web Site

Mobile Express provides inexpensive and flexible access to most of the data in Dynamics CRM. However, it does include some limitations (such as the inability to access data offline and lack of integration with the telephony components of your mobile device). Fortunately CWR Solutions, a third-party developer, has developed a very robust mobile access add-on for Dynamics CRM that fills these gaps. See the Web site for a link to learn more about CWR Mobility from CWR Solutions.

Managing Connection Roles and Relationship Roles

As you learned in Chapter 17, relationships are *formalized* links between entities. You can use the connections or relationships entities to set up informal or ad-hoc relationships between records. Here is a quick rundown of the options for using the connections and relationships entities to link records in Dynamics CRM:

- Connections Entity: The connections entity, new in Dynamics CRM 2011, allows you to make a connection between any two entities for any purpose. Each connection is assigned a "role" for that connection. A few examples include:

  - For organizations that use distributors to sell products, a connection can be created between two accounts. The distributor would have a role of "Distributor" and the buyer would have a role of "Buyer." When viewing either account, the connection between these two accounts will be very clear.

  - For organizations that work directly with consumers, a connection can be created between two contacts. The first contact may be assigned a role of "Parent" and the other contact may be assigned a role of "Child." The parent may have multiple children assigned. Furthermore, the children can all have connections to the other children, both having a role of "Sibling." Although the organization may have different relationships with each family member, they can also see all the other family members during every interaction. This can help organizations to understand the full extent of the relationship when servicing their customers.

- Some businesses work with very complex relationships. For example, business brokerage firms buy and sell businesses. Frequently, they buy and sell businesses that are held by private equity firms. These private equity firms own a number of businesses — sometimes they may be a buyer, other times they may be a seller. The business brokerage firms may wish to see every business that these private equity firms are connected to as either a potential buyer, a current owner, or an active seller. Connections can make this type of complex relationship possible to track.

- Relationships Entity: The relationships entity is still available in Dynamics CRM 2011 to remain compatible with prior versions. However, this has been replaced with the functionality of the connections entity and should no longer be used. In addition, the relationships entity should not be confused with creating a formal relationship between two entities (for example a 1:N, N:1, or N:N relationship as discussed in Chapter 17).

Adding connections to entities

Before using connections with an entity, you need to first make sure that connections have been enabled for that entity. To do this, navigate to the customization area (go to Settings and then choose either Customizations or Solutions, depending on which solution you wish to customize). Use the Navigation pane and click on the entity you want to enable connections for. On the General tab, scroll down and make sure that the check box next to Connections has been selected. Save and publish the update.

Configuring connection roles

A Connection Role is the type of relationship that exists between two records. Or, put another way, it is the role that each record plays in that connection. Dynamics CRM includes a number of potential roles out of the box. You can also create your own roles using the procedure below:

1. Navigate to Settings ⇨ Business Management and click on Connection Roles in the main window. Note that this will create new roles in the default solution. If you wish to create roles in another solution then navigate to Settings ⇨ Solutions, choose the solution you wish to customize, and then navigate to Connection Roles in the navigation pane.

2. Click the New button to create a new role. You are presented with the connection role data entry form (see Figure 19.5).

3. Complete each area of the form as follows:
   - Step 1: Enter the name of the role (such as Partner, Manufacturer, Developer, Vendor, and so on), the category of the connection (note that new categories can be created by editing the option set), and a brief description.
   - Step 2: Choose which record types this connection role will be available for. It may be tempting to choose All — but by carefully selecting only the relevant record types, you will save users some data entry time.
   - Step 3: List the roles that are available to match to this role. In other words, if you created a role named, "Parent" then the only matching role may be "Child." Although this step is optional, it is worth taking the time to do. Matching connection roles will improve the efficiency and quality of data entry by limiting the available options.

The connection role data entry form

Working with CRM Extensions

In Chapters 16 through 19, we have focused on how to customize and extend Dynamics CRM without writing code. In the next section of the book, we will focus on the tools that developers can use to further extend Dynamics CRM. It is important to point out, however, that Dynamics CRM makes it possible for non-coders to collaborate with developers to tap into advanced extensions. Non-coders can develop portions of the Dynamics CRM customizations, while developers create the portions that require custom coding. This approach maximizes the value that each individual contributes to the final deliverable.

In this section, we briefly discuss some of the possibilities that are available when using code to create extensions to Dynamics CRM. In the next group of chapters, we dive deeper into how to create some of these extensions.

Extending forms

Figure 19.6 illustrates a form in Dynamics CRM that has been customized using both non-code and code-driven changes. After the figure is a description of the code-driven customizations that are included in the form.

FIGURE 19.6

A form in Dynamics CRM that has been customized using custom code

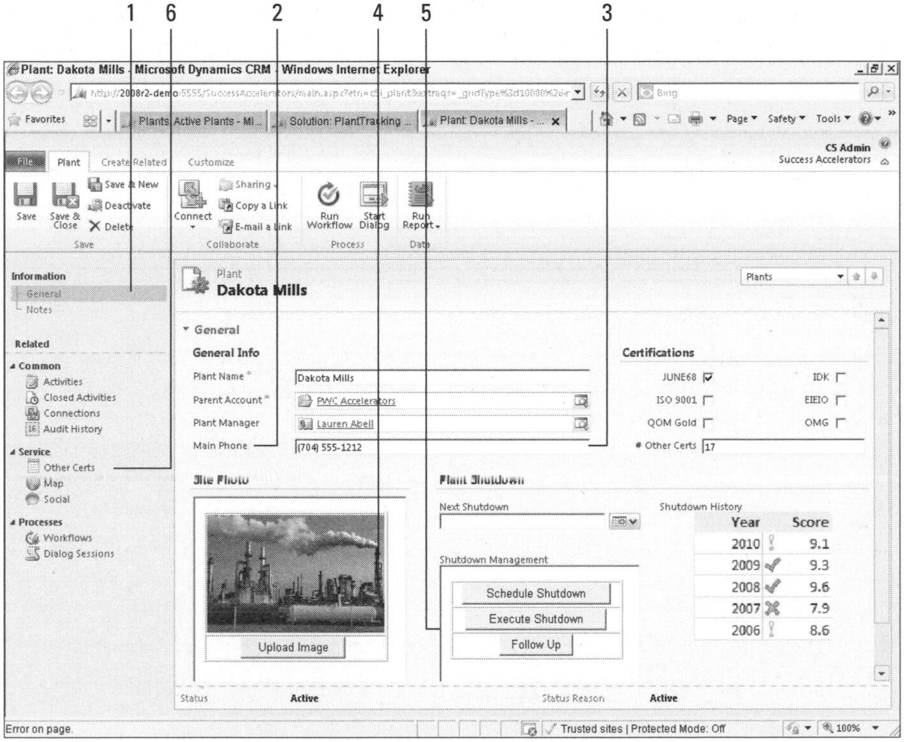

1. **Custom entity:** The system customizer created a custom entity called "Plant." This entity is used to manage a list of manufacturing plants that their service team provides support to. As described in earlier chapters, the entity, form, views, and charts were all created without writing code.

2. **Auto formatted phone number:** The phone number field on the form is automatically formatted for the user. The user can simply type in the numeric for the phone number and, when they tab out of the field, the phone is formatted automatically. This is managed through a JScript Web resource. The system customizer did not have to write this code, they only had to install a custom solution that contained the code and then add it to the form and to the field. See the nearby "On the Site" note for information on how to try this on your own.

3. **Calculated field:** This field is automatically calculated by counting the number of active certifications from the Other Certifications entity. There are a number of ways to calculate fields in Dynamics CRM; several are described below.

    -   **Plug-in assembly:** Plug-in assemblies are code that can be run automatically when certain events take place in Dynamics CRM (such as when a record is updated). These are powerful because they are written in .NET and can perform an almost unlimited array of functions — but they do not interact directly with the user (for example, they cannot update forms). Think of plug-in assemblies as a more powerful version of a workflow.

- **JScript:** JScript can also be used to calculate fields. The advantage of using Jscript to calculate fields is that the calculated values can be immediately visible to the end user. The disadvantage is that these calculations only run when the form is being displayed. In the case of our example form, Jscript would not be a useful choice because the calculation needs to be changed whenever a case is closed.

- **Workflow:** Workflows have the ability to perform simple calculations. For example, a workflow can increment a counter field by 1 every time a case is closed. Workflow calculations, however, are fairly limited unless they are extended using workflow extensions (more on that later).

4. **HTML Web resource:** The site photo is presented using an HTML Web resource. The HTML page includes a button to upload an image and an area to display the image. When the system customizer created this form, she created a placeholder for this item and then asked a developer to write the HTML code for her. Once the code was written, she could easily insert it into the form.

5. **Custom buttons:** Manufacturing plants typically shut down once a year for maintenance. There are certain procedures that must be followed by support during this time. The system customizer was able to create dialogs for these actions, but she wanted the dialogs to be available via a button embedded directly into the form rather than relying on users remembering to click the Start Dialog button in the Ribbon menu. Another HTML Web resource was used for this purpose that contained the necessary buttons. Note that the Ribbon menu itself can also be customized This is covered Chapter 21.

6. **Custom navigation items:** The system customizer also created a navigation link to a map of the facility and another link to a custom application used to track internal SharePoint social media and external social media related to the plant. These applications were developed outside of Dynamics CRM and are linked to using the Navigation pane links.

As you can see, the form was created and designed without writing any code at all. The form components that required custom code were developed separately. The coded elements were then added to the form and manipulated by a nondeveloper. This approach enables a system customizer to do much of the design work on the application and rely on a developer only for the components that require custom coding. Custom add-ons can also be downloaded from the Dynamics Marketplace.

On the Web Site

The CRM Bible site includes a custom solution for phone number formatting as well as a description of how to install and set up the solution to format phone numbers in Dynamics CRM.

Extending dashboards

Dashboards can be customized in a similar manner to forms. Using Web resources and Iframes, dashboards can be enriched with additional information and can interact directly with end users. Figure 19.7 is an example of a dashboard that has been extended using custom code (note that the Navigation pane and Ribbon menu have both been minimized to show more of the dashboard). After the figure is a description of how it has been extended.

1. **HTML Web resource:** The Facebook integration uses an HTML Web resource. This could be used to display updates posted to a public Facebook page. You could also use this area to display a search of a Twitter account or a search of social media sites for manufacturing plants that your organization does business with.

2. **Iframe:** This frame displays a search of the SharePoint site for the term "CRM 2011" (it could just as easily have displayed a search for the term "manufacturing plants"). The result is a set of all documents, discussions, or other information that has been tagged with the selected search term. The search was converted into an RSS feed and displayed in an Iframe. RSS feeds can also be read by Silverlight applications and displayed in a dashboard.

3. **HTML Web resource:** The map displayed in the dashboard is an HTML Web resource. An HTML page was written to post CRM data to a Bing map — representing each plant as a pushpin.

Extending processes

Dynamics CRM processes (workflows and dialogs) can also be extended using custom code. These extensions appear as new steps available in the list of steps when creating or modifying a process. Examples of workflow extensions may include:

- Record sharing: To automatically share records with other users when certain criteria are met

- Add to campaign: To automatically add records to specified campaigns when defined criteria are met

- Team alerts: To notify the members of a team (for records that are team-owned)

- Advanced assignment and escalation rules: To apply advanced filtering rules to the assignment or escalation of records

Caution

At the time of this writing, workflow extensions can only be used in Dynamics CRM On-Premise (they cannot be used in Dynamics CRM Online).

A dashboard with code-driven extensions

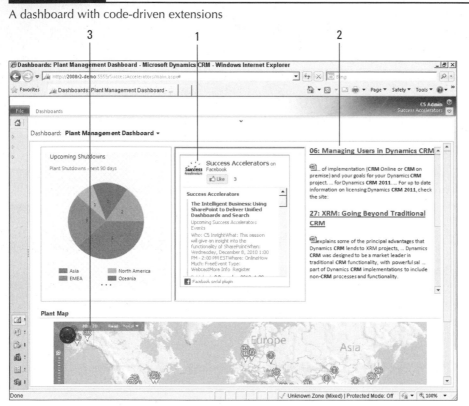

Summary

The customization options we cover in this chapter provide the ability to manage picklists (or option sets) that appear on multiple forms, create queues for managing and distributing workload, provide visibility into Dynamics CRM on mobile devices, and create ad-hoc connections between records.

Also covered was the concept of further extending Dynamics CRM using components that are coded by a developer. The flexible customization framework included with Dynamics CRM means that nondevelopers can install and utilize custom-coded components as part of their customization responsibilities.

CHAPTER 20

Understanding the Development Options

Up until this point in the book, we have focused on customizing Dynamics CRM without coding. You have learned about the broad range of customization options that are available to you through the user interface. These options can be combined with "coding" options that range from simple to very sophisticated. This chapter introduces you to the development options without yet getting into writing code (which comes in later chapters). Later in the chapter we discuss the options for deploying a development environment — an important topic that is often overlooked.

Our goal in this chapter is to provide content to three audiences. First, for the system customizer who has no intention of writing code, our goal is to aid you in understanding the options so you can better partner with a developer when needed. Secondly, for administrators who want to do a bit of coding, we want to lay a foundation to prepare you to begin writing code yourself. Lastly, for the experienced developer, our objective is to familiarize you with the development options as well as some of the best practices for drawing the line between using the built-in tools and writing code.

A recurring theme you will hear in this chapter is the idea of "leveraging the framework." The idea is that most customization needs can be addressed through the user interface rather than writing code. Writing unnecessary code can result in customizations that are costly to implement and maintain. If you flipped directly to this chapter of the book without first understanding the customization framework available within Dynamics CRM, we strongly encourage you to first read through the preceding section of the book.

IN THIS CHAPTER

Understanding development terminology

Envisioning custom solutions

Selecting the best development tools for your project

Setting up a development environment

Understanding Development Options

As you have discovered in preceding chapters, there are a wide variety of ways available to extend the application without writing code. As you discover in this and subsequent chapters, a dizzying variety of options are available for extending Dynamics CRM by writing code (or by updating "code-like" files, such as XML). The concept of extending the functionality of Dynamics CRM is referred to as extensibility. Figure 20.1 illustrates the extensibility options.

As illustrated in the above diagram, there is a hierarchy of customization options available to organizations that use Dynamics CRM. A best practice is to leverage this hierarchy as you consider how you will plan to customize the application. If a simple option is available to achieve your desired ends, then this should typically be the approach that you take. This is commonly referred to as leveraging the framework, meaning that you should write as little code as possible when customizing Dynamics CRM. This approach has a number of benefits:

FIGURE 20.1

Extensibility options available in Dynamics CRM

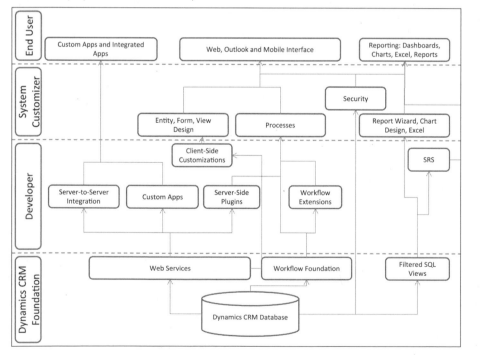

- It keeps developers focused on their core competencies. Skilled developers are in demand. By enabling developers to focus on discrete areas of coding that specifically require their skills, they can deliver value on a larger number of projects.

- It lowers costs and speeds deployment. Customizing the application through the user interface is faster and easier to maintain than writing custom code.

- It is easier to upgrade or transport. Customizations made through the user interface will be supported in future versions of Dynamics CRM. These customizations are also compatible with both the Online and On-Premise versions.

Envisioning the possibilities

Virtually anything can be accomplished using the supported methods for extending Dynamics CRM. In fact, the limitations have more to do with "how" things can and should be done rather than "what" can be done. This section provides a walk-through of some of the more advanced customizations available by writing code. Figure 20.2 is an illustration of a highly customized Dynamics CRM form using both custom code and user-interface-based customizations.

FIGURE 20.2

A Dynamics CRM form using a custom entity, customized Ribbon menu, Silverlight Web resource, HTML Web resource, a custom navigation bar item, plug-in for calculating aggregate values, and custom chart

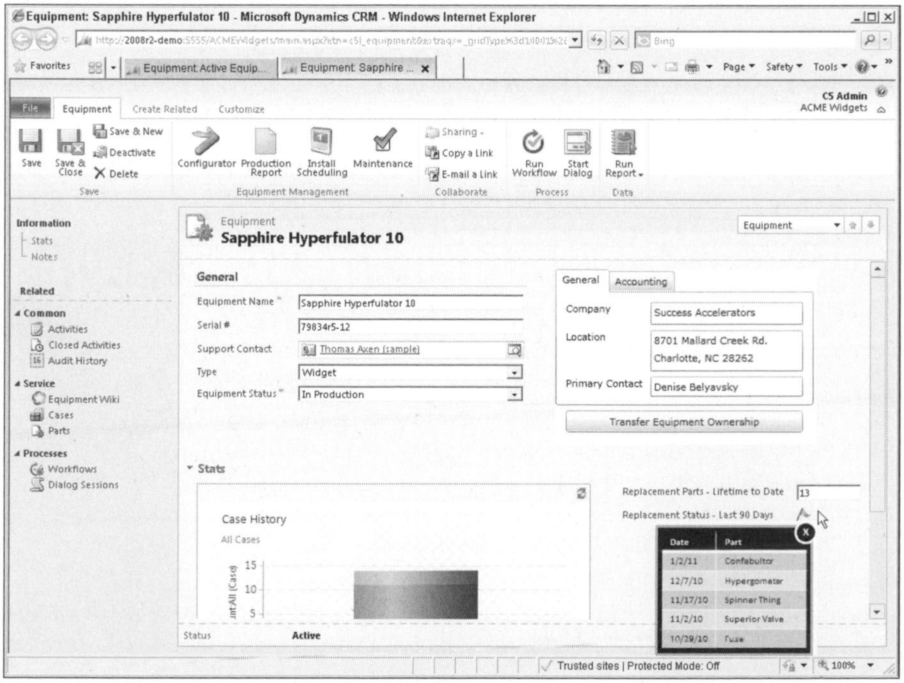

This form includes the following customizations:

- **Custom entity.** The form is for a custom entity called Equipment. This is used for a manufacturer of custom equipment that needs to track each piece of equipment in Dynamics CRM from the time that it is ordered, through installation at the user site, through service incidents, and through final decommissioning.

- **Custom chart.** Users indicated a preference for a 3-D chart to show the service history for this type of product. The initial chart was developed as a stacked bar chart in Dynamics CRM and exported as an XML file. The XML was then edited using a standard text editor, and options were sent to render it as a 3-D chart. The XML was then reimported as a new chart.

- **HTML Web resource.** A custom flag was developed to show as red if the number of cases for this piece of equipment in the last 90 days is more than ten; yellow if the number is three to nine; and green if it is two or fewer. This Web resource uses a combination of HTML, FetchXML, and Jquery to interact with the user presenting the ability to zoom in for a recent list of parts that were installed on the piece of equipment.

- **Silverlight Web resource.** Data from the parent Account that this piece of equipment is related to is presented within a Silverlight form. This can also be been presented as an HTML Web resource or in an Iframe to a custom application.

- **Plug-in.** A custom plug-in was created to aggregate values from the parts entity. The add-in, a .dll file, is loaded into Dynamics CRM using the plug-in registration tool. This is custom .NET code that was registered to run whenever a new part is added with a status of "replacement."

- **Customized context sensitive ribbon.** A custom section was added to the ribbon that appears only when the Equipment form is being viewed. Buttons can be added to or removed from any ribbon menus. The buttons on this custom ribbon perform as follows:

  - Configurator: Launches a custom application, hosted on the Azure platform, that interacts with Dynamics CRM. Custom applications can be integrated within Dynamics CRM (such as the Silverlight component described above) or can be launched in separate windows with the Ribbon menu.

  - Production Report: Loads the production report for the organization by calling the URL for the report.

  - Schedule Installation and Schedule Training: This button open a new service activity form automatically populating the fields with the appropriate information about the customer, subject, and service type. This is accomplished by calling a JScript Web resource when the button is clicked. The JScript can use an Odata REST endpoint to populate the relevant fields with data.

  - Annual Maintenance Checklist: This uses a URL to open a dialog process. The dialog is customized based on the type of equipment. This is used by field service representatives to perform annual maintenance services on equipment.

This organization uses a SharePoint Wiki site to maintain documentation for the equipment that they manufacture. A separate Wiki library is maintained for each type of equipment. A link in the Navigation pane automatically links to the correct library by passing the equipment type as part of the URL (see Figure 20.3).

The above images and narratives provide some context for understanding the variety of ways in which you can customize Dynamics CRM. Combine this with what you have already learned in the book and you have an idea of the range of customizations that are possible when blending customizations available with and without writing code. This should also give you a sense that some customizations that require code are more difficult to develop than others. Even nondevelopers can usually learn enough about JScript and XML to handle many of these customizations without the assistance of a professional developer. On the other hand, developing custom applications using C#, Silverlight, and other professional development technologies usually requires the expertise of an experienced developer. With Dynamics CRM, however, a nondeveloper can lay much of the foundation first, and a developer can focus only on the "spot development" that is required to finish out a solution.

FIGURE 20.3

A custom Navigation pane link to a SharePoint Wiki site

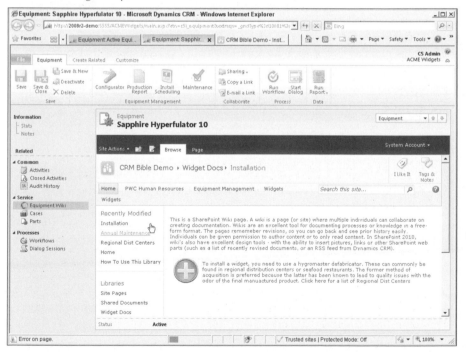

Understanding the fundamentals

If the concept of developing computer code is new to you, be warned that it brings with it a large, new vocabulary. Microsoft and other development companies are also constantly rolling out innovative new development systems and standards — so the vocabulary continues to expand. In this section, we will take a look at the fundamental items that you should understand as a Dynamics CRM administrator — even if you never intend to write a line of code. We also provide a glossary of a broad range of the terminology as a reference point.

Client-side and server-side customization

Customizations (or extensions) made to Dynamics CRM fall into one of two categories for the most part: client-side or server-side customizations. In Web applications, the term client refers to the computer (and, more specifically, the browser) that is being used to access a Web site, whereas server refers the computer that is hosting the Web site.

Client-side customizations are items that "run on the client." What this means is that computer code is passed to your Web browser (in the case of Dynamics CRM, the browser will always be Internet Explorer) and the browser executes the code. By running in the browser, client-side code allows Dynamics CRM to interact directly with the user. A simple example is adding the values in two fields together and storing the value in a third field (as illustrated in Figure 20.4). The value is calculated when the user tabs out of the second field and is instantly available in the third field. This code was written in a language called JScript. Client-side customizations run only when the user is interacting with the application. In our example of a calculated field, if the values in the first two fields were updated by a workflow, the value in the third field would not be updated because a user did not interact with Dynamics CRM to update the first two fields. Client-side customizations refer to any items that are sent to the browser for processing. Chapter 21 focuses on client-side customizations.

Tip

In general, client-side customizations are a much easier starting point for new developers to work with than are server-side customizations.

FIGURE 20.4

A client-side customization that calculates the value in field 3 by adding the values in fields 1 and 2

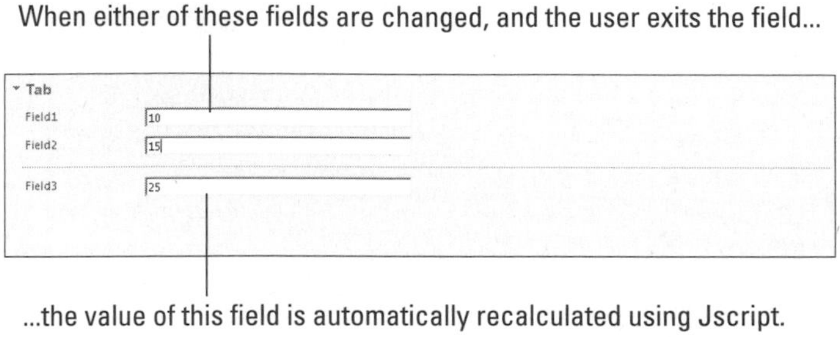

When either of these fields are changed, and the user exits the field...

...the value of this field is automatically recalculated using Jscript.

In contrast, server-side customizations run only when the user submits a request to the server (that is, when a user submits a form or clicks a button) or when a condition on the server is met (for example, when a record in the database is updated). Server-side customizations can generally leverage a greater breadth and depth of development tools and options, but they are limited in that they cannot interact directly with the end user in real time. In our example from the previous paragraph, a server-side customization could run whenever a record is updated in the table; the customization would add the values in field 1 and field 2 and store the result in field 3. This server-side customization, however, would not run until the updated record is saved to the database — so users would not see the number calculated in real time as they interact with the form. Chapter 22 focuses on server-side customizations.

In recent years, the line between client-side and server-side has become increasingly blurred. For example, programming languages such as Silverlight include components that run on both the client and the server side. The Silverlight code that is running client-side can interact with the server, which then runs server-side code and sends updated data to the client.

Caution

The terms client-side and server-side can appear with different suffixes that have different meanings. In general, the suffixes of customization or extensions (that is, client-side extensions) broadly refer to any customizations (even those that do not require code) that are run on the client. The suffixes programming, coding or development (meaning server-side development) specifically refer to computer code that runs either on the client or the server.

Dynamics CRM development terminology

Table 20.1 is a reference guide to the terminology you are likely to hear in relation to writing custom code to extend Dynamics CRM. This is intended to be a reference for nondevelopers or a starting point for developers who may be new to the Dynamics CRM extensibility framework. Keep in mind that entire books have been written on some of the terms in the list below, so the brief definitions only scratch the surface.

TABLE 20.1

Dynamics CRM Development Terminology

Term	Definition
.NET Framework	This is a software framework developed by Microsoft. It allows applications to be developed in multiple languages and deployed to the Web, computers, mobile phones, and other devices.
AJAX	Asynchronous JavaScript and XML (AJAX) is a set of client-side Web development methods that enable applications to interact with users. It allows data to be exchanged between a browser and a server, which allows Web applications to run faster.
Application Ribbons	Ribbon menus seen at the top of the Dynamics CRM interface. Also known as Ribbon menus, these were introduced with Microsoft Office 2007

continued

TABLE 20.1 (continued)

Term	Definition
Asynchronous	In the case of Dynamics CRM, this refers to processes (such as workflows) that run independently of other processes. A Dynamics CRM process that runs asynchronously waits for system resources to become available — as a result it does not interact directly with the user and may take a period of time to begin and complete running.
Client Extensions	In Dynamics CRM, the client extensions components refer to the site map (the navigation structure) and the application Ribbons (menu ribbon) that can be customized by exporting the components, editing their XML, and reimporting them.
Client-Side	This term generally refers to programs that run "in the browser." All of the information needed for the program (such as HTML and JScript code) is sent to the "client" browser by a server and the browser runs the code, displaying the results in the browser window.
Cascading Style Sheets (CSS)	CSS is a language that describes the look and feel of a Web page. The CSS Web resource in Dynamics CRM is intended to support the Web page (HTML) Web resources. You can create an HTML Web resource that references a CSS resource to derive its formatting settings.
DHTML	Dynamic HTML refers to a set of technologies and browser features that make Web sites more interactive, so that a Web page can be dynamically updated after it is loaded (without having to load a new page).
FetchXML	FetchXML (or "Fetch") is a querying language that was developed specifically for Dynamics CRM. FetchXML is used behind the scenes for some components of Dynamics CRM (such as charts and reports). It can also be embedded into JScript code to return query results.
HTML	Hypertext Markup Language is the language of the Internet. Although the familiar ".htm" or ".html" suffix on Web pages has become less common as Web developers have switched to more dynamic Web content systems, HTML is still the language that pages are rendered in when they display in your browser window. Dynamics CRM enables you to load HTML as a Web resource that can then be displayed in forms or dashboards.
Image Resources	Image resources are a customization component of Dynamics CRM. They include images in PNG, GIF, ICO, JPG format. Image resources can be displayed as icons in the navigation pane, on forms or in dashboards. They can also be included in HTML Web resources.
ISV	Independent Software Vendor refers to third parties that develop and sell applications. In the case of Dynamics CRM, ISVs sell add-on components that extend the core functionality. Dynamics CRM On-Premise includes an "ISV folder" that allows third-party applications to be installed on the Dynamics CRM Web server. However, this option is not available for Dynamics CRM Online implementations and is expected to be deprecated in future versions of Dynamics CRM On-Premise. We recommend the use of Azure to manage applications.
Jquery	Jquery is a library that extends JavaScript (or JScript) with user interaction and animation capabilities.
JScript / JavaScript	JScript is the client-side coding language supported in Dynamics CRM. Many other programming languages and methods can be integrated with or accessed from JScript such as Jquery, AJAX, and FetchXML. JScript and JavaScript were developed by two different organizations (Microsoft and Netscape); over time they have converged and are almost synonymous.

Term	Definition
JSON	JavaScript Object Notation is based on the JavaScript programming language and is typically used to transfer data from a server to a browser — similar to XML.
LINQ	Language Integrated Query is a Microsoft method for including queries in code. LINQ queries can be embedded in computer programs (such as C#) and can be run against data in SQL — including Dynamics CRM or SharePoint data.
OData	Open data protocol is an open-source standard for reading and updating databases using only parameters appended to a URL.
Plug-In	In Dynamics CRM a plug-in is a compiled computer program (with a .dll extension) that is started when an event is triggered. This event, for example, can be the creation of a record, or updating a field. The event is not "fired" until the database is updated — so plug-ins do not interact directly with the user.
REST	Representational State Transfer is an approach to developing Web services (see definition below). It was developed more recently than SOAP (see definition below) and focuses on using protocols that are simpler and more established than SOAP. REST can simplify application development and speed network traffic, but in some cases SOAP may be a better approach for reasons of security or detailed data transmission.
REST endpoint	This is a "point" at which a REST service is available to communicate with other services across the Internet. It is generally expressed as a URL.
Sandbox	In development, a sandbox is often another name for an environment in which developers can write and test code that is isolated from the production environment.
Sandbox Service	In Dynamics CRM 2011, the sandbox service was introduced. This is a service that runs on the Dynamics CRM Server (Online or On-Premise) that enables custom plug-ins to be registered and to run on the server.
SDK	The software development kit (SDK) is a collection of tools, documents, and code samples used as a guide for developers to learn how to develop extensions for Dynamics CRM.
Server-Side	This term refers to processes or code that run on the server-side of a Web application. In contrast to client-side, this code is never loaded into the browser and runs exclusively on the server. As such, this code does not interact directly with the user.
Silverlight	Silverlight is a development platform included in Visual Studio. It includes a plug-in that works with multiple browsers. It is similar to Adobe Flash in that it provides a strong set of interactive capabilities the enables interaction with users on Web sites.
Site Map	In Dynamics CRM, the site map is an XML file that contains the navigation system for the Dynamics CRM Web site. The site map appears in the list of solution components under the heading Client Extensions. The site map can be customized by exporting it, modifying the XML, and reimporting it.
SOAP	Simple Object Access Protocol is a way for computer programs to communicate with one another over the Internet.
SSIS	SQL Server Integration Services is an application that enables data to be extracted (exported) from one system, transformed (values can be aggregated, subtotaled, and so on), and loaded (imported) into another system.

continued

TABLE 20.1 *(continued)*

Term	Definition
SSRS	SQL Server Reporting Services is report generation software included with SQL Server. SSRS reports are rendered as Web pages. This is the reporting tool that is used to render reports for Dynamics CRM.
Synchronous	In the case of Dynamics CRM, this refers to processes (such as dialogs) that run immediately and/or interactively with other processes. A Dynamics CRM process that runs synchronously executes immediately without waiting for system resources to become available. As a result, it can immediately calculate fields or interact with the user.
URI	A uniform resource identifier (URI) identifies the name of a resource on the Internet. This enables the resource to be accessed over the Internet and, potentially, to be integrated with other resources.
VBScript	VBScript is a client-side language for Web sites that was developed by Microsoft. It is not supported in Dynamics CRM.
Visual Studio	Microsoft Visual Studio is a suite of programming languages and tools. Visual Studio and its extensions can be used to develop Web applications, windows programs, SQL Server reports, and Web services in a variety of programming languages.
Web Resource	Web resources are components that can be uploaded to the Dynamics CRM server to extend the application. This includes image resources, script, HTML, Silverlight, and other resources. All Web resources are assigned a URL. Web resources are only available to licensed CRM users.
Web Services	Web services methods allow computer programs to share information over the Internet. For example, an accounting application may use Web Services to update data in Dynamics CRM. SOAP and REST are different approaches to developing Web services.
Windows Azure	The Windows Azure platform provides a way to build and run applications, including underlying data, in the cloud. Included is SQL Azure, a cloud-hosted version of SQL Server.
Windows Azure AppFabric	This cloud-based technology enables applications to authenticate, connect, and exchange data across the Internet regardless of where they are hosted. It includes the Windows Azure AppFabric Service Bus.
Windows Communication Foundation (WCF)	WCF is a framework used to send messages from one service endpoint to another. It is included in many of the technologies associated with Dynamics CRM including WF, Silverlight, and Windows Azure.
Windows Workflow Foundation (WF)	WF is a technology from Microsoft for managing workflows. It is included with the .NET framework. Workflows can be designed in Visual Studio. WF is used to run workflows built in Dynamics CRM.
Workflow Extension	A workflow extension is server-side code used to extend the functionality of workflows in Dynamics CRM by making more steps available that can be added to workflows.
WSDL	Web Services Definition Language is a language for describing Web services. It is based on XML.
XAML	XAML is a language derived from XML. In the case of Dynamics CRM, it is used to describe workflows.

Term	Definition
XSL	XSL is a style sheet similar to CSS (see definition) that describes how an XML document should be styled.
XML	Extensible markup language (XML) is a language used to exchange data. It has been the foundation of many related languages (such as XAML, XSL, WSDL, and others). XML is a hierarchical language that is well suited to organizing information. The language can be thought of as an outline, with each topic and subtopic in the outline having a beginning and ending tag. XML is available as a Web resource in Dynamics CRM solutions. Using XML as a Web resource is not a good option for data that changes frequently. However, it can be a helpful way to store data that changes only periodically.

Using the Software Development Kit (SDK)

The Software Development Kit (SDK) is a set of documentation provided by Microsoft that explains how to extend the application using programming and other available tools. It includes code examples, references, tutorials, and other information to aid you as you learn to extend the interface. In general, the SDK is designed for developers to aid in learning to extend Dynamics CRM and to serve as a reference. However, many examples included in the SDK are good learning tools for non-developers. The SDK is an important part of your Dynamics CRM administrator's library.

The SDK can be downloaded from Microsoft at no cost. To find the SDK, go to www. microsoft.com/downloads and search for CRM 2011 SDK. You can also check the Web site for the book, where we will maintain a link to the SDK: www.dynamicscrmbible.com.

Making smart development decisions

With such a diverse array of customization options available to you, it can be difficult to select the right tools for any given project. As we have pointed out several times in this chapter, the first rule when deciding how to approach your project is to "leverage the platform" — that is, do as much as you can without writing custom code.

Once you have come to the conclusion that custom code is required for your project, your next decision is to decide what kind of coding technologies should be used. In large part, this will be dictated based on user requirements. You should also, however, consider the strengths of the team (or individual) that will be delivering the code. If the individual is strong in JScript and Jquery, but has no experience with Silverlight, then that should play a role in your decision making. While it is optimal to extend Dynamics CRM by using other Microsoft technologies, it is also an option to use other development platforms too. With that said, if Dynamics CRM is a mission critical application, we strongly urge you to consider adopting the Microsoft suite of development tools to manage your customizations.

In short, you should first leverage the strengths of the platform. Then, once you move into code-based customizations, you should seek to leverage the strengths of the team performing the customizations.

Avoiding unsupported customizations

Dynamics CRM does not support some methods for customization that are familiar to a number of developers. It is important to understand what the unsupported methods are in order to avoid making customizations that could cause Dynamics CRM to become unstable or that could cause incompatibilities with future versions of Dynamics CRM (making upgrades time-consuming and expensive).

SQL Server is the database engine used by Dynamics CRM. Developers who are familiar with SQL Server may be tempted to make direct updates to the tables and other information in the Dynamics CRM database. However, making updates of any kind directly to the SQL Server database (including simply updating data) is unsupported. Rather than directly writing to the SQL Database, you should use the methods outlined in the SDK to make updates. These methods are outlined in Chapters 20 through 22 of this book. Making changes directly to the SQL Server tables can result in serious issues with your instance of Dynamics CRM.

Tip

There are a few supported instances in which making changes to SQL Server tables is permissible. These are outlined in the Microsoft Knowledge Base (an online repository of articles for resolving issues with Microsoft software). Authorized Microsoft support personnel may also ask you to make changes to tables in certain cases. Other than that, you should refrain from making any changes directly to tables in SQL Server.

You also should not update the ASPX pages or other application files in the Web root folder of the Dynamics CRM application. These changes can cause issues with the performance of the application and can make upgrades difficult. Moreover, when Microsoft occasionally releases updates, the changes made to these files may be overwritten.

In general, the fundamental user interface for Dynamics CRM cannot be changed at this time. This includes the basic look and feel of the Ribbon menu, Navigation pane, usage of grids throughout the application, and the overall layout of forms. While some tweaking of the interface is possible through JScript or other means, these are not generally supported or recommended. Keep in mind that while the "skin" cannot be changed for these items, the "content" can be changed.

There are many opportunities to customize the user experience using JScript. Not all of these, however, are supported. Chapter 21 provides an introduction to JScript and other client-side customizations. However, if you will be spending significant time customizing Dynamics CRM with JScript, we urge you to familiarize yourself with the Dynamics CRM SDK (referenced earlier in this chapter) after you use this book to get up to speed with the basics. In general, directly accessing and manipulating the DOM using JScript is not supported.

Developing for CRM Online usage

Dynamics CRM On-Premise allows developers access to some customization methods that are not available when using Dynamics CRM Online. As a best practice, we recommend that businesses customize Dynamics CRM so that it can be used either online or on-premise. Technology industry analysts are predicting that a substantial portion of IT applications will be migrated to the cloud in the coming decade, so investing in an architecture that can be easily migrated to the cloud is a wise move. Customization methods available for CRM On-Premise that should be avoided because they are not supported in CRM Online include:

- Using SQL Filtered Views for Reports: Dynamics CRM includes the ability to develop custom reports. When using Dynamics CRM On-Premise, it is permissible to directly read the certain views in SQL Server in order to develop reports. In Dynamics CRM Online, however, the SQL Server database is not available for this kind of direct access. For this reason, we recommend using FetchXML queries to manage your report querying.

- Uploading Custom Workflow XAML Files: Workflows can be exported from Dynamics CRM and edited in Visual Studio. This approach can allow you to visually make changes to your workflow that you can't make through the Dynamics CRM user interface. The exported XAML file can then be loaded back into Dynamics CRM where it will run like any other workflow (although it can no longer be edited within Dynamics CRM). While this can deliver more options for customizing your workflows, it also is not supported in Dynamics CRM Online. We recommend creating custom workflow extensions that will run in either Dynamics CRM Online or On-Premise.

Setting Up Development and Testing Environments

Most organizations that implement Dynamics CRM (or any new CRM solution) begin with an initial period of heavy customization prior to the time that any users are actively updating records. During this initial phase of customization, it is perfectly acceptable to have only a single instance of Dynamics CRM available.

Most organizations tend to continue to customize Dynamics CRM after the initial rollout. During this process of continuous improvement, it is important to establish an environment (and procedures) for development and testing that mitigate the risk that your production environment is disrupted with unexpected changes.

In this section, we look at the technologies, processes, and procedures for ensuring a safe and efficient development and testing strategy. Figure 20.5 illustrates a simplified view of the multiple instances of Dynamics CRM that are required for a robust development and testing environment. Some of the terminology in the diagram and that you may hear as you discuss this with your team is outlined below the diagram.

- **Development:** The development environment is sometimes shortened to DEV (in both verbal and written communications). The development instance of Dynamics CRM is where initial customizations are made by both systems customizers (nondevelopers) and by experienced developers. The environment includes the tools required for development (such as Visual Studio). Users do not access the development environment for day-to-day operations. It is not critical that the development environment exactly mirror the production environment — this is the job of the test environment.

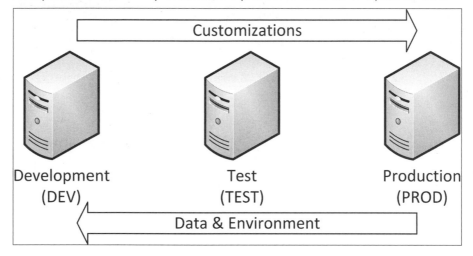

FIGURE 20.5

A simplified view of development, test, and production instances of Dynamics CRM

- **Test:** The test environment is where all customizations are tested prior to putting them into production. Changes are migrated from the development environment to the test environment and are tested there. It is important that the test environment very closely mirror the production environment so that customizations can be tested in exactly the same manner as they will work in production. The test environment is constantly refreshed to mirror the data and environmental settings of the production environment. No customizations should be made directly to the test environment; they should only be migrated from the development environment.

- **Production:** The production environment is sometimes shortened to PROD (in both verbal and written communications). The production environment is where actual work is getting done with Dynamics CRM. As a result, it is a highly dynamic environment with records constantly being updated, created, and deleted. Once testing of customizations is completed in the test environment, they can be migrated to the production environment. No changes should ever be made directly to the production environment.

Setting up development and test environments is a bit like making sure that your computers are backed up regularly. Businesses don't tend to budget the time and expense for it until they experience a failure. The need for this type of environment is even more important when more than one individual will be making customizations to Dynamics CRM.

Paved with Good Intentions

Examples of the need for not only a development environment but also process and governance around managing changes to Dynamics CRM are easy to find. In one recent case, a business completed customizing an XRM application that significantly extended the capabilities of Dynamics CRM for global users. One of the key users of the new XRM application was a technically inclined individual who requested an administrator account so he could make some of his own customizations. The well-intended manager of the project granted him this access level. Within a short time, most of the customizations had been supplanted with poorly designed forms that no longer met the long-term needs of the organization. As a result, much of the value that the business had invested in was lost.

Development teams long ago learned the importance of setting up processes and environments to avoid exactly these kinds of issues. Extensible frameworks like Dynamics CRM (and others, such as SharePoint) suffer from this issue regularly because they are so easy for "the business" to customize that they often end up being managed by individuals unfamiliar with the risks. Learn a lesson at the expense of the businesses above and take the time to configure your development environment correctly, and establish processes, before there is a meltdown.

Establishing processes, procedures, and governance

Few organizations want to think about processes, procedures, and governance at the beginning of their CRM projects. In the excitement to quickly set up and become productive with a new piece of technology, these steps seem to be a distraction. Sadly, this issue is often amplified by organizations that are anxious to sell software licenses (choose your partner carefully).

Establishing policies for rolling out customizations does not need to be a laborious and overly complex undertaking. You should establish a leadership team that reviews and prioritizes all customizations before work is begun (this can be a team of just a few individuals for small businesses). Documentation should be drawn up that includes a "pre-flight checklist" prior to rolling out any new customizations (and each individual should be held accountable to their part in working through the list — not just the project manager). You should include a decision about how your development environment will be set up and what the rules will be related to making customizations as a part of this process. You should also determine how your customizations will be rolled out (see the discussion of managed solutions in Chapter 16 for some thoughts on this).

On the Web Site

Check the book Web site (www.dynamicscrmbible.com) for an example "pre-flight checklist" that can be used to aid you in rolling out customizations for your Dynamics CRM implementation.

Testing: Plan Your Work and Work Your Plan

Large organizations are familiar with the concepts related to testing computer software. Smaller organizations that are unfamiliar with best practices for testing can often run into bad surprises that don't appear until days, weeks, or even months after a change has been rolled out. Organizations that adopt Dynamics CRM may think that an environment that can be customized without writing code will protect them from making mistakes, but this is not true.

Take, for instance, a workflow that is developed by a savvy administrator. Without realizing it, the administrator may create a workflow that calls itself repetitively. This can potentially result in mistakenly sending out e-mails or updating records. Or, the workflow may simply stop working (Dynamics CRM includes safeguards that stop workflows that loop endlessly) without the user knowing.

A full discussion of a testing plan is beyond the scope of this book. But one helpful rule of thumb is to carefully think through two areas: (1) What is every conceivable way that a customization can be used, and what is every conceivable path that it can take; (2) What could possibly go wrong with a customization. If you start with those items in mind and develop a checklist to test every possible outcome, you'll be on your way to a thorough approach to testing that will mitigate the risk of unforeseen consequences.

Using the right development tools

As you may expect, Dynamics CRM has strong ties to the Microsoft development toolset. If you plan extend Dynamics CRM by writing code, we strongly encourage you to invest in Visual Studio and related tools. Here are some suggestions for a development toolbox that are based directly on your budget and how deep you plan to go with customization:

- **Client-Side Only:** If you plan to customize XML files and update JScript, but you're not planning on developing any compiled code, then some free resources should work just fine for you. You will need a good text editor as the most important tool. You can start with something as simple as Notepad (the free text editor that comes with Windows). However, we recommend a text editor that can format your code for you (making writing and debugging code much easier) and that can work with XSD files to help you with intellisense for your code. Free text editors with these capabilities include Notepad++, XML Notepad, and Visual Web Developer Express. This latter option is our recommended free option and is downloadable from Microsoft.

- **Server-Side Coding:** If you plan to write code that can be compiled and executed on the server (server-side code) or if you plan to develop significant Web resources (such as Silverlight, HTML, or JScript resources) then you should consider an investment in a professional development environment. This includes the most recent version of Visual Studio and may also include a development version of SQL Server.

- **Enterprise Development:** Enterprises with multiple developers that will work on code at the same time should consider a team development environment and the appropriate tools. We discuss this in more detail in the section "Configuring an enterprise class development environment."

Planning and configuring your environment

The best approach to configuring a development and testing environment will vary depending upon the size and complexity of your organization and your goals. In this section, we will break recommendations down based on three different levels of complexity, as illustrated in Figure 20.6. The costs for a simple environment are relatively low, but it carries a higher risk of downtime.

Time and risks associated with various development environment configurations

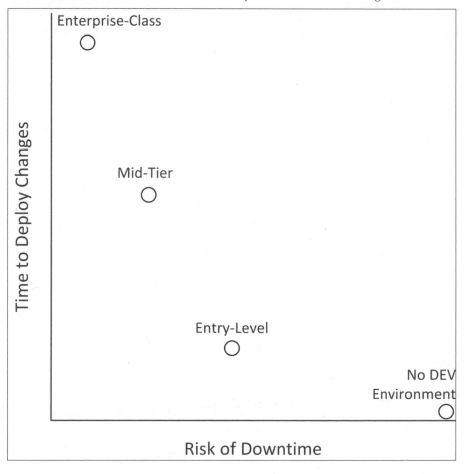

When most organizations plan their development environment, they assume that the level of sophistication should be in alignment with the number of users. In reality, your development environment will have more to do with the complexity and criticality of your Dynamics CRM implementation. We have worked with relatively small CRM projects with fewer than 100 users that have a mission critical role and a complex set of customizations that required a sophisticated development environment. Conversely, we have also worked with some organizations with thousands of users, but that are leveraging a very simple setup that can suffice with a mid-tier environment. Keep that thought in mind as you review the recommendations. We have also included a fourth variation for organizations that are using Dynamics CRM Online.

On the Web Site

This section provides some high-level recommendations for setting up and automating development and testing environments. A complete how-to guide for setting up these environments is beyond the scope of this book. We will, however, post helpful links and information on the Web site: www.dynamicscrmbible.com**.**

Configuring an entry level development environment

An entry level development environment is generally best for organizations that have a simple Dynamics CRM deployment (very few code-based customizations) and has one one or two individuals who are permitted to make any customizations to the system. In general, this is also a better solution for small businesses with fewer than 50 users of Dynamics CRM because a small amount of downtime across a large group of users can be costly. In general, these organizations will not be using "developers" to regularly update their Dynamics CRM implementation — most updates will be made through the user interface and not by writing code. After you have programmers regularly making updates to your Dynamics CRM implementation, we highly recommend that you move to a mid-tier or enterprise class development environment.

Organizations meeting the above description can set up a virtual environment with a copy of Dynamics CRM Server and all of their customizations installed. A virtual environment can be hosted on a server or on your local PC. Virtual environments also isolate your development environment from the production version of Dynamics CRM — giving you a safe area to test changes. After you are satisfied with your changes, you can export them as a solution and import them into your production environment. If you are working with an outside partner to handle most of your customizations, then they may be able to host a virtual environment of this type for you. This virtual development environment is illustrated in Figure 20.7.

Keep in mind that, although this development environment is simple, process and procedure is still critical — perhaps even more important than in a more sophisticated development environment. Changes should always be made and tested in your development environment and then migrated to production. Configuration changes should never be made directly to your production server. After changes are migrated to your server, they should again be tested immediately after publishing them.

A virtual development environment for simple Dynamics CRM implementations

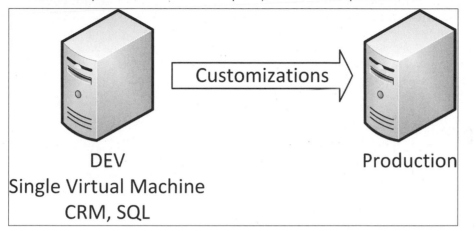

On the Web Site

A number of different software options are available to create a virtual environment including VMWare, VirtualBox, and Microsoft Hyper-V Server. We will include links to these options on the site. Another virtual option, Virtual PC, is free from Microsoft and is simple to set up. However, at the time of this writing, Virtual PC is not capable of running a 64-bit operating system (which is required for Dynamics CRM Server), so you will want to go with one of the aforementioned virtual options. We will post links to virtual environments on www.dynamicscrmbible.com.

In the past, Microsoft has made a virtual copy of Dynamics CRM freely available for download for testing and development purposes at no cost. This version often includes some of their "solution accelerators" (free add-ons) that may be interesting for your team to test to see if they might play a role in your Dynamics CRM project. We anticipate that they will continue this practice with Dynamics CRM 2011. If not, they also generally make it available for subscribers to TechNet (a service from Microsoft that permits customers to download software for development purposes at a very low cost). Although the configuration of this virtual copy may not exactly mirror your production environment, it will be far easier for a small business to configure and install than performing a full installation in a virtual environment.

Some organizations of this size manage to get by with no "true" development environment. They test their customizations out as thoroughly as possible before publishing them, and immediately retest them in production. While this may suffice in some cases, it is not optimal and runs a high risk of unanticipated problems.

Configuring a mid-tier development environment

This configuration suits the purposes of the vast majority of businesses that have implemented Dynamics CRM. It is designed for businesses that have more than one system customizer, with one or two developers regularly deploying new code, and a fairly complex configuration supporting 50 users or more. For those organizations that will have multiple developers working on complex customizations as a team, we recommend moving up to the enterprise class environment. For most others, the mid-tier environment will suffice.

On the Web Site

Check www.dynamicscrmbible.com **for links to Web articles with detailed information on how to set up this type of environment.**

As with the entry level environment, this environment can also be run using a single virtual server. Unlike the entry level environment, however, you should set up this environment to closely mirror your production environment and to allow multiple users to access the development environment concurrently. Specifically, we recommend the following configuration:

- Microsoft Hyper-V Server: You need to install this on a server at your location or hosted by a partner.

- Server OS: You should install the same version of Windows Server in your development environment as you are using to host Dynamics CRM Server — this includes the same patches and software.

- Server Software: You should install Dynamics CRM Server, SQL Server (including SQL Reporting Services and SQL Server Integration Services if you are using that), SharePoint, and any other software that you are running in your production environment. Server software should be installed manually (rather than downloading a preconfigured server as with the entry level environment). All of these should be running the same versions and updates as you are running in production. You may install all of this software on the same virtual server. In this sense, it will not be an exact mirror of your production environment, but this balances the costs and benefits associated with a mid-tier environment.

- Development Software: Development software should also be installed in the development environment. This includes Visual Studio, the Dynamics CRM SDK and Azure development extensions (such as the Azure SDK, Azure AppFabric SDK, and Azure Tools for Visual Studio), and any other development tools that your team wishes to use. Again, this means your development environment will not precisely mirror production, but it will provide a close approximation at a reasonable cost.

- Testing Software: You may want to install other software required to fully test your customizations. This may include Microsoft Office (including Outlook) and the Dynamics CRM Outlook client. Once again, this is not an exact mirror of your production environment, but it will be very similar.

When configuring your development environment, you can set up two separate instances of Dynamics CRM (because Dynamics CRM is multitenant, it is possible to run two instances on the same server). The first instance can be used for development and the second can be used for testing. The test instance can be removed and refreshed with production data periodically. This ensures that your DEV/TEST environment closely mirrors your PROD environment.

From a process standpoint, you should follow the same basic steps as defined in the entry level environment. Customizations should be made only to the development environment, and after testing, be migrated into production (or first to testing if you choose to set up a TEST instance on your DEV virtual server). Figure 20.8 illustrates this environment. Keep in mind that your development environment will not exactly mirror your production environment — so retesting in production is still critical.

FIGURE 20.8

A mid-tier development environment with a single virtual server

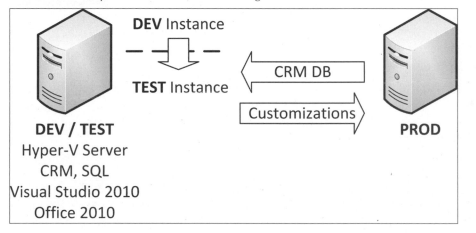

If you have multiple individuals who may be making customizations concurrently, then it will be important that you have proper controls in place to avoid potential conflicts. You can manage work by clearly communicating which portions of the application each customizer or developer is working on at any given time. Keep in mind, however, that there can still be conflicts. Clear communication, disciplined processes, and an understanding of the solution architecture included with Dynamics CRM 2011 (Chapter 16) will help to mitigate the risks of conflict.

Configuring an enterprise class development environment

This configuration is focused on organizations with complex configurations that must support multiple concurrent developers. The first priority for an enterprise development and testing environment is to mitigate the risks of any problems with the production environment. In these situations, Dynamics CRM is a mission critical application supporting a large proportion of the individuals across the organization. A short period of downtime can result in lost profits, dissatisfied customers, or even legal risks such as exposing confidential data.

An enterprise class development environment will use at least three different environments — development, testing, and production. The development environment is optimized for rapidly developing new customizations, with relatively little effort focused on mirroring the production environment. The testing environment is designed to very closely match the production environment so that testing will result in near certainty of the quality of customizations prior to migrating them to production.

The largest enterprises often include a fourth development environment called the staging area. Changes are migrated from the test environment to the staging area as a final testing step so that the migration can be replayed into production to reduce the risk of unexpected issues. As a result, the staging area should mirror the production environment as precisely as possible.

Environments of this complexity can be configured in any of a number of different ways. Figure 20.9 depicts one potential approach. As with the other environments, all customizations should be made to the development environment only. If customizations fail in the testing environment, then they should be revised in development and remigrated to testing. The development and testing environments should be configured as follows:

- Development. In general, this should be configured similarly to the mid-tier development environment. However, you should also provide access to source control and team development tools (such as the Microsoft Team Foundation Server) to better support concurrent development and proper version management for code-driven customizations. Alternatively, development tools may be installed on individual developer machines and on a developer server (for team tools), as illustrated in Figure 20.9.

- Test. The test environment should be configured as close to the production environment as possible. This includes setting up individual servers for related server software (such as SQL Server) that reflects the setup of the production environment. Data and systems configurations from the production environment should regularly be used to refresh the test environment so the environment will very closely mirror the production environment to ensure that testing produces the same results that will be experienced in production.

In the case of enterprise class development environments, governance and process are critical. Procedures should be developed, documented, and followed carefully. Specifically, a plan for migrating customizations from development to test should be documented and verified with each iterative update. Processes for testing should be documented and also verified prior to migration to production. In addition, processes for updating the test environment to properly mirror the production environment should also be documented and followed. In complex enterprises, frustrations more often have to do with a lack of discipline around documenting and following processes than they do with technology failures — avoiding these issues requires strong technology project leadership.

FIGURE 20.9

An enterprise class development environment

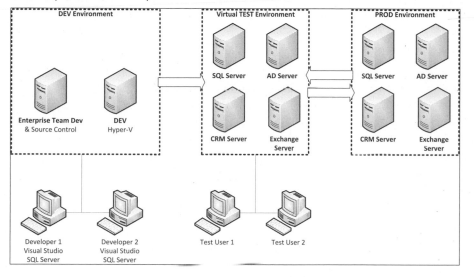

Large enterprises often take additional steps to automate their development and testing environments. Custom automation can be developed around rebuilding the test environment from production to ensure that it is always an accurate representation of production. This process can either be fully automated or partially automated using available tools and documenting appropriate supporting procedures. Continuous integration software can also be employed to speed the testing process. Continuous integration is the process of regularly integrating changes made by multiple developers into a single test environment. This can aid in identifying potential errors prior to entering a formalized testing phase. If your organization is already using continuous integration software, or if you are experiencing bottlenecks during software testing, then you may want to consider using a continuous integration approach in your development environment.

On the Web Site

Microsoft and third-party vendors have released a number of tools that improve the speed and quality of development in Dynamics CRM 4.0. Dynamics CRM 2011 includes improvements that will remove the need for many of these tools. However, we expect to see improvements to existing tools and new tools become available to aid with development in Dynamics CRM 2011. Check the site for links to these tools: www.dynamicscrmbible.com.

Configuring a CRM Online development environment

At the time of this writing, Dynamics CRM Online does not yet include a method to rapidly deploy a robust development or testing environment. We expect to see this emerge in future versions of Dynamics CRM (or perhaps even in updates made to Dynamics CRM 2011 Online). In the meantime, for businesses using Dynamics CRM Online, this section is designed to offer some helpful suggestions.

Your organization can deploy a development environment similar to the one described in the three preceding scenarios. Because this development environment would be an On-Premise deployment of Dynamics CRM, there would be some significant variances between the development and production environments. As such, your organization will want to take measures to make sure that customizations are tested for Dynamics CRM Online prior to migrating them. Keep in mind if you set up a DEV/TEST environment on-premise (either on physical on virtual servers) and you are using CRM Online, then some methods of customization will be available to you that are not available in CRM Online — so you will not be able to fully test your customizations until they have been installed in a CRM Online environment

To fully test customizations, some organizations may choose to purchase a second copy of Dynamics CRM Online specifically for testing purposes (perhaps using fewer user licenses than the production environment). Changes can be migrated from DEV to TEST to ensure that they are compatible with Dynamics CRM Online before being migrated into production.

Once Microsoft provides a way to rapidly "mirror" a Dynamics CRM Online production environment into an exact image for development and testing purposes, it will save significant time for businesses that require this kind of environment. This will present another compelling reason to migrate applications to the cloud using Dynamics CRM Online — maintenance of these environments will be significantly simplified.

Summary

The idea of "leveraging the framework" has been a recurring theme throughout this chapter. Another way to put this is, "if you're a hammer, everything looks like a nail." If you're approaching Dynamics CRM as a developer, then it may not be readily apparent to you that many problems that have traditionally required code to solve can now be solved without writing any code at all. Before diving deep into learning how to write customizations that extend Dynamics CRM, make sure you understand what can be accomplished without writing code. This knowledge will be a tremendous boost to accelerating the speed and success of your Dynamics CRM project.

As you begin to explore extending Dynamics CRM using programming tools, take the time to get clarity on your desired outcomes. Use some of the methods described in earlier chapters of the book to document your requirements. Once the "blueprint" has been written, determine which members of the team will provide which skills and customizations. As a model driven development framework, much of the "design" work can be done by an individual who does not have any development skills at all. Development work can then be plugged into the design.

Take the time to understand which customizations are not supported. People naturally gravitate to familiar work habits. In the case of development, this can mean making customizations to Dynamics CRM or to the underlying SQL Server database that can result in causing the system to become unstable. If working with Dynamics CRM On-Premise, assume that you are developing for Dynamics CRM Online. This will not only make your code more portable but will result in customizations that are supported by Microsoft (since it is relatively difficult to make unsupported changes to Dynamics CRM Online).

After you begin to make the investment in "deep" customizations to Dynamics CRM, it is important that you set up a development environment that can handle the complexity of your needs. Programming code can sometimes deliver unexpected results, so having an environment that is isolated from your production environment is important. In addition to a development environment, you should invest the time to document and follow disciplined development processes that mitigate the risk of costly downtime to your Dynamics CRM users.

Working with Client-Side Customizations

I n this chapter, we take a look at how to write client-side code and
work with other customizations on the client-side of Dynamics CRM.
We provide some examples for the newcomer to coding and we offer
some ideas for experienced programmers to get them moving along
with client-side customizations in Dynamics CRM.

For Web applications, the term "client" refers to the user computer
that is viewing the Web application, and the term "server" refers to the
computer that hosts the Web application.

In Dynamics CRM, the term "client-side" refers to information that is
sent to your browser for processing. Customizations that are made to
the client-side include any items that are processed by the browser. This
may include Web pages or it may include computer code. Computer
code that runs client-side (it is run by the browser) can interact directly
with the user. For example, it can pop up a message when a user enters
an incorrect value into a field. Server-side, on the other hand, refers to
code that only runs on the server and is never loaded to your browser.

The line between server-side and client-side is becoming increasingly
blurred. For example, client-side code can send a request to the server
that causes server-side code to execute, which, in turn, sends more
information to the client to display in a popup window without opening
a new Web page.

For purposes of this chapter, we will focus on customizations that
can be made to Dynamics CRM without having to use a development
environment (like Visual Studio). We leave those more traditional
computer programming concepts to Chapter 22.

IN THIS CHAPTER

Getting started with coding

Using code without writing code

Working with other client-side customizations

If you're a CRM administrator with little or no experience with coding, but you'd like to dive in and work with some code, then spend plenty of time reading this chapter and working through the code samples. If your focus is on learning what the possibilities are and how to communicate your requirements to a professional developer, then preview this chapter and the next one to gain an understanding of the concepts.

Tip

Much of the content in this chapter is covered extensively in the SDK. The SDK, however, is focused on a technical audience. In this chapter, we focus on simple examples focusing on common tasks to get you started. Use this chapter to form a foundation. After you are ready to go deeper with developing client-side customizations, use the Microsoft Dynamics CRM 2011 SDK (freely downloadable from Microsoft) to take the next step.

Getting Started with Coding in CRM

In this section, we're going to dive right into writing JScript code and HTML code. We present some simple examples that serve no purpose other than to ground you in the fundamentals, and we'll share some practical examples that you can use in your Dynamics CRM implementation to make users more productive.

This is by no means a comprehensive reference on client-side coding, but it is a good starting point for the newcomer. If you want to go deeper, we recommend working through the SDK (see Appendix B or the site `www.dynamicscrmbible.com`). You can also invest in books on HTML, JScript, and related topics — and a few Web searches will produce dozens of good tutorials and sample code sites on the Internet.

Understanding Web resources

Web resources are components that you use to add client-side code to Dynamics CRM. Web resources are available within the customizations area of Dynamics CRM as illustrated in Figure 21.1. When you add a Web resource file, it is hosted on the server with Dynamics CRM, so there is no need to host the code on a separate server. Web resources can include HTML files, CSS files (that are usually used in combination with HTML files), JScript libraries, image files, and Silverlight (discussed in the next chapter). We provide examples of creating Web resources throughout this chapter.

One significant benefit of Web resources is that you can load them once, and they can be reused many times in your Dynamics CRM system. For example, you may load a Web resource that formats phone numbers. You can load this Web resource only once and use it across the Lead, Account, Contact, and any other entities that use phone numbers.

Understanding events

To understand how code-based customizations work in Dynamics CRM, it is important to first understand the idea of events. Events are "triggers" that can cause code to be launched.

If you worked through the chapter on processes in Dynamics CRM, then you're familiar with the idea of events. With processes, an event is something that happens with a record (for example, a new record is created, or a field is changed) or something a user intentionally triggers (an on-demand workflow). When writing client-side code, you work with a different set of events, so it's time to take a bit deeper dive into events.

Once you've read about the different events, you can check out the "Hello world" example in the "Writing JScript" section of this chapter for some examples you can quickly run to understand exactly how events work.

Form onLoad and onSave events

Form events are triggered based on the status of a form. In Dynamics CRM, you can set up code that runs immediately after a form is loaded or immediately after the user clicks the save button (or save and close button) on a form. To run code when a form is loaded, you call it from the onLoad event. Similarly, the onSave event is used to execute code after clicking one of the save buttons. Some practical uses of form events include:

FIGURE 21.1

The Web resources list in the customizations area of Dynamics CRM

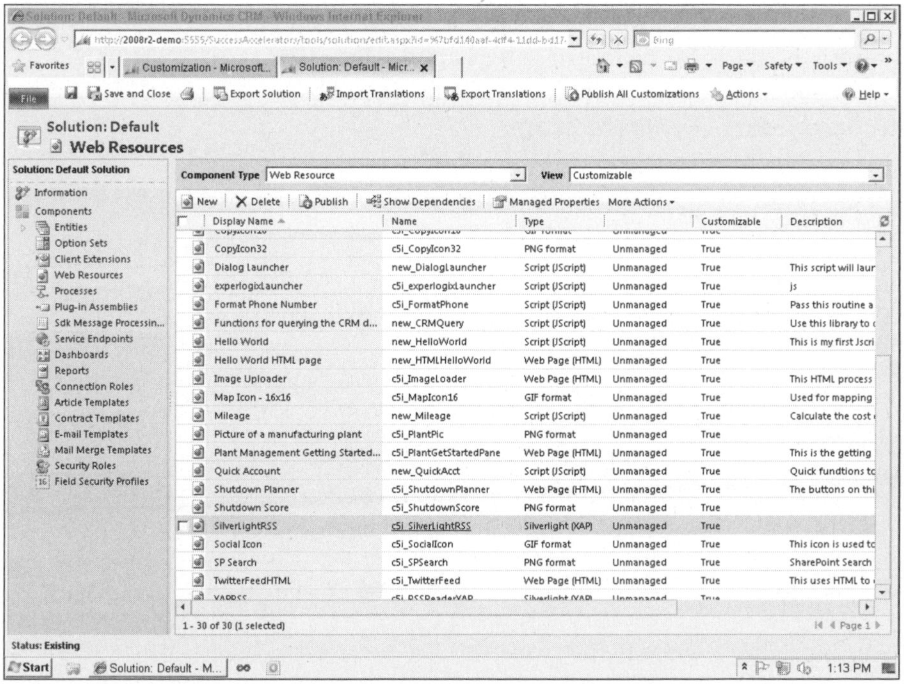

- When a user initially loads a form for an Account record, you may wish to check the credit status for the customer and show a warning if they are on credit hold. The onLoad event is the perfect time to do this. When the form is loaded the code runs, and if the credit status is "on hold," then an alert dialog box can be programmed to pop up, letting the user know about the status.

- Before a Lead record is saved, you may want to check to ensure that the user has entered all of the correct information. While you can set some fields to be required without writing code, you cannot create complex business rules. For example, you may want to ensure that at least one contact method has been entered for a Lead, either phone number, e-mail address, or mailing address. Code that executes onSave can check to ensure that at least one of these pieces of information exists before it allows the user to save the record.

Field onChange event

The onChange event occurs whenever the value in a field is changed and the field loses focus (for example, after a user updates a field and then either tabs out of the field or clicks on another field). The onChange event is often used to format data (for example, to apply standard formatting to a phone number) or trigger a change on a form based on the value entered in a field (for example, to hide a tab on the form when a certain value is selected in a picklist).

Tab TabStateChange event

This event occurs whenever a tab display changes (a tab is expanded or collapsed). This can be used to refresh the content of an Iframe contained within the tab.

Iframe OnReadyStateComplete Event

This event occurs when the content of an Iframe has finished loading. This can be used to wait for the content of an Iframe to finish loading, and to then run script against the content of the Iframe.

Ribbon control events

Ribbon controls include a number of events. Each of these events can be used to execute code associated with actions that the user performs on a ribbon. We take a closer look at how to modify a ribbon later in this chapter.

Database events

Database events happen on the server side rather than on the client side. This includes record updates and other changes made to the data within the database. Database events can trigger workflows (discussed in Chapter 18) and plug-ins (discussed in Chapter 22).

Writing JScript

JScript is the client-side programming language for Dynamics CRM (you may also hear it referred to as JavaScript — the two are not exactly the same, but close enough that you can consider them to be synonymous for purposes of this book). JScript is a common programming language used behind many Web sites and Web applications. JScript code can be as short as a few lines long or many thousands of lines long.

Understanding JScript libraries

Dynamics CRM 2011 enables developers to write libraries of JScript code and to load these as Web resources. These libraries contain functions that can be called from within forms, Ribbon menus, and from other JScript functions. Multiple functions can be included in a single library. For example, a JScript library called Field Formatting might contain two functions: the first reformats telephone numbers so users don't have to type in punctuation when entering a phone number; the second reformats postal code fields.

On the Web Site

We have included some free JScript libraries on the Web site `www.dynamicscrmbible.com` that you can use as learning tools and to enhance your Dynamics CRM implementation.

Hello world

A "Hello World" program is a simple way to take a first step into a new programming paradigm. It doesn't serve any function other than to help someone new to an area of coding to grasp the fundamental concepts quickly. We use the hello world approach to look at a few different client-side customizations throughout this chapter. We also provide some real-world applications.

Caution

When following along with the examples in this chapter, we suggest that you do this work in a development environment (see Chapter 20 for information on setting up a development environment) to avoid any risk of disrupting the users of your Dynamics CRM system. Many client-side customizations cannot be tested without first publishing them — which could risk causing some frustration to your users if you are working in a production environment.

In this particular case, we use a hello world application to demonstrate not only the fundamentals of JScript, but also to help you understand the events that can trigger your JScript to run. Use the steps below to create and run your first JScript code:

1. Navigate to the customizations area of Dynamics CRM (Settings ⇨ Customizations ⇨ Customize the System).

2. In the navigation pane, click on Web Resources, then click on the New button above the grid.

3. You are presented with the Web resources data entry form. Fill the form out as illustrated in Figure 21.2 (you won't be able to fill in the URL field; Dynamics CRM can do that for you when you save the record).

4. When you are done filling out the form, click the button labeled Text Editor. You are presented with a blank form for entering code.

5. Enter the code illustrated in Figure 21.3 and click the OK button. Remember that JScript is case sensitive, so enter everything exactly as you see it in the image.

6. Save and close the form. Congratulations — you've just written your first JScript code for Dynamics CRM! Now all you have to do is tell Dynamics where you want the code to run.

FIGURE 21.2

The Web resource data entry form

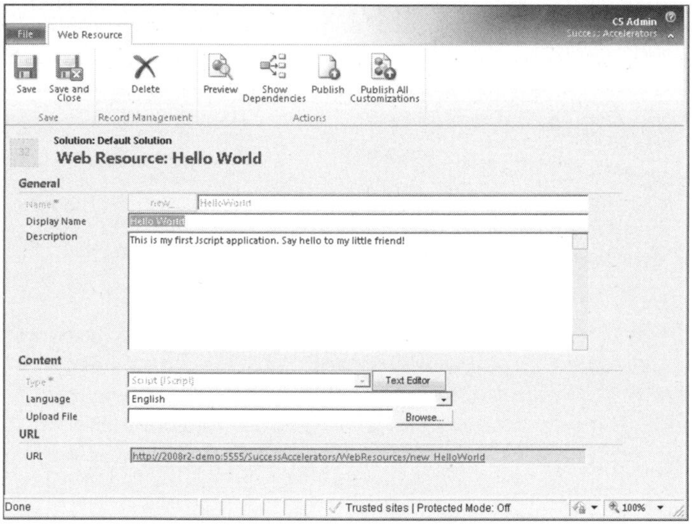

FIGURE 21.3

The text editor for entering JScript code

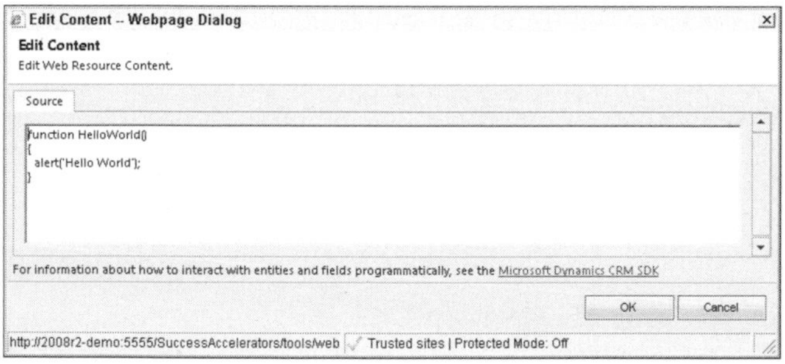

7. Still in the customization area, use the navigation pane to navigate to the list of forms for the Account entity. Open the main form and then click the Form Properties button in the Ribbon menu. You will be presented with a list of form libraries as illustrated in Figure 21.4 (note that your list may not contain any libraries — ours contains some libraries used for the book).

8. Click the Add button above the list. From the list, choose the Hello World Web resource that you just created and click the OK button.

9. Back in the Form Properties dialog (Figure 21.4) scroll down a bit to the section titled Event Handlers. Click the Add button for this section. You are presented with the Handler Properties dialog box.

FIGURE 21.4

The list of form libraries for the Account form

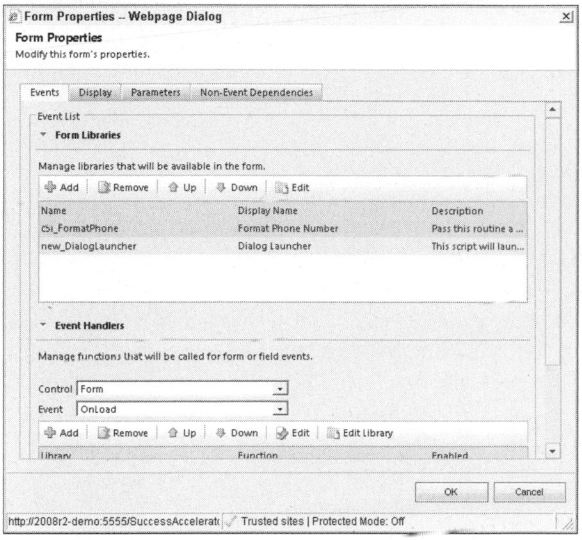

10. Fill out the form as it is illustrated in Figure 21.5. You have just told Dynamics that your JScript should run whenever the form is initially loaded. Click OK to return to the Form Properties dialog box.

FIGURE 21.5

The Handler Properties dialog box

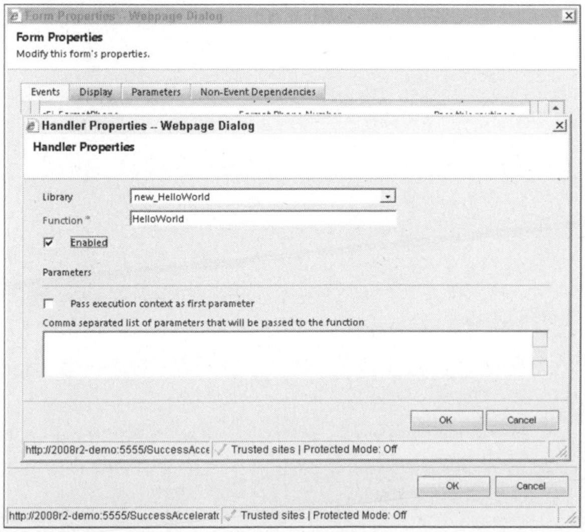

11. On the Form Properties dialog, click the Event picklist (it is likely set to OnLoad). Change it to OnSave.

12. Click the Add button again and fill out the form in the same manner as Figure 21.5 again. Click OK when you have finished completing the form.

13. Click OK again to close the Form Properties dialog box. You should now be on the form designer.

14. Click on the Account Name field and then click on the Change Properties button in the Ribbon menu.

15. You are presented with the Field Properties dialog box. Click on the Events tab (Figure 21.6).

16. In the Event Handlers section, click the Add button. Once again, you are presented with the Handler Properties dialog box. Once again, fill it out as you did in Figure 21.5 and click the OK button. You have just told CRM to run your JScript when the user changes the Account Name field and then moves to another field.

17. Save and Close the form.

18. Click the Publish All Customizations button.

FIGURE 21.6

The Field Properties dialog box with the Events tab selected

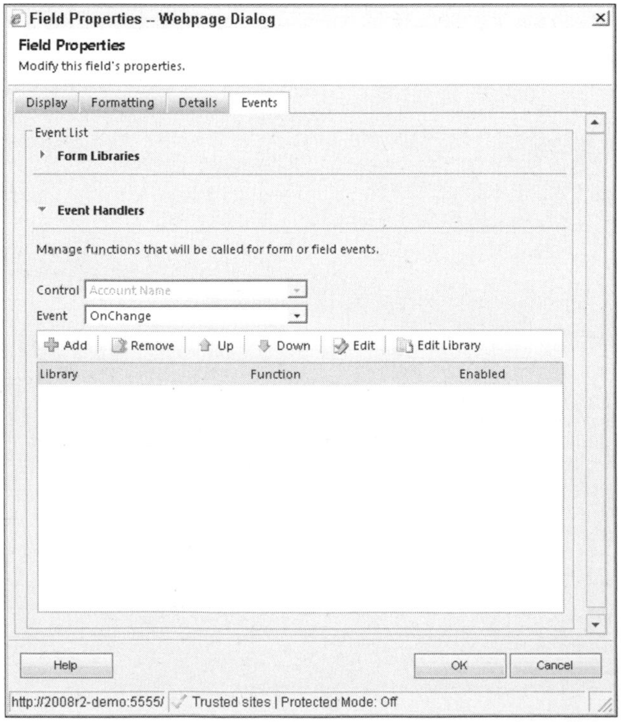

Your code has now been published! Let's go have a look at what it does.

Close the customizations area of CRM. Navigate to the Accounts list (Workplace ⇨ Accounts). Open any account in the list. If your code is written and working correctly, you will immediately see the dialog in Figure 21.7. This is the JScript that you wrote in Step 6, executing in the onLoad event that you set up in Step 8.

FIGURE 21.7

A dialog box that was created by JScript code

Click OK to close the dialog box. Change the account name (you can just add a single letter to it). Tab to the next field. Up comes the dialog box again. This is using the onChange event for the Account Name field that you set up in Step 16.

Click the OK button to close the dialog box. Click Save and Close. The dialog box comes up one more time. This is the onSave event that you set up in Step 12.

How the JScript code works

The code (in Figure 21.3) begins with the word "function." This tells the code that the next word is the name of a function (in this case, "HelloWorld"). The name provided here is the name that will be used in events (such as onChange) to call the code. The function can also be called by name in other JScript code. Immediately after the function is a pair of parentheses. If you were to "pass" a value to this function, then you would insert a variable here to capture what you are passing (you'll see samples of this a bit later).

Next is an opening curly bracket. JScript uses curly brackets to indicate segments of code that belong together. In this case, the opening curly bracket after the function statement is saying, "everything between here and the closing curly bracket belongs to this function." This is useful because a single JScript Web resource may have multiple functions, so you need a way to delineate which code goes with which function and where one function ends and another begins.

The next line, with the "alert" statement, is the main portion of our code. An alert statement tells JScript that whatever comes next should be placed into a dialog box so that the user can see it. The statement ends with a semicolon, which is how most lines of JScript code should end.

On the Web Site

JScript is a programming language used in millions of Web pages. It includes a diverse range of statements for writing code. A full tutorial cannot be covered in this book. However, we will post links to some recommended online tutorials on www.dynamicscrmbible.com. If you are interested in going deep with JScript, then the Dynamics CRM SDK is another document that you should take the time to read through.

Options for loading your JScript code

You may have noticed that on Step 5 (Figure 21.3), you could have clicked the browse button to load a JScript file from your computer rather than using the text editor to create your JScript. If you're just writing a few lines of JScript code, using the text editor built into Dynamics CRM is a convenient way to quickly enter the code. But if you're developing JScript that will be hundreds of lines long, you will want to use a different editor to create your code. Options for editing code are outlined in Chapter 20.

Additional JScript code examples

In this section, we quickly cover a number of additional JScript code examples. We go over a number of functions that are useful for Dynamics CRM applications and will explain a few other features of the JScript language in the process. We won't take the time to explain the code line-by-line, so if you'd like to learn exactly how the code works, then spend a bit of time researching it on the Internet. Use the instructions from creating the "hello world" script if you need a little help with remembering how to add the JScript to Dynamics CRM.

On the Web Site

The code examples in this section can all be found on the www.dynamicscrmbible.com Web site. From the site, you can download solutions and import them directly into Dynamics CRM to eliminate the need to type in all of the code below.

Format a phone number

We've referenced the idea of using JScript to format phone number fields a number of times throughout this book; now it's finally time to show you how to make this happen. Use the procedure below to create the required JScript and call it from the Account form.

1. Create a JScript Web resource named Format Phone.

2. Insert the following JScript into the resource:

```
function FormatPhone(context) {
// The above "context" parameter is being passed the context
// of this function from the onChange event.
// This means we can call the same function from multiple
// different phone number fields - each phone number field
// will pass in information about itself. Remember to check
// the "Pass execution context as first parameter" box in
// order to pass in the context.

// This line extracts the value from the field that was passed
// in the context parameter. In other words, the value
```

```
// "strPhone" now contains whatever the user typed into the
// phone number field.
var strPhone = context.getEventSource().getValue();

// If the field is null, then there is no reason to try to
// format it. Exit the function without doing any more
// work and return to processing other input from the user.
if (strPhone == null)
 return;

// This code segment tests to see if the phone number has
// an "x" within it. If so, this is interpreted to
// be an extension. The code places everything to the right
// of the "x" into a new variable called strExt.
// Everything to the left of the "x" is kept in the
// strPhone variable.
var booExt = false;
 if (strPhone.indexOf("x") > 0) {
 var strExt = strPhone.split("x");
 booExt = true;
 strPhone = strExt[0];
 }

// Next, we will remove any characters that are not numbers
// from the phone number. We store the result in a new field
// called strCleanPhone. The ".replace" is a function that is
// called on the string "strPhone". In effect, this removes
// all non-numeric characters from the strong by replacing
// them with "". See online Jscript tutorials to learn more
// about the replace function.
 var strCleanPhone = strPhone.replace(/[^0-9]/g, "");
 var strNewPhone;


// The switch statement executes the case statement that
// matches the result of the switch. In this code, the
// switch statement checks the length of the phone number
// with everything except for the numbers removed from it.
// It then executes the case statement that returns the
// same length. The subsequent three case statements execute
// to format the phone according to the number of digits
// entered by the user.
 switch (strCleanPhone.length)
 {
 case "17048952500".length:
  strNewPhone = "1(" + strCleanPhone.substr(1, 3) + ")" +
   strCleanPhone.substr(4, 3) + "-" + strCleanPhone.substr(7, 4);
  break;

 case "7048952500".length:
```

```
   strNewPhone = "(" + strCleanPhone.substr(0, 3) + ")" +
     strCleanPhone.substr(3, 3) + "-" + strCleanPhone.substr(6, 4);
   break;

 case "8952500".length:
   strNewPhone = strCleanPhone.substr(0, 3) + "-" + strCleanPhone.
     substr(3, 4);
   break;
 }

// If the original phone number had an extension, then this
// code segment will add the extension to the end of the
// newly formatted phone number.
if (strNewPhone != null) {
 if (booExt) {
 strNewPhone = strNewPhone + " x" + strExt[1];
 }}
 else {
 strNewPhone = strPhone;
 }

// This line of code uses the original context that was passed
// in when the code was called to update the phone number field
// to the formatted value.
context.getEventSource().setValue(strNewPhone);

 }
```

3. Save and publish the Jscript Web resource.

4. Customize the main form on the Account entity.

5. On the Ribbon menu, click the Form Properties button.

6. Add the Web resource to the form libraries according to Figures 21.8.

7. Double-click on the Main Phone field on the form. Under the events tab, add the FormatPhone function to the OnChange event according to Figure 21.9. Note that you should check the Enabled box and the "Pass execution context as first parameter" (this second check box tells the function which field you were on when the function was called — see the comments in the code for more information).

8. Repeat Step 7 for each phone field on your form.

9. Save and Close the form.

10. Publish the customizations.

Open an account record and change some phone numbers by typing in just a string of numbers (with either no punctuation, or just an x to delineate the extension). Notice how the JScript automatically reformats the phone numbers when you tab out of each field.

FIGURE 21.8

Adding the Format Phone Web resource to a form

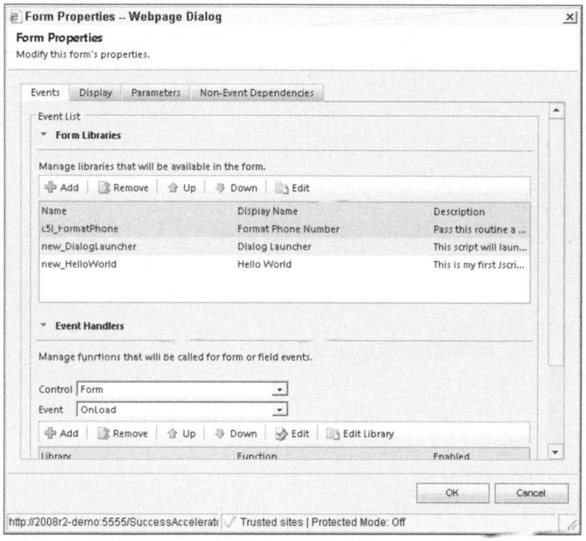

FIGURE 21.9

Adding the FormatPhone function to the OnChange event

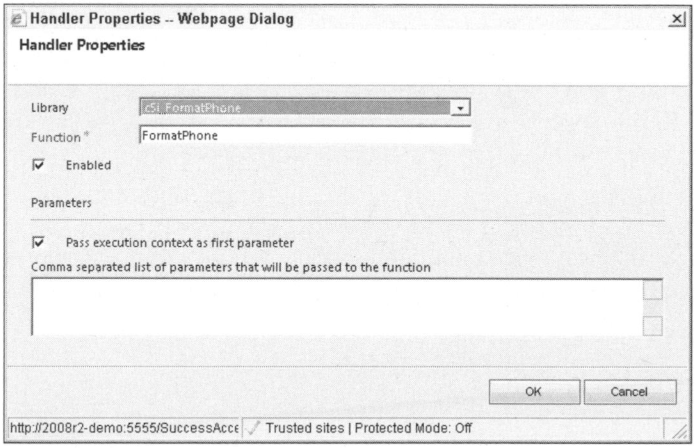

Tip

See the double slash in the code above? In JScript, that means that the remainder of the text on the line is a comment. This enables you to document your code so that when you look at it six months later, you will remember what you were trying to accomplish. Doing a good job of documenting your code is an important part of developing a solution so that it will be easy to maintain.

Calculate a field

When working with data on forms, it is frequently desirable to calculate a field. Use the process below to calculate the mileage reimbursement rate when entering the mileage into a custom field called "Miles" (an integer field) that has been added to the task entity. You need to add the Miles field to the Task entity before you start (see Chapter 17 if you need help adding a field to a form).

1. Create a Web resource called "Mileage" and paste the following code into it.

```
function CalculateMileageCost(intMiles, curRate) {
// This function multiplies intMiles by curRate and
// creates a pop up alert displaying the product. It
// could also store the rate in a field on the form
// if desired.

// This illustrates how to do math functions using
// JScript. It also illustrates how to pass
// additional arguments into a Jscript function
// from a Dynamics CRM event.

// This line multiplies the two values that were passed
// into the function.
    var curTotalAmount = intMiles * curRate;

// This line displays the product in a pop-up alert.
// Replace this with a line that writes the product back
// to a field on the form if you prefer.
    alert ('Total reimbursement amount: ', curTotalAmount);

}
```

2. Add the Web resource to your Task form as a form library (see Step 6 in the preceding section if you need help remembering how to do this).

3. Add a call to the function "CalculateMileageCost" to the OnChange event of the Miles filed according to Figure 21.10 (note that we are passing in the value from the Miles field here as well as the cost per mile). Wondering where the term "Xrm.Page.data. entity.attributes.get("new_miles").getValue()" came from? You can learn more about it in the section "The XRM page model."

4. Save and close the form and publish all customizations.

Open a task and enter a value into the mileage field, then tab out of the field. The popup alert tells you the total cost for the mileage. If you wanted to get fancy, you could create a custom solution with a configuration page in which the mileage rate is entered. Using this approach, an administrative user could update the mileage rate periodically without having to edit the function call. Of course, you can also put the calculate field into another field rather than a popup box (which may be quite a bit more useful for reporting purposes).

FIGURE 21.10

Calling the CalculateMileageCost function from the OnChange event for the Miles field

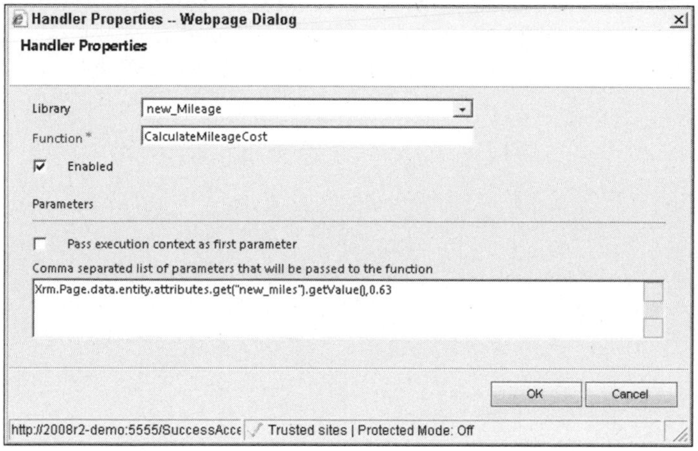

Even more JScript code

Sometimes finding that "one line of code" can be a frustrating and time-consuming process. To help you get started with some of the more common JScript statements for Dynamics CRM, we've listed a number of them below. These were all written and tested using the Account entity and the default form — you may need to adjust them a bit to work with your forms.

```
// Determine the entity that the currently displayed
// form is related to. You can use this to setup different
// behaviors depending on which entity the function is
// called from.
Xrm.Page.context.getValue();

// Read the value in the field named "name"
Xrm.Page.data.entity.attributes.get("name").getValue());

// Hide a field
Xrm.Page.ui.controls.get("accountnumber").setVisible(false);

// Hide one item in a picklist.
Xrm.Page.ui.controls.get("new_quickpick").removeOption(100000000);

// Set a field to required.
Xrm.Page.data.entity.attributes.get("accountnumber").
    setRequiredLevel("required");

// Change the color of a field.
```

```
// CAUTION: This code is unsupported - meaning that it works at
// the time of this writing, but may not work in future versions
// Dynamics CRM.
crmForm.all.name.style.backgroundColor = "#FFB6C1";

// Hide a section
Xrm.Page.ui.tabs.get("general").sections.get("address").
   setVisible(false);

// Hide a navigation item
Xrm.Page.ui.navigation.items.get(0).setVisible(false);

// Switch to another form
Xrm.Page.ui.formSelector.items.get(0).navigate();
```

How to Calculate a Field

When calculating a field (or updating any data in Dynamics CRM) a number of options are open to you. Each has its pros and cons.

- **JScript code:** You can do some very helpful things with JScript code. But remember that this code only executes when a user is interacting with Dynamics CRM. If you want to calculate a field every time a record is changed, and if those records can change without user input (for example, if a workflow changes the record), then the JScript that calculates the field will not run — resulting in an inaccurate calculation stored in the database. This in turn may produce inaccurate information in reports, charts, and views.

- **Workflow:** You can use workflows to calculate fields as well. The built-in capabilities are limited, but you can perform basic calculations. The benefit to this approach is that you can be certain that the calculation will run whenever the record is updated (assuming you set the workflow triggers properly and assuming that workflow remains published). The downside is that the value is not updated immediately, so users may be confused if they don't see the right value while editing the record.

- **Workflow Extensions:** Workflow extensions can be written that provide more advanced calculation capabilities in workflows. The downsides for this approach are the same as mentioned for workflows.

- **Plug-Ins:** Plug-ins can be written and added to Dynamics CRM that run immediately when values are changed in the database. These also have a tremendous amount of flexibility and can generally calculate anything you like. The downside is that plug-ins require the skills of a professional developer, and they still do not interact directly with the end user (a record needs to be saved before the calculations can be run).

Determining how you calculate a field in Dynamics CRM is based on a number of factors. Consider how you want to interact with the user, how complex the calculation is, how else your database is being updated, and what level of expertise your Dynamics CRM customizations team has.

A nearly limitless list of statements is available in JScript, so the list is by no means comprehensive. Other sources you can turn to for help include (the below referenced sites are linked to on the book site: www.dynamicscrmbible.com):

- The Dynamics CRM 2011 software development kit (SDK). This is freely downloadable from the Microsoft Web site. It contains an enormous volume of reference materials and code samples.

- The Microsoft Dynamics CRM forums. This is an online discussion group that you can use to ask questions and search to see if others have experienced the same issues.

- Dynamics CRM blogs. There are many individuals and companies that publish blogs specifically on writing code for Dynamics CRM. These can be great references. Search for terms like "Dynamics CRM JScript" and you'll see what I mean.

- JScript blogs. Because JScript is a language used on millions of Web pages, there are also thousands of other examples of JScript that are not specifically written for Dynamics CRM but that can be integrated into your own Dynamics CRM customizations. Spend a bit of time searching the Internet when you're trying to solve a problem with JScript and you'll be surprised at how much information you can find.

The XRM page model

JScript statements that retrieve data from Dynamics CRM forms or that interact with the user or with form design are based on something called the XRM page model. This is a hierarchical way that Microsoft describes the structure of forms (pages) in Dynamics CRM. When you're trying to solve a problem with JScript and you're not sure how to formulate a statement, the XRM page model (illustrated in Figure 21.11) is a good place to start.

You can use the page model to formulate the first parts of a JScript statement and look up the last portion of the statement in the SDK. As an example, if you wanted to hide a tab from the user view, you would work from the top of the XRM page model down to come up with something like Xrm.Page.ui.tabs. You may then search the SDK for specific "methods" you can use to complete your statement. For additional examples of how the XRM page model is used to develop JScript statements, check the previous section, "Even more JScript code."

Testing your JScript code

While developing your JScript code, you are likely to go through many iterations before your code is complete and ready for production. Here are a few things that we recommend to simplify the process a bit.

- Develop your form first. Although it is possible to edit your JScript from directly within your form, this can be a bit time-consuming and frustrating. Work on developing your form first. Create any libraries that you might need, and insert event handlers wherever necessary (including function calls), but leave the functions empty while you are designing your form. After you have completed your form design, save, and publish the form.

FIGURE 21.11

The XRM page model

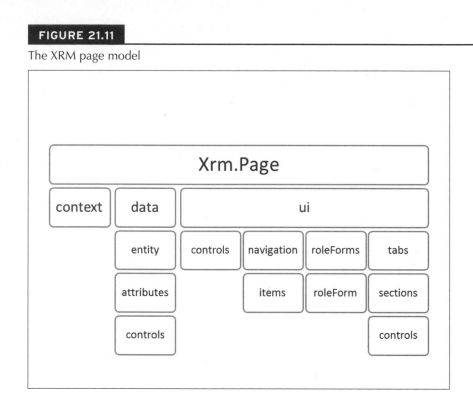

- Work on your code one library at a time. As you modify the code, save and publish it and then try it out in production. You can keep both the Web resource page and the grid page for the entity that you're working on open at the same time so you can quickly toggle back-and-forth between modifying and publishing your code, and opening a form to test it.

- Remember that your published JScript code will not go into effect with any forms that are already open for data entry because the JScript is loaded when the page is initially loaded. So after you make changes to your JScript and publish it, you'll have to open a new form to test your code.

- Remember that (at the time of this writing) the only straightforward way to test your JScript in Dynamics CRM will be to publish it — so it will be in production. This could cause a lot of complaints from your users if you make any mistakes. We highly recommend a development environment to mitigate this potential problem.

Converting your Dynamics CRM 4.0 JScript

If you have worked with JScript in Dynamics CRM 4.0, then you've probably noticed some pretty big changes in how it works in 2011 — both in terms of how your code is managed and in terms of how the code is now written. The good news is that most of your code from

4.0 will still work in 2011 with relatively little modification. However, some items that you are used to using (such as the crmForm statement) have been deprecated. This means that they still work, but Microsoft has said that they do not plan to continue to support them in the future.

If you upgrade from 4.0 to 2011 following the normal process, then much of your code (assuming it was supported) should upgrade without a problem. A free tool has been published on www.codeplex.com called Infusion JavaScript converter that should help with code that doesn't convert. If you wrote unsupported code, then you may have to work through a manual process to upgrade it — the good news is that most of the code that will no longer work in 2011 can be replaced with UI based tools.

Supported and unsupported JScript

It is important to note that, although you may be able to get some things to work in JScript, it does not necessarily mean that your code is "supported." Unsupported code, in essence, means that Microsoft does not intend to make sure that the code will update to future versions and will not provide support on the code. There was some outstanding code available for Dynamics CRM 4.0 that, while not supported, provided some excellent new functionality. Some of that code won't upgrade to 2011, but for the most part there are ways to replace it that are improvements over the unsupported code. Expect the same to be true in 2011. You will likely come across code that you can download from blogs that works well in 2011, but it may be unsupported and may not upgrade to future versions properly. You'll need to decide if this is an acceptable risk to take.

Working with Web pages

Web pages can be integrated into your Dynamics CRM solution as Web resources (self-contained HTML or Silverlight files hosted on the Dynamics CRM server) or as Iframes (Web pages that are not hosted on your server but that appear in a "window" within CRM). These pages can appear in a variety of locations throughout your application including within forms, in dashboards, as part of the main navigation structure of the application, or as related navigation items in data entry forms.

Using HTML Web resources

HTML Web resources are created and managed in the Web resources list just like JScript. HTML Web resources enable you to create HTML Web pages that can be embedded directly within a form, into the site navigation, or that can be called from JScript on a form. The HTML is stored on the Dynamics CRM server so it is easy to export with a solution and import into another instance of Dynamics CRM. Because the code is on the server, it executes only Dynamics CRM security context (only users can access the sites). HTML Web resources are also available offline. This section provides an outline of these resources, using a similar approach to the previous section.

HTML Web resources can be coupled with CSS or the various image Web resources (PNG, GIF, or JPG) items in order to format the content delivered in the HTML resource.

Hello world

If you're unfamiliar with HTML code, then let's start by creating our "hello world" program again — this time to be displayed in an HTML Web resource within the form. Use the steps below to create this program:

1. In the customize area, navigate to the Web resources list and choose to add a new Web resource.

2. Fill out the Web resource as in Figure 21.12.

3. Click the text editor and enter "Hello World" in to the rich text tab of the editor. Click the Source tab to see how it looks. Click OK when you are done.

4. Save the form, publish it and then close it.

5. Edit the main form for the Account entity.

6. In the Ribbon menu, select the Insert tab and then select Web Resource. Browse to the resource you just created and fill out the rest of the form as shown in Figure 21.13. Click OK when you are done.

7. Place the HTML Web resource wherever you like on your form.

8. When you are done, save and close the form and then publish your customizations.

You're done! Now open the form to check out your handiwork.

FIGURE 21.12

Configuring an HTML Web resource

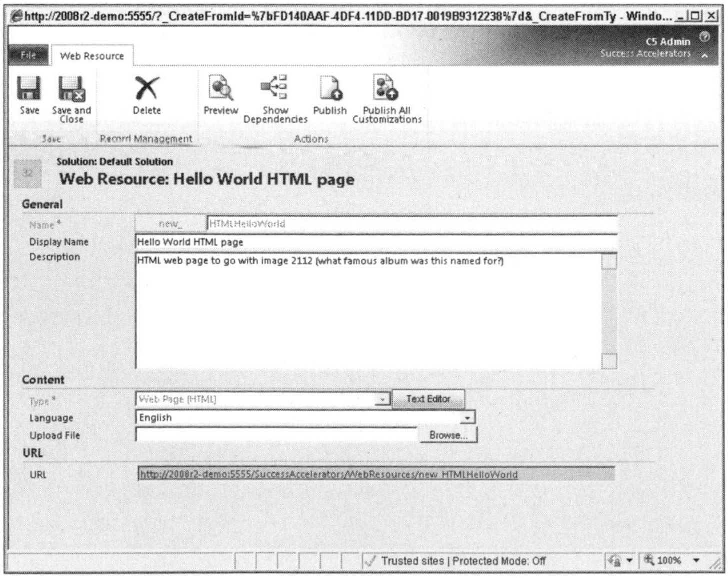

Creating mash-ups with Iframes

Iframes work in a manner similar to HTML Web resources. The difference is that Iframes are a "window" into a Web application or Web site that is running elsewhere. This, for example, could include a SharePoint Web site, a mapping application (such as Bing maps), or a distributor portal run by a manufacturer that your organization partners with.

FIGURE 21.13

The Add Web Resource dialog box

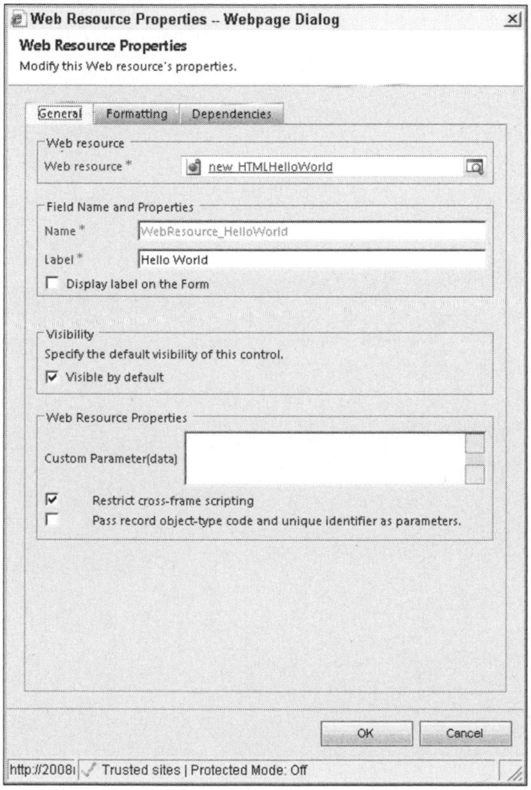

Data from Dynamics CRM can be passed into an application within an Iframe. For example, if you place an Iframe onto the Account form, the account number could be used when loading the page within the Iframe. This enables you to create a type of integration called a "mash-up" where your Dynamics CRM application is "mashed up" against another application. The data between the applications is not synchronized, but a small amount of data is exchanged (via the URL) at the time that the Web page is displayed that enables the application inside of the Iframe to respond by displaying relevant information.

A popular mash-up is to integrate Dynamics CRM with a mapping application. The address from an Account record is passed in to the Iframe and the address is mapped on Microsoft Bing maps in the Iframe. Figure 21.14 demonstrates this type of Iframe integration. Below the figure are the steps required to integrate this with the Account entity in Dynamics CRM. This same approach can be used to integrate with your accounting application (assuming it is Web-based), produce information about a company from a Web search, and pass information into SharePoint.

FIGURE 21.14

An Iframe mash-up to produce a Bing Map for the Account entity

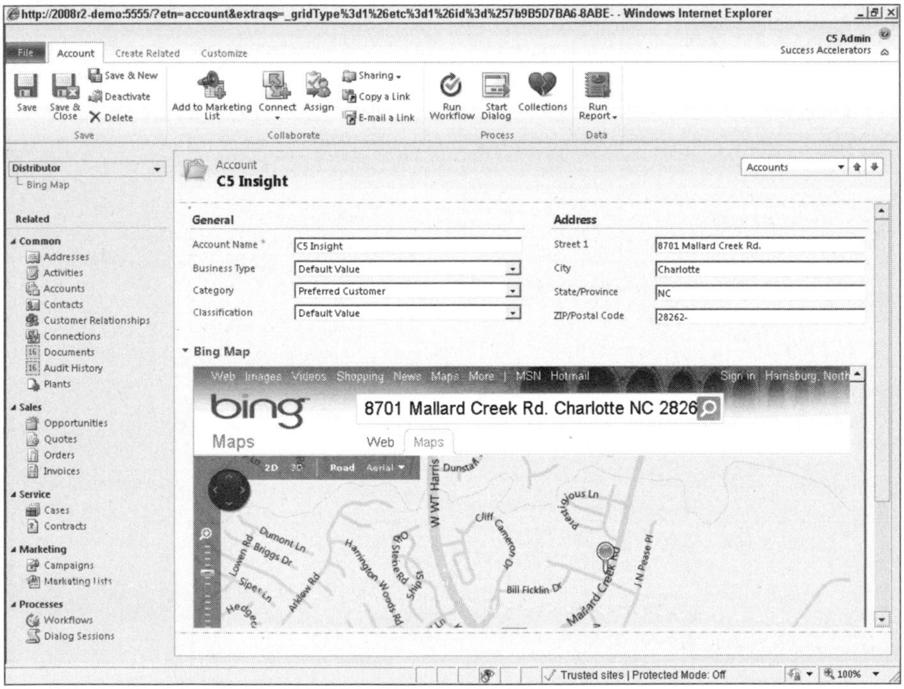

1. Create a JScript Web resource using the code below.

```
function BingMap (strStreet, strCity, strState, strZip)
// This function will map the address that is passed
// to it to an Iframe containing a Bing Map that is
// on the same page as the form and is named:
// IFRAME_BingMap
//
// You may want to add to this code a test to ensure that
// the tab the map is displayed in is expanded, and on
// the form you can collapse the tab by default and
// remove this code from the OnLoad event. This will
```

```
// result in only loading the map when the tab is
// expanded.
{
 var IFrame = Xrm.Page.ui.controls.get("IFRAME_BingMap");
 strURL = "http://www.bing.com/maps/?v=2&where1=" + strStreet +
   "%20" + strCity + "%20" + strState + "%20" + strZip +
   "&encType=1";
 IFrame.setSrc(strURL);
}
```

2. Edit one of the forms on the Account entity. In our case, we want the map on the form called "Distributor" for the Account entity, so this is the form that we will edit.

3. Add a tab to the form that will hold the map. Set this tab to be visible and give it a descriptive title such as "Bing Map." Note that, after you initially follow this process, you may want to set the tab to be invisible by default and require the user to expand the tab before the map is refreshed.

4. Add an Iframe to the tab on the form. Use the settings in Figure 21.15.

FIGURE 21.15

The Iframe Properties dialog box

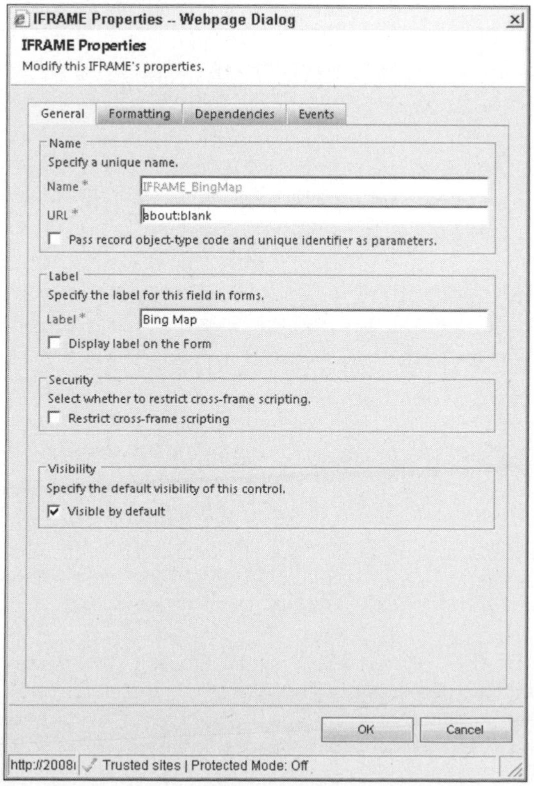

- **Name:** This is a unique name of your choice. You are referencing this in a JScript resource, so make a note of it.

- **URL:** You can use "about:blank" to start with in this case. We will use JScript code to update this when a mailing address is present on the form.

- **Pass record object-type code and unique identifier as parameters:** We will leave this unchecked in this case. This can be a useful feature if you want to pass context information to the Iframe that can be used to render data properly. This can also be useful if the application in your Iframe uses the Dynamics CRM Web service to retrieve information about the Account (or related records) directly from Dynamics CRM.

- **Restrict cross-frame scripting:** This restricts scripts interacting with the site in the Iframe. If your Iframe will contain a link to a site that is outside of your firewall and does not need to interact with your Dynamics CRM form, then it is wise to leave this box checked to avoid potential security issues.

- **Dependencies tab:** It is a best practice to add any fields from your form that the Iframe is dependent upon. This will prevent these fields (in this case the address fields) from being deleted from the form if the Iframe is still on it.

- **Events tab:** This contains an event for Iframes called OnReadyStateComplete. This event fires when the site within the Iframe finishes loading. You can use this to call JScript functions when a page loads within the Iframe.

5. In the Ribbon menu, click the Form Properties button. Add the JScript Web resource that you created in the first step to the form as a Form Library. Add the same JScript Web resource to the Event Handler for the form OnLoad event as well, using the settings in Figure 21.16.

6. On the tab that contains the Bing Map, add the same event handler to the TabStateChange event as you did for the form OnLoad event (including passing in the same four fields). You could have added this function to the OnChange event to each address field, but this may result in distracting reloads of the map as the user is entering data. By attaching the JScript to the TabStateChange event, the user can collapse and then re-expand the tab and the map will be refreshed with any new address data that was entered after the form was opened.

7. Save and publish the form and the Web resource. Open an Account to view the map.

A number of options are available for further customizing this type of mash-up. The tab containing the map can be hidden until enough address information exists to show it. Rather than embedding the map into the form, it can be behind a custom navigation link or behind a button in the ribbon menu. The map can be set up as a dashboard that maps out multiple addresses. When setting up Iframe integration, it is important to understand the needs of your users and to then design it to work the way that your team works.

FIGURE 21.16

FIGURE 21.16

The Event Handler settings for the form OnLoad event

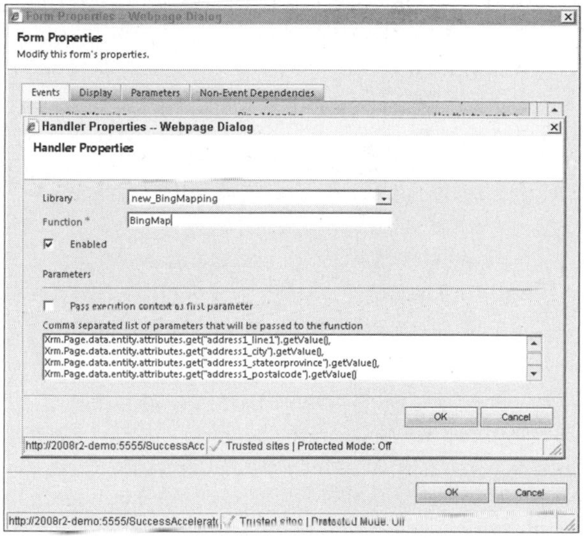

Other Customizations

A variety of other client-side customizations can be made to Dynamics CRM that have not been discussed in-depth elsewhere in the book. Some of these require some level of coding, and others can be accessed as simply as calling a URL. This section outlines some of these other useful customization options.

Calling CRM functions with URLs

Because Dynamics CRM is a Web application, almost everything in it can be accessed by calling a URL. This can be a very useful and simple way to quickly execute functions without having to write code. Below are a few examples of items you can access with URLs and some concepts for where this might make a valuable contribution to your Dynamics CRM setup.

Copying or sending a URL link

To copy or send a link from Dynamics CRM, navigate to the view or record that you want to send the link to. Look for the buttons labeled "Copy a Link" and "E-mail a Link" in the Ribbon menu as illustrated in Figure 21.17. Click on either of these according to your preference.

Every record and view in Dynamics CRM has a unique ID (called a GUID). This ID is embedded into the URL. When a URL is passed in, it can decipher which specific record (or view) that you are requesting and can display it properly.

FIGURE 21.17

Using the Ribbon menu to share a link

Launching dialog processes with a URL

The process for launching a dialog process with a URL is a bit more complex. That's because Dynamics CRM needs to know not only which dialog you want to launch but also which record in Dynamics CRM you will be launching it for.

If you want to send an e-mail that contains a link to launch a specific dialog for a specific record in Dynamics CRM, you can copy the URL right out of the address bar in Internet Explorer. To do this, start by navigating to the record in Dynamics CRM that you want to run the dialog for. Click the Start Dialog button in the ribbon menu and then click the name of the dialog you want to run. When the dialog starts, copy the URL out of the address bar. Close the dialog without running it. Now you can paste the link to this dialog into an e-mail. Remember that this will run the dialog for the specific record that you were on and will only work when clicked by users licensed for your instance of Dynamics CRM.

Creating links in JScript or processes

When customizing Dynamics CRM, you will often encounter a need to send a link to a record, or to launch a process, as part of a workflow or dialog process. You may also want to launch a dialog directly from the Ribbon menu or even when a user makes a change to a field on a form.

Use the following JScript to dynamically create a link that can launch a dialog (note that we reuse this JScript when talking about modifying the Ribbon menu a little later in this chapter).

1. Create a new JScript Web resource.

2. Insert the JScript code, below, into the resource:

```
function LaunchDialog (context,strDialogGUID)
// This function will launch a dialog for the
// record that is currently being viewed in
// Dynamics CRM. The GUID for the desired
// dialog should be passed in as the
// strDialogGUID parameter. Note that the
// dialog must be associated with the proper
// record type or this procedure will throw
// an error.
{

  // These initial lines of code are used to
  // get the information required in order
  // to formulate the complete URL for
```

```
// the selected dialog.
strOrgURL = Xrm.Page.context.getServerUrl();
strEntityName = Xrm.Page.data.entity.getEntityName();
strRecordID = Xrm.Page.data.entity.getId();

// This concatenates all of the above into a
// single URL
strDialogURL = strOrgURL + "/cs/dialog/rundialog.
  aspx?DialogID=%7b" + strDialogGUID + "%7d&EntityName=" +
  strEntityName + "&ObjectID=" + strRecordID;

// This opens the dialog in a new window.
window.open(strDialogURL,'Dialog')
}
```

3. In the form designer, click the Form Properties button in the Ribbon menu. Add the JScript Web resource you created above as a Form Library.

4. You can now call this function from an OnChange event or from the Ribbon menu.

When working with a workflow or dialog process, you may also want to dynamically generate a link. In this case, the link may be embedded in an e-mail and may link to a either a record (such as a Case) or to a dialog. Retrieving the required GUID fields is not directly supported when designing workflow and dialog processes. However, a workflow plug-in can be created that can retrieve the GUID for you and can make it available as a "data slug" that you can use in e-mails or other records generated by a process. See the next chapter for information on creating workflow plug-ins.

Modifying XML files

Dynamics CRM generates a number of XML files to manage configuration settings. To change these settings, you export the XML file, make changes to the file, and then reimport it. When editing XML files, we highly recommend the usage of a text editor that can format XML files (such as Notepad++). A better option is to use a text editor that also includes schema validation using an XSD file, which will provide intellisense to help you edit the code in the files. These options are discussed in detail in Chapter 20.

Caution

Editing the XML files often requires certain files from the SDK. If you have not yet downloaded the Dynamics SDK from Microsoft, we strongly encourage you to do so now. A link to download the SDK will be published on the site for the book (www.dynamicscrmbible.com).

Modifying the site map

The site map that appears in the left Navigation pane throughout the application can be customized. Items can be added, moved, or removed. In addition, you can set items to appear only in the Outlook or Web interface, or to be restricted based on security settings. Two factors to consider before updating the site navigation are:

1. Many items in site navigation can be modified using security roles or entity settings. For example, custom entities can be moved between areas by changing the entity settings. These settings are much easier to maintain than are customizations made directly to the sitemap.xml file, so you should use these when possible.

2. Updating sitemap.xml only relates to the main site map. It does not affect the navigation menu that appears on forms. The form navigation menu can be updated directly while editing the form (see Chapter 17).

Two updates that organizations often want to make to the site navigation are to move unused functions out of the Workplace group and to create a new item that exposes SharePoint functionality through the Dynamics CRM user interface. We will be moving the Imports navigation link out of the My Work area, and we will create a new area called Admin for it. We will also be adding a new link called CRM SharePoint where users can share tips and tricks for working with CRM with each other. Use the following steps to move the first navigation item (creating a new group in the process) and to create a new navigation link.

Tip

If you want to add another Web site to your Dynamics CRM site map without having to update any XML files at all, you can create a dashboard with only an Iframe. In the Iframe, you can display any Web site you want to. This may not provide the exact user experience you are looking for, but it is a quick way to deliver some functionality without any coding know-how at all.

1. You need to create a Web resource to handle the icon for your new SharePoint menu item. This should be a 16x16 image in GIF, PNG, or JPG format. Make a note of the URL to the Web resource. We will be using a company logo and our file will be named: c5i_c5logo.

2. Export a solution that contains the site map. The site map can be found in the list of system configuration components under the heading Client Extensions. Under this heading, you add the Site Map to the solution that you will export. You can export any solution that contains the Site Map, but to make your job of editing the file simpler, we recommend you create a custom solution that contains only the Site Map. Check Chapter 16 if you need some insight on exporting solutions.

3. The solution is exported in a ZIP file containing three files. Make a copy of the original file in case you make changes that you wish to reverse. Extract the ZIP file to a separate directory. You will be working on the file named customizations.xml.

4. Open the file for editing. As mentioned above, we highly recommend a text editor that supports both formatted XML and XSD validation.

5. Begin by creating a new group to use for administrative functions. This group is a part of the Workplace area. To do this, enter the code in Figure 21.18. In the figure, I have collapsed some of the sections of XML to make finding the correct place to insert the code a bit easier (this is using Visual Web Developer). Below the figure is a description of the various settings that I have entered.

FIGURE 21.18

Adding a new group called "Admin" to the Workplace area

```
<Templates />
<SiteMap>
  <SiteMap>
    <Area Id="Workplace" ResourceId="Area_Workplace" ShowGroups="true" Icon="/_imgs/workplace_24x24.gif" DescriptionResourceId="Wor
      <Group Id="MyWork" ResourceId="Group_MyWork" DescriptionResourceId="My_Work_Descrip">...</Group>
      <Group Id="Customers" ResourceId="Group_Customers" DescriptionResourceId="Customers_Descr">...</Group>
      <Group Id="SFA" ResourceId="Area_Sales" IsProfile="true" DescriptionResourceId="Sales_Descripti">...</Group>
      <Group Id="MA" ResourceId="Area_Marketing" IsProfile="true" DescriptionResourceId="Marketing_Descr">...</Group>
      <Group Id="CS" ResourceId="Area_Service" IsProfile="true" DescriptionResourceId="Customer_Servic">...</Group>
      <Group Id="SM" ResourceId="Area_Scheduling" IsProfile="true" DescriptionResourceId="Scheduling_Grou">...</Group>
      <Group Id="Extensions" ResourceId="Group_Extension">...</Group>
      <Group Id="Admin" Title="Admin" IsProfile="true" >

      </Group>
    </Area>
    <Area Id="SFA" ResourceId="Area_Sales" Icon="/_imgs/sales_24x24.gif" DescriptionResourceId="Sales_Description">
```

- **Group:** Each group in the navigation pane (such as My Work and Customers) is defined by a group tag in the XML.

- **Id:** Each group must be assigned a unique ID. When creating a new group, ensure that the ID you use is not already used elsewhere.

- **Title:** This is the title that shows up in the user view. Existing groups do not use a title. If you want to change the title for an existing group, add the Title value to the XML code and give it whatever title you like.

- **IsProfile:** Setting this value to true will enable the user to use a check box in their profile to determine if this group will be visible to them or not. This is only valid for the Workplace area.

6. Now we move the Imports navigation from the My Work area down to the Admin area that you just created. Using the illustration in Figure 21.18, uncollapse the My Work section. Highlight everything beginning with '<SubArea Id="nav_import" icon' and the matching '</SubArea>' at the end of it. Cut this text. Scroll down to the section you just created and paste just below the line that begins, 'Group Id="Admin" Title'. Your code should now appear as below.

```
<Group Id="Admin" Title="Admin" IsProfile="true" >
<SubArea Id="nav_import" Icon="/_imgs/area/18_import.gif"
Entity="importfile" ResourceId="Homepage_Import"
DescriptionResourceId="Imports_Description"
AvailableOffline="false" GetStartedPanePath="Imports_Web_User_
Visor.html" GetStartedPanePathAdmin="Imports_Web_Admin_Visor.
html" GetStartedPanePathOutlook="Imports_Outlook_User_Visor.
html" GetStartedPanePathAdminOutlook="Imports_Outlook_Admin_
Visor.html">
<Privilege Entity="import" Privilege="Read" />
</SubArea>
</Group>
```

7. You can now create a new navigation link (in the XML file, these are tagged as SubAreas) for our SharePoint site dedicated to supporting Dynamics CRM 2011. In the XML file, make sure that the Group ID "MyWork" is expanded so you can see all

of the sub-areas below it. The last sub-area ID should be nav_news. Insert a blank line under this and enter the following code (this should be a single line of code, and you should update the URL to match a site you can access):

```
<SubArea Id="nav_spcrm" Url="https://sp.c5insight.com/it/default.
    aspx?isdlg=1" Title="SharePoint CRM" Icon="$webresource:c5i_
    c5logo"/>
```

- **Id:** This is the unique ID value that you are assigning to this sub-area.
- **Url:** This URL points to a Web site. If this were a Web resource (such as an HTML page or a Silverlight application), you would prefix the address with $webresource. In this case, we are calling a SharePoint site on our Internet, and we're directing it to show up as a dialog (stripping the normal SharePoint navigation elements from it).
- **Title:** This is what will show up in the Navigation pane as the name for our link.
- **Icon:** This is the icon that you loaded as a Web resource in Step 1. If you do not assign an icon, then a default icon will be assigned. Working with a default icon while in the design and development cycle is a good practice. However, before you put your changes into production, you should consider a custom icon to deliver a professional touch to the user experience.

Tip

When adding to the Site Map, or any XML file, a helpful starting point can be to copy and paste a section of XML that is similar to what you are trying to create. If you do this, keep in mind that ID elements must be unique and not all elements from the system navigation items are required for custom items.

8. Save your changes to the customizations.xml file. Copy the file into the original ZIP file that you exported from Dynamics CRM (this overwrites the original file, so make sure you keep your backup file available in case there are any problems).

9. Back in the Dynamics CRM interface, import your solution (see Chapter 16 if you need pointers on importing a solution). Be sure to publish all of your changes after you have completed the import.

To see all of the changes to the Site Map, you may need to click the refresh button in Dynamics CRM and then go to File ⇨ Options and select to show the new Admin group. Figure 21.19 shows the new site map with the SharePoint page visible inside of Dynamics CRM.

Tip

When making multiple changes to an XML file (such as a site map or a Ribbon menu) we recommend making a single change at a time and uploading the file. This will aid you in troubleshooting any mistakes that you make in modifying the XML.

Customizing the getting started pane

The getting started pane, the "helper" area that you see at the top of most CRM pages that can be minimized, can be customized to show a custom pane for a navigation item. This can be a helpful way to add training information related to a custom entity that you develop. The getting started pane can use HTML or Silverlight Web resources to display content. You also have the option of setting up different getting started panes for the Web client and for the Outlook client. In addition, you can have a different pane available for administrators if desired (for example, you could set up a pane that allows administrators to add more links to the getting started pane).

Note that a getting started pane cannot be added to items on the site map that use a URL (such as an outside Web site or an HTML Web resource). You can, however, create your own getting started area with those resources prior to integrating them into the Dynamics CRM site map.

Changing the getting started area is done in the same manner, and on the same file, as modifying the site map. You can embed one or more of the four attributes in the example below into the appropriate sub-area of the site map to customize the getting started area. For purposes of the sample code, we have created a custom getting started pane for the custom Plant entity that we created in Dynamics CRM. These attributes point to a Silverlight or HTML Web resource — so remember to create those resources and include the path to them along with the attribute.

```
<SubArea Id="c5i_plant" Entity="c5i_plant" GetStartedPanePath="$webre
    source:c5i_PlantGetStartedPane" GetStartedPanePathAdmin="$webreso
    urce:c5i_PlantGetStartedPane" GetStartedPanePathOutlook="$webreso
    urce:c5i_PlantGetStartedPane" GetStartedPanePathAdminOutlook="$we
    bresource:c5i_PlantGetStartedPane"/>
```

FIGURE 21.19

Updated Dynamics CRM navigation with embedded SharePoint site visible

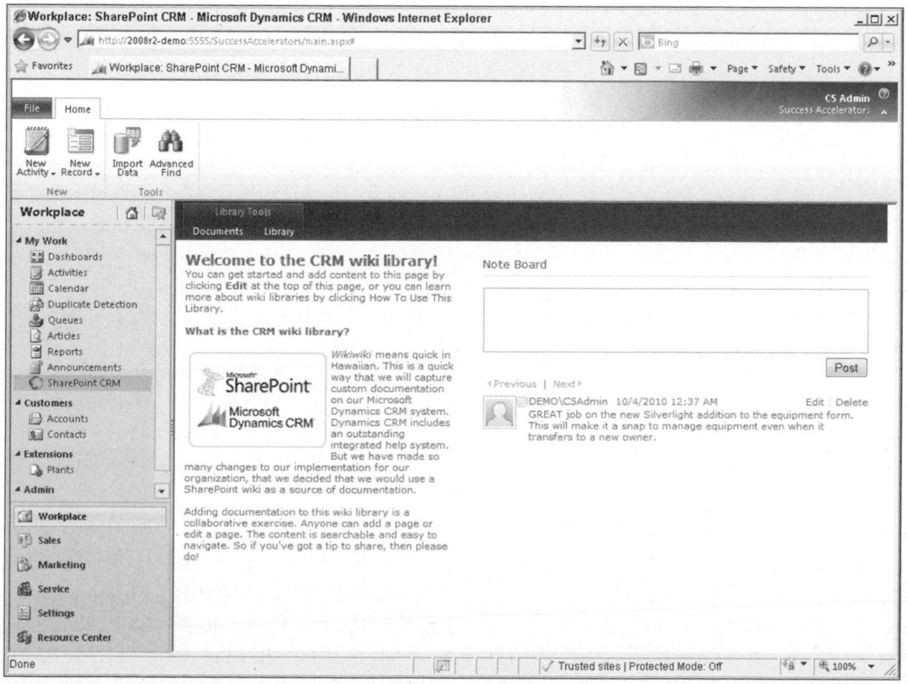

As you can see, we made four entries for the pane that all point to the same Web resource. If you want to present a different view to administrators, or to users of Outlook, you can change the Web resources accordingly. Using this approach, you can provide administrative access to revise the pane, and you can provide a different set of instructions to Outlook users and Web users.

Modifying the Ribbon menu

The Ribbon menus that appear throughout the application can be customized in a manner similar to the site map. Ribbon menus allow a large range of flexibility, but be forewarned that this flexibility carries with it some additional complexity in understanding the XML files. We will cover a couple of examples here, and you can also consult the SDK for a comprehensive overview. The basic options for extending Ribbon menus include:

- Adding new buttons or hiding existing buttons
- Adding custom groups (buttons within a section of a tab) to menus
- Updating ribbons at the entity, or application level
- Adding custom tabs to menus

Caution

Although it is possible to hide buttons from the ribbon menu, directly updating the menu is not always the appropriate option. For example, if you want to prohibit a user from sharing Account records with other users, you can set this up with the correct usage of security roles. Be sure to fully understand the requirements and the capabilities of Dynamics CRM before modifying the ribbon through the use of XML files.

The Ribbon menu is maintained in an XML file. To modify the Ribbon menu, you export the XML file, modify it using a text editor, and then reimport it into Dynamics CRM. In the procedure below, we add a custom button to the Account tab that will automatically launch a dialog. For purposes of this exercise, we will be adding a button to the ribbon for both the Account grid and the Account form. We will be adding it to the processes group to the right of the Dialog button.

1. There are a number of settings you will need to have on hand before you begin making edits to the menu. These settings will tell the menu where you want your button displayed, how it will behave, and what action you want it to perform. You'll need to gather this information from a file in the SDK directory:

   ```
   SDK\SampleCode\CS\Client\Ribbon\ExportRibbonXml\ExportedRibbonXml.
       For this exercise, we will be looking at the accountribbon.xml
       file. Open this file (ideally in an XML editor).
   ```

2. In the above referenced file, we will be looking for the IDs in the process section (which, although it is named process in the user interface, is actually named workflow in the XML file). When you initially open the XML file to peruse it for the proper IDs, it may look a little intimidating. You can, however, expand and collapse sections on the left-hand side of the screen (assuming you are using the Visual Studio or similar editor) to find just the section that you're looking for. In Figure 21.20 I have found the appropriate sections and left them expanded so you can see them. The IDs that we are looking for are:

- Template attribute value for the form and homepage workflow group: Mscrm. Templates.Flexible

- Workflow Control ID in the homepage: Mscrm.HomepageGrid.account.MainTab. Workflow.Controls (you will add ._children to this)

- Workflow Control ID in the form page: Mscrm.Form.account.MainTab.Workflow. Controls(you will add ._children to this)

FIGURE 21.20

The accountribbon.xml file in Visual Studio / Visual Web Developer Express

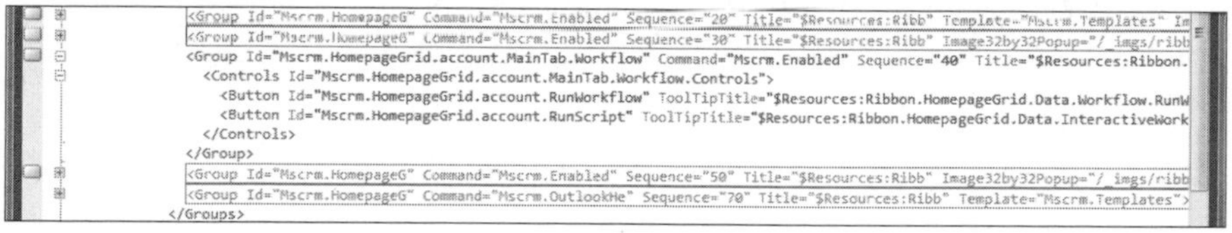

3. For our project, we want to place our button to the right of the Dialog button (called RunScript in the XML) that is in the workflow group of the ribbon menu. So you will need to find the sequence number for that button. Still in the accountribbon.xml file, you'll need to search for button sequence number. It's in the same section that you found the IDs in, just a bit farther down.

- The sequence number for the homepage: 50

- The sequence number for the form: 25

4. Also still in the accountribbon.xml file, you should take note of the TemplateAlias value for other controls in the group. This is on the same line as the sequence numbers that you found in Step 6. Note that different sizes of buttons use different templates. Large buttons use template "o1" and small buttons use template "o2." Note that the leading character is a lowercase letter O (not a zero). You are done with the accountribbon.xml file now — you can safely close it.

5. Now you need to create the Web resources required for your button. In the previous section, we created a JScript Web resource that we will use. You'll also need to create a 16x16 and 32x32 image to use in the button (these can be in any of the graphics formats supported in the Web resources area). Make a note of the URL for your image files and for the JScript resource that you created (replacing the full path with the $webresource attribute). Our files are as follows (yours will vary depending on what you named them):

- JScript: $webresource:c5i_CollectionsDialog (note that we made changes to the code to include the Dialog GUID so we don't have to pass it in from the ribbon menu)

- Small (16x16) Icon: $webresource:c5i_BrokenHeartSmall

- Large (32x32) Icon: $webresource:c5i_BrokenHeartLarge

6. The next step is to export a solution that contains the Account entity (or whichever entity you want to customize the ribbon for). You can export any solution that contains the Account entity, but to make your job of editing the file simpler, we recommend you create a custom solution that contains only the Account entity. Check Chapter 16 if you need some insight on exporting solutions.

7. The solution will be exported in a ZIP file containing three files. Extract the ZIP file to a separate directory. You will be working on the file named customizations.xml.

8. Open the file for editing. As mentioned above, we highly recommend a text editor that supports both formatted XML and XSD validation. For more information on how to configure Visual Web Developer Express, see the SDK (search for the topic Exporting, Preparing to Edit, and Importing the Ribbon).

9. Locate the node called RibbonDiffXml. All of your edits will be made to this node.

10. The finalized RibbonDiffXml node will contain quite a bit of additional code (a full copy of the code can be found on the Website `www.dynamicscrmbible.com`). Creating the code requires modifying the following four sections of the XML file:

   - The RuleDefinitions node defines when the buttons will be displayed and any rules related to disabling the buttons under certain circumstances. The rules we set here ensure that the button does not appear on a new record until it has been saved, that the buttons only appear in the Web version of Dynamics CRM (not Outlook), and that only one record can have the button applied to it at a time.

   - The LocLabels node defines how the buttons will be labeled and what tooltip will be presented when the user hovers over the button. If you are using a multilingual configuration, then you can set up labels for each installed language.

   - The CommandDefinitions node groups together and enables multiple RuleDefintions. It also points to the action (our JScript file) that should be performed.

   - The CustomActions node defines the icons, location, and sequence of the buttons. You use the values you obtained in earlier steps of this procedure to plug into this node.

The above instructions are for updating a ribbon for an entity. You can follow a similar procedure to update an application ribbon. For application ribbons, you will export a solution that contains the Application Ribbon under the Client Extensions component. Again, the SDK offers a comprehensive reference guide to the Ribbon menus that you should use when making any modifications.

Updating chart XML

In other chapters, we discussed designing charts by using the controls built into the user interface in Dynamics CRM. You can also export the chart XML and make changes to charts beyond what can be accomplished in the user interface. Once completed, you can reimport your charts to display the new functionality. Charts can be created (or modified) to add a second axis to a chart, create a new chart type (such as a doughnut), or change the formatting and coloring of a chart.

To export the XML for a chart, begin by navigating to the entity with the chart you wish to update. Be sure that the chart is displayed next to the grid. Next, click the view tab in the ribbon menu and click the Export Chart button. Save the XML to your desktop and open it in an XML editor. Figure 21.21 illustrates a pie chart that was created in Dynamics CRM that was then exported and transformed into a doughnut chart.

Tip

Some of the charts included with Dynamics CRM include functionality that cannot be re-created directly through the user interface. You can export these charts and review the XML to get an idea of the possibilities.

Tip

Charts in Dynamics CRM use the ASP.NET charting controls included in the .NET framework. You can download or view the documentation for this online to give you some ideas of how you can further customize the charts.

FIGURE 21.21

A doughnut chart created by updating the chart XML file

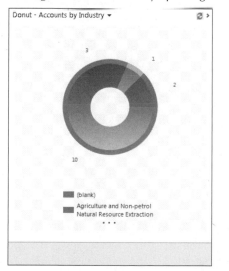

Updating process XAML

The Dynamics CRM process engine is built using the Microsoft Windows Workflow Foundation. This is the same toolset that is used to manage processes in SharePoint and to build processes using the .NET development platform. Because processes use this foundation, you can export them into a file (called a XAML file) and import them into .NET. Once they have been imported into .NET, you can make additional customizations to them that cannot be made directly within the Dynamics CRM user interface. This opens up additional functions for use within your processes. Figure 21.22 is an example of a workflow that was exported from Dynamics CRM and opened in .NET.

Caution

Processes that have been modified in .NET cannot be imported into Dynamics CRM Online at the time of this writing.

FIGURE 21.22

Modifying a process using Visual Studio .NET

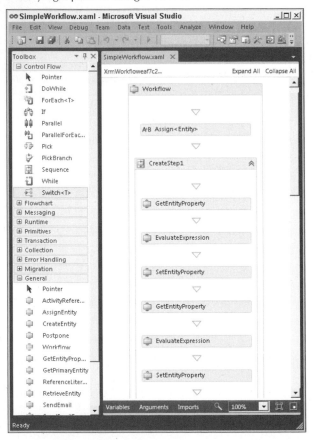

Summary

In this chapter, we have presented an overview of the possibilities available to you through client-side customizations. With all of the example code provided, we have only just scratched the surface of the possibilities. If you want to go deeper with coding, then once you are comfortable with the concepts in this chapter, spend some time reviewing the SDK. You will also benefit from doing some Web searches on "Dynamics CRM JScript" and similar terms.

If, on the other hand, your preference is to steer clear of writing code, then you should at least be familiar with the concepts presented in this chapter. As a system customizer, you can align yourself with qualified developers and have them write code for you while you focus on the design components of the Dynamics CRM user interface. By understanding this chapter (and the next) you will know what kind of development options are available and the kind of code to suggest to your developer.

When using all of the different client-side customization options available, there is literally a limitless range of functions that you can configure Dynamics CRM to deliver. When combined with other extension possibilities through server-side customization (covered in the next chapter) and SharePoint integration, organizations can meet virtually all of their data management and business process automation needs.

Working with Server-Side Customizations

A s previous chapters show, Microsoft has released an incredibly powerful and extensible platform that can be tailored to an endless variety of business processes through GUI-based configuration tools and client-side techniques familiar to many Web technologists. The company has also incorporated a robust and flexible server-side programming architecture, enabling developers to tap into the power of the Dynamics CRM platform in order to supplement the system's functionality or build entirely new functionality in a supportable and scalable manner. The goal of this chapter is to introduce you to the concepts and techniques used to extend the functionality of the Dynamics CRM platform with server-side technologies.

As far back as version 3.0, Dynamics CRM started to emerge as a compelling platform for applications that had little to do with traditional customer relationship management. Still, many developers were stymied by some of the quirks of developing with Dynamics CRM. For example, some of the system's custom data types didn't behave the same way as their standard .NET counterparts. The many little quirks compounded together sometimes made for a steep and unpredictable learning curve.

With version 4.0 the idea of XRM really took hold. The application programming interface (API) and the Software Development Kit (SDK) had matured significantly. New and improved features, such as an improved plug-in model, a new Asynchronous Service, and advances in leveraging the .NET Framework, among other improvements, made it possible to build custom line-of-business applications with advanced functionality in a fraction of the time that it would take to develop them from scratch.

Cross-Reference

An exploration of XRM — also known as eXtended Relationship Management — is covered in Chapter 27, including some example scenarios that combine many of the customization techniques described in this and other chapters.

With the release of Microsoft Dynamics CRM 2011, Microsoft has made tremendous strides toward providing a standards-based development experience on a world-class, powerful platform. Microsoft refers to the platform architecture and capabilities in Dynamics CRM as the XRM platform to distinguish it from the customer relationship management functionality that has been the hallmark of the application. This distinction provides an important insight into the development model for Dynamics CRM.

In addition to expanding upon its ability to leverage newer versions of the underlying technologies such as Visual Studio 2010, the .NET 4.0 Framework, Silverlight, LINQ, and the Windows Workflow Foundation, Microsoft Dynamics CRM 2011 has also been significantly re-architected to use newly emerging technologies such as OData and Azure cloud services. Microsoft's aim with this redesign of the platform was to make it possible to maintain parity between the application's codebase regardless of where it is installed. Whether hosted in the cloud (Microsoft Dynamics CRM Online or partner-hosted) or installed on your company's servers, this version of Dynamics CRM was built to provide programmers with as similar a development experience as possible across all deployment models.

With these improvements to the development experience, ISVs (Integrated Software Vendors), Microsoft partners, and .NET developers can use their existing development skills to quickly begin extending Dynamics CRM.

Note

To successfully create and deploy server-side customizations requires an understanding of .NET development languages such as Visual C#, as well as familiarity with common Microsoft server technologies, tools, and development practices. In addition to this chapter, read the Microsoft Dynamics CRM SDK, a free download, to understand how these technologies can be used in the context of Dynamics CRM. The SDK contains many useful tools, resources, samples, and guides for developing server-side customizations.

Becoming Familiar with Dynamics CRM's Architecture and Development Model

Dynamics CRM is built on Microsoft's .NET development framework, which provides base classes, utilities, and a common language runtime. Microsoft Dynamics CRM 2011 runs on version 4 of the .NET Framework, leveraging many of the improvements in its core components such as the Windows Communication Foundation and Windows Workflow Foundation, and data services. The .NET Framework 4 includes improved support for the latest technologies for rich Web applications like RESTful data operations, improved performance, and enhanced developer experiences.

Cross-Reference

Chapter 20 contains a comprehensive introduction to the SDK, as well as instructions for setting up a development environment. You can also find a lot of useful information, extensions, and code samples by visiting the Microsoft Dynamics CRM Developer Forum, Codeplex (Microsoft's open-source project site), and the Microsoft Dynamics CRM Team Blog. See Appendix B for links to these and other developer resources.

Some of the changes that will be immediately apparent to developers who have worked with previous versions of Dynamics CRM are:

- The Metadata and CRMService Web services interfaces have been combined into one Web service, the IOrganizationService. This enables a simpler and more streamlined interface to speed development, simplify troubleshooting, and improve performance.

- A new assembly that you can reference in your solutions, Microsoft.Xrm.Sdk.dll, provides the main access to the IOrganizationService. Microsoft.Xrm.Sdk provides the primary classes that developers will use to leverage the security, metadata, data, and services operations within Dynamics CRM.

- Where possible, Dynamics CRM data types have been replaced with native .NET data types (see the "New data types in Microsoft Dynamics CRM 2011" sidebar).

Exploring the Extensibility Architecture

In addition to making use of the improved .NET framework components, Dynamics CRM's own extensibility has been redesigned to provide a more standards-based development experience, relying heavily on the Windows Communication Foundation (see the "What is WCF?" sidebar). The system uses a state-of-the-art service-oriented application (SOA) architecture, shown in Figure 22.1, with a synchronous and asynchronous services platform at its core, accessed via a Web services API.

Dynamics CRM's extensible architecture consists of the following components:

- **Web Services API.** The Web services interface includes three distinct APIs: the Deployment Web service, the Discovery Web service and the IOrganization Web service.

- **Microsoft.Xrm.Sdk and the CrmSvcUtil.exe.** The Xrm.Sdk assembly provides the platform classes for custom code, and the CRM Service Utility is used to generate classes specific to customized metadata.

- **Event Framework.** An event pipeline framework where messages sent through the API can be sent to custom plug-ins, including the Azure Service Bus, or custom workflow assemblies.

- **Platform Services.** The platform provides synchronous and asynchronous processes; a sandbox service that provides isolation and the ability to run custom plug-ins on Dynamics CRM Online.

FIGURE 22.1

Dynamics CRM's architecture provides a robust development model that leverages a Web services API to enable developers to extend the platform's functionality and integrate with custom applications.

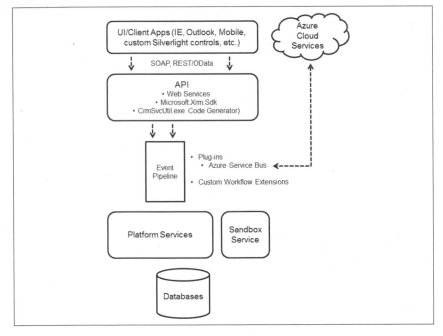

New Data Types in Microsoft Dynamics CRM 2011

Microsoft Dynamics CRM 2011 has updated attribute data types, replacing custom CRM types with native .NET data types where possible. Removing this layer of abstraction makes it easier for .NET developers new to Dynamics CRM to begin programming, as well as provides a minor performance improvement. Additionally, changes in the API such as the new Entity class have resulted in several updated data types that are specific to Dynamics CRM.

Dynamics CRM 4.0 Data Types Replaced by Native .NET Data Types

4.0 Data Type	2011 Data Type
CrmBoolean	System.Boolean or bool
CrmDateTime	System.DateTime
CrmDecimal	System.Decimal or decimal
CrmFloat	System.Double or double
CrmNumber	System.Integer or int
Key or UniqueIdentifier	System.Guid

Updated Data Types

4.0 data type	2011 Data Type
DynamicEntity	EntityCollection
activityparty	EntityCollection or ActivityParty
Customer, Lookup, and Owner	EntityReference
CrmMoney	Money
Picklist	OptionSetValue
Status	OptionSetValue or int

In addition to the changes to data types, Microsoft Dynamics CRM 2011 also introduces new, separate formatted values for some attribute types. For example, an int attribute such as the duration field in a contract might contain a value of 1000. The formatted value — which could be addressed like this in custom code: (contractEntity.FormattedValues["duration"]) — would return the value with the comma: 1,000.

Numerous options are available for tapping into these pieces of the platform, either as part of the platform operations or from custom client applications:

- **SOAP.** SOAP calls are the primary method that the application layer and clients interact with the platform layer. SOAP stands for Simple Object Access Protocol and is the standard protocol for interacting with Web services.

- **REST.** In Microsoft Dynamics CRM 2011 there is a new REST endpoint that uses the OData protocol to interact with data and platform operations. OData is an emerging open standard syntax for working with data via strings passed in a URL to the REST endpoint.

- **Plug-ins.** Plug-ins are custom assemblies (DLL files) that are registered with the Dynamics CRM platform, and which essentially act as part of the platform. Plug-ins can be fired on a wide variety of messages. As the message traverses the event pipeline, the custom logic is fired.

- **Azure AppFabric.** Azure, Microsoft's cloud-based computing platform, provides application hosting and storage, SQL database services, and a processing platform that can be used to host highly scalable applications. Dynamics CRM has built-in support for interacting with Azure via Azure's AppFabric, the service that provides access control and messaging between applications.

- **Custom workflow extensions.** Developers can create custom assemblies to extend the functionality of the built-in process and workflow tools, and register these with the Dynamics CRM platform. Custom workflow assemblies are not supported in Dynamics CRM Online.

What Is WCF?

The Windows Communication Foundation was released with version 3.0 of the .NET Framework. Its purpose was to simplify the connection between Web services endpoints by providing a standard set of components to handle the binding between clients and services. WCF is the key element in Microsoft's framework for building service-oriented applications.

Put simply, a service-oriented application (SOA) is designed to take advantage of the processing, logic and data from one or more services, whether on the Web, a server, or a client device. Service-oriented applications typically use the channels, protocols, and languages of the Web. In other words, they use Web services to exchange information.

In order for these sometimes disparate services to work together, the client and service components need to know three things: 1) where to find one another; 2) how to talk to one another; and 3) what type of communication is desired and allowed. These three items are often referred to as the ABCs of service-oriented applications: the Address, the Binding, and the Contract.

SOA architecture design is intended to enable interoperability between different systems, including different operating systems, different programming languages, and different protocols. This approach to application design provides many benefits, but it can also present developers with incredible complexity. WCF helps to overcome this complexity by providing developers with an extensible library of .NET classes that enable interoperable Web services, messaging communications, and data access — essentially wrapping up the underlying .NET technologies.

In Microsoft Dynamics CRM 2011, the contract that WCF accesses is the IOrganizationService, the new Web service that combines the metadata and data in the organization deployment.

See Appendix B for links to more information about WCF.

Developing Server-Side Extensions for Different Deployment Scenarios

There are a number of different options for adding server-side code to your Dynamics CRM system, depending on where your code will be deployed, when it will be triggered, and what its intended function is. Custom code can be stored in the Dynamics CRM database, on the server disk, as part of the server's global assembly cache (GAC), or even in the cloud. In some cases, server-side extensions can be configured to work even when a user is using the Outlook client in offline mode. And, with Microsoft Dynamics CRM 2011, server-side code can now be used with Microsoft's hosted Dynamics CRM Online. This section explores these deployment options in detail.

Deciding where to store your custom server-side code

Microsoft has provided a great deal of flexibility to developers on where custom server-side plug-ins can be stored. When registering plug-ins to the platform, developers are provided with three options for storing the plug-in assemblies:

- **Database:** This is the preferred and default location for plug-in assemblies. When a plug-in is stored in the database, the platform can synchronize the code to client applications, and the plug-in will be replicated across all the SQL Servers in the deployment. This is the only option for Dynamics CRM Online.

- **The server disk:** This option is generally used during development to simplify debugging. Deploying custom assemblies to the disk means that the assemblies will not be copied to other servers in the deployment automatically.

- **The server's global assembly cache (GAC):** Typically, plug-in assemblies are not registered to the GAC. However, if your custom code has dependencies on other assemblies, the other assemblies must be copied to the GAC (located at `C:\ Windows\assembly`).

Deploying code for offline use

Because plug-ins can be registered to the database, they can also synchronize to the Outlook client and perform their functions even when the Outlook client is offline. Plug-ins can be registered to run online, offline, or both. However, care must be taken when creating a plug-in that will be registered to run offline to ensure that it does not get triggered a second time when the client synchronizes with the server. When the Outlook client is brought back online, the synchronization process plays back the changes that were made offline, potentially causing plug-ins to fire on the server that have already fired on the offline client. To avoid this, your code can check two properties:

- IsExecutingOffline: This is a property of the ExecutionContext method which can be used to see if the code is being called while offline.

- IsOfflinePlayback: This property can be used to check if code has already run offline to avoid running it again during playback.

Microsoft Dynamics CRM 2011 has simplified the process of adding custom code that will run on the client by incorporating Web resources that can be called from events on the application's forms. However, these Web resources are limited to client technologies like HTML and JavaScript, and cannot be used to store server-side code like ASPX pages. Version 4.0 introduced the ISV folder in the Dynamics CRM Web site root on both the server and the offline client. The ISV folder is a convenient place to store application files and resources so they can run in the context of Dynamics CRM's security and processes.

The ISV folder is still available in the latest version of Dynamics CRM, though it is being deprecated. However, it is still a favorite option for developers who wish to deploy server technologies to offline clients. The ISV folder on the offline client is not automatically synchronized with its server counterpart, so developers must create an installation or updating process to place application files in offline clients. The default location of the folder for offline clients is `<drive>:\Program Files\Microsoft Dynamics CRM \Client\ res\web\ISV`. Custom assemblies can be placed in the bin folder on the client, located at `<drive>:\Program Files\Microsoft Dynamics CRM\Client\res\web\bin`.

One of the reasons that the ISV folder is being deprecated is that Microsoft is encouraging greater use of new technologies such as Azure cloud services. Azure is Microsoft's cloud computing platform. Using Azure to host ISV applications allows Microsoft to maintain parity between codebases for the different deployment models, since both on-premise and hosted deployments can leverage Azure-hosted applications. For offline use, Azure has recently introduced a client synchronization framework, Azure Data Sync, that incorporates the Sync Framework to provide an experience with Azure databases and applications that is similar to working with Outlook in offline cached mode. Potentially, developers could use Azure Data Sync to create cloud-based, integrated applications that work both online and offline, and therefore can interact with Dynamics CRM clients while offline.

Comparing the sandbox service to non-isolated mode

As Microsoft has moved to make their hosted Dynamics CRM Online offering more extensible, and in keeping with the goal of maintaining parity between the codebase for different deployment models, the company has incorporated a new, isolated processing service called the sandbox service.

The sandbox service enables custom server-side plug-ins to be deployed to Dynamics CRM Online, essentially allowing custom code to become part of the platform, without the risk of interfering with other organizations' deployments. Partners who offer hosted Dynamics CRM may also limit their customers to the isolated sandbox service in order to offer server-side extensibility in a multitenant environment.

When a plug-in is registered in the sandbox service it runs in an isolated mode, its access to system files, network resources, and machine registries is restricted. Additionally, interactions with external services, such as an application or database, rely on using the Azure AppFabric Service Bus to handle communication between the isolated plug-in and the external service.

The isolation of custom code in the sandbox service also means that custom plug-ins cannot write to log files. Therefore, the platform handles the recording of each execution of a plug-in (whether sandboxed or non-isolated) in a table in the database called PluginTypeStatistic Base. There are also views (PluginTypeStatistic and FilteredPluginTypeStatistic) provided that can be read with code (for Dynamics CRM Online) or in a report (for on-premises deployments). A summary of the plug-in's outcome, failure rate, and other statistics is recorded in the statistic record.

Tip
The sandbox service is only used for running plug-ins in isolation. For on-premises deployments of Dynamics CRM, if you do not wish to run custom code in an isolated fashion, you can disable the sandbox service on the Dynamics CRM server. The service can be disabled from the Services snap-in.

Creating plug-ins for the sandbox

Because the sandbox service was created to enable server-side code to run in Dynamics CRM Online, there are certain requirements for how sandbox plug-ins must be designed as compared to non-isolated plug-ins:

- They must use the current API. Sandboxed plug-ins can only use the 2011 version of the Dynamics CRM interface. The older APIs which are included in Dynamics CRM to support backwards compatibility are not supported in assemblies running in the sandbox service.

- Strong-naming. Any assemblies that will be registered in the sandbox must be strong-named. Strong-naming an assembly ensures that the assembly contains a unique name made up of the assembly's name, version number, and a public key. Microsoft will maintain a list of untrusted publishers for Dynamics CRM Online and check the strong-name of a custom assembly against this list. If the public key is on this list, the assembly cannot be registered to Dynamics CRM Online.

Setting up users to deploy plug-ins

Certain privileges are required in order to register plug-ins with Dynamics CRM. These privileges vary slightly depending on whether the plug-in will be registered in the isolated sandbox service or in a non-isolated mode.

To register a plug-in in either mode, users must have create privileges on the entities in the following list (see Figure 22.2). The System Administrator and System Customizer roles contain these privileges by default.

- Plug-in Assembly
- Plug-in Type
- Sdk Message Processing Step
- Sdk Message Processing Step Image
- Sdk Message Processing Step Secure Configuration

In order to register a plug-in to run in non-isolated mode, the user must also be a Deployment Administrator. The user account that was used to install Dynamics CRM is automatically created as a Deployment Administrator and can therefore run the Deployment Manager in order to add other Deployment Administrator users. (There is no way to set up a user as a Deployment Administrator within the Dynamics CRM interface.)

If a user who is not a Deployment Administrator attempts to register a non-isolated plug-in, an error is thrown stating that the user does not have the privileges required to complete a create operation on an SDK entity.

Users registering sandboxed plug-ins do not need to be Deployment Administrators, because this would obviate the purpose of the sandbox service, which is to enable server-side code to be deployed to Dynamics CRM Online. However, they must have the privileges listed above.

FIGURE 22.2

In order to register a plug-in, a user's security role must have certain privileges.

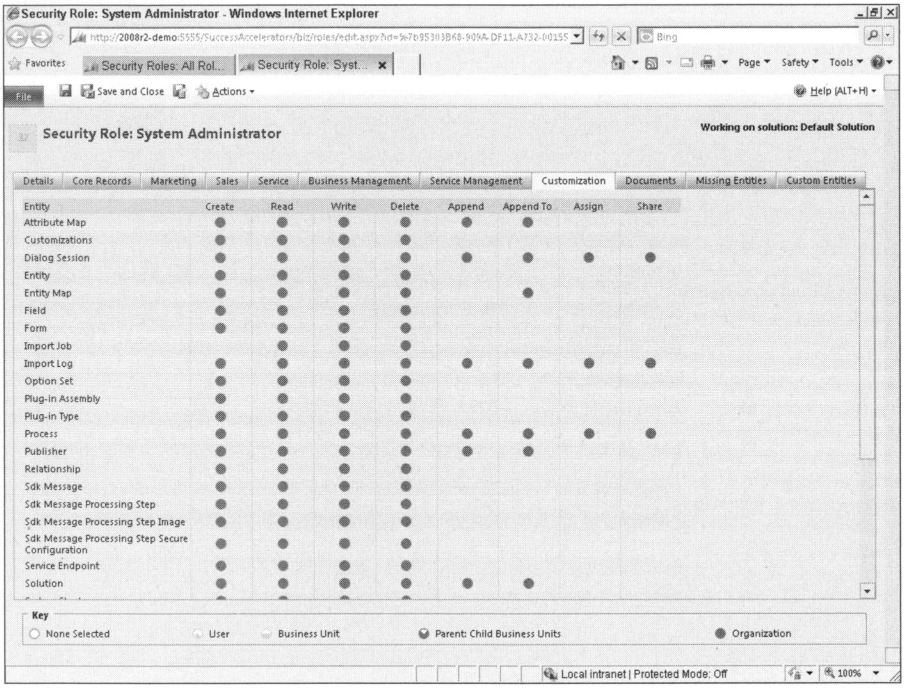

Interfacing with Dynamics CRM

The primary means of interfacing with the Dynamics CRM platform is through SOAP messages passed from the client application to the Web services. However, unlike previous versions that used a dynamically generated WSDL as the endpoint, Microsoft Dynamics CRM 2011 incorporates a new development model. The WSDL endpoint is still available for backwards compatibility and for use from non-.NET applications, but applications using this endpoint will not be able to leverage new functionality.

Understanding the Web services

There are three main Web services that developers can use to extend the Dynamics CRM platform:

- **Deployment Web service:** The deployment Web service provides an interface to the services and operations that Deployment Administrators can use to create or import organizations, enable and disable organizations, add deployment administrators, configure internet-facing deployment and claims-based authentication, and other operations.

- **Discovery Web service:** The discovery Web service helps to identify the organization that a developer's custom code will be working with. The discovery service identifies the organizations that are available in a deployment.

- **IOrganizationService:** The main interface in Microsoft Dynamics CRM 2011 is the IOrganizationService. This is the new, combined Web service endpoint that includes both the data and metadata that in previous versions were accessed through the CrmService and the CrmMetadataService, respectively. The combined interface provides a more streamlined development experience and faster response when the service is instantiated.

In addition to using SOAP messages against these Web services, the new WCF interface also enables a REST interface, making it easier to create AJAX or Silverlight client applications that interact with the Dynamics CRM Web services.

Accessing the Web services

The primary API under the new development model is a WCF interface that introduces the concepts of late-bound and early-bound programming. Late-bound programming is loosely typed and is an approach that can be used for plug-ins and extensions that do not depend on the specifics of an organization's data model. For example, a plug-in may be developed that performs certain business logic on the create event of any entity against which it is registered. Early-bound programming, on the other hand, means that the developer knows the entity and attribute names within an organization, and the code references these specifically.

For late-bound development, Microsoft Dynamics CRM 2011 provides the Microsoft.Xrm.Sdk and the Microsoft.Crm.Sdk assemblies. Adding references to these assemblies in your custom code provides access to all the classes needed to work with the Dynamics CRM platform in a late-bound fashion.

To create an organization-specific endpoint that includes the details of customizations for early-bound development, Microsoft has provided the CRM Service Utility, which is used to generate an output file that can be referenced in custom code. Referencing this output file enables IntelliSense and creates a class for each system and custom entity in the organization. The utility is run from a command line with parameters specifying the organization name and the desired name of the output file.

To run the CRM Service Utility for an on-premises deployment, follow the steps below. For a Dynamics CRM Online organization or an IFD organization, refer to the SDK for the correct URL format for Step 3.

1. The CrmSvcUtil.exe and the Microsoft.Xrm.Sdk.dll files must be in the same folder. They are available with the Microsoft Dynamics CRM 2011 SDK. The CrmSvcUtil.exe file is in the /Tools/CodeGen folder in the folder where you installed the SDK. Copy the Microsoft.Xrm.Sdk.dll from the SDK's Bin folder to the same folder.

2. Open a command prompt and navigate to the folder where the two files are located.

3. Run this command, replacing the items in brackets with values appropriate for your deployment:

```
CrmSvcUtil.exe /url:http://[crmserver]/[OrgName]/XrmServices/2011/
    Organization.svc /org:[OrgName] /out:[ClassFileName].cs /
    username:[user] /password:[password] /domain:[domain]
```

4. Depending on the amount of customization in your organization, the utility may take several minutes to run. When it is finished, a message will appear confirming that the code was written to the file specified.

5. To use the classes in a solution, copy the output file to the project folder, and launch Visual Studio. In Visual Studio, right-click the solution name in the Solution Explorer panel and choose Add ⇨ Existing Item. Select the class file and click Add.

Plugging-in to the Platform

Plug-ins are one of the primary ways the platform is extended. They are deep custom extensions that essentially run as part of the Dynamics CRM platform. Microsoft Dynamics CRM 2011 introduces a number of improvements to plug-in architecture:

- **Sandbox service.** As discussed earlier in this chapter, because plug-ins run in the same process context as the platform and, prior to the release of Microsoft Dynamics CRM 2011, there was no separation between the custom code and the core operations of the platform, they were unable to run on Dynamics CRM Online. The new sandbox service resolves this dilemma, opening the potential for platform extension to a far greater audience.

- **Transaction participation.** In previous versions, plug-ins could not participate in database transactions, meaning that if the custom code failed at some point, operations that had already been performed were committed and the entire transaction could not be rolled back. Now, developers can group operations to take advantage of transaction rollback in case of a failure. The concepts of the Parent and Child Pipelines are also deprecated.

- **Query enhancements.** Query operations have been enhanced in Dynamics CRM. Developers can now query both an entity and records related to it, returning attributes from both entities. The resulting records can be sorted by columns from the related entities.

- **Entity class replaces DynamicEntity.** The DynamicEntity class is being deprecated and replaced with the new Entity class. Custom classes inherit from the Entity class, making it possible to have greater uniformity across your code.

- **Enhanced LINQ provider.** Microsoft Dynamics CRM 2011 includes an improved and expanded version of the LINQ provider that was introduced in an update to the version 4.0 SDK. LINQ queries are automatically converted by the platform into Dynamics CRM-specific query expressions. This means that developers can create LINQ queries with standard types in their custom code, accessing WCF Data Services.

- **Tracing.** Microsoft Dynamics CRM 2011 now includes a diagnostic tracing functionality (the ITracingService interface) that can be incorporated into plug-in code to provide exception detail.

Looking at how Dynamics CRM incorporates plug-ins

Plug-ins participate in the platform operations of Dynamics CRM. The pipeline is organization specific. Plug-in operations follow this general pattern:

1. A client application sends a message to the Dynamics CRM Web services interface.

2. The message raises an event such as Create, Assign, or Retrieve.

3. This message creates an event pipeline, which consists of four stages.

4. Plug-in code is registered to fire on one of these stages. It can run synchronously or asynchronously.

5. The plug-in uses the IPlugin interface in the Microsoft.Xrm.Sdk assembly to access the Dynamics CRM API.

Message support for plug-ins

Dynamics CRM's API supports a large number of messages. Messages that are frequently used in plug-ins include:

- Assign
- Create
- Delete
- Execute
- Retrieve
- RetrieveMultiple
- Send
- SetState
- Update

The complete list of messages that can raise the event pipeline is included in an Excel file that comes with the SDK. Each entity has its own implementation of the messages, so, for example, a plug-in might be registered on the Update of the Contact entity. Update messages for other entities would not trigger the plug-in.

Event pipeline stages

There are four stages in the event pipeline:

- Pre-Stage (Outside Transaction)
- Pre-Stage (Inside Transaction)

- Post-Stage (Inside Transaction)
- Post-Stage (Outside Transaction)

These stages allow plug-in operations to occur either before or after the transaction, or as part of the transaction. Pre-Stage events trigger the plug-in code before the operation hits the platform, and Post-Stage plug-ins are fired after the operation. For example, a Pre-Stage plug-in that is fired on the Create message of an Account entity would carry out its custom business logic before the Account record is actually created in the platform.

Synchronous and asynchronous execution modes

Plug-ins that are registered to run synchronously will execute along with the core platform operation. The operation will not be considered complete until the synchronous plug-in is completed. Plug-ins that are registered for asynchronous execution are queued and processed by the Asynchronous Service. The platform operation completes regardless of the state of the plug-in operation.

Walking through a sample plug-in

The SDK contains many code samples and a few plug-in examples. The following section walks through the steps involved in creating a simple plug-in using code snippets and examples based on examples from the SDK. The code in this section will create a plug-in that will be registered to fire when an account is created. When that happens, a task is created to remind the user to follow up with the account. (The sample code for this plug-in is available in the Dynamics CRM SDK.)

Cross-Reference

Chapter 20 provides instructions for acquiring the SDK and setting up a development environment, including the tools needed to follow the steps in this section.

1. Launch Visual Studio 2010.

2. On the Start Page, click the link to create a new project. In the New Project dialog (see Figure 22.3), select Visual C# and click on the Class Library project template. Make sure the project template is set to use the .NET Framework 4. Name the project CRMBiblePlugin and set a location for it to be stored. Click OK.

3. Add a reference to the required assemblies (Microsoft.Xrm.Sdk, System. ServiceModel, and System.Runtime.Serialization). In the Solution Explorer in Visual Studio, right-click on References and select the Add Reference... option.

4. In the Add Reference dialog box, click on the Browse tab and navigate to the bin folder under the SDK installation path (see Figure 22.4). Select the Microsoft.Xrm. Sdk.dll application extension and click OK. Repeat this step to add a reference to the System.ServiceModel and System.Runtime.Serialization assemblies, which are part of the .NET Framework 4 and are responsible for implementing WCF classes.

FIGURE 22.3

Use the project templates in Visual Studio to start building a plug-in for Dynamics CRM. This example starts with a C# Class Library project template.

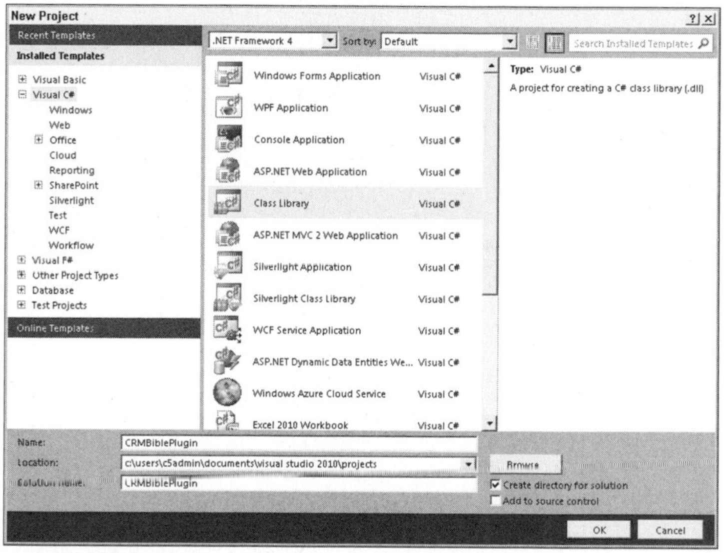

FIGURE 22.4

Adding a reference to the Microsoft.Xrm.Sdk.dll assembly, located in the bin folder of the SDK, and the .NET assembly System.ServiceModel

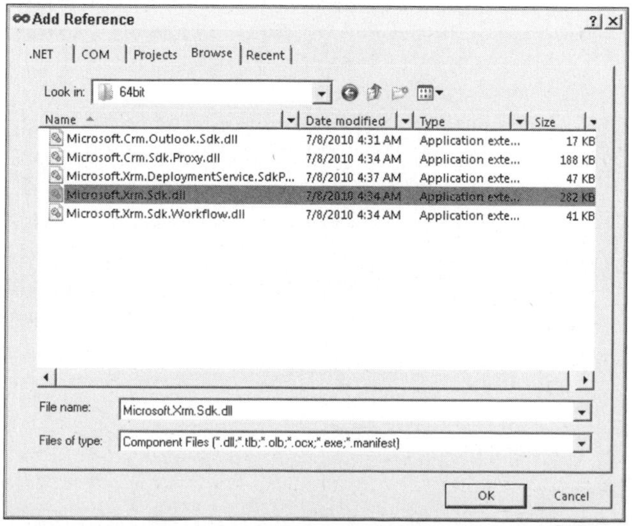

5. In the Class1.cs file, add a using directive for the System.ServiceModel and the Microsoft.Xrm.Sdk.

6. Next, call the IPlugin interface by adding ": IPlugin" after Class1 public class. The Class1.cs file should look like this after you have completed this step:

```csharp
using System;
using System.Collections.Generic;
using System.Linq;
using System.Text;
using System.ServiceModel;
using Microsoft.Xrm.Sdk;

namespace CRMBiblePlugin
{
    public class Class1: IPlugin
    {
    }
}
```

7. We are now ready to add our custom business logic from the SDK sample. Inside the IPlugin interface, type the following code:

```csharp
public void Execute(IServiceProvider serviceProvider)
        {
            IPluginExecutionContext context =
    (IPluginExecutionContext)serviceProvider.GetService(typeof(IPlu
ginExecutionContext));
            IOrganizationServiceFactory factory =
    (IOrganizationServiceFactory)serviceProvider.GetService(typeof(
IOrganizationServiceFactory));
            ITracingService tracer = (ITracingService)
serviceProvider.GetService(typeof(ITracingService));
            tracer.Trace("START: IPlugin.Execute");
            Entity entity = null;
            if (context.InputParameters.Contains("Target") &&
context.InputParameters["Target"] is Entity)
            {
                entity = (Entity)context.
InputParameters["Target"];
                if (entity.LogicalName != "account")
{
return;
}
            }
            else
            {
                return;
            }
            try
            {
                Entity followup = new Entity("task");
```

```
                        followup["subject"] = "Follow-up with new
account";
                        followup["description"] = "Introduce company to
the new account.";
                        followup["scheduledstart"] = DateTime.Now.
AddHours(72);
                        followup["scheduledend"] = DateTime.Now.
AddHours(72);

                        if (context.OutputParameters.Contains("id"))
                        {
                            Guid regardingobjectid = new Guid(context.
OutputParameters["id"].ToString());
                            string regardingobjectidType = "account";

                            followup["regardingobjectid"] = new EntityRefe
rence(regardingobjectidType, regardingobjectid);
                        }
                        IOrganizationService service = factory.CreateOrgan
izationService(context.UserId);
                        service.Create(followup, null);
                    }
                    catch (FaultException<OrganizationServiceFault> ex)
                    {
                        throw new InvalidPluginExecutionException("An
error occurred in the AccountCreateHandler plug-in", ex);
                    }
                    tracer.Trace("END: IPlugin.Execute");
                    if (entity["name"].ToString().ToUpper().
Contains("THROW"))
                    {
                        throw new InvalidPluginExecutionException("THROW
ING AN EXCEPTION THAT IS VISIBLE IN THE TRACE FILE IF TRACING
HAS BEEN ENABLED.");
                    }
                }
```

8. You must now sign the code before building the assembly. To sign the assembly, right-click on the solution name and choose Properties.

9. In the Properties page for the plug-in, click the Signing tab (see Figure 22.5). Select the Sign the assembly option and from the drop-down menu choose <New...> to create a new strong name key file. The Create Strong Name Key dialog box opens.

10. Provide a name and password that you wish to use to sign your assembly (see Figure 22.6). Then save and close the Properties page. You are now ready to build the plug-in to create the DLL file that you will register against the Dynamics CRM platform.

11. In the Solution Explorer panel, right-click the project name and select "Build" from the context menu. The code will be compiled and the DLL file will be placed in the Debug folder of the project's bin.

FIGURE 22.5

Sign the assembly in Visual Studio before building the project.

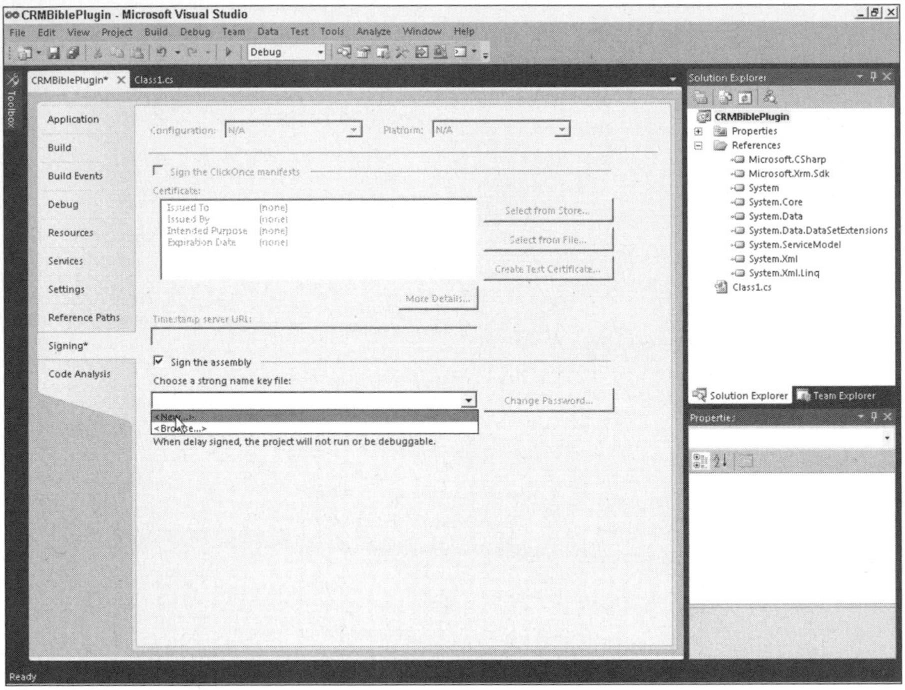

FIGURE 22.6

Provide a name and password to create a strong name key for your plug-in assembly.

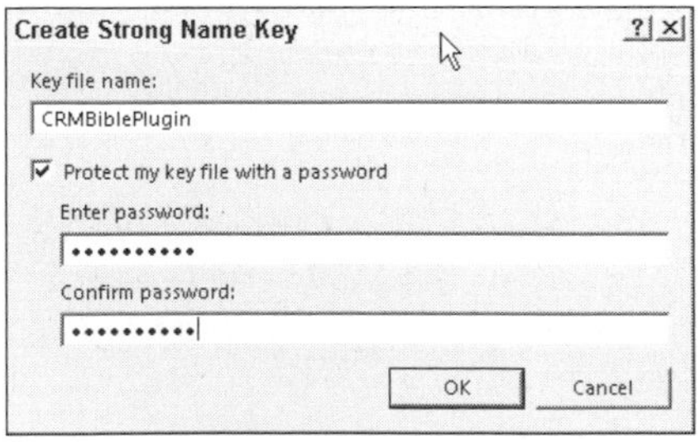

Deploying a plug-in

After your custom code has been compiled and the DLL has been created, you can proceed to registering the plug-in with the Dynamics CRM platform. To register the plug-in you must use the Plug-In Registration Tool, which is available as part of the Dynamics CRM SDK. The Plug-in Registration Tool must be compiled before it can be run. (Microsoft provides the

Plug-in Registration Tool as a Visual Studio project so you can investigate and learn from the code behind the tool, which uses completely supported SDK methods.) Follow the instructions in the SDK to build the tool. Then, follow these steps to register your custom plug-in assembly:

1. Open the Plug-in Registration Tool by double-clicking the executable file in the SDK\ Tools\PluginRegistrationTool\bin\Debug folder.

2. When the tool launches, click the Create New Connection button (Figure 22.7).

FIGURE 22.7

You must first create a new connection in the Plug-in Registration Tool.

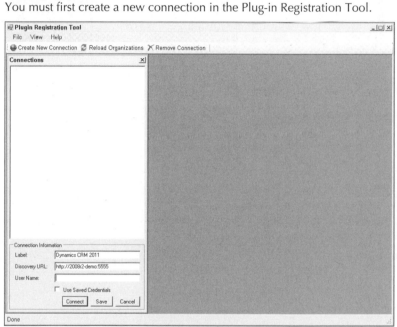

3. Enter a convenient label for the connection, and the address of the discovery service server. If you are running the registration tool on the Dynamics CRM server, you can enter a username and select Use saved credentials to automatically use Windows authentication to connect to the discovery service. Otherwise, leave these options blank. Click the Connect button.

4. After connecting to the discovery service, the Plug-in Registration Tool displays the organizations available. Select an organization from the list and click the Connect button again to connect to the organization's Web service API. The tool now displays the registration panel (see Figure 22.8).

5. To register the assembly, click the Register button and choose Register New Assembly or press Ctrl + A. The Register New Plugin dialog box opens, as shown in Figure 22.9.

The Plug-in Registration Tool, displaying a connection to a selected organization, and the registration panel

6. Click the Load Assembly button to navigate to the location of the DLL file for your plug-in. Select the isolation mode and the location that the plug-in should be stored. Then click the Register Selected Plugins button. When the plug-in has been registered, an information dialog box will appear. Click OK to close the information box.

7. Next, you must specify on which entity message the plug-in will fire. Expand the assembly in the registration panel and right-click on the plug-in. Select Register New Step, shown in Figure 22.10.

8. In the Register New Step dialog box (see Figure 22.11) set the following options. Note that the message and entity names are case-sensitive. Leave the defaults for the remaining options and click the Register New Step button.

   - Message: Create
   - Primary Entity: account

9. The plug-in is now registered. To test this plug-in, create a new account record and check to see if a task is created as specified.

FIGURE 22.9

The "Register New Plugin" dialog box allows you to select the assembly, specify the isolation mode, and select the storage location for a plug-in.

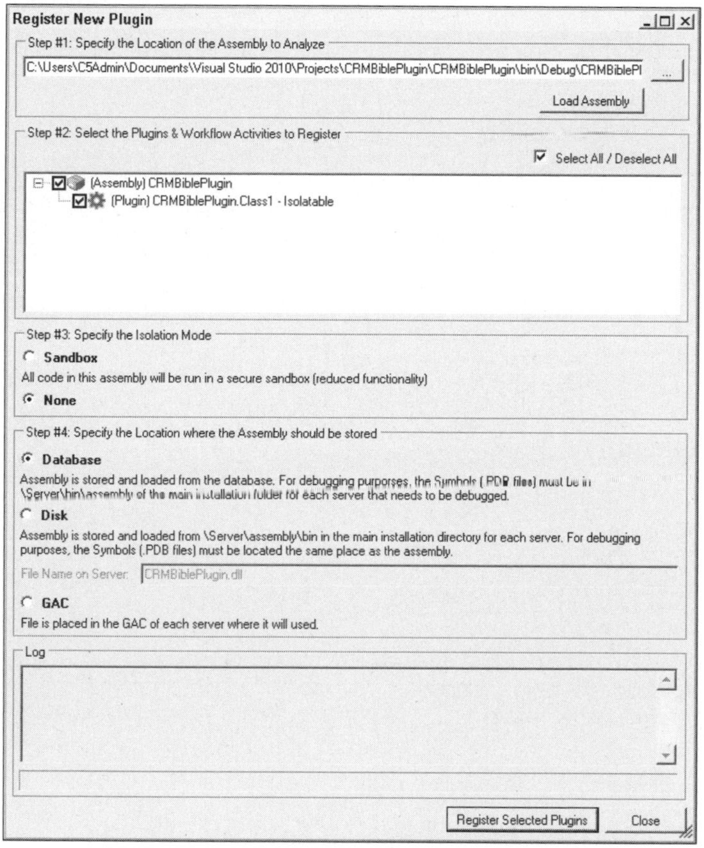

Custom plug-ins that are registered with an organization can also be viewed and managed within a solution in the Dynamics CRM web client interface, where the steps for each plug-in can be deactivated and reactivated. To view the plug-ins that have been registered as part of a solution, in the Dynamics CRM Web client, navigate to the Settings area and open the Solution. The left-hand list of solution components includes a link to view the Plug-in Assemblies and the Sdk Message Processing Steps.

FIGURE 22.10

Select the plug-in and register a new step to specify which entity message the plug-in will be fired on.

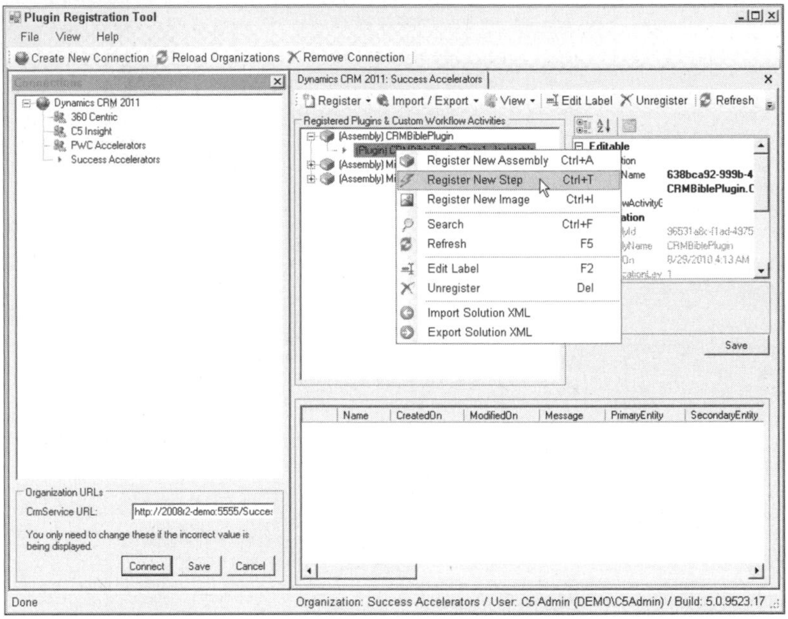

FIGURE 22.11

Specifying the message and entity for the plug-in.

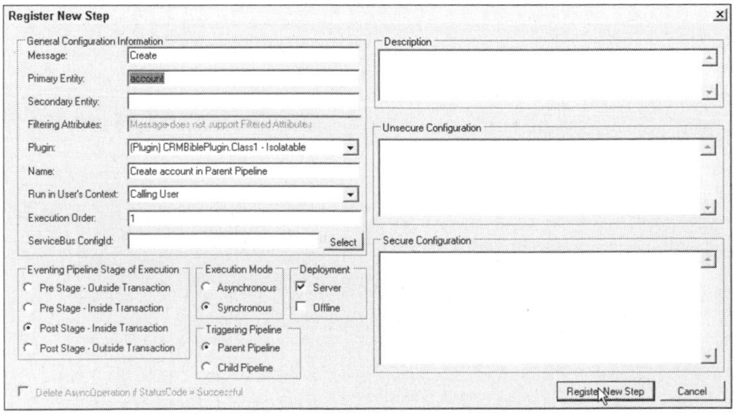

RESTing with Dynamics CRM

REST is a major addition to the methods that can be used to interface with Dynamics CRM. REST, an acronym for Representational State Transfer, is a way of making CRUD operations possible through HTTP by simply appending querystring parameters to the URI of the REST endpoint. Because of its ease-of-use and flexibility, REST is poised to become a ubiquitous feature in many business and consumer applications. A RESTful API was one of the significant improvements in SharePoint 2010, and popular consumer Web sites like Netflix and Flickr. Microsoft SQL Azure and SQL Server 2008 R2 Reporting Services also have RESTful interfaces.

A RESTful endpoint enables developers to connect Web-based systems together using a variety of Web technologies like AJAX (Asynchronous JavaScript and XML), JSON (JavaScript Object Notation), or Silverlight.

REST can be implemented using a variety of technologies and protocols. Depending on the protocols used, RESTful endpoints can also be incorporated in server-side applications.

Microsoft has used the OData protocol to implement a RESTful API for Dynamics CRM. OData, short for the Open Data Protocol, is an open-source implementation of Microsoft's data services architecture that provides a standard syntax for querying and updating structured data. WCF Data Services enables .NET Framework 4 applications to use the OData protocol. OData returns data that is requested in an atom feed format (just like an RSS feed — in fact, your Web browser interprets the results as an RSS feed). When querying Dynamics CRM using the OData service, the platform interprets the request as a standard Dynamics CRM query expression.

Querying Dynamics CRM's OData service

The REST endpoint for Microsoft Dynamics CRM 2011 is available at a URI in the following format:

```
http://<crmserver>/<orgname>/xrmservices/2011/organizationdata.svc
```

In Dynamics CRM, browsing to the endpoint above returns a list of data collections (see Figure 22.12).

Tip

By default, Internet Explorer displays this data as a nicely formatted RSS feed. To see the underlying XML, disable the feed reading view from the Internet Options dialog. Click the Content tab and, in the Feeds and Web Slices section, click the Settings button. Deselect the Turn on feed reading view option.

Appending the name of one of the collections, or sets, to the endpoint URI will return a feed of the first 50 records in that collection. For example, adding /AccountSet will show the XML for the first 50 accounts in the organization's database. If there are more than 50 records, the end of the XML will contain a link reference with a special querystring parameter that can be used to skip to the next 50 records in the set:

```
http://<crmserver>/<orgname>/xrmservices/2011/organizationdata.svc/AccountSet?$s
    kiptoken=guid'91e8833a-e7da-db11-a47d-00065bf3e4c3'
```

FIGURE 22.12

Browsing to the organizationdata.svc endpoint returns the list of data sets in Dynamics CRM's REST API.

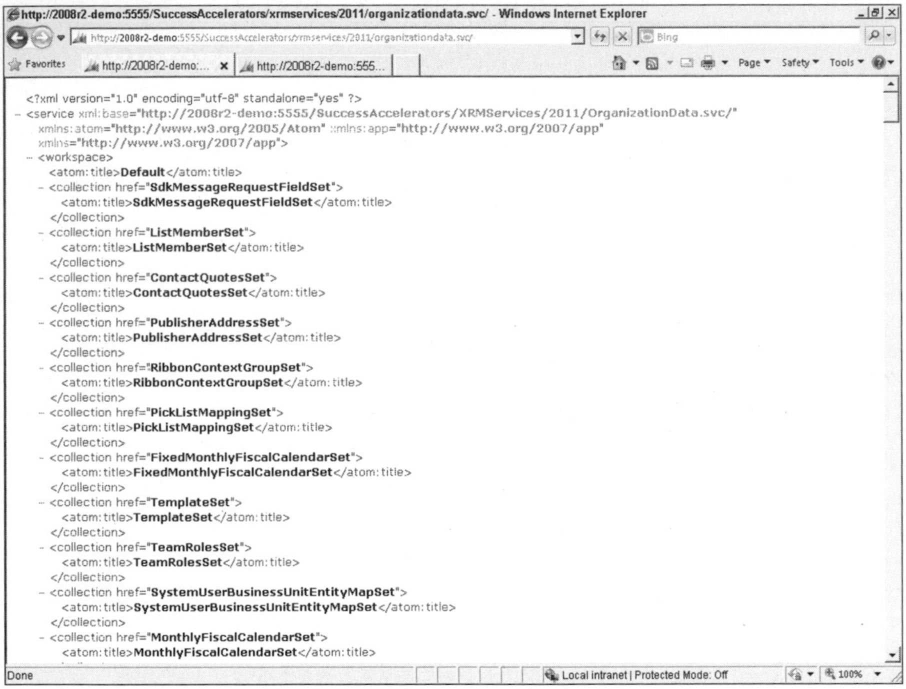

To access the metadata for an organization, append the metadata token to the endpoint URI:

```
http://<crmserver>/<orgname>/xrmservices/2011/organizationdata.svc/$metadata
```

Query operations are performed by addressing a set and appending the querystring parameters to the end of the URI in the format $parameter. Microsoft has implemented a subset of the OData query operations. The SDK includes a list of all of the support query operations, such as select, filter, and top, that can be used together to return data.

To return the properties for an account named Advanced Components, use query similar to the following:

```
http://<crmserver>/<orgname>/xrmservices/2011/organizationdata.svc/
    AccountSet?$filter=Name eq 'Advanced Components'
```

To specify the properties you wish returned, use the $select parameter. When combining the $select and $filter operations, place the $select parameter first. Figure 22.13 shows the results of this query:

```
http://<crmserver>/<orgname>/xrmservices/2011/organizationdata.svc/AccountSet?$s
    elect=AccountNumber,Address1_City&$filter=Name eq 'Advanced Components'
```

FIGURE 22.13

You can combine query operations to return only the desired properties of a specific record.

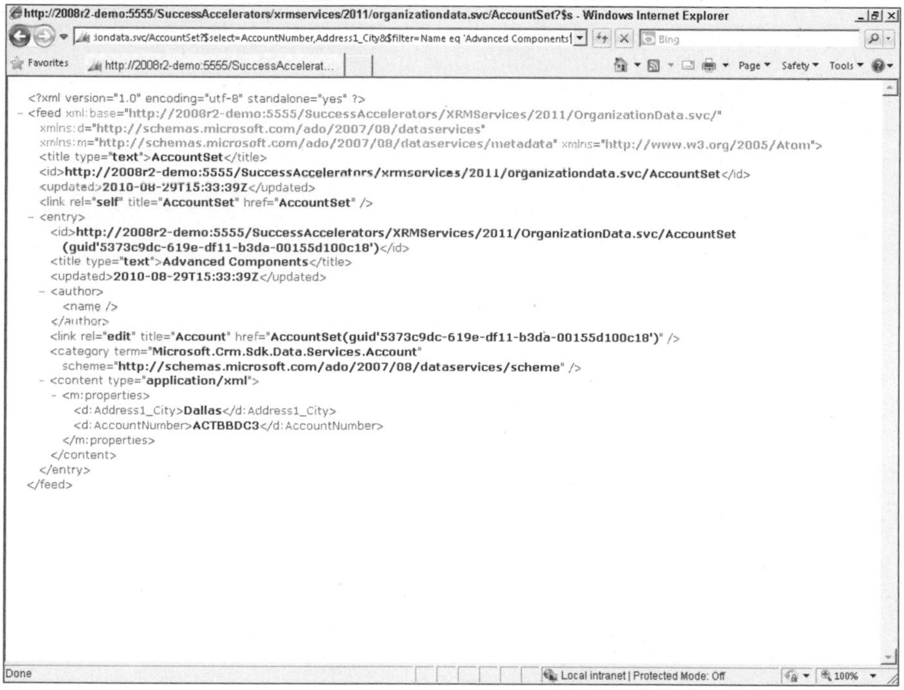

Note

In addition to query operations, client applications built with technologies like JavaScript or Silverlight that can send HTTP messages (GET, POST, PUT, and DELETE) can use the OData service to create, update, and delete records in Dynamics CRM. While not as robust as the SOAP interface, the OData interface is lightweight and easy to implement, and therefore lends itself to client-side extensions. The SDK contains comprehensive documentation on using the OData service from client extensions and Web resources.

Using the OData endpoint in Visual Studio

The OData service in Dynamics CRM does not permit authentication from external applications. (An exception to this is if the external application uses the Azure AppFabric Service Bus to pass messages between it and Dynamics CRM's OData service.) However, a Web resource such as a Silverlight XAP file or a JavaScript file that is hosted in a Dynamics CRM solution can use the OData service as a data source.

To use the OData endpoint in a Silverlight Web resource, follow these steps:

1. Open your project in Visual Studio. In the Solution Explorer, right-click on Service Reference and select "Add Service Reference..."

585

2. In the Add Service Reference dialog box (Figure 22.14) navigate to the metadata collection service endpoint for your organization. (This will be in the format of `http://<crmserver>/<orgname>/xrmservices/2011/organizationdata.svc/$metadata`.)

FIGURE 22.14

Adding the data service endpoint as a service reference in a Visual Studio project

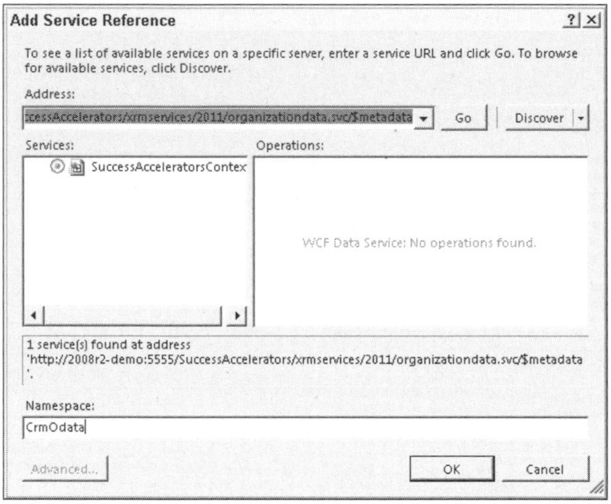

3. Provide a namespace for the reference and click OK.

After adding the service reference to the OData service, you will also need to add a reference to the System.Data.Services.Client if it is not already referenced by your project. This assembly contains classes that allow use of WCF Data Services classes in .NET applications.

In your code, add a using statement in the form of ProjectName.ODataReferenceName (where ProjectName is the name of your Visual Studio solution, and ODataReferenceName is the name you gave to the service reference). This will enable Intellisense when referencing your organization's metadata.

Connecting to the Cloud with Azure

Azure is Microsoft's cloud-based computing platform, consisting of service hosting, storage, SQL database services, access control, and other components. It provides all the components needed for an n-tier application as a highly scalable and inexpensive service. In industry parlance, Azure is known as a PaaS application: Platform-as-a-Service. The same n-tier approach to systems architecture that is at the heart of Dynamics CRM is available as a service. Integrating Azure, Dynamics CRM, and other platforms like SharePoint can provide powerful solutions to enterprises and organizations of all sizes.

One of the main components of Azure is AppFabric. Azure AppFabric handles the access and communications between cloud-enabled applications like Dynamics CRM. The two core components of AppFabric are the Service Bus and Access Control:

- **Service Bus.** The Service Bus is the messaging bus that transports messages between two systems. The systems sending messages across the AppFabric Service Bus can be anywhere — they don't need to be in Azure. The Service Bus helps applications negotiate network boundaries in a secure manner. Even if an application is behind a NAT'ed firewall, as long as it has internet access, the Service Bus can be used to connect it to other applications in public or private clouds.

  Microsoft Dynamics CRM 2011 includes built-in support for the AppFabric Service Bus via a Service Bus plug-in that has been incorporated into the platform (Figure 22.15).

FIGURE 22.15

Microsoft Dynamics CRM 2011 includes a built-in Service Bus plug-in to integrate with Azure services.

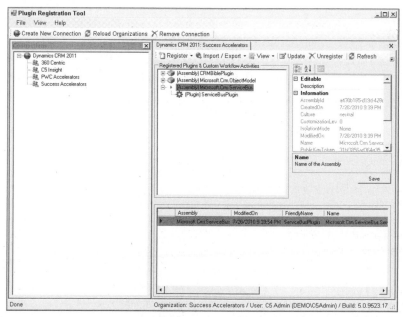

- **Access Control.** Access Control Services provides a way to manage and federate identity providers across cloud-enabled applications. Using Access Control enables Dynamics CRM to pass messages on the Service Bus to other systems.

In relation to Dynamics CRM, Microsoft Azure services support for core scenarios:

- Dynamics CRM On-premise ⇨ External/Cloud-hosted system
- On-Premise Line-of-Business system ⇨ Dynamics CRM Online
- Dynamics CRM Online ⇨ External/Cloud-hosted system
- Dynamics CRM (On-premise or Online) ⇨ Dynamics CRM (On-premise or Online)

Note

The SDK contains detailed instructions for using Azure integration with Dynamics CRM. The focus of this section is to provide complementary guidance to assist administrators and beginner developers with understanding and implementing Azure integration.

The basic steps of preparing to use Azure integration with Dynamics CRM are:

1. Sign up for the Azure services your organization needs.
2. Set up the Azure project and namespace on the AppFabric Web site.
3. Configure your development environment to work with Azure (see Chapter 20).

The SDK provides guidance and examples for completing these steps:

1. Set up a certificate and install it in the Dynamics CRM database.
2. Create a custom application that prepares a message for the Azure AppFabric Service Bus and register it with the Dynamics CRM platform.
3. Configure the Service Bus to listen for and accept the messages sent by your custom application.

Signing up for Azure services

For people who are new to Microsoft's Azure service offerings, it can be a little confusing as to what services are needed for a particular application, how much they cost, and how to sign up for them. The Azure platform consists of three primary components that can be purchased and used independently or in combination with one another:

- Windows Azure: Storage, computing, and application hosting
- SQL Azure: A relational database service based on SQL Server
- AppFabric: Communications and access control service

Dynamics CRM integrates directly with AppFabric via the Service Bus plug-in. There are no other direct or inherent integrations with Windows Azure or SQL Azure. If your organization wishes to host a database-driven .NET application in the cloud, Azure is worth investigating. However, for the purposes of a Dynamics CRM administrator, it is primarily important to understand AppFabric.

Microsoft offers Azure services through a variety of payment models, including a pay-per-use plan and bundled packages. The pay-per-use plans are typically less economical than the bundled services, but they are helpful in beginning to understand the costs involved. As of this writing, the pricing for AppFabric is as follows:

- Access Control: $1.99 per 100,000 transactions
- Service Bus: $3.99 per connection on a "pay-as-you-go" basis
  - Pack of 5 connections $9.95
  - Pack of 25 connections $49.75
  - Pack of 100 connections $199.00
  - Pack of 500 connections $995.00

The pricing for the other Azure services is based on factors such as bandwidth, database size, and CPU usage. For more information, refer to the Microsoft Azure Web site.

Once you have decided which services to subscribe to, you can initiate the purchase process directly from the Azure Web site. You will need a Windows Live ID in order to complete the subscription process. When signing up for AppFabric services, you will need to provide a project name that is used in provisioning your service. Once you have completed the subscription process, the services are provisioned immediately.

Setting up your AppFabric services

After completing the sign-up process for Azure AppFabric, log in to the Azure Web site (`https://appfabric.azure.com`). Follow these steps to prepare AppFabric for use:

1. On the AppFabric summary page, click the project name that you created during the sign-up process. This opens the Project page (see Figure 22.16).

2. On the Project page, click the Add Service Namespace link. You must create a namespace that will be referenced by the Access Control and Service Bus configurations. This is a global namespace and must be validated as unique.

3. Select a region that is close to your current location. (If you have an application that makes use of multiple pieces of the Azure platform, configuring them all to use the same region helps Microsoft provide optimal performance as they work together.)

4. Select a connection pack. Connection packs specify the number of simultaneous connections your application can have on the Service Bus.

5. After the namespace has been created, go to the namespace management page and copy the management key. This key is needed when you configure access for the Service Bus application.

Your AppFabric service is now set up and ready to be configured for use with Dynamics CRM.

FIGURE 22.16

The Azure AppFabric Project page

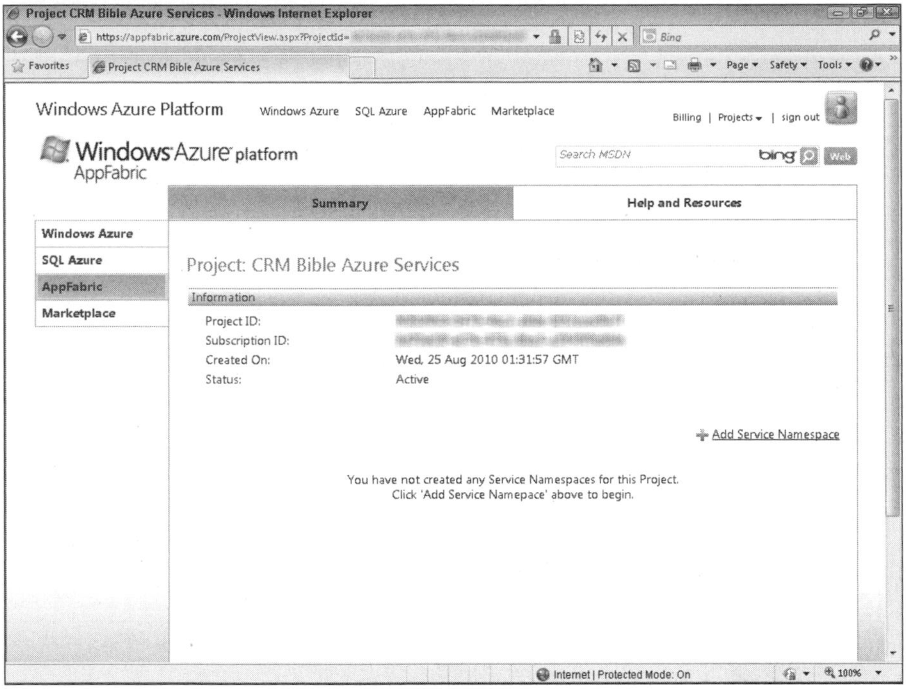

Cross-Reference
Developing solutions that integrate with Azure can be quite complex and require that you have the correct tools and SDKs installed. In addition to the Dynamics CRM SDK, you will need the Azure SDK, the Azure AppFabric SDK, and Azure tools for Visual Studio. Detailed guidance for setting up your development environment is included in Chapter 20.

Getting started with an Azure-enabled solution

Building an Azure-enabled solution requires performing a number of configuration steps before registering the custom plug-in. To understand these configurations, a metaphor of a bus trip can serve as a helpful illustration. If an individual (message) is going to take a bus (service bus) somewhere, he needs to have a place to get on the bus (issuer) and a destination (the other application or system to be interacted with). He also needs a ticket (permissions/contract) and some official identification (certificate). When he arrives at his destination, a friend (listener) will meet him and take him into town.

In terms of our bus trip metaphor, we have already established the bus company by signing up for Azure AppFabric services and creating a project and a namespace. We must now carry out the remaining configurations to complete the trip:

1. **Certificate.** The first step is to acquire and install a public key certificate for the Dynamics CRM server. This certificate establishes the identity of the server (see Figure 22.17). Because the messages passed through the Service Bus originate in the context of the platform, the certificate must also be installed in the MSCRM_CONFIG database. In the case of Dynamics CRM Online, the certificate has already been created.

FIGURE 22.17

Managing a self-signed certificate in the Microsoft Management Console

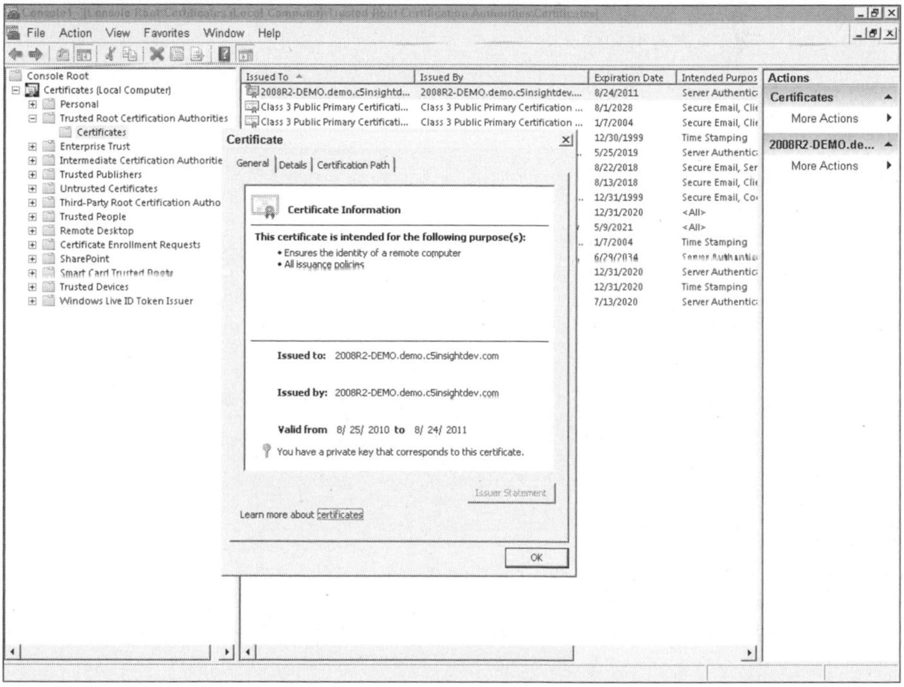

2. **Listener.** The next step is to write an event listener using the IRemotePlugin interface that implements a WCF Service Contract. The listener will receive the SAML token created by the Access Control services configuration in order to establish authentication with the Service Bus.

3. **Permissions.** Use the Access Control services management utility to configure permissions. The utility, acm.exe or ACM, is a tool installed as part of the AppFabric SDK. The permissions take the public key certificate information and unique identifiers from your AppFabric service as inputs to create the "ticket" that the message will need for the Service Bus. In the language of AppFabric, the Dynamics CRM server becomes an "issuer" and the ACM tool sets rules for how the issuer will interact with the Service Bus.

4. Service Bus. When a pipeline event is raised, your custom plug-in containing the message must be registered as a step in the Service Bus plug-in on the Dynamics CRM platform in order to send the message on the Service Bus (see Figure 22.18).

Registering a step in the Service Bus plug-in using the Plugin Registration Tool, part of the Dynamics CRM SDK, requires entering certain configuration details.

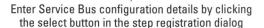

Enter Service Bus configuration details by clicking the select button in the step registration dialog

Creating an Azure project

In addition to using the AppFabric Service Bus to handle communication between Dynamics CRM and other applications, you may decide to use Azure to host cloud-based solutions that integrate with your system in other ways. Follow the instructions included here to set up the Azure tools in Visual Studio and start a new cloud-based project.

To install the Azure tools for Visual Studio 2010, if you haven't already done so, follow these steps:

1. Open Visual Studio and start a new project.

2. From the New Project window, select the Cloud template under Visual C#. If the Azure tools are not already installed, you see an option, Enable Windows Azure Tools. Select this option and click OK.

3. Visual Studio takes you to a page with a link to download the tools. Click the link to go to the Microsoft Downloads site and begin the download.

4. When the download completes, close Visual Studio and click Run to launch the Windows Azure Tools for Microsoft Visual Studio Installation Wizard.

When creating a new cloud project, the first task that Visual Studio will require is that a Web role for the application be selected. A Web role is a designation of what role the application will be playing. Will it be a Web site that people will visit and interact with? Will it be a data service? Or will it provide computing power as a worker role? To create a simple Web page hosted in Azure, choose the ASP.NET Web Role.

To host a Web site in Azure, you must subscribe to the Windows Azure service. If your Web application requires a database, you can use the SQL Azure service. Azure applications can be deployed directly from Visual Studio or by logging into the Azure Web site and uploading the packaged application.

Extending Dynamics CRM Workflow

Dynamics CRM includes powerful tools called workflows and dialogs to automate business processes. These processes run on the platform's Asynchronous Service using the Windows Workflow Foundation (WWF), which is part of the .NET Framework 4.

The workflow tools have flexible and user-friendly graphical interfaces in the Web client that enable administrators and users to create workflow rules that can be triggered manually, on certain events, or as subroutines nested in other processes.

Out of the box, workflow rules can create or update records, send e-mail, assign record ownership, start other workflows, or change the status of records (see Figure 22.19).

Cross-Reference

In Microsoft Dynamics CRM 2011, workflows have been complemented by dialogs, synchronous wizard-like interactions that can automate and streamline business processes. Collectively, workflows and dialogs are referred to as processes. Chapter 18 includes detailed instructions for working with workflow and dialog processes in the Dynamics CRM Web client process designer interface.

Developers have two basic options for extending workflow functionality in Dynamics CRM:

- Add custom logic that can be used in the Web client's workflow rule designer.
- Create or modify complete workflow rules and import them into the solution.

The main distinction between custom workflow activities and plug-ins is that workflows run asynchronously, whereas plugins can be registered to execute synchronously with an operation.

FIGURE 22.19

The Web client provides a rich interface for building workflow processes. Workflows can perform a wide variety of functions without any custom code.

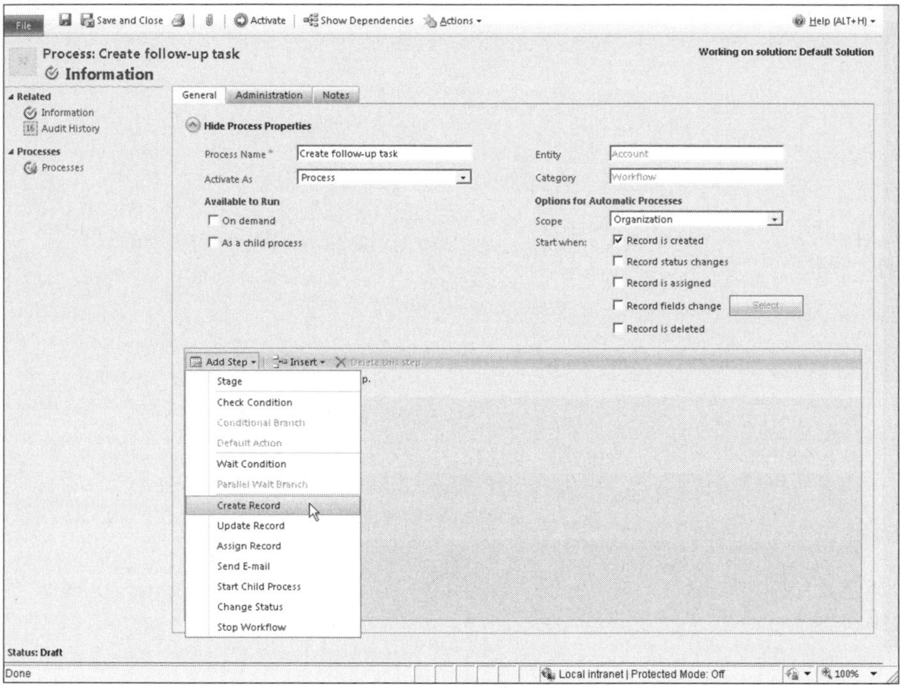

Creating custom steps for use in building workflow rules

Because these tools are built using WWF, they can be extended with custom steps. Using the Visual Studio Workflow Designer, developers can use visual tools to create custom workflow extensions without writing any code. The custom XAML files can be compiled and registered to the platform using the Plugin Registration Tool. Once a workflow assembly has been registered, it will appear on the list of available workflow steps in the client interface.

Note

Custom workflow extensions cannot be run in the isolated Sandbox mode. Therefore they are not supported in Dynamics CRM Online.

Workflow steps accept input parameters, and then result in output parameters. Custom assemblies use this same paradigm, taking inputs from the context of the triggering event in the execution pipeline (the event that triggered the workflow), processing it with your custom business logic, and then creating output parameters that can be used in subsequent steps of the workflow process. For example, a custom workflow step might be able to multiply two integers. If a workflow is running against an Opportunity record, the custom step can take the Opportunity's Estimated Value and Probability as inputs, multiply the two numbers, and provide the result as an output.

To create a custom workflow activity to extend the built-in Dynamics CRM functionality, follow these steps:

1. Open Visual Studio 2010 and start a new project by selecting the Activity Library template.

2. Add references to the Microsoft.Xrm.Sdk.dll and the Microsoft.Xrm.Sdk.Workflow. dll. These DLLs are available in the bin folder where you have installed the SDK.

3. Remove the Activity1.xaml file and replace it with a class file (.cs) to hold your custom code.

4. Add using directives that reference the assemblies from Step 2, as well as the System.Activities assembly from the .NET Framework 4. Your custom code should inherit from the CodeActivity class and use the Execute method.

5. When you are finished designing the custom logic, build the solution.

6. Register the DLL file by using the Plugin Registration Tool. There is no need to register any steps for the custom assembly.

7. In the process designer interface in the Dynamics CRM client, create a new workflow rule. Click the Add Steps button to add your custom activity (see Figure 22.20).

Tip

The SDK includes instructions for adding the built-in Dynamics CRM workflow steps to the Visual Studio toolbox, enabling you to incorporate them in the visual activity designer. In the toolbox's general category, right-click and select "Choose Items. . .". From the System.Activities tab, browse to the location of the Microsoft.Xrm.Sdk.Workflow.dll assembly and select it. This will enable you to add the activities to the toolbox.

Creating or modifying a complete workflow rule

In addition to adding custom steps to the workflow rule designer, developers can also create complete workflow rules or modify rules that were created in the Dynamics CRM Web client.

The process for creating a custom workflow rule is similar to the process of creating custom steps for workflows. Instead of replacing the XAML file with a .cs class file and compiling the project, however, the developer will create the custom workflow rule in the XAML file (see Figure 22.21). The XAML file will then be imported either as part of a solution or via an SDK import tool.

Workflow rules customized or created in Visual Studio can use built-in Dynamics CRM workflow activities or the entire range of Windows Workflow Foundation activities. They can also reference external resources and data, making them a powerful point of extensibility.

FIGURE 22.20

Custom workflow activities that are properly registered will be available in the built-in workflow rule designer in the Dynamics CRM Web client. In this figure, a custom workflow called "Share Record" has been added to the list of steps under the Utilities submenu.

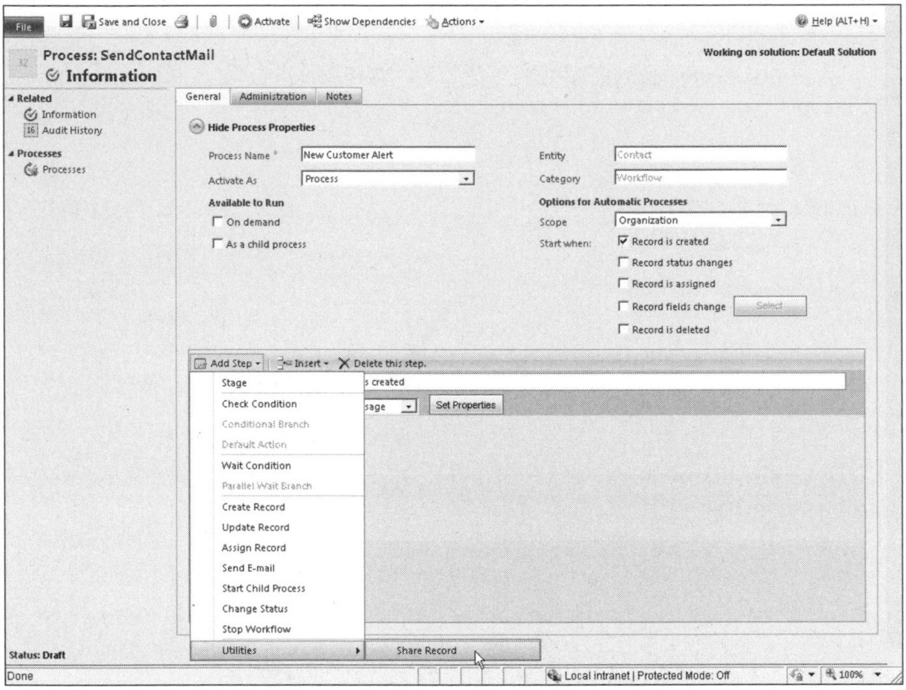

To export a rule that was created in Dynamics CRM, export the solution that contains it. Unzip the exported solution and locate the Workflows folder. Each workflow rule will be in a subfolder named with the workflow rule name and its GUID. Inside this folder will be the actual XAML file that can be edited in Visual Studio.

After making the desired modifications, the XAML file must be reimported into Dynamics CRM. In order to import a modified workflow rule, it must be saved as an XAML file and a user with Deployment Administrator privileges must perform the import process. The file can then be placed back into the folder and zipped back up with the solution for reimport. To simplify this process, Microsoft has released a tool with the SDK that can be used to import XAML files directly into the system. The tool must first be built and is operated from a command prompt. See the SDK for more information.

After importing a workflow rule, it must be published and activated before it will be executed.

FIGURE 22.21

This workflow rule was exported from a Dynamics CRM solution. The XAML file was added to an Activity Library project so it could be edited in Visual Studio. The SDK contains instructions for modifying existing workflow rules.

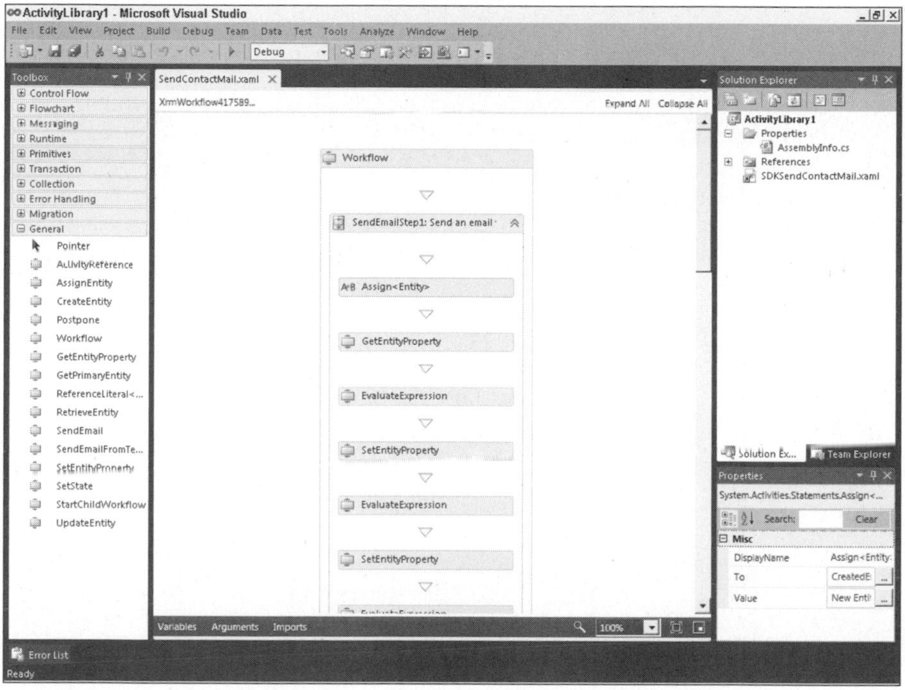

Caution

Workflow rules that are created in Visual Studio, or which are exported from Dynamics CRM and modified in Visual Studio, cannot be viewed or edited in the Web client workflow rule designer interface. However, you can still manage the execution of instances of customized workflow rules by pausing, canceling, or resuming them.

Summary

Microsoft Dynamics CRM 2011 provides a mature platform for custom development with well-defined APIs, and a robust architecture supports a variety of deployment models, extension methods, and technologies.

With this version of Dynamics CRM, the application has taken a significant step toward providing a true development platform that can be tailored well beyond traditional customer relationship management functionality to support an infinite variety of business processes.

This chapter reviewed the architecture and technologies that make this level of customization possible, including the new WCF services framework, the OData endpoint, plug-in architecture, and the basics of Azure integration.

Considered as a whole, Microsoft has delivered in Dynamics CRM a flexible deployment model and an open architecture, providing programmers with a powerful platform for developing custom line-of-business applications.

Part VII

Visualizing Your Dynamics CRM Data with Charts, Reports, and Dashboards

A recent survey of IT managers and other businesspeople responsible for making software purchases found that one of their top priorities was to add business intelligence (BI) and analytics capabilities to their stable of tools. Businesses of every stripe are finding that the challenges of collecting and storing data quickly yield to the greater challenge of making sense of these vast stockpiles of information. And beyond making sense of the data, they want the data to inform intelligent decisions to guide their organizations' tactical and strategic direction.

Microsoft's response to this trend in its latest Dynamics CRM offering is to incorporate an arsenal of BI and analytics weapons, surfacing a bevy of reports, charts, dashboards, and analytical tools for users of every skill level.

Using the Built-in Reporting Tools

Business intelligence (BI) is an increasingly important facet of any business application, and Dynamics CRM is no exception. BI is a general term that describes reporting and analyzing business data in a way that enables the organization to make smart decisions. Of course, in order for BI efforts to be successful, the data going into the business application needs to be accurate and relevant, a subject we discuss in other chapters dealing with data management and using the Dynamics CRM application.

Microsoft has built several tools right into Dynamics CRM to simplify reporting and analysis:

- Views
- Visualizations
- Dashboards
- Report Wizard
- Export to Excel

In addition to tools built into the application, there are a variety of external BI tools that can be used to develop and deliver compelling intelligence to users of Dynamics CRM. Chief among these tools is the Business Intelligence Development Studio (BIDS), which uses the Visual Studio interface and SQL Server Reporting Services to enable developers to create rich custom reports.

For a more user-friendly, Office-like experience, Microsoft offers a free report application called SQL Server Reporting Services Report Builder 2.0 (Report Builder). Report Builder is a happy medium between the advanced toolset available in BIDS and the built-in Report Wizard.

IN THIS CHAPTER

The Advanced Find tool

Using the reports that come with Dynamics CRM

The Report Wizard

Reporting with Excel

Microsoft SharePoint also delivers a rich BI experience that can tap into Dynamics CRM data to display KPIs (key performance indicators) and other intelligence.

Cross-Reference

This chapter focuses on the built-in tools that require little to no development expertise and that enable a rich self-service reporting experience for administrators and users. Chapter 24 provides greater detail about dashboards and visualizations, and Chapter 25 provides comprehensive guidance on advanced reporting with Microsoft Business Intelligence Development Studio.

Because Dynamics CRM uses Microsoft SQL Server for its database, you can also use many other enterprise reporting tools like Crystal Reports or Cognos to develop custom reports.

Note

The built-in reporting tools discussed in this chapter all respect the Dynamics CRM security model, meaning that users will see only the data in these reports that they would otherwise see in the application.

Leveraging Dynamics CRM's Business Intelligence Capabilities

Before we go further, it will be helpful to define what a report is in the context of Dynamics CRM. A report is a way to query and display data. Many people who are new to using Dynamics CRM are surprised to learn how easy it is to gather and present information in a useful way. In fact, what many people consider reports can often be accomplished with simple list views of records using system views or the Advanced Find tool.

Using Advanced Find as a reporting tool

Dynamics CRM is designed with the goal of giving users tools to consume data how and when they want. Advanced Find is a powerful querying tool that can be used to modify system views or create new personal views that users can save and share.

Views, whether systemwide or saved as personal views from the Advanced Find tool, provide up-to-date lists of records that can include columns from related record types. Views can be printed, and links to views can be E-mailed to other Dynamics CRM users. In short, for organizations moving to Dynamics CRM from less-capable systems, views can often replace hosts of spreadsheet "reports" that might have previously required a great deal of manual effort.

Let's look at a typical scenario where Advanced Find can be used as a reporting tool, and walk through an example of creating Advanced Find views.

Example 1: Creating a view of important customers in a salesperson's territory

In our first example, a salesperson is planning a trip to Dallas to visit a customer and wants an up-to-date report showing all his customers who are also located in Dallas. He already has a view called "My Active Accounts" that he could filter to show only those in Dallas, but he also wants to view the mobile phone number of each accounts' primary contact. He can accomplish this by using the Advanced Find tool.

1. From the Accounts list, select the "My Active Accounts" view.

2. On the Ribbon menu, click the Advanced Find icon to launch the Advanced Find tool.

3. If the button at the top of the query says "Show Details," click it to expose the detailed view of the query rows. (Users can set this to default to show or hide details in their personal options settings.) If the button says "Hide Details" skip this step. The screen should now resemble the screen shown in Figure 23.1.

4. In the third row of the query, click the Select link to reveal the available fields. Select the "Address 1: City" field. Note that the operator next to the selected field automatically defaults to "Equals" which is the desired option for this example.

5. Click on the "Enter Value" link and type Dallas.

FIGURE 23.1

The Advanced Find tool is context-aware.

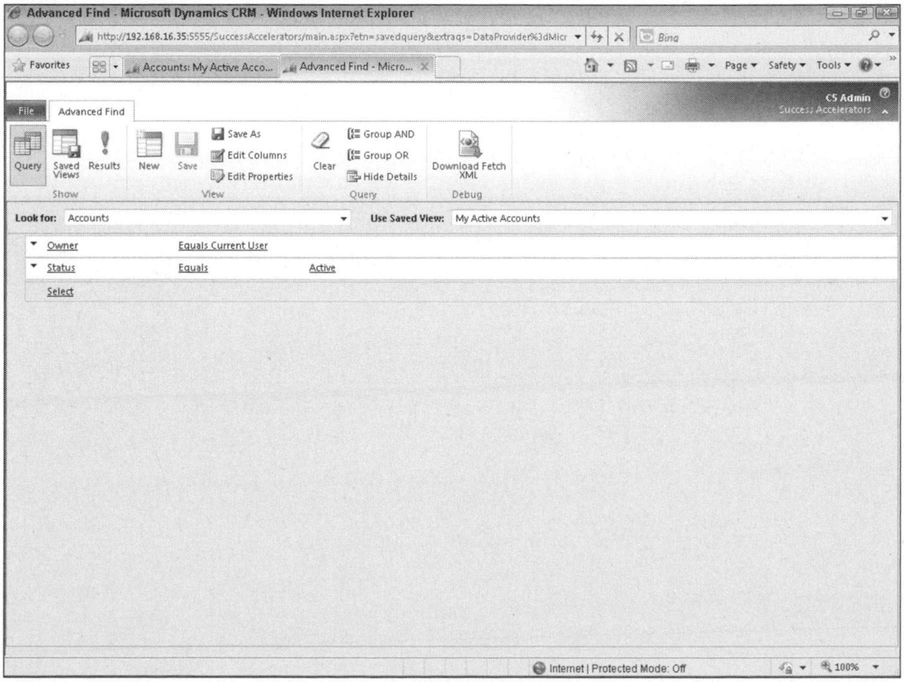

6. Add another row to the query by selecting the "Relationship Type" field and clicking the ellipsis button to look up the available options. In the Select Values dialog, double-click "Customer" to add it to the Selected Values box and click OK to set this value for the query.

7. You can test the results of the query by clicking the Find button on the bottom right. (Remember that your system may not have data that matches this query.) After previewing the query, click the "Back to Query" button on the bottom right of the results screen.

8. Because the salesperson wants to see columns from a related entity (Contacts) we will add these to our results screen. On the query screen, click the "Edit Columns" button to open the Edit Columns window.

9. Click Add Columns. At the top of the Add Columns dialog, select "Primary Contact (Contact)" from the Record Type picklist.

10. Place a check mark next to Mobile Phone and click OK.

11. Click OK to close the Edit Columns dialog.

12. Click the Find button on the Advanced Find query page to see the results (Figure 23.2).

13. To print the results, click the printer icon to open a Print Preview screen. From the Print Preview screen you can print the view.

14. To save the results of this Advanced Find, go back to the query screen and click the "Save As" button. In the Save As dialog, enter a name for the view and click OK.

Tip

By default, Advanced Find treats each row in a query as an AND condition, unless you group two rows using an OR condition. If you do not specify the OR condition, only records that meet all of the query criteria will be returned.

Example 2: An advanced Advanced Find view

Advanced Find is also capable of querying the values on related entities and grouping queries in complex ways. For this scenario, a senior vice president wishes to make some spot calls to large customers to see how satisfied they are with the recent sales they've participated in. He's particularly interested in the performance of the salespeople who report to a recently hired sales manager. The SVP is going to want to see:

- Active customer Account records

- Where an opportunity has either closed this month OR is scheduled to close this month

- Where the opportunities' values were greater than $100,000

- And where the opportunity owner's manager is the recently hired sales manager

Here's how he would build this Advanced Find:

1. Navigate to the Active Accounts list view and click the Advanced Find icon.

2. Click the button to Show Details if necessary.

FIGURE 23.2

The Advanced Find tool can be used to modify existing views or build new views. Views can also show columns from related records.

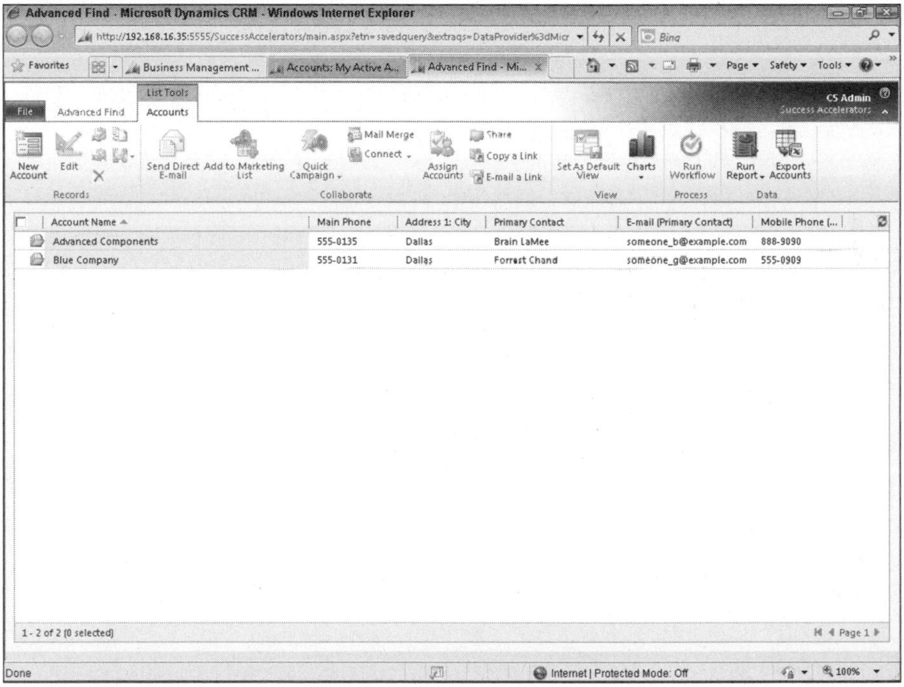

3. Click the Select link to reveal the list of fields you can query, and scroll down to the "Related" entities (see Figure 23.3). Select "Opportunities (Potential Customer)."

4. Select the Actual Revenue and Actual Close Date fields with the criteria shown in Figure 4, and click the triangle to the left of each row to select it. With both rows selected, click the "Group AND" button at the top of the query to group the two criteria. Repeat this step for the Est. Revenue and Est. Closed Date fields.

5. Once both groups have been made, you can click the triangle next to each group to select it, and then click the "Group OR" button to group both groups together as illustrated.

6. Next, click the Select link under the Opportunities groupings, and select the "Owning User (User)" option from the related items.

7. Under the Owning User, select the Manager, with an operator of Equals, and look up a user record for a manager. See Figure 23.4 to build the Advanced Find criteria.

8. Click the Find button to preview your results.

FIGURE 23.3

In addition to building queries using an entity's fields, the Advanced Find tool can query against related entities.

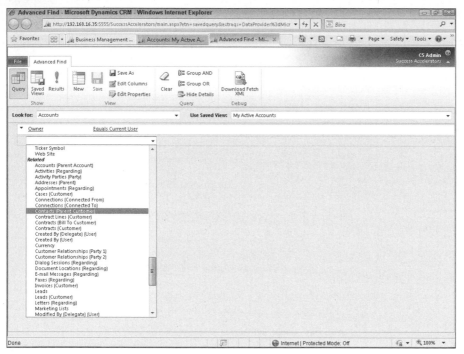

As these examples show, the Advanced Find tool is very powerful and can help properly trained users locate the precise records they need in order to make meaningful business decisions — all without using any external reporting tools.

Note

Some queries are not possible using Advanced Find, which uses FetchXML, an XML-based query language Microsoft developed for an earlier version of Dynamics CRM. FetchXML, though powerful, is unable to form certain query structures, such as a query that returns records that are NOT IN a defined set. For example, you cannot use Advanced Find to build a view of accounts with no associated opportunities. For this type of query, you will need to use a reporting tool capable of more advanced SQL queries.

Getting the most from the included reports

When views and Advanced Finds are insufficient, more advanced reports may be necessary. Dynamics CRM includes two dozen built-in reports that cover many traditional CRM reporting needs. Additionally, many of these canned reports include subreports, filtering, and parameter selection capabilities that allow users to "slice and dice" the data in numerous ways, multiplying the power of these 24 reports several times over. The reports are grouped according to the default reporting categories of Administrative, Marketing, Sales. and Service. Some of the reports are associated with more than one category. The embedded subreports allow users to drill into the first page of the canned reports, which often include informative charts, to view the underlying data.

The built-in reports are available in the Workplace area, by clicking on the Reports link. Many of them are also available from the Ribbon menu above the entity lists with which they are associated, and from individual records.

Note

Installing a new language pack on the Dynamics CRM server also installs a new set of canned reports in the new language. Users will see the list of included reports in the language they have set in their personal options.

Administrative reports

There is one built-in report, the User Summary report, that is categorized as Administrative. Another report, called Activities, is not categorized by default but is often used administratively to gauge user adoption.

FIGURE 23.4

To select a row in order to add it to an AND or OR group, click the triangle to the left of the row.

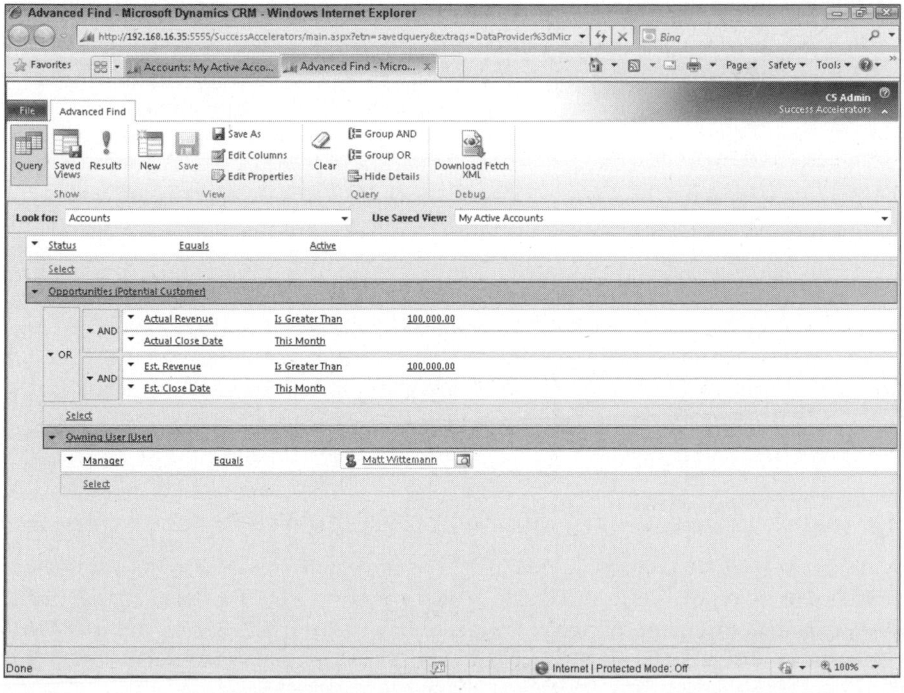

User Summary

The User Summary report is a quick way to see which users are grouped in which Business Unit, and which security role each has been assigned. This is extremely helpful when conducting a review of your business unit structure and consumed licenses.

Activities

The Activities report shows counts of activities that users have completed in Dynamics CRM. The chart it renders can be grouped by user, activity type, and other options. Clicking on parts of the chart reveals lists of the underlying activities. This report is frequently used by managers to see how actively their employees are using the system.

Marketing reports

The built-in marketing reports provide insight into the effectiveness of campaigns and lead sources, as well as existing accounts.

Account Distribution

The Account Distribution report, which also appears under the Sales category, displays the top accounts that have driven revenue, and can be grouped by parameters like the account's industry, territory, or size. This report helps marketers understand which customer segments are most likely to become customers.

Account Overview

The Account Overview report is designed to be run from within an individual account record, though you can also run it from the reports area, setting the account to report on in the filter. This report is a one-page overview of an account including an account profile, all recent activity for the selected account, including recent and upcoming sales opportunities, service cases, communications, planned meetings, and notes. This report is an excellent one for salespeople preparing for a client meeting.

Account Summary

The Account Summary pulls roll-up information from accounts and sub-accounts to reflect sales opportunities, activities and notes in a chronological order. This report is helpful to users trying to familiarize themselves with the history of an organization's relationship with an account.

Campaign Activity Status

This report gives marketers a view of the status of recent campaign activities, special types of activities that are generated during marketing campaigns. This is a good tool for marketing managers wishing to get an overview of the progress of the execution of multiple campaigns.

Cross-Reference

In order for the built-in marketing reports to provide relevant business intelligence, it's important to understand Dynamics CRM's marketing functionality, including campaigns, quick campaigns, campaign responses, and marketing lists. Chapter 13 covers Dynamics CRM's marketing functionality in great detail.

Campaign Comparison

Comparative reports are among the most powerful BI tools that marketers can use when planning future marketing efforts. The Campaign Comparison report enables the user to view the impact of two campaigns side-by-side. When running this report, select two campaigns in the report filter, and then, in the report view, select one of the campaigns for the Campaign A column, and the other for the Campaign B column, and click the View Report button.

Campaign Performance

When the built-in marketing functionality is fully utilized, the Campaign Performance report is a gold mine for marketing professionals. It is a comprehensive report that details the effort and expense that have gone into a campaign as well as the response rate, cost per response, and the return on investment (ROI). This report serves to bridge the gap between marketing and sales, and is a powerful tool to help marketers analyze their work.

Lead Source Effectiveness

Another tool to help marketers gauge the impact of their marketing investments is the Lead Source Effectiveness report. This report shows opportunities that have resulted from each of your system's lead sources (as indicated on the lead records). Marketers can run this report to determine where their lead-generation efforts are best focused.

Tip

Scheduling reports: If you have installed Dynamics CRM on-premises, and properly configured the SRS Data Connector and SQL Reporting Services, you will be able to schedule reports from the report list Ribbon menu. This feature is not available for Dynamics CRM Online.

Sales reports

Some sales reports are also in the marketing category and have been described above. The following reports are only in the sales category by default.

Competitor Win Loss

This report displays how your sales team stacks up against the competition. In order for this report to provide useful intelligence, competitors should be tracked on each opportunity, and, when an opportunity is lost to a competitor, it should be recorded in the opportunity close activity.

Neglected Accounts

This report will show accounts that have not had any activities logged against them during a specified time period. When running the Neglected Accounts report you can set the parameter for the minimum days an account has been neglected. The results can be grouped by the length of neglect, owner and category. The report also allows the user to select whether to include sub-contacts and sub-accounts. This report helps sales users to ensure that they are maintaining communication with existing customers.

Neglected Leads

Similar to the Neglected Accounts report, this report shows Leads with no activities during a set time period.

Products By Account

If your organization uses the product catalog built into Dynamics CRM, this report will show the products that have been associated with accounts' orders or opportunities. This is helpful to determine which products a customer has already ordered in order to identify upsell or cross-sell opportunities, and product trends.

Products By Contact

Similar to the above report, if your organization sells to contacts (as opposed to accounts), this report will show you the products your customers have purchased.

Sales History

Sales History shows both earned and lost opportunity revenue, grouped by owner, month, territory, or customer category or industry. This is a rearward looking report that helps sales users and managers gauge performance and evaluate how accurately they have recorded estimated revenues and probabilities.

Sales Pipeline

Perhaps the most powerful and useful report that is included with Dynamics CRM, the Sales Pipeline report (see Figure 23.5) is commonly used by sales manager and salespeople alike to view anticipated sales that have been logged as opportunities. In order for the Sales Pipeline report to function, a sales process workflow must be designed and applied to opportunities. The sales process workflow must use workflow stages, waiting for certain tasks or conditions before advancing to the next stage. Each stage in the sales workflow is then available in the Sales Pipeline report as a step in the pipeline.

Cross-Reference

Quotes, orders, and invoices are tightly related to one another in Dynamics CRM, both in terms of functionality and business processes. Many organizations that use these entities will integrate them with an ERP system which may be better-suited for processing transactions, using the Dynamics CRM records to display the transactions in account histories. More detail about using quotes, orders, and invoices is in Chapter 12.

Quote, Order, and Invoice reports

The Quote, Order, and Invoice reports are all nicely formatted reports meant to be customer-facing documents. Users who use the sales functionality to assemble a quote with products, quantities, taxes, and so on can run this report and export it as a PDF or Word document to send to the customer for approval. The user can select which columns to display in the report, such as quantity, discount, and price. When the quote is accepted, it can be converted to an order in Dynamics CRM, and then to an invoice, with each corresponding report serving as a customer-facing document. Many organizations will modify these reports to include a company logo and other formatting.

FIGURE 23.5

With a properly designed sales process workflow, the Sales Pipeline report becomes a powerful way to visualize anticipated sales figures.

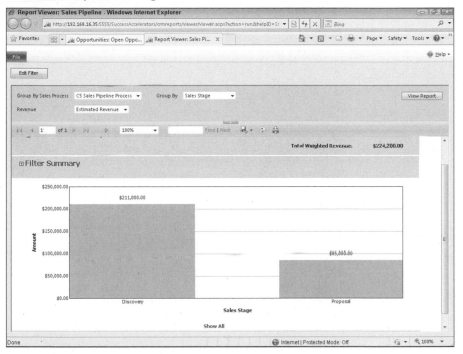

Invoice Status

This report is used to display the payment status of invoices and can be grouped by time period. Drilling into the chart reveals details for the underlying invoices for each status visible, and clicking on these details will open the relevant invoice record.

Service reports

The service reports that are not included in the sales and marketing categories deliver insight into the status of service cases, service activities, and the most frequently used knowledge base articles. Dynamics CRM has robust service functionality: cases are commonly used to track support requests and the resolutions; service activities can be used to schedule resources like people and equipment; and knowledge base articles are a handy means of capturing institutional knowledge and sharing it in a structure format.

Case Summary Table

The Case Summary Table is a multidimensional report that service managers can use to analyze the performance of service workers, trends in support requests, customer satisfaction, and case volume. To fully utilize this report, cases should have appropriate subjects and/or products associated with them, and customer satisfaction should be recorded before a case is resolved. Users can select from a variety of groupings when running this report in order to analyze the data from multiple perspectives.

Neglected Cases

This report is often used by service managers to determine which support requests have been overlooked or have gone unresolved over a period of time. When running this report, enter a period of days in the "Minimum Days Neglected" parameter to view cases with no associated activities during that time period.

Service Activity Volume

This report displays the number and duration of service activities, grouped by time period, resource, or customer. For those organizations that use the service scheduling tools in Dynamics CRM, this report is helpful in gauging utilization of resources such as personnel and equipment.

Top Knowledge Base Articles

Knowledge base (KB) articles can be attached to cases as a means of documenting the steps used to resolve a customer issue. Dynamics CRM keeps track of how frequently a KB article is used, and this report displays the top number of articles specified by the user. This report helps to identify recurring problems with product or subject categories, and is also useful when compiling an FAQ for customers to assist with self-service.

Using the Report Wizard

In keeping with Microsoft's emphasis on empowering users to consume data how and when they want it, Dynamics CRM has a simple, yet powerful, Report Wizard built in. The Report Wizard enables users to quickly create professionally formatted reports with charts, tables, and drill-through capabilities in just a few minutes and fully supports custom entities and fields.

The reports are generated as RDL files, the native format of Dynamics CRM's reporting engine, SQL Server Reporting Services. They can be shared with the entire organization and made context-sensitive so they can be run from the lists and forms of the underlying entities. Report Wizard reports can also be downloaded for further editing and customization in advanced reporting tools like Microsoft's Business Intelligence Development Studio.

Creating your first report with the wizard

In this example, we will build a report using the Report Wizard that displays the top ten accounts in our pipeline based on the size of the estimated revenue for open opportunities. Users with appropriate permissions may create this report using the Report Wizard by navigating to the Reports list in the Workplace area, clicking the New button, and following these steps:

1. By default the Report Type field is set to Report Wizard Report and the Report Wizard button is enabled. Click the button to launch the wizard.

2. On the Get Started screen, accept the default option to start a new report and choose the Language for which the report should be rendered (if multiple language packs are installed). Click Next.

3. On the Report Properties screen, enter the following values:
   - Report name: Top 10 Accounts in Pipeline
   - Report description: Top accounts currently in the pipeline
   - Primary record type: Accounts
   - Related record type: Opportunities (Potential Customer)

4. Click Next.

5. The next screen allows you to specify filtering criteria for the report. Filtering criteria narrow the scope of the report, reducing the number of records returned. Clear the criteria under the Accounts heading to run the report against all available accounts. Set the Opportunities filtering criteria to show only those opportunities with a Status that equals Open. Click Next.

Cross-Reference

The filter screen uses query criteria in a similar way as the Advanced Find tool, covered earlier in this chapter. Refer to the Advanced Find section to learn more about how to create complex queries.

6. On the Lay Out Fields screen, click the box at the top-left labeled Click here to add a grouping.

7. In the Add Grouping dialog set the following selections:

   Record type: Accounts

   Column: Account Name

   Sort order: Ascending

   Column width: 100 pixels

   Summary type: None

8. Click OK to close the Add Grouping dialog.

9. Next click the box labeled "Click here to add columns" and add the Opportunity's Topic column. Set the column width as 200 pixels.

10. Add another column with the Opportunity's Est. Close Date column. Set the column width to 75 pixels.

11. Add a third column with the Opportunity's Probability field. For the Summary type, choose Average, as shown in Figure 23.6.

12. Add a fourth column for the Opportunity's Est. Revenue. For the Summary type setting, choose Sum.

FIGURE 23.6

When adding columns to a report in the Report Wizard, you can summarize certain types of fields. Here we are calculating the average probability for an account's opportunities.

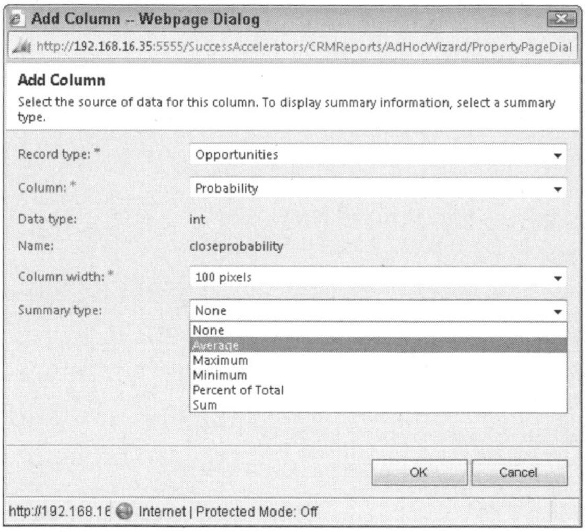

13. Still working on the Lay Out Fields screen, select the Set Top or Bottom Number... option. In the dialog that opens, set the number of groups to display as the top ten based on the Sum of Est. Revenue, as shown in Figure 23.7.

FIGURE 23.7

Setting the number of groups to display based on a calculated field in a Report Wizard report

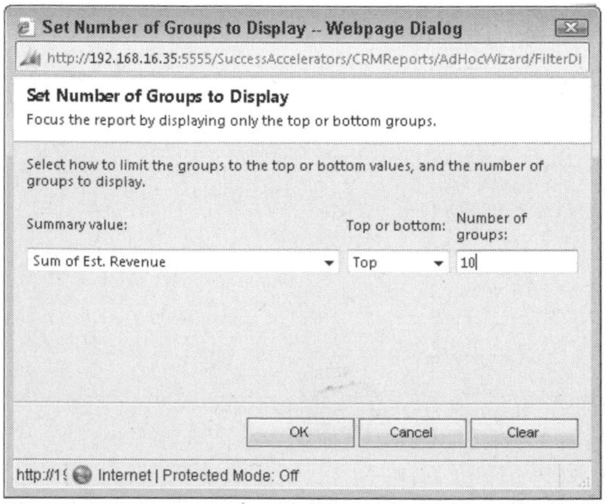

14. After laying out the fields, click the Next button to move to the Format Report screen. Format the report to display both a chart and a table, and select the option that reads Show chart. To view data for a chart region, click the chart region. Click Next.

15. Choose the Pie Chart option on the Select Chart Type screen and click Next.

16. Accept the defaults for the chart format. The slices data should come from the Account Name field, and the values from the Sum of Est. Revenue. Leave the check marks next to the labels and legend options and click Next. A Report Summary is displayed. Click Next again, and then Finish to complete the wizard.

17. The main report form will now be updated to reflect the values you entered in the Report Wizard. Set the categories option to Sales, and add Opportunities to the related record types. Click the Run Report button to preview the report (Figure 23.8).

On the Web Site

The RDL for this report is included on the companion Web site, in the file entitled Top 10 Accounts in Pipeline. rdl. If you are using Dynamics CRM on-premise or through a hosting provider that allows custom reports to be uploaded, you can create a new report using an existing file, and upload this file. Once uploaded you can edit it in the Report Wizard.

FIGURE 23.8

The custom report "Top 10 Accounts in Pipeline" created with the Report Wizard. Follow the steps in this section to create this report.

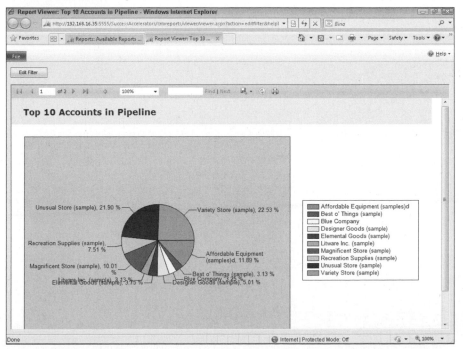

Tip

You can also create a report from an existing report that was created using the Report Wizard. This is a good practice if you want to experiment with a new version of a report you created using the wizard without altering the original. Once you are satisfied with your changes, you can unpublish the original by reverting it to a personal report. Trying to use the Report Wizard to modify the built-in reports or other custom reports not made with the wizard is likely to cause errors as the underlying query and data structure is not likely to be compatible with the wizard.

Setting default filters and report options

After creating a report with the Report Wizard or uploading a custom report, it will be set as a personal report by default. To make the report available to your organization's users:

1. Select the report in the reports list view and click the Edit button on the Ribbon.

2. Click the Actions menu item on the report property form and click Make Report Available to Organization. You can also use this menu to revert the report to personal.

You can edit the other properties of existing reports to tailor them to your organization. For example, if your organization will not be using the product catalog, follow these steps to hide the product reports from your organization:

1. Select the Products by Account report and click the Edit button to open its properties form.

2. Click the ellipsis next to the Categories field and remove the Sales Report category option. Click OK.

3. In the Display In field, remove all of the options so this field is empty. Save and close the report properties form.

Repeat these steps for the Products by Contact report. The reports will still be visible in the "All Reports, Including Sub-Reports" view, should you wish to make them available to your users again.

Using Excel as a BI Tool

One of the great advantages of Dynamics CRM is its tight integration with other Microsoft products, especially the ubiquitous Office program, Excel. Excel is, in fact, the world's most popular business intelligence and analysis tool, and, combined with Dynamics CRM, it can provide an incredibly powerful reporting platform.

Exporting data to Excel

The Export to Excel icon shows up at the top of nearly every list view in Dynamics CRM, including those for custom entities. There are several options for how the export should be formatted:

- **Static worksheet with records from this page.** This option exports the current page of the selected view to Excel with no link back to the live Dynamics CRM data. (Static worksheets can also be used to update and reimport data back into Dynamics CRM.)

- **Static worksheet with records from all pages in the current view.** This option is available only if there is more than one page of records in the currently selected view.

- **Dynamic PivotTable.** This option opens Excel with a preformatted pivot table and a dynamic query back to Dynamics CRM that can be refreshed. Users can select which columns will be available to use in the Excel pivot table.

- **Dynamic worksheet.** This option creates an Excel spreadsheet with a list of live data. If the data in Dynamics CRM is updated, refreshing the worksheet in Excel will reflect the updated records.

Caution

Some organizations may not want to allow data to be exported to Excel since this provides a simple way for large datasets to be copied to a common file format. The ability to export data to Excel can be restricted by a simple setting in users' security roles.

The Dynamic PivotTable option is the most commonly used for ad hoc reporting of Dynamics CRM data with Excel and will be the focus of this section. It provides a powerful example of combining these two Microsoft tools for business intelligence and analysis.

When exporting Dynamics CRM data to Excel, users can select the columns they wish to include in the export. Columns available for selection are not simply those of the presently viewed entity, but also those of entities that have an N:1 relationship with the present entity. An N:1 relationship means there is a lookup from the present entity to a "parent" entity. Columns from these parent entities are available for export.

When exporting to a Dynamic PivotTable, Dynamics CRM launches Excel and preformats an empty pivot table in the Excel 97-2003 Worksheet file format. which is compatible with nearly all versions of Excel in use today.

Note

Pivot tables are a way to view summaries of related data in a cross-tab format that is queried from the SQL Server database. While users can sometimes be intimidated by pivot tables, Dynamics CRM makes them very easy to create. Exporting to a pivot table can help users quickly summarize Dynamics CRM data, with automatically calculated counts or totals, nested and selectable groups, and compelling charts.

Creating useful reports with Excel

In order to create useful pivot tables to analyze your Dynamics CRM data, it is essential to select columns that make sense in a cross-tab format. Because pivot tables automatically summarize data, it often makes sense to select columns that have numerical values, as well as columns that represent logical groupings like categories or record owners.

In the following example, you can use the steps to create a pivot table and chart that display the estimated revenue of open opportunities by salesperson and by relationship type.

1. Navigate to the Opportunities list view in the Sales area and select the Open Opportunities view.

2. Click the Export to Excel button on the Ribbon menu.

3. Select the Dynamic PivotTable option (see Figure 23.9) and click the Select Columns button.

In this dialog, select the Dynamic PivotTable option to create a dynamic data link between Excel and Dynamics CRM and set up a pivot table in Excel.

4. In the Select PivotTable Columns dialog, with the Opportunity set as the Record Type, place check marks next to the following fields: Est. Revenue, Owner, and Probability. Remove check marks from other Opportunity fields. Do not close the column selection dialog.

5. Change the Record Type to Potential Customer (Account) and select the Relationship Type column as shown in Figure 23.10. Click OK.

6. Back on the Export Data to Excel dialog, click the Export button.

7. You will receive a File Download prompt asking if you want to open or save the Excel file. Save the file to your desktop, and then open it. Excel will prompt you with a warning that the file is in a different format than specified by the file extension. This is normal. Click Yes to open the file.

FIGURE 23.10

You can select columns from related record types when exporting data to Excel.

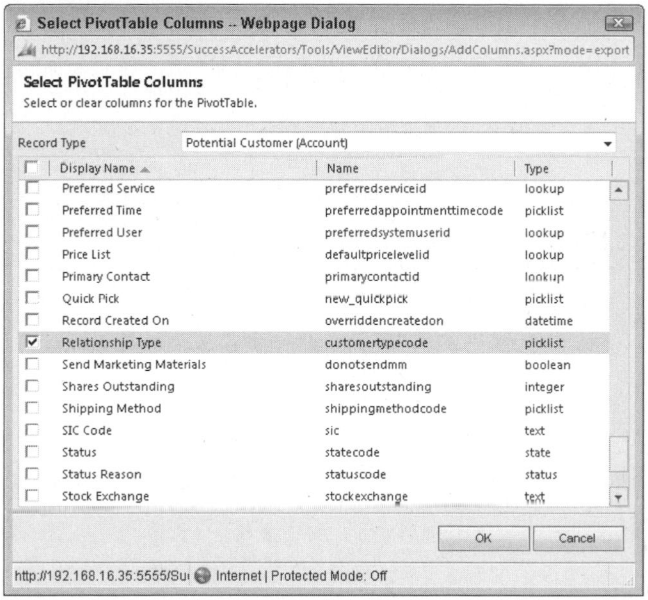

8. Click the Enable Content button to disable the security warning and permit the dynamic connection to the database. (This step may vary depending on the version of Excel you are using and your computer's security settings.) The file opens with an empty pivot table, and the Excel pivot table field list (see Figure 23.11).

When the Dynamics CRM for Outlook client is not installed, you cannot see this data.

1. Click on the Owner field in the field list and drag it to the box in column A, where it says Drop Row Fields Here.

2. Drag the Probability field next to the Owner field to create a nested grouping.

3. Drag the Est. Value field to the box labeled Drop Value Fields Here.

4. Drag the Relationship Type field to the box labeled Drop Report Filter Fields Here.

5. Your pivot table should now have data with automated summaries as shown in Figure 23.12.

6. To add a chart, place your cursor in one of the data cells in the pivot table, and click the Insert menu in Excel. Select a pie chart of your choosing. The results should look similar to Figure 23.12.

7. Save the Excel file and close it.

FIGURE 23.11

The export process includes commands which set up an empty pivot table in Excel and open the Excel PivotTable Field List panel. You may need to enable the content if you receive a security warning.

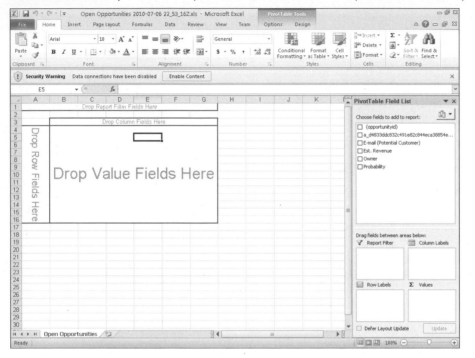

Making the pivot table available to other users

The pivot table and chart created in the previous exercise contains a dynamic link to the data in Dynamics CRM. If you reopen the pivot table, it will automatically refresh with the latest data in the system. The dynamic link uses a data query in Excel that uses special views in Dynamics CRM to maintain data security. Users will only be able to see data in pivot tables that they would otherwise be able to see in Dynamics CRM. This makes pivot tables a great way to quickly build interesting reports that can be shared with other users.

To share the pivot table with other users:

1. Navigate to the reports area in the Workplace and click the New button.

2. In the report properties form, highlight the picklist drop-down for the Report Type field and select Existing File.

3. In the File Location box that appears, browse to the location where you saved the pivot table Excel file.

FIGURE 23.12

The completed pivot table report includes a chart.

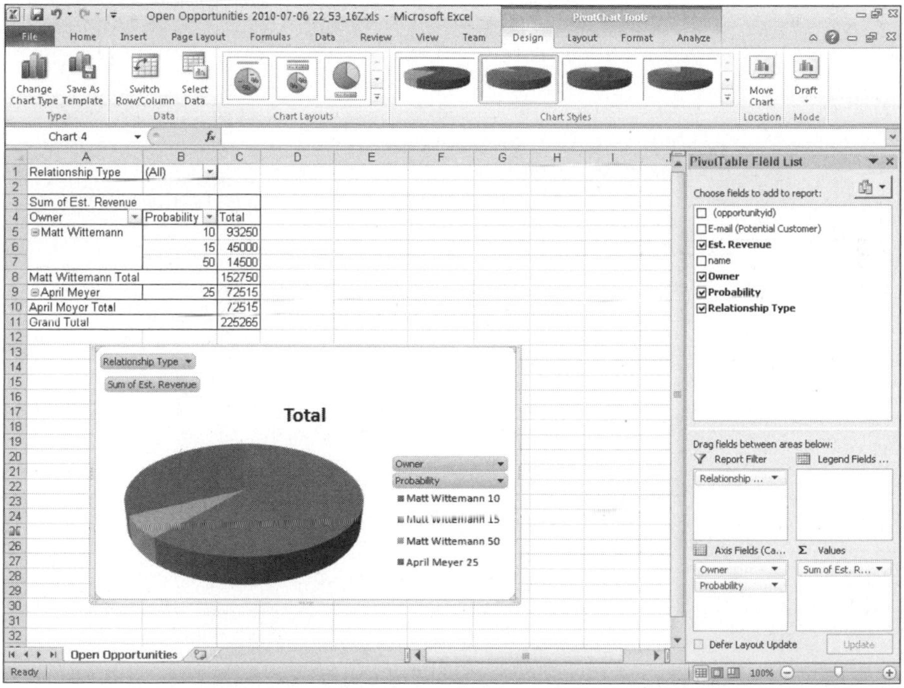

4. The report name will be pre-populated based on the filename. You may modify this if you wish.

5. Set the category, related record types, and the areas of Dynamics CRM where you wish the report to appear, and click the Save button. Do not close the report properties form.

6. On the Actions menu at the top of the report properties form, select Make Report Available to Organization.

7. Let your users know about the new report and where they can find it. When they run the report, Dynamics CRM will launch Excel (and may give them similar security prompts as you received when you designed the pivot table), and automatically update with the latest data their security roles permit them to view.

Summary

This chapter introduced the concept of Business Intelligence (BI) and the variety of ways that Dynamics CRM makes BI easy for users, lessening their reliance on busy IT departments or costly consultants.

Dynamics CRM is designed to make it easy for users to consume and analyze data when and how they want, with built-in tools that are both powerful and intuitive. Some of the quickest ways that users can begin to create their own reports are through the Advanced Find tool, the Report Wizard, and by using Excel for analysis. There are also a couple dozen reports included with Dynamics CRM for analysis of traditional customer relationship management functions.

Often what users call reports can be provided via system views. Some users may also avail themselves of the Advanced Find tool, which can create very complex queries to locate precise sets of data and display them dynamically in views that can be saved and shared among users.

The built-in reports deliver great value if your organization uses Dynamics CRM for traditional sales, service, and marketing. The 24 reports include many subreports and can be sliced and diced to display data in dozens more ways, multiplying the reports to effectively provide 75 or more ways to analyze your organizations data and performance.

The Report Wizard is easy to use and provides nicely formatted, professional looking reports with charts, pre-filtering and drill-through capabilities. Users can create reports in under five minutes and save them for reuse and sharing.

Finally, the power of Excel is brought to bear on Dynamics CRM as demonstrated through powerful pivot tables. Pivot tables automatically summarize data, and Dynamics CRM sets up live data links between itself and Excel so data is automatically refreshed when the pivot table file is opened.

Working with Visualizations: Charts and Dashboards

O ne of the most significant features introduced with Dynamics CRM 2011 is visualizations. Visualizations (charts and dashboards) enable users to quickly summarize information from thousands of records into snapshots. But visualizations go beyond static graphical pictures — they also enable users to interact with them. This interactive experience with visualizations means that users can move from summary data to detailed actionable information in a few clicks.

Visualizations can be created by users for personal use, or by administrators for distribution systemwide. Users can share their user visualizations with others. Charts and dashboards presented by visualizations honor each user's security settings to ensure that data is protected.

The visualization framework can also be expanded if desired. Organizations can create their own visualizations or Microsoft and third parties can offer new visualizations over time. Some visualization expansions may include new chart types, geographic mapping, SharePoint and social media integration, Gantt charts, gauges for tracking goals, and advanced data analysis through statistical modeling.

Cross-Reference

In addition to the visualizations discussed in this chapter, you can also use Excel and SQL Server Reporting Services (SSRS) to create and publish other types of visualizations. For more information, see Chapters 23 and 25.

IN THIS CHAPTER

Using and creating charts

Advanced charting with the SDK

Using and creating dashboards

Working with Charts

Charts are a way to visualize information that is in Dynamics CRM views. Charts enable you and others in your business to quickly summarize information that may be contained in hundreds, thousands, or millions of records in Dynamics CRM.

If you think of a Dynamics CRM view as an Excel spreadsheet (with rows and columns), then you can think of a chart as an Excel chart that summarizes data from the spreadsheet. As you find out later, charts share many other characteristics with views.

Cross-Reference

To work with charts, you should have a good understanding of views and advanced find. For more information about working with views, see Chapter 10. For information about using advanced find and creating custom views, see Chapter 17.

Using charts

Dynamics CRM includes a number of charts out of the box. You can quickly display and interact with these charts to analyze the information within Dynamics CRM.

Viewing charts

Wherever you see a grid in Dynamics CRM you can view a chart to visualize the data in the grid. This includes areas such as accounts, opportunities, and cases. Figure 24.1 is an example of the opportunity grid with a funnel chart displayed next to it.

The steps for viewing charts are the same in the Outlook and Web versions of Dynamics CRM. Note, however, that the screens will look a bit different depending upon which version you are using. Use this process to view a chart:

1. Navigate to the grid that you would like to visualize as a chart. For example, to view a chart of opportunities, navigate to Sales ⇨ Opportunities.

2. If you do not already see a chart near the grid, then in the Ribbon menu select the View option and click on Charts (see Figure 24.2).

3. Select Right or Top depending on where you want the chart to be displayed (to the right of the grid or above the grid). The chart is displayed in the selected position.

4. Above the chart is a picklist containing all of the charts available for this Dynamics CRM entity. Click the picklist to choose the desired chart.

Tip

You can also view charts in sub-grids by following the same instructions as above. There are some differences and limitations with using charts on sub-grids. For more information see the section later in this chapter, "Using charts on forms."

Opportunity grid with a funnel chart

Clicking the Charts button on the view tab of the Ribbon menu

Interacting with charts

After a chart is displayed next to a grid, there are a variety of ways that you can interact with it. We describe some of the basic methods first, and then we spend a little more time discussing how you can use the drill-down feature to go deeper when analyzing data in Dynamics CRM.

Basic chart interactions

This section summarizes some simple methods for interacting with your charts to get a quick understanding of the data in Dynamics CRM.

- **Change the chart type.** You can use the picklist just above the chart to view different charts.

- **Changing the view.** You can change the view for the grid and the chart will be refreshed to summarize the data in the current view. For example, you can switch from the My Open Opportunities view to the Open Opportunities view and the data will be refreshed to reflect the new view.

- **Changing the chart layout.** You can move the layout of the chart by clicking the Chart button in the Ribbon menu and selecting a new location for the chart.

- **Collapsing and expanding the chart.** If you would like to see more of the data in the grid, but still have easy access to the chart, you can click the collapse button. You can click the button again to expand the chart.

- **Hiding the chart.** If you decide that you would prefer not to display a chart for a grid at all, you can navigate to the View tab in the ribbon Ribbon menu, click the Charts button, and select Off. Clicking this button again will allow you to redisplay the chart. Note that at the time of this writing, charts can be turned off completely in Outlook, but not in the Web version of Dynamics CRM.

Drilling down

In addition to the above options, you can also drill-down into the data in your charts. Drilling down lets you select a portion of a chart to create another chart with more details about the selected section of a chart and also update the view grid to display only the selected records. The drill-down functionality works in a similar manner for all chart types. Use the procedure below to drill down into a chart:

1. Navigate to the chart that you wish to drill down into.

2. Using the mouse pointer, click on the section of the chart that you want to drill into. For example, this can be an individual bar in a bar graph, a section of a funnel (as illustrated in Figure 24.3), or a slice in a pie chart.

3. You will be presented with a popup dialog box asking for information on how you want to drill into the data. Fill in the dialog box and click the OK button.

   - In the View By box, select the field that you wish to use for the chart in your drill down.

   - In the Chart Type box, select the type of chart that you wish to use to present the data. The chart and the grid are refreshed to show only the records you selected for your drill down.

You can repeat this process to drill farther and farther down into your data for increasing levels of detail. As you drill deeper into your data, you can use the breadcrumbs to back up through earlier steps in your drill-down iterations if you like.

FIGURE 24.3

Drilling into a funnel chart

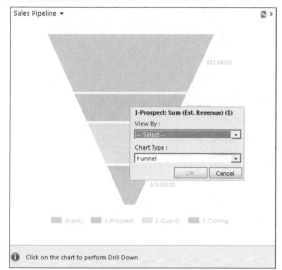

Managing charts

In addition to using the included charts, you also have the option of creating new charts or modifying existing charts. The Dynamics CRM user interface makes it fast and easy to create new charts. If you need even more options to customize your charts then you can export an existing chart, modify it externally, and import it back into Dynamics CRM.

Creating charts

Users can create new charts whenever they wish. These charts are available to the user for personal use or to selectively share with other users. Follow the steps below to create a new chart:

1. Navigate to the grid that you wish to create a chart for. For example, if you would like to create a chart of opportunities, navigate to Sales ➪ Opportunities.

2. If charts are not displayed for this entity, then follow the instructions under Viewing Charts (covered earlier in this chapter) to display a chart.

3. Click the View tab in the Ribbon menu and then click the New Chart button. The chart you were viewing will be replaced with the chart designer (see Figure 24.4) and some new options will become available in the Ribbon menu.

4. Back in the Ribbon menu, make sure you are now on the Design tab and choose the type of chart you wish to display from the Charts area.

FIGURE 24.4

The chart designer

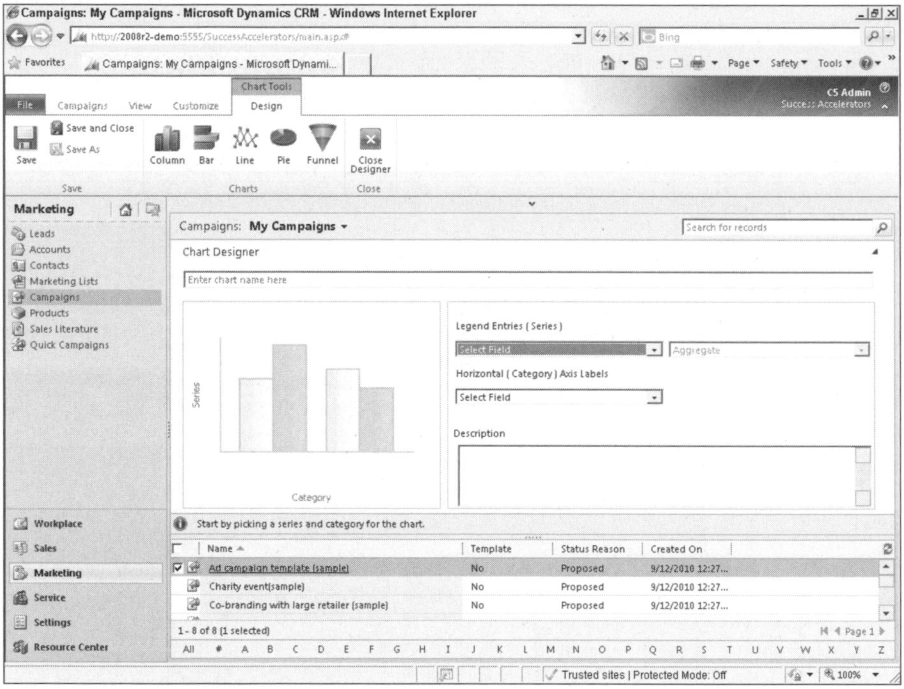

5. Using the chart designer, fill in the fields to design your chart. Options include:

- **Chart Name:** Fill in the box above the chart with a descriptive name for your chart. If you leave this field blank, it will be auto-populated based on what you enter into remaining fields.

- **Legend Entries (Series):** These two fields determine the field that will be used as the "scale" on the chart and the operator that will be applied to this value. For example, your chart can display the sum of all estimated revenues or the average of all estimated revenues. Alternatively you can display a count of the number of records by category (if you wish to display only a count, then you can select any field for the first value and then choose count).

- **Horizontal (Category) Axis Labels:** This is the category that will be used to subdivide the chart into individual bars, slices, or sections of a funnel. Depending on what you enter in this field, you may also be presented with an option for how to group your data. For example, if you enter a date field here, you will have the option to group dates by month, day, and so on.

- **Description:** Optionally, you can enter a description here that provides more information about the purpose and usage of your chart.

- **Advanced Options:** Clicking the Show link next to Advanced Options allows you to display only the top or bottom records based on the selected legend. This can be useful for charts that display the top ten customers, for example.

6. When you are satisfied with the design of your chart, go to the Design tab in the Ribbon menu and click Save and Close. The chart designer closes and your chart is updated.

7. Your saved chart is added to the picklist of charts for the entity in Dynamics CRM under the heading of My Charts (see Figure 24.5).

FIGURE 24.5

The My Charts" area of the charts picklist

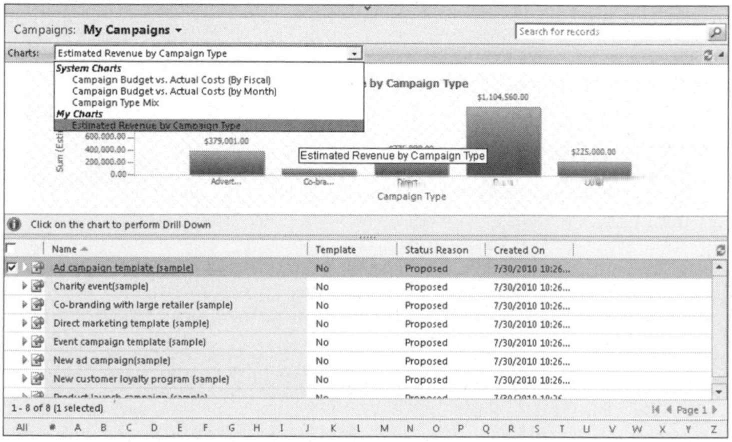

Everyday use of Drill Down

There are a number of ways that the drill-down functionality can enhance how you make decisions and how quickly you can respond to customers and prospects. Here is one example:

Lauren is the Director of Customer Service. Using Dynamics CRM, she has a view of all cases that her team is actively working. Her department promises a follow-up date after each customer call, and they are measured by how well they meet those expectations. So Lauren has set up a view of past due cases and (1) a chart that shows the day that they were due for follow-up. This gives her an at-a-glance perspective on the number of past due follow-ups and how far past due they are. She then drills into the past due items with (2) a pie chart based on the priority of the items. From here, she (3) can drill deeper into the high-priority items by customer. Using the list in her grid, she can then assign relevant items to senior support technicians for follow-up.

continued

continued

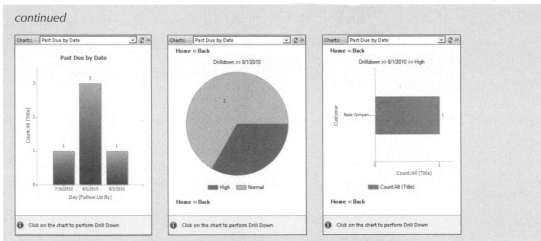

Three drill-downs for case follow-up planning

Lauren could also use drill down to analyze which service reps have the largest backlog of items for follow-up, customer satisfaction with completed cases, and so on.

Now that you have designed a chart, there are some other options that you may want to use in the Chart area of the View tab of the Ribbon menu while the chart is being displayed:

- **Edit, Save As, Delete Chart:** You can edit the current chart, or delete the chart. Note that you cannot edit system charts from here, but you can click the Save As button and save a copy of a system chart and you can then edit the saved copy.

- **Assign:** You can assign the chart to a different user as the owner. This can be a helpful feature if a colleague asks you to design a chart. Note that if you do not first share the chart with yourself, then the chart will no longer be visible to you after you assign it to someone else.

- **Share this Chart:** Similar to assign, this allows you to share a chart with a colleague while also enabling you to determine if the colleague can edit the chart or only view it. Sharing charts is very similar to sharing other records in Dynamics CRM. For more information on sharing records, see Chapter 10.

- **Import/Export Chart:** Your chart can be exported to a file that can then be updated externally with some features that are not available in the chart designer.

System Charts versus User Charts

Charts can be created as either system charts (charts that are available for everyone in your organization) or as user charts (charts created by an individual user and that can be shared selectively with other users). System charts are created in the Settings area and user charts are created next to the grid that the chart will be associated with. For purposes of this section, we are creating user charts. For more information on creating system charts, see Chapters 16 and 17.

Using charts on forms

As mentioned earlier in this chapter, charts can be presented within your Dynamics CRM forms. Viewing and interacting charts within forms is done, for the most part, in the same manner as has been described earlier. However, there are a few items to be aware of:

- Charts can only be made visible where there are grids or sub-grids. When viewing a form, grids are visible where you see related items in the navigation pane. Sub-grids can be embedded directly into forms without using the Navigation pane and these, too, can have charts associated with them.

- The form designer can restrict how sub-grids work with charts. Depending on how a form was designed will determine if you can use charts with sub-grids. Figure 24.6 illustrates a sub-grid that has been configured to allow charts and sub-grids to be displayed.

Importing and exporting charts

As mentioned earlier, charts can be exported into an XML format. Once it is exported it can be modified and reimported into Dynamics CRM. Exporting and importing charts can also be handy if you want to move a chart from one instance of Dynamics CRM to another or convert a user chart into an organization chart.

To export a chart:

1. Navigate to the page containing the chart you wish to export.
2. Select the chart that you want to export from the picklist above the currently displayed chart.
3. In the Ribbon menu, select the View tab and then click Export Chart.
4. Save the file to a convenient location.

Use the same process to import a chart, clicking on the Import Chart button in the Ribbon menu rather than Export Chart. If the chart appears to be a duplicate, you will have the opportunity to either overwrite the duplicate chart or create a new one.

FIGURE 24.6

A chart displayed as part of a form by using a sub-grid

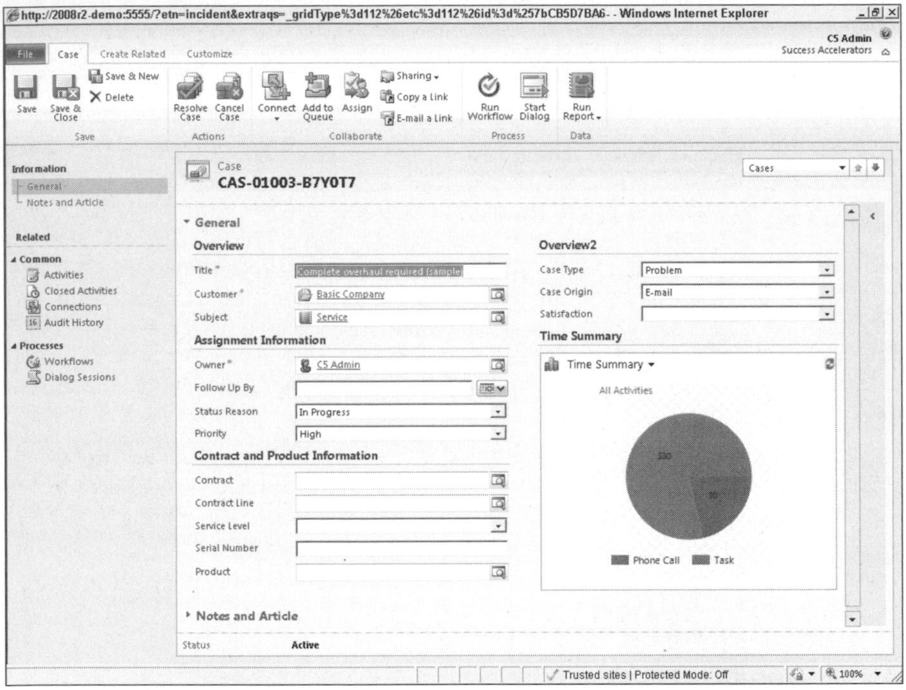

Modifying charts with the software development kit (SDK)

Exported charts can be edited to add options not available from the chart designer in Dynamics CRM. Editing an exported chart requires some understanding of XML (specifically FetchXML), which is documented in the Dynamics CRM software development kit (SDK).

Cross-Reference

The software development kit (SDK) is a set of documentation that provides instructions on methods for extending Dynamics CRM. The SDK can be freely downloaded from Microsoft. For more information on the SDK and on extending Dynamics CRM, see Chapter 20.

If you would like to experiment with updating the FetchXML for a chart, then export the chart that you wish to update. Open the chart in a text editing tool (such as Windows Notepad) to view the code. Here are a few simple changes you can make to the chart by editing the FetchXML:

- Change the chart type: Charts support some chart types that you cannot access from the Dynamics CRM user interface. Replace the text after "Chart Type=" with values such as Doughnut, StackedColumn and Pyramid.

- Change fonts and colors: Wherever you see a font or color, you can customize it to your liking. Colors can be standard colors such as "blue" or can be RGB colors.

- Imitate other charts: Dynamics CRM includes a number of charts that contain formatting that is not available for charts created through the user interface. Export these charts and review the FetchXML for them to understand how to change these settings in your charts.

Once you have completed making your changes, import them back into Dynamics CRM to see how they look. Keep in mind that editing FetchXML requires precision — if there is anything that you revised that Dynamics CRM does not understand, then it will not allow you to import the chart.

Cross-Reference
Writing code in FetchXML is covered in more detail in Chapters 20 and 21.

On the Web Site
Check the Web site (www.dynamicscrmbible.com) for a few examples of charts that you can develop by editing the FetchXML. Use them as a starting point to learn how to update the XML to create your own custom charts.

Working with Dashboards

A dashboard combines multiple grids, charts, Iframes, and Web resources into a single page in Dynamics CRM. In addition, using the Iframe, Dynamics CRM reports can also be incorporated into dashboards. These different types of visualizations can be grouped into sections, and sections can be grouped into tabs to organize all of the elements of a dashboard. Figure 24.7 illustrates the elements that can be combined to create dashboards.

Note
At the time of this writing, you cannot control the sections and tabs on dashboards. However, control for these elements may be included in future updates to Dynamics CRM 2011.

Dashboards are powerful because they combine multiple elements into a single screen. Dashboard elements can be set up for users so that most of the information that they need to organize their day, be responsive to customers, and track their work can be available in just a few screens. Because they're interactive, users can get work done directly from their dashboards.

Multiple dashboards can be accessed in the dashboards area of Dynamics CRM. Like charts, dashboards can be delivered to all users systemwide, or they can be developed by a single user for personal use. Also like charts, user dashboards can be shared among different users.

FIGURE 24.7

The structure of a Dynamics CRM dashboard

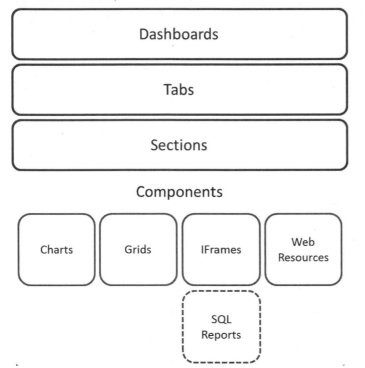

Using dashboards

Dynamics CRM includes a number of dashboards for immediate use out of the box. You may find that the visualizations included in these dashboards are sufficient to handle the needs of many of the individuals within your organization.

Viewing dashboards

Dashboards are found in the Workplace area of Dynamics CRM as the first available link in the Navigation pane. Navigating to the dashboards area will bring up your default dashboard. Use the functions described below to set up and manage your dashboard view:

- **Change dashboards:** There is a picklist located just above the dashboards and below the Ribbon menu. Use this to navigate to different dashboards.

- **Set as Default:** Click this option in the Ribbon menu to set the dashboard that you are currently viewing to be your default. The next time you return to the dashboards area, the selected dashboard will be the first one that you see.

- **Refresh All:** Click this option in the Ribbon menu if you want to see updated information in the dashboard. This enables you to see up-to-the-minute information in the dashboard without having to navigate away from the page and then back again. This can be helpful if you tend to monitor a dashboard without otherwise interacting with Dynamics CRM.

Interacting with dashboards

Dashboards can be made up of four different types of components or visualizations. How you interact with each component varies depending upon the component itself.

- **Charts:** If you are comfortable interacting with charts, then you already know the fundamentals of interacting with charts in dashboards. In addition to drill downs (see the section "Interacting with charts") charts presented within dashboards also allow you to zoom in, view the grid behind the chart, or refresh the chart. These options become visible as icons when you move the mouse pointer over the chart area. Figure 24.8 is an example of interaction icons on a dashboard.

FIGURE 24.8

Interaction icons in a chart on a dashboard

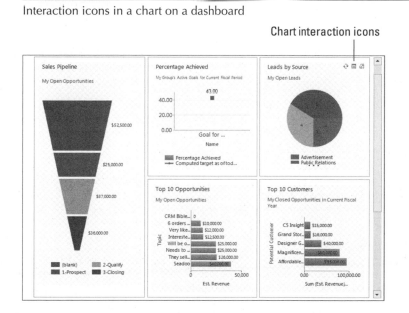

- **Grids:** Grids presented in charts behave in almost exactly the same manner as grids presented in other areas of Dynamics CRM. You can open records from within the grid, search and sort the grid; you can even display a chart of the grid data to the right of the grid if the dashboard creator has included this functionality.

- **Iframes and Web Resources:** Iframes and Web resources display information from other Web sites or customizations you have installed for Dynamics CRM. How you interact with these items will vary depending upon the nature of the site or application. See Chapter 21 for more information on iframes and Web resources.

Managing dashboards

Dynamics CRM allows users to create their own dashboards and allows system administrators to create dashboards that can be distributed across the organization. The process for creating either type of dashboard is identical with the exception of where you go to start the process of creating a dashboard.

- User dashboards are created in Workplace ⇨ Dashboards.
- Systemwide dashboards (also called organization owned dashboards) are created in Settings ⇨ Customizations.

Instructions are provided for creating user dashboards in this chapter. For information on how to make systemwide customizations, see Chapters 16 and 17.

Creating dashboards

Follow these instructions to design a dashboard in Dynamics CRM:

1. Create the necessary views and charts. Dashboards in Dynamics CRM are made up mostly of charts and views. Prior to creating a dashboard, you must prepare the charts and views required for your dashboard. For information on creating charts, see the appropriate section earlier in this chapter. For information on creating views, see Chapter 10 for the basics and Chapter 17 for information on using advanced find.

2. Navigate to the dashboards area of Dynamics CRM by going to Workplace ⇨ Dashboards.

3. Click the New button in the Ribbon menu.

4. You will be presented with the Dashboard Layouts dialog box (see Figure 24.9). Select the layout closest to your desired design.

5. Each component on the dashboard page has four icons in it. You can click on the desired icon to add a chart, grid, Iframe, or Web resource. For your initial charts, select either a chart or a grid for each component (for more information on Iframes and Web resources, see the next section).

   - If you choose to add a chart, you then need to select the record type, view, and chart for this component of the dashboard. Figure 24.10 is an example of the dialog box for setting up a chart in a dashboard.

   - If you choose a grid, you will then be asked for the record type and view for your grid. After adding a grid to a dashboard, you can double-click it to open the sub-grid properties dialog box and make changes to the settings for the grid.

6. You can insert new components into the dashboard or change the layout of the dashboard by using the options in the Ribbon menu.

7. Click Dashboard Properties in the Ribbon menu and give your dashboard a name.

8. When you have completed designing your dashboard, click Save and Close.

FIGURE 24.9

Dashboard Layouts dialog box

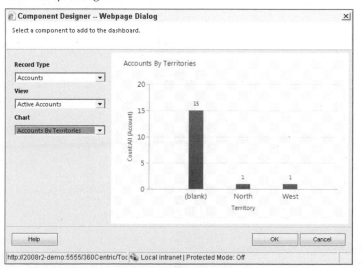

FIGURE 24.10

Chart setup dialog box

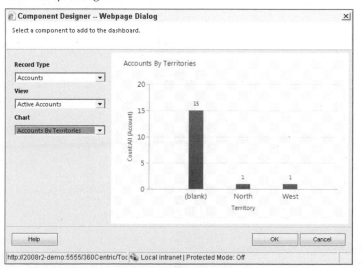

Understanding iframes and Web resources

Dashboards can be extended by using Iframes and Web resources to embed additional functionality into them. Iframes stand for internet frames. They frame up information from other Web sites and make it available inside a window of another Web application (such as Dynamics CRM). Web resources are stored directly on the Dynamics CRM server and are assigned a URL and can include HTML pages, Silverlight applications, images, JScript code, and other files.

Any number of extensions can be added to Dynamics CRM using these tools including:

- Mapping applications to visualize data geographically
- Social media connectors to display social interactions within the dashboard
- Integration with other systems within your organization
- SharePoint integration to share announcements and other information from SharePoint inside of Dynamics CRM

Cross-Reference
For more information on Iframes and Web resources, see Chapter 21.

Summary

Visualizations in Dynamics CRM present a snapshot of your data in a quick and easy-to-understand format. The included design tools can be used by either end users to develop personal visualizations or by system administrators to develop organization-wide charts and dashboards. Charts and dashboards can be extended programmatically with custom functions if desired.

Microsoft designed visualizations in Dynamics CRM to be interactive. Users can work with charts and dashboards to move from analysis to action in fewer steps because they don't have to navigate to one part of the application to see charts and another part to see detailed records. Through the use of grids, charts, and interactivity, many users can manage their work directly from a few dashboards rather than having to navigate to other areas of Dynamics CRM for routine tasks.

CHAPTER 25

Custom Reporting for Dynamics CRM

In spite of the tremendous improvements to the built-in reporting tools in Microsoft Dynamics CRM 2011, there may still arise a need for more complex or customized reports. When custom views or visualizations, dashboards, Excel pivot tables, and Report Wizard reports do not provide the flexibility your organization requires, it is time to turn to custom report development.

The goal of this chapter is to provide you with the knowledge you will need to begin creating custom reports for Dynamics CRM, beginning with an introduction to the architecture of Dynamics CRM's reporting engine. We then provide an overview of the tools you can use to develop custom reports for both on-premises and online deployments, recommendations for creating professional, useful reports that meet your users' needs, and a walk-through of the report development process.

In the most general sense, a report can take many forms. A report can be any organized view of data, including lists, charts, and tables. Reports can be rendered as dynamic views, printed lists, spreadsheets, or any number of formats. The focus of this chapter, however, is on the concepts and technologies used to create reports that are powered by SQL Server Reporting Services. These custom reports are launched from the reports list view in the Dynamics CRM Workplace area or from the report icon on view and record toolbars.

Examining the Anatomy of Dynamics CRM Reporting

Dynamics CRM uses Microsoft's SQL Server Reporting Services (SSRS) as the engine that delivers a rich and interactive report experience. SSRS is a component that is included in most versions of SQL Server, and should be installed and configured prior to installing Dynamics CRM.

SSRS is an n-tier Web application, with a browser-based user interface, a Web services API, a processing platform, and a data layer housed in SQL Server. The SSRS application can be installed from the SQL Server installation media on the same server as the SQL Server databases, or on a separate server.

Depending on the underlying query and the amount of data to be returned, running an SSRS report can be a resource-intensive operation that can cause high memory and CPU utilization. Therefore, organizations that expect high demand for custom reports may wish to install SSRS on its own server.

Cross-Reference

Custom reports built using SQL Server Reporting Services are only one of the ways to create reports. More information on the built-in tools that can be used for business intelligence and data analysis is included in other chapters of this book. Chapter 23 includes details on using Dynamics CRM's dashboards and inline visualizations. Chapter 24 covers the other built-in reporting tools, including the Report Wizard and Excel.

Taking a look at how Dynamics CRM interacts with the report server

The Report Manager Web site and the Report Server Web site are the two primary Web interfaces for SSRS. The Report Manager Web site , shown in Figure 25.1, is the main Web interface for SSRS, designed to provide administrators with an interface that can be used to manage reports and report server settings. The Report Manager Web site's address by default is `http://<servername>/Reports`.

As shown in Figure 25.1, when Dynamics CRM is installed, a folder is created in the SSRS Web site using the name of the organization database. In a multitenant deployment, each organization has its own folder within the SSRS Report Manager Web site.

The Report Server Web site is the root URI of the SSRS Web services API and is primarily used by applications that use the SSRS reporting engine. You must specify the Report Server address (`http://server/reportserver` by default) when installing Dynamics CRM. Installing Dynamics CRM or creating a new organization creates a folder for the organization within the Report Server. The folders for each Dynamics CRM organization are represented as text links in the Report Server Web site (see Figure 25.2).

FIGURE 25.1

The SSRS Report Manager Web site is used to manage reports for Dynamics CRM organizations as well as SSRS settings.

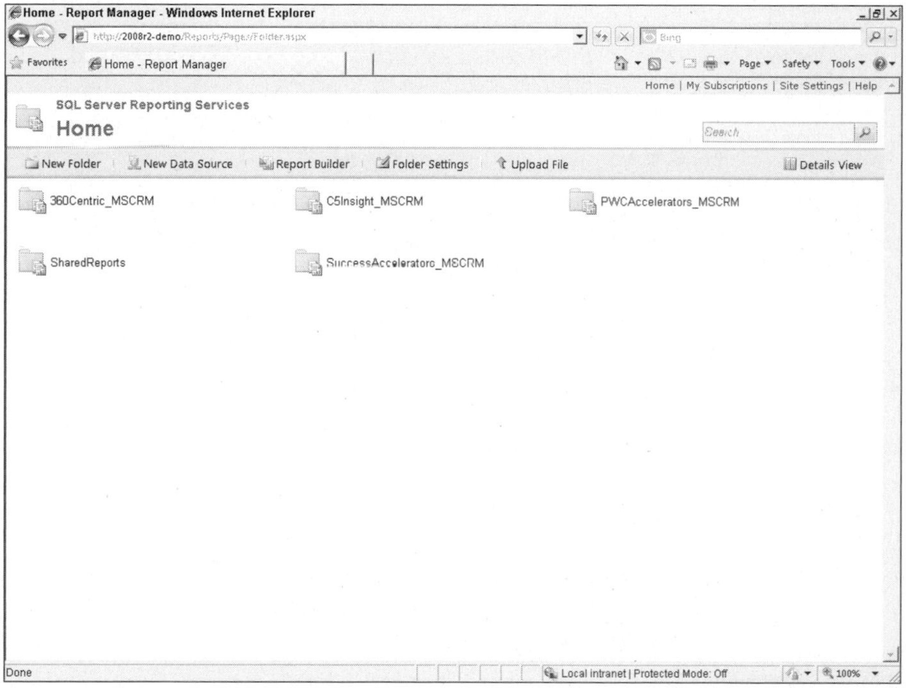

The installation or organization creation process also creates the data sources that SSRS needs to connect to the Dynamics CRM organization databases and publishes the included reports to a Shared Reports folder in the SSRS Report Manager. Two data sources are created for each organization: a SQL Server data source and a Fetch data source. The SQL Server data source enables reports to use a standard SQL connection string to query the tables and views within an organization database. The Fetch data source is a special data source that was developed to enable custom reports to be developed for Dynamics CRM Online, since direct access to the SQL Server tables and views in Microsoft's data centers is not permitted. When an SSRS report is run through Dynamics CRM, it uses the appropriate data source, ignoring the data source that was used during report development.

Serving a report through Dynamics CRM

When a client requests a report from Dynamics CRM, the request is passed to the Dynamics CRM application layer (the Dynamics CRM Web site), and then to the SQL Server Reporting Services application. The report server passes the query to the SQL Server database for the organization and then processes the results of the report request (see Figure 25.3).

FIGURE 25.2

The SSRS Report Server Web site, with links to each organization's reports

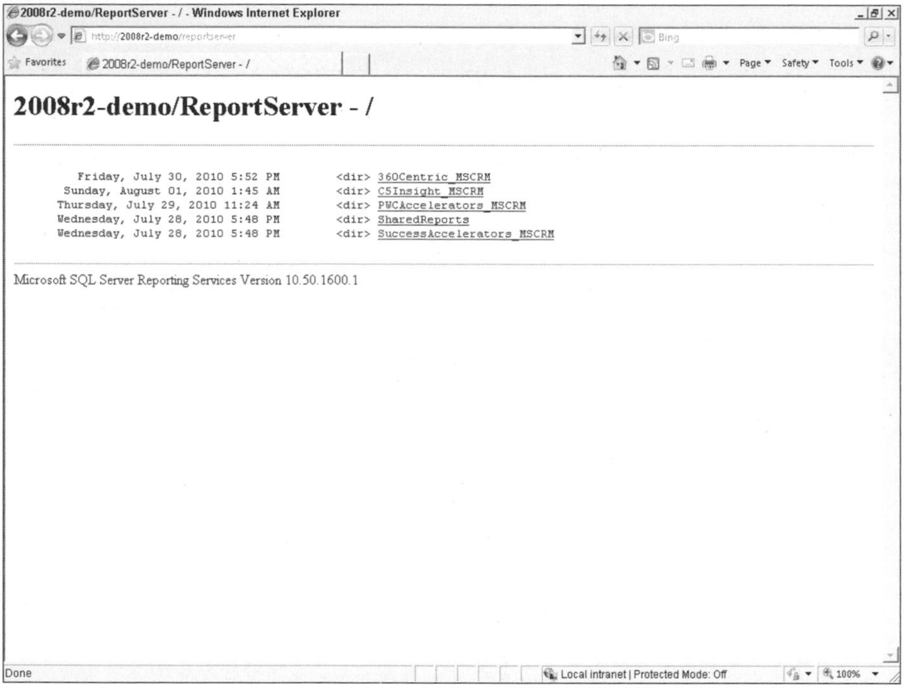

The report is then rendered in Dynamics CRM using a report viewer control. The report viewer control displays the report to the requesting user inside the Dynamics CRM interface.

Authentication needs to traverse all of these layers as well — from the client to the Dynamics CRM application to the report server. Normally, when a client makes a request of an application that uses SSRS as its report engine, SSRS authenticates to the database to retrieve the data. Because the data returned in a Dynamics CRM report is dependent on the security role privileges of the user, the credentials of the user must be used by SSRS to retrieve the data. This is known as a double-hop, and might be a point of failure if the credentials are not handed off between the applications. In order to overcome this inherent challenge, Microsoft provides an application extension called the Reporting Extension for SSRS. (See Chapter 4 for more information on this extension and how to install and configure it.)

Report file format

SSRS reports can be created by any tool that can generate XML that complies with Microsoft's Report Definition Language (RDL). Report files have the .rdl file extension. RDL files are uploaded into the Dynamics CRM report entity, where they are stored in the organization database and synchronized to the report server. Because the code in the RDL file is stored in the Dynamics CRM database, reports are transported with the organization database if it is redeployed, and they can be run by users with the Outlook client while offline. They can also be exported as part of a solution along with other customizations.

The Dynamics CRM application passes report requests to the SQL Server Reporting Services service, which retrieves the data from SQL Server and handles the layout and report rendering, which is delivered to the Dynamics CRM report viewer control.

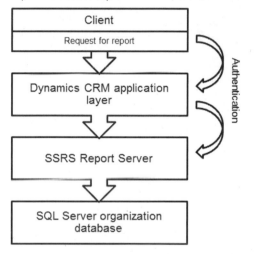

Working with the report

Designing useful reports for Dynamics CRM requires an understanding of more than report design. Reports interact with the Dynamics CRM interface in a variety of ways that make them more contextual and useful for users. We recommend that you review some of the key elements in the user's report experience in the Dynamics CRM interface in order to help your users get the most out of the system's robust reporting functionality.

Selecting the records to report on

Users can run a report from three places in Dynamics CRM: the report list view in the Workplace, the ribbon at the top of an entity list view, and from a record form. Running a report from each of these areas has slightly different implications:

- Report list view. Typically if a built-in or custom report is run from the report list view, the user will need to supply parameters so the report server knows which record or records to include in the query.

- Ribbon on entity list views. Running a report from the list view of an entity requires the user to select a record or records to be used by the report server as parameters in the report.

- Ribbon on a record form. Running a report from a record's form typically means the report will be run against only the currently viewed record.

Filtering a report

Many reports include filtering options that enable users to run a report on a specific set of records that is relevant to them (see Figure 25.4). A report can include default filters, and users can use an Advanced Find-like interface to modify the filter before running the report. Filtering also helps to improve report performance by limiting the amount of data that is returned.

Using report controls

In addition to prefiltering a report, many reports include textboxes, picklists, or calendar controls that enable users to set parameters within a report (see Figure 25.5). (Reports often contain hidden parameters as well, a topic that is discussed later in this chapter.) Parameters can allow users to change the way the report is displayed by changing groupings or further filtering data.

The report viewer control also includes a toolbar with navigation, search, export, and print controls. Reports can be exported to a variety of formats including PDF files, Word, and Excel.

FIGURE 25.4

The default filter on the built-in Case Summary Table report. Users can adjust the filter to suit their needs before running the report. In this case, the default filter also limits the data to those active cases created in the last month, helping to make sure the result of the report query is not too large.

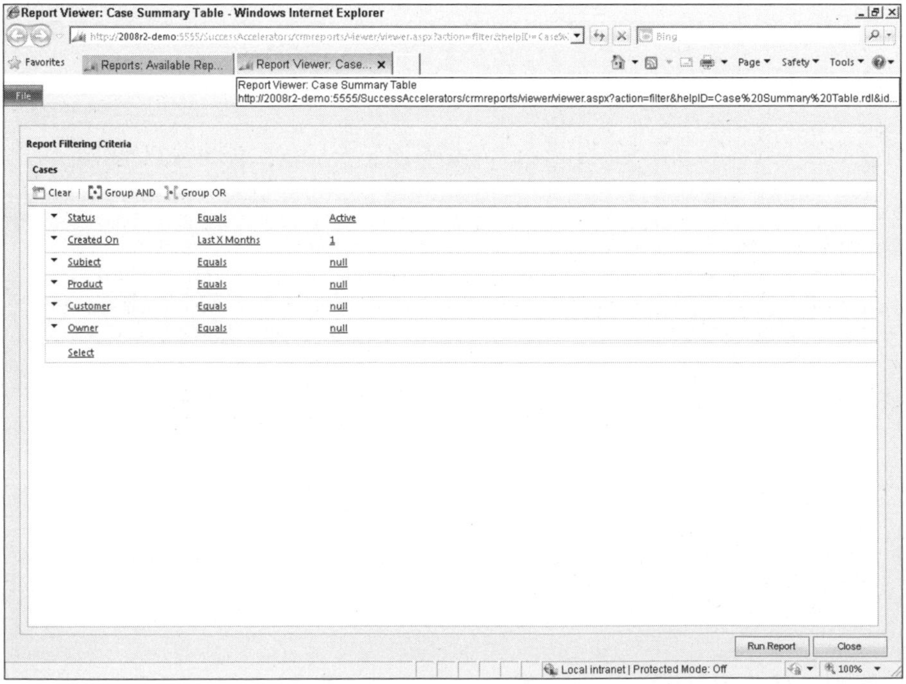

The report viewer control in Dynamics CRM can be used to provide interactivity to users, including custom parameters, navigation, search, and the ability to export reports into various formats.

Selecting the Right Report Development Tools

A number of development tools that can be used to create custom SSRS reports in the RDL format. In this section, we take a look at two that are freely available from Microsoft: the Business Intelligence Development Studio and SQL Server 2008 Report Builder 3.0.

Business Intelligence Development Studio (BIDS)

In spite of its name, Business Intelligence Development Studio, or BIDS, is not a stand-alone product. It is actually the Visual Studio 2008 development environment, but is installed as an option when installing SQL Server 2008. BIDS includes project templates for use with SSRS, as well as for creating SQL Server Analysis Services (SSAS) and SQL Server Integration Services (SSIS) solutions (see Figure 25.6).

Note

Visual Studio 2010 is not currently supported for the Business Intelligence Development Studio, which is part of the SQL Server 2008 and SQL Server 2008 R2 products. Visual Studio 2010 can be installed on the same computer with Visual Studio 2008/BIDS.

You can use BIDS to create a new, empty report server project or choose to use the Report Server Project Wizard to create the project. The Report Server Project Wizard walks through the steps to set up a data source and a query, and select the layout for the initial report.

After a report project is created, BIDS allows a report project to be set up with a default target report server as the deployment target so you can publish reports without leaving the development environment. However, when creating reports for Dynamics CRM, it is not necessary to use this feature since reports must be uploaded through the Dynamics CRM interface. For this reason, you should not publish reports from BIDS directly to the organization's folder on the report server. You can use this feature to publish reports to a test report server or a test folder on the report server.

FIGURE 25.6

The Business Intelligence Development Studio project templates enable report development using the Visual Studio 2008 shell.

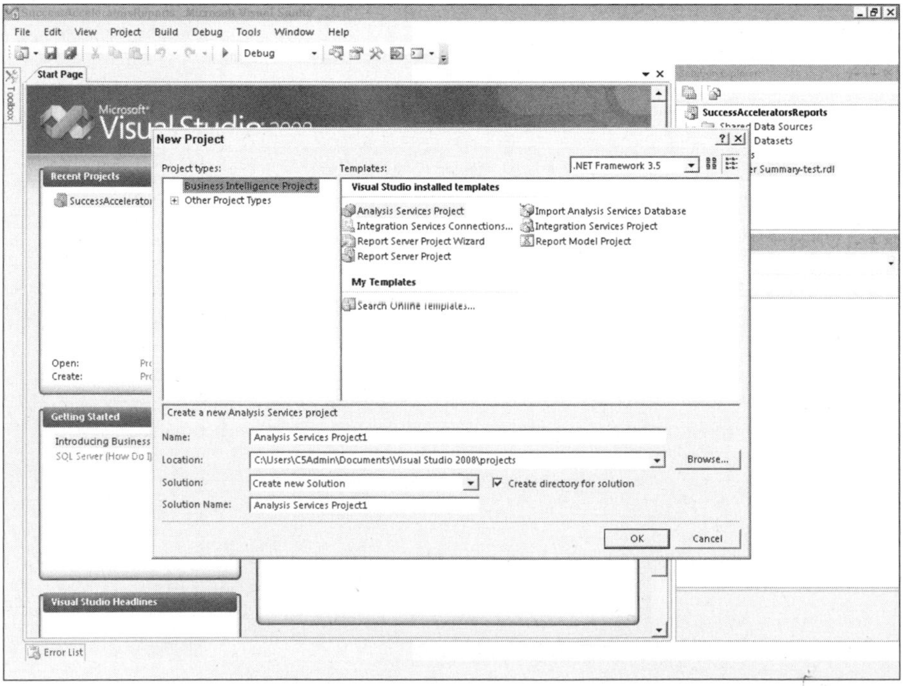

Visual Studio, and, by extension, BIDS, stores projects and related files in the user's Documents library by default, setting up a convenient path to locate them. A report project may contain multiple separate RDL files which can be uploaded individually to Dynamics CRM. To locate an RDL file stored in the default project folder, navigate to the appropriate folder in your Documents\Visual Studio 2008\Projects directory.

The Visual Studio/BIDS interface provides the following:

- A report design and preview area
- A toolbox panel with common report objects like tables, matrixes, charts, and lists
- The Report Data panel with datasets, parameters, and fields
- The Solution Explorer and Properties panels

Using BIDS, you can also reference custom Visual Basic code or assembly references that you have embedded in the report properties (see Figure 25.7).

FIGURE 25.7

You can embed custom code in a report's properties, and reference the code in expressions.

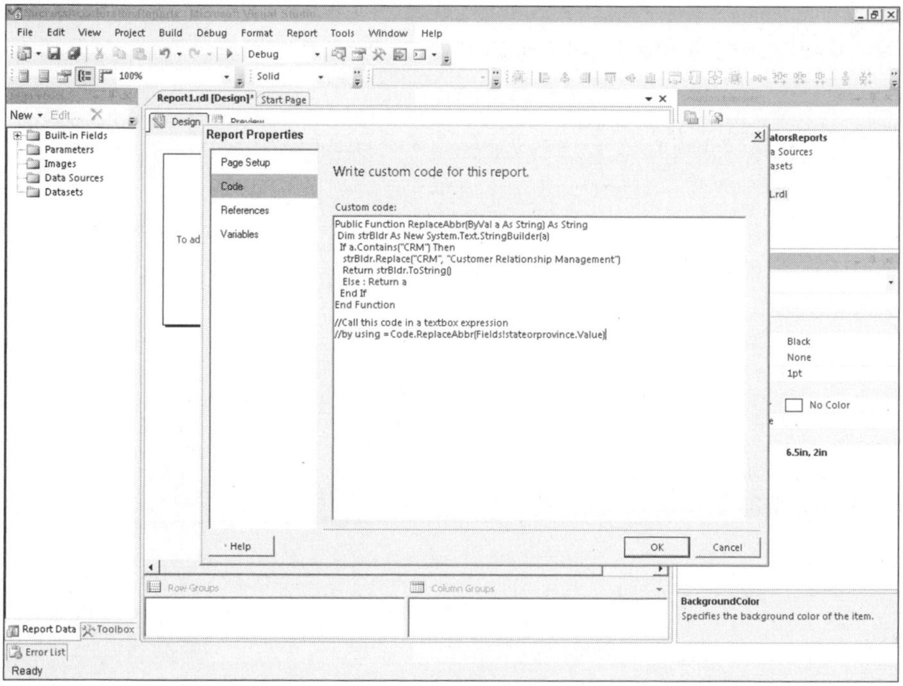

SQL Server 2008 R2 Report Builder 3.0

Microsoft SQL Server 2008 R2 Report Builder 3.0 (Report Builder) is a very user-friendly report design environment, with an interface that is similar to an Office application (Figure 25.8). It includes most of the same tools and capabilities as BIDS, and is available as a free download from the Microsoft Downloads Web site.

Microsoft SQL Server 2008 R2 Report Builder 3.0 offers a familiar Office-like interface with most of the same powerful report development tools as BIDS.

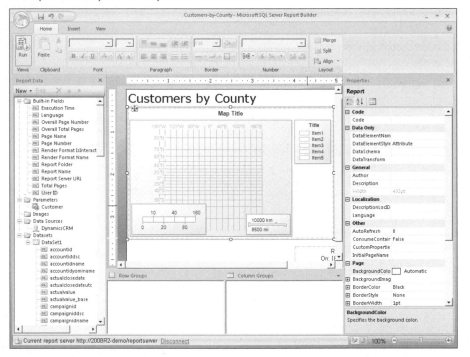

The Fetch Provider for Dynamics CRM Online

Prior to Microsoft Dynamics CRM 2011, it was not possible to upload custom reports to Dynamics CRM Online. This limitation was due to the fact that Microsoft did not allow direct connections to the SQL Server databases. This restriction from directly querying the views and tables in Dynamics CRM Online's databases is still in effect. To overcome this and enable custom RDL report files to be uploaded to Dynamics CRM Online, Microsoft has made available the Microsoft Dynamics CRM Fetch Extension.

Fetch XML is an XML query language developed by Microsoft for Dynamics CRM, and is the native query language that tools like Advanced Find and the Report Wizard use.

The Fetch Extension is a tool that plugs into the Visual Studio/BIDS environment that allows BIDS to connect to and consume the Fetch data source, which is exposed in Dynamics CRM Online and created in on-premises deployments during installation. When creating a report in BIDS, select the data source type "Microsoft Dynamics CRM Fetch" and enter your logon credentials when prompted.

The Fetch Extension makes it possible to use all of the report design features in BIDS to create professional reports and upload them to Dynamics CRM where they can be accessed by your organization's users. It creates standard RDL files that contain a custom Fetch data source and your FetchXML query.

The extension handles authentication against Dynamics CRM Online and enables you to query metadata and data during the report development process. You can even preview live data in the BIDS environment.

The Microsoft Dynamics CRM Fetch Extension does not help report designers to create the Fetch XML query. However, there are several ways to start writing custom fetch queries:

- Using the Advanced Find tool, you can build a query and test it. Then use the Download Fetch XML button on the Advanced Find's ribbon to download a copy of the query XML.

- Extracting the FetchXML that is embedded in chart definitions.

- Creating a report in the Report Wizard, downloading it, and copying the FetchXML query from the RDL file, then hand-editing it.

An example of a Fetch query that returns a list of open opportunities for customers in the state of North Carolina with an estimated value that is greater than ten thousand dollars:

```xml
<fetch version="1.0" output-format="xml-platform" mapping="logical"
  distinct="false">
 <entity name="opportunity" enableprefiltering="1">
   <attribute name="name" />
   <attribute name="estimatedvalue" />
   <attribute name="estimatedclosedate" />
   <attribute name="customerid" />
   <attribute name="opportunityratingcode" />
   <attribute name="closeprobability" />
   <attribute name="opportunityid" />
   <order attribute="name" descending="false" />
   <filter type="and">
     <condition attribute="statecode" operator="eq" value="0" />
     <condition attribute="estimatedvalue" operator="gt" value="10000" />
   </filter>
   <link-entity name="account" from="accountid" to="customerid"
  alias="ab">
     <filter type="and">
       <condition attribute="address1_stateorprovince" operator="eq"
  value="NC" />
     </filter>
   </link-entity>
 </entity>
</fetch>
```

continued

continued

Tip

Empower the users to use the built-in filtering mechanism on reports by enabling prefiltering in your Fetch-based custom reports. To enable prefiltering for Accounts, use <entity name="account" enableprefiltering="1"> in your Fetch XML query.

The FetchXML query language has some limitations and is not as powerful as T-SQL. Many of the language's limitations can be overcome by using the tools available in BIDS. For example, FetchXML has predefined date groupings such as week, year, fiscal period, and so on. If these groupings are not sufficient for your report, rather than attempting to group the data in the query, use the grouping options in the report designer to create a custom grouping.

To learn more about the FetchXML query language, refer to the links for this chapter in Appendix B.

With SQL Server 2008 R2, the Report Builder is also available as a one-click installation directly from the Report Manager Web site (see Figure 25.9).

FIGURE 25.9

Users can install the Report Builder directly from the SQL Server 2008 R2 Report Manager Web site.

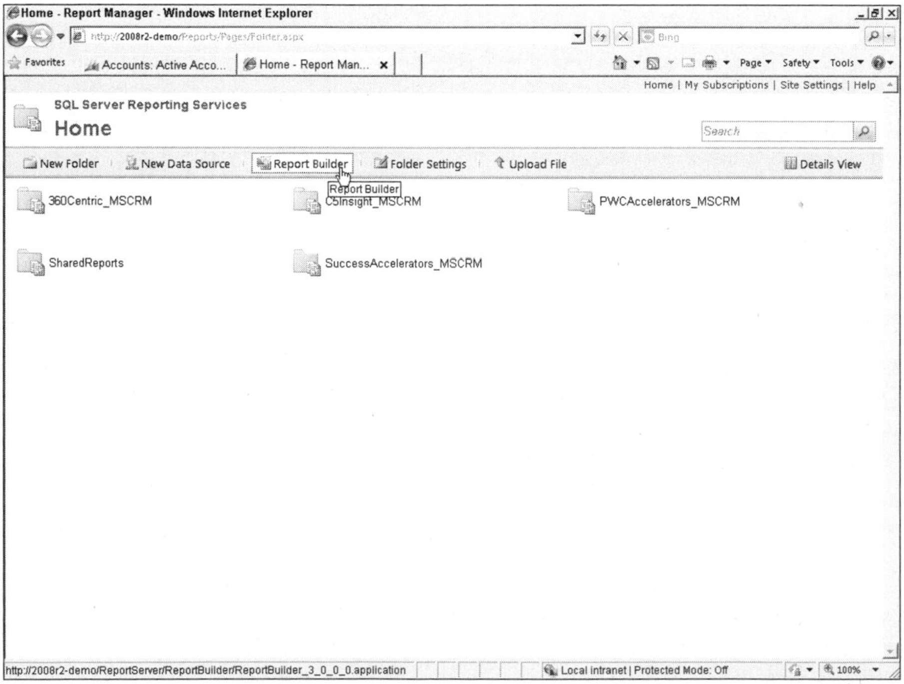

Designing Professional Reports

BIDS and the Report Builder make it easy to create powerful reports. But creating reports that are useful and easily understood by users takes some practice. Follow the best practices recommendations in this section when creating custom reports for Dynamics CRM.

Starting at the beginning

Good report design starts before you ever open the report development tool. You must begin with a clear understanding of the end user's needs. When gathering requirements for a report, ask users to provide examples of existing reports that will be replaced by the Dynamics CRM report. If there are no existing reports, ask users to mock up the report they need in Excel or PowerPoint. Find out what types of summaries and calculations are required.

Keep in mind that the reporting tools in Dynamics CRM are designed to allow users to provide self-service, so reports should be designed with that goal in mind. Find out what entities and processes they are going to want to report on, and plan the report design to be as broad as possible with the goal of allowing the user to modify the scope and slice and dice the data at runtime.

Using filtered views

Dynamics CRM provides automatically generated "filtered" views for all entities (system and custom). Filtered views enforce users' security role permissions when running reports against Dynamics CRM data. When using the SQL Server data source type, it is recommended to always use the filtered views in your report queries, rather than the tables or nonfiltered views to ensure that users are not accidentally granted access to restricted data. Filtered views also provide an easier structure to query against since they incorporate the attributes from the underlying tables into one view.

The Fetch XML query language automatically translates queries to enforce security by using the filtered views.

Empowering users

When designing a report, do as little grouping and filtering in the query as possible. Instead, incorporate prefiltering and user-selectable parameters in the report:

Enabling prefiltering

Configuring prefiltering in a report enables users to change the scope of the dataset before running a report, and it also allows the report to be published as context-sensitive, meaning it can be run against one or more selected records in a list view or from a record form.

To enable prefiltering when using the SQL Server data source type, specify an alias for the filtered view in your query with a prefix of "CRMAF_", a special prefix that the Dynamics CRM platform will interpret:

```
SELECT          *
```

```
FROM            FilteredOpportunity AS CRMAF_FilteredOpportunity
```

For reports that use the Fetch data source type, enable prefiltering as follows:

```
<entity name="opportunity" enableprefiltering="1">
```

In order to avoid a performance impact, be sure to specify the default filters for the report after uploading it to Dynamics CRM.

When using prefiltering, you should also include the filter options on the rendered report so users can see what filtering options they chose. To display the prefiltering options, you must use a special hidden string parameter called CRM_FilterText. The parameter should allow null values. Place a textbox in the header of the report with the value set to following expression:

```
=Parameters!CRM_FilterText.Value
```

Creating user-selectable parameters

After a user narrows the query with prefiltering, they might also wish to change the view of the report data by changing groupings or selecting a subset of the returned records. The following steps show an example of adding a parameter to allow users to change the grouping on an opportunity report to be grouped by either the customer or the owner:

1. Create a report with a table that contains opportunities. Make sure your query includes the customerid and ownerid fields.

2. In the Report Data panel in the report designer, right-click on Parameters and add a new parameter called GroupBy.

3. In the Report Parameter Properties, click the Available Values tab and specify the following values:
   - Label: Customer; Value: customerid
   - Label: Owner; Value: ownerid

4. Right-click the table in the report and select Properties. In the group properties for the table, enter the following group expression:

```
=Fields(Parameters!GroupBy.Value).Value
```

When the user runs the report, they will be presented with a "Group By" drop-down menu. They can select either Customer or Owner. When the report is refreshed the results will be grouped based on the selection.

Configuring dynamic sorting

Users often want to change the order in which records are sorted. SSRS enables columns in a table to be interactively sorted. To enable interactive sorting, right-click the text box at the top of a column to open the text box properties dialog. Click the Interactive Sorting section (see Figure 25.10) and select the Enable interactive sorting on this text box option. You can also select which parts of the table should be sorted, and if you'd like to sort based on a different attribute from your query.

Localizing a report

Many values in the Dynamics CRM database are displayed to end users with formatting options that are set in the application. To use these formatting options in your reports, create a separate dataset in the report with the following query:

```
SELECT * FROM dbo.fn_GetFormatStrings()
```

This returns format settings for dates, time, languages, numbers, and currency. To use the format values that are returned, reference them in a report text box's format settings as an expression. For example, use the following expression as a custom number format in a currency value:

```
=First(Fields!CurrencyFormat_2_Precision.Value, "FormatDataset")
```

FIGURE 25.10

Setting interactive sorting on a column in an SSRS report table

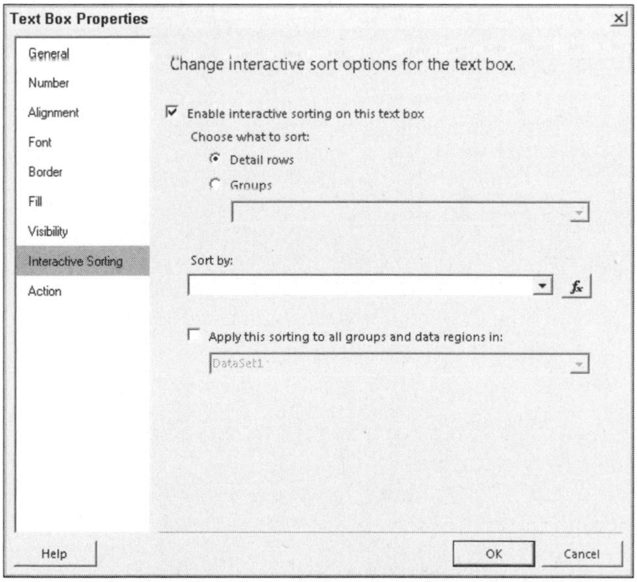

Using global values

Since reports might end up being printed or exported to PDF, it's always a good practice to include helpful information in the report footer about when the report was run, and by whom. These values are automatically available in SSRS as built-in fields. Built-in fields include the execution time (which can be formatted according to the Dynamics CRM format settings as shown above), the report language, page numbers, and user ID. These values can be dragged into the report footer from the Report Data panel.

Formatting for print layout

Controlling print layout can be problematic in BIDS and Report Builder. While the page orientation and page size can be set in the Report Properties dialog, any part of a table that extends beyond the margins will be printed on separate pages. Test your reports by exporting them to PDF and Word, and by printing them out. Adjust the contents of the report so the layout fits the standard paper size.

Refer to the SDK

Microsoft includes a an extensive reporting section as part of the Dynamics CRM SDK. The SDK makes a number of recommendations on report performance and navigation that are helpful when designing a custom report. This includes instructions for adding drill-through links and other helpful report features for your users. The SDK also includes a reporting best practices page that you should refer to when working with Dynamics CRM custom reports.

Developing Your First Custom Report

The following section is a walk-through to create a custom report for Dynamics CRM that displays all of the Field Security Profiles that belong to each user. This example uses the BIDS report environment to introduce the core concepts needed for connecting to Dynamics CRM, building a query, and laying out the report.

1. Open Business Intelligence Development Studio. If you installed this as part of your SQL Server installation, this is available at Start ➪ All Programs ➪ Microsoft SQL Server 2008 R2 ➪ SQL Server Business Intelligence Development Studio.

2. Create a new report project. In the New Project dialog, click on the Business Intelligence Projects and select the Report Server Project template. Give your project a name and click OK.

3. In the Solution Explorer, right-click the Reports folder and select Add New Report. The Report Wizard opens.

4. Select the Data Source. Specify a data source name. (Do not use a shared data source. Dynamics CRM reports do not support shared data sources since the data source connection will be over-ridden during report publishing.) You can select either the Microsoft SQL Server or Microsoft Dynamics CRM Fetch data source type (see Figure 25.11). If you select the Fetch data source type you will be prompted for the login credentials and URL. For this example, select the Microsoft SQL Server data source type.

5. Enter the connection string, or click the Edit button to open the Connection Properties dialog. For the SQL Server connection, you will select the SQL Server name and the organization database (orgname_MSCRM), and use Windows authentication. Your connection string will look like this:

```
Data Source=SQLSERVERNAME;Initial Catalog=OrgName_MSCRM
```

6. Click Next to proceed to the query design screen.

7. In the query design screen, enter a T-SQL or FetchXML query, or, for SQL Server data source connections, use the Query Builder to design a query. For this example, paste the following query into the query string box and then click Next:

```
SELECT CRMAF_FilteredSystemUser.businessunitidname, CRMAF_
    FilteredSystemUser.fullname, CRMAF_
    FilteredFieldSecurityProfile.name, CAST(CRMAF_
    FilteredSystemUser.systemuserid AS char(36)) AS UserId
FROM FilteredFieldSecurityProfile AS CRMAF_
    FilteredFieldSecurityProfile INNER JOIN
    FilteredSystemUserProfiles ON CRMAF_
    FilteredFieldSecurityProfile.fieldsecurityprofileid =
    FilteredSystemUserProfiles.fieldsecurityprofileid INNER JOIN
    FilteredSystemUser AS CRMAF_FilteredSystemUser ON
    FilteredSystemUserProfiles.systemuserid = CRMAF_
    FilteredSystemUser.systemuserid
```

8. On the Select the Report Type screen, select the Tabular report and click Next.

9. On the Design the Table screen, add the businessunitidname to the Group box, and the fullname and name fields to the Details box (see Figure 25.12) and click Next.

FIGURE 25.11

Select either the Microsoft SQL Server or Microsoft Dynamics CRM Fetch data source type.

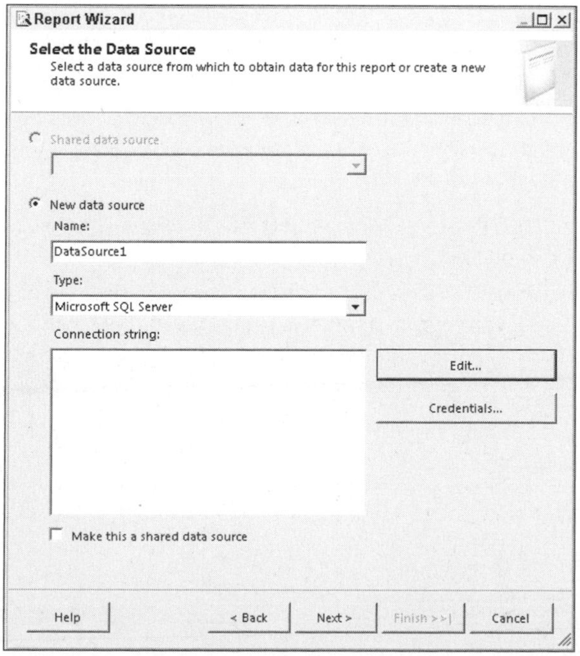

FIGURE 25.12

Use the Report Wizard to help design the table groupings and details.

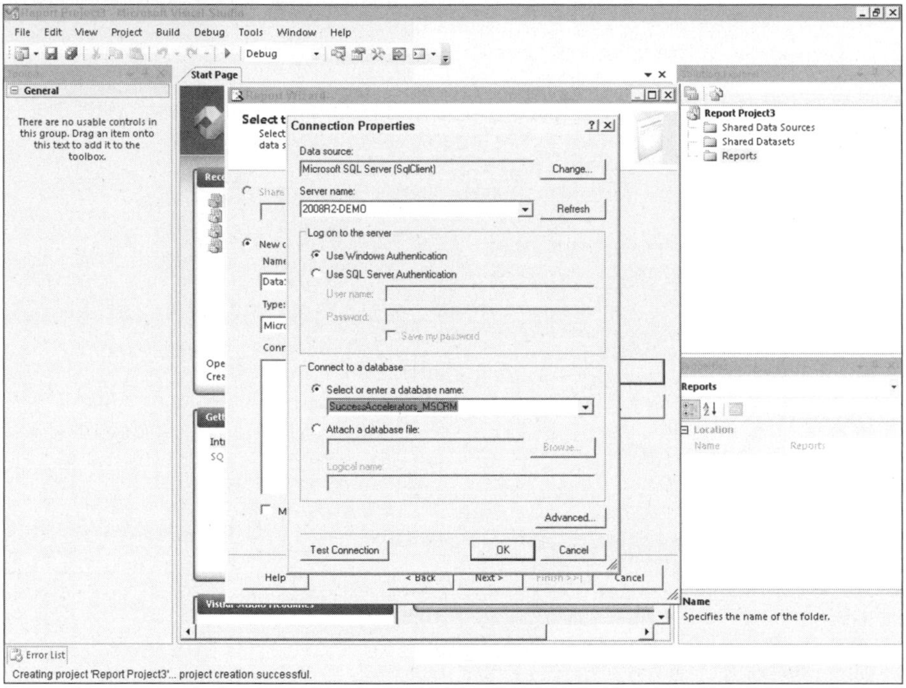

10. On the Choose the Table Layout screen, leave the Stepped option selected, and click Next.

11. Select a table style and click Next.

12. Enter a name for the report, leave the checkmark in the "Preview report" checkbox, and click the Finish button to complete the wizard. The report is displayed in preview mode, as shown in Figure 25.13.

13. In the report design area, click the Design tab to leave the preview.

14. Take a few minutes to refine the report layout. Rename the column headings and change the width of columns to use the space better. Add interactive sorting to columns to enable users to change the sort order at runtime. Remove the systemuserid column from the table. Use the preview tab to see how the report looks.

15. Add the parameters needed to make this report useful to a Dynamics CRM user. In this example, add the parameter needed to display the prefiltering values that are used when the report is run from Dynamics CRM. Allow this parameter to accept null values so you can preview the report in the development environment:

CRM_FilterText — a hidden parameter

FIGURE 25.13

The result of the Report Wizard

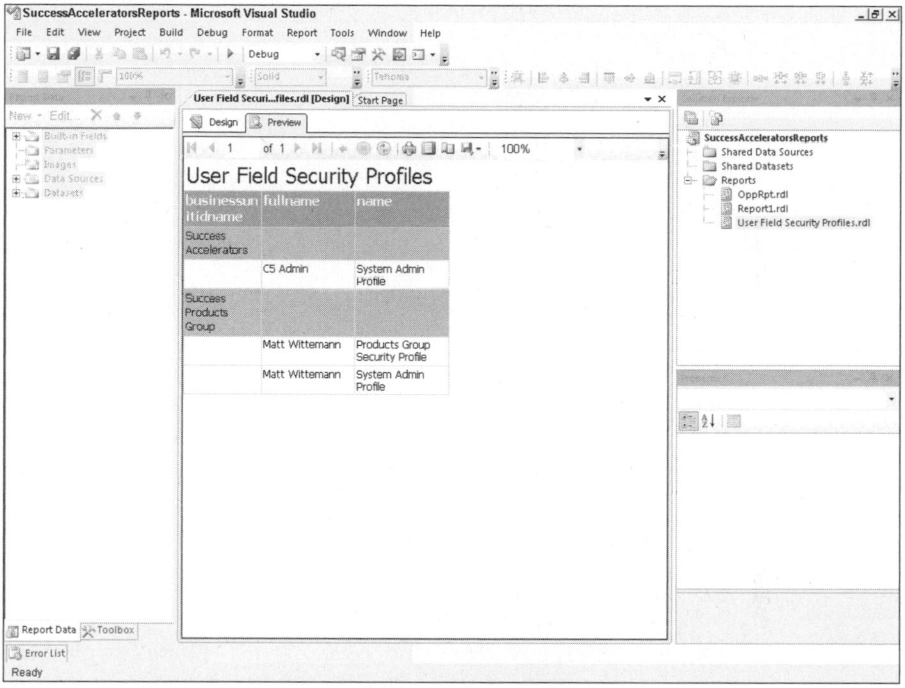

16. Add a header to the report. With the design tab open, click on Report in the BIDS/ Visual Studio menu and select Add Page Header. Drag the text box containing the report title into the header. Drag the CRM_FilterText parameter into the header as well.

17. Add a new dataset so you can refer to the formatting from the Dynamics CRM organization in the report design. Right-click on the Datasets folder in the Report Data panel and choose Add Dataset. In the Dataset Properties dialog, select the Use a dataset embedded in my report option. Select the data source that you created in Step 4. In the query box, paste the following:

```
SELECT * FROM dbo.fn_GetFormatStrings()
```

18. Add a footer to the report and drag the built-in Execution Time and UserID fields into it. You can also put the page number in the footer. Right-click the Execution Time text box and open its properties dialog. On the number section of the Text Box Properties dialog, select the Custom category (see Figure 25.14). In the Custom format use the following expression (where "CRMFormats" is the dataset name created in the previous step:

```
=First(Fields!DateFormat.Value, "CRMFormats")
```

FIGURE 25.14

Setting a custom format for the Execution Time text box

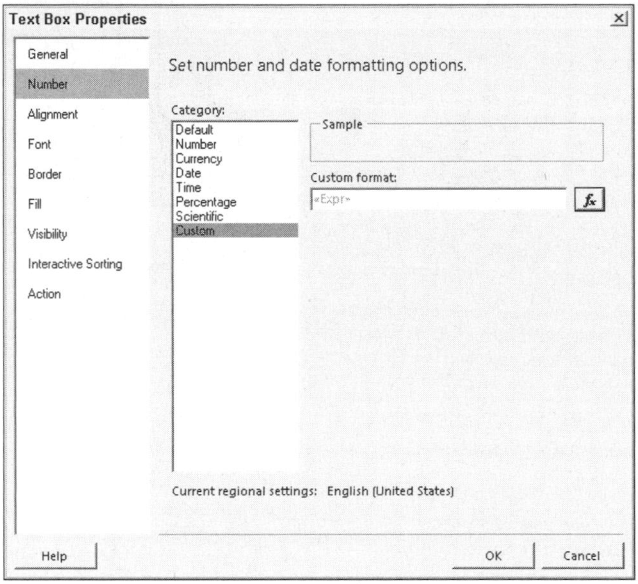

19. Set up drill-through to the user records. In the text box properties for the fullname field, click on the Action area and select the Go to URL option. Add the following expression, replacing the server address and organization name for your own:

```
="http://crmserver/orgname/CRMReports/viewer/drillopen.
    aspx?OTC=8&ID=%7B" & Fields!UserId.Value & "%7D"
```

20. Test the report by running it in the preview. You should be able to click on a username and open the user's record in the Dynamics CRM Web client from the preview pane.

21. When you are satisfied with the layout, design, and function of your report, save your work and close Visual Studio.

Tip

To jump-start your report development you can create a report in Dynamic CRM using the Report Wizard or make a copy of a built-in report, then download it and edit it in BIDS or Report Builder. To download a report from Dynamics CRM, select the report in the Reports list view, and click the Edit button on the ribbon menu. In the report edit window, click the Actions menu item and select Download Report. Save the RDL file to your local machine, then open the RDL file in Report Builder or open a report project in BIDS and add the report to the project by right-clicking the report folder and selecting Add⇨ Existing Item.

When editing a report downloaded from Dynamics CRM, before previewing it, you may need to change the data source. In the Report Data panel, expand the Data Sources folder and right-click the CRM data source and open the properties dialog. In the connection string, change the data source to your Dynamics CRM SQL Server and the initial catalog to the organization database you are working with. By default, reports that are included with Dynamics CRM have a data source of localhost and are set to use the AdventureWorksCycle_ MSCRM database as the initial catalog.

Once you have changed the data source, you should be able to preview the report and then begin making modifications to it. Of course, make sure to change the name of the report so when you upload it to Dynamics CRM you do not overwrite the original report.

Sharing Custom Reports

After completing the development of a custom report, you must share it with the users by publishing it to Dynamics CRM. In addition to being able to upload RDL files, you can also upload other existing files, such as Excel files to the reports list or link to a Web page. If your organization uses a reporting tool other than SQL Server Reporting Services, you can experiment with uploading its report files to Dynamics CRM. Essentially you are creating a link to the report for your users, so they must have the tools needed to render the report.

Publishing a report to Dynamics CRM

Reports are a full-fledged entity in Dynamics CRM, meaning they have privileges and permissions associated with them. In order to publish a SQL Reporting Services report to Dynamics CRM, users must have a security role with the appropriate permissions, as shown in Figure 25.15:

- Publish Reports (prvPublishRSReport)
- Report — Create (prvCreateReport)
- Report — Append (prvAppendReport)
- Report — Append to (prvAppendToReport)

The System Administrator and System Customizer security roles have these privileges by default.

To upload a report to Dynamics CRM and make it available to the organization's users, follow these steps:

1. In the Workplace, navigate to the Reports list view and click the New button on the Ribbon menu.

2. In the new report form (Figure 25.16) from the Report Type drop-down menu, select Existing File.

3. Browse to the location of the RDL file and enter the path in the report form. The report's name will be automatically populated. You can change it if you wish, add a description, and then save the report by clicking the Save icon.

FIGURE 25.15

Uses who wish to publish an SSRS report must have a security role with the relevant privileges.

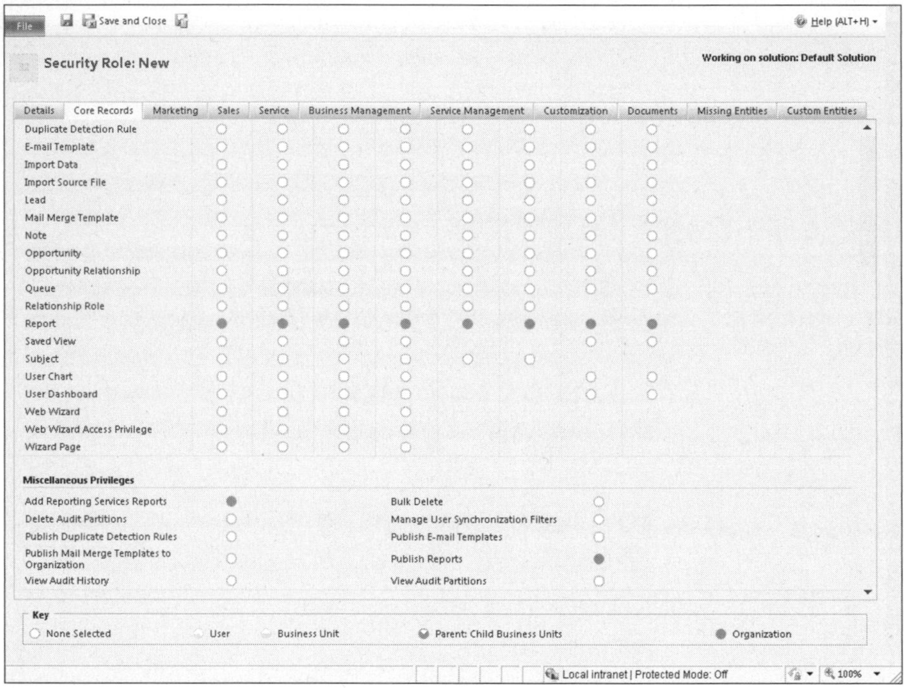

Note

If your report contains one or more subreports, upload the parent report first. Then upload the subreports. When uploading the subreports, Dynamics CRM should automatically detect the parent report and set its link in the report form.

By default, a newly uploaded report is not visible to other users. It is considered a personal report until it has been share with the organization. To share the report with other users:

1. In the report edit form, click the Administration tab, as shown in Figure 25.17.

2. In the Viewable By radio button control, select Organization. Save and close the report.

Setting other report options

After publishing a report to Dynamics CRM and making it viewable to the organization, there are several other settings that you can configure to make the report easy to access for your users.

FIGURE 25.16

The report form. Specify an existing file and provide a report name and then click the Save icon.

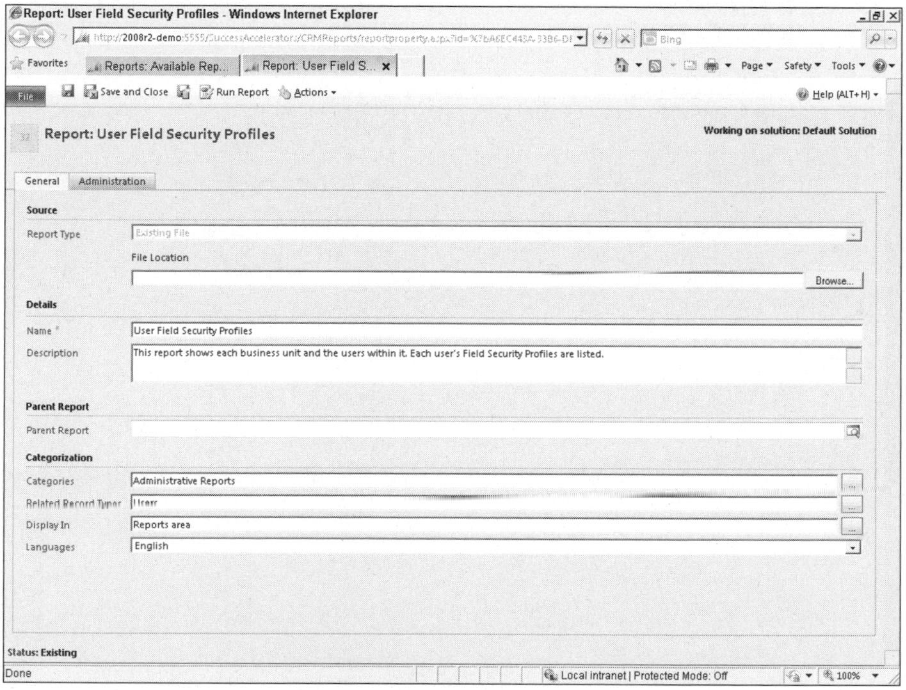

Adding report categories

The report record includes a Categories field where you can look up and select from the available categories. This is especially helpful if your organization has a large number of custom reports. Default categories include:

- Administrative Reports
- Marketing Reports
- Sales Reports
- Service Reports

Additional categories can be added in the settings area by navigating to Settings ⇨ Administration and clicking on the System Settings link. The System Settings dialog contains a Reporting tab where you can add, edit, and reorder the report categories.

FIGURE 25.17

Reports are only viewable by the user who uploaded them until they are shared with the organization.

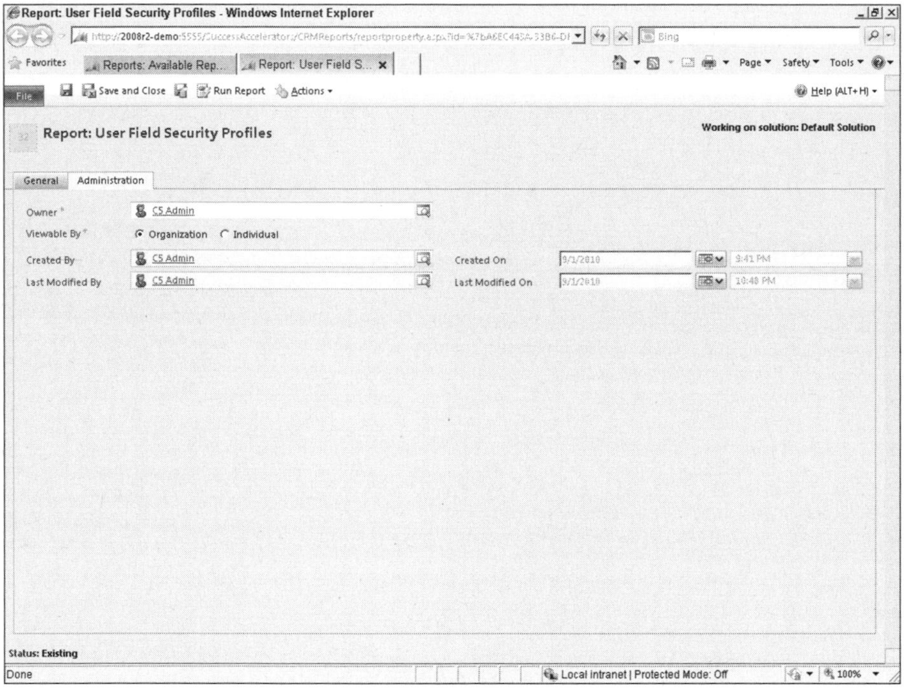

Cross-Reference

After adding a report category, it is a good idea to create a view for reports that is filtered on that category. Custom views can be added in the solution that contains the report. See Part V for information on customizing views and working with solutions.

Making reports context-sensitive

Earlier in this chapter we walked through the use of a special prefix (CRMAF_) in report queries, and, in the case of reports that use the Fetch extension, the element needed in the XML (enablefiltering = "1"), to enable prefiltering in a report. Setting this special configuration in the query of a report also enables the report to be made context-sensitive. A context-sensitive report can be run from a list view when one or more records are selected, or from a related record's form. The Dynamics CRM platform handles passing the record's ID to the report as an internal parameter.

The report form contains a "Related Record Types" field where you can specify the entities to which the report relates (see Figure 25.18). While you can technically add any entity you wish to this field, the SSRS report will only be able to receive the IDs for entities that are enabled for prefiltering in the underlying report query.

You must also specify where the report should be displayed. Options include:

- Reports area. This is the default setting. A report with this display option is available in the reports list view.

- Lists for related record types. Selecting this option makes the report available from the Reports Ribbon menu item on the list views for related record types.

- Forms for related record types. This option makes the report available from the related record types' Ribbon menu Reports item.

Setting the related record types and the areas for the report to be displayed in will make the report context-sensitive. If the report's query is configured for prefiltering, the platform will automatically pass the record ID to the report as a parameter so it is run against only the selected report.

Related Record Types	Users	
Display In	Forms for related record types;Lists for related record types;Reports area	

Summary

This chapter covered the concepts and techniques necessary to begin creating custom reports for Dynamics CRM:

- The architecture of SQL Server 2008 Reporting Services (SSRS) - SSRS, like Dynamics CRM itself, is an n-tier application, with a presentation layer, a processing platform, and a data layer. Dynamics CRM uses SSRS as its reporting engine.

- In Microsoft Dynamics CRM 2011, a shared folder is created in the report server Web site for the standard Dynamics CRM reports. When installing Dynamics CRM or adding an organization through the Deployment Manager, a new folder is created for the organization within the report server. Custom and customized reports are placed in the organization's folder.

- The Dynamics CRM platform is designed to empower users to access, consume, and analyze data when and how they need to. There are many ways that the platform supports custom report developers to build reports that enable self-service. Reports can be designed to be context-sensitive, to enable prefiltering, and custom slicing and dicing. This chapter introduced some of these techniques.

- There are two tools available from Microsoft that can be used to create custom SSRS reports: the Business Intelligence Development Studio (BIDS) and the SQL Server 2008 R2 Report Builder 3.0 (Report Builder). This chapter presented the features of these tools and instructions for accessing and using them.

- Microsoft Dynamics CRM 2011 introduces a new extension for BIDS to enable developers to create custom reports that use FetchXML queries. SSRS reports that use the FetchXML provider can be developed for Dynamics CRM Online.

Part VIII

Extending and Integrating Dynamics CRM

Among the most compelling factors that probably influenced your decision to tackle Microsoft Dynamics CRM 2011 is its ability to integrate with a wide range of other systems, and to support an endless variety of business processes.

Entire books, veritable tomes, have been written about integrating Dynamics CRM with other systems and extending its functionality into other corners of your business. Big topics indeed! In this final part of the book we attempt to cover everything an administrator needs to know about these two complex topics.

Connecting to Other Systems: Migration and Integration with Dynamics CRM

Our goal with this chapter is to provide an administrative overview of the types of integrations that are frequently implemented with Dynamics CRM, as well as a summary of various integration techniques, best practices, and useful integration technologies.

Whether you implement Dynamics CRM for traditional customer relationship management or as a platform for a line-of-business application, it will undoubtedly play a central role in your organization's daily operations. As a sales, marketing, and service application, Dynamics CRM is the primary tool for facilitating interactions between your organization and your customers. As a LOB platform, it may be used to track the key functions of your organization's core competencies.

Because of this central role, it is often necessary to integrate Dynamics CRM with other business systems. Integration typically refers to sharing data between systems, such as an accounting system and your CRM system. Increasingly, however, as services-oriented applications have become more prevalent, and with the advent of distributed platforms such as cloud-based services, integration needs include not just sharing data between systems but also leveraging the services of one application from another.

Dynamics CRM is frequently integrated with the data and services of systems such as:

- ERP and accounting systems like Dynamics GP, NAV, and AX, as well as third-party systems like SAP, QuickBooks, and many others
- CTI/Telephone systems like Cisco and Avaya
- Line-of-business applications, such as manufacturing process management systems and shipping systems

- Internal and external-facing Web sites, from simple contact or help request forms through full portal and e-commerce integration
- File and data repositories and directories
- External data sources used for lead generation and market research, such as Dun & Bradstreet, Hoover's, or Dodge Reports

Recognizing the need for these kinds of integrations, Microsoft has designed Dynamics CRM to be an incredibly flexible and extensible system with many points for integration. Microsoft Dynamics CRM 2011 is itself an integrated system, each tier of the system having multiple integration points, as shown in Figure 26.1, and natively integrating with other systems, such as SQL Server Reporting Services, Active Directory, Microsoft Office (primarily Outlook, but also Word and Excel), Exchange Server, SharePoint, and AD FS 2. It is built to enable an endless variety of integration options.

FIGURE 26.1

Dynamics CRM provides numerous points for integrating data and services.

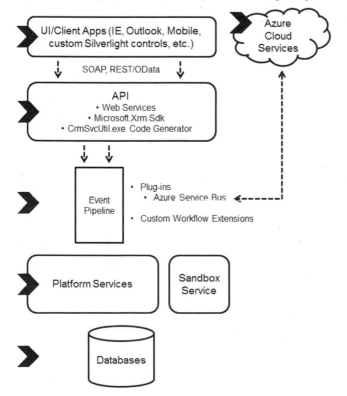

Microsoft Dynamics CRM 2011 provides the fundamental architecture needed to develop scalable and secure data and services integration with external systems, including:

- Web services and WCF APIs
- Messaging and event pipeline
- Service Bus plug-in
- Platform services
- Database views

Note

It is typically not recommended to use data layer integration approaches (other than reading from the database views), since this would bypass the application layer's business logic and security — as well as placing your Dynamics CRM implementation into an unsupported state.

Most data exchange typically takes place using the Web services API, but as this list shows, there are numerous ways to interact with Dynamics CRM's data and services.

Preparing for Integration

You should begin preparing for integration early in your implementation planning for Dynamics CRM. When defining the objectives your organization has in using Dynamics CRM, capture the goals for bringing data into Dynamics CRM on a one-time basis (migrating data), such as when replacing an older system, as well as when data and/or services need to be shared at regular intervals or on a near real-time basis (integrating data).

Due to the complexity of data migration and integration, we recommend getting the basics of your Dynamics CRM implementation done right. Capture your migration and integration requirements and incorporate them into your implementation planning for Dynamics CRM, but make sure that the priority of your implementation plan is a focus on designing optimal business processes and configuring Dynamics CRM to support them. Consider starting with "swivel-chair" integration — that is, integration that relies on users to manually input data from one system into another. This approach can help to make sure the business process is properly designed before you set about automating it. If the business process itself is flawed, automating it will only make your organization more efficient at making mistakes.

Developing an integration solution for Dynamics CRM is likely to require some or all of the following skills:

- Familiarity with the Dynamics CRM data model
- Web services and SDK knowledge
- .NET programming skills
- SQL Server administration and operation skills

Looking at the benefits of integration

With the above caveats in place, if your organization's goals have been well understood and Dynamics CRM has been carefully customized to support them, it may well be time to begin integration. Integrating data and services can provide many significant benefits to your organization. Integration can:

- Tremendously simplify the use of Dynamics CRM by providing timely and relevant access to pertinent information and functionality

- Increase user adoption by reducing repetitive actions and data entry

- Increase the accuracy of information, improving forecasting and responsiveness to a changing marketplace

- Assist your organization in responding to scenarios more intelligently, providing a better picture of customer relationships and business processes

The value of Dynamics CRM hinges on the quality and relevance of its data. Tying Dynamics CRM data into other business systems can have a multiplying effect on that value to your organization.

Considering the challenges of integration

Integration is often the most complex part of any technology project and can therefore be time-consuming and costly. Interdependencies and unknowns about existing data can create tremendous challenges for integrators. When developing an integration with Dynamics CRM and other systems, prioritize the data that must be integrated and start simple, incorporating additional data and services integration in steps.

Be sure to have a thorough understanding of your organization's business processes. Eliminate any gray areas and maintain clear documentation of the processes. Your documentation should include complete descriptions of each system that supports the business processes, the inputs and outputs for each step of the processes, and a data model definition.

Figure 26.2 shows an example of a business process that requires Dynamics CRM to be integrated with an accounting system. In this illustration, Dynamics CRM supports the sales process by keeping track of the customer's Account record, the Opportunity, and the Quote. When the Quote is accepted, the integration solution creates an Order in the accounting system. When the order is invoiced, a cumulative sales total field on the Dynamics CRM Account record is updated.

Implement the data model within Dynamics CRM first, and test the processes manually first before proceeding to integration. Create any entities and fields that will be needed to support data that will be coming in from integrated systems. Also, because records in Dynamics CRM can be user- or team-owned, make sure to have appropriate user and team records created beforehand so that ownership of integrated data can be appropriately assigned.

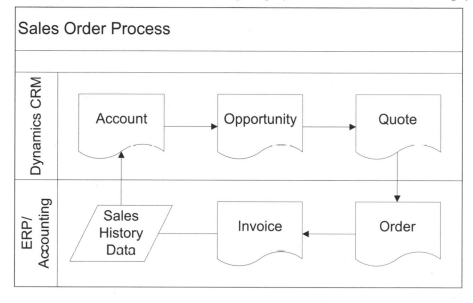

FIGURE 26.2

An example of a process that relies on integrating Dynamics CRM with an accounting system

Caution

The Dynamics CRM Web services API does not enforce validation of data formatting. For example, if you have included a client-side script (as a Web resource) to format phone numbers, passing a phone number through the Web services API will not trigger this validation. You must design this type of formatting and validation into your integration process.

Defining Migration and Integration Scenarios

As we noted above, there are two broad categories of integration: data and services. Although there are occasions where these two categories may both be involved in an integration project, they are the core ingredients that can be shared between Dynamics CRM and other systems. *Process integration* is another term that is frequently used to describe integration categories when the objective of the integration is to provide a comprehensive solution to accomplish certain tasks. In the context of this chapter, we are focusing on the ways that data and service integration can help accomplish this type of process integration.

Integrating data

Integrating data is the most common category of integration that most people think of when considering integration. For example, it is often helpful to have customer information such as account numbers, credit limits, and order histories shared between Dynamics CRM and an accounting system, as shown in Figure 26.3.

This example also underscores the concept of master data as opposed to transactional data. Master data is data that changes infrequently, and to which other types of data are related. In this illustration, the customer account record is treated as master data. Transactional data represents the more frequent or regular interactions between systems, such as orders or invoices.

FIGURE 26.3

An account's account number and credit limit are examples of non-transactional or "master" data, whereas orders and invoices are examples of transactional data.

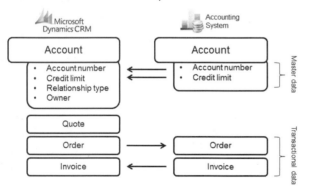

Another consideration when designing a data integration solution is to consider which system will be the *system of record* for a given piece of master or transactional data. For example, an accounting system may generate the account number and also be the system of record for customer credit limit amounts, in which case these fields might be set to read-only in the Dynamics CRM forms.

Note

ETL is an acronym commonly used when discussing data migration and integration. It stands for extract, transform, and load. These basic steps are involved in any process that moves data from one system to another.

Integrating services

SOA systems like Dynamics CRM provide many opportunities to incorporate the services or functionality of external systems, or to share Dynamics CRM services with an external application. Authentication is a good example of how Dynamics CRM natively integrates the services of another system, such as Active Directory or a federated authentication provider, in order to control access to data and resources.

Another example of integrating an external service into Dynamics CRM is using a cloud-based address validation service. Dynamics CRM does not have a built-in ability to verify a contact's street address, but there are third-party providers that will compare an address against the postal service's database and validate or reject the address (see Figure 26.4). In this scenario, a custom add-on can be developed to incorporate this cloud-based service into the Dynamics CRM application to provide new functionality to users that is not native to the platform.

FIGURE 26.4

An example of using an integrated external service to validate an address for a Dynamics CRM contact record

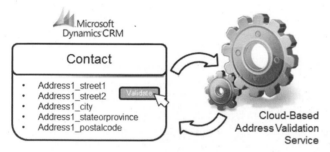

Migration and integration techniques

The following key data integration techniques are available:

- Migrating data
- Application/presentation layer integration
- Batch integration
- Real-time or near real-time integration

In the following sections, we cover these techniques in greater detail.

Migrating data

Loading data into Dynamics CRM on a one-time or occasional basis is a common scenario. Integrating data in this manner is referred to as data migration. Dynamics CRM provides a powerful import API, as well as the Import Data Wizard, that can be used for these types of ETL operations. (Previous versions of Dynamics CRM included a free Data Migration Manager utility that has been replaced by the enhanced functionality of the Import Data Wizard.) The API and the wizard support the migration of single files as well as multiple related source files (see Figure 26.5). There are also a number of third-party tools that use the Web services API for data migration.

FIGURE 26.5

The import process in Dynamics CRM can support importing multiple source files at a time.

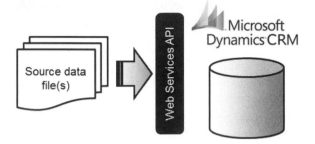

Regardless of what type of data you are migrating into Dynamics CRM, the migration process follows several common steps:

1. Clean and normalize the data in the source system. When possible, clean the data in the source system by removing duplicate or irrelevant records, and standardizing data formats.

2. Export data from the source system. Many data systems provide a way to export data, often into a comma-separated format (.csv) or other delimited format. Make sure to include unique identifiers, record owner names, and relational information, when available.

3. Prepare data for import. Often, you will need to perform further data cleansing and manipulation in order to prepare it for import into Dynamics CRM. Microsoft Office Excel is often one of the most powerful and simple tools that can be used for data preparation.

4. Perform test imports. Using a small number of representative records, perform test migrations. This will help you format the source data and refine the data map.

Presentation-layer integration

The simplest and most common integration technique is implemented on the presentation layer, or user interface. As a Web application, Dynamics CRM can incorporate external data and services as mash-ups to display the external system in an integrated fashion. With presentation-layer integrations, the data or service is accessed during a user session and typically does not persist beyond the session.

Typically, presentation-layer integrations rely on passing parameters as query strings in the external system's URL. Because much of the Dynamics CRM application is URL-addressable, it also lends itself to this form of integration into other systems.

Examples of presentation layer integration that incorporate external systems into the Dynamics CRM interface include:

- Sitemap links to other web applications

- Dashboards and forms that incorporate i-framed Web applications, such as maps, social media sites, or other information

- ISV buttons linking to external resources

Examples of presentation layer integration that incorporates Dynamics CRM into other applications:

- Displaying Dynamics CRM list views in a frame, such as a webpage viewer Web part on a SharePoint page

- Adding links to create new Dynamics CRM records, such as cases, to an intranet

One disadvantage of presentation-layer integration is that, since it typically does not transfer data between systems, users cannot leverage some of the built-in functionality in Dynamics CRM to act on the external system's data, such as the Advanced Find tool, Report Wizard, or workflow rules.

The following code sample illustrates embedding a map in an Iframe on a contact form (see Figure 26.6). This code would be saved in a Web resource and called on the OnLoad event of a contact form with an Iframe called 'IFRAME_contact'.

```
function mapCont()
{
var street = Xrm.Page.data.entity.attributes.get("address1_line1").getValue();
var city = Xrm.Page.data.entity.attributes.get("address1_city").getValue();
var province = Xrm.Page.data.entity.attributes.get("address1_stateorprovince").
   getValue();
var zip = Xrm.Page.data.entity.attributes.get("address1_postalcode").getValue();
var ContactFrm = Xrm.Page.ui.controls.get("IFRAME_contact");
if(city != null) {
var newTarget = 'http://mapq.st/embed?q=' + street + '+' + city + '+' + province
   + '+' + zip;
ContactFrm.setSrc(newTarget);
}
}
```

Cross-Reference

Chapter 21 includes details on incorporating client-side customizations to extend the Ribbon menu and site map to incorporate external Web applications into the Dynamics CRM user interface.

Batch integration

Batch integration is when ETL processes are automated and run on a schedule or regular interval (see Figure 26.7). Batch integrations can include the insert, update, or delete operations going one-way — from an external source to Dynamics CRM, or vice versa — or two-way.

FIGURE 26.6

Embedding maps in Iframes is a common use of presentation-layer integration.

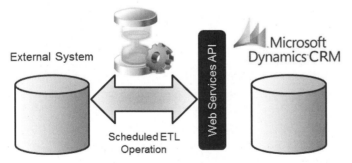

FIGURE 26.7

Batch integrations automate the process of extracting, transforming, and loading data, and typically run on a scheduled interval.

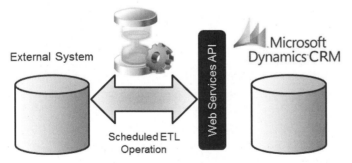

Setting up a batch integration requires many of the same steps as a data migration, though the process of cleansing and preparing data must be automated. After the extraction and transformation of the data is automated, the loading must be scheduled. This requires that source data is accessible at a predictable location and in a standard format at the right time.

Batch integration techniques are well suited for keeping master data such as account names and numbers synchronized between systems. (Master data is defined as data that does not change frequently, and which does not represent transactions.) Batch integration jobs may also be well suited for integrating large data sets, since they can be scheduled to run during off-peak hours.

Using scheduled batch jobs for integration also typically requires less complex infrastructure and error-handling mechanisms than real-time integrations, which can often require robust failover and rollback capabilities.

Real-time or near real-time integration

Real-time, or near real-time, integration techniques are typically employed for integrating data and services that change frequently or are transactional in nature. Like batch integration, real-time integration can go one way or two ways, and requires an automated ETL process. Unlike batch integration, however, real-time integration is usually event-driven. This type of integration often incorporates a message queuing function, which is why it is sometimes referred to as "near real-time" integration because data exchanges may occur asynchronously.

Real-time integrations can be more complex and difficult to maintain since business critical processes require a method to handle failover and transaction rollback capabilities. Failover is necessary in case one piece of the integration solution suffers an outage, and rollback functionality is needed in case there is an error in a piece of the integrated data.

The events that trigger the integration process can be either platform-level events or user-initiated events. Some examples of common implementations of real-time integration include order and invoice processing that is triggered by an opportunity being closed, and Web-to-lead arrangements that take data submitted on Web site contact forms and pump it into Dynamics CRM to create lead records. The Azure Service Bus plug-in is a good example of a real-time service integration that leverages the services of an external system to augment Dynamics CRM functionality.

Selecting an integration model

Depending on your organization's requirements, there are three basic approaches to consider when designing an integration solution: point-to-point, the data hub model, and the enterprise service bus. A variety of tools and technologies (discussed later in this chapter) can be used to implement these models.

Cross-Reference

See Appendix B for links to informative articles and resources that can help you select an appropriate integration approach.

Point-to-point

Point-to-point integration is usually the simplest to develop, integrating one system with one other system. This method is the quickest integration model to implement, but it can become overly complex as additional systems are added to the integrated environment, as shown in

Figure 26.8. Each successive integration creates new interdependencies that can cause unexpected behavior between systems.

FIGURE 26.8

Point-to-point integrations can be the simplest and quickest to develop (A), but can become unwieldy as new systems are added to the mix (B).

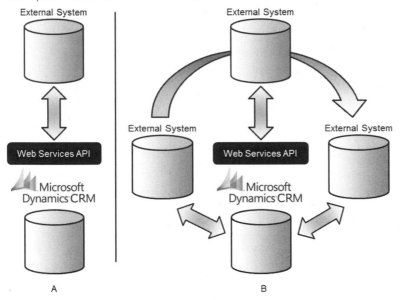

Another challenge with point-to-point integration is that each system's interface may differ, meaning that as additional systems are added to the integration, and existing systems are replaced or upgraded, the connections must often be redesigned and reimplemented. Point-to-point integration is typically a tightly coupled integration, meaning that the integrated systems become dependent on one another in order to operate.

Data hub

A hub and spoke approach to integration overcomes some of the limitations of the point-to-point integration by creating a central point to which all systems are integrated, minimizing the complexity and providing a standard interface for systems to interact with one another. Using a data hub for integration can help to avoid the interdependencies of a point-to-point integration when multiple systems are integrated.

This approach requires more design and planning up front, but provides less interdependency, more scalability and maintainability in the long run. If your organization will only be integrating Dynamics CRM with one other system, this is probably not a cost-effective solution.

The hub model, which can be illustrated as a central hub with source and target systems comprising the spokes (see Figure 26.9), is implemented by extracting common data from all the relevant systems and federating the data in the hub in the formats needed for the target systems. The hub then serves the data to the requesting applications. May not be as efficient or timely, because a lot of processing may need to take place in order to extract and transform data from multiple systems.

FIGURE 26.9

A hub and spoke integration model, where Dynamics CRM is connected to other business systems through a central data hub

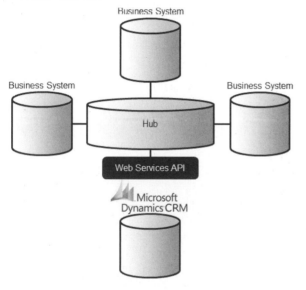

Enterprise service bus

An enterprise service bus (ESB) integration provides a platform for a services-oriented architecture with each system receiving (subscribing) and transmitting (publishing) one or more messages via a messaging pipeline, or service bus (Figure 26.10). ESB has many advantages over other methods of integration, including presenting a standard layer of abstraction for systems to plug into in a loosely coupled fashion as well as a scalable architecture. Unlike a hub and spoke integration, an ESB model does not have a single point of failure, making it a more stable architecture in a large enterprise environment.

The ESB model enables each application's interfaces to be completely independent of the others, as long as they can support the messaging system. ESB integration demands a more modern architecture and a unified messaging model, and relies on well-defined and well-managed processes with known inputs and outputs at each stage.

This can be the most complex and advanced integration model, but for large enterprises with business systems that operate on different platforms, this can be the most effective way to integration operational data and services.

FIGURE 26.10

The enterprise service bus model relies on a common messaging protocol to standardize integration of disparate systems.

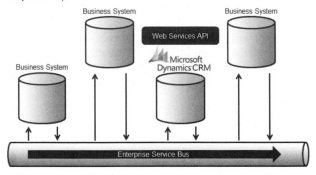

Adhering to Best Practices for Migration and Integration

Migration and integration projects focus on the very heart of your business: the intersection between processes, data, and services applications, and user interactions like inputting data and conducting analysis through reports or other BI tools. Because of this critically important juncture of people, processes, and technology, it is incumbent on the integration implementer to carefully adhere to best practices while designing, developing, testing, and deploying an integration solution. Forthwith are some key recommendations to consider as you develop your integration solution:

- Weigh cost versus need. When gathering requirements from the business users, it is easy for each requirement to be given "top priority." However, you must carefully evaluate the criticality of each requirement, focusing on developing integrations that can provide a clear return on investment, and where the costs, risks, and benefits are clearly understood.

- Keep it simple. Use the simplest techniques where appropriate, mixing and matching approaches to fit the scenario and the type of data or service that is being integrated. For example when integrating both master data and transactional data, consider synchronizing master data using a batch integration technique, but implement a UI mash-up for transactional data. In the simplest scenario, opt for swivel chair integrations at first, automating them later after the process has been proved out.

- Keep it stable. Avoid single points of failure and complex interdependencies by using a loosely-coupled integration model when possible.

- Maintain data quality. Data is one of your organization's most valuable assets. The goal of data quality in your Dynamics CRM implementation should include ensuring that the data is accurate, relevant, timely, complete, and consistent. Inevitably, data will be imperfect — especially in a sales environment where prospect and opportunity information is constantly changing — but imperfect data is not necessarily poor quality data. The data's quality is acceptable if it meets the aggregate needs of the organization and the specific needs of users. For example, a particular opportunity record's estimated value may not be precisely accurate to the penny, but as a means of tracking a sales pipeline and adjusting forecasts, imperfect data may be sufficient. Poor data quality, on the other hand, can impede your organization's use of Dynamics CRM as well as significantly reduce its effectiveness. If your users don't trust the data, they will stop using Dynamics CRM. To avoid this, engineer your integrations to have quality built into the process.

Some tips for maintaining high-quality data:

- Define your organization's data quality standards. Data quality is an important metric for gauging the success of your Dynamics CRM implementation. Develop the definitions for your organization of what constitutes the timeliness, accuracy, relevance, and completeness of your data.

- Provide users with ways to measure the accuracy and quality of your data using reporting and analytics tools. (For example, help to surface duplicates or neglected records and assign owners to merge, update, or deactivate the records.)

- Design data entry to minimize the margin of error. This applies to all points of entry — whether users or integrated systems. Define standards for formatting data (US or U.S.A.?), and implement validation techniques to ensure formats are enforced.

- Minimize the repetition of data. For example, use links to other records instead of having a value repeated. Use picklists and lookups where appropriate to minimize manual entry. Augment data that is input by users with data retrieved from reliable external system and resources, such as address validation or postal code lookup services.

- Control bulk imports/migrations. Use security roles in Dynamics CRM to restrict which users can import data. For those users who are authorized to import data, provide regular training on preparing data for import and using the import tools.

- Practice good data management. Use tools like the Duplicate Detection jobs and record merging to eliminate poor data.

Tip

When external parties (such as customers or partners) have an incentive to keep their data up to date, it may be valuable to give them the ability to modify their data through the use of an external-facing portal, for example. With Microsoft Dynamics CRM 2011's built-in auditing feature, your users can monitor changes to customer data.

- Monitor performance. Integrations that involve a large amount of data may require additional optimization tuning. Where possible, only transfer net changed data between systems to maximize performance. Include integration performance monitoring in your regular maintenance and administration tasks.

- Plan for problems. Make sure your integration solution includes a way to identify and handle failures or exceptions.

Selecting Tools for Migration and Integration

After deciding on an integration model and the techniques you will use to implement the integration, you must evaluate and select the tools you will use to develop the integration. In some cases, the Import Data Wizard may be sufficient. In situations that require automated data extraction, cleansing, validation, transformation and loading, a custom SDK solution or third-party tools may be required. This section provides an overview of the different tools that are available for migration and integration. Figure 26.11 presents a summary of the integration scenarios and the tools discussed in this chapter that are best suited for each scenario.

FIGURE 26.11

The integration tools best-suited for the various integration scenarios discussed in this chapter

	Presentation Layer/UI Mashups	Migrations	Scheduled Batch/Real-time Integrations		
			Point-to-point	Hub and spoke	Enterprise Services Bus
Import Data Wizard		✓			
SDK/Custom Code	✓	✓	✓		
Scribe Insight		✓	✓		
Pervasive Data Integrator		✓	✓	✓	
Microsoft BizTalk Server					✓

Developing a custom SDK import solution

The Dynamics CRM SDK provides complete methods and code samples for using the Web services API to develop custom migration and integration solutions. Using the SDK can have many benefits, but it also requires a deep technical skillset to develop and maintain a robust solution. Custom code can also be difficult to scale and support over time.

The Web services API can be used to perform data imports that can't be done with the Import Data Wizard. If your organization or partner has the right skillset, consider using the SDK to develop custom import processes when you need to:

- Include transformations in custom data maps
- Automate imports from the command line or via scripts
- Incorporate customized user mapping to set record ownership
- Perform on-the-fly data validation during import

Using the SDK, you can import one or more files at a time, parsing the data and transforming it with a map. You can use the SDK or the Import Data Wizard to create data maps. Keep in mind that the default maximum size for a data import using the Web services API is 32 MB. This can be modified by changing the maxRequestLength attribute in the web.config. The SDK provides complete documentation on parsing source data files, creating data maps, configuring lookup, and picklist mappings, and transforming data.

Dynamics CRM includes XML data maps for use with the Import Data Wizard. These maps can also be copied and modified to meet your precise needs, and leveraged via the API when creating a custom migration solution. The data maps included with Microsoft Dynamics CRM 2011 are:

- BCM 2010. A map for importing data from Microsoft Business Contact Manager 2010.
- Generic Map for Contact and Account. This map can be used if you are importing a flat file that contains both account and contact data. For example, if you have a CSV file that lists contacts with company names, such as you might export from Outlook or another e-mail application, use this map.
- Salesforce.com maps. Dynamics CRM includes three maps specifically formatted to simplify importing data that has been exported from Salesforce.com:
  - For Full Data Export.A map for data exported using the Salesforce.com Data Export utility.
  - For Account and Contact Report Export. If you run a Salesforce.com Account and Contact Report and export the data, this map can be used to import the data into Dynamics CRM.
  - For Report Export. This map can be used for records exported using the Report Export in Salesforce.com.

To edit a map, export it from the Dynamics CRM by navigating to the Data Management page and clicking on Data Maps. Select the map from the list and click the Export button. The maps are stored as XML. The map XML includes entity and attribute (field) elements that define the name values for the source and target fields. You can also specify mapping values for picklists and other field types in the XML. The SDK provides a complete guide for the data map schema.

When using the Import Data Wizard or leveraging the API's import method with custom code or a third-party tool, you can monitor the import job's progress in the Dynamics CRM user interface. The import process is an asynchronous process, and the Imports list view shows the status of the import jobs as well as successes and failures.

Cross-Reference

The Import Data Wizard is well suited for one-time or ad hoc data loads. In Microsoft Dynamics CRM 2011 the wizard's ability to import related data, update existing records, and save and reuse data maps make it very powerful. Chapter 8 includes details on using the Import Data Wizard to import data, create, and modify data maps and import relational data from multiple files.

Microsoft integration tools

Microsoft provides a variety of tools and functionality that can be used in migration and integration projects. Two SQL Server components that are sometimes used in Dynamics CRM integrations are SQL Server Integration Services (SSIS) and SQL Server replication. Microsoft also sells BizTalk Server. Microsoft also provides a limited number of prebuilt connectors for Dynamics products.

SQL Server Integration Services

SSIS is part of the Standard and Enterprise versions of SQL Server 2008. SSIS is the evolution of Data Transformation Services from previous versions of SQL Server. SSIS is part of the Business Intelligence Development Studio (BIDS) that is used in the Visual Studio 2008 interface. Using BIDS, you can create SSIS projects that connect to a data source, perform embedded logic, and load data in the target database. SSIS can connect to Web services APIs as a data source by using script components, as shown in Figure 26.12.

To use SSIS to connect to a Web services API like Dynamics CRM's, add a script component to the SSIS project. Edit the script component by adding a Web reference to the Dynamics CRM organization endpoint, and then add a using statement to the script component's CS file (see Figure 26.13). Refer to the SSIS documentation for instructions on consuming a Web service in an integration solution.

SQL Server replication

Many factors make SQL Server replication a complex solution not well suited to most integration scenarios. In some cases where the schema of the data in both the source and the targets are closely aligned and transformation is not required, SQL Server replication techniques can be used for data integration between Dynamics CRM organizations and/or external systems. Microsoft's Enterprise Engineering team released a whitepaper and build guide with information about using replication to integrate multiple Dynamics CRM Version 4.0 organizations. (See Appendix B for links to download these resources.) Using replication does not typically allow for transformation of data. Instead, subscribing databases typically receive data from the publishing database as is.

FIGURE 26.12

A script component in the SSIS designer interface in Business Intelligence Development Studio

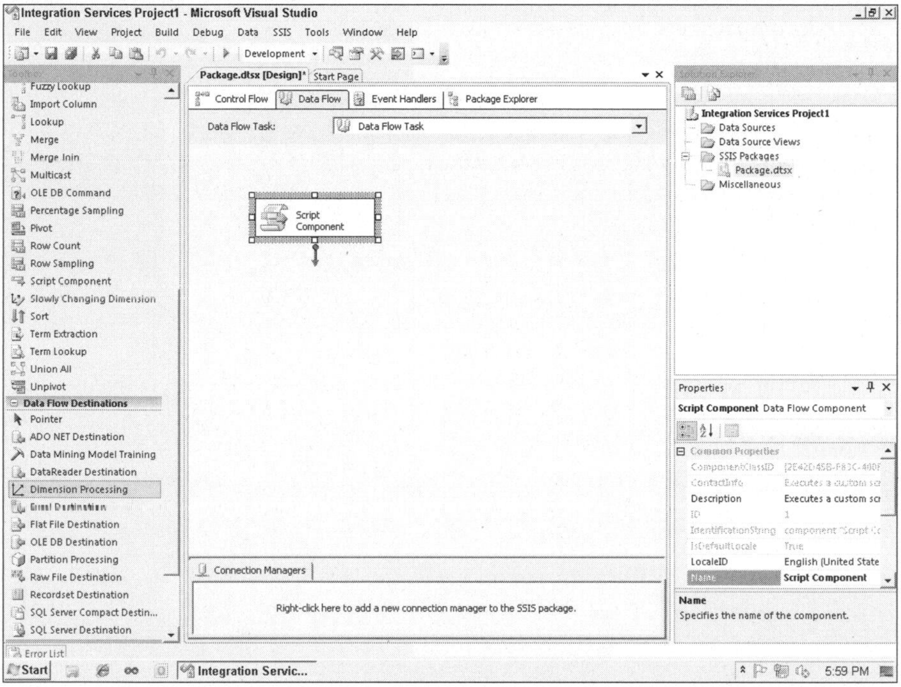

Microsoft BizTalk Server

Microsoft BizTalk Server is Microsoft's flagship enterprise integration solution, with deep functionality that supports a variety of integration techniques and models. BizTalk enables an enterprise service bus (ESB) integration model, supporting connectivity, data integration, and services integration with a robust toolset and messaging platform.

Microsoft releases connectors for BizTalk that enable standard connectivity to other applications. A connector for Dynamics CRM 4.0 was released in 2009 for BizTalk 2006 and 2009. At the time of this writing, a connector for Microsoft Dynamics CRM 2011 is planned.

BizTalk is an enterprise-level server product that uses the Visual Studio IDE to develop integrations. It includes a rules processing engine to automate processes, as well as a message broker to handle communications between systems.

It is designed to allow business analysts to define the integrated processes using visual tools, which developers can then implement in code. BizTalk also includes power business activity monitoring (BAM) capabilities that can capture data from integrated processes and systems and make it available for analysis and reporting. BizTalk also allows for reliable message routing in case of transmission failures or disruptions, providing a high level of continuity in critical integrations.

FIGURE 26.13

The script component's CS file will need a Web reference pointing to the Dynamics CRM Web services endpoint and a using statement for the reference.

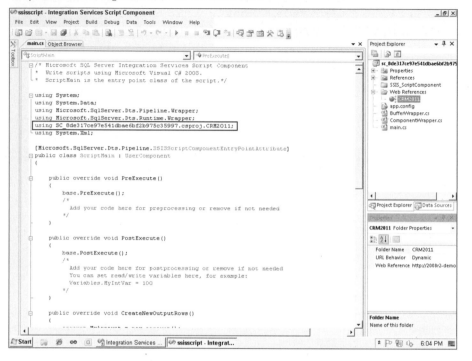

Dynamics CRM Adapter for Dynamics GP

Microsoft's business products include Dynamics GP, a popular accounting and ERP system aimed at mid-market businesses. Microsoft has released integration adapters for several versions of Dynamics CRM and Dynamics GP which automate the synchronization of business data between the two systems.

The adapter, which is a complete integration solution, enables the synchronization of Dynamics GP's customer records, sales items, invoices, orders, and other entities with corresponding Dynamics CRM entities. The Dynamics CRM Adapter for Dynamics GP consists of a Windows service to process integrations, a client used to configure and customize the integration maps, a database that stores the integration configurations, map templates, and a transformation engine.

The adapter is available through your Microsoft Dynamics partner.

Scribe Insight

Scribe Software provides Scribe Insight, one of the most widely used third-party integration toolsets for Dynamics CRM. Scribe Insight lends itself to point-to-point integrations and complex migrations. Scribe Insight includes a strong GUI-based solution for migration and integration, and works with both on-premises and online implementations of Dynamics CRM. The Enterprise licensing for Scribe also uses Windows clustering to enable integration failover support.

Scribe Insight has connects natively to a variety of data sources including ODBC, MySQL, Oracle, and, of course, SQL Server. Integration implementers can use it to perform extraction, transformation, updates, inserts, and deletes as part of either batch or real-time integration jobs. Scribe can also monitor for files being dropped in a directory or modified, and use them as the data source.

Scribe Insight architecture

Scribe Insight is composed of three primary components: the integration server, a workbench, and a console.

- Scribe Integration Server. The Scribe Integration Server can be installed as a stand-alone server for high-volume integrations, or installed on an existing application server to share resources. The Integration Server is the software component where the orchestrations take place and are processed.

- Workbench. The Workbench is the user interface component used to design mappings and transformations between the source and target. Scribe makes use of adapters to connect to the API of a large number of systems, including an adapter that is certified by Microsoft for use with the Dynamics CRM Web services API. They also provide adapters for other Dynamics products including GP and NAV.

  After using adapters in the Workbench to connect to the source and target systems, you can begin designing the mappings and transformations in the easy-to-use interface.

  After the mappings and transformations have been designed they can be saved as templates for reuse and portability. Predesigned templates are available from Scribe's Web site to speed up your integration development, including templates for ACT!, QuickBooks, and GoldMine. The Scribe Workbench also has these characteristics:

  - It can be used to do data cleansing to prepare the source data, incorporate custom logic and design formulas to transform data. For example, using the Workbench you can create validation parameters to ensure consistent data formatting.

  - The Workbench allows you to perform lookups and preview Dynamics CRM picklist values, as well as work with entity relationships.

  - The Workbench can be used to design the integration process flow in a series of steps that can branch into subprocesses based on the output of each step. This is enabled in a graphical, drag-and-drop process design area of the Workbench.

- Using the Workbench, you can create custom functions using a variety of common programming languages.

- The Workbench also lets you preview the integration for testing purposes so you can develop in an iterative manner and deploy the solution quickly.

- Scribe Console: The console is used to control the triggers and/or schedules used to initiate integration processes. It also provides monitoring capabilities and can send alerts based on business activity or system conditions. For example, the console can be configured to send an e-mail alert with a summary of the number of daily order records processed by the integration solution. The console is also responsible for monitoring directories for file drops. The Scribe Console provides error tracking and displays the history of integration jobs.

Pervasive Data Integrator

Pervasive Software is a long-time player in the data integration market, and an up-and-comer in the Dynamics CRM space. Pervasive's solution, Data Integrator, is certified for Microsoft Dynamics CRM and works with on-premises as well as cloud integrations. Pervasive delivers Data Integrator as traditional installable software or as an on-demand service.

Pervasive Data Integrator has a strong graphical user interface, but tends to be more complex than Scribe, with a somewhat steeper learning curve, but this is perhaps offset by the software's ability to handle more complex integration scenarios. Pervasive Data Integrator can be used to create robust point-to-point integrations and to perform one-time or ad hoc migrations. Coupled with the Pervasive Integration Hub, the Pervasive Data Integrator is an ideal solution for hub and spoke integration models.

Pervasive does an excellent job of extracting data from multiple sources with connectors to hundreds of data sources including Oracle, Sybase, SQL Server, DB2, and many others. The software includes connectors for a variety of ERP and business applications, including Dynamics CRM. Pervasive also provides an advanced scripting language (RIFL) that can handle complex transformations.

Given the importance of data quality to an integration solution, one of the most powerful features of the Pervasive offering is the Data Profiler, which helps to maintain data quality by identifying problematic or erroneous data.

Pervasive Data Integrator architecture

There are several core components to the Pervasive Data Integrator:

- The Pervasive IDE (Integrated Development Environment). The IDE includes tools to configure connections, design integration processes, create mappings, and develop transformations. The Pervasive IDE provides a graphical interface to lay out the integration's flow of steps and branches, and also has a map designer with drag-and-drop mapping. The Join Designer utility in the IDE allows you to connect multiple data sources together to act as a single source for data mapping.

- Repository Manager. The Repository Manager is used to package up integration solutions and reusable components and to store them for access and deployment. Pervasive stores all metadata about integrations as XML files, making them easy to edit and reuse.

- Data Profiler. The Data Profiler component assists in analyzing data for errors and inconsistencies, helping to ensure high-quality data. It can be used to identify data that violates business rules or contains null values.

- Pervasive Integration Engine. The Integration Engine is a lightweight processing and transformation engine designed for high throughput. It can be executed via event triggers, scheduling, or scripting, and handles batch and transaction integration processing. The Integration Engine can be controlled through COM and Java APIs, command line instructions, or via the Integration Services API.

- Integration Services. Integration Services is a Web services API for the Pervasive integration system enabling the entire platform to be leveraged as a service by SOA systems.

Integrating Dynamics CRM with a Web Site

Many scenarios require organizations to integrate Dynamics CRM with one or more Web sites or Web applications. Among the most common scenarios are simple contact forms, interactive portals, and intranet. There are numerous Web technologies that can be integrated with Dynamics CRM including custom ASP.NET Web sites, Azure applications, SharePoint, and, of course, many non-Microsoft technologies.

Web site form integration

Web-to-lead forms and similar integrations are Contact Us type forms found on most Web sites. Organizations frequently want the data that a visitor submits through these forms to create a new lead or contact record in Dynamics CRM. These types of forms can be used to submit lead info, create a case, or for a variety of other reasons. This simple integration can be very powerful when combined with workflows for automated responses, assigning leads, or routing cases.

Creating simple Web-to-lead type integrations between a Web site form and Dynamics CRM can be achieved in a number of ways:

- Synchronously via direct input through the Dynamics CRM Web services create and/ or update methods (Figure 26.14). Direct Web form integration requires that the external Web site can access the Dynamics CRM server, whether it is hosted or deployed on-premises, in order to post the submitted information to the API. On-premises installations must therefore have an exposure to the Internet, either through IFD or some other means. This type of direct integration has the benefit of being straightforward and simple to implement. However, it may pose security risks depending on the configuration, and the Dynamics CRM server's performance could be impacted if the submissions from the website form are sufficiently numerous.

> **FIGURE 26.14**
>
> A simple Web-to-lead integration uses a direct synchronous connection to the Dynamics CRM Web services API.

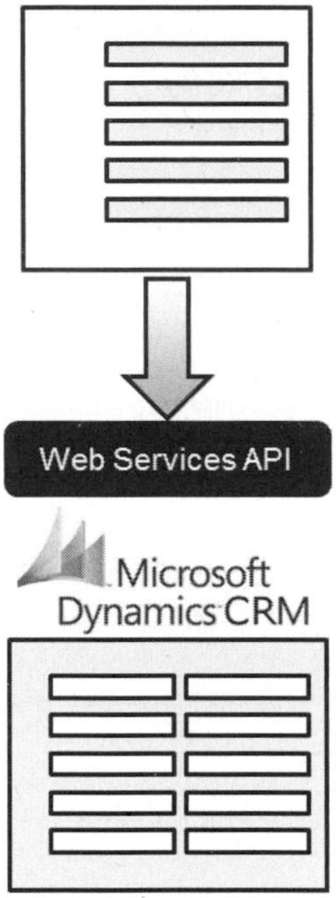

- Asynchronous indirect input via a service (Figure 26.15). In this scenario, the Web form's output is temporarily stored in a drop file or intermediate database, where it is later retrieved asynchronously by a service, such as an integration application or custom code, transformed, and input into the Dynamics CRM system. This method typically requires additional architectural considerations and custom components, but it has the advantage of mitigating security concerns and potential performance impacts.

Web portals

Portals are often made available for customers or partners so an organization can more easily share information with them in a relevant way. A portal, or extranet, typically requires visitors to log in to the Web site, where they can update their profiles, view records, submit requests for information or support, and so on. In some cases, administration of the portal users' access is simplified by allowing Dynamics CRM users to initiate invitations and grant access levels directly from within Dynamics CRM. Portals that are integrated with Dynamics CRM might also be used to display knowledge base articles, sales literature, or lists of any other type of record.

FIGURE 26.15

A service can be developed that monitors an intermediate file drop location or database, retrieves the submitted data, and loads into Dynamics CRM via the Web services API, creating a lead record.

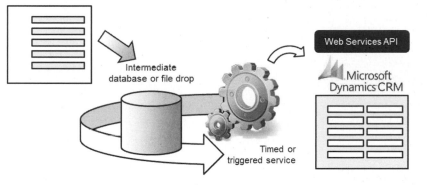

Microsoft periodically releases free, open-source CRM Accelerators that serve as functional examples of ways to extend Dynamics CRM functionality using supported development methods and technologies. They typically include customized solutions that can be imported into your Dynamics CRM instance, custom code, and installation and use instructions. Accelerators are available for download from within the Marketplace.

One such accelerator is Microsoft's Portal Accelerator. The Portal Accelerator is designed to be hosted on your own servers or in the cloud with Azure. The accelerator installs a custom solution that integrates with the portal Web site, enabling Dynamics CRM to be used to control the portal, including content management and portal user administration. The Portal Accelerator provides the foundation for customer and partner portals, and can be further customized for your business scenario.

Note

When implementing a Web portal that is integrated with Dynamics CRM, Microsoft may require an External Connector License if nonemployees are accessing live Dynamics CRM data. Please refer to your licensing agreements and related documentation to be sure that your organization remains in compliance.

Cross-Reference

In addition to external-facing portals, many organizations wish to share information and extend processes within the organization but beyond the group of Dynamics CRM users. In these cases, it is often helpful to integrate the system with an intranet system such as SharePoint.

SharePoint and Dynamics CRM are natural partners, complementing one another's functionality to provide a comprehensive platform for managing the artifacts and activities of tailored business processes. Dynamics CRM includes built-in integration with SharePoint document libraries, creating them on-the-fly and linking to them in hierarchical fashion. There are lots of ways to use SharePoint and Dynamics CRM together: displaying Dynamics CRM list views in SharePoint pages, for example, or using metadata from Dynamics CRM entities to create the column headers on SharePoint lists. Appendix A includes a few more examples and walk-throughs for using these two technologies together.

Adding Functionality with Integrated ISV Solutions

The acronym ISV stands for Independent Software Vendor and is a term that Microsoft uses to refer to software developers and partner organizations that make custom applications to extend the functionality of Dynamics CRM. Microsoft relies on the special skills and industry expertise of ISVs to deliver niche solutions and functionality that are not native to the Dynamics CRM platform.

The reason that ISV solutions are pertinent to the present discussion of integration is twofold: First, many ISV solutions — especially those that are certified for Microsoft Dynamics CRM — are excellent examples of the types of applications that can be integrated into Dynamics CRM using the supported SDK methods. Second, there are many ISV solutions available that provide specific data and service integration with minimal customization in order to support many common business processes like sales, marketing, and customer service. For example, there are ISV solutions that provide e-mail and postal address validation, graphical data imports, and complete line-of-business functionality.

Finding ISV solutions

Microsoft has introduced a new, centralized app store for Microsoft Dynamics CRM 2011 called the Marketplace. The Marketplace is accessible directly within the system from the Settings area. ISVs and other Microsoft partners have posted in the Marketplace many prebuilt solutions that you can download, install and evaluate, and new apps are being posted regularly. This is the primary place for an administrator to visit to locate an ISV solution. Solutions that marked as being Certified for Microsoft Dynamics have passed a rigorous set of tests and reviews to ensure not only that they work as advertised, but that they conform to supported methods for extensibility and security.

Some notable examples of ISV solutions

Microsoft has long cultivated a diverse ecosystem of partners for many of its software titles, and Dynamics CRM is no exception. There are many ISVs that have been working with Dynamics CRM since its earliest versions, and new ISVs are emerging every day. It would be difficult to list all of the ISV solutions, or even to list all of the *best-of-breed* ISV solutions available. However, in our experience, the following ISV solutions do a great job of fulfilling some of the most common functional requirement gaps for organizations implementing Dynamics CRM.

Data2CRM from CRM Innovation

CRM Innovation's Data2CRM is a great example of a state-of-the-art extension for Dynamics CRM. It allows subscribers to easily import data via the API using a graphical, drag-and-drop interface that takes just minutes to learn (see Figure 26.16). Data2CRM is also a great example of a cloud-based solution that incorporates a Silverlight interface.

FIGURE 26.16

The Data2CRM interface provides an easy-to-use graphical way to map, transform, and import data to Dynamics CRM.

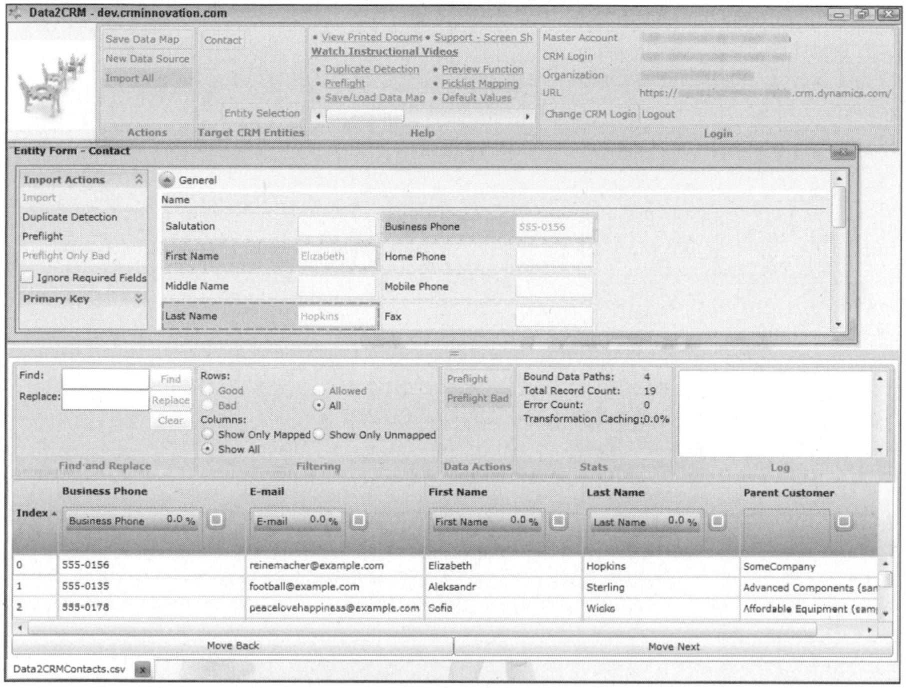

Users can upload CSV files, graphically edit the mappings, apply a variety of transformations, and import data into Dynamics CRM. The Silverlight interface mimics the layout of the target entity's form, and provides the user with a preview before executing the import. Its real-time pre-flight checks the data for potential errors and allows users to fix them directly in the interface. Data2CRM also enables users to create new picklist values on the fly, set default values, and maintain relationships between imported files, such as accounts and contacts.

CWR Mobility

Microsoft Dynamics CRM 2011 includes a mobile client interface, Mobile Express, that is highly configurable and browser-neutral. With an IFD deployment, it fits the bill for mobile access for many organizations. However, it does have some limitations, chiefly the fact that the Mobile Express interface is only available online — meaning the mobile device must have an internet connection to access it.

CWR Mobility is an ISV that develops mobile client applications exclusively for Dynamics CRM. Currently, their stable of mobile clients include apps for the iPhone, many BlackBerry models, and the Microsoft mobile platforms Windows Mobile and Windows Phone 7.

CWR's mobile clients for Dynamics CRM provide complete functionality offline, as well as an enterprise-class administrative interface directly within the Dynamics CRM Web client (see Figure 26.17). The administrative interface allows organizations to define security parameters, profiles, form layout, and site maps for the mobile clients. It also enables Dynamics CRM data to be wiped from mobile devices remotely in the event of loss or theft.

CWR Mobility's ISV solutions are certified for Microsoft Dynamics, and the company has won numerous prestigious industry awards and recognition from Microsoft.

Experlogix

Many organizations face the challenge of needing to quickly develop quotes and orders for customers using their own products list and business logic. Dynamics CRM does an excellent job of enabling salespeople to create and manage quotes, but it is well suited only for organizations with a small number of SKUs and low volume of quotes. Dynamics CRM does not provide any product configuration rules either.

FIGURE 26.17

The administrative interface for the CWR Mobile CRM extension

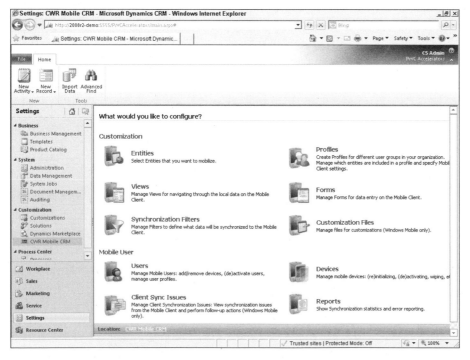

To fill this gap and provide a powerful, intuitive product configurator experience for developing quotes and orders, an ISV called Experlogix has developed a sophisticated and easy-to-use configurator that is certified for Dynamics CRM. It incorporates your organization's custom business logic, as well as system and custom attributes, in order to formalize product rules.

The Experlogix Configurator is launched from a custom button on the Quote entity's Ribbon (see Figure 26.18). Another button allows quotes and the configured products to be copied automatically.

Experlogix's configurator makes liberal use of images and color coding to aid users in visually assembling the products for a quote or order, and provides seamless integration with the Dynamics CRM system. Its interface (see Figure 26.19) provides users with a simple, guided method to quickly configure professional quotes.

FIGURE 26.18

The Experlogix Configurator is tightly integrated with the user interface and the functionality of Dynamics CRM.

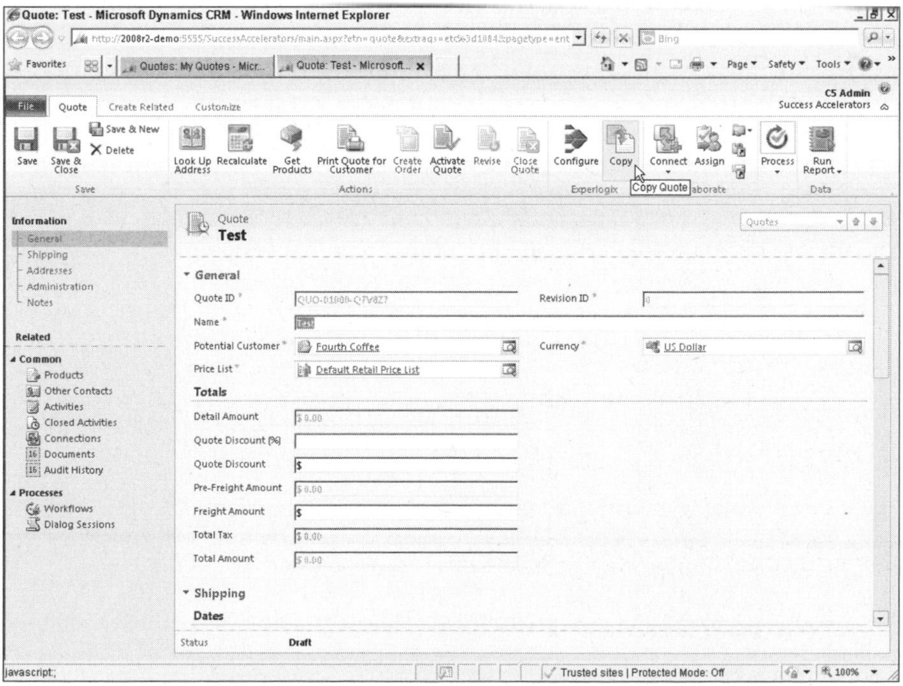

FIGURE 26.19

The Experlogix Configurator incorporates product images and business rules to guide salespeople through the process of building quotes.

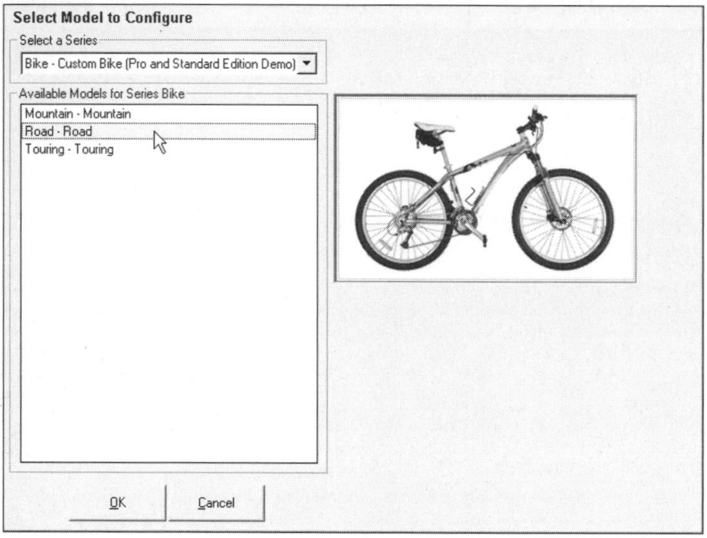

Summary

This chapter provided an overview of common integration scenarios, the techniques, strategies, and tools that can be used to accomplish them, and a look at some of the solutions available from Independent Software Vendors on Microsoft's Marketplace.

Many organizations implement Dynamics CRM with the goal of integrating it with their accounting systems, VoIP/CTI systems, Web sites, and a variety of other data and services.

Dynamics CRM has been designed to accommodate these types of integration needs, providing numerous integration points for user-interface mash-ups, data, and service integration.

Integrating LOB systems and Web applications with Dynamics CRM can simplify users' jobs and automate end-to-end business processes. It can improve user adoption and boost the return on your investment in Dynamics CRM.

Depending on the type of integration you are trying to achieve, there are a number of tools and methods you can use. There are built-in tools, like the Import Data Wizard, that can be used to quickly migrate data. There are also custom applications and third-party solutions that can be used to perform more complex batch and real-time integrations. And there are many partner organizations and ISVs with powerful prebuilt solutions that can extend the functionality of Dynamics CRM.

XRM: Going Beyond Traditional CRM

XRM — it's a buzzword in the Dynamics CRM market that has been gaining ground for a few years now. Although the buzzword may be occasionally overused, the concept is unlocking incredible value and power for businesses in every industry across the globe.

This chapter defines XRM and its place in your business, explains some of the principal advantages that Dynamics CRM lends to XRM projects, and walks through a complete XRM solution from beginning to end, illustrating some of the ways that the concept can be applied.

Exploring XRM

XRM is not the name of a software product or even the exclusive domain of Microsoft Dynamics CRM. But it is primarily Microsoft's Dynamics CRM product that is the driving force behind the XRM phenomenon.

What does XRM mean, and why is Dynamics CRM at its core? How will it benefit your organization? These are some of the questions we will address before jumping in to an example of XRM in action.

Defining XRM

The acronym itself has been variously described as the abbreviation for "eXtensible Relationship Management," "eXtended Relationship Management," or simply "Anything Relationship Management" with the X being represented with a small x indicating the reader can substitute anything for the first letter.

So what is XRM? Simply put, it is the practice of developing a custom line-of-business application using Dynamics CRM as a foundation.

Over the years since Microsoft first released its Customer Relationship Management product, the software has evolved. This evolution has seen improvements in both the system's native functionality and its programmability. From its inception, Dynamics CRM was designed to be a market leader in traditional CRM functionality, with powerful sales, marketing, and customer service functionality. The software was also designed to be extensible.

As it began to take hold in the marketplace, creative customers and partners began expanding this highly customizable software to address other business needs. Because Dynamics CRM provides the tools needed to formalize and automate business processes with a great deal of flexibility, it very quickly became evident that it could do more than track leads, customers, cases, and marketing campaigns.

The software began to emerge as a platform, a foundation upon which an endless variety of business applications could be built. This idea started to blossom with Version 3.0, and by the time Version 4.0 hit the market, it was an increasingly common part of Dynamics CRM implementations to include non-CRM processes and functionality.

Partners started to build solutions on Dynamics CRM to track vehicle fleets for large corporations, machines for manufacturers, citizen relationships and service requests for municipalities, research projects and materials for laboratories, and much more. A small sampling of XRM solutions include:

- Employee management
- Event management
- Asset management
- Compliance management
- Vendor and partner management
- Property management

With the introduction of Microsoft's hosted Dynamics CRM Online, suddenly this powerful platform was available in the cloud for a low cost of entry. Microsoft had entered the Platform-as-a-Service (PaaS) market. Instead of simply delivering a nicely packaged, albeit functional, application as a service (Software as a Service, or SaaS), the extensible nature of Dynamics CRM translated into a full-on PaaS play in this emerging market.

Understanding why Dynamics CRM is a good platform

Dynamics CRM isn't always the best platform for custom line-of-business applications. There are certainly trade-offs when it comes to developing on a platform as compared to creating a custom application from scratch in which every detail can be (and must be) custom developed. However, Dynamics CRM lends itself to XRM development for many reasons:

- It has an open architecture. Dynamics CRM's n-tier architecture provides developers and implementers with many ways to tap into its functionality. The application programming interfaces are built using technologies that are widely adopted and widely understood, with a large pool of existing partners, developers, and customers already employing the skills needed to extend it. Using graphical customization tools, workflow rules, custom reports, ISV add-ons, Web resources, plug-ins, and other methods, Dynamics CRM's component functionalities can be tapped into in countless ways.

- It enables declarative design. Because of the simplicity of adding custom entities, fields, views, workflows, and other elements directly within the user interface, Dynamics CRM allows a declarative or model-driven design approach. It's not necessary to manually create a table in a database, specifying SQL column types and table relationships, and business logic. Instead, a user or implementer can use a few clicks and drag-and-drop functionality to quickly build an interface that has business logic and functionality behind it inherently.

- It is familiar to end users. As a Microsoft product, XRM applications can leverage the familiar Microsoft look and feel, taking advantage of the user-experience design and know-how of the world's largest software maker.

Understanding the value of platform development

With the variety of development technologies and tools available today, why should a business opt for a platform — why build a line-of-business application on top of Dynamics CRM?

Among the most compelling reasons that businesses are opting for platform-based solution development are the incredible time and cost savings (see Figure 27.1). In today's fast-paced and constantly changing business environment, it's increasingly important to get a solution into users' hands quickly and at as low a cost as possible. And once the solution has been delivered, it must be flexible enough to adapt to new factors in the environment. A platform solution like Dynamics CRM becomes a competitive advantage.

What are these foundational elements that Dynamics CRM provides and which otherwise would have to be coded up from scratch in order to deliver a functional business application?

- Access and authentication: Built-in Active Directory, Live ID and claims-based authentication provide flexible and standards-based sign-on capabilities out-of-the-box.

- A robust and flexible security model: A mixed record ownership model with organizational, team and user ownership enables incredibly granular fine-tuning of the XRM solution's security implementation. Add to that the concepts of business units and field-level security, and Dynamics CRM's security model can be fit to nearly any requirements.

- Offline capability. With native Outlook synchronization of system and custom entities, offline reporting, and full offline application functionality, Dynamics CRM provides XRM solutions with functionality that most LOB applications would never achieve otherwise.

FIGURE 27.1

Developing an application from scratch means a lot of time and effort must be spent in building the foundational architecture of the application, as well as on creating custom code to support business processes.

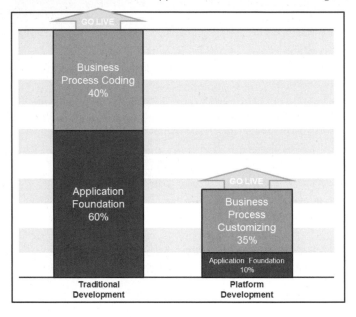

- Calendar, schedule, and task management. Both natively to Dynamics CRM and integrated with Outlook, these functions are core components to most business applications and are immediately available to an XRM solution.

- Business and contact management. Most business applications have some relation to customers, whether businesses or individuals. Dynamics CRM of course has built-in support for these types of records, including address tracking, leads management, and more.

- Activity tracking. Dynamics CRM does an excellent job of organizing and tracking activities, such as e-mails, phone calls, and even custom activity types. Activities can be "regarded" to system and custom entities, adding a powerful dimension to XRM solutions.

- Service management. Whether it's help desk type inquiries, user support, knowledge base articles, or scheduling service, the service management functionality of Dynamics CRM is complementary to a variety of LOB processes.

- Built-in maintainability. One of the biggest challenges with homegrown applications is that they tend to be difficult to maintain and upgrade. Often, the inner workings of the application are known to only a few individuals whom the business rapidly becomes dependent on to keep the system updated. Microsoft Dynamics CRM 2011 incorporates the Windows Update mechanisms that are common to the Windows operating system and Office applications, meaning that your XRM solution will also benefit from this continual maintenance and level of supportability.

- Localization. Dynamics CRM supports localization to support multilingual and multi-currency organizations. Language packs can be downloaded and installed freely, and customizations can include translated labels, allowing users to select their preferred languages for the user interface. For XRM solutions that will record money values, Dynamics CRM's multi-currency support will be indispensable.

- Simple customization. Another advantage that Dynamics CRM has over homegrown solutions for LOB applications is that Dynamics CRM is built for customization and extensibility whereas homegrown applications typically are built to fit a fixed set of requirements. Dynamics CRM's customizability means that as your business needs change, your XRM solution can keep pace.

- Office integration. Many business users rely on the ubiquitous Microsoft Office applications to get their work done. Whether it is Outlook, Word, or Excel, your XRM solution built on Dynamics CRM can immediately take advantage of this tightly integrated suite of applications.

- SharePoint document management. Many LOB applications require document management capabilities. Quotes, proposals, bills of lading, and countless other documents are key elements of LOB processes. An XRM solution can take advantage of the built-in SharePoint document management integration.

- BI/Analytics. Process automation and data management are only two of the many facets of a mature LOB application. Business intelligence and analytics are also integral to most such applications. The native reporting functionality with the Report Wizard and SQL Server Reporting Services, Advanced Find, and inline visualizations provide a complete set of BI tools for your XRM solution.

- Community contributions. There is a mature and extensive ecosystem of partners, developers, ISVs, and others who share their knowledge about Dynamics CRM on blogs, forums, user groups, and many other venues. A custom-coded LOB application can't compete with this global product knowledge.

- Processes. Built-in workflow design and automation, and interactive dialogs are powerful enablers of tailored business processes. Dynamics CRM includes these tools and surfaces them in a way that doesn't require a developer or system administrator to configure. Processes work with custom entities, can be saved as templates, and create a viewable history for users.

- Mobile access. It goes without saying that today's workforce is more mobile — and more dependent on mobile devices — than ever before. Microsoft Dynamics CRM 2011 includes configurable mobile functionality out-of-the-box.

- Data management. Even line-of-business applications need data, and Dynamics CRM's data management tools — the Import Data Wizard, and duplicate detection rules and jobs — are yet another piece of the foundation that can speed an XRM application's time-to-value.

The list above presents many important functional areas that make Dynamics CRM a compelling platform for custom business applications. Add to this mix the extensible architecture and SDK, and the advantages of XRM compared to a custom-coded LOB applications are clear.

Walking Through a Typical XRM Scenario

To illustrate the capabilities of Dynamics CRM to deliver a line-of-business application in a shorter time and with a fraction of the custom code needed for a custom application, let's take a look at a common business process that has little to do with the functional areas of traditional customer relationship management software: Human Resources management.

As we walk through the implementation of this scenario for a fictitious company, PWC Accelerators, we will illustrate the configuration, customization, extension, and implementation of the Dynamics CRM platform.

Setting up the scenario

PWC Accelerators manufactures and sells personal watercraft through a network of national retail outlets. PWC's Human Resources department is responsible for a wide range of services for job applicants, employees, and management. Many of the HR department's processes currently rely on manual data entry, spreadsheets, and paper forms. The department wants to improve its efficiency and its ability to track, manage, and measure the way it delivers its services. Due to the confidential nature of HR data, the department also must comply with certain corporate privacy and security requirements.

PWC Accelerators has evaluated off-the-shelf Human Resources applications, but has been unable to find one that fits the company's requirements for supporting a complete end-to-end employee lifecycle, and which can easily integrate with existing systems. They also considered developing an application from scratch, but ruled that out due to cost and complexity. As a result, they have turned to Dynamics CRM as a development platform.

The original process for managing the employee lifecycle

In order to understand the needs that PWC has for a new HR solution, let's briefly examine the current processes the company follows to support its employees, as shown in Figure 27.2.

PWC Accelerators has retail outlets across the country that employ sales and service associates. During the busy summer months, they must often increase their sales team quickly. Regional managers, who each oversee from five to ten stores, independently advertise job openings. Currently, when someone responds to a help wanted ad, or inquires at a retail outlet about openings, the stores have been using a combination of paper applications and e-mail to handle the application process.

FIGURE 27.2

This chapter explores the business processes of a hypothetical company's HR department, and how an XRM application can be built on the Dynamics CRM platform to support them.

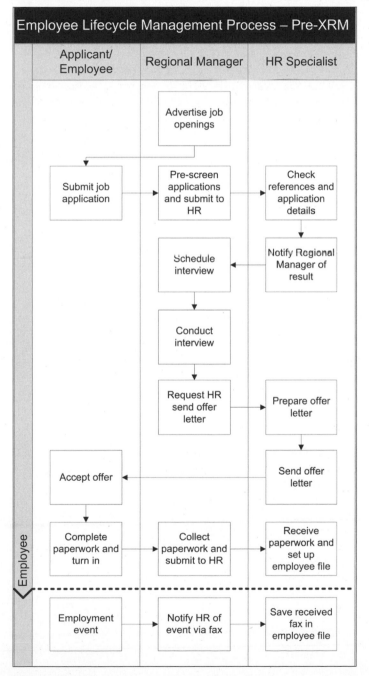

When an application is received, a regional manager is required to do the initial screening while the corporate HR department lends support by background checks and validating application details. Much of the communication for this process is handled via email and telephone, and a regional manager who is hiring sales associates for multiple retail outlets can often be overwhelmed trying to keep up with the status of an application.

HR notifies the regional manager when the reference checks and other details have been verified, and the manager schedules and conducts an interview with the candidate.

When the interview has been completed the regional manager may decide to extend an offer to the applicant. This is currently handled by requesting the HR department to send an offer letter to the candidate.

Candidates who accept the job offer are supposed to complete a packet of new hire paperwork and an orientation session, but in practice, this process is not always carried out. The HR department would like to be able to ensure that this process is followed at each retail outlet.

During the course of an individual's employment with PWC Accelerators, the HR department is responsible for maintaining a file with the employee's information, and recording events like leaves-of-absence, paid time-off, promotions, incidents, and termination of employment. Currently, the department relies on regional managers and store managers to fax in documentation for these types of events. The faxes are received electronically and stored on a shared drive.

This process presents the HR department with a number of challenges. Many of the steps require manual data entry and filing, and there is no shared visibility for managers or HR personnel into the process, and as a result there is often confusion about who is responsible for the next step of the process, or indeed what the next step is for a given candidate. As the company has grown, this manual process has become burdensome and a hindrance to the company's growth.

The XRM solution

PWC Accelerators engaged an experienced Dynamics CRM partner to help redesign this process and to implement a streamlined XRM solution to overcome these challenges and shortcomings. The XRM solution described here performs all of the steps required by the HR department and adds a number of significant improvements.

By incorporating many of the methods described in this book, Dynamics CRM was used as a platform to create a unique, line-of-business application that closely fit the requirements of the PWC Accelerators' HR department. Let's examine the elements that were brought together to deliver this solution.

The solution interface

PWC Accelerators chose Microsoft Dynamics CRM 2011 as the foundation for their XRM solution partly because of the familiar interface that the system provides. Leveraging this familiarity in the Web and Outlook clients, the solution interface makes use of the following techniques:

- Sitemap customization
- Custom dashboard
- Custom charts
- Web resources

The main navigation has been tailored to display only the elements that are of interest to the Human Resources department by modifying the site map (see Figure 27.3). The sales, marketing, and customer service areas were removed from the left-hand navigation and replaced with a single Human Resources area. A link to the payroll system was added to the Workplace, using a Web resource for the icon. A custom group was created to display employee records.

FIGURE 27.3

An XRM solution, built on Dynamics CRM, streamlines and automates PWC Accelerators' hiring and human resources management processes.

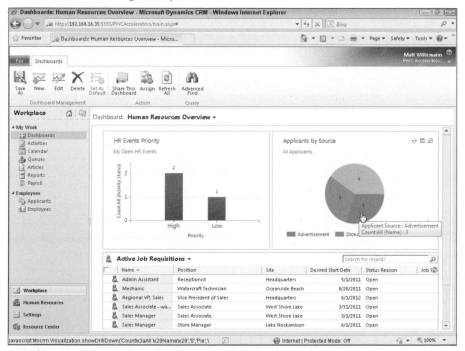

A custom dashboard was built to display some of the key metrics for the HR department, such as high-priority employee incidents, the performance of various job advertising channels, and a list of active job requisitions.

The Job Requisition process

In the manual process that regional managers had to follow in the past, when a position opened up in one of their stores, they had to write up a help wanted ad and find places to advertise. They were left to their own devices, and results were inconsistent across the company. The managers also had difficulty in keeping track of which job openings had received applications.

The job requisition process implemented as part of the XRM solution uses a combination of the following customization options and methods:

- Custom entities
- Workflow rule
- Queue
- Solution Accelerator from Microsoft
- Security Roles
- Field Security Profiles
- Custom SDK code

The XRM solution has incorporated a new entity called the Job Requisition as shown in Figure 27.4. Regional managers need only submit a new job requisition through the XRM solution. The job requisition contains a lookup to a library of job descriptions (housed in the Position entity), a lookup to the Site where the job is available, and several radio buttons that allow an authorized HR approver to post the job automatically to the company's Web site and social media sites.

The Position entity contains information about the types of jobs that are performed at PWC Accelerators, including the position title, a job description, a pay band to indicate the compensation level for the position, and the type of location at which the position is typically located (see Figure 27.5).

FIGURE 27.4

The job requisition form. A regional manager submits the form to the HR queue, from where it is reviewed and automatically published to the company Web site and social media.

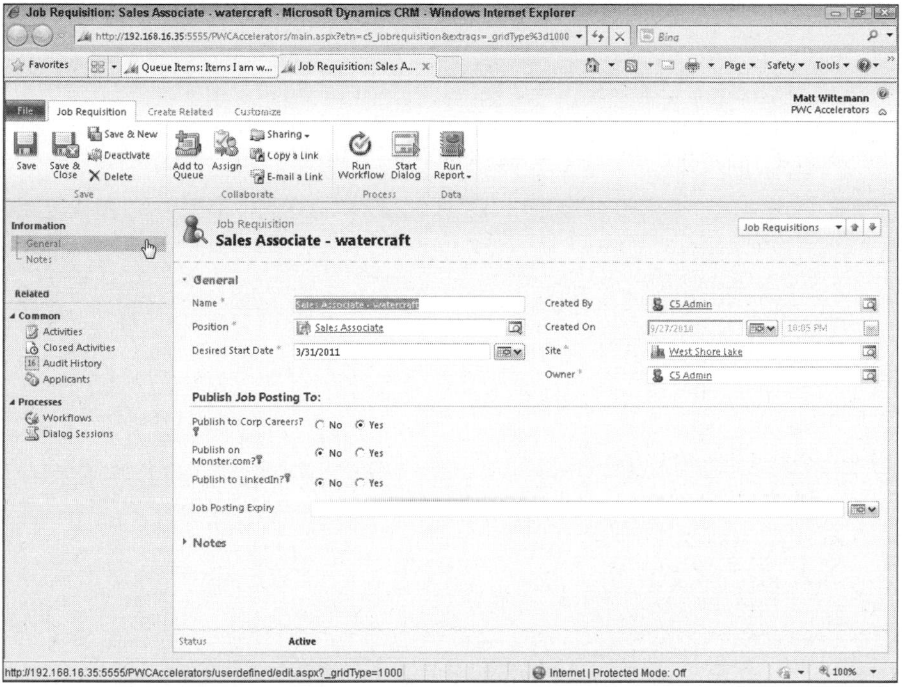

When the job requisition is created, it is automatically routed by workflow rules to the HR queue, where an HR Specialist reviews it. If the requisition is approved, the HR Specialist can select where the job should be posted. Using the example provided by the Portal Accelerator (see Chapter 26), the job posting is published to the company's Web site. If selected, it is also posted to social media sites (see Figure 27.6) using custom code that leverages the SDK.

As applications are received for the requisition, the regional manager can view the list called My Active Job Requisitions to monitor the applications received for each position.

FIGURE 27.5

The position record contains standard job titles and descriptions. Users of the XRM solution can also views applicants who have applied for the position, as well as employees who currently hold the position.

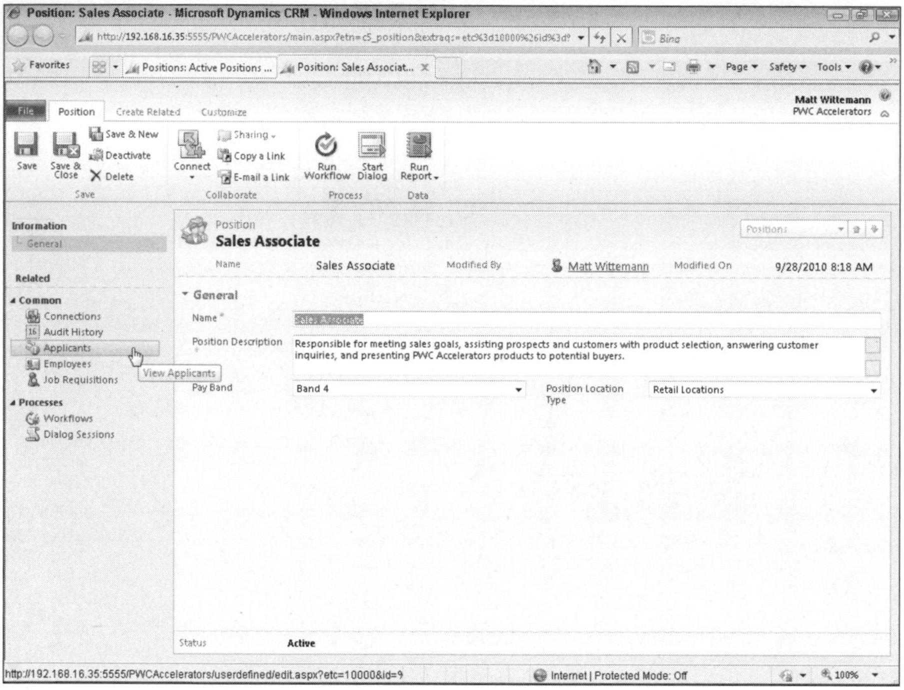

The application process

PWC Accelerators has relied on a paper application process that is growing unwieldy as the company expands. Paper applications had to be mailed or faxed to the corporate office for review, leaving the regional managers awaiting a response and unsure if the applications had been received or were being reviewed.

The XRM solution developed to streamline this process incorporates a number of key elements and builds on the job requisition process:

- Microsoft InfoPath form
- Web-to-lead type form
- Renamed system entity
- Integration of external Web service
- Built-in "lead" conversion functionality

FIGURE 27.6

The job requisition process incorporates custom entities, workflow processes, queues, field security profiles, and custom code based on Microsoft's portal accelerator.

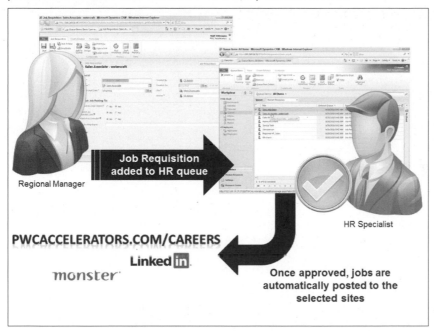

To make it easier to apply for a job, and to capture the application information directly in the XRM system, PWC Accelerators has installed kiosks in their stores that provide access to an electronic application. Applications are also available on the company's Web site.

When using the in-store kiosks, interested individuals can select the position they wish to apply for from the list of available jobs. This list is pulled from Dynamics CRM's list of approved job requisitions, which is populated into SharePoint using Business Connectivity Services (BCS). Because SharePoint BCS enables CRUD operations on connected data, they've opted to use an InfoPath form hosted in SharePoint to allow the data entry for the application, as shown in Figure 27.7. When the application is saved, the BCS connection creates the application record in Dynamics CRM.

FIGURE 27.7

An InfoPath form on the company's SharePoint site is used as an electronic application. The applications can be filled out at kiosks in the PWC Accelerators stores.

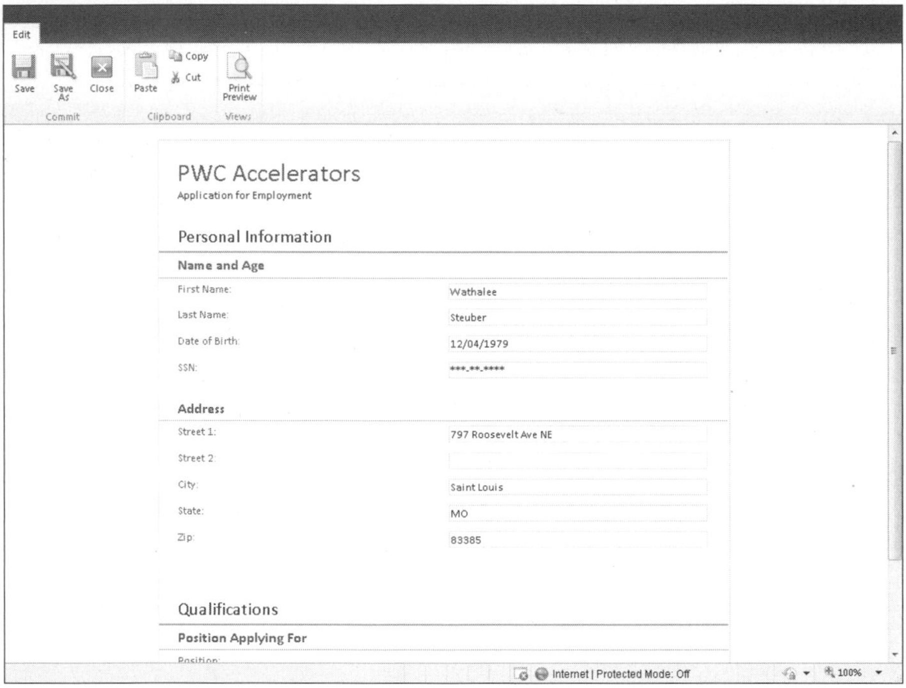

Cross-Reference

See Appendix A for more on using BCS to allow create, read, update, and delete operations on Dynamics CRM data from within SharePoint.

The electronic application submits data to the Applicant entity in Dynamics CRM, which is simply the renamed Lead system entity.

Repurposing system entities in Dynamics CRM by changing their names and modifying other entity features can be a quick way to leverage the platform's built-in functionality. This strategy should be carefully evaluated to make sure it will support your current and anticipated requirements. Repurposing system entities was more common in earlier versions of Dynamics CRM that were less flexible in their customization options. With Microsoft Dynamics CRM 2011, the extensibility of the platform makes it possible to duplicate many of the built-in features. Still, there are some advantages to repurposing system entities and functionality, such as the native integration between Outlook contacts and activities and Dynamics CRM contacts and activities, and a quicker development process.

In this instance, it made sense to reuse the Lead entity since new applicants follow a similar qualification process as Leads. The HR department also wished to keep applicants separate from the employee lists.

The default view of applicants is set to All Applicants and shows the status reason of applicants for positions at PWC Accelerators. It also shows another key metric that the HR department is concerned with: the number of applicants per position (see Figure 27.8).

Figure 27.9 shows the repurposed Lead form, now called the Applicant. Custom buttons on the ribbon menu allow HR Specialists to submit applicant information to one of two Web-based background verification services. Clicking the buttons passes the pertinent applicant data to a custom ASPX page, which connects to the Web services APIs of the verification services. The results are displayed and accepted by the HR Specialist in order to complete the background check process.

FIGURE 27.8

Using inline charts, Dynamics CRM can present users with key metrics alongside the records they are viewing.

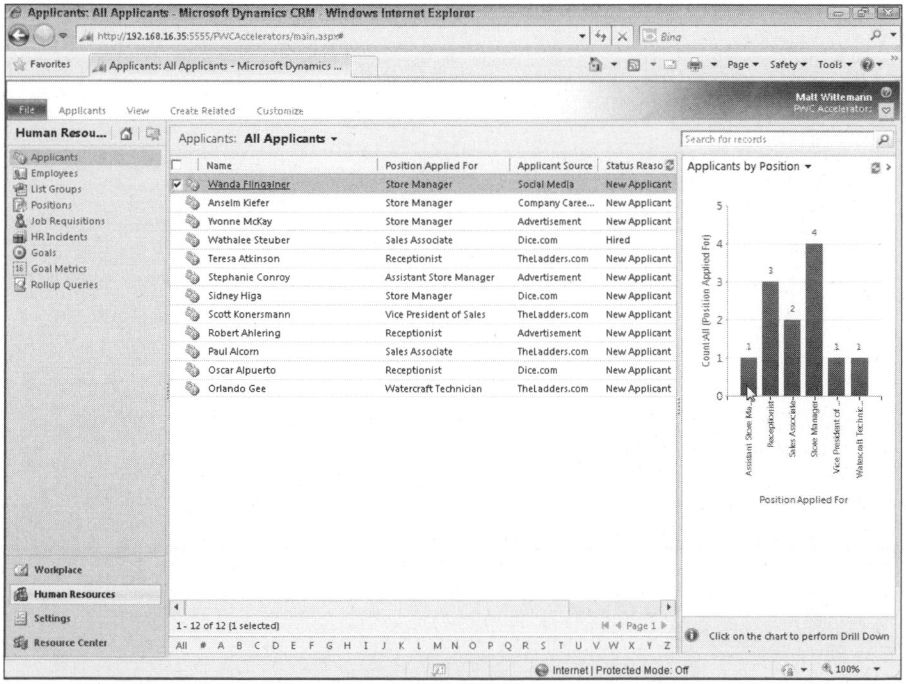

FIGURE 27.9

Custom external services can be integrated seamlessly into the Dynamics CRM interface using the Ribbon menus.

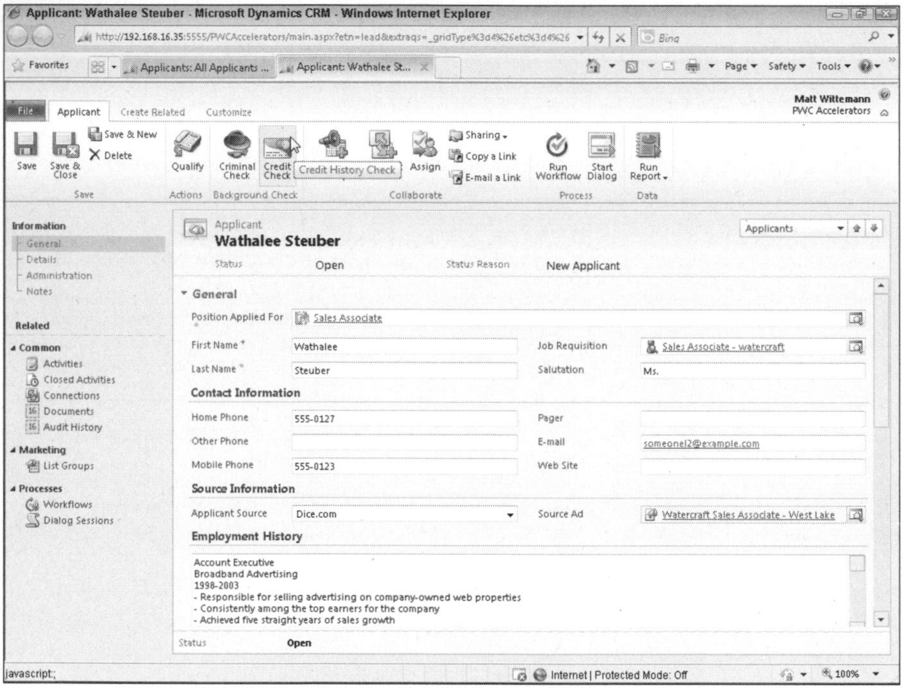

In addition to the custom functionality that has been layered on to this renamed system entity, we've leveraged some of the built-in functionality that the Lead entity supports for scheduling interview appointments and converting the applicant to an employee using the conversion dialog.

HR Specialists contact the applicants to arrange interviews and create appointment activities within Dynamics CRM, setting the applicant and the regional manager as required attendees. Dynamics CRM automatically sends out meeting requests by e-mail to the attendees.

The conversion dialog will allow the HR Specialist to deactivate the lead and either create a new Employee record if the applicant is hired or mark the applicant as disqualified and indicate the reason (see Figure 27.10).

FIGURE 27.10

By repurposing the lead entity, PWC Accelerators' XRM solution can take advantage of some built-in functionality like this conversion dialog box.

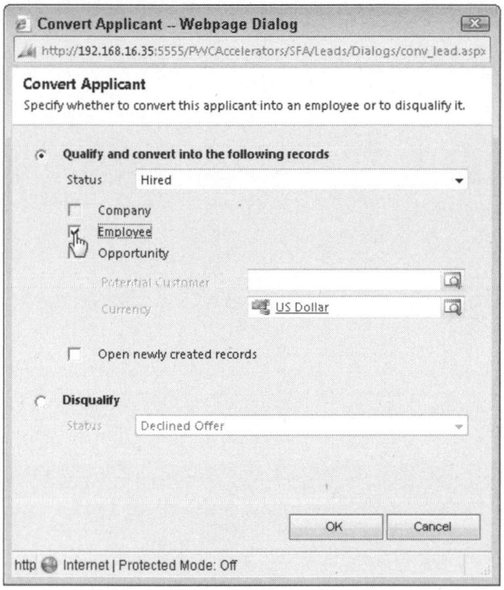

The on-boarding process

PWC Accelerators' previous process for bringing on new employees involved a standardized checklist of tax forms, employee agreements, a handbook, an orientation video, and other paperwork that had to be completed. These elements are still required, but several components of Microsoft Dynamics CRM 2011 lend themselves to facilitating a more automated and standardized process. The XRM solution for the on-boarding of newly hired employees includes:

- A custom plug-in
- Workflow automation
- Outlook integration
- SharePoint integration

When a new employee is hired, the first thing that the HR department must do is assign a unique employee number that can be used by the payroll system and other integrated systems to track information related to the employee. A custom plug-in was used in the PWC Accelerators XRM solution to generate a new Employee ID number when a new Employee record is created (Figure 27.11). (The plug-in that generates the employee ID is based on the account number plug-in example in the SDK.)

FIGURE 27.11

A plug-in is used to create an employee number each time a new employee record is created.

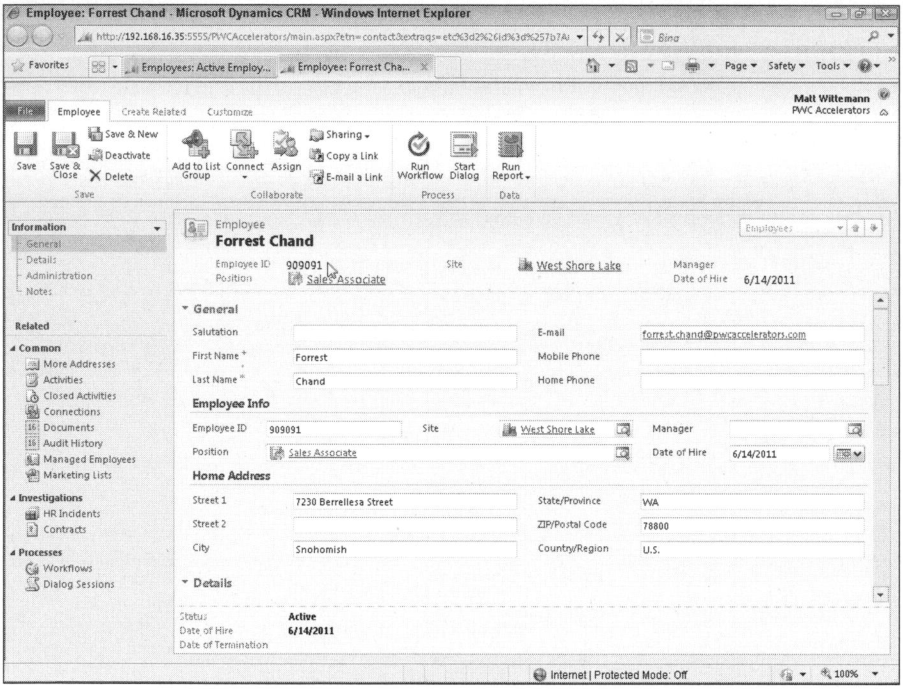

When the new employee record is created, in addition to generating an employee ID, the XRM solution uses a workflow rule to generate a number of tasks that the HR Specialist must complete to ensure the on-boarding process is completed. The tasks are displayed in the Activities list, synchronized to the HR Specialist's Outlook task list, and are visible from the new employee's open activities related list (see Figure 27.12).

FIGURE 27.12

A workflow process automatically creates tasks to guide the HR Specialist through the new employee on-boarding process.

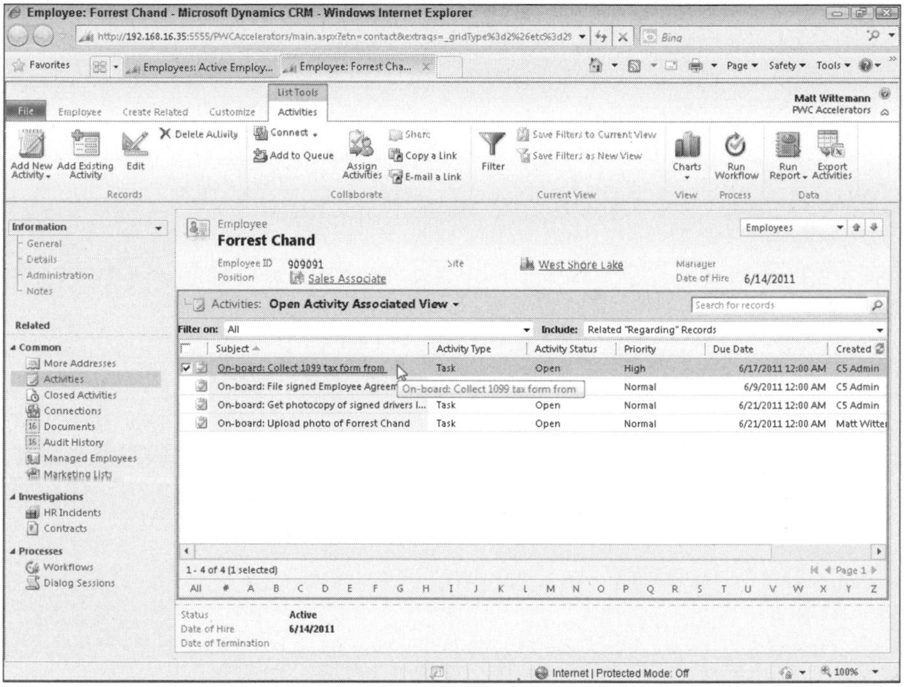

Employee photographs can be added using the native functionality of Outlook contacts (see Figure 27.13). Synchronization and integration with Outlook is another built-in feature that the PWC Accelerators HR solution leverages automatically.

FIGURE 27.13

The Outlook client for Dynamics CRM provides a view of an employee's record as well as a photo and the Outlook people pane.

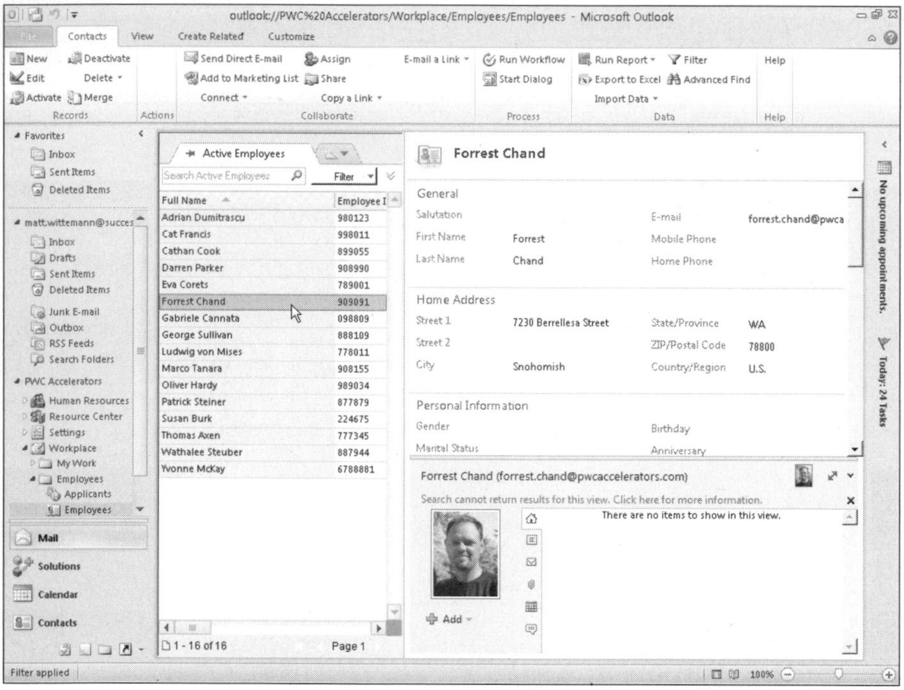

All of the documents that are gathered during the on-boarding process used to be filed on a shared network directory, or as paper documents in old filing cabinets. With the new XRM solution built on Dynamics CRM, the on-boarding documents are stored using the SharePoint document management integration (see Figure 27.14). Documents can be uploaded directly to SharePoint by the regional manager or to the Employee record in Dynamics CRM by the HR Specialist.

Employee management process

One of the main responsibilities of the HR department is to keep accurate records for each employee, recording the details around a variety of different types of events and activities, such as promotions and disciplinary actions. The process that PWC Accelerators followed for this prior to implementing Dynamics CRM involved recording events on paper forms and storing them in files, and in some cases, storing electronic documents in a shared directory.

FIGURE 27.14

To handle the HR department's documents, PWC has implemented SharePoint integration for storage and version control.

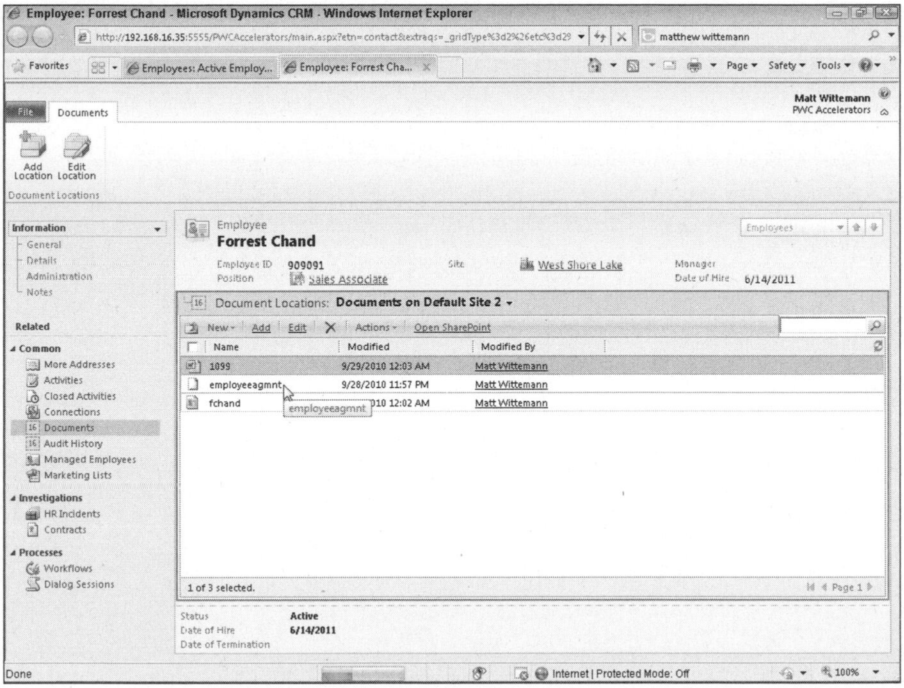

The challenge with this process is that it took some time to assemble all of the documentation that was needed to review an individual's employment history. If a regional manager was planning on conducting an annual review of the employees at a given store, it was often too difficult to get the pertinent information.

Similarly, recording these events was not done in a standard way, resulting in oversights and mistakes in documenting important human resources issues. Regional managers typically spend much of their work lives on the road, visiting the stores in their regions and performing other duties. As a result, they often called in issues to the HR department, which was a distraction to the duties of the HR Specialists. More often than not, many employment related matters did not get recorded in employees' files.

To overcome these challenges, the XRM solution implements the following Dynamics CRM components:

- Custom activity
- Mobile Express
- Report Wizard
- Auditing

A custom activity called an HR Event (see Figure 27.15) was created in the XRM solution to be used for recording events, inquiries, and other types of interactions that should be recorded in an employee's record. The HR Event records capture the date, time and type of event, as well as a description. A custom option set allows users to select the type of event to record:

- Absent without leave
- Annual Review
- Assault
- Employment Agreement Violation
- General Inquiry
- Harassment
- Hired
- Illegal Activity
- Insubordination
- Leave of Absence/FMLA
- Pay Dispute
- Payroll Inquiry
- Promoted
- Recognized
- Rehired
- Suspended
- Tardy
- Terminated
- Theft
- Transferred
- Verbal Warning
- Written Warning

Dynamics CRM allows workflow rules to be triggered when custom activities are created. Based on the type of HR Event, workflow rules route the activity to the appropriate HR Specialist for follow-up. In some cases, the events are simply for record-keeping and the workflow automatically closes the custom activity, marking it as complete.

FIGURE 27.15

The XRM solution incorporates a custom activity called the HR Event which captures significant events in an employee's record.

In addition to being able to file these HR Events through the Web or Outlook interface, the Employee form and activities have been published through Mobile Express, Dynamics CRM's built-in mobile client (see Figure 27.16). Now the highly mobile regional managers can record changes to employee records and HR Events from their mobile devices.

FIGURE 27.16

The Mobile Express mobile Employee form allows regional managers to access important records while traveling.

Regional managers are responsible for conducting annual reviews with each employee. The XRM solution makes pulling together each employee's information simple. Using the Report Wizard, one regional manager created and shared a report that he uses to conduct annual reviews. He likes to conduct the reviews for all employees at a given store on the same day, so he runs the report by opening the site record for the store and navigating to the associated list of employees. He selects all the employees and runs the report directly in context against the selected records (see Figure 27.17).

FIGURE 27.17

Contextual reports enable users to quickly get precisely the information they need. Reports created with the Report Wizard are automatically added to the Reports menu for related entities.

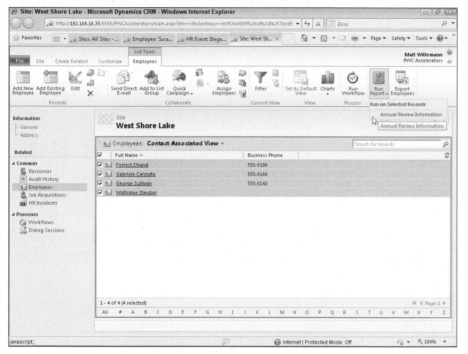

Since regional managers are frequently on the road, the HR Specialists sometimes assist them in preparing for annual reviews by running the report for them, exporting it to PDF and e-mailing it to them (see Figure 27.18).

FIGURE 27.18

Dynamics CRM's reporting capabilities allow for flexible delivery of reports.

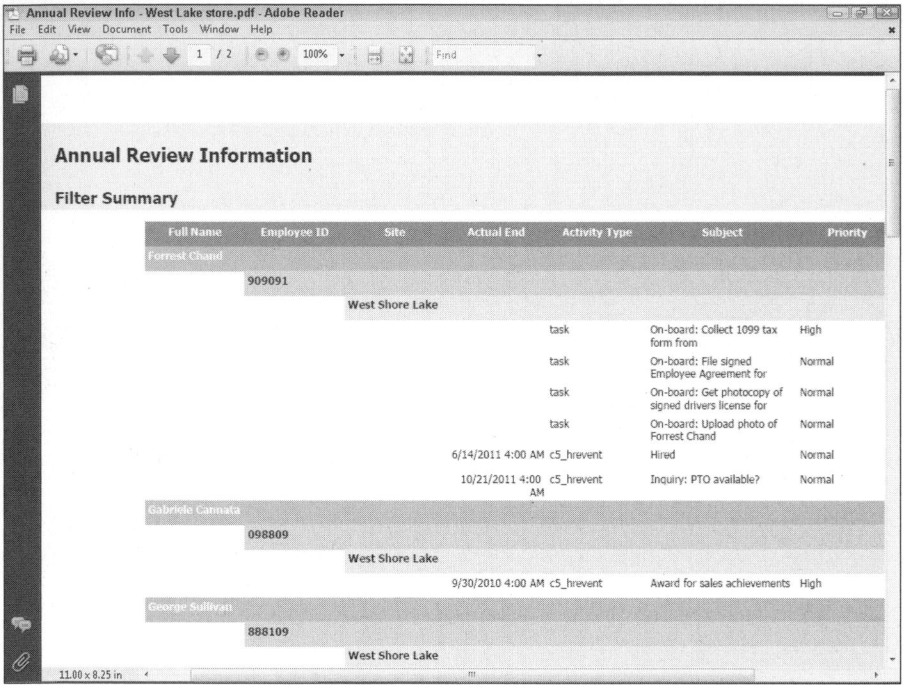

An important function of any HR system is being able to track over time what changes have been made to employee records. The XRM solution for PWC Accelerators makes use of the built-in auditing features in Dynamics CRM in order to capture and display these changes. Any change to an employee record is automatically tracked (see Figure 27.19). Dynamics CRM's security roles and field-level security are used to restrict visibility of these sensitive records to only those users who are authorized.

Employee HR Incident process

Occasionally, the HR department is called upon to investigate serious incidents involving the company's employees. These investigations often involve highly confidential information and legal matters.

FIGURE 27.19

The audit functionality in Dynamics CRM lends itself to the employee management process at PWC Accelerators.

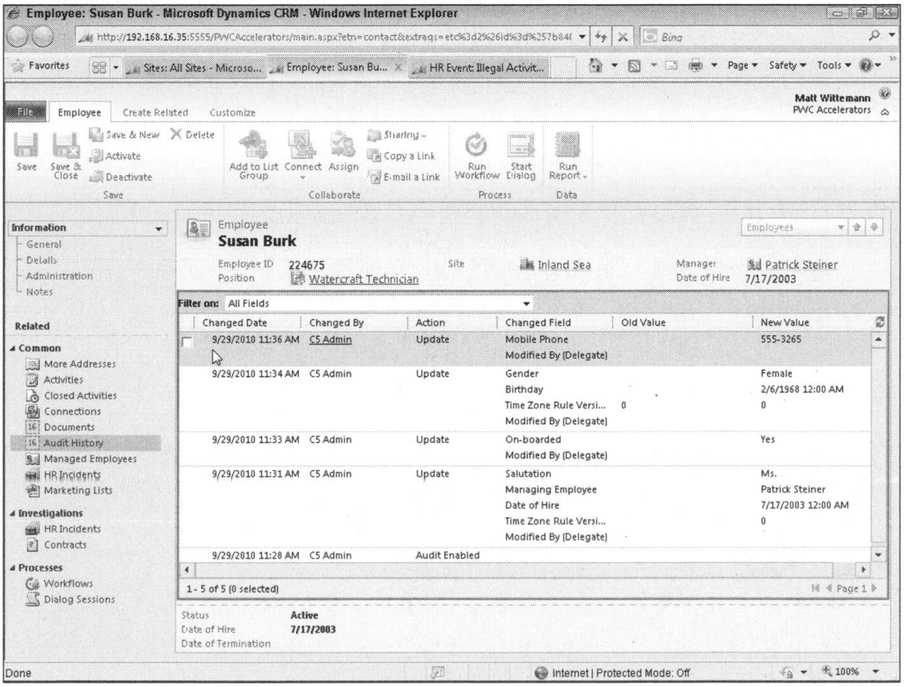

Without a system for handling these issues, PWC Accelerators relied on a manual process to track these types of issues. The manual process increased the company's risk of legal repercussions since it was easy for details to be overlooked or investigations neglected. The company was in need of an enforceable, standardized process.

The XRM solution made use of the following platform elements in order to help the company deal with these sensitive employee issues:

- Built-in conversion of custom activity
- Renamed system entity
- Dialog process

Once again, a system entity was repurposed to support this critical process. The Case entity was renamed to HR Incident (see Figure 27.20). One of the benefits of using the Case entity is that it has three state codes, whereas most entities can only have two: Active and Inactive. The case entity's three states are: Active, Resolved, and Canceled. This maps well to PWC's processes, where HR Incidents can be active investigations, resolved, or canceled for various reasons. Each state can have its own list of status reasons:

- Status: Active
  - In Progress
  - Referred to Legal
- Status: Resolved
  - Disciplinary Action
  - No Action
- Canceled
  - Misreported Incident
  - Insufficient Information

Using the Case entity also enables the HR Department to take advantage of other built-in features, such as the Neglected Case report, the resolution activity that records the time and status reason of a resolution, and the ability to associate and embed knowledge base articles directly into the form for reference.

Investigations of employee incidents typically start with the reporting of an issue using the HR Event custom activity. For this reason, the process that the HR Specialists follow takes advantage of the built-in ability to convert an activity into an HR Incident (see Figure 27.21). When an HR Specialist determines that an issue must be escalated to an investigation, he can convert it to an HR Incident manually. This process closes the HR Event custom activity and stores it in the history of the HR Incident record for reference.

In order to make sure that details of the incident are captured properly during the investigation, the XRM solution uses the new Dialogs feature of Dynamics CRM to guide HR Specialists through the process of conducting the initial phone interview to start the investigation (see Figure 27.22). This ensures that all of the legally required information is covered in a uniform manner during the initial investigation of the incident.

The Case entity was renamed to HR Incident and is used in the XRM solution to track investigations into serious employee issues.

Converting a custom activity into an HR Incident. This process allows issues to be escalated and tracked using the built-in service case management functionality of Dynamics CRM.

FIGURE 27.22

A dialog process is used to guide the investigating HR Specialist through the initial information-gathering for an HR Incident.

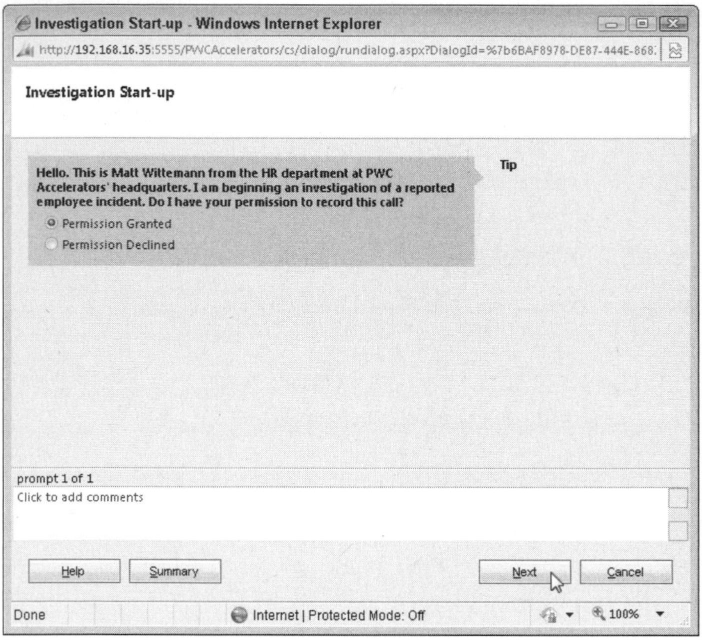

One of the nice features of the dialog process in Dynamics CRM is that it records each instance, or session, that the dialog is used (see Figure 27.23). This is perfect for managers in the HR department to ensure that the HR Specialists are complying with procedure, and also to be able to re-create what happened during an investigative call should questions later arise.

Localization

PWC Accelerators is experiencing tremendous growth and has recently opened stores throughout Latin America. Fortunately, the custom solution developed for the HR department was built on the Dynamics CRM platform, meaning the company can take advantage of the localization features of the system:

- A MUI (multilingual user interface) pack
- Translated labels

FIGURE 27.23

The "history" of a dialog process session is viewable during and after the session so it can be referenced later, a critical auditing component of a compliant HR system.

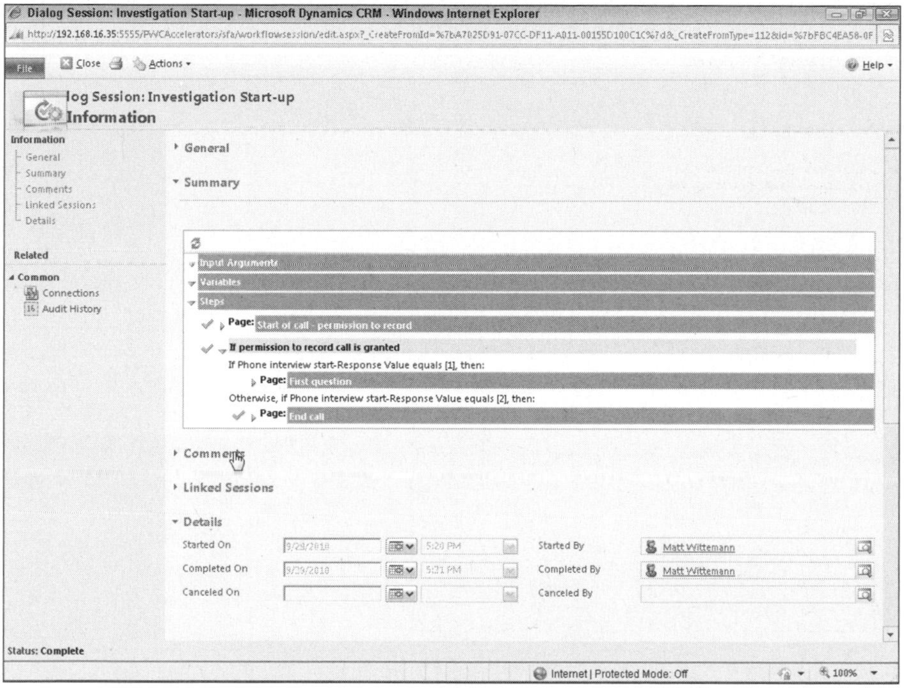

The Spanish language MUI pack was downloaded, installed, and activated for the PWC Accelerators' XRM organization. After adding the language pack, custom labels were translated, and the system's site map were updated to accommodate the new language settings.

HR Specialists at the company's offices in Latin America were then able to select the Spanish language option in their personal settings in order to use the system in their native tongue (see Figure 27.24).

FIGURE 27.24

The employee form with the Spanish language MUI pack installed and selected

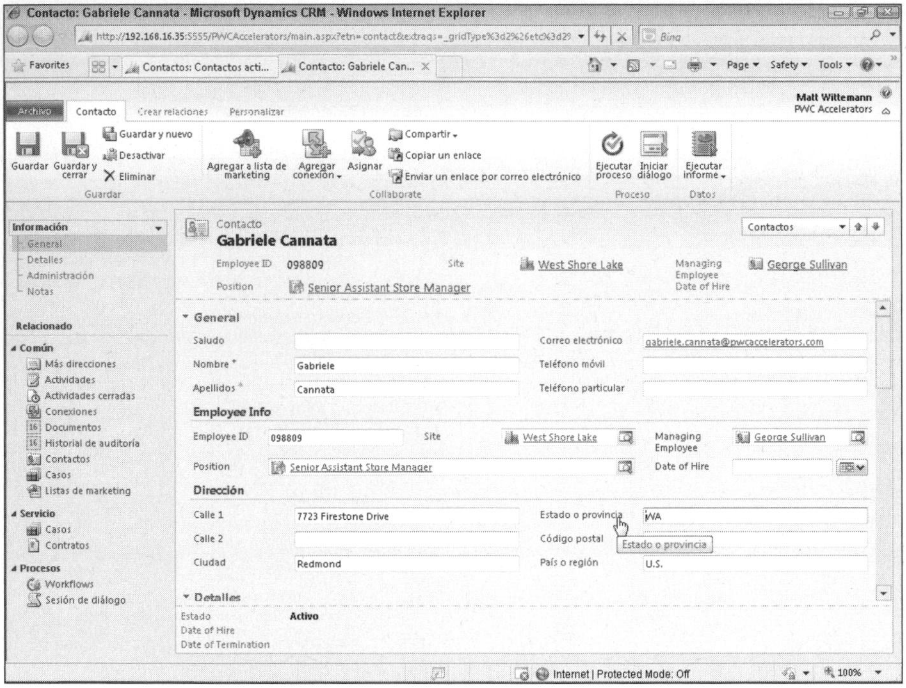

Maintenance and extensibility

PWC Accelerators is a fast-growing company undergoing lots of changes. Its processes and systems are continuously undergoing changes and refinements. To accommodate these changes, the XRM solution incorporates:

- Windows Updates
- Role-based forms
- Solutions

After deploying the tailored Dynamics CRM system for managing the company's HR processes, PWC Accelerators' small IT team wants to make sure the system remains stable and secure. When installing the Outlook clients, the users opted in to automatically download Windows Updates for Dynamics CRM (see Figure 27.25).

FIGURE 27.25

FIGURE 27.25

Windows Updates are a new feature for Microsoft Dynamics CRM 2011, and another compelling factor when considering the platform for XRM solution development.

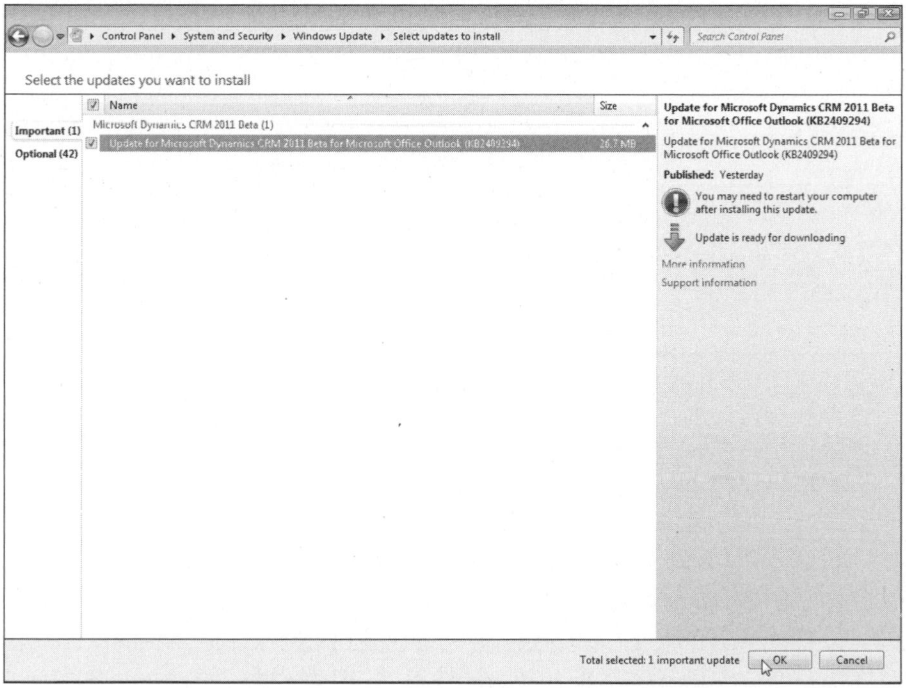

As the company grows, the responsibilities of the HR department change and grow as well. The company has decided to begin using the XRM solution to track employee benefit enrollment as well. A benefits administrator has joined the team, and a new form will be added to the Employee entity that is tailored to the benefits administrator's responsibilities (see Figure 27.26). A security role was created for the HR Benefits Administrator and the form was associated with this role.

FIGURE 27.26

Associating a form with a custom security role allows flexibility in designing a role-based interface for an XRM solution.

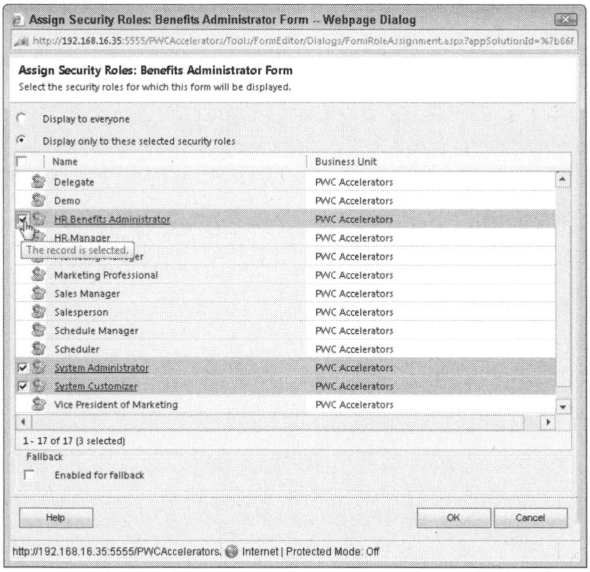

As PWC Accelerators grows, they may modify their infrastructure by adding new, more powerful servers — or even by migrating to the cloud. Fortunately, Dynamics CRM offers XRM developers with great flexibility to handle these types of migrations and redeployments. By packaging the Human Resources XRM customizations, extensions, and other components into a solution (see Figure 27.27), the entire system becomes easy to deploy between environments.

Imagining the possibilities: Other XRM scenarios

The walk-through of the human resources XRM solution provided a large number of illustrations of how the Dynamics CRM platform can be tailored to address a number of nontraditional, non-customer-centric business processes. The ISV community and other Microsoft partners are assisting organizations across the globe to develop a wide variety of XRM solutions to support the line-of-business needs for industry, government, and educational institutions.

Here are a few ideas of the types of XRM solutions that Dynamics CRM makes possible:

- Asset Management. Dynamics CRM can be tailored to track company assets like furniture, projectors, and office equipment. The assets can be tracked in a custom entity that is associated with a site to indicate its physical location. Responsible individuals can be indicated as the asset "owner" and information like purchase dates and usage history can also be tracked.

- **Expense Management.** Either as an add-on to a traditional customer relationship management implementation, or as a stand-alone implementation for a large organization, Dynamics CRM provides all the tools needed to track expense reporting, receipt storage in integrated SharePoint document libraries, workflows to support approval and payment processes, and the ability to enforce business rules and security.

- **Customer Loyalty Programs.** For organizations that use loyalty cards or points systems to track customers' purchases and reward them for repeat business, Dynamics CRM could be customized to catalog purchase histories or points awarded, and use the built-in automation and marketing tools to notify loyal customers of their status. Portal integration would enable allowing customers to log in and review their loyalty points balances or purchase history. If the organization has a large number of retail stores, the different stores could transmit data to a cloud-based application hosted in Azure, which would act as a federated database, aggregating the data and transferring it to the XRM solution periodically.

The list of potential XRM scenarios really is as endless and varied as the needs of businesses and other organizations.

FIGURE 27.27

The PWC Accelerators XRM system was designed to be packaged up as a solution that contains all of the components needed to easily deploy it to a new environment if necessary.

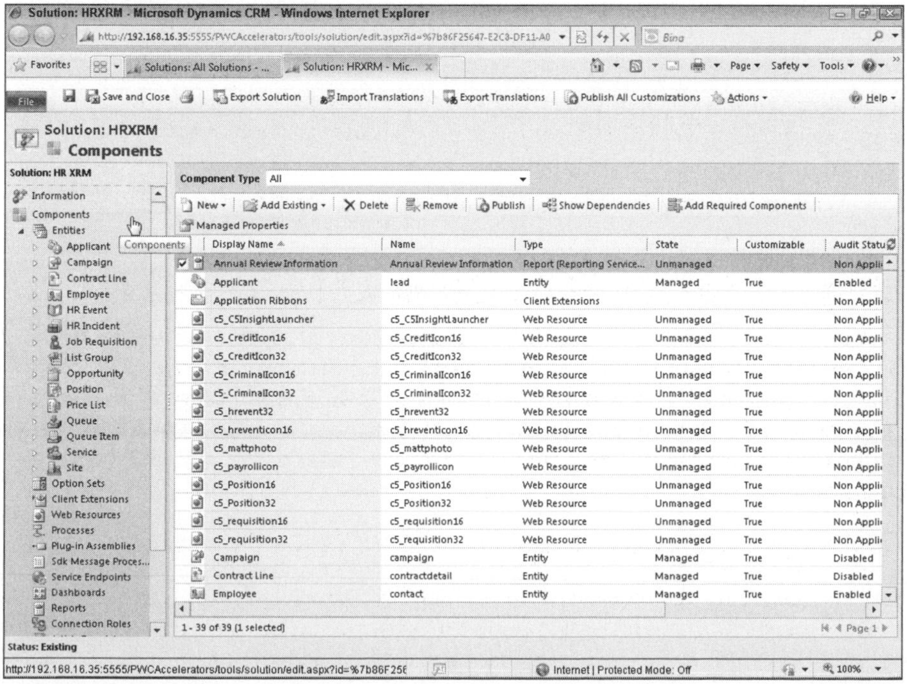

Summary

In this chapter, we defined the buzzword XRM and discussed its evolution in the CRM industry. The chapter also presented a number of reasons why Dynamics CRM makes such a compelling platform for line-of-business application development, and why platform development makes sense compared to traditional custom development.

We walked through a Human Resources XRM solution that served to illustrate how the concepts covered throughout this book can be employed to quickly develop a powerful and highly tailored application.

Microsoft Dynamics CRM 2011 includes many features and powerful functionality that take it well beyond the realm of customer relationship management. Its extensibility and model-driven design environment, coupled with a deep API, translate to a system full of limitless possibilities.

Part IX

Appendixes

Advanced Integration with SharePoint 2010

Written By: Curtis Hughes, www.asksharepoint.com

I n this Appendix to the *Microsoft Dynamics CRM 2011 Administrators Bible*, SharePoint expert Curtis Hughes shares some of the powerful ways you can integrate Dynamics CRM with SharePoint 2010. Microsoft has raised the bar with the latest releases of these two platforms, and they naturally complement each other to deliver a versatile development platform.

Integrating with SharePoint

If you're ready to jump into the *how* of integrating CRM with SharePoint, then this Appendix is for you. I promise to delve into the how very shortly, showing two real-world examples of value that can be derived from integrating Dynamics CRM 2011 and SharePoint 2010. However, I believe the more important question with which to start is, "Why should you integrate with SharePoint?"

SharePoint 2010 is a large application with many facets to uncover. SharePoint covers the vast areas of: Sites, Communities, Content, Search, Insights, and Composites. Although I certainly won't have time to probe all of these areas, my goal for this Appendix is to get you and your team thinking about the abundance of integration points between Microsoft Dynamics CRM 2011 and SharePoint 2010. In addition, I hope that this Appendix will point you in the right direction with some practical examples of integration between these two platforms.

With robust platforms such as Dynamics CRM and SharePoint, there are virtually limitless possibilities for integration. To begin, it helps to understand which version of SharePoint you have within your organization. What many organizations do not realize is that Microsoft Windows Server includes licensing for the basic version of Microsoft SharePoint 2010, aptly named *Microsoft SharePoint Foundation 2010*. Therefore, one obvious reason to integrate with SharePoint is the fact that the basic functionality is free and likely already available within your organization.

Many businesses can benefit from formalizing and automating their business processes, including task-oriented processes and knowledge or collaboration-oriented processes. While there are other document management and collaboration platforms besides SharePoint, there are powerful synergies between Dynamics CRM and SharePoint that make integrating these two systems very appealing to businesses and developers. Here are just a few of the reasons why the integration between these two products makes so much sense:

- Microsoft brand and a large community and support network
- Seamless Microsoft Office integration
- Standards-based platforms (XML, XHTML, REST, SOAP, WCAG)
- Shared skillsets for both platforms (.NET, WCF, REST, SOAP, JavaScript, Workflows)
- Both platforms have native support for cloud technologies (Azure, OData)
- Both platforms utilize the same backend data repository (Microsoft SQL Server)
- Dynamics CRM and SharePoint are very complimentary (think structured data versus unstructured data)

Note

This Appendix focuses on Microsoft Dynamics CRM 2011 and SharePoint 2010. Although there are certainly many levels of integration with previous versions of these tools, my focus is strictly on the latest versions of these products.

Areas of integration

Now that you understand the *why* of integrating with SharePoint, take a brief look at a few areas of integration between Dynamics CRM and SharePoint 2010. Although space constraints do not allow me to explore examples for all of these integration possibilities, I hope this section begins to reveal the power and possibilities of integrating these two platforms.

You can use a number of different ways to integrate Dynamics CRM and SharePoint. These methods span from minimalist integrations (such as using an Iframe or Page Viewer Web Part to integrate Dynamics CRM and SharePoint pages) to more elaborate integrations (such as writing custom code to perform detailed actions based on events from one or more systems).

In the preceding chapters, you have certainly seen the power of Dynamics CRM, so approaching this from a SharePoint perspective, the examples in Table A.1 provide a brief listing of some common areas where you can integrate Dynamics CRM with SharePoint. Beginning in the next section, I jump directly into two real-world examples.

TABLE A.1

Common Places to Integrate Dynamics CRM with SharePoint 2010

CRM Integration	Example
Business Connectivity Services	Create external list to CRM entity with read/write capability
SharePoint Client Object Model	Interact with CRM data from an external list
Microsoft Office Client	Consume data directly from CRM or a BCS external list
PerformancePoint Services	Run dynamic, analytical, and ad hoc reports on CRM data
Search	Use BCS or Federated Search to include CRM data
Social Activity Feed	Consume and subscribe to events from CRM
Web Parts	Show CRM data within any SharePoint page
REST / Web Services	Automatically create customer sites/libraries in SharePoint

Integration Examples

Within every organization, no matter the size, there is an inherent need for information workers to access data residing in disparate software systems. Additionally, these systems can range from large, enterprise applications such as ERP and CRM to smaller, less structured systems, such as Microsoft Office, Microsoft SharePoint, custom Internet application, blogs, and social networking sites.

Accessing Dynamics CRM with Business Connectivity Services

Microsoft Business Connectivity Services (BCS), recently released with Microsoft SharePoint Server (SPS) 2010, provides a set of features and functionality which help streamline the integration of external data into the SharePoint environment. By leveraging tools such as SharePoint Designer, Microsoft Office, and Visual Studio you can create solutions that range from simple to advanced, and span every system in your organization.

External Content Types

External Content Types are an essential concept to grasp when working with Business Connectivity Services. The functionality of external content types is behind nearly every BCS implementation, and is a critical part of leveraging the full power of BCS in SharePoint 2010. In short, external content types define the connectivity information, data structure, and overall behaviors that you wish to implement for your external data. What makes these gems even more attractive is the fact that external content types are reusable once they have been defined. For example, you may want to work with your Dynamics CRM opportunities in a SharePoint list, offline in Microsoft Outlook, or allow users to select an opportunity as a metadata field within SharePoint. In this case, you would create the opportunity external content type once, and then be able to reuse it for any application or project.

Showing external data

As mentioned above, SharePoint is one of the most obvious places to leverage external content types. Besides being an out-of-the-box feature of SharePoint Server 2010, BCS has presentation features which provide a nice interface to your external data. A few areas where external data can be shown in SharePoint 2010 include:

- External list
- External data column
- Business data Web part
- External content type picker
- External item picker
- Profile pages

Note

It is important to mention that Business Connectivity Services are included with Microsoft SharePoint Foundation (SPF) 2010. As mentioned above, this version is available as part of the standard Windows Server licensing. Note that although BCS functionality is available with SharePoint Foundation, there are some important feature differences when using BCS in SharePoint Foundation, SharePoint Server Standard, or SharePoint Server Enterprise. To see a listing of these differences, visit http://msdn.microsoft.com/en-us/library/ee556390.aspx.

Creating an external content type from a CRM entity

Many of the external content type examples discussed in the previous section can be created without writing a single line of code. However, certain aspects of Dynamics CRM require a bit of code to accurately define the more complex data structures and entities. Remember that as I stated above, external content types are where the data structures and behaviors are defined. As you can imagine, describing a customer, account, or opportunity in simple terms is virtually impossible. Because of this, you have to write a bit of code to effectively "wrap" the complex structures from Dynamics CRM with simple structures for the Create, Read, Update, and Delete (CRUD) functions.

For this example, I utilize Visual Studio 2010 to assist with the creation of the Business Data Connectivity (BDC) Model based on an Account entity in Dynamics CRM. Although this Appendix is entitled "Advanced Integration with SharePoint." the overall book is focused on the Dynamics CRM administrator, so I won't get too deep into the .NET code. However, this Appendix is provided to show scenarios and provoke ideas for integration between Dynamics CRM and SharePoint 2010. All code samples will be posted on the book's Web site at www.dynamicscrmbible.com.

The first step is to create a new BDC Model project in Visual Studio 2010 (Figure A.1).

FIGURE A.1

Create new BDC Model project in visual Studio 2010

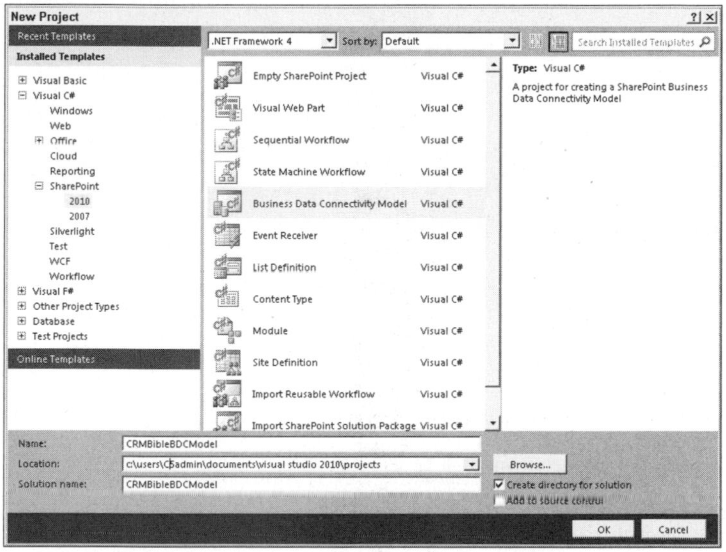

[Figure: New Project dialog in Visual Studio 2010 showing Installed Templates with Visual C# > SharePoint > 2010 selected, and "Business Data Connectivity Model" highlighted in the template list. Name: CRMBibleBDCModel, Location: c:\users\CRMadmin\documents\visual studio 2010\projects, Solution name: CRMBibleBDCModel]

After the project has been created, the BDC Model will be shown and you can begin defining the Identifiers, Operations, Filters, and Parameters that you would like for this external content type to have. By default, a single identifier and two methods are created to get you started.

Identifiers are the fields that uniquely define an instance of the external content type. Without such an identifier, the BDC service cannot identify an entity instance.

By default, the ReadList and ReadItem methods are created. In this case, the external content type needs to be able to Create, Read, Update. and Delete from Dynamics CRM. Begin by using the BDC Explorer UI to define each of the methods listed above, as seen in Figure A.2 below.

FIGURE A.2

Viewing the BDC Model using the BDC Explorer UI

Note that because this method leverages the Dynamics CRM Web services for connectivity into Dynamics CRM, you need to add a Web reference to these Web services. After this is complete, you will be able to write code against Dynamics CRM-specific methods.

After the Web service reference has been added, it is necessary to define the In, Out, and Return parameters for each CRUD method (Create, Read, Update, Delete). With the Web service added under Web References, you can retrieve these parameters and names from the Web service using the Object Browser.

With the parameters defined, you are now ready to write the code for each individual CRUD method. Below is the Create method that was created for allowing creation of a new Dynamics CRM Account record.

```
public static CRMAccount Create(CRMAccount newCRMAccount)
{
CrmService crmWebService = GetCRMWebService();
   account crmAccount = new account();
   crmAccount.name = newCRMAccount.Name;
   crmAccount.address1_city = newCRMAccount.City;
   Guid id = crmWebService.Create(crmAccount);

   newCRMAccount.AccountID = id.ToString();
   return newCRMAccount;
}
```

With the code written for each CRUD method, you are now ready to deploy the external content type to SharePoint. However, before doing so, ensure that you have completed the following task in Visual Studio:

- Set the Site URL for the BDC Model project properties to the SharePoint site to which you want to deploy the external content type (see Figure A.3).

To deploy the external content type to SharePoint, right-click on the project name and select Deploy as shown in Figure A.4 (you can also select Deploy from the Build menu in Visual Studio).

FIGURE A.3

Setting the Site URL property for the external content type

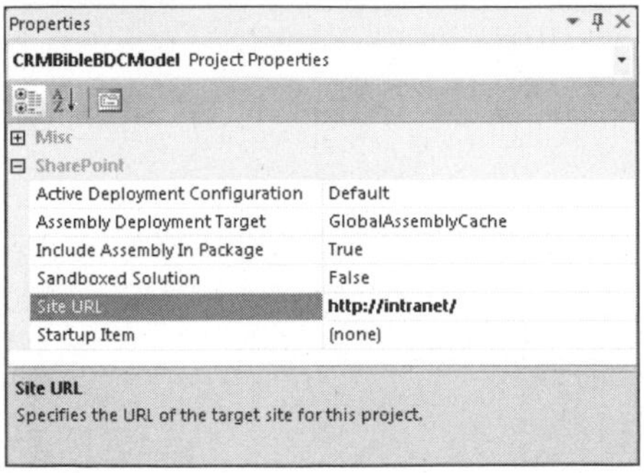

Deploying the solution to SharePoint from Visual Studio 2010

When the deployment is complete, you can then navigate to Central Administration on your SharePoint server and view the external content type that you just deployed. To get to the external content types in SharePoint 2010 Central Administration, open Central Administration and navigate to Application Management, select Manage service applications, then select Business Data Connectivity Services, and you will see your external content types as seen in Figure A.5.

External content types shown in Central Administration after deployment

With the external content type deployed, you can now create custom actions via Central Administration, as well as manage permissions for which users can execute and modify data via the external content type.

Once created, you can also work with this external content type in SharePoint Designer. SharePoint Designer allows advanced users and developers alike to rapidly create no-code SharePoint solutions that cover a variety of business needs. If you open SharePoint Designer and navigate to the site to which you just deployed the external content type, you will see the new external content type listed as seen in Figure A.6 below.

External content type shown in SharePoint Designer

By double-clicking the Account external content type, you will be able to see the configuration options available within SharePoint Designer. From this screen you can create an external list by clicking the Create Lists and Form menu item on the top Ribbon. Alternatively, now that the external content type is created and configured, you can also create a new external content type directly from SharePoint as you would any other list (Figure A.7).

FIGURE A.7

Creating an external list via the SharePoint UI

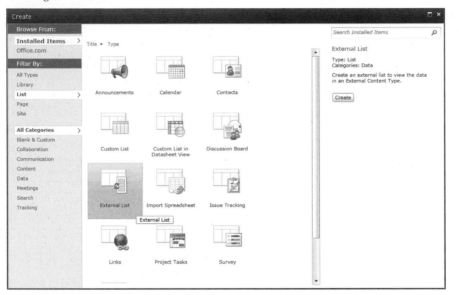

Finally, with our external content type and external list created, we can now leverage all that SharePoint has to offer to its native lists and libraries. SharePoint now recognizes this external list as a SharePoint list. To be more specific, this means you can now:

- Create custom views and rollups for this list
- Add, edit, and delete list items (external data) directly from this list
- Work with this list data (CRM data) offline in SharePoint Workspace
- Search this list
- Consume RSS feeds from this list
- Subscribe to alerts from this list
- Tag and write notes for these CRM list items (they now become part of your social taxonomy)
- Use native SharePoint Web parts for this list

Showing CRM data in the Social Activity Feed

One of the most highly anticipated features of SharePoint 2010 is the Social Activity Feed. Social activity feeds can be considered part of SharePoint's new suite of Social features.

A few of these features include:

- My Sites
- Profiles
- Tagging
- Note Board
- Bookmarking
- Ratings

For more information about the social activity feed, visit the following Web sites:

- `http://httpcode.com/blogs/PermaLink,guid,b3af80e2-4e6f-41d6-ae93-61950a332a39.aspx`
- `http://msdn.microsoft.com/en-us/library/ff426884.aspx`

The goal for this integration example is to get you and your team thinking about the many ways you can surface Dynamics CRM data in other applications. One myth that we hear is that social activity feeds are only good for use within SharePoint. And while this *is* true, part of the power in social activity feeds lies in the fact that all feeds are exposed via universal standard formats, ATOM 1.0 or RSS 2.0. This opens the door for any social activity feed to be consumed by a number of different applications such as Microsoft Outlook, iGoogle, Windows desktop gadgets, Web browsers, and any other RSS or ATOM feed reader.

What we hope to demonstrate over the next few pages is how to leverage SharePoint as a *platform* for pulling together activities that take place across your organization. What better place to start than with Dynamics CRM, which is at the center of many organizations.

As with the previous integration scenario, this example also involves writing a bit of code to complete the integration. However, what we demonstrate can be applied to nearly all systems across any organization, and will be highly repeatable and very powerful. Again, the sample code is posted to the book's Web site at www.dynamicscrmbible.com.

To begin, it is important that you understand the core concepts and components that are behind the Social Activity Feed in SharePoint 2010.

Activity Manager

The Activity Manager contains a collection of Activity Application and Activity Type objects. Every implementation of an Activity Feed must begin with an Activity Manager.

Activity Application

The first element that every social activity feed needs is an Activity Application. This simply defines a grouping of Activity Types, which we will discuss in more detail next. An Activity Application can be anything you would like, but it makes sense to think about this logically. For a small organization, you may only have one Activity Application, for example your company name, and all Activity Types could belong to this organization Activity Application. For larger organization with many integration points, you may wish to define an Activity Application per line-of-business system, for example CRM, ERP, and so on.

Activity Type

An Activity Type is the first element you will define and see in the SharePoint user interface. This is the activity to which you will subscribe or opt-into via the Newsfeed settings of your SharePoint user profile. As you might imagine, there can be many Activity Types per Activity Application. An Activity Type has various properties which allow you to specify whether or not it can be published, consolidated, and so on. An example of an Activity Type would be New Campaign Response with an Activity Application of Dynamics CRM.

Activity Template

The Activity Template defines the formatting of the Activity Type. Typically names and templates are stored in a resource file (.resx) under the Resources folder for SharePoint 2010. An example of an Activity Template would be:

```
{Publisher} has created a new opportunity in CRM: {Link}
```

By default there are a few template variables available for use. These are:

- {Link}
- {Value}
- {Publisher}
- {Size}

Activity Event

The Activity Event is the core component of the Social Activity Feed. This is the actual event which is published to the newsfeed. Each Activity Type can create any number of Activity Events. The Activity Event also allows you to set specific properties such as the privacy level of the event (public/private) as well as the publisher, owner, and so on. It is here where you also set the variables mentioned above which are ultimately injected into the predefined Activity Template.

Activity Feed Gatherer

The final component is the Activity Feed Gatherer. While admittedly not the most intuitive object, the Activity Feed Gatherer contains the functions to write events to newsfeeds. This includes publishing to a colleague's newsfeed, batch updating events, and so on.

Step 1: Setting-up an Activity

Please see the sample code on the book's website for the complete example.

As I mentioned, the first step is to define and set up our Activity Application and Activity Type. Since this is typically a one-time setup, to keep the example below simple, the instructions show how to create a console application to set up an Activity. In practice, you would do this via a Feature and Feature Receiver, then package and deploy via a SharePoint Solution (WSP).

In Visual Studio 2010, begin by creating a new console application project. Once created, you will need to add references to the following SharePoint 2010 assemblies which will allow the application to interact with the activity feed object model:

- System.Web.dll
- Microsoft.SharePoint.dll
- Microsoft.Office.Server.dll
- Microsoft.Office.Server.UserProfiles.dll

In addition, you will need to add the following/ Using directives to the top of your code:

```
using Microsoft.SharePoint;
using Microsoft.Office.Server.ActivityFeed;
using Microsoft.Office.Server.UserProfiles;
```

At this point, you are ready to begin coding for the activity setup. The sample used in this integration example is an Activity Type that represents a new Dynamics CRM opportunity. This Activity Type enables users to follow any new opportunities that are added in the Dynamics CRM system.

The code below accesses the context of the SharePoint site, creates a User Profile Manager, then creates the Activity Manager object and finally creates a pointer to the resource file.

```
string mySites = "http://mysites";
using (SPSite aSite = new SPSite(mySites))
{
SPServiceContext context = SPServiceContext.GetContext(aSite);
m_UPM = new UserProfileManager(context);
m_Admin = Environment.UserDomainName + "\\" + Environment.UserName;
UserProfile p = m_UPM.GetUserProfile(m_Admin);
m_ActivityManager = new ActivityManager(p, context);
m_ResourceFile = "CRMBibleActivitySample";

bool hasrights = m_ActivityManager.PrepareToAllowSchemaChanges();

//Activity Application
ActivityApplication app = m_ActivityManager.ActivityApplications["
    CRM2011"];
```

```
if (app == null)
{
app = m_ActivityManager.ActivityApplications.Create("CRM2011");
        app.Commit();
            }

//Activity Type
ActivityType activityType = app.ActivityTypes["NewCRMOpportunity"];
if (activityType == null)
            {
activityType = app.ActivityTypes.Create("NewCRMOpportunity");
activityType.ActivityTypeNameLocStringResourceFile = m_ResourceFile;
activityType.ActivityTypeNameLocStringName = "ActivityFeed_NewCRMOpp_
    Type_Display";
        activityType.IsPublished = true;
        activityType.IsConsolidated = true;
        activityType.Commit();
            }

//Activity Template
ActivityTemplate TemplateSV = createType.ActivityTemplates[ActivityTe
    mplatesCollection.CreateKey(false)];
if (TemplateSV == null)
            {
        TemplateSV = createType.ActivityTemplates.Create(false);
        TemplateSV.TitleFormatLocStringResourceFile = m_
    ResourceFile;
        TemplateSV.TitleFormatLocStringName = "ActivityFeed_
    NewCRMOpp_Template";
        TemplateSV.Commit();
            }
}
```

After this code has been successfully executed, a new activity is available in your newsfeed settings labeled "New CRM Opportunity" as shown in Figure A.8.

FIGURE A.8

New Activity Type listed in the user profile newsfeed settings

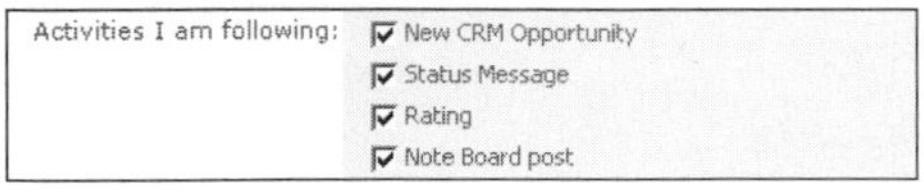

```
Activities I am following:   ☑ New CRM Opportunity
                             ☑ Status Message
                             ☑ Rating
                             ☑ Note Board post
```

Step 2: Gathering Activity Events

The next step after configuring and setting up the activity is to monitor and gather events which meet the criteria of the activity. This example is concerned with new Dynamics CRM opportunities, so the application needs to notify the activity type of any new activity events, in this case new Dynamics CRM opportunities.

While the methods to set up and create the activity type are limited to only a few, the approaches to gather and compile the events are typically numerous, and often depend on the system with which you are integrating.

In this example, SharePoint is integrating with Microsoft Dynamics CRM 2011, so there are a few options for initiating the gathering process:

- Dynamics CRM event triggered on save of a new opportunity
- Dynamics CRM workflow initiated with the creation of a new opportunity
- Dynamics CRM plug-in
- SharePoint timer job
- Windows service
- A Console or WinForms application scheduled with Windows Task Scheduler

There are likely many more that you can think of, but the idea is that there is more than one way to gather the events, and careful consideration should be taken when selecting an option for gathering activity events. Just a few items you should consider are:

- Performance. How many events might there possibly be in the future? Will the gatherer cause any performance issues for other systems (database locks, file locks, and so on)?
- Reliability: What are the chances that the gatherer becomes unavailable? Do you need high-availability for this activity?
- Maintainability: Is the gatherer code easily maintained with the rest of the system? If there are multiple activity types, should the gatherers for all activities use the same code and gathering method?
- Knowledge: What skillset do you have at your disposal for writing the gatherer? Would one method be easier to implement within your organization?

Once a decision has been made on the method for gathering activity events, the next step is to begin coding the gatherer. The structure for a gatherer is fairly logical and straightforward and from a high level, consists of the following sections:

- Identify the last update date and time for this Activity Type
- Gather all events that have occurred since the last update time
- Create an Activity Event for each event that has occurred
- Publish or broadcast the events to users' newsfeeds
- Write the events to the SharePoint 2010 social database
- Update the last update time for the Activity Type

The code below could be placed in any .NET project and assumes we have successfully queried Dynamics CRM for all new opportunities that have been created since the last update time.

```
//Get the owner and publisher profile.
Entity ownerMP = new MinimalPerson(ownerProfile).
CreateEntity(activityManager);
Entity publisherMP = new MinimalPerson(publisherProfile).
CreateEntity(activityManager);

//Create the activity event and set its properties
ActivityManager am = new ActivityManager();

foreach (Opportunity crmopp in Opportunities)
{
      ActivityEvent activityEvent = ActivityEvent.
CreateActivityEvent(am, activityType.ActivityTypeId, ownerMP,
publisherMP);

      activityEvent.Name = activityType.ActivityTypeName;
      activityEvent.ItemPrivacy = (int)Privacy.Public;
      activityEvent.Owner = ownerMP;
      activityEvent.Publisher = publisherMP;

      //Create the link for the activity.
      Link link = new Link();
      link.Href = CRMOpportunityURL;
      link.Name = CRMOpportunityName;
      activityEvent.Link = link;

      //Save
      activityEvent.Commit();
}
```

Finally, after you have gathered and created the activity events, you need to publish the events to the newsfeed and write the events to the social database in a batch fashion.

```
//Get the colleagues of each publisher so we can publish to their
newsfeed
ActivityFeedGatherer.GetUsersColleaguesAndRights(m_
ActivityManager, publishers, out owners, out colleaguesOfOwners);

//Multicast the events to our colleagues
ActivityFeedGatherer.MulticastActivityEvents(m_ActivityManager,
m_ActivityEvents, colleaguesOfOwners, out eventsPerOwner);

//Create a list of events that need to be written to the
database.
ActivityFeedGatherer.CollectActivityEventsToConsolidate(eventsPer
Owner, out eventsToWrite);

//Batch write events to the database
ActivityFeedGatherer.BatchWriteActivityEvents(eventsToWrite,
startIndex, m_ActivityManager.MaxEventsPerBatch);
```

Note

To protect user privacy, you must have administrative permissions for the User Profile Service Application to create activity events and insert them into users' newsfeeds.

Once the gatherer is in place, upon entering a new opportunity, the newsfeed will be updated as shown below in Figure A.9.

FIGURE A.9

New activity event shown in Recent Activities on SharePoint 2010

I hope that these two integration examples give you a good understanding of what is possible. There is no one-size-fits-all approach and every integration idea should fit squarely in your overall business vision and road map for Dynamics CRM and SharePoint.

Summary

This Appendix aimed to quickly cover the full spectrum of integration between Microsoft Dynamics CRM 2011 and SharePoint 2010. Although I could not cover every detail in a single Appendix, I certainly hope that I have opened the door for you to begin thinking about how to integrate these two great products within your organization. I believe the true power in both of these platforms is yet to be realized. Organizations with a vision and strategy for increasing value will find that both of these solutions deliver on so many levels, and when combined, allow ordinary products to become extraordinary.

Accessing and Using Online Resources

Throughout the book, we have referenced a variety of resources, tools, documents, and information that are available on the Web. Table B-1 presents these online resources, along with the chapters in which they were referenced, and a brief description.

For more convenient access to these links, visit the companion Web site for the book at www.dynamicscrmbible.com.

TABLE B.1

Links to Online Resources

Chapters	URL	Description
2, 19	`www.cwrmobility.com`	CWR Mobility: independent software vendor that provides mobile clients for Dynamics CRM for the iPhone, Windows Phones, and BlackBerry
2	`www.tendigits.com`	Ten Digits: independent software vendor that provides mobile clients for Dynamics CRM for the iPhone, Windows Phones, and BlackBerry
3	`www.microsoft.com/downloads/details.aspx?FamilyID=3bf7ecda-7eaf-4f1c-bbfe-cae19bc8bb78&displaylang=en`	Suggested hardware for deployments of up to 500 users (Version 4.0)
3	`www.microsoft.com/dynamics/crm/using/deploy/clusteringssrs.mspx`	SQL cluster configuration for Dynamics CRM
3	`http://go.microsoft.com/fwlink/?LinkID=200050`	Dynamics CRM Implementation Guide (Beta)
3, 20, 21, 24	`http://go.microsoft.com/fwlink/?LinkID=200082`	Dynamics CRM Software Development Kit (SDK) (Beta)
4	`http://technet.microsoft.com/en-us/library/ff356872(WS.10).aspx`	Network load balancing with Forefront Identity Manager
4	`http://technet.microsoft.com/en-us/library/cc732230(WS.10).aspx`	Configuring server certificates in IIS 7
4	`www.microsoft.com/downloads/details.aspx?FamilyID-118c3580-9070-426a-b655-6cec0a92c10b&displaylang=en`	AD FS 2.0 download
4	`http://technet.microsoft.com/en-us/library/cc772128(WS.10).aspx`	Configuring AD FS 2.0 for claims-based authentication
4	`http://msdn.microsoft.com/en-us/library/cc287610.aspx`	Information about Microsoft's federation gateway
4	`www.microsoft.com/downloads/details.aspx?FamilyID=e17e7f31-079a-43a9-bff2-0a110307611e&DisplayLang=en`	Download the MAPI client data objects (a prerequisite for the Rule Deployment Wizard)
5	`http://msdn.microsoft.com/en-us/library/0h88fahh(VS.85).aspx`	Locale IDs (LCIDs) to determine the language code associated with multilanguage packs
5, 9	`www.microsoft.com/en-us/dynamics/customersource.aspx`	CustomerSource: Microsoft Dynamics' portal for customers
9, 21	`http://social.microsoft.com/Forums/en-US/category/dynamics`	Microsoft forums location for Dynamics CRM

Chapters	URL	Description
9, 22	`http://blogs.msdn.com/b/crm/`	Microsoft Dynamics CRM Team Blog
9	`www.codeplex.com/crmperftoolkit`	Microsoft Dynamics CRM Performance and Scalability Toolkit
9	`www.microsoft.com/downloads/details.aspx?FamilyID=ba826cee-eddf-4d6e-842d-27fd654ed893&DisplayLang=en`	Microsoft Dynamics CRM Tuning and Optimization whitepaper
9	`http://technet.microsoft.com/en-us/library/bb496810.aspx`	TechNet library for Dynamics CRM
9	`http://mscrmtools.blogspot.com/`	Troubleshooting and configuration tools from Dynamics CRM MVP Tanguy Touzard
9	`http://support.microsoft.com`	Microsoft's support Web site
9	`http://support.microsoft.com/kb/907490`	Knowledgebase article with instructions for enabling tracing in Dynamics CRM
9	`www.microsoft.com/downloads/details.aspx?FamilyID=823fa114-5fb1-4fc2-9ea3-8282ff38964d&displaylang=en`	How to use BitLocker drive encryption to secure Dynamics CRM for Outlook
9	`http://technet.microsoft.com/en-us/library/cc771692(WS.10).aspx`	Instructions for using Windows Reliability and Performance Monitor
9	`www.microsoft.com/downloads/details.aspx?FamilyID=ba826cee-eddf-4d6e-842d-27fd654ed893&displaylang=en`	Whitepaper about optimizing and maintaining Dynamics CRM (Version 4.0)
9	`http://rc.crm.dynamics.com/rc/regcont/en_us/default.aspx`	The Dynamics CRM Resource Center
9	`http://blogs.msdn.com/cfs-file.ashx/__key/CommunityServer-Components-PostAttachments/00-09-97-27-69/CrmDiagTool4.zip`	Dynamics CRM DiagTool download
9	`www.fiddler2.com/fiddler2/`	Fiddler Web debugger
9	`http://msdn.microsoft.com/en-us/library/ms156500.aspx`	How to enable trace logging for SQL Server Reporting Services
9	`www.stunnware.com/crm2/topic.aspx?id=tracelogviewer`	Stunnware Trace Log Viewer
10, 21	`http://blogs.c5insight.com`	C5 Insight blogs on Dynamics CRM and SharePoint

continued

TABLE B.1 *(continued)*

Chapters	URL	Description
13, 22	`www.codeplex.com`	CodePlex: Microsoft's site for open source and community software development
17	`http://crm4activities.codeplex.com/`	A workflow extension for data manipulation and calculation
20, 21	`www.microsoft.com/express/Web/`	Visual Web Developer Express download
20	`http://notepad-plus-plus.org/download`	NotePad++ download
20	`www.microsoft.com/downloads/en/details.aspx?familyid=72d6aa49-787d-4118-ba5f-4f30fe913628&displaylang=en`	XML Notepad download
21	`http://crm2011scriptconvert.codeplex.com/`	Dynamics CRM 4.0 to 2011 JavaScript Converter
21	`http://jquery.com/`	jQuery download and documentation
21	`http://w3schools.com/`	Online learning resources for HTML, JavaScript, XML, and more
22	`http://msdn.microsoft.com/en-us/dynamics/crm/default.aspx`	Microsoft Dynamics CRM Developer Center on MSDN
22	`http://social.microsoft.com/Forums/en-US/crmdevelopment/threads`	Microsoft Dynamics CRM Developer forum
22	`http://msdn.microsoft.com/en-us/library/ee958158.aspx`	What is WCF?
22	`www.odata.org`	Open Data protocol
22	`www.microsoft.com/windowsazure/`	Microsoft Windows Azure
22	`www.microsoft.com/windowsazure/offers/default.aspx`	Microsoft Windows Azure pricing information
25	`http://msdn.microsoft.com/en-us/library/ms173767.aspx`	Business Intelligence Development Studio information
25	`http://msdn.microsoft.com/en-us/library/bb930489.aspx`	FetchXML schema reference
25	`http://blogs.msdn.com/b/dynamicscrmonline/archive/2009/06/17/fetch-it-part-2.aspx`	FetchXML query examples
25	`www.microsoft.com/downloads/details.aspx?FamilyID=d3173a87-7c0d-40cc-a408-3d1a43ae4e33&displaylang=en`	SQL Server 2008 R2 Report Builder 3.0 download

Chapters	URL	Description
25	`http://technet.microsoft.com/en-us/library/ee706623.aspx`	TechNet Report Builder 3.0 reference
25	`http://prologika.com/CS/blogs/blog/archive/2009/11/23/report-parts.aspx`	Instruction for publishing and reusing report parts
25	`http://blogs.msdn.com/b/crm/archive/2008/11/10/reports-for-crm-4-0-using-sql-server-2008-and-report-builder-2-0.aspx`	Tutorial on using report builder
25	`http://edgewatertech.wordpress.com/2010/06/28/step-by-step-creating-microsoft-dynamics-crm-4-reports-using-silverlight-ria-services-and-visifire/`	Silverlight chart report example for Dynamics CRM 4.0
26	`http://blogs.msdn.com/b/crm/archive/2008/05/07/integrating-crm-using-sql-integration-services-ssis.aspx`	Using SSIS to perform integrations with Dynamics CRM
26	`http://msdn.microsoft.com/en-us/library/aa480046.aspx`	Evaluating Integration solutions
26	`www.microsoft.com/downloads/en/details.aspx?displaylang=en&FamilyID=584531fe-796e-4ffe-8881-65c1f94207ae`	Sharing Data Between Dynamics CRM Organizations (whitepaper)
26	`http://en.wikipedia.org/wiki/Enterprise_application_integration`	Overview of Enterprise Application Integration (EAI)
26	`www.microsoft.com/biztalk/en/us/default.aspx`	Microsoft BizTalk Server
26	`http://crmaccelerators.codeplex.com`	Dynamics CRM Accelerators from Microsoft
27	`www.xrmshowcase.com/solutions?view=latest`	XRM Showcase
Appendix A	`http://sharepoint.microsoft.com`	SharePoint 2010
Appendix A	`http://office.microsoft.com/en-us/sharepoint-help/`	SharePoint 2010 help and documentation
Appendix A	`http://technet.microsoft.com/en-us/sharepoint/ee263917.aspx#tab=1`	SharePoint 2010 Resource Center
Appendix A	`http://technet.microsoft.com/en-us/evalcenter/ee388573.aspx`	Download SharePoint 2010
Appendix A	`http://sharepoint.microsoft.com/en-us/product/related-technologies/pages/sharepoint-designer.aspx`	SharePoint 2010 Designer

continued

TABLE B.1 *(continued)*

Chapters	URL	Description
Appendix A	`http://msdn.microsoft.com/en-us/library/ee557253.aspx`	SharePoint 2010 SDK
Appendix A	`http://msdn.microsoft.com/en-us/library/ee556826.aspx`	SharePoint 2010 Business Connectivity Services documentation
Appendix A	`http://msdn.microsoft.com/en-us/library/ee557271.aspx`	SharePoint 2010 user profiles and social data

Index

Numerics

1:N (one-to-many) relationship, 426
64-bit operating system, 36, 81

A

Account Distribution report, 608
Account Overview report, 608
Account Summary report, 608
accounts, defined, 7
actions
    behavior, 428–429
    dialog, 475–477
    workflow, 465–466
activities
    alerts, 268
    campaign, 320–321
    completing, 268
    creating, 265–266
    defined, 7–8
    general discussion, 261–263
    planning, 320
    types of, 263–265
    viewing, 266–267
Activities list sub-area, 266–267
Activities report, 608
Activity Application, 744
Activity Event, 744
Activity Feed Gatherer
    gathering activity events, 746–749
    overview, 744
    setting-up activity, 745–746
Activity Manager, 743
Activity Monitor, SQL Server, 218–219
Activity Template, 744
Activity Type, 744
administration, Dynamics CRM, 15
administrative reports, 607–608
Advanced Find tool, 602–606

advanced integration, SharePoint 2010
    accessing Dynamics CRM with Business Connectivity
        Services, 737–742
    areas of, 736–737
    showing CRM data in Social Activity Feed, 743–749
alerts, activity, 268
AppFabric services, 589–590
application process, XRM solution, 708–713
articles. *See* knowledge base articles
asynchronous execution mode, plug-ins, 574
auditing, defined, 45
Auditing field, field customization form, 422
Auditing tab, System Settings dialog, 130
authenticating users, 154–156
automating
    leads, 303–304
    queues, 486–487
    synchronization, 296
Auto-Numbering dialog, 134
Azure
    AppFabric services, 589–590
    Azure-enabled solution, 590–593
    defined, 39
    signing up for, 588–589

B

Back End Server, 68
backing up
    additional server components, 211–212
    database maintenance plan, 205–209
    Dynamics CRM application, 209–211
backup administrator, 124–125
balanced organization, 141
baseline report, 213–215
batch integration, 675–677
BCS. *See* Business Connectivity Services
behavior, relationship
    behavior actions, 428–429
    cascading behavior rules, 429–430
    types of, 430

Index

Index

Index

Index

Index

M

mail merging
    marketing lists, 327
    with Microsoft Word, 357–363
maintaining Dynamics CRM
    backing up
        additional server components, 211–212
        database maintenance plan, 205–209
        Dynamics CRM application, 209–211
    monitoring
        counters, 215–217
        creating baseline report in Windows reliability and Performance Monitor, 213–215
    simplifying updates, 204–205
managed properties, solutions, 386–389
managing data
    Bulk Deletion Wizard, 201–202
    detecting duplicates, 195–201
    Import Data Wizard, 189–195
    overview, 187–189
manual synchronization, 296
many-to-many (n:n) relationship, 427
mapping
    fields between relationships, 433
    users, Deployment Manager organizations, 176–178
marketing functions
    campaigns
        adding products and sales literature to, 324–325
        campaign activities, 320–321
        campaign responses, 321–324
        creating first campaign, 319
        defined, 10–11
        overview, 318–320
        planning activities, 320
        quick, 325–326
        templates, 320
    Internet marketing, 328
    marketing lists
        defined, 11
        managing list members dynamically, 327
        managing list members manually, 326–327
        using mail merge documents with, 327
    overview, 317
    sales literature list, 12, 328
    third party add-ons, 328–329
marketing reports
    Account Distribution, 608
    Account Overview, 608

    Account Summary, 608
    Campaign Activity Status, 608
    Campaign Comparison, 609
    Campaign Performance, 609
    Lead Source Effectiveness, 609
Marketing tab, System Settings dialog, 131–132
marketplace, solutions, 393
mash-ups, creating with Iframes, 543–547
MDD (model driven development), 374–375
merging duplicate records, 275–276
Microsoft BizTalk Server, 685–686
Microsoft ecosystem, XRM, 20
Microsoft Excel
    creating useful reports with, 617–620
    exporting data to, 352–353, 616–617
    integrating CRM, 13
    making pivot table available to other users, 620–621
    overview, 351
    publishing pivot tables as SharePoint dashboards, 368
    updating existing records from, 354–357
Microsoft Integration tools
    Dynamics CRM Adapter for Dynamics GP, 686
    Microsoft BizTalk Server, 685–686
    SQL Server Integration Services, 684
    SQL Server replication, 684–685
Microsoft Office. *See also* Microsoft Word
    Microsoft Excel
        exporting data to, 352–353
        integrating, 13
        overview, 351
        updating existing records from, 354–357
    Microsoft Outlook, 12–13
Microsoft Word
    integrating CRM, 13
    mail merging with
        creating template, 357–360
        using template, 360–363
mid-tier development environment, 516–517
migration
    best practices for, 680–682
    data, 673–674
mobile device
    Mobile Express, 277
    Outlook synchronization, 277
    overview, 276
    third-party options, 277
Mobile Express, 58–59, 277, 488–490
model driven development (MDD), 374–375

Index

Index

T

TabStateChange event, 526
tags, SharePoint 2010, 368–369
team ownership of records, 44, 259
teams, 146–147, 159
templates
    campaigns, 320
    contracts, 338–339
    data import, 191–192
    e-mail, 272–274
    knowledge base articles, 336–337
    mail merge, 357–363
    process automation, 478
    sending from Outlook, 297
terminology
    basic, 7–9
    customizing CRM, 372–373
    development options, 503–507
    marketing, 10–12
    service and call center, 9–10
testing
    JScript, 539–540
    security, 149
    upgrade, 87–88
    user connectivity, 149
third-party options
    marketing functions, 328–329
    mobile device, 277
tools
    development
        Business Intelligence Development Studio, 645–647
        SQL Server 2008 R2 Report Builder 3.0, 648–650
    enhanced data management, 41
    Microsoft Integration
        Dynamics CRM Adapter for Dynamics GP, 686
        Microsoft BizTalk Server, 685–686
        SQL Server Integration Services, 684
        SQL Server replication, 684–685
    reporting
        business intelligence, 602–612
        Excel, 616–621
        overview, 601–602
        Report Wizard, 612–616
tracing
    enabling for Dynamics CRM, 236–238
    enabling logging and finding logs for other
        components, 239–240
    enabling logging for E-mail Router, 239

tracking
    Outlook records
        converting Outlook record to Dynamics CRM
            opportunity, lead or case, 294–295
        e-mail threads, 292
        navigating to Dynamics CRM records from
            Outlook, 294
        setting connections, 294
        setting regarding, 291–292
        untracking and re-regarding, 293–294
    time, cases, 333
triggers
    dialog, 471
    workflow, 461–462
troubleshooting
    developer errors (DevErrors), 232–236
    Dynamics CRM for Outlook, 290
    event logs, 231–232
    resources, 229–230
    tracing, 236–240
Type field, field customization form, 423–424

U

units, product, 307
unsupported customizations, 508
unsupported JScript, 541
unsupported relationship, 427–428
untracking, 293–294
update rollup, 127
updated fields, 45
updated queues, 47
updating
    chart XML, 556–557
    entity icons, 418–419
    existing data, 193
    process XAML, 557–558
    records from Microsoft Excel, 354–357
    synchronized records, 296
    workflows, 469
upgrading server
    checking current system, 81
    installing deployment that connects to existing
        database, 86–87
    migrating Version 4.0 organization database, 82–84
    moving to 64-bit hardware, 81
    Outlook clients, 82
    overview, 80

Index

The books you read to succeed.

Get the most out of the latest software and leading-edge technologies
with a Wiley Bible—your one-stop reference.

978-0-470-55419-7

978-0-470-56813-2

978-0-470-50909-8

978-0-470-55481-4